1990 Which? W

1990 Which? Wine Guide

Edited by Roger Voss

Published by Consumers' Association and Hodder & Stoughton

Which? Books are commissioned and researched by
The Association for Consumer Research and published by
Consumers' Association, 2 Marylebone Road, NW1 4DX and
Hodder & Stoughton, 47 Bedford Square, London WC1B 3DP

British Library Cataloguing in Publication Data

Which? wine guide. – 1990 –
  1. Wines. Buyers' guides – Serials
  2. Great Britain. Wines trades.
  Directories – Serials
  641.2'2'0294

ISBN 0 340 51143 5

Researchers   Mary Redgate and Gina Copparelli
Cover   Linda Schwab
Cover typography   Philip Mann (ACE Ltd)
Illustrations   Caroline Drew

Cartography by GEOprojects (UK) Ltd
Henley-on-Thames, Oxfordshire

Typesetting by Page Bros (Norwich) Ltd

Printed and bound in Great Britain
by Collins, Glasgow

Contents

Part I Where to buy

Part II What to buy

CONTENTS

Introduction

Since the first appearance of *Which? Wine Guide*, the world of wine – both in Britain and abroad – has moved a long way. Quite apart from being a good excuse to celebrate, this tenth edition of *Which? Wine Guide* is an opportunity to reflect on the changing trends in the wine market and to anticipate developments in the nineties.

The trends highlighted in the introduction to the first Guide show how much has changed since the early eighties. More people are drinking wine; wine is drunk on more occasions; it is more socially acceptable; and, in these health-conscious days, it is considered by many a safer bet than spirits. Drinking wine at home on a regular basis has become much more prevalent in the context both of high restaurant prices and the drink-drive laws.

It would be fascinating to speculate on how much this change has been affected by the increasing 'middle classing' of Britain, higher incomes, and the growing influence of Europe on our behaviour, but whatever the causes more and more people are fascinated by the subject: reading about it, talking, visiting the vineyards and searching out unusual wines.

Who has been doing the educating? Much of it has spilled out from newspaper and magazine columns, and from the wealth of books, including this Guide, which have been published during the past decade. But, equally, much of the work has been done by the wine retailers recorded in these pages. The supermarkets and wine warehouses have led the way in the demystification of wine, while wine merchants have presented us with an unrivalled range from which to choose, from everyday pleasure to the finest and rarest bottles – and everything in between. And, as fuel to the increasing interest, the price of wine has fortunately risen much more slowly than inflation.

Concentrating power

With the spread of wine purchasing into supermarkets and its continuing place in the high street off-licences, merchant power has been concentrated in a few hands. It is said that only ten people need turn up to a wine trade tasting for it to be a success – provided those ten are the buyers of the major supermarkets and wine warehouses.

Such a quasi-monopoly could easily be a worry. In practice, competition between the giants has tended to keep that concern at bay. A potentially more serious monopolistic situation has been in the realm of the high street off-licences, with their vast numbers of stores (the largest boasting 800 or 900) and their strategic situations in prime shopping areas.

It is no coincidence that all these major chains are owned by firms with brewing interests. Just as with pubs, brewers look on a high number of outlets as an essential part of their sales policy. The value of the property also appeals to their accounts-led managements. This means that they have a potential stranglehold on sales through their off-licences every bit as tight as on sales through their pubs (and will continue to have after the collapse of the Monopolies and Mergers Commission attempt in 1989 to force them to sell off pubs).

Yet for some reason (lack of imagination? toeing the company line? ineptitude? trying to spread themselves too thinly over the whole area of alcoholic drinks, as well as sweets and tobacco?), the off-licences have had less effect on wine sales than their potential warrants. But at long last there are signs that some of the chains are pulling themselves together with the launch of up-market shops in competition more with traditional wine merchants than with the supermarkets, and the dedication of selected branches specifically to wine.

What about the independents?

The growth of the major supermarkets and warehouses in wine retailing has inevitably led to a continuing series of question marks over the place of the independents. How can they survive against the power of the big boys? Look, after all, at the fate of the corner shop in the face of the competition in food sales from supermarkets. In the context of wine, though, a better parallel would seem to be restaurants rather than food shops, since independent restaurants at all levels continue to flourish despite the huge power of the big chains.

The individual wine merchants, like the restaurants, have survived because they provide some things that the giants cannot – and do not profess – to offer: a level of service which ranges from regular newsletters and mailings to the ability to find a special wine or to rush an order through in an emergency. Many have sought increasingly to supply companies, to set themselves up as specialists in a particular area and to import many of their wines direct, thus keeping their range exciting and improving their competitiveness. Tim Atkin further explores the reasons why good merchants are flourishing in our feature on page 43.

This year's Guide – what's new

This year we are launching a series of eight regional awards.
These single out independent merchants who, we feel, are doing
most to promote the cause of high quality wine their area.
Details of the awards are on page 15. These are followed by the
roll call of our regular awards for good value, quality of wines,
breadth of range and high standard of service. Further
celebration marking our tenth issue is our recognition of those
merchants – national chains and independents alike – who have
been in the Guide every year since its inception. And, as last
year, we pick out on pages 21-26 the very best of our Best Buys
for your enjoyment over the coming months.

What of the future? Apart from James Ainsworth's
lighthearted look at the world of wine fashion on page 54, our
own crystal ball reveals that certain trends of the 1980s, such as
alarm at the effects of alcohol on health and concern for the way
our food and drink is made, are going to be more and more
important during the next decade. Wine, the most civilised and
civilising of all alcoholic drinks, will, we are sure, continue to
benefit from both trends. And organic wines will inevitably
make a greater impact as we look for safer food and drink.
Maureen Ashley picks up on this theme in her article on page
37, in which she looks at all the additives that can be used in
wine-making that organic wine-makers are trying to abandon.

And what of the wines themselves? More varietally labelled
wines are a certainty (even the French are recognising that
'Chardonnay' sells better than 'Burgundy'). There will be a
continuing search for good value white wines, always more
difficult to find than red because they are more expensive to
make. Demand for decent low-alcohol wine is set to increase
(see also Joanna Simon's review on page 49). And – after a
decade in which every country in the world has been combed
for likely wines – there will be a return to Europe, as France,
Italy, Spain, Portugal and Germany reassert their traditional
dominance, having assimilated the lessons of the New World.

A case of confusion

Which? Wine Guide is published jointly by Consumers'
Association and Hodder & Stoughton. Increasingly during the
past two years there has been confusion on the part of both
readers and the wine trade between this Guide and *The Good
Wine Guide*, published by *The Sunday Telegraph*. We would like
to point out that there is no connection between the two books.

ROGER VOSS

11

South African wine

The Council of The Association for Consumer Research, parent body of Consumers' Association, has a policy of not reporting on South African wine in *Which? Wine Guide*. We are founder members of the International Organisation of Consumer Unions, which is vigorously opposed to discrimination against any group of consumers on grounds of race, creed, gender or nationality. As a matter of moral principle, therefore, we have not included South African wine in the guide and will not do so while the citizens of that country are denied basic human and consumer rights by virtue of their colour.

How to use this Guide

Which? Wine Guide is divided into two major sections, both designed to help you get the best out of your wine buying. One section – WHERE TO BUY – tells you which wine merchants we consider to be the best. The second – WHAT TO BUY – is our report on what is happening in the world of wine and where the best buys are to be found at the moment.

But first, right at the beginning of the book, we list our Awards and Best Buys – our choice of the best wine merchants and wines for 1990.

Part I – Where to buy

This is our directory of the top wine merchants all over the UK (and, in one case, in the Republic of Ireland). We include supermarkets, high street off-licences and wine warehouses as well as individual wine merchants, delicatessens and department stores. They are in the Guide because they sell an exciting range of wines or because they offer particularly good value. Generally they score well on both counts. We have investigated many more wine merchants than have finally gained entry into these pages: some may have even slipped through our net (in which case we would be delighted to hear from our readers about them – use the report forms at the back of the book if you like), but most merchants who are not in the Guide are not, in our opinion, good enough.

Directory entries

Before the main text, a directory entry will give you the following information:

1 Name of the firm – generally the name of the shop.

2 The address of the place where you can order or buy wine. For chains with a number of branches, we give the head office only – phone them for your nearest branch.

3 Any special awards that the merchant has won – see page 16.

4 Case sales – an indication of whether the merchant is licensed to sell a minimum of twelve bottles.

5 Open and closed – the opening hours and days on which the shop or order office is closed.

6 Credit cards – which ones are accepted; whether you can open a personal or business account. Most merchants operate on 30-day credit if you have an account – but always read the small print in the list or ask if you are planning to open an account. Some merchants now charge interest on overdue accounts.

7 Discounts – what discounts are offered (generally on unmixed cases). This information does not include any special offers.

8 Delivery – what delivery terms the merchant offers. It pays to read these closely, because even if a merchant seems expensive, free delivery can make quite a difference to the final bill.

Part II – Guide to wines

The second principal reference section is a review of what's happening in the vineyards of the world, the WHAT TO BUY section. Each regional entry is organised like this:

1 An introductory section giving up-to-date information on new styles of wine, new trends and what to watch for over the coming year.

2 A glossary of terms used in that region to describe wines.

3 A directory of principal producers, merchants and estates in the region, with information about British stockists.

4 Best buys – our choice of the wines we would buy over the next year from that region.

5 Specialist stockists – wine merchants who specialise in the wines of the region. Unless the address is printed there, details of the merchants will be found in the WHERE TO BUY merchants directory.

More help?

Other sections of the Guide are also designed to help you bring a wine and merchant together or find a merchant in your area.

1 WHO'S WHERE – the gazetteer on page 61 – lists all the merchants in the WHERE TO BUY directory by town or village and by county. Use this if you want to find a good local wine merchant. The gazetteer cannot, however, include all the branches of chains, high street off-licences or supermarkets – you will need to contact the head office for this information (see page 67).

2 The index of wines – if you want to find where a wine is mentioned in the WHAT TO BUY section, turn to page 699.

Regional awards

 New to the Guide this year are our regional awards. The eight awards are available only to individual merchants and have been made in recognition of those whom we consider offer the best all-round service – in terms of range, quality and value for money.

Scotland

Peter Green

North of England

D Byrne & Co

The Midlands

Tanners Wines

East Anglia

Lay & Wheeler

South-West England

Christopher Piper Wines

South-East England

The Upper Crust

Greater London

Bibendum

The award for **Wales** has not been made this year.

1990 Which? Wine Guide awards

Awards are made on the basis of the quality of the wines sold, the range of the list, the prices of the wines and the service offered. This year, we have five four-symbol and seventeen three-symbol award winners – all achieving, in our view, the high standards we have set.

Key to symbols

🐷 **Low mark-up on wine** Awarded to merchants who offer a wide range of wines at prices which are more modest than most. Good value may be obtained from merchants without this symbol if you are prepared to pay more for service.

❀ **Wine quality** Awarded to merchants whose wines are of a consistently good quality across the range.

🏳 **Wine range** Awarded to merchants with an unusually wide choice of good wines, whether from one country or the whole world.

☞ **Service** Awarded to merchants who give exceptional service, whether it is in the form of personal advice, or through newsletters, tastings or informative lists.

Ad Hoc Wine Warehouse		🏳	
Adnams	❀	🏳	☞
James Aitken & Son		🏳	
Alastair's Grapevine	🐷		
H Allen Smith	❀		
Les Amis du Vin	❀		
John Armit Wines	❀		
Asda	🐷		
Averys of Bristol	❀		☞
David Baillie Vintners		🏳	☞
Ballantynes of Cowbridge	❀		
Adam Bancroft Associates		🏳	

16

	Pig	Rosette	Bottle	Hand
Nigel Baring		✽		
Barnes Wine Shop		✽		☞
Benson Fine Wines		✽		
Berkmann Wine Cellars/Le Nez Rouge		✽	◁	☞
Berry Bros & Rudd		✽		☞
B H Wines	🐷			
Bibendum	🐷	✽	◁	☞
Booths		✽		
Bottle & Basket			◁	
The Butler's Wine Cellar			◁	
Anthony Byrne Fine Wines		✽		☞
D Byrne & Co	🐷	✽	◁	
Cadwgan Fine Wine Merchants		✽	◁	
Champagne House		✽		
Chesterford Vintners				☞
City Wines			◁	
Claridge Fine Wines				☞
Classic Wines		✽		
Corney & Barrow		✽		☞
Restaurant Croque-en-Bouche			◁	
Davisons Wine Merchants				☞
Domaine Direct		✽	◁	
Eldridge Pope		✽	◁	
Philip Eyres Wine Merchant		✽		
Farr Vintners		✽		
Farthinghoe Fine Wine and Food				☞
Alex Findlater		✽	◁	☞
Findlater Mackie Todd			◁	
Fine Vintage Wines		✽		
Friarwood		✽		
Fulham Road Wine Centre			◁	☞
Gare du Vin			◁	
Goedhuis & Co		✽		
Andrew Gordon Wines	🐷		◁	
Grape Ideas Wine Warehouse	🐷			
Great Northern Wine Company			◁	
Peter Green	🐷	✽	◁	☞

	Pig	Flower	Bottle	Hand
Green's				☞
Gerard Harris		✸		
Roger Harris			◁	
John Harvey & Sons				☞
Haughton Fine Wines			◁	
Haynes Hanson & Clark		✸		☞
Hicks & Don	🐷	✸		☞
High Breck Vintners	🐷			☞
Hilbre Wine Company			◁	
J E Hogg	🐷		◁	
Hungerford Wine Company		✸		☞
Ingletons Wines		✸		
S H Jones		✸	◁	☞
Justerini & Brooks		✸		☞
Kurtz & Chan Wines		✸		
Lay & Wheeler		✸	◁	☞
Laymont & Shaw		✸	◁	
Laytons		✸		☞
O W Loeb		✸	◁	
London Wine Co	🐷			
Lorne House Vintners	🐷			
Majestic Wine Warehouses	🐷		◁	☞
Marks & Spencer		✸		
Martinez Fine Wine			◁	☞
Master Cellar Wine Warehouse	🐷		◁	
Andrew Mead Wines	🐷			
Millevini			◁	
Moreno Wines			◁	
Morris & Verdin		✸		
Morrisons	🐷			
Nickolls & Perks		✸		
The Nobody Inn			◁	
Oddbins	🐷	✸	◁	☞
Pavilion Wine Company		✸		
Thos Peatling			◁	☞
Christopher Piper Wines		✸	◁	☞
Premier Wine Warehouse	🐷			

	🐷	❀	🏳	☞
Arthur Rackhams	🐷		🏳	
Raeburn Fine Wines and Foods	🐷	❀	🏳	☞
Reid Wines		❀	🏳	
La Reserva Wines			🏳	
La Réserve			🏳	
Howard Ripley		❀		
William Rush	🐷			
J Sainsbury	🐷		🏳	
Seckford Wines			🏳	
Selfridges		❀	🏳	
Edward Sheldon		❀		
Sookias and Bertaut			🏳	☞
Stapylton Fletcher	🐷			
Tanners Wines		❀	🏳	☞
Tesco	🐷			
Thresher			🏳	
Turville Valley Wines		❀		
T & W Wines		❀	🏳	
Ubiquitous Chip Wine Shop			🏳	
The Upper Crust		❀	🏳	☞
Valvona & Crolla		❀	🏳	
Helen Verdcourt Wines		❀		☞
La Vigneronne		❀	🏳	☞
Waitrose	🐷		🏳	
Wessex Wines	🐷			
Willoughbys				☞
Windrush Wines		❀	🏳	☞
The Wine House	🐷	❀	🏳	☞
The Wine Society		❀	🏳	☞
Winecellars	🐷	❀	🏳	
Wines from Paris			🏳	
Wines of Westhorpe			🏳	
Wizard Wine Warehouses	🐷		🏳	
Peter Wylie Fine Wines		❀		
Yapp Brothers		❀	🏳	☞
Yorkshire Fine Wine Company		❀	🏳	☞

Wine merchants of the 1980s

To mark our tenth edition, we have awarded all those merchants who have appeared in every guide with a congratulatory star. This appears in their entry alongside any other awards they may have won this year.

Adnams
Les Amis du Vin/
   Christopher & Co
Arriba Kettle
Averys of Bristol
David Baillie Vintners
Balls Brothers
Barwell & Jones
Berry Bros & Rudd
Bordeaux Direct
Corney & Barrow
Davisons
Davy's of London
Peter Dominic
Eldridge Pope
Ellis Son & Vidler
Farr Vintners
Farthinghoe Fine Wine
   and Food
Ferrers le Mesurier
Findlater Mackie Todd
Fortnum & Mason
Andrew Gordon Wines
Green's
Gerard Harris
Roger Harris
Harrods
John Harvey & Sons
Haynes Hanson & Clark
Hicks & Don

High Breck Vintners
Hungerford Wine Company
S H Jones
Justerini & Brooks
Lay & Wheeler
Laymont & Shaw
Laytons
O W Loeb
Lorne House Vintners
Majestic Wine Warehouses
Marks & Spencer
Oddbins
La Réserve
Russell & McIver
J Sainsbury
Selfridges
Edward Sheldon
André Simon
Stapylton Fletcher
Tanners Wines
Thresher
T & W Wines
Victoria Wine Company
Waitrose
Windrush Wines
The Wine Society
Wines of Westhorpe
Yapp Brothers
Yorkshire Fine Wines

Which? Wine Guide Best buys for 1990

White sparkling wines

AUSTRALIA

Seaview Blanc de Blancs 1986 (*Oddbins*)
Yalumba D (*Les Amis du Vin; Drunken Mouse*)

FRANCE

Blanquette de Limoux Fleur de Lys (*Les Amis du Vin*)
Crémant de Bourgogne, Cave de Viré (*Alex Findlater; Haynes Hanson & Clark; Marks & Spencer*)

ITALY

Ca' del Bosco Franciacorta (*Adnams; Valvona & Crolla*)
Mompiano Brut, Pasolini (*Adnams; Winecellars*)

SPAIN

Codorníu Chardonnay 1986 Cava (*Harrods; Oddbins*)
Freixenet Carta Nevada, Cava (*Bottle and Basket*)
Raimat Chardonnay Cava (*Victoria Wine Company*)

Grapey sweet sparkling white wines

FRANCE

Clairette de Die Tradition Demi-Sec, Achard-Vincent (*Vinceremos; Yapp Brothers*)

ITALY

Asti Spumante Fontanafredda (*widely available*)
Asti Spumante Viticoltori dell'Acquese (*Winecellars*)
St Michael Asti Spumante (*Marks & Spencer*)

Champagnes

Albert Le Brun Carte Blanche NV (*Champagne House*)
Emile Hamm Brut Réserve Premier Cru (*Bottoms Up*)
Lanson Black Label NV (*widely available*)
Laurent Perrier Brut NV (*widely available*)
Lay & Wheeler Extra Quality Brut (*Lay & Wheeler*)
Mailly Grand Cru Champagne (*Oddbins*)
Massé NV Brut (*Classic Wine Warehouses*)
St-Gall 1985 (*Marks & Spencer*)
De Telmont Réserve NV (*Majestic*)

Pink sparkling wines

FRANCE

Bouvet Ladubay Saumur Rosé (*Master Cellar Wine Warehouse; Thos Peatling*)
Crémant de Bourgogne Rosé, Caves de Bailly (*Fullers; Upper Crust; Waitrose; Wines from Paris*)
Sainsbury's Crémant de Bourgogne Rosé (*J Sainsbury*)

Pink Champagnes

FRANCE

Landragin NV (*Oddbins*)
Mercier Rosé NV (*Unwins; Wizard Wine Warehouses*)
Sainsbury's Rosé NV (*J Sainsbury*)
Taittinger Comtes de Champagne (*Oddbins; Selfridges*)

Bone dry white wines

FRANCE

Bergerac Sec Blanc 1983, Domaine de Grandchamp (*Peter Green; J Sainsbury*)
Listel Domaine de Villeroy Blanc de Blancs sur Lie (*William Addison; Chaplin & Son; G M Vintners*)
Muscadet de Sèvre et Maine 1988, Guy Bossard (*Asda; Hampden Wine Company*)
Savennières 1987, Clos St-Yves, Jean Baumard (*La Réserve*)
Ch Thieuley Sauvignon, Bordeaux (*widely available*)

NEW ZEALAND

Montana New Zealand Sauvignon Blanc 1988 (*widely available*)

PORTUGAL

Vinho Verde Quinta do Tamariz (*La Reserva Wines*)

USA

Fumé Blanc 1985, Ch Ste Michelle, Washington State (*David Baillie Vintners*)

Fruity (but dry) white wines

FRANCE

Riesling d'Alsace Cave Vinicole de Turckheim (*widely available*)
Vins de Pays des Côtes de Gascogne, Domaine de Rieux, Grassa (*widely available*)

GERMANY

Sainsbury's Baden Dry (*J Sainsbury*)

Full white wines

AUSTRALIA
Jacob's Creek Dry White, Orlando (*widely available*)

FRANCE
Côtes du Lubéron, La Vieille Ferme (*widely available*)
Sauvignon Blanc 1986, Gallo (*Gare du Vin; Rex Norris; Wessex Wines*)

ITALY
Cellaro Bianco, Sicily (*Rose Tree Wine Co; Winecellars*)
Soave Classico 1988, Guerrieri-Rizzardi (*widely available*)
Tocai di San Martino della Battaglia 1988, Zenato (*Davisons*)

White wines with some wood flavours

AUSTRALIA
Hollydene Chardonnay 1987, South Australia (*Majestic*)

FRANCE
Bourgogne Blanc Chardonnay, Cuvée du Muguet 1987, Patrick Javillier (*Peter Green*)
Bourgogne Chardonnay 1987, Domaine Ste-Claire (*Thresher*)
Sirius Blanc 1987, Bordeaux, Peter Allan Sichel (*widely available*)
Vin de Pays d'Oc Chardonnay, Hugh Ryman (*Majestic*)

SPAIN
Monopole Seco Blanco 1985, CVNE (*Hungerford Wine Company*)

Medium white wines with fragrant fruit

FRANCE
Ch de Moncontour Vouvray 1986 (*Winecellars*)

GERMANY
Bernkasteler Bratenhof Kabinett 1982, Reichsgraf von Kesselstatt (*Anthony Byrne Fine Wines*)
Winkeler Hasensprung Riesling Kabinett 1983, Deinhard (*Christchurch Fine Wine*)

Sweet white wines

FRANCE
Ch de Berbec 1983, Premières Côtes de Bordeaux (*Safeway*)
Ch des Coulinats 1982, Ste-Croix-du-Mont (*D Byrne & Co; Winelines*)
Coteaux du Layon Chaume 1987, Ch de Suronde (*Edward Sheldon*)

GERMANY

Trierer St Mattheiser Riesling Spätlese 1983, Max Erben (*Averys of Bristol*)

Light dry red wines

FRANCE

Beaujolais Régnié 1988, Georges Duboeuf (*Morrisons*)
Bourgogne Passetoutgrains 1986, Jayer (*Raeburn Fine Wines and Foods*)
Bourgogne Pinot Noir 1985, André Ropiteau (*Safeway*)
Brouilly 1988, Ch des Tours (*Christopher Piper Wines*)
Chinon 1987, Domaine de la Noblaie (*Chesterford Vintners*)
Gamay de Touraine 1988, Henry Marionnet (*Bibendum*)
Vin de Pays de Charentais Cabernet/Merlot 1985, Sornin
(*B H Wines*)

ITALY

Valpolicella Classico Superiore 1986, Vigneti Marani, Boscaini
(*Safeway*)

Medium weight red wines

BULGARIA

Plovdiv Cabernet Sauvignon, Bulgaria (*widely available*)

CHILE

Concha y Toro Cabernet Sauvignon 1984 (*Balls Brothers; Chiswick Wine Cellar; Ellis Son & Vidler*)

FRANCE

Ch du Grand Caumont 1986, Corbières (*Fulham Road Wine Centre*)
Ch de Méaume 1986, Bordeaux Supérieur (*Majestic*)
Ch de Mirefleurs 1986, Bordeaux Supérieur (*J Sainsbury*)
Ch Pitray 1986, Côtes de Castillon (*John Armit Wines; The Wine Society*)
Corbières 1985, Dame Adelaide (*Oddbins*)
Domaine de Limbardie 1988, Vin de Pays des Coteaux de Murviel (*Adnams; Majestic*)
St-Julien 1985, Léoville-Barton (*Marks & Spencer*)

ITALY

Chianti 1987, Fattoria dell'Ugo (*Pimlico Dozen*)
Chianti Rufina Banda Blu, Grati (*Ellis Son & Vidler; Winecellars*)

LEBANON

Ch Musar 1980 (*widely available*)

RUMANIA

Classic Rumanian Pinot Noir (*Booths; Ubiquitous Chip Wine Shop*)

USA

Glen Ellen Merlot 1986, Sonoma (*Oddbins*)

Full-bodied red wines

AUSTRALIA

Penfolds Dalwood Shiraz/Cabernet 1984, Barossa Valley (*Chaplin & Sons; J E Hogg; Oddbins*)
St Michael Shiraz Cabernet, Penfolds (*Marks & Spencer*)

BULGARIA

Asenovgrad Mavrud 1983 (*widely available*)

FRANCE

Coteaux des Baux en Provence, Mas de Gourgonnier 1986 (*Haughton Fine Wines; Organic Wine Company*)
Coteaux du Tricastin 1986, Domaine de Vieux Micocoulier (*Gerard Harris*)
Côtes du Rhône, Ch du Grand Moulas 1987 (*widely available*)
Côtes du Ventoux, Domaine des Anges (*Bibendum; Pavilion Wine Co*)
Côtes du Ventoux, La Vieille Ferme (*widely available*)
Crozes-Hermitage, Domaine de Thalabert 1986, Jaboulet Aîné (*widely available*)
Madiran 1983, Ch Peyros (*Eaton Elliot Winebrokers*)

ITALY

Dolcetto d'Alba 1987, Ascheri (*Oddbins; Winecellars*)
Rosso Cònero 1982, Vigneto San Lorenzo, Umani Ronchi (*Oddbins; Wizard Wine Warehouses*)
Rosso di Montalcino, Villa Banfi 1985 (*J E Hogg*)
Salice Salentino Riserva 1982, Taurino (*Oddbins; Wine Growers Association*)

PORTUGAL

Garrafeira 1974, Paula da Silva (*Unwins*)
Quinta da Abrigada 1984 (*Oddbins*)
Reguengos de Monsaraz Tinto Velho 1983 (*Tesco*)

SPAIN

Castillo di Alhambra Tinto 1988 (*Martinez Fine Wines; Oddbins*)
Raimat Abadía 1986 (*Gare du Vin; Victoria Wine Company*)
Rioja Gran Reserva Campo Viejo 1978 (*widely available*)
Tudela del Duero 1984, Mauro (*Fulham Wine Centre; Master Cellar Wine Warehouse*)

Valdepeñas Señorio de Los Llanos Gran Reserva 1978 (*widely available*)

USA

Lost Hills Red, San Joaquin Valley, California (*Bibendum*)

Fortified wines and other wines of similar type

AUSTRALIA

Baileys Founders Award Liqueur Muscat, Glenrowan (*Whiteside's of Clitheroe*)
Josephine Doré, de Bartoli (*Oddbins*)
Ch Reynella 10-year-old tawny (*Waitrose*)

MADEIRA

Tesco Malmsey Madeira (*Tesco*)

PORTUGAL

Dows Crusted Port Bottled 1985 (*Oddbins*)
Niepoort Colheita Port 1975 (*Premier Wines*)
Quinta da Ervamoira 10-year-old tawny, Ramos Pinto (*Berkmann Wine Cellars/Le Nez Rouge; Lamb Wine Co*)

SPAIN

Apostoles Oloroso Abbacado, Gonzalez Byass (*Del Monico*)
Sainsbury's Premium Sherries (*J Sainsbury*)
Tanner's Mariscal Fino (*Tanners*)

What's best in the French hypermarkets

Mindful of those wonderful wines and prices that so many of us encounter during holidays abroad and of the growing trend towards shopping expeditions to the north French coast, we decided to look into the realities of taking a day excursion to a hypermarket in Calais or Boulogne. We bought a mixed case of 12 bottles in each of four hypermarkets to enable us to compare the prices, the quality of the wines and the choice available in each. The wines chosen reflected popular tastes in the UK. GORDON BROWN *investigates.*

It is surprisingly difficult to obtain advance information in order to plan such a trip. The French government marketing organisation in London, Food and Wine from France, are concerned only with French goods into, and on sale in, Britain, and the French Embassy, if approached, will refer you to Food and Wine from France. Do check French public holidays with the Embassy, however, since it could mean an expensive, shoppingless trip if you arrived in France when all the stores were closed. The brochures can, and do, get it wrong: Sealink's Summer 1989 day excursion leaflet had two incorrect French holiday dates. If you check with any of the Sealink Travel Centres, insist that someone check directly with French counterparts or the company's Service Planning Manager.

Although you may be able to do little planning on board ship (no free maps or ad hoc shopping leaflets on the P & O ferry, at least), if you come across *Daytripper* magazine you will see advertisements for two hypermarkets with simple maps and directions. Also, the purser may be able to help. Once in the store's environs, follow the countdown of advertising billboards by the roadside – 'Mammouth, 5 km', 'Auchan, Direction St-Martins' etc. This works quite well but you should build in time to miss a few turnings in the search for the stores. In smaller markets (such as Intermarché), and even those with up to 50 check-outs, paying and leaving takes time because almost everybody has full trolleys, sometimes two or three of them. Allow a minimum of 40 minutes' queuing time, even on a weekday mid-afternoon. Bar-code systems are the rule and they often cause further delay by breaking down.

You need a 10-franc coin for each trolley. Slot it into the handle to release it from the link-chain, and when shopping is over, link the trolley back into the chain to get back your 10 francs (worth about £1). Empty boxes to carry wines away tend not to be available because most stores sell fold-up, open-top cartons (9 francs) for the purpose. The cartons hold plenty of bottles but are a bit unwieldy with a full load and have no internal spacers to avoid glass-against-glass contact – *very* important for the car or coach journey home – so bring some from home.

The stores

The hypermarkets we visited were Auchan, Intermarché and Leclerc outside Boulogne, and Mammouth on the outskirts of Calais.

Auchan is a fairly typical hypermarket – enormous (10,000m^2), with 50 check-outs, a range of 350 wines, including 40 Champagnes, and over 70 brands of beer. It has a bureau de change by the entrance and a wide range of other merchandise, and is open from 9am to 10pm daily except Sunday. It accepts Visa and Mastercard and incorporates an arcade with 35 other single-business shops – in all, a hypermarket in the fullest sense.

Intermarché, at least the one in Boulogne, is not. It is smaller, mainly a food and drink supermarket, with no ancillary departments such as clothing or household appliances. It has a more restricted, downmarket and unexciting range of wines, with reds and whites confusingly intermingled. There were some good wines but they were largely confined to single bottles and a small range of crus bourgeois clarets. Intermarché's opening hours are: 9-12, 2.30-7.30 (Mon to Fri), and 9-7.30 with no lunch break on Saturdays and Sundays; all branches accept all credit cards.

Leclerc is on the same scale as Auchan and, in a good range of wines, had an excellent in-depth selection of clarets – petits châteaux, crus bourgeois and grands crus classés – from recent and back vintages. Opening hours are: 9-12, 2-7.15 (Mon to Thur and Sat), and 9-12, 2-8 (Fri); all branches are closed all day on Sunday. All credit cards are accepted.

Mammouth is large and modern with a hairdressing salon and several other shops in the foyer area, including snack facilities. The store accepts all credit cards as well as sterling currency and is open from 9am to 9pm (Mon to Sat). There's a wide selection of sweet wines, including Asti Spumante at £1.89, a separate beer store, and a good range of Champagnes. There is a wide-ranging claret selection here, too, with greater emphasis overall on red wines and marginally less choice of whites – no white vins de pays, for example.

The wines

We set out to buy the following representative shopping basket:

Sparkling: Basic Champagne.

Still white: Vin de pays; Vouvray; basic Muscadet-sur-Lie; Alsace Riesling; basic Chablis or white Burgundy; Sancerre.

Still red: Vin de pays; Corbières or Roussillon; basic Côtes du Rhône; basic claret; petit château claret.

The wines from each category were chosen from the lowest price bracket at each store. Where a wide choice was available, such as vins de pays and Côtes du Rhône, an extra franc or two was spent for better presentation, since we felt that the bottles should not look too basic on a dinner table. Prices are given in sterling, based on 10.57FF/£, the exchange rate current when the wines were bought.

Basic Champagne

All the stores had a choice of both unknown names at under £5.68, and established marques. Ayala cost £7 (*Auchan*), Mercier £7.24 (*Leclerc*) and £7.43 (*Auchan and Mammouth*), Moët et Chandon £9.13 (*Auchan and Leclerc*) and £9.70 (*Mammouth*), Canard Duchêne £6.99 (*Mammouth*), Mumm's Cordon Rouge £10.40 (*Auchan*) and £9.70 (*Mammouth*).

Although our tasting sample of Rothschild NV was bought at Auchan, Intermarché stocked three different Rothschild Champagnes. The Jeanmaire marque was available at Mammouth in large six- and three-litre bottles for £107.85 and £52.51 respectively, as well as in standard bottles at £6.62.

Tasted: All four of the non-vintage Champagnes tasted were fresh, pleasant and authentic in character with little quality variation except the **Alfred Rothschild Grande Réserve Brut** (*Auchan £6.24*), which showed elegance, a restrained, yeasty nose and a mature taste. **Récamier Brut** (*Leclerc £5.38*) was the best of the rest with more yeasty fruit impact and a soft, creamy finish. **Vallès Brut** (*Mammouth £5.67*) had slightly fuller, straight fruit style with nice mousse and alert acidity, while **Veuve Rueff Blanc de Blancs** (*Intermarché £5.99*) had a light, fresh Chardonnay nose, nicely mature palate and vervy finish. All were acceptable examples of what they should be.

Best: Although all four had authentic attributes, down to greater or lesser bready/yeasty signature, the best combination of fruit, mousse and balanced finish came from the **Rothschild Grande Réserve**, which also had a definite elegance that was less evident in the other three.

White vins de pays

There was no lack at most of the stores of very cheap blended wines, with prices starting at 56p a litre. The wine may be blowsy and coarse or jammy and cordial-like, but it is rarely unpleasant these days. By spending a few extra francs you buy a bit more individuality, an identifiable geographical style, perhaps even a specific grape-type. Since appellation contrôlée wines are available from about 66p not all the lesser wine designations are offered: Auchan, for instance, had no white vin de pays, and Intermarché didn't have any breadth of choice.

Tasted: **Cépage Sauvignon Jean Beauquin nv** (*Leclerc £1.02*) had authentic, grassy, gooseberry Sauvignon nose and flavour, was refreshing, well made and showed good acidity and fruit. **Gros Plant du Pays Nantais nv** (*Mammouth 94p*) was quite clean, still with some fruit, but it was dull, with none of the bite you expect from Gros Plant. **Blanc de Blancs Fief des Lois nv** (*Intermarché 66p*) had a chemical nose, no fruit and hardly any acidity. Very dull.

Best: This is a category where no producer can afford the very best vinification methods. If your grapes and your techniques are right, you come out with pleasing, tasty wine and **Cépage Sauvignon Jean Beauquin** was just that – positive and outgoing.

Vouvray

Much of the Vouvray sold is demi-sec but it can be a surprise
package varying in style from dry to fully sweet, sparkling or
still, and you will not necessarily know much about your chosen
bottle until you taste it. The sparkling style with mushroom cork
is, of course, easily recognisable and it usually has a style
statement on the label, but this is much less common with the
still versions. The Vouvrays we tasted were not of a great
standard.

Tasted: Domaine de la Pouvraie 1987 (*Auchan £1.89*) had very
little nose, Chenin or otherwise, and had a slightly petrolly note
instead of clean fruit flavour. It was perhaps already too tired
(1987). **Jean Beauquin 1988** (*Leclerc £1.58*) had a touch of sulphur
on the nose but was gentle with a decent fruit core. Some
typical Chenin bitterness was apparent despite a lack of acidity.
Félicien Brou Blanc de Blancs nv (*Mammouth £1.89*) is a
sparkling version, fizzy and cheerful with a very perfumed
Chenin nose, and very approachable if you like this light, frothy
style. **Sica de Brenne et Cisse Tête de Cuvée** (*Intermarché £2.85*),
demi-sec and sparkling, had no great Chenin nose, but the
grape showed up on flavour and finish.

Best: Even allowing for the diversity of style and sweetness/
dryness, none of the wines was sufficiently attractive to be
nominated as best.

Basic Muscadet-sur-Lie

Some stores offered a choice of Muscadet, even of 'sur lie'
brands (from £1.09 upwards). At this basic level, don't buy
anything that is more than two years old.

Tasted: Château de la Malonnière 1987 (*Auchan £1.70*) was
spritzy, quite clean, with nice depth of fruit and pleasant, ripe
flavour. It had a good balance between acidity and fruit and, if
anything, was a little on the light side. **Grapiloire 1987** (*Leclerc
£1.22*) had a stern, slightly unpleasant nose from too much
sulphur, and what little fruit there was did not balance what
would otherwise have been an appropriate tartness. **Ch La
Cormerais-Cheneau 1988** (*Mammouth £1.89*) had a soft, greenish
nose, some bite and rather thin fruit. It was surprisingly tired
for a 1988, rather stern in overall aspect and faintly edged with
sulphur. **Domaine de la Pièce du Bois 1987** (*Intermarché £1.66*)
had an authentic, yeasty, mellow nose with soft fruit flavour
and strangely separate acidity.

Best: None was outstanding in a group which showed the main
Muscadet pitfalls of old age and residual sulphur smells, but **Ch**

de la Malonnière had enough concentration and maturity to stand out.

Alsace Riesling

The usual range of Alsace wines was well covered in the four stores and often we had a choice or producers. We tasted Riesling because it is the Alsace grape-type most familiar to the British palate.

Tasted: **Kolb 1987** (*Auchan £1.89*) displayed an unusual, ersatz nose and acidity was poor. Apart from a flowery aspect to the taste, the palate was quite muted. **Réserve Personnelle 1986, Vieux Celliers** (*Leclerc £1.78*) seemed very inexpensive for its age although 1986 was a difficult year in Alsace. Its deep, fragrant nose was not followed through on the palate. **Cave d'Obernai 1987** (*Mammouth £1.94*) showed a good, fruity, generous nose and a nice zest on the tongue – very rich for a Riesling, and excellent value at this price. **Hauller 1987** (*Intermarché £1.79*) – in comparison with the Mammouth sample tasted immediately before it, this was fuller, with quite concentrated tart flavour but lacking breadth.

Best: These wines were light, approachable and, on the whole, quite elegant. They showed that it was possible to be inexpensive and really rather good, especially **Cave d'Obernai**.

Basic Chablis/white Burgundy

All the stores had put some thought into offering a good-to-very-good choice of white Burgundies. Auchan in particular had two Chablis – a 1987 and a 1988 – at £4.75, a Bourgogne Chardonnay at £3.31, a Mâcon Villages at £3.50 and a Bourgogne Aligoté at £2.55, while Mammouth stocked a good low-priced Petit Chablis. While Chardonnay is the best-known white wine grape in Burgundy, Aligoté is the other, more modest variety used there.

Tasted: **Paul Reitz 1988** (*Auchan £4.73*) – quite tangy, with the acidity perhaps too dominant for the available fruit. Not a lot of character but it is still a little young. **Louis Chèdeville 1988** (*Leclerc £3.96*) had a very perfumed nose of apples and greengage and a steely core. The tartness of youth will balance up with a bit more time, but the wine was already pleasant, with very good length. **Cave des Vignerons Petit Chablis 1987** (*Mammouth £3.55*) had a forthright, farmyardy nose with gentle fruit matching the acidity. Well-rounded, Burgundian taste, and a tangy, yeasty finish with a little wood. **Vignerons de Buxy Bourgogne Aligoté 1987** (*Intermarché £2.46*) showed little fruit on the palate, just a vinous tang.

Best: The overall standard was good although some sulphur showed through on more than one of the wines, and the lack of development had also to be taken into account. The youthful promise of the **Caves des Vignerons Petit Chablis** and the fruity assertiveness of the **Louis Chèdeville** made them joint best buys.

Sancerre

Authentic Sancerre character is likely to be smokily aromatic, herby and earthy with full fruit presence and a dry, crisp finish. The wines are best drunk between seven months and two years although the top wines last up to five years from good vintages. Auchan stock two Sancerres at £3.60.

Tasted: **Domaine Louis Martin 1988** (*Auchan £3.60*) was quite perfumed but with a nettly, vegetal nose. The gooseberry acidity on the palate was more to be expected but overall it was a rather dull wine. **Les Champtins 1988** (*Leclerc £3.95*) had a good fruity taste but was a bit on the soft side. **La Moussière 1988** (*Mammouth £3.49*) opened up with a lovely, gooseberry/grassy nose and the concentrated fruit impact continued right through it against a lovely, smoky background. Good acidity, nicely balanced and clean. **Domaine des Roussières Touraine Sauvignon 1987** (*Intermarché £1.79*) – it may have been unfair to rope in this lesser appellation, but Intermarché did not stock a Sancerre and this one was from a single property. In the event the bottle was out of condition.

Best: Polarised impressions between a pair of approachable but too young wines which may be fine in another six months' time, and a solitary positive, well-adjusted one made **La Moussière** an easy choice.

Red vins de pays

The choice is vast, particularly if you include VDQS and even some of the more obscure and rustic appellations contrôlées in this category. Styles are from big plummy essences to more restrained, traditional styles, plus all points in between. We tasted two reds from Auchan in this category (but not the Thatcher Rouge 1986 for £1.89) since they had no white vin de pays.

Tasted: **Vaucluse Terradou nv** (*Auchan 94p*) – red, as opposed to purple, and quite a mature nose and taste which included hints of strawberry. Very light, soft fruit, pleasant and innocuous. **Coteaux de l'Ardèche les Muletiers nv** (*Auchan 88p*) was purple, fruity and quite tannic with an acid/alcoholic tang slightly apart from the rest. It was a bit closed but had a dash of pepper at the end. **Bouches du Rhône Vieux Colombier nv** (*Leclerc 66p*) – purple, hard and tannic but, more importantly, redolent of damp floors. **Pyrénées-Orientales la Villageoise nv** (*Mammouth 94p*) was big and purple, plummy on the nose, rich and round on the tongue. A bit of acidic bite, too, with a spot of tannin. **Sables du Golfe du Lion Scep nv** (*Intermarché 90p*) had deep, opaque purple colour but little nose. Its rich, stewed fruit/ cinnamon flavour was a little baked. An enormous, almost brutish, wine, easily dilutable at lunchtime.

Best: The relative sedateness and togetherness of the 'real wine' styles here – the **Vaucluse Terradou** and **Les Muletiers** – as against the upstart raucousness of the others, came over well, making them joint best.

Corbières and Roussillon

Tasted: **Corbières Domaine Peyrière 1987** (*Auchan 92p*) – purple, hard wine, closed on the nose, very tannic and 'grippy'. Time could help a bit but the fruit is possibly under-ripe. **Corbières Classique 1987** (*Leclerc £1.12*) – quite an elegant nose, then tarry, tangy and tannic. A solid, slightly austere style which appeals to some and not others. **Côtes du Roussillon Jean-Jean 1987** (*Mammouth £1.47*) – rich, soft and very attractive wine with concentrated, jammy nose and warm, velvety flavour, with the correct tannic tang through to the finish. **Corbières Château d'Olivery 1987** (*Intermarché £1.02*) had a hot nose, opaque purple colour and coarse and assertive flavour.

Best: These wines may be over the top but at least they have their own positive attributes and they do grow on you. The softness and richness well merged with the tannin made the **Côtes du Roussillon Jean-Jean** stand out.

Basic Côtes du Rhône

The choice in the stores ranged from wide to none – hence the presence here of Côtes du Ventoux as a stand-in from Leclerc's shelves. Côtes du Rhône prices start at about 94p, which buys you a young, light, fruity style; the more you pay the closer you get to velvety roundness, spicy, mature fruit and perhaps even a bit of oak-ageing.

Tasted: **Honoré Lavigne Cuvée Spéciale 1988** (*Auchan £1.61*) – stern nose leading to rather acid wine, lacking in fruit. Dry and cheerless despite very chic packaging. **Côtes du Ventoux les Réclauzes AC 1987** (*Leclerc £1.32*) – stylish, full, almost heavy wine with quite high acidity, well made, elegant, rather Dão-like in its smooth, gamey fruit and weight. **Domaine de la Meynarde 1986** (*Mammouth £1.59*) – no great nose but clean, round, with rich fruit and a good, earthy flavour. Almost elegant, pleasingly balanced style and finish – very drinkable. **Les Celliers Rhodaniens Réserve 1988** (*Intermarché £1.13*) – vinous nose and quite round, warm flavour, and a nicely tart, spicy finish.

Best: With one exception this was a consistent category that gave excellent value for money. The **Côtes du Ventoux Réclauzes** was best overall (and look at the price!) and the best Côtes du Rhône was the **Domaine de la Meynarde**.

Basic claret

A basic claret has come to mean just that with prices here as low as 84p yet still qualifying for an allegedly prestigious denomination.

Tasted: **Versant Royal 1986** (*Auchan £1.60*) – pleasant nose and quite firm fruit; some tannin but a soft, slightly gamey style. **Sica nv** (*Leclerc 84p*) – oxidised, toffee-ish, over-ripe nose. **Prieuré St-Laurent nv** (*Mammouth £1.20*) – young, stalky aroma and flavour. Grassy fruit, good straight style, with some tannic bite at end. **Baron des Gravelines nv** (*Intermarché £1.08*) – very young and purple but traditional claret style. Lots of tannin, too little fruit, but gutsy and acceptable through to a decent finish.

Best: Perhaps we aimed too low here, not realising how cheap 'real' claret can be. Given the fixed bottling and transport costs, plus some margin, how much money can possibly be available from 84p to make even acceptable wine, never mind to vaunted AC standards? **Prieuré St-Laurent** was marginally the best but it would be more rewarding to spend more in order to raise expectations in any important category.

Petit château claret

All the stores had good-to-excellent selections of petits châteaux and crus bourgeois. There is even scope to seek your favourite commune if you have one. All our single-property purchases cost much less than simple generic claret in the UK.

Tasted: **Ch Fronsac, AC Fronsac 1984** (*Auchan £2.34*) – rich, mellow, gamey nose, fruit a little short but some acidity on the palate. As a 1984, perhaps it is as good now as it is going to be. **Ch Meilhan AC Médoc 1986** (*Leclerc £2.65*) – dumb nose, quite tannic but ripe and tarry on the palate. A little austere, but mellow right at the end. **Ch Moulin Rouge, AC Côtes de Castillon 1986** (*Mammouth £2.45*) – strangely spicy nose, followed through on palate. Good, rich, tannic fruit, too. Could still improve with a bit more time. **Ch Maillard, AC Graves**

1986 (*Intermarché £2.12*) – nice astringent nose, moving on to soft, grassy fruit taste and good acidity. Spicy, tannic, cigar-box fragrance. Will improve.

Best: A satisfactory showing by all four, two rather good and two quite acceptable. The spicy individuality and better balance of the **Ch Moulin Rouge** enabled it to stand out as the best of the four.

Conclusion

The same types of wine bought duty-paid at a UK specialist off-licence would cost about £46.40. However, remember that there may be duty to pay depending on how much wine you buy (don't forget your duty-free allowance). Duty is currently £8.60 to £9.22 per case of 12 bottles depending whether each is 70cl or 75cl. Mushroom-corked bottles of sparkling wine, including Champagne, cost more. A typical day excursion from Dover to Calais or Boulogne costs £56 for a car and four occupants.

Best store: *Mammouth* offered the best combination of quality, merchandise, choice, fair prices and best buys. The cost of the basket was £27.15, second-highest of the four, giving the best quality/spend ratio. Next in terms of best buys was *Auchan*, but the total cost there was the dearest, £28.59. Relative to Auchan, *Leclerc* showed well with almost the same number of best buys, but the cost of the basket was over £3 less, £25.52. *Intermarché* fared poorest of all with no best buys, the basket costing £22.55. (Check your receipt: on this sortie three of the four stores made mistakes – two of them to their own benefit - arising because of discrepancies between the shelf price and the bar-code data.)

With only about £6 differential between the best and worst in buying 12 bottles of wine, buying as cheaply as possible is not a good idea and would be a waste of time, effort and money. Intermarché would seem not to be an appropriate store for this kind of exercise because of its lack of range and low-quality/risky stocking policy, whereas the others all offer possibilities of rewarding and inexpensive wine shopping expeditions. You would be wise to spend at least £26 on this particular range of wine types. The nearer the total spent to £30-plus, however, the more exciting and reliable the selection is likely to be.

On a final note, a good wine department will be thronged with people most of the time so if that is what you see on your arrival, join in. If not, drive on to the next one.

That something extra

Wine isn't just fermented grape juice – it contains quite a few little extras. There are the additives, like sulphur, used to make the wine stable, and there are the clarifiers, like egg whites, which make it look crystal-free and clean. MAUREEN ASHLEY explains why they are all there, suggests that perhaps we don't need as much or as many of them as the producers think we do, and wonders why we are not told about them on wine labels.

'Eye of newt and toe of frog...' – well, not quite, perhaps, but you may well have seen hardly less appetising ingredients, such as fish bladders and ox blood, not to mention various lethal-sounding chemicals, quoted as permitted wine-making additives. Just as disquieting is the fact that wine remains one of the few processed consumables on sale which does not have to declare any substances that have been added to it during its transformation from grapes. Indeed, by some vicissitude of EC law, to give this information, for the time being at least, is banned. So the consumer who wants to know whether he or she is drinking solely fermented grape must or the output of a medium-sized laboratory, can't. And secrecy can only bring about scare stories of the witches' cauldron type on the one hand and sweeping assurances of virginal purity on the other. Neither, of course, is the case.

It *is* possible to make wine without any additives at all. It *is* possible, just, to make stable wine without any additives at all. But it is not possible to produce the wide range of styles of wines at the sorts of prices we are accustomed to without at least some recourse to the clarifiers, anti-oxidants and so on that practically all wine-makers use. The broad aim, therefore, has to be to reduce the use of these to a minimum while pursuing all the research possible to find ways of managing without them.

Winemaker's Dettol

For example, possibly the greatest bugbear of all in wine is sulphur dioxide, or 'winemaker's Dettol', as it has been sympathetically termed for years. No other substance has been found which can so simply, inexpensively and comparatively non-toxically emulate its functions. Wine, left to its own devices, will oxidise or become acetic, or both. Sulphur dioxide effectively nips in the bud any such attempts at self-destruction, while at the same time inhibiting the action of any stray yeast cells, so preventing a re-fermentation in bottle. Unfortunately, such a boon is not without its disadvantages. If used to excess – and apart from any legal restrictions the level at which it becomes excessive is extremely variable, depending mainly on the sensitivity of the individual – it is pretty unpleasant, causing sneezing, coughing or eye-watering. Many people also firmly believe that it bears a large responsibility for the morning-after head. Worse, though, may be its long-term effects; sulphites, formed by sulphur dioxide in solution, have long been under the health lobby's microscope (particularly in the US) and have been condemned as A Bad Thing: a danger to asthmatics, inducer of hypersensitive reactions and possibly carcinogenic. It is clear that sulphur dioxide cannot just be sloshed around willy-nilly.

Would that there were an alternative, though. The restraint of recalcitrant yeasts can be, and sometimes is, achieved with sorbic acid – particularly in the case of some lower-priced wines with residual sugar where the risks of refermentation are higher – but, apart from the fact that sorbic acid itself isn't completely harmless and there are limits on its use, it doesn't work properly unless sulphur dioxide is present too. More acceptable ought to be the adoption of ultra-tight filtering techniques and super-clean working conditions to prevent even one minute micro-organism lurking in the finished wine. Much work is being carried out in developing more and more sophisticated filters: cross-flow filters are the latest wheeze to have caught wine-makers' attention. These may be fine for everyday wines, but both producers and consumers of more complex, finer wines have yet to be convinced that filtering doesn't strip their wines of taste as well as the odd clarity-spoiler or bug.

Oxidation can be held at bay by ascorbic acid. There's nothing unpleasant about that: it is simply vitamin C. The only problem is that it only really works well as an extra precaution at the bottling stage and is not successful as a complete replacement for sulphur dioxide. Alternatively, one could keep the wine away from even a sniff of air throughout its life. Everything – storage, racking, fining, filtering, bottling – would have to be done in a completely inert atmosphere. Apart from the immense physical difficulties (and concomitant expense) of achieving this, a wine which is so completely reduced (the opposite of oxidised) doesn't necessarily taste too good either. And once such an oxygen-protected wine was exposed to the air when opened it would have no resistance at all and succumb to oxidation horrifyingly quickly.

Learning to do without

If no sensible alternatives to sulphur dioxide yet exist, what about learning to make wine without it (or at least with much less of it)? Great strides have, indeed, been taken in limiting its use in recent years by astute producers once they realised that often the more sulphur dioxide that is added, especially at the early stages of wine-making, the more a wine needs. The chemical gets combined with constituents of the wine and so loses its protective properties, which it possesses only when uncombined, or *free*. An additional effect is that sulphur dioxide helps create aldehydes in an embryonic wine. These do not help its flavour – although arguably we are already used to the style in numerous wines. Another realisation has been that an oxidised must does not necessarily yield an oxidised wine. Fermentation itself is so strongly reductive a process that it can reverse the effect of oxygen on the must. In fact, numerous experiments have been carried out where the must is deliberately and completely oxidised before fermentation. The resultant wine is not exactly the same as from an oxidation-prevented must, but it is not *per se* inferior, nor itself oxidised, and may well have better resistance to oxygen than a wine from non-hyper-oxygenated musts.

Once it was accepted that there was no need to add sulphur dioxide before fermenting wine (preventing premature fermentation during *débourbage*, or settling, could be achieved with refrigeration) and that this could reduce the amount that had to be added later, the battle was on – among those who cared – to reduce the use of sulphur dioxide to a minimum, if not eliminate it altogether. One or two claim to have succeeded in the latter and a few even to be 'almost there'. Numerous wine-makers now produce wines without using any sulphur dioxide at all until bottling but have to add a little at this final stage.

Unfortunately, only a very small minority of bottles currently on our shelves comes from these pioneers. The producers tend to be small 'boutique' wineries, often committed to the organic ideal, who can lavish plentiful care and attention on their wine-making. Alternatively, they may be large, successful companies intent on the highest quality image. What they share is the ability to invest comparatively large sums in equipment to ensure that their sulphur needs remain as low as feasible and to keep up to date with current relevant researches. Apart from the majority who are unable, or can't be bothered, to follow such a crusade, it is distressing to discover that far too many producers are still apparently ladling the sulphur dioxide in as if subscribing to the old premise that if a little is good for you a lot will be better.

A question of semantics

Of course, sulphur dioxide and its alternatives are not the only additives permitted in wine. Yet which of the other thirty-odd substances the EC allows wine-makers to employ should truly be termed additives is not as straightforward as you might think. An additive is, after all, something that is added. But it is also, one assumes, something that was not there in the first place and something that once added stays there. Tartaric acid, for example, may be used to help balance musts which lack acidity. But tartaric acid is also the principal acid occurring naturally in grapes. At the same time, over-acidic musts may be toned down by the addition of calcium carbonate or potassium bicarbonate. But in the very act of achieving the required de-acidification, they get broken down to calcium or potassium tartrate which are not only formed in wine anyway, but will usually be precipitated out, eventually, as 'tartrates'. Then, of course, sugar is one of the commonest additives, used in chaptalisation to increase the alcoholic degree. Concentrated grape must is an alternative 'enricher', but who would cite this as an additive if it were made from a batch of the very same wine?

After fermentation, which may have been controlled by the addition of cultured yeasts, themselves encouraged by the addition of growth stimulants, conditions may convince the wine-maker to encourage the malolactic fermentation by addition of an appropriate lactic bacterium and later to keep the wine protected against oxygen by the addition of a nitrogen blanket. And so on. But possibly the most contentious use of the word comes when considering fining agents. It is here that there is greatest scope for recoil. After all, even egg white can seem a pretty eccentric substance to add to wine (particularly in the salmonella era) for those as yet uninitiated into the finer points of traditional claret vinification, let alone gelatine and stranger-sounding substances such as a clay from Wyoming (bentonite), casein (milk protein) and the much trumpeted dried ox blood (no longer permitted) and isinglass (from fish membranes).

Clarifying the question

Anyone who has made a home brew or even clarified stock probably understands that the principle of fining is not to add something but to take something away. The irreplaceable benefit of fining is to remove colloids: tiny agglomerates of molecules which are just too big to form a real solution but too small to be visible, even under a microscope, but which can, in certain circumstances, form a light haze. And even if the highly sophisticated filters now developed can remove the hazes if they do appear (goodness knows what else they would remove at the same time), they can't remove the colloids (proteins are a prime example, tannins another) that are naturally present which could recreate them. A fining agent's role is to attach itself to the colloids, thereby making them bigger so that they form particles heavy enough to fall as a sediment, from which the wine can be racked and/or filtered.

A fining agent, therefore, does not remain in the wine but passes clean through it, dragging other bits and bobs along too, like some microscopic set of magnets. The use of the term additive is, therefore, hardly appropriate – 'subtractive' seems more apt. Yet it would be a brave soul who could swear with one hundred per cent certainty that not one single molecule of bentonite or whatever remained in a wine, however unlikely it seemed. There are no alternatives to fining until we are prepared to accept that any wine we buy, cheap or expensive, may be a bit murky. The only wines that might escape the drag net are those which have already spent over a year in vat, subjected to both warmth and coolness, have fallen bright naturally and appear to be stable – not a large group.

The liberty to tinker

Another group of substances permitted in wine-making could loosely be termed 'fault correctors'. An example is potassium ferrocyanide which is used, according to strict rules to allow no residue to remain in the wine after treatment, to eliminate traces of iron and copper, usually picked up by contact with piping made from these metals. Nowadays, with the proliferation of stainless steel in any winery with an image to nurture, the need for its use is becoming less and less common.

Without the permitted use of such additives wine prices would have to rise to cover the increased wastage from batches of faulty wines which could not be put right. Of course, it might just encourage greater care in the cellar. There's nothing like knowing that a remedy is at hand if things should go wrong to prompt a somewhat bolder attitude to wine handling: no matter if the grapes come in a little late, we can always bump up the acidity; no matter if we rack a little over-enthusiastically, sulphur dioxide will snaffle the oxygen; no matter if the colour is a bit deep, we can filter through charcoal; and so on. Indeed, a glance through the three pages' worth of treatments the EC does permit shows that most eventualities seem to be catered for and that, although a few substances have been eliminated in recent years, the list seems to be growing.

Such apparent liberty to tinker benefits the over-conscientious wine-maker as much as the slapdash, but over-conscientious in the sense of having a rigid idea of what his or her wine should be like and using every treatment necessary to ensure that the wine meets the ideal in every aspect. The cheap, technology-reliant, fault-free, identikit wine is as much a product of the additive age as the cheap and nasty.

The right to know

The rights and wrongs of using additives, all of them or just some, generally or in specific cases, can – and should – be argued incessantly. The consumer, though, for whose ultimate benefit, in theory at least, these substances are used, should surely at least be able to decide which ones he or she can and cannot accept. The only way to achieve that is by listing additives on the bottle – once an agreed definition of 'additive' in the context of wine can be agreed. And all additives should then be listed (not just 'sulfites', which are now compulsorily declared in the US) to give a clear indication of which wines are more reliant on the chemist and which on a sympathetic understanding of making wine. After all, there is no stronger stimulus than falling sales for a producer to convert to 'minimum additive' wine-making, whatever the costs.

Maureen Ashley *is a Master of Wine, a wine writer and a wine consultant. She is a regular member of* Which? Wine Monthly *tasting panels.*

Do we get a good deal from the wine trade?

There has been a revolution in wine retailing in Britain in the ten years since this Guide was launched. Are the supermarkets and high street multiples that dominate the market giving us proper service and choice - or just what they decide we want? And what place have the independent merchants in this scheme of things?
TIM ATKIN *investigates.*

The British wine trade has undergone a revolution in the last two decades. The image of the chinless, pinstriped half-wit selling a few cases of claret at the end of a boozy, four-hour lunch is no longer appropriate. Once a repository of idle bons viveurs, the wine trade has become a sophisticated, computer-driven, international business in which only the most competitive can survive. Nowadays the talk is of bottom lines, not waistlines.

For the wine consumer, this is not the unalloyed boon it might seem. On the positive side, more people in Britain are drinking wine than ever, even if we remain a nation of beer, or more specifically lager, drinkers. And thanks to technological improvements in the cellar, the wine we buy is on the whole cleaner, fresher and more stable than it was 20 years ago.

At the same time, good wine has started to emerge from some unlikely sources – Bulgaria, New Zealand, Zimbabwe and the Lebanon, for instance – which are hardly traditional wine-producing countries. Britain's status as a valuable export market with only a small, if undervalued, wine industry gives us a greater choice of bottles than any other country in the world.

One-stop shopping

That's the good news. The down side is that in attempting to remain competitive – and profit margins in the wine trade are unbelievably low – many of the more unusual, independent merchants are being forced to shave off corners, for, increasingly, the wine business is being dominated by a dozen or so companies. Foremost among these are supermarkets like Sainsbury, Tesco, Safeway, Asda and Gateway and the brewery- or multinational-owned high street chains: Victoria Wine Company (Allied), Thresher (Whitbread), Peter Dominic/ Bottoms Up (Grand Met), Augustus Barnett (Bass) and Oddbins (Seagram).

Three-quarters of the wine consumed in Britain is sold through what is known as the 'off-trade' (supermarkets and cash-and-carries, independent merchants, wine warehouses and off-licences) as opposed to the 'on-trade', where you consume wine on the premises, such as at a hotel, restaurant or wine bar.

That 75 per cent covers a multitude of outlets, from the dingy corner shop with a couple of bottles of Piat d'Or on the top shelf, to the rapid turnover of Sainsbury's, the country's single largest wine retailer (10.9 per cent of all households buy their food and drink at one of its 280 stores).

It is difficult for traditional merchants to compete with the pre-packaged slickness of what Americans call 'the one-stop shopping phenomenon'. You wheel your trolley past the bacon and cornflakes, pausing to pick up a couple of bottles of wine on your way to the check-out. All terribly simple.

Bulk buying

But what if you want to ask someone about the grower who made the wine, or when it ought to be drunk? If you can't find what you're after on the back-label you are unlikely to have your questions answered. For the consumer, lack of service is the greatest drawback of buying wine in a supermarket. So is depth, as opposed to breadth, of choice. No problem if you want a decent Muscadet, or a bottle of claret, but if you're after a line-up of ten single estate Chiantis, you'd be better off at one of the specialist Italian merchants included in the Guide.

Supermarkets have done a tremendous amount to popularise wine-drinking in Britain. Waitrose, Sainsbury and Tesco led the way, to be followed more recently by Marks & Spencer, Asda and Safeway. It is possible to find some very individual wines in these stores – a top Pinot Noir from California or Chardonnay from Washington State – but by and large they are catering for lowest common denominator tastes.

With the exception of Waitrose, who have avoided proprietory 'own-label' brands, the big supermarkets major on their own wines. A relationship between a small Burgundian domaine and a supermarket is unlikely to be beneficial, simply because the domaine will not be able to supply sufficient quantities of wine. Bar-coding and labelling are not worth the trouble for three cases of wine.

Popular own-label lines (Muscadet, Champagne, Liebfraumilch and claret, for example) are often bought from more than one source, so individuality is not what a buyer is looking for from his or her supplier; far more important are reliability and the potential to make wine to strict specifications.

The breadth of a supermarket wine list makes it impossible for a buyer to spend a lot of time developing, and indulging, a knowledge of any one wine region. Cold calls, whereby a team from a major supermarket descends upon Chinon, say, to knock on a hundred cellar doors, are not economically viable. Purchasing is generally done by tasting lots of samples in Britain, and by relying on the advice and expertise of local brokers.

This can lead to lazy decisions – buying all your Burgundies from one négociant, for instance. Similarly, at least six supermarkets buy a white Vin de Pays des Côtes de Gascogne from the same source, Grassa. The amount of residual sugar may vary, but the base wine is the same in each case.

One big advantage of buying wine in a supermarket is that as turnover of stock is relatively fast, you are unlikely to be sold a wine that is past its best. Nevertheless, Tesco and Safeway are to be congratulated for printing a 'best by' date on their wine labels, but others may say rather lamely 'consume within six months of purchase', which is of little use to the consumer if the bottling date is not specified.

Staff training

If lack of wine advice is excusable in a supermarket, where cheese and meat are more important in terms of turnover than wine, it is less forgivable in high street off-licence chains. Of course it is unfair to ask for the moon here, especially as wine may account for a relatively small part of a shop's profit (Victoria Wine, for instance, is the country's largest tobacconist), but a basic knowledge of what is on the shelves would be a start.

The retail trade as a whole pays its employees poorly, and wine is no exception. In fact, it is probably one of the worst offenders. Low pay does little to attract enthusiastic or qualified staff. Quite why the brewers should not be willing to invest more of their profits in training is a mystery. There seems little point in refitting your shops, only to employ staff who think that Beaumes-de-Venise is in Italy. Huge improvements must be made here. Badly informed employees are a rarity at places like Majestic, Oddbins and Wizard Wines, for instance, so it is surely not unreasonable to expect the same level of expertise elsewhere.

To be fair to the brewers, they are offering a greater and more inspiring range of wines than they were five years ago (though things could only improve). Nevertheless, the success of Oddbins is, in one sense, a reflection of how uninspired the competition is. Their list of more than a thousand wines is consistently interesting.

The two largest chains, Victoria Wine and Thresher, both buy some of their wines from the same source, European Cellars. This is a service company set up by parent companies Allied and Whitbread as a way of offering wine to both chains. The two of them stress their independence, but it is a fact that about 75 per cent of Victoria Wine's purchases is made through European Cellars. Thresher are a little more coy, saying only that 'a decreasing proportion' of their wines comes from European Cellars. There is, apparently, no obligation to buy, but the very existence of European Cellars must place certain limits on the wines that the two are able to stock.

Independent merchants make a great deal of the service they can offer. But each merchant is only as good as its staff. Wages are no higher in this sector of the wine trade. A graduate joining one of the more reputable London wine firms would be expected to start as a van driver on £6,500 a year. Rising interest rates and the impending Poll Tax will not make attracting personable staff, preferably with languages, any easier.

Staying afloat

But service must be good because the independents cannot hope to compete with the supermarkets, off-licence and wine warehouse chains on price. Cellaring, advice, delivery, letting customers taste before they buy and informative wine lists are all things that a supermarket cannot offer. And so is in-depth expertise in one area – for instance, Burgundy at Domaine Direct, Spain at Laymont & Shaw, California at Les Amis du Vin, the Rhône and Loire at Yapp Brothers or Bordeaux at the Hungerford Wine Company.

The number of merchants who go out and scour the world in search of new wines is, nevertheless, small. Visiting a place like California to look for a couple of undiscovered wineries is costly and beyond the pocket of most small independent wine merchants. Getting to know a region like Burgundy is a lifetime's work on its own, so it is not surprising that merchants rely on the services of négociants and brokers rather than going direct. Majestic are rare in buying 90 per cent of their wine at source.

Merchant Vintners is the response of one group of companies to the problem of buying direct. This co-operative venture, which celebrated its 25th anniversary in 1989, pools information and resources. Its 19 members include some of the best merchants in the country – S H Jones, Lay & Wheeler, Tanners and Adnams, to name but four. Each is responsible for one region or country, and then buys on behalf of the group. The result is that they have some wines in common (at different prices), as well as stocking a few finds of their own. All are in different parts of the United Kingdom, so in theory they are not in competition.

Feel the quality

One way of looking at this area of the market is to consider the best independents as one would a Savile Row tailor: they may not provide suits for everyone, but they do use the best cloth. You should get what you pay for. Problems arise when the merchant fails to fulfil his or her side of the bargain – certainly independents are not always the most reliable sources of fine wine.

Can the independents survive? Part of the answer must lie in their ability to continue to provide service and to increase their margins. To do so they will have to convince the customer that a £1.99 wine is not necessarily better value than one at £2.99. After all, duty and freight are fixed charges, so on the more expensive bottle, you are actually getting more wine for your pennies. The competition from other areas of the business will not make their task any easier, but the more of it there is, the better the prospects for the consumer.

Tim Atkin is wine correspondent for The Guardian.
He was previously editor of the wine trade's monthly magazine, Wine & Spirit.

Is there hope for low-alcohol wines?

Low-alcohol wines have been billed as the driver's alternative to the Real Thing. But how can they be, when they taste nothing like it? JOANNA SIMON *decides that, at the moment, wine drinkers would prefer mineral water or fruit juice, but reveals that things may be about to change.*

If you have ever tried low-alcohol or no-alcohol wine and been horribly disappointed, read on.

For more than two years we have been bombarded with new products – not all of them entitled to the designation 'wine', but all of them dressed up like bottles of wine and all of them purporting to be non-alcohol, low-alcohol or 'light' substitutes for the real thing. And so far the most positive thing that can be said is that some of them (but only some) are fresh, grapy and clean – but not like wine.

So what is the problem?

The trouble may be partly, as the buyer for one of the UK's national wine chains has said, that most of these wines (together with the wine-like drinks – see later – which are not

49

allowed to be called wine) haven't been designed with the wine lover in mind. Instead, they've been 'created in marketing departments by people who have no idea who this country's wine drinkers are, nor any clue about what they want.'

The main problem is undoubtedly the technology: scientists and wine-makers just haven't clinched it yet. They are capable of removing alcohol from wine (de-alcoholising it, in the jargon) and they can also make a product (which they can't call wine) from fresh grapes which never reach the fully alcoholic stage because they have been allowed to ferment only partially – but neither process produces a beverage that could, when tasted, be mistaken for real wine with alcohol.

The most common criticisms of low-alcohol and no-alcohol wines are that they taste thin and hollow and/or too sweet. They seem hollow because they are deprived of the body (or weight) that alcohol gives, but another reason is that when alcohol is removed from a fully fermented wine other flavour-giving substances are invariably lost in the process. The excess of sweetness comes from two sources. In the de-alcoholised wines producers often try to use sugar to fill in the holes left by the loss of alcohol, or to mask unpleasant cooked, burnt or bitter flavours that some of the processes seem to leave. In the partially fermented wines, unfermented (or residual) sugar remains – hence the sweetness of these.

It is significant that so far the most successful – or least awful – of the low- and no-alcohol 'wines' have been the lightweight, naturally grapy and/or medium sweet styles of wine – Italian Moscatos, Lambruscos and one or two Germanic types. At the other end of the scale are red wines, where using the sugar disguise is out of the question and where, when the alcohol is absent, the tannin seems to stand out even more astringently.

Yet things have actually improved, as anybody who tasted some of the even more appalling products of three or four years ago will know. Originally there was only one sort of product: de-alcoholised wine in which the alcohol had been removed by distillation. It tasted exactly as you might expect from wine that had literally been cooked. Nowadays, a handful of different techniques for removing alcohol from wine exist – competition is always good for consumer choice – as well as the growing category of drinks (not allowed to be called wine) that are made either from grape must that has been only partially fermented, or from grape juice, wine and water blended together, or from partially fermented must and de-alcoholised wine combined. (To ferment must partially you stop the fermentation at the required level of alcohol by chilling it, then filter and/or centrifuge very thoroughly to remove every trace of yeast. This is important because the presence of unfermented sugars means that the risk of fermentation starting up again is high.)

The nitty-gritty

Looking more closely at the de-alcoholising technology, the distillation method is still used but it has been refined somewhat by bringing the wine to boiling point at a lower temperature (either by means of a vacuum or by spreading the wine across a large surface area). The effect, however, is still to cook the wine, which tends to come through on the taste, and to lose other flavours.

A better method using heat, but considerably less of it, is the centrifuge, which has been used to clarify wine for many years, but has only recently been used to remove alcohol. At its most basic it spins the alcohol out and, it is hoped, nothing else along with it. But a more sophisticated version, called in Australia the spinning cone, separates out all the component parts of the wine, including the alcohol, and wine is then 'rebuilt' without the alcohol. It may sound rather brutal, not to say manufactured, but many producers consider it a relatively delicate and controllable process, used, for example, by Penfolds working in South Australia on behalf of Oddbins.

The other two methods devised in the last two or three years are essentially very refined forms of filtration - unfortunately rather expensive ones. With reverse osmosis, pressure is used to force the alcohol in a wine to migrate through a membrane into a lower alcohol or de-alcoholised wine on the other side. Results are considered reasonably good, although some other substances migrate alongside the alcohol, with the inevitable loss of flavour. Dialysis, in which wine is run along the other side simultaneously, results in fewer of these substances being lost.

The men in white coats are pretty pleased with these three techniques – spinning cone, reverse osmosis and dialysis – and current research seems to be concentrating on refining these to produce better results. But they have yet to convince the real wine drinker. The 'wines' and 'drinks' are mostly very unpleasant and the labelling seems to have been designed for people who can't find enough cryptic crosswords to do. Dr Richard Smith of the *British Medical Journal* has even said that wine drinkers who turn to low-alcohol wine may be classed with vegetarians who eat imitation meat or men who have sex with inflatable rubber women.

A glimmer of hope

The future, however, looks slightly more promising. Oddbins hope to have a low-alcohol dry white wine made in Australia from Semillon grapes on the shelves by Christmas. They claim that it will taste of wine – and not just wine, but oak-aged wine. It is the brainchild of buyer John Radcliffe, who thought that oak (from oak chips, not expensive new barrels) might provide what he calls 'the middle-mouth feel' which so far is missing from all other low- and no-alcohol wines and drinks. He chose Semillon because he thought the fatter, 'waxier' style of wine,

---

Labelling lunacy

While low-alcohol products are made in a number of different ways, the labelling at least ought to be easy. But it isn't. Why?

Well, for a start, you end up with all sorts of differing alcoholic contents between 0.05 and 5.5 per cent – just as you do with normal table wine, which is anything from 6 to 15 per cent. But the problem with the low- and no-alcohol stuff is that a ridiculously confusing nomenclature has been allowed to evolve to take in these differing alcohol levels.

Starting at the bottom, alcoholically speaking, alcohol-free or non-alcohol wine may contain a maximum of 0.05 per cent alcohol. The next category is de-alcoholised wine – 0.05-0.5 per cent – followed by low-alcohol wine which must be under 1.2 per cent alcohol. There is no excise duty on any of these. But, note, they *are* called wine.

At 1.2 per cent alcohol we move into the Chancellor's orbit, but out of that of British Food Labelling Regulations and into those of the EC instead. This means that, on the one hand, excise duty begins to be levied, on a sliding scale according to alcohol content; on the other hand, the products can't be called wine – only 'drink' – because the EC says that wine has to have at least six per cent alcohol. Where appropriate the label has to state 'partially fermented' or 'grape must in fermentation'.

Just to add to the complications, 'reduced alcohol', which you may have seen on labels, isn't actually permitted (but it hasn't been declared illegal either). In fact, it could usefully be applied in the 1.2-5.5 per cent area of 'drinks', since these are as bereft of nomenclature as the categories under 1.2 per cent are overloaded. We shall see.

---

together with its ability to develop in bottle, would be an advantage once the alcohol was removed, and wine-makers Penfolds are thinking of putting a little older Semillon in as well, to give it a bit more depth. Red wines are not in the pipeline yet - the tannin is still the hurdle – but if the Semillon works, it will retail at about £2.49 and will join the oak-aged French white already being sold by Marks & Spencer. Together, they should herald a new era of drinkable low- or no-alcohol wines. Fingers crossed, please.

Joanna Simon is wine correspondent of The Sunday Times *and Contributing Editor to* Wine *and* Wine & Spirit.

In vino, in fashion

Last year it was Australia and Chardonnay. This year, maybe Chile, certainly Sauvignon Blanc. And next year? JAMES AINSWORTH does a little crystal ball gazing as he speculates on changing fashions.

What will be this season's fashionable favourite: something light and frivolous, or bold and brassy? And the colour: purple, garnet, brick?; lemon, buttercup, gold? And the hemline: above £3.50 or below?

Wine never stays the same. The Málaga, Madeira and Marsala of our grandparents look positively dated beside Carneros Pinot Noir, Hunter Valley Semillon and Marlborough Sauvignon Blanc. By next week they in turn could easily be overtaken by a Bolivian Barbera, Paraguayan Port or Zimbabwean Zinfandel.

Two wines can be equally deserving of fame and fortune, but a quirk of fate will turn one into a chic, glossy, sexy, front-cover star, while the other will remain on the sidelines, neglected. What makes one wine throw in the towel while another – Tignanello perhaps, or Vega Sicilia – drapes it seductively about itself in such a way that every drinker wants some?

Unpredictability

The microcosmic world of the restaurant illustrates the insubstantial mechanics of fashionography. You order a bottle of Bourgogne Aligoté because you enjoyed one on holiday. Half an hour later you look up and see that every single table has a bottle of Bourgogne Aligoté. Russell Grant, Uri Geller and Doris Stokes combined couldn't have predicted such demand. The only sure thing is that the restaurant will not sell another bottle for a month. Drinkers seem to have a collective whim of iron.

Such total uncertainty, complete unpredictability and utter randomness do not stop certain people claiming credit for initiating fashion, guiding it and putting in a bill for their services. Wine writers think of themselves as 'opinion formers', sifting and tasting carefully through hundreds of wines, trying to be the first in print with a new recommendation. Many take themselves so seriously that a new discovery becomes 'their' wine, as if the chap who made it hardly mattered.

On the supply side, producers also believe they have some influence, although on what evidence it is difficult to see. Look at blush wine. California tried to make rosé take up its bed and walk but the miracle never happened.

The truth is that we only have fashion because we get bored easily. Muscadet on holiday in Brittany is brilliant, but nobody would dream of drinking it every week back home. A supply of Muscat de Beaumes-de-Venise in the fridge is one of life's essentials, except that by the third bottle you are wondering how to turn the other nine into sorbet.

Boredom, plus a dollop of envy, makes fashion possible. A fashionable wine is just beyond reach, something we aspire to a lot, but only drink a little, something wanted by more people than can have it. It should be in *fairly* short supply or *moderately* expensive. The have-nots should feel that only another month's wages (or, in the case of the Burgundy, a year's salary) stands between them and a dozen bottles of fulfilment.

To take an example: both Montana and Cloudy Bay make world-class Sauvignon Blanc, but Cloudy Bay is twice the price, and you have to put your name down for it a year ahead. Montana is for when you want a drink because it is such good value. Cloudy Bay is for when you want to be *seen* to be drinking; fashion demands spectators.

Fashion also implies a certain exclusivity and an element of the hand-made about it, which militates against branded wines, vins de pays, and supermarkets' own-labels. But it has to be credible too, so Opus One, and Châteaux Pétrus and Yquem are out because they are too expensive actually to drink. They are more collectors' items; indeed, they might just as well be stamps as far as most of us are concerned. But that still leaves a lot of candidates in the middle, and to explain their fashionability we must look outside the world of wine.

Current preoccupations

Personal health was a fashionable pre-occupation not long ago, fuelled by diet books, Sunday supplement exercise regimes, food labelling and the anti E-number lobby. This, coupled with concern about drinking and driving, led to a 'trading down' in alcoholic degree, although de-alcoholised wines seem to have rather overdone it. Then, as attention widened to focus on the health of the planet in general, so organic wine-making became a fashionable pursuit. Not only did new wine-makers take up organic methods, but a host of others, who previously couldn't spell 'environmentalist', suddenly discovered that they had been using organic principles all along.

Pétillant de Raisin embodies these notions: it has even less alcohol than beer, is produced organically, and is frothy (fizz is never out of fashion). It seems to have everything. Unfortunately, though, an own-goal by the producer keeps it out of the limelight. It is under £3. Whatever can Listel be thinking of? Put it up to £7.50 in easy stages – about a penny a day is a fashionable rate of increase – and it would clean up.

It is difficult to anticipate what global issues will galvanise the nation next, and therefore which, of the hundreds of wines waiting for the appropriate *Zeitgeist*, will shoot to prominence. But knowing where the eligible wines are likely to come from should help smart drinkers keep one step ahead of their fashion-unconscious peers.

Where next

First, it might be a new country. There has been a rash of them in recent years: Australia, India, New Zealand, Chile. For some, like Bulgaria, it was the one opportunity to shine on the world stage: East European cars, luggage and perfume stand absolutely no chance of getting into *Vogue*. The only danger is that, as with coal, the supply is finite and we shall eventually run out of new countries. But there are rich seams to be mined before that happens. Russia, for example, the world's third largest wine producer, is a dead cert. The only question is when. Given the pace of Gorbachev's reforms, it could well have started to happen by the time you read this.

China might have been a (more distant) possibility, but we are now hardly likely to be over-subscribed with Chinese wine bars. If Japan wasn't such an economic whizz-bang hot-shot already, there might be a place for it on the vinous catwalk; but it simply doesn't need the foreign currency badly enough to export any to us. Brazil is more likely: it will have to do *something* with the desert created by chopping down the rain forests.

But, just as renewable and familiar resources like wind and wave could well be the key to long-term power supplies, so it is remarkable how much energy is still released in places that have long been taken for granted. There remains ample scope for classic regions. Remember 'real' Burgundy a few years back, and then 'super seconds' from Bordeaux? Just when you think it has been KO'd by the New World, suddenly France gets up and fights another round. Perhaps, one day, even Alsace will jump into the ring. Never under-estimate France: it seems to have an inexhaustible supply of tricks up its sleeve. A country that can make Beaujolais Nouveau run for more than ten years is capable of anything.

Italy, too, has limitless potential. Yesterday it was the 'super-Tuscans', Alto Adige, and 'real' Soave. Today there is new Barolo. Tomorrow, perhaps some Australian wine-maker will marry an Italian girl, go to live in Puglia, and do for it what Peter Bright has done for Portugal.

Looking further ahead, the real sensation of the 21st century will be Scottish wine. Once the greenhouse effect has warmed up the climate, melted the ice-caps and flooded East Anglia, the viticultural fulcrum will move north. Iberia, the South of France and most of Italy will be desert, while Caithness Cabernet, Peebles Pinot, Mull Merlot and Stirling Sauvignon will be regularly topping *Which? Wine Monthly*'s tastings.

James Ainsworth is wine correspondent for Punch, *and editor of* The Wine Times, *the newsletter of the Sunday Times Wine Club.*

Part I

Where to buy

Who's where
- *a county-by-county guide to individual wine stockists* 61
- *chains and supermarkets* 67

Specialist merchants, chains and supermarkets 68

Wine at auction 311

Buying wine en primeur 317

Who's where

This is a gazetteer of individual wine stockists listed in the Guide. See also the directory of chains and supermarkets on page 67.

London

E2
Balls Brothers 86

EC1
Cantina Augusto 115
Corney & Barrow 129
Old Street Wine
 Company 227

EC2
Corney & Barrow 129
Ellis Son & Vidler 149
Pavilion Wine
 Company 230

EC3
Champagne and
 Caviar Shop 118
Russell & McIver 249

EC4
Corney & Barrow 129

N1
The Market 301

N6
Bottle and Basket 106

N7
Berkmann Wine
 Cellars/Le Nez
 Rouge 94

N8
Heywood Wines 150

N21
Howard Ripley 246

NW1
Nigel Baring 88
Bibendum 98
Richard Kihl 200
Laytons 204

NW3
H Allen Smith 78
Madeleine Treharne
 Partners 271

NW6
Grape Ideas 156, 170

NW10
Wine Growers
 Association 295

SE1
Davys of London 134
Green's 173
Kurtz & Chan Wines
 201
O W Loeb 205
Mayor Sworder & Co
 214
Russell & McIver 249

SE10
Ravensbourne Wine
 Co 240
Wines Galore 304

SE11
Alex Findlater 154

SW1
Berry Bros & Rudd 95
Farr Vintners 152
Gardner Martens Fine
 Wines 161
Harrods 178
John Harvey & Sons
 179
Jeroboams 196
Justerini & Brooks 198
Morris & Verdin 221
Pimlico Dozen 233
André Simon 204
Stones of Belgravia
 263

SW3
Bibendum 98
Gare du Vin 162
Nicolas 224
La Réserve 244

SW4
Wine Rack 297

SW5
Nicolas 224

SW6
Caves de la Madeleine
 116
Elite Wines 147
Friarwood 158
Fulham Road Wine
 Centre 158
Harbottle Wines 186
Haynes Hanson &
 Clark 181
Premier Wine
 Warehouse 235
Le Sac à Vin 244

SW7
Gare du Vin 162
Jeroboams 196
La Vigneronne 278

SW9
Ad Hoc Wine
 Warehouse 71

SW10
London Wine Co 206
Luigi's Delicatessen
 208
Stones of Belgravia 263
Le Viticulteur 238

SW11
Battersea Wine
 Company 92
Goedhuis & Co 167

SW12
Benson Fine Wines 93

SW13
Barnes Wine Shop 88

SW15
Drunken Mouse 143
Sookias & Bertaut 260

SW18
Supergrape 265
Winecellars 301

SW19
Esprit du Vin 151, 268

W1
H Allen Smith 78
Les Amis du Vin 79
Adam Bancroft
    Associates 87
English Wine Shop
    150
Esprit du Vin 151, 268
Fortnum & Mason 157
Nicolas 224
Selfridges 255
André Simon 204
Villandry 279

W2
Champagne House
    119
Moreno Wines 220
Le Picoleur 244

W4
Chiswick Wine Cellar
    123

W5
Freddy Price 264
Wine Rack 297

W8
Haynes Hanson &
    Clark 181
Nicolas 224
The Vintner 238

W9
Moreno Wines 220
The Winery 79

W11
John Armit Wines 80
Corney & Barrow 129
Nicolas 224

W14
Queens Club Wines
    238

WC1
H Allen Smith 78
Domaine Direct 141

WC2
Findlater Mackie Todd
    155
Kiwifruits 200

England

Avon

Batheaston
Luxembourg Wine
    Company 208

Bristol
Averys of Bristol 84
Bin Club 100
John Harvey & Sons 179

Hallatrow
Reid Wines 242

Bedfordshire

Lilley
Smedley Vintners 258

Berkshire

Eton
M & W Gilbey 164

Hungerford
Hungerford Wine
    Company 193

Maidenhead
David Alexander 77
Helen Verdcourt Wines
    276

Mortimer
Nalders Wine Agency
    186

Reading
Bordeaux Direct 104
Vintage Roots 282
Wine Club 104, 294

Sunninghill
Marske Mill House 211

Whitchurch
Col G P Pease 186

Buckinghamshire

Amersham
Demijohn Wines 136

Aston Clinton
Gerard Harris 176

Coleshill
Philip Eyres 151

Gerrards Cross
William Rush 248

Great Missenden
Turville Valley Wines
    271

High Wycombe
Organic Wine
    Company 228

Cambridgeshire

Cambridge
Barwell & Jones 91
Oxford & Cambridge
    Fine Wine 229

Cottenham
Pond Farm Wines 235
Wines of Argentina 235

Ramsey
Anthony Byrne Fine
    Wines 110

Cheshire

Alderley Edge
Eaton Elliot
    Winebrokers 144

Chester
Classic Wine
    Warehouses 127
George Dutton & Son
    292

Chorley
Haughton Fine Wines
    180

Hale
Cadwgan Fine Wine
    Merchants 113

Nantwich
Rodney Densem Wines
138

Stockport
Millevini 217

Wilmslow
Willoughbys 292

Cornwall

St Austell
Del Monico's 135

Truro
G M Vintners 165
Laymont & Shaw 203

Cumbria

Burgh-by-Sands
B H Wines 97

Cockermouth
Garrards 163

Grange-over-Sands
A L Vose 283, 299

Kendal
Frank E Stainton 261

Penrith
Cumbrian Cellar 131

Derbyshire

Buxton
Mi Casa Wines 217
Pugsons Food and
Wine 237

Swadlincote
Colombier Vins Fins
128

Devon

Doddiscombsleigh
Nobody Inn 224

Exeter
David Baillie Vintners
85

Marsh Barton
G M Vintners 165

Ottery St Mary
Christopher Piper
Wines 234

Plymtree
Peter Wylie Fine Wines
308

Dorset

Bridport
Wessex Wines 287

Christchurch
Christchurch Fine
Wine Co 123

Dorchester
Weatherbury Vintners
285

Leigh
Sherborne Vinters 257

Shillingstone
CCG Edwards 145

Durham

Darlington
John Armit Wines 80

Essex

Chelmsford
Welbeck Wine 286

Chigwell
Classic Wines 127

Coggeshall
Peter Watts Wines 284

Colchester
Lay & Wheeler 202
Snipe Wine Cellars 259

Great Chesterford
Chesterford Vintners
122

Maldon
Ingletons Wines 195

Gloucestershire

Cheltenham
J C Karn 199
Rose Tree Wine Co 247

Cirencester
Windrush Wines 293

Greater Manchester

Chadderton
Willoughbys 292

Manchester
Cadwgan Fine Wine
Merchants 113
Gare du Vin 162
Willoughbys 292

Hampshire

Basingstoke
Berry Bros & Rudd 95

Headley
High Breck Vintners
186

Portsmouth
John Harvey & Sons 179

Winchester
Godrich & Petman 166

Hereford & Worcester

Cleobury Mortimer
Hopton Wines 190

Hereford
Tanners Wines 266

Honeybourne
Arriba Kettle 81

Kidderminster
Touchstone Wines 269
Wine Schoppen 299

Malvern Wells
Restaurant Croque-en-
Bouche 130

Hertfordshire

Bishop's Stortford
Hedley Wright 182

Odsey
Pennyloaf Wines 232

St Albans
Desborough & Brown
Fine Wines 139

Stevenage
The Wine Society 300

Ware
Sapsford Wines 252

Humberside

Hull
Wine Cellars 270

Willerby
Willerby Manor Wine
Market 270

Kent

Cranbrook
Perfect Partners 126

Eccles
Douglas Henn-Macrae
183

Hawkenbury
Claridge Fine Wines
126

Maidstone
Stapylton Fletcher 262

Otford
Reid Wines Warehouse
242

Tunbridge Wells
Gare du Vin 162

Lancashire

Clitheroe
D Byrne & Co 111
Whiteside's 290

Samlesbury Bottoms
Borg Castel 105

Tunstall
Redpath and Thackray
Wines 241
Vessel du Vin 241

Leicestershire

Coalville
R T Wines 299

Leicester
G E Bromley 108

Loughborough
George Hill of
Loughborough 188

Wigston
Drinksmart 142

Lincolnshire

Ludborough
Lincolnshire Wine
Company 228

Spalding
J H Measures & Sons
108, 216

Merseyside

Liverpool
Thomas Baty & Sons
292
Hilbre Wine Company
187

Middlesex

Twickenham
Winelines 302

Norfolk

Beeston St Lawrence
Beeston Hall Cellars 186

Harleston
Barwell & Jones 91

North Elmham
Hicks & Don 184

Norwich
Adnams 72
Barwell & Jones 91
City Wines 124

Thetford
T & W Wines 272

Weston Longville
Roger Harris 177

Northamptonshire

Earls Barton
Summerlee Wines 264

Farthinghoe
Farthinghoe Fine Wine
and Food 152

Titchmarsh
Ferrers le Mesurier 153

Northumberland

Wooler
Graham MacHarg Fine
Wines 195

Nottinghamshire

Askham
Askham Wines 83

Newark
Ian G Howe 191

Oxfordshire

Banbury
S H Jones 197

Blewbury
Sebastopol Wines 254

Oxford
Fine Vintage Wines 156
Grape Ideas Wine
Warehouse 170

Thame
Hampden Wine
Company 175

Wallingford
Lamb Wine Company
207

Shropshire

Bridgnorth
Tanners Wines 266

Lilleshall
William Addison
(Newport) 70

Newport
William Addison
(Newport) 70

Shrewsbury
Tanners Wines 266

Somerset

Bishop's Lydeard
Châteaux Wines 121

Yeovil
Abbey Cellars 69

Staffordshire

Marchington
Wines of Westhorpe
305

Stafford
William Addison
(Newport) 70

Suffolk

Bury St Edmunds
Hadleigh Wine Cellars
174

Halesworth
Alex Findlater 154

Ipswich
Barwell & Jones 91
Burlington Wines 109
Champagne de Villages
118
Wines of Interest 305

Martlesham Heath
Seckford Wines 254

Needham Market
Snipe Wine Cellars 259

Southwold
Adnams 72

Woodbridge
Barwell & Jones 91

Surrey

Buckland
Ben Ellis and Associates
148

Cranleigh
A & A Wines 68
Lorne House Vintners
207

Croydon
Master Cellar Wine
Warehouse 213

Dorking
Andrew Gordon Wines
168

East Horsley
Upper Crust 274

Kingston-upon-Thames
Bentalls of Kingston 93

Pirbright
West Heath Wine 288

Richmond
Richmond Wine
Warehouse 245

Surbiton
Hurt & Daniel 194

Wallington
Wine House 296

Woking
Gare du Vin 162

Sussex (East)

Alfriston
English Wine Centre
150

Brighton
The Butler's Wine
Cellar 110

Haywards Heath
Rex Norris 225

Lewes
Cliffe Cellars 149

Sussex (West)

Billingshurst
Charles Hennings 184

Chichester
Pallant Wines 229

Midhurst
Duras Direct 144

Petworth
Charles Hennings 184

Pulborough
Charles Hennings 184

Rudgwick
J Dudley 186

Worthing
A G Barnett 186
Chaplin & Son 120

Tyne & Wear

Newcastle upon Tyne
Dennhöfer Wines 137
Richard Granger 169

Warwickshire

Leamington Spa
Alastair's Grapevine 75

Shipston-on-Stour
Edward Sheldon 256

Stratford upon Avon
C A Rookes 246

Warwick
Broad Street Wine Co
107

West Midlands

Lye
Greenwood & Co 223

Moseley
Vinature 281

Stourbridge
Nickolls & Perks 223

Sutton Coldfield
Jacqueline's Wines 196

Walsall
Whittalls Wines 291

Wiltshire

Mere
Yapp Brothers 308

Westbury
Hicks & Don 184

Yorkshire (North)

Copmanthorpe
Fine English Wine
Company 156

Harrogate
Martinez Fine Wine 212

Nun Monkton
Yorkshire Fine Wine
Company 309

Oswaldkirk
Patrick Toone 101

Skipton
Wright Wine Co 307

York
Cachet Wines 112

Yorkshire (South)

Huddersfield
Pennine Wines 299

Rotherham
Toone House & Cellars
101

Sheffield
Bin 89 Wine Warehouse
99
Michael Menzel 216
Wine Schoppen 232,
299

Stainforth
Wine Warehouse 299

Yorkshire (West)

Halifax
Classic Wines 299

Huddersfield
Grapehop 243
Pennine Wines 232

Ilkley
Martinez Fine Wine 212

Leeds
Cairns & Hickey 114
Great Northern Wine
Company 171
Vinceremos Wines 281

Linthwaite
La Reserva Wines 243

Scotland

Ayr
Whighams of Ayr 289

Biggar
Villeneuve Wines 280

Coldstream
Alba Wine Society 76

Dundee
James Aitken & Son 74

Edinburgh
Peter Green 172
J E Hogg 189
G Hush 194
Irvine Robertson Wines
195
Justerini & Brooks 198
Raeburn Fine Wines
and Foods 239
Valvona & Crolla 275
Whighams Young &
Saunders at Jenners
289
Wine Emporium 295
Wines from Paris 303

Glasgow
d'Arcy's 132
Ubiquitous Chip Wine
Shop 273

Moffat
Moffat Wine Shop 219

Peebles
Villeneuve Wines 280

Perth
Matthew Gloag & Son
164

Stevenston
Premier Wines 236

Wales

Hawarden
Ashley Scott 253

Llanblethian
Ballantynes of
Cowbridge 86

Presteigne
Andrew Mead Wines
215

Swansea
Celtic Vintner 117

Welshpool
Tanners Wines 266

Channel Islands

Longueville, Jersey
Victor Hugo Wines 192

St Brelade, Jersey
Victor Hugo Wines 192

St Helier, Jersey
Victor Hugo Wines 192

Northern Ireland

Belfast
Direct Wine Shipments
140
Duncairn Wines 140

Republic of Ireland

Dublin
Mitchell & Son 218

CHAINS AND SUPERMARKETS

Space does not permit us to list the addresses of all the branches of each chain, but details at the head of the entry include the address and telephone number of the company's head office, from whom you will be able to find out your nearest branch.

Asda 82
Augustus Barnett 89
Blayneys 102
Booths 103
Bottoms Up 107
Davisons 133
Peter Dominic 142
Eldridge Pope 146
Fullers 160

Majestic Wine
  Warehouses 209
Marks & Spencer 210
Morrisons 222
Oddbins 226
Thos Peatling 231
Arthur Rackhams 238
Safeway 250
J Sainsbury 251

Tesco 267
Thresher 268
J Townend & Sons 270
Unwins 274
Victoria Wine
  Company 277
Waitrose 284
Wizard Wine
  Warehouses 306

A & A Wines

Smithbrook Kilns, nr Cranleigh, Surrey GU6 8JJ   TEL (0483) 274666

CASE SALES ONLY   OPEN Mon–Fri 9.30–5.30; Sat 10–2   CLOSED Sun, public holidays   CREDIT CARDS None accepted; personal and business accounts DISCOUNTS 5% on 10+ cases   DELIVERY Free in Surrey (min 1 case) and Sussex, Hampshire, Kent, Berkshire and Greater London (min 5 cases); elsewhere negotiable   GLASS HIRE Free with any case order TASTINGS AND TALKS Generally monthly tastings in-store; to groups on request   CELLARAGE Not available

While there has been an extension to the range of wines from France – especially Bordeaux – in this merchant's list, it is to Spain and Italy that we continue to turn for the main interest.

In Spain, there is a wide selection of Riojas, including the excellent value wines of Campo Viejo and Faustino Martinez, wines from Bodegas El Coto and Bodegas Riojanas, plus the top quality wines of Marqués de Murrieta (Murrieta Blanco 1984 at £5.99, the rare Castillo Ygay 1942 at £40.25). Other areas of Spain that are well treated include Penedés with a good selection of Torres wines, the Palacio de León wines from León and the fruity and inexpensive reds of Viña Albali (Reserva 1983 at £2.75). While in the Iberian peninsula, it is also worth noting the mature vintages of Pasmados Portuguese red from J M da Fonseca (1978 at £3.95 is a bargain).

Moving to Italy, interest centres on Tuscany, with Chiantis from La Pagliaia, the Amarone Recioto Valpolicella of Tedeschi, and a range of Barolos from La Brenta d'Oro. Good quaffing wines come from Settesoli in Sicily. In Australia, look for wines from Lindemans, Hardy and Wyndham Estates.

To France: in Bordeaux, there are a few good-value 1985 St-Emilions, and from the South of France (Domaine de Montariol Côtes du Roussillon at £2.75 and the Minervois Ch Millegrand 1987 at £2.65).

Best buys

Chianti Classico La Pagliaia 1987, £3.65
Settesoli Rosso 1986, £2.49
Pasmados 1978, J M da Fonseca, £3.95
Faustino V White 1987, Rioja, £4.40

Prices were current in summer 1989 to the best of our knowledge but can only be a rough indication of prices throughout 1990.

Abbey Cellars

The Abbey, Preston Road, Yeovil, TEL (0935) 76228
Somerset BA21 3AR

CASE SALES ONLY OPEN Tue–Fri 10–6; Sat 10–3 CLOSED Mon, Sun, public
holidays CREDIT CARDS Access, Visa; business accounts
DISCOUNTS Negotiable (min 1 case) DELIVERY Free within 30-mile radius
of Yeovil and central London (min 1 case); elsewhere at cost; mail order
available GLASS HIRE Free with 1-case order
TASTINGS AND TALKS Tastings held 3 times a year; to groups on request
(max 20–25 people) CELLARAGE £3 per case per year

A newcomer to the Guide, this firm has been in business since
1988. Judging by their early lists, they choose small but careful
selections of wines from right round the world.

So, for instance, we find a good range of French country
wines (including Vin de Pays des Côtes de Gascogne of
Domaine de Rieux at £2.80 or the Côtes du Marmandais 1986, Le
Mardelon at £2.85. Well-priced clarets hover around the £3 to £4
mark (look for the ready-for-drinking 1985s). Robert Sarrau
provides the Beaujolais, while further south the wines of La
Vieille Ferme (including the Muscat de Beaumes-de-Venise) are
of interest.

Spain has the Añares Riojas (1984 vintage of the red is £3.85),
while Italy offers the Chianti Classico of Castello di Lucignano
1986 at £3.95. Australia fares well, with wines from Wyndham
Estates at good prices and the Western Australian wines of
Plantagenet at Mount Barker (Shiraz 1985 at £6.90).

Best buys

Côtes du Roussillon 1985, Domaine du Mas Sibade, £2.75
Ch Verdelet 1986, Bordeaux, £3.45
Wyndham Estates Cabernet Sauvignon Bin 444 1985, £4.45
Añares Blanco 1985, Rioja, £3.75

Special awards

means bargain prices (good *value* may be obtained from
merchants without this symbol, of course, if you wish to pay for
service)

means that the wines stocked are of consistently high quality

means that the merchant stocks an above-average range

means that extra-special service is offered; helpful advice,
information lists and newsletters, tastings etc.

William Addison (Newport)

HEAD OFFICE AND THE WAREHOUSE

The Warehouse, Village Farm, Lilleshall, Newport, Shropshire TF10 9HB	TEL (0952) 670200 (24-hour answering service (0952) 670300)
67 High Street, Newport, Shropshire TF10 7AU	TEL (0952) 810627
35 Mill Street, Stafford, Staffordshire ST16 2AJ	TEL (0785) 52735

OPEN Mon–Sat 9–5 CLOSED Wed pm (Stafford), Mon (Newport), Sun, public holidays CREDIT CARDS Visa; personal and business accounts DISCOUNTS Not available DELIVERY Free in Shropshire (min 1 case); elsewhere at cost; mail order available GLASS HIRE Free with wine order TASTINGS AND TALKS To groups on request CELLARAGE £3.45 per case per year

A classically safe range, with emphasis on Bordeaux and Burgundy, both of which are covered well. In Bordeaux, for instance, there are big selections from most of the vintages of the 1980s (especially 1982 and 1985), with wines in most price areas (in 1985 for example you can choose from wines between Ch Litay at £4.47 (prices on the list do not include VAT, but we have added it here) up to Ch Palmer at £28.69. In Burgundy, we find a carefully chosen range featuring many well-known domaine names (Jean Germain, J Prieur), with négociant wines from Antonin Rodet and Chanson among others. There is also a special selection of Georges Duboeuf Beaujolais.

The main interest in the Rhône centres on wines from Ch de Beaucastel in Châteauneuf-du-Pape (both red and white), and while the Loire is less exciting, the wines of Louis Sipp in Alsace and the top quality Ch Vignelaure in Provence are both high points.

Beyond France, Germany – as we noted last year – seems unfortunately bereft of producers for many of the wines (although they do look worth investigating). There are a couple of English wines, Riojas from Marqués de Cáceres and Siglo Saco (Bodegas Age), and a good range of California wines from Robert Mondavi. In Australia, Brown Brothers and Rouge Homme are the star turns, while the Italian selection only just touches the acceptable mark. However, the range of Champagnes is big and interesting (house Champagne is Charles Bonnaire at £9.18) and includes some large bottles, and there's an equally comprehensive range of vintage Ports.

Send us your views on the report forms at the back of the book.

Best buys

House Claret, Nathaniel Johnston, £2.95
Muscat d'Alsace 1985, Louis Sipp, £4.79
Rully Blanc, Ch de Rully 1987, £7.89
Midi wines from Listel

Ad Hoc Wine Warehouse   ⊫

363 Clapham Road, London SW9 9BT   TEL 01–326 1799
(warehouse)
TEL 01–274 0988 (office)

OPEN Mon–Fri 9.30–7.30; Sat 10–7.30; Sun 11–6   CLOSED Public holidays
CREDIT CARDS Access, Visa; personal and business accounts
DISCOUNTS 5% on 10 cases   DELIVERY Free in London area and UK (for
25+ cases); otherwise at cost   GLASS HIRE Free
TASTINGS AND TALKS Tastings held 2–3 times per year; to groups on
request   CELLARAGE Not available

This is becoming more and more of a good all-round range of
wines, the previous interest in Spain and Italy maintained but
enhanced by more from the French regions and Bordeaux and a
wide choice of Bulgarian wines.

In France we find wines from Bergerac such as the familiar Ch
La Jaubertie (the red Reserve 1985 is £5.45), rubbing shoulders
with rarities such as Irouléguy from St-Etienne de Baigorry deep
in the South-West of France. There's also good quality from
Languedoc and Provence (Coteaux Varois Ch St-Estève 1986 at
£2.85, or Vin de Pays des Bouches du Rhône Sélection Philibert
at £2.25). And in the classic areas an excellent cross-section of
wines covers the cheapest house claret from Lebègue at £2.49 up
to classed growths from vintages back to 1966. While
Burgundy's listing is shorter, it does offer interest with wines
from Faiveley (that firm also supplies Beaujolais), and the Rhône
has wines from Guigal (including the top quality Côtes du
Rhône at £5.75) as well as Ch de Beaucastel Châteauneuf-du-
Pape. Alsace has wines from the co-ops at Obernai and
Ingersheim, while the Loire offers a representative selection
from the major areas along the river.

Italy is a star performer with the best sections from Piedmont
and Tuscany (Chiantis from Rocca delle Macie, Castello
Vicchiomaggio and Antinori, Barbera from Prunotto, Barolo
from Cavalotto and Fontanafredda). Further south, we find the
splendid white Bianco d'Arquata from Adanti (1986 vintage at
£4.45) and Regaleali from Sicily.

Bulgarian wines feature strongly as well, at the usual good-
value prices, with the top quality Controliran wines at £3.35
down to the basic Country Wine range at £2.05. And, on to

71

Spain, where there is a big collection of Riojas from top bodegas such as CVNE and La Rioja Alta and a large Torres offering from the Penedés; a few vintages of Vega Sicilia as well. Portugal has wines from the top two firms of João Pires and J M da Fonseca.

Then we move to the New World, with Australian wines from Penfolds, Rosemount, Brown Brothers and Orlando, while New Zealand has Nobilo and Delegats wines and California a serious selection of famous names (Trefethen, Mondavi, Clos du Bois among them). There are plenty of Champagnes, Ports from Messias, and Madeira from Henriques and Henriques.

Best buys

Jacob's Creek Red and White, Orlando, Australia, £2.99
Côtes du Lubéron, Cellier de Marrenon Blanc, £2.35
Riesling d'Alsace 1987, Cave d'Obernai, £3.29
Ch Bois Malot 1983, Bordeaux Supérieur, £4.29
Montepulciano d'Abruzzo 1987, Umani Ronchi, £2.89
Bulgarian wines
Messias 10-year-old tawny Port, £7.69

Adnams Wine Merchants   ❀ ⊡ ☞ ☆

The Crown, High Street, Southwold, Suffolk IP18 6DP	TEL (0502) 724222
The Cellar & Kitchen Store, Victoria Street, Southwold, Suffolk IP18 6DP	TEL (0502) 724222
The Grapevine, Cellar & Kitchen Store, 109 Unthank Road, Norwich, Norfolk NR2 2PE	TEL (0603) 613998

OPEN (The Crown) Mon–Fri 9–1, 2–5 (mail order); (Cellar & Kitchen Store) Mon–Sat 10–6.30 (Southwold), 9–9 (Norwich)   CLOSED Sun, public holidays   CREDIT CARDS Access, Visa; personal and business accounts   DISCOUNTS 5% on 1 case (min)   DELIVERY Free on UK mainland (min 2 cases); elsewhere at cost; mail order available   GLASS HIRE Free with 1-case order   TASTINGS AND TALKS Up to 30 wines always available for tasting in Southwold store; to groups on request; series of wine breaks in the winter months   CELLARAGE £3.16 per case per year

---

Adnams have become the first wine merchant in the country to charge for their wine list and mail shots. If any wine list is worth it, Adnams' list must qualify as one of the most likely contenders, because not only does it contain one of the best wine ranges in this guide but it also has some of the most interesting comments and information (coupled with a fascinating set of regional recipes) which make it as much a good read as a means of selling wine.

There has been one other change at Adnams this year. They have opened a branch in Norwich which sells the combination of wine and kitchen equipment that has been such a success in their Southwold Cellar and Kitchen store since it opened two years ago.

But in case purchasers of Adnams' wines begin to feel that the wines themselves are taking second place, they can be reassured. What is on offer is still very much the same variety of mainstream classic wines and enthusiasms generated by wine buyer Simon Loftus, which take the list into byways such as Recioto Valpolicellas from Italy, a collection of old Tokays, and a long German list in these days when interest in fine German wines is usually distinctly lacking.

To begin at the beginning, a fine collection of vintage Ports, a short but sound selection of Sherries and a sadly depleted selection of Madeiras makes way for an enormous range from Bordeaux which covers the full price spectrum (look especially for wines from the 1985 vintage) and goes back in years to a couple of representatives from 1978 – strange that a wine merchant of this calibre lists nothing older. On to Burgundy, and here we are in with the great domaine wines with a vengeance: red is marginally more interesting than white.

For many, the Rhône will be the star area. The northern Rhône in particular is very well served, with wines from Guigal, Jaboulet Aîné, Emile Florentin in St-Joseph, Guy de Barjac, Robert Jasmin in Côte Rôtie – in other words the great, good and exciting from around the region. The southern part of the Rhône is surprisingly less well treated. The Loire has as its particular interest the Vouvrays of Foreau and Huet, while Alsace features the wines of P Blanck in profusion. Champagnes are present in reasonable quantity, too, but there is just as much interest in other sparkling wines, such as the Indian Omar Khayyam.

Attention now turns to the range from Italy. This features much of the excitement in wines that this country is currently generating: Valpolicella from Quintarelli, Tiefenbrunner wines from the Südtirol, some very serious Barolos including wines from the late Renato Ratti, Chianti from Castello di Volpaia, Soave from Tedeschi. Spain has offerings which include the much acclaimed Pesquera from Ribera del Duero, while Portugal features wines from J M da Fonseca, and Quinta do Côtto red from the Douro.

Germany still stands strongly in this list, and blazons many famous estate names including Dr Bürklin-Wolf, Deinhard, Friedrich Wilhelm Gymnasium – now at bargain prices simply because there is so little demand. Over in the New World,

California features as strongly as Australia, both offering smaller boutique wines, as well as more famous names (look for instance for Carneros Pinot Noir from Saintsbury in California, or Andrew Mitchell's Shiraz from Clare Valley in South Australia).

Best buys

Domaine de Belvert 1987, Côtes du Vivarais, £3.50
Cuvée Vincent Vin de Table Blanc, £3.85
Gris Fumé, Vin de Pays du Jardin de la France, £3.30
Lieserer Schlossberg Riesking Kabinett 1983, Bischöfliches Priesterseminar, £6.60
Ch du Grand Moulas 1987, Côtes du Rhône, £3.60
Domaine de Limbardie 1988, Vin de Pays des Coteaux de Murviel, £3.40
Martinez Fine Crusted Port, £7.25

James Aitken & Son ✉

53 Perth Road, Dundee DD1 4HY   TEL (0382) 21197

OPEN Mon–Fri 8.30–5.45; Sat 8.30–5   CLOSED Sun, public holidays
CREDIT CARDS None accepted; personal and business accounts
DISCOUNTS 5% on 1 case   DELIVERY Free in city of Dundee and district; otherwise by arrangement; mail order available   GLASS HIRE Free with appropriate order   TASTINGS AND TALKS To groups on request
CELLARAGE Free for wines purchased from premises

France tends to remain the mainstay of this range but there is increasing interest in other wine regions of the world as well. It seems to reflect a careful combination of caution and adventure: caution (in the best sense) in the range of clarets, adventure in the long (well, 12 is long in this context) listing of Greek wines.

France is covered thoroughly. Clarets go back to the odd 1970 wine, with the greatest concentration in 1983 and 1982. In Burgundy, we find a mix of négociant wines (from Faiveley in particular) and domaine wines, with Beaujolais from Georges Duboeuf. The Rhône has wines from Jaboulet Aîné. There is not much of interest on the Loire, but look for the Alsace wines of Dopff et Irion and Dopff au Moulin. French country wines abound, and include Bergerac Blanc from Domaine de Grandchamp, good Corbières from Domaine de St-Maurice (1987 vintage at £3.19) and Ch Aussières (1987 vintage here at £3.29). Pommery is the featured Champagne house.

Germany continues to have a sensible selection of wines from some top estates (look especially for wines from the State Domaine on the Mosel, and Dr Bürklin-Wolf on the Rheinpfalz.

In other European countries, look at the Riojas from Spain (and the wines of Torres) and the attractive set of Italian bottles (Barolos from Fontanafredda, Chianti from Antinori and Rocca delle Macie) – and those Greek wines, which include good things like the wines of Calliga as well as cheap and cheerfuls like Amalia red and white at £2.75.

Elsewhere, Australia has Brown Brothers and Rosemount wines, and New Zealand wines from Montana. There are Mondavi wines from California, and Ch Musar from the Lebanon. Ports have a speciality corner in Dow's tawnies.

Best buys

Valdepeñas Gran Reserva 1978, Señorio de los Llanos, £4.30
Coteaux du Languedoc 1986, Abbaye de Valmagne, £3.80
Barolo 1983, Casa Vinicola Nicolello, £5.80
Ch Rébouquet la Roquette 1985, Première Côtes de Blaye, £4.35
Amalia Red, Greece, £2.75

Alastair's Grapevine

2 Upper Grove Street, Leamington Spa,   TEL (0926) 339032
Warwickshire CV32 5AN

OPEN Mon–Fri 9.30–6.30; Sat 9.30–5.30   CLOSED Sun, public holidays
CREDIT CARDS Access, Visa   DISCOUNTS 5% on 1 case   DELIVERY Free within 35-mile radius (min 2 case); otherwise 1–5 cases £5, 6–10 cases £2.50 per case; mail order available   GLASS HIRE Free with 2-case order (minimum £50 order)   TASTINGS AND TALKS Two main tastings annually; Saturday morning tastings in-store; to groups on request
CELLARAGE Not available

Alastair Macbrayne seems to have a very healthy view of his aims: 'to provide excellence and bring enjoyment of wine to ordinary people so that they are not intimidated by attitudes of people who make out they know more than they do.' He might have been writing about *Which? Wine Guide*.

Certainly his list (which will be even more use when his mail order business starts up early in 1990) is full of encouragement for those who wish to experiment, finishing as it does with the classics of Bordeaux, but starting with basic French vins de table, wines from Greece, and two unusual ranges of wines from Italy (vini da tavola from Sicily at a good-value £2.69 and Friuli wines at under £4).

Under the heading 'Discovering France' Mr Macbrayne introduces us to the delights of the deliciously fruity Sornin Vin de Pays de Charentais (a blend of Merlot and Cabernet Franc), a Sauvignon de St-Bris, and two Burgundies from top Châlonnais producer Emile Voarick (both at under £5). The Bordeaux listing sticks sensibly to middle-priced wines and doesn't attempt the heady heights of classed growths. Alsace wines from Louis Gisselbrecht join some good single domaine Beaujolais, and some rarities from the South-West of France (a sweet white Rosette from the Bergerac area, Ch Puypezat-Rosette 1986 at £4.99).

Outside France, there is yet more interest in the Hunters wines from New Zealand (coupled with examples from Delegats and Brookfields). German producers' names in many cases are still lacking from the list so it is difficult to determine how good the wines are but in Italy there are Franciacorta wines from the Contessa Martinoni and Chiantis from Frescobaldi. A special treat is a big selection of Madeiras from Rutherford & Miles.

Best buys

Franciacorta Rosso 1987, Contessa Martinoni, £3.99
Campo Seco 1985, Jumilla, £2.99
Vin de Pays de Charentais 1988, Sornin, £2.99
Isonzo Pinot Grigio, £3.99
Rutherford & Miles Reserve Madeiras, £7.99

Alba Wine Society

MAIL ORDER
Leet Street, Coldstream, Borders
TD12 4BJ
TEL (0890) 3166

CASE SALES ONLY   OPEN Mon–Fri 8–7   CLOSED Sat, Sun
CREDIT CARDS Access, Visa; personal and business accounts
DISCOUNTS Not available   DELIVERY Free on UK mainland (min 3 cases); £2 for less than 3 cases; £3 to the islands   GLASS HIRE Not available
TASTINGS AND TALKS Tastings and talks given regularly throughout Scotland (charge for samples only)   CELLARAGE £2 per case per year

After a somewhat muddled start with a distinct lack of information for members, the Alba Wine Society now looks as if it is going places as a distinctively Scottish mail order business. Details of membership will be found in the section on FIND OUT MORE ABOUT WINE (page 669).

At first sight the list seems cast in the traditional mould (with, for example, plenty of domaine Burgundies and clarets) but it strikes out in more unusual ways as well, with featured estates or producers. For instance, from Spain there is a wealth of Riojas from CVNE, Penedés wines from René Barbier, Navarra wines from Ochoa and Sherries from Garvey, all listed in depth. From Portugal, there's a delicious-sounding rosé wine (Passal Rosado at £3.20). Producers are featured in Germany, too: Louis Guntrum, Reichsrat von Buhl, Prinz zu Salm-Dalberg in the

Nahe, the estate of Castell in Franconia. Featured producer in
Italy seems to be Frescobaldi, but there are other treats as well
(Chianti from Ripanera, wines from Lungarotti). An interesting
display of Austrian wines makes this merchant the largest seller
of Austrian wines in the Guide, while Hungary provides a
number of great Tokays.

Outside Europe, look for wines from small wineries like
Sanford and Newton in California, and Texas Vineyards. All the
Australian wines come from Brown Brothers, and New Zealand
offers Stoneleigh Vineyards wines.

Best buys

Madiran 1985, Caves Quercynoises, £3.45
René Barbier Tinto 1986, Penedés, £3.25
Vinho Verde Paço de Cardião, £4.95
St Lorenzi Grüner Veltliner, Co-operative of Wachau, £3.95

David Alexander

69 Queen Street, Maidenhead, Berkshire   TEL (0628) 30295
SL6 1LT

OPEN Mon 10–7; Tue–Thur 10–8.30; Fri, Sat 10–9; Sun 12–2   CLOSED Chr
Day, 26 Dec   CREDIT CARDS All accepted; personal and business
accounts   DISCOUNTS 5% on 1 case   DELIVERY Free locally and along M4
corridor (min 1 case); mail order available   GLASS HIRE Free with order
TASTINGS AND TALKS By invitation to customers on mailing list (every 8–10
weeks); to groups on request   CELLARAGE £5 per case per year

This continues to be a wide-ranging list, touching on most areas
of the wine world, with Australia and New Zealand the star
areas.

For instance, in Australia we find wines from Lindemans, the
superbly old-fashioned wines of Ch Tahbilk (Shiraz 1985 at
£4.99), Rothbury, Brown Brothers, Rosemount, Cape Mentelle,
Pirramimma – a mix of smaller and larger firms. The same is
true in California, where Monticello, Clos du Val and Buena
Vista are listed together with the highly-reputed wines from the
Jordan winery in Sonoma.

The French collection consists of a rather pricy set of clarets
and Burgundies from négociants (Moillard, Labouré-Roi,
Delaunay); Délas wines represent the Rhône, and Guy Saget the
Loire. Germany offers very little (and no producers' names),
while Italy has Chianti from Pagliarese and Valpolicella from
Tedeschi (and a similar paucity of producer information). Spain
features Torres wines, and Portugal those of J M da Fonseca.

Best buys

Ch Tahbilk Shiraz 1985, Victoria, Australia, £4.99
Domaine du Bosquet Canet Cabernet Sauvignon 1985, £4
Chablis 1987, Geoffroy, £5.99

H Allen Smith

24–25 Scala Street, London W1P 1LU — TEL 01–637 4767
56 Lamb's Conduit Street, London WC1N 3LW — TEL 01–405 3106
29 Heath Street, London NW3 6TR — TEL 01–435 6845

OPEN Mon–Fri 9.30–6.30 (W1), 9–7 (WC1), Mon–Sat 10–8 (NW3); Sat 10–1 (W1 & WC1)   CLOSED Sun, public holidays   CREDIT CARDS All accepted; personal and business accounts   DISCOUNTS 5% on 1 case (if payment is by cash or cheque)   DELIVERY Free in central London (min 1 case); otherwise 1 case £7.50, 2–5 cases £4.50 per case, 6–10 cases £3.15 per case; mail order available   GLASS HIRE Free with 1-case order
TASTINGS AND TALKS Regular quarterly tastings in-store, evening tastings at each branch; wine school at Scala Street branch; to groups on request   CELLARAGE Available

This is the firm that regularly gives us the year's first 'new wine' – the Early Bird red and white from Hardy's in Australia (the white is generally better than the red). It's also the firm that imports the splendid wines of J M da Fonseca in Portugal, Tiefenbrunner wines from Italy and Reichsrat von Buhl wines from Germany.

That is quite a good start. But H Allen Smith have also been concentrating more on France in the past couple of years, and their listing from that country is now quite extensive. They have a few country wines (including a good Ch La Baronne from Corbières at £3.35), but their main thrust has been on Bordeaux, with a selection, mainly of finer wines, which they have sensibly divided into wines for drinking now and wines for laying down. We can recommend their house Champagne (La Justice Brut at £9.95), as well as the Hardy's sparkling wines from Australia (Grand Reserve Brut at £6.25) and the Cava from Cavas Hill in Penedés.

H Allen Smith have made something of a speciality of the Iberian peninsula, and their range has interest both from Spain (with Monte Ory wines from Navarra, Valdepeñas Viña Albali and the Cabernet Sauvignon of Marqués de Griñon) and from Portugal (with wines from João Pires as well as J M da Fonseca and Champalimaud in the Douro). In Italy, the star producers are Tiefenbrunner, Castello di San Polo in Rosso in Tuscany, and Aldo Conterno in Piedmont (look for his Barbera d'Alba 1985 at £6.95).

From Australia, the Hardy range also includes the wines of its consultant winemaker Geoff Merrill as well as top names like the Shiraz Nottage Hill (1985 vintage at £4.65), and wines from the Ch Reynella estate in South Australia.

Best buys

Marqués de Gastanaga 1988, Valdepeñas, £2.80
Santa Marta 1988, Alentejo, João Pires, £3.35
Gamay d'Auvergne 1987, £2.45
Hardy's Premium Classic White, South Australia, £4.25
Delamonte Cava Brut, £4.65
Ch Pigoudet 1985, Coteaux d'Aix-en-Provence, £4.25

Les Amis du Vin

MAIL ORDER ONLY
19 Charlotte Street,   TEL 01–636 4020
London W1P 1HB
SHOPS
The Winery, 4 Clifton Road, London   TEL 01–286 6475
W9 1SS
Les Amis du Vin, 51 Chiltern Street,   TEL 01–487 3419
London W1M 1HQ

OPEN Mon–Fri 10.30–8.30 (W9), 10.30–7 (W1); Sat 10–6.30 (W9), 10.30–5 (W1) CLOSED Sun, public holidays CREDIT CARDS All accepted; personal and business accounts DISCOUNTS 5% for unmixed cases DELIVERY Free in London (min 1 case) and elsewhere (min 2 cases or orders of £75+); mail order at 19 Charlotte Street GLASS HIRE Free with case order from shops only TASTINGS AND TALKS Monthly tastings through Les Amis Wine Club CELLARAGE £4.75 per case per year

Since the link-up with Christopher and Co, the Les Amis du Vin list has taken on the best aspects of both businesses, so you get a greatly enhanced range of French wines (the Christopher contribution) coupled with treasure troves from California and Australia.

While there is a useful range of clarets from vintages of the 1980s (which mainly concentrates on classed growths), there are also some interesting sweet white Bordeaux (look for the old vintages of Ch Gilette (1950 at £34.99 a bottle). In Burgundy, Ropiteau Frères is the main supplier of wines, but there are also domaine wines from Leflaive and Marcel Vincent in Pouilly Fuissé. As so often, red Burgundy is more interesting than white.

While the Loire sparkles only with wines from Marc Brédif, the Rhône shines with Guigal and Ch de Beaucastel, and there's more in the French regions (Vin de Pays des Collines Rhodaniennes 1986 – a blend of Marsanne and Roussanne – is £3.05, and the wines of La Vieille Ferme feature strongly).

In Italy, the featured producer is Frescobaldi, whose wines are represented by Christopher and Co in Britain, but there are also wines from a number of top producers round the country (influenced by the fact that one of the major Italian importers is an associate company of Les Amis du Vin). Spain offers Torres and Marqués de Riscal, while much further afield Chilean wines come from Cousiño Macul.

And so to the star areas of Australia and California, for which another associate of Les Amis du Vin is the importer. We find from California Mondavi, Clos du Bois, Ch St Jean, Acacia, Heitz Cellars, Chalone Vineyards, Joseph Phelps, Firestone – and many more. And in Australia the list includes Yalumba, Rothbury, Petaluma, Pewsey Vale and Bannockburn.

Best buys

Campo ai Sassi 1985, Rosso di Montalcino, £5.12
Sancerre Blanc 1987, Michel Thomas, £6.20
Pewsey Vale Rhine Riesling 1985, Australia, £4.49
Chardonnay 1987, Edna Valley Vineyards, California, £8.50
Blanquette de Limoux Fleur de Lys, £6.25

John Armit Wines

190 Kensington Park Road, London W11 2ES   TEL 01–727 6846

NORTHERN OFFICE, The Imperial Centre, Grange Road, Darlington, Co Durham DL1 5JG   TEL (0325) 381478

CASE SALES ONLY   OPEN Mon–Fri 9–5.30   CLOSED Sat, Sun, public holidays   CREDIT CARDS None accepted; personal and business accounts   DISCOUNTS Not available   DELIVERY Free for 3+ cases; mail order available   GLASS HIRE Not available   TASTINGS AND TALKS Tastings held 2–3 times annually; to groups on request   CELLARAGE £4 per case (inc insurance)

A brand new company, set up by John Armit, who was long associated with Corney & Barrow (see separate entry), and who did much to pioneer the way for the wines of Pomerol in this country. He has produced a list heavily weighted in favour of France (with, incidentally, some startling illustrations), which homes in on the finer wines from classic areas.

There is, therefore, considerable representation from the areas of Bordeaux which Mr Armit knows well – Pomerol and more recently Fronsac. But there are also wines from the Médoc, mainly of classed growths. For such a new company, such a quantity of mature wines from the 1978 vintage is a matter for congratulation.

In Burgundy, they have gone for domaine wines, and have focused on certain estates such as Olivier Leflaive, Domaine Dujac and Trapet, with a few wines from négociant Faiveley. Little is cheap here, but prices are reasonably competitive. In other areas of France, there is a small selection from Sancerre, much more from the Rhône (with wines from Guigal, Jaboulet Aîné), and Châteauneuf-du-Pape from Domaine de la Roquette. Alsace wines come from André Kientzler.

Outside France, there are small nods in the direction of California (Clos Pegase, a small winery in the Napa Valley), Oregon (Eyrie Vineyards), Australia (Cape Mentelle and Hardys) and Spain (Pesquera Ribera del Duero).

Best buys

Ch Hervé Laroque 1986, Fronsac, £4
Pinot Blanc d'Alsace Domaine des Loups, £4.17
Bourgogne Blanc Les Setilles, Olivier Leflaive 1987, £5.42
Ch Pitray 1986, Côtes de Castillon, £4.08

Arriba Kettle

MAIL ORDER ONLY
Buckle Street, Honeybourne,
Nr Evesham, Hereford & Worcester
WR11 5QB

TEL (0386) 833024
(24-hour telephone
answering service)

CASE SALES ONLY   OPEN 24-hour telephone answering service
CREDIT CARDS None accepted; business accounts DISCOUNTS From £1.50 on 3 cases to £2.75 on 11+ cases; £1 per case collected DELIVERY Free on UK mainland (min 2 cases) GLASS HIRE Free in West Midlands, north Cotswolds and Central London TASTINGS AND TALKS For mail order customers in November held in Birmingham and north Cotswolds; to groups on request CELLARAGE Not available

---

This is a list that stays almost entirely in Spain, with a particular concentration on the wines of Rioja. Owner Barry Kettle imports a number of Riojas directly, including Cosecheros Alavesas (the basic Rioja Tinto Artadi at £3.49 is worth considering), Martinez Bujanda, a family-owned bodega in Haro and the small bodega of Viña Salceda (Viña Salceda 1985 at £4.63). There are plenty of other Riojas in the list, including wines from Bodegas Bilbainas and La Rioja Alta.

Outside Rioja, interest centres on Penedés, with wines from Manuel Sancho (who also make the Cavas on the list) and

81

Torres. There are also wines from Señorio de Sarria in Navarra and from the co-operative of Ribera del Duero, plus almacenista Sherries from Lustau, a few Ports and – a new departure – Babich wines from New Zealand.

Best buys

Rioja Artadi Tinto 1988, Cosecheros Alavesas, £3.49
Mont Marçal Brut Cava, £5.41
Valdepeñas Señorio de los Llanos Gran Reserva 1978, £4.13
Amontillado Fino de Jerez, Almacenista Dr Faustino Gonzalez Aparicio, £7.80

Asda

HEAD OFFICE
Asda House, South Bank, Great Wilson Street, Leeds, West Yorkshire LS11 5AD   TEL (0532) 435435/ 418047
130 licensed branches nationwide

OPEN (Generally) Mon–Sat 9–8   CLOSED Sun, public holidays (vary from store to store)   CREDIT CARDS Access, Visa   DISCOUNTS, DELIVERY, GLASS HIRE Not available   TASTINGS AND TALKS Regular in-store tastings of promotional lines   CELLARAGE Not available

There's a two-tier selection in operation at this chain of supermarkets. While all the stores stock wines from the main own-label list, larger stores also carry a selection of fine wines displayed on special racks.

The standard range, while covering most areas briefly, does have some interesting concentrations, such as plenty of vins de pays from France (all excellent value at under £2), a good set of wines from the South of France (including bottles from more unusual areas such as St-Chinian in the Midi), a number of the good-value wines from Bulgaria, and two terrific Australians (Shiraz/Cabernet Sauvignon at £2.75; Rhine Riesling at £2.35).

On the Fine Wine list, there is a particularly strong showing of Champagnes, some very classy clarets, mainly négociant wines from Burgundy (including those from Jaboulet-Vercherre and Antonin Rodet), a most impressive set of dessert wines (try a half-bottle of Andrew Quady's Essensia, an Orange Muscat wine from California at £4.99). Serious things crop up in Italy (Brunello di Montalcino Val di Suga 1981 is £7.99), next to Montana wines from New Zealand and some Mondavis from California. More good Australian value is to be found with the Orlando Cabernet Sauvignon 1986 at £4.55.

Best buys

Vin de Pays des Côtes de Gascogne, Asda, £1.99
Côtes de Duras, Asda, £2.19
St-Chinian, Asda, £2.45
Cava, Asda, £3.95
Australian Shiraz/Cabernet Sauvignon, Asda, £2.75

Ashley Scott

See under Scott.

Askham Wines

Askham, via Newark, Notts NG22 0RP   TEL (077 783) 659

CASE SALES ONLY   OPEN Mon–Fri 9–6; Sat 9–12   CLOSED Sun, public
holidays   CREDIT CARDS None accepted; business accounts
DISCOUNTS Occasionally to businesses   DELIVERY Free on mainland UK
(min £50 order); mail order available   GLASS HIRE Free with 1-case
order   TASTINGS AND TALKS Two main tastings a year; to groups on
request   CELLARAGE Not available

A workmanlike range of wines, of which shortness on quantity
is made up for by the quality of each wine. The list starts firmly
in France, but there are treats from right round the world.

Those treats include a very interesting collection of wines
from smaller wineries in California (Stag's Leap, Hawk Crest,
Round Hill, Cuvaison), Washington State (Snoqualmie and
Salishan Vineyards) and Idaho (Rose Creek Vineyard). Also in
the New World, look for Rouge Homme wines from Coonawarra
in Australia and Delegats wines from New Zealand.

In France, we find that it is the regions, as much as the classic
areas, which give the satisfaction. For instance, there are the
Val-Joanis wines from the Côtes du Lubéron, Touraine wines
from the Confrérie des Vignerons at Oisly-et-Thésée, wines
from Jaboulet Aîné on the Rhône and Alsace wines from Zind-
Humbrecht, and the co-operative of Turckheim.

In Bordeaux, there is a good price spread across recent
vintages (back to 1978), while in Burgundy, it is Chablis which
offers the most interest. Champagnes come from the small house
of Billecart-Salmon, and there are Sherries from Gil Luque and
Hidalgo, with Ports from Churchill.

Best buys

Ch Val-Joanis 1986, Côtes du Lubéron, £4.17
Vin de Pays des Côtes de Gascogne, Cépage Colombard,
Producteurs Plaimont, £2.78

Hawks Crest Cabernet Sauvignon 1985, Napa Valley (California), £5.94
Dry Moscato Palmela 1987, João Pires, £3.79

Averys of Bristol

7 Park Street, Bristol, Avon BS1 5NG   TEL (0272) 214141

OPEN Mon–Fri 9–6; Sat 9–5   CLOSED Sun, public holidays
CREDIT CARDS Access, Visa; personal and business accounts
DISCOUNTS Available   DELIVERY Free on UK mainland (min 1 case within 5-mile radius of Bristol, 2 cases elsewhere); otherwise £5.50 for under 2 cases; £5 per case for Isle of Wight, Orkney and Shetland; mail order available   GLASS HIRE Free with £15+ order (with refundable deposit)
TASTINGS AND TALKS Regional tastings through Avery Bin Club; to groups on request   CELLARAGE £2.50 per case or part-case per year

A major change at this traditional wine merchant over the past two years has been its diversification into what the wine trade calls 'agency business'. This means that many of the wines they sell are bought direct from the producers. They also act as agents by selling the wines on to other merchants.

One of Averys' most interesting agencies is for the Madeiras of Cossart Gordon, and they now list a good selection of this producer's five- and ten-year-old Reserves and 15-year-old Exceptional Reserves. In France, they act as agents for the wines of Remoissenet in Burgundy, for Ch Bonnet in Beaujolais (Beaujolais Villages 1987 at £4.76), for Domaine Jacques Morin in Bourgueil and Chinon, and for Ch de la Tuilerie in Costières du Gard.

But there are many other French wines to consider. A particular strength is the range from Bordeaux, with vintages back to 1970 (limited supplies of these, we are told), but equal interest can be found in Burgundy, where négociant wines are much to the fore (as well as Averys' own bottlings, which often represent very good value for money). Other areas of France are less well served, although the wines from the co-operative of Ribeauvillé in Alsace are worth looking out for.

Beyond Europe, Australia offers wines from Tim Knappstein, Rouge Homme and Tyrrells (also try the Liqueur Muscats from Chambers in Rutherglen). There is a complete range of Nobilo wines from New Zealand, and a wide-ranging collection of wines from a number of smaller boutique wineries in California (Alexander Valley, Freemark Abbey, Rutherford Hill and Sonoma-Cutrer). Averys also represent the wines from the Inniskillin Winery at Niagara in Canada, regarded as one of the best wineries in that country at the moment. Look, too, for the traditionally produced Undurraga wines of Chile.

Best buys

Rouge Homme Shiraz/Cabernet 1984, Australia, £5.12
Viña Undurraga Cabernet Sauvignon 1987, Chile, £3.38
Ch de la Tuilerie 1987, Costières du Gard Rouge, £3.88
Domaine de Baudare, Vin de Pays du Comté Tolosan 1986, £3.11
Trier St Mattheiser Riesling Spätlese, Max Erben 1983, £4.36
White Cloud Müller-Thurgau, Nobilo, New Zealand, £3.97

David Baillie Vintners   ▱ ☞ ☆

At the Sign of the Lucky Horseshoe,   TEL (0392) 221345
86 Longbrook Street, Exeter, Devon EX4 6AP

OPEN Mon–Sat 9–6   CLOSED Sun, public holidays   CREDIT CARDS Access,
Visa; personal and business accounts   DISCOUNTS Available (min 2
cases)   DELIVERY Free on UK mainland (min 2 cases); otherwise at cost;
mail order available   GLASS HIRE Free with order
TASTINGS AND TALKS Talks for diploma courses held at local college; to
groups on request   CELLARAGE £2.87 per case per year

In this interesting and traditional list, it is the classic areas of
France that fare best (with exceptions such as the wines from
the Pacific North-West of the United States). Clarets go back to
1975, with the biggest concentrations in 1985; in Burgundy, it is
domaines such as Tollot-Beaut, Jean Monnier, Jacques Germain
and Henri Clerc which dominate the (in-depth) list, and there
are smaller selections from the Rhône and the Loire.

Outside France, look for German estate wines, an increasing
interest in Italy (especially in Tuscany with fine wines from
Castello Vicchiomaggio and Antinori), while in Spain the stars
are Riojas from CVNE.

When we get to the New World, the traditional mould cracks
to let in a big range of wines from Washington State (Columbia
Crest, Ch Ste Michelle and Farron Ridge). In Australia, there is a
good spread of estate wines (Jim Barry in Clare, Rothbury Estate
and St Huberts in the Yarra Valley). Other areas of interest
include the Madeiras of Cossart Gordon and the vintage Ports.

Look also for special offers such as en primeur wines from
Bordeaux, and Sauternes and German wines.

Best buys

Galestro 1988, Antinori, £3.89
Merlot Val d'Orbieu, £2.91
Fumé Blanc 1985, Ch Ste Michelle, Washington State, £3.89
Manzanilla Pasada de Sanlúcar, Herederos Argueso, almacenista,
£6.33

Ballantynes of Cowbridge

MAIL ORDER
Stallcourt House, Llanblethian,
Cowbridge, South Glamorgan CF7 7JU

TEL (04463) 3044

CASE SALES ONLY   OPEN 24-hour answering service   CREDIT CARDS None
accepted; personal and business accounts   DISCOUNTS Not available
DELIVERY At cost   GLASS HIRE, TASTINGS AND TALKS Not available
CELLARAGE Approximately £3.45 per case per year (in bond)

This is a serious fine wine list, concentrating on Bordeaux and
Burgundy and featuring rare bottles of old vintages, as well as
larger collections from more recent years. So a recent list offered
us 1929 Ch Lafite Rothschild at £378 for the bottle, moving
down to earth (in their terms) with a single bottle of Ch Canon
1985 at £185, in between covering most of the great and some of
the useful vintages.

Similar riches are apparent in Burgundy, although here, on
the recent list, reds started in 1945 and whites in 1973. There are
a few interests from other regions of France, the Rhône in
particular as well as sweet white Bordeaux. Vintage Ports and
Champagnes come as no surprise. Bear in mind that such a list
changes constantly as stocks are always very limited.

Best buys

Rare and old wines

Balls Brothers ☆

Balls Brothers Wine Centre,
313 Cambridge Heath Road,
London E2 9LQ

TEL 01–739 6466

OPEN Mon–Sat 10–6   CLOSED Sun, public holidays   CREDIT CARDS Access,
Visa   DISCOUNTS Not available   DELIVERY Free on UK mainland (min 2
cases); mail order available   GLASS HIRE Free (4 glasses per bottle
purchased)   TASTINGS AND TALKS Annual tasting for regular customers;
tastings for groups of 20+ by arrangement   CELLARAGE £1.80 per case
per year

This traditional City wine merchant also runs wine bars. But
forget the image that this conjures up of pinstripes and a list
composed entirely of claret and Burgundy.

There *are* clarets (with a good selection back to 1977, and with
strong points in the mid-price range of the 1985 and 1983
vintages), and Burgundies (mainly from négociants such as
Faiveley, Chanson, Louis Latour and Mommessin), but also
Beaujolais from Loron and Sarrau. And while the Loire is dull,

there is interest from the Rhône with a good set of wines from producers such as Guigal, Jaboulet Aîné and Ch du Grand Moulas. Alsace offers wines from Blanck and the Midi and Provence come up with a useful range.

But even outside France there is considerable interest: see for instance the interesting Italian section (Chianti from Castello Vicchiomaggio and Frescobaldi, plus Orvieto from Antinori and Brunello di Montalcino of Castelgiocondo). From Spain, there is Remelluri Rioja and Viña Ardanza of La Rioja Alta. Germany suffers from a common problem among wine merchants – no producers' names. Outside Europe, look for Lebanese wines from Ch Musar, Australian wine from Tyrrell and Chilean bottles from Concha y Toro.

Best buys

Ch du Grand Moulas 1987, Côtes du Rhône, £3.85
Ch de Brondeau 1986, Bordeaux Supérieur, £3.90
Concha y Toro Cabernet Sauvignon 1984, Chile, £3.60
Ch Moulin de Launay 1987, Entre-Deux-Mers, £3.30
Gold Cap, Very Fine Old Tawny Port, £8.75

Adam Bancroft Associates   ✉

Gresham House, 4–7 Great Pulteney   TEL 01–434 9919
Street, London W1R 3DF

CASE SALES ONLY   OPEN Mon–Fri 9.30–6   CLOSED Sat, Sun, public holidays   CREDIT CARDS None accepted; personal and business accounts DISCOUNTS Not available   DELIVERY Free within London (min 1 case) and within UK (min 3 cases); otherwise 2 cases £8.05, 1 case £5.75; mail order available   GLASS HIRE Free   TASTINGS AND TALKS Irregular tastings 2–3 times per year; to groups on request   CELLARAGE Possible

This is a fascinating list. It is chosen, as Adam Bancroft describes it, on the basis of quality, regardless of whether the choices actually produce a balanced whole. It leads to some curiously satisfying results.

For instance, 11 red wines from the Loire are listed, a region much more familiar to us for whites (of which Adam Bancroft lists only nine). Of those reds, the Bourgueils of Boucard and the Chinon of Michel Page are fine examples of the appellation.

Though the list is French throughout, it avoids the biggest regions – Bordeaux, the South of France, Provence – completely. Rather, the range is chosen from the Loire (as we have seen), Champagne, Burgundy and Beaujolais.

In Burgundy, Michel Barat is the supplier of Chablis, while Jean-Luc Joillot is the name connected with Beaune and Pommard; there's also Pouilly-Fuissé from Michel Forest. And from Beaujolais, look for the wines of a whole clutch of estates, which, like every other wine in this list, are otherwise unavailable in this country.

Best buys

Sauvignon de Touraine 1987, Alain Marcadet, £3.45
St-Nicolas de Bourgueil 1987, Claude Vallée, £4.54
Bourgogne Clos de Chenoves 1986, Noël Perrin, £6.04
St-Véran 1987, Domaine des Deux Roches, £5.69

Nigel Baring

20 Ranston Street, London NW1 6SY — TEL 01–724 0836

CASE SALES ONLY   OPEN Mon–Fri 9–5   CLOSED Sat, Sun, public holidays
CREDIT CARDS None accepted; personal and business accounts
DISCOUNTS 2.5% on minimum quantity of £5,000   DELIVERY £1 per case in London (min £5), £3 per case outside London (min £10) plus VAT; mail order available   GLASS HIRE Not available   TASTINGS AND TALKS Major classified claret vertical tasting held; to groups on request   CELLARAGE £4 per case per year

This firm deals mainly with fine clarets and Burgundy, and makes regular offers of claret en primeur. But there are a few other areas of interest as well. Look for a selection of top quality Italian wines from producers like Antinori, Bruno Ceretto, Gaja, Castello Vicchiomaggio. Also look for vintage Ports, some vintage Champagnes and an unusual set of early landed Cognacs (Cognacs which are shipped in cask, matured in England and then bottled after some years – English maturation is supposed to change the taste, some say to improve it).

Best buys

Fine clarets and Burgundies

Barnes Wine Shop

51 Barnes High Street, London — TEL 01–878 8643
SW13 9LN

OPEN Mon–Sat 9.30–8.30; Sun 12–2   CLOSED Public holidays
CREDIT CARDS Access, Visa; personal and business accounts
DISCOUNTS 5% on 1 case; larger discounts for larger orders   DELIVERY Free in London (min 1 case); otherwise £4.80 for 1 case up to £14.25 for 5 cases; mail order available   GLASS HIRE Free with wine order
TASTINGS AND TALKS In-store tastings available daily; organised Saturday tasting four times a year; Barnes Wine Festival held May/June; to groups on request   CELLARAGE £2.60 per case per year

A simple-looking shop it may be, tucked tidily into Barnes High Street in south-west London. But Barnes Wine Shop continues to expand its list, so that it is now a highly sophisticated range of wines, where each bottle makes itself felt. While there may not be much under £3.50, the quality of wines at around the £4 to £5 mark is extremely high. The list is sensibly arranged by country within colour – white wines first.

Australia first, where a range from many small, top class estates as well as some more familiar names such as Rosemount and Wynns are brought together. Although France comes next, it is relatively overshadowed by the wines from countries like Italy (look for the Friuli wines of Jermann or the excellent value of the Bardolino of Ca' Bordenis (1986 vintage at £3.99), or by the splendid set of wines from Ch Musar in the Lebanon (vintages back to 1961 at a modest £13.95 for a half-bottle of such quality). There's much pleasure to be had, too, from the California wines – look, for instance, for the the wines of the small ZD Winery in Napa, or the inexpensive range from Glen Ellen in Sonoma (Merlot 1986 at £4.39).

In France itself, interest centres on the Alsace wines from the Turckheim co-operative, a sensible mid-priced set of clarets, and on a splendid range of Champagnes. And don't forget one of the most enticing collections of pudding wines offered by any wine merchant.

Best buys

Ch de Lastours 1986, Corbières, £3.99
Tokay Pinot Gris 1987, Cave Vinicole de Turckheim, £3.95
Casato Bianco, Rocca delle Macie, £3.45
Ch Laurette 1986, Sauternes, £4.79
Bleasdale Verdelho, 6 years old, £7.95
Ch Musar 1970, Lebanon, £19.50
Rioja 1987, Viña Cumbrero, £3.65

Augustus Barnett

HEAD OFFICE
North Woolwich Road, Silvertown,   TEL 01–476 1477
London E16 2BN
641 Branches nationwide

OPEN Varies from store to store; most outlets open 10–10 on weekdays
CREDIT CARDS Access, American Express, Visa; personal and business
accounts DISCOUNTS Available on non-promoted lines DELIVERY Free
from selected outlets (dependent on size of order) GLASS HIRE Free with
large orders TASTINGS AND TALKS Monthly tastings in selected stores; to
groups on request CELLARAGE Not available

Radical changes in the quality of the wines offered by this national group of off-licences, prompted by the appointment of a Master of Wine as wine buyer, have led to the beginning of the restoration of Augustus Barnett to the position they once occupied when they were owned by the eponymous Mr Barnett.

Then they were the source of amazing bargains as well as some parcels of fine wines. Now they are the place where you can buy a rapidly improving all-round range, which perhaps still includes some tired old warhorses, but also has room for some good representatives of the world's wines.

The list is not long – not necessarily a bad sign. But we find, for instance, some well-chosen clarets which occupy the mid-price range very satisfactorily, alongside a less impressive set of Burgundies (mainly from the Beaujolais négociant firm of Pasquier-Desvignes). On the Loire, there are some treats among some rather dull wines – try the Sancerre Les Montachins 1988 of Fouassier Père et Fils at £5.49 or the Muscadet Ch de la Ragotière at £4.29. Delas Frères supply Châteauneuf-du-Pape at £6.49, and the Cave Coopérative de Ribeauvillé produce the Alsace wines. The other French regions offer such treats as Mas de la Dame from Coteaux des Baux-en-Provence (1987 vintage at £3.49), as well as an unusual Madiran, Prestige de Gascogne (1986 vintage at £3.59).

While Germany is still stuck in the Liebfraumilch era, Italy is progressing, with wines from Lageder in the Südtirol, and Villa Banfi's Rosso di Montalcino. Spain has the excellent value Rioja of Campo Viejo as well as Ribera del Duero wines from Peñalba. There are a couple of wines from J M da Fonseca in Portugal.

When we move to the New World, there are more treats. Glen Ellen produces some good, mid-priced California wines (Cabernet 1987 at £3.99), while in Australia, there's Jacob's Creek red and white, Wolf Blass, Penfolds and Lindemans wines. From New Zealand come the Montana wines.

Best buys

Glen Ellen Cabernet Sauvignon 1987, California, £3.99
Montepulciano d'Abruzzo 1987, Tollo, £2.79
Peñalba 1985, Ribera del Duero, £3.99
Listel Gris de Gris, Vin de Pays des Sables du Golfe du Lion, £2.99

Special awards

is for bargain prices   is for a very good range of wines

is for high quality wines   is for exceptional service

Barwell & Jones ☆

HEAD OFFICE
24 Fore Street, Ipswich, Suffolk IP4 1JU   TEL (0473) 231723
OFF-LICENCES
118 Sprowston Road, Norwich, Norfolk   TEL (0603) 484966
NR3 4QH
70 Trumpington Street, Cambridge,   TEL (0223) 354431
Cambridgeshire CB2 1RJ
3 Redenhall Road, Harleston, Norfolk   TEL (0379) 852243
IP20 9EN
The Cross Inn, 2 Church Street,   TEL (03943) 3288
Woodbridge, Suffolk IP12 1DH
94 Rushmere Road, Ipswich, Suffolk   TEL (0473) 727426
IP4 4JL

OPEN Hours vary from branch to branch   CREDIT CARDS Access, Visa;
personal and business accounts   DISCOUNTS Available   DELIVERY Free
locally; elsewhere charges negotiable; mail order available
GLASS HIRE Free with case order   TASTINGS AND TALKS To groups on
request by arrangement with individual managers   CELLARAGE Not
available

This small group of shops is now owned by the Whyte &
Mackay Scotch whisky firm, and it is early days to know
whether the new owners will be making any changes.

At the moment, the list is strong on wines that the firm
imports direct, such as the organic Veneto wines of Guerrieri-
Rizzardi in Italy, Burgundies from Jaboulet Vercherre and
Coron, Alsace wines from Pierre Sparr, the Muscadet of
Domaine des Dorices, the wines of Domaine Sarda-Malet in
Côtes du Roussillon, and Riojas of Bodegas Montecillo (Viña
Cumbrero Tinto 1985 at £4.38).

But there are also plenty of clarets from vintages of the mid-
1980s, a few Australian wines (look for the Middlebrook wines
from McLaren Vale), domaine Burgundies, Ports from Burmester
(another firm whose wines they import) and Barolos from
Giacosa Bruno.

Best buys

Vacqueyras Domaine de la Brunely 1986, £4.56
Ch Cantegrive 1986, Côtes de Castillon, £4.44
Chiarretto del Garda Classico 1988, Guerrieri-Rizzardi, £3.93
Rioja Montecillo Cumbrero 1985, Bodegas Montecillo, £4.38

Please write to tell us about any ideas for features you would like to see
in next year's edition or in *Which? Wine Monthly*.

The Battersea Wine Company

4 Battersea Rise, London SW11 1ED   TEL 01–924 3631

OPEN Mon–Fri 12–9; Sat 10.30–9; Sun 12–2, 7–10, public holidays 12–9
CLOSED Christmas   CREDIT CARDS Access, Visa; personal and business
accounts   DISCOUNTS Up to 10% on 1 case (may be mixed)
DELIVERY Free in Battersea, Clapham, Wandsworth, Fulham, Chelsea and
City (min 1 case); elsewhere £5 per case for 1–4 cases   GLASS HIRE Free
with 1-case order   TASTINGS AND TALKS Monthly tastings held in
basement function room; Battersea Wine Appreciation Course (10 two-
hour sessions, cost £150); to groups on request   CELLARAGE Not available

A new company and a new entrant to the Guide, the Battersea
Wine Company's list is helpfully divided into red and white
(with a few rosé wines in the middle), and offers a careful
balance between France and the rest of the world.

Thus, although there are sound selections of claret (including
a goodly number of wines from vintages of the 1970s) and a
sensible selection of domaine wines from Burgundy, the balance
within France takes in a useful section of everyday drinking
wines (La Vieille Ferme Côtes du Lubéron white or the red
Faugères from Val d'Orbieu are good examples). This section of
everyday wines also includes a range from around the world,
such as Bulgarian wines and a good simple quaffing Rioja
(Señor Burges 1985 at £3.10) and a white from the Valdadige in
northern Italy (Valdadige Bianco Delle Torre 1987 at £2.95).

Outside France, the offerings continue to strike a good price
balance. There are Chilean wines at under £4 (from Torres and
Viña Linderos), more serious wines from Australia and
California (including the fabled Dominus of Christian Moueix at
£39.50 per bottle for the 1984 vintage). And to round off the
collection are various dessert wines, from inexpensive Croix du
Mont to Ch d'Yquem 1976 at £110 a bottle (and including halves
of many of the wines – not the Yquem).

Best buys

Viña Linderos Cabernet Sauvignon 1983, Chile, £3.75
Valpolicella Classico Superiore Vigneti di Marano 1985, £4.27
Faugères Etiquette d'Argent, Val d'Orbieu 1986, £2.70
Sauvignon de Touraine, Guy Saget 1987, £3.35
Verbesco 1987, Duca d'Asti, £3.99

Prices are only a rough indication, and were current in summer 1989.

Thomas Baty & Sons

See Willoughbys.

Benson Fine Wines

96 Ramsden Road, London SW12 8QZ   TEL 01–673 4439

OPEN Mon–Fri 10–6   CLOSED Sat, Sun, public holidays
CREDIT CARDS None accepted; personal and business accounts
DISCOUNTS Not available   DELIVERY Free in London; elsewhere at cost
GLASS HIRE Not available   TASTINGS AND TALKS To groups on request;
Wine & Dine Society   CELLARAGE Not available

'We specialise in fine, rare and obscure wines,' writes owner
Clare Benson. This is where to come if you are looking for 1874
Ch Lafite in a Scottish bottling; or 1928 Louis Roederer vintage
Champagne; or pre-first-world-war vintages of red Burgundy; or
1912 Taylors Port. And, considering the obscure, how about a
1930 red wine, Nectar Pierides from Nicosia in Cyprus? The list
just describes it as 'very rare': we believe it.

Best buys

Rare and old wines

Bentalls of Kingston

Wood Street, Kingston upon Thames,   TEL 01–546 1001
Surrey KT1 1TX

OPEN Mon–Wed, Fri 9–5.30; Thur 9–9; Sat 9–6   CLOSED Sun, public
holidays (except Good Friday)   CREDIT CARDS Access, Bentalls Privilege
Chargecard, American Express, Visa; personal and business accounts
DISCOUNTS 5% on 1 case   DELIVERY Free anywhere on UK mainland for
Bentalls Privilege Chargecard (min 1 bottle), otherwise south-west
London and Surrey (min £10); elsewhere at cost; mail order available
GLASS HIRE Free   TASTINGS AND TALKS Bentalls Wine Fair in May and
November; Bentalls Privilege Wine Club; to groups on request
CELLARAGE Not available

Optimistic signs are emerging from this department store. Their
list, which had threatened to shrink almost to nothing, has been
expanding again. And a refurbishment programme for the
whole store promises a splendid new wine department in the
summer of 1990.
    The first sign of expansion is in the wide range of
Champagnes, which includes many grande marque brands, as
well as wines from smaller houses such as Jacques Selosse and
Barancourt. If Champagne is not what is wanted, there is a good

selection of sparkling wines, including the unusual but good Omar Khayyam from India, and the more familiar Freixenet Cava from Spain.

There is a well-balanced list of clarets (starting at £2.95 and going up to £63), but a small, rather disappointing selection of mainly négociant Burgundy. As compensation, there is plenty to interest among the Beaujolais cru wines. More disappointments on the Rhône and Loire, but, again, compensations in Alsace with wines from Louis Gisselbrecht and Trimbach. Some familiar names in the French regions include the Vin de Pays des Côtes de Gascogne of Tariquet, and Domaine Cauhapé from Jurançon.

Outside France, the greatest interest is in the Veneto wines of Guerrieri-Rizzardi from Italy, CVNE Riojas from Spain, and Joseph Phelps, Robert Mondavi and Monterey Vineyard in California.

Best buys

Señorio de los Llanos, Valdepeñas 1981, £2.89
Bardolino Classico 1986, Guerrieri-Rizzardi, £3.59
Tyrrells Long Flat White 1987, Hunter Valley, Australia, £3.99
Champagne, Barancourt Réserve NV, £10.99
Monterey Vineyard Classic Red 1984, California, £3.89

Berkmann Wine Cellars

12 Brewery Road, London N7 9NH   TEL 01–609 4711
OPEN Mon–Fri 9–5.30; Sat 10–4   CLOSED Sun, public holidays
CREDIT CARDS Access, Visa   DISCOUNTS Available   DELIVERY Free to London postal districts (min 1 case); mail order available
GLASS HIRE Free with 2-case order   TASTINGS AND TALKS Tutored tastings monthly on average; to groups on request   CELLARAGE £3.75 per case per year or part year (unmixed cases purchased through Le Nez Rouge club only)

This firm lists only wines that it imports direct, almost all from France, and with a number of famous names among them.

The most famous of all is perhaps Georges Duboeuf, who supplies the Beaujolais on the list, and it is obvious that with these wines, and the impressive range of domaine-bottled Burgundies, this part of France is an area of major interest. Apart from Duboeuf, look for estates such as Domaine Guy Roulot, Albert Morey, Hugues de Suremain in Mercurey, or Alain Michelot in Nuits St-Georges.

Other French areas come out well. Alsace has the wines of Gaston Bec, including some of their estate wines, there are Rhône wines from Vidal-Fleury, a big range of Provençal wines

from Les Maîtres Vignerons de St-Tropez, Champagnes from
Bruno Paillard, Muscadet from Sauvion et Fils and Pineau des
Charentes from Ch de Beaulon.

Outside France, look for Petersons wines from Australia,
Morton Estate from New Zealand and the elegant Ports of
Ramos Pinto.

Best buys

Quinta de Ervamoira 10-year-old tawny, Ramos-Pinto, £8.75
Le Fronsac, Jean-Pierre Moueix, £4.65
Ch de Pampelonne Rouge 1988, Maîtres Vignerons de St-Tropez,
£4.65
Paillard Brut 1976, Dégorgé 1986, £19.70

Berry Bros & Rudd

3 St James's Street, London SW1A 1EG

TEL 01–839 9033
(answering machine
01–930 1888)

The Wine Shop, Hamilton Close,
Houndmills, Basingstoke, Hampshire
RG21 2YH

TEL (0256) 23566

OPEN Mon–Fri 9.30–5 (London), 9–5 (Basingstoke); Sat 9–1 (Basingstoke)
CLOSED Sat (London), Sun, public holidays   CREDIT CARDS Access, Diners
Club, Visa; personal and business accounts   DISCOUNTS 3% on 2 cases
minimum, 5% on 5–10 cases; 7.5% on 10+ cases   DELIVERY Free on UK
mainland (min 1 case); £1.25 per case for Northern Ireland; mail order
available   GLASS HIRE Hire charge of £1.15 per dozen together with wine
order   TASTINGS AND TALKS Bi-annual tasting by invitation in Basingstoke
cellars; to groups on request   CELLARAGE £3.59 per case per year

---

In keeping with the traditional air of their panelled St James's
Street shop, Berry Bros & Rudd maintain an essentially
traditional list, strong on claret, Burgundy and Port, short on the
rest of Europe, but, interestingly, discovering the New World in
a serious way.

Really, though, customers come here for their claret, Burgundy
and Port. From Berry's Good Ordinary Claret (currently at £3.35
a bottle) up to the great first growths and back to vintages such
as 1971, this covers the great and the good in depth. If there are
gaps, they are in the middle price ranges. But compensation is
to be found in the splendour of the sweet white Bordeaux list,
which includes some bargains (Ch des Tours, Ste-Croix du
Mont 1983 at £3.25 for a half-bottle) as well as vintages of Ch
d'Yquem.

Burgundy sticks principally with négociant wines from houses
such as Moillard, Prosper Maufoux and Doudet-Naudin. There

95

is Beaujolais from Thorin, and Chablis from Albert Pic and Moreau. The Rhône is strongest in the northern vineyards, where Chapoutier is the principal supplier, but also look for the Lirac of Domaine Maby and Côtes du Rhône of Guigal. On the Loire the treats are Chinon from Couly-Dutheil and the Vouvray of Ch Moncontour, while in Alsace, famous houses such as Trimbach and Kuentz-Bas supply the wines. The Champagne list is long and serious and dwells on vintages of grandes marques.

In keeping with their traditional role, Berry's have a strong German range, with a reminder in their current list that German wine was once more expensive than white Burgundy – before the First World War. Now they have a fine range of estate wines, at prices which would make a Burgundian blush. Other than Germany, though, Europe is sparsely covered, but with points of interest in Italy, such as the Barolos of Ceretto, plus Riojas from Marqués de Cáceres, a few English wines, but nothing much else. Except, of course, for the vintage Ports, which contain a satisfying section on single quinta wines; and the Madeiras, including some old vintage wines (back to 1906 currently).

We turn to the New World for further inspiration. In Australia, considerable expansion of the list throws up many famous names – Brown Brothers, Hill-Smith, Quelltaler, Penfolds and Yalumba. New Zealand's contribution of wines from Matua Valley and Stoneleigh Vineyard is very representative, while the California section, though shorter, offers Wente Brothers, Trefethen and Iron Horse.

Don't forget the good range of sample cases which reveal many aspects of Berry's range in one box of 12 bottles.

Best buys

Good Ordinary Claret, £3.35
Ch des Tours 1983, Ste-Croix du Mont, £3.25 half bottle
Hochheimer Hölle Riesling Kabinett 1983, Geh'rat Aschrott, £6.45
Ch Respide 1981, Graves (Berry Bros bottling), £3.95
Crown Old Tawny Port, £7.70
Bourgogne Pinot Chardonnay, Berry's Own Selection, £4.95

We have tried to make the *1990 Which? Wine Guide* as comprehensive as possible, but we should love to hear from you about any other wine merchants you feel deserve an entry, or your comments on existing entries. Write to us either by letter or using the report forms supplied at the back of the book.

B H Wines

Boustead Hill House, Boustead Hill, TEL (0228 76) 711
Burgh-by-Sands, Carlisle, Cumbria
CA5 6AA

CASE SALES ONLY   OPEN 'All reasonable hours', but advisable to phone
before calling   CREDIT CARDS, DISCOUNTS Not available   DELIVERY Free
within Carlisle/North Cumbria area (min 1 case) and outside this area
for larger orders; otherwise by negotiation   GLASS HIRE Free with 1-case
order   TASTINGS AND TALKS Free tastings twice yearly; participate in
'Wine at The Sands' – Carlisle's wine tasting society; to groups on
request   CELLARAGE Not available

Along with a few other, much-to-be-encouraged wine
merchants, B H Wines organises its list according to colour. This
means, for example, that the first wine we meet on the list is a
red from Argentina (the Andean Vineyards Mendoza Cabernet
Sauvignon 1979 at £4.27); we then plunge into a varied and
serious selection of Australian reds (balanced later by an equally
impressive set of whites) from firms such as Orlando, Tyrrells,
Leasingham, Simon Whitlam, plus small wineries such as Evans
& Tate in Western Australia.

It is also worth considering the range of California wines
(including Firestone and Clos du Bois), the Chilean Cabernet
Sauvignon from Viña Linderos, and the New Zealand wines
from Cooks.

In the Old World, we find plenty more of interest from this
firm, which combines a sound range with good prices. France
has an excellent clutch from the South and Provence – look, for
example, for the Coteaux des Baux en Provence wine of
Domaine de Trévallon (1984 vintage at £6.29), Alsace wines from
the Turckheim co-operative, the fascinating dry white
Savennières of Domaine de la Bizolière (1985 vintage at £4.80 –
keep it a few years before drinking). In Burgundy and
Bordeaux – as befits a modern wine list – there is a small
selection which puts these classic areas firmly in perspective.

Italy offers some good Piedmontese wines (Barolo from
Fontanafredda, Dolcetto d'Alba from Borgogno); Spain has Rioja
from CVNE, and there is a representative set of Bulgarian
wines. Also look for the set of Ports from Ramos Pinto.

Best buys

Huapai Semillon 1985, New Zealand, £4.70
Santa Rita Reserva Cabernet Sauvignon, Chile, £4.25
Vin de Pays de Charentais Cabernet/Merlot 1985, £2.25
Navarra Gran Reserva 1978, Gran Plané, £3.36
Mark West Chardonnay 1981, California, £6.30

Bibendum

WHOLESALE
113 Regent's Park Road, London NW1 8UR   TEL 01–586 9761

RETAIL
The Conran Shop, 81 Fulham Road, London SW3 6RE   TEL 01–584 3577

OPEN (NW1) Mon–Sat 10–8; (SW3) Mon–Sat 9.30–6   CLOSED Sun, public holidays   CREDIT CARDS Access, Visa; personal and business accounts   DISCOUNTS Negotiable   DELIVERY Free within London postal districts (min 1 mixed case); elsewhere £3.95 per consignment; mail order available   GLASS HIRE Free with 1 mixed case order   TASTINGS AND TALKS Wines always available for tasting at NW1; range of wines available every weekend; series of regular monthly tastings; to groups by arrangement   CELLARAGE £4.82 per case per year (inc insurance)

Which? Wine Guide is normally sceptical of claims such as that which Bibendum makes for itself. 'Bibendum is a pursuit of excellence', they write when asked what their aims are. But, for once, we have to agree with the claim, because Bibendum's range, quality, prices and service are such that they consistently win all the awards we make. What makes Bibendum so special is that they are not just fine wine merchants, whose floors are piled high with cases of the best claret, but they seem to be able to search out wines from a surprisingly wide area of the vinous world at all price levels, while keeping a uniformly high quality.

What of the wines themselves? Strong areas that we would highlight in a very comprehensive list include the French regions (with plenty of wines from areas such as the South-West (Madiran from Domaine Damiens 1987 at £3.75, or Bergerac from Ch Court-les-Mûts), Provence (try the wines of Domine d'Astros in the Vin de Pays des Maures – white and red at £2.98). In other parts of France, there is a star-studded set of domaine wines from Burgundy, equal interest from the Loire (wines of Gaston Huet in Vouvray, Henri Natter in Sancerre or Henry Marionnet in Touraine), and more of the same quality from the Rhône (St-Joseph of Florentin, Hermitage at Marc Sorrel, the Côtes du Rhône and Côtes du Ventoux of Domaine des Anges, and Châteauneuf of Paul Avril). Champagne does pretty well, too, as does Alsace with the wines of Rolly Gassmann. Bordeaux is not quite so exciting, although in their en primeur offers, Bibendum offer a larger selection of classed growths, and stock a fascinating set of larger bottles of claret.

Outside France, Germany receives short shrift, but Italy blossoms: there are wines from all over the country, but especially from Piedmont (look for the Barolo of Clerico, the Dolcetto of Chionetti or that of Maria Feyles). Spain's contribution is much shorter, while Portugal has a brief look in with the wines of Champalimaud in the Douro.

In the New World, we turn first to the expansive range of Australian wines from a big range of smaller estates – Tim Adams in Clare, Moss Wood in Margaret River, Basedow in the Barossa, Richard Hamilton in McLaren, Yarra Burn in Yarra Valley, Sutherland in the Hunter Valley. New Zealand has a small set of wines from Collard Brothers, while California features Lost Hills winery and Stag's Leap Wine Cellars.

It is a pity that the selection of fortified wines (especially the wood-aged Ports and Sherries) does not live up to the same quality.

Best buys

Coteaux du Languedoc 1986, Alain Roux, £4.78
Bergerac Blanc 1988, Ch Court-les-Mûts, £3.77
Gamay de Touraine 1988, Henry Marionnet, £3.98
Côtes du Ventoux 1987, Domaine des Anges, £3.65
Mâcon Bray 1988, Domaine de la Combe, £4.89
Champagne Albert Beerens Reserve, £9.55
Sangioveto del Borgo, Carlo Citterio, £4.50
Lost Hills Red, San Joaquin Valley, California, £3.43

Bin 89 Wine Warehouse

89 Trippet Lane, Sheffield, South Yorkshire S1 4EL   TEL (0742) 755889

CASE SALES ONLY   OPEN Tue–Fri 11–6; Sat 10–5   CLOSED Mon, Sun, public holidays   CREDIT CARDS None accepted; personal and business accounts DISCOUNTS 5% on 5 cases (min)   DELIVERY Free in Sheffield and North Derbyshire (min 2 cases); elsewhere at cost; mail order available GLASS HIRE Free with 1-case order   TASTINGS AND TALKS Two in-store tastings per year by invitation; to groups on request   CELLARAGE £3 per case per year

This is a list which seems to offer a little of everything, but with some areas treated in more depth. A new wine bar is promised on the premises where it should be possible to sample the wines.

The range is strongest in France: good and well-priced petit château clarets, Alsace wines from Lucien Albrecht and the co-operative of Turckheim, and the French country wines section (look for Ch La Gordonne from Provence, a red organic wine at

£3.50 for the 1987 vintage, or the Côtes du Frontonnais Ch La Palme 1986 at £4.25).

Strengths are also apparent in Italy, with Pieropan and Portalupi two of the top Veneto producers represented, and the Torre Quarto red from Puglia; and Australia, with wines from small estates like Pirramimma in McLaren Vale and Hopwood Estate in Victoria. Look for the inter-continental pairing of Clos du Val in California and Taltarni in Australia, run by brothers; or for the Ports from Smith Woodhouse and Warre.

Best buys

Ch de Parenchère, Bordeaux Supérieur 1982, £4.95
Morgon 1985, Vincent Vial, £5.95
Gewürztraminer 1987, Charles Grass, £4.15
Dalahaye Brut Champagne NV, £8.95

The Bin Club

Wickwar Trading Estate, Station Road,   TEL (0272) 277641
Wickwar, Glos GL12 8NB
All business is mail order

OPEN Mon–Fri 9–6 (office), 9–4.30 (cellars) – visits by appointment
CREDIT CARDS, DISCOUNTS Not available   DELIVERY At cost   GLASS HIRE, TASTINGS AND TALKS Not available   CELLARAGE £2.76 duty paid; £3.45 in bond

This is a club aimed principally at expatriates who want to build up a cellar for enjoyment when they return home. But you don't have to live overseas to join – it's open to anyone who wants a cellar planned for them. Offers are made regularly to members (for details of membership see FIND OUT MORE ABOUT WINE), who receive frequent updates on the development of bottles they have purchased.

A recent offer included a number of 1986 clarets, the odd red Burgundy, and Côtes du Rhône of Guigal. For whites, there were Australian and California Chardonnays, white Burgundy and Chablis and a Savennières from the Loire (perfect for laying down for years).

The Wine & Spirit Education Trust is the body in charge of educating those in and on the fringes of the wine trade. They offer a series of courses right up to Master of Wine level, the more basic of which are open to non-trade members who can convince the Trust of their intention to enter the wine trade. Contact them at: Five Kings House, Kennet Wharf Lane, Upper Thames Street, London EC4V 3AJ; TEL 01-236 3551.

Bin Ends

Toone House & Cellars, 83–85 Badsley   TEL (0709) 367771
Moor Lane, Rotherham, South
Yorkshire S65 2PH
ASSOCIATED OUTLET
(By the case only), Patrick Toone   TEL (04393) 504
Personal Wine Merchant, Pavilion
House, Oswaldkirk, York, North
Yorkshire YO6 5XZ

OPEN (Bin Ends) Mon–Fri 10–5.30; Sat 9.30–12.30   CLOSED Sun, public
holidays   CREDIT CARDS Access, Visa; personal and business accounts
DISCOUNTS 5% on 1 unmixed case, 7.5% on 3+ mixed cases (does not
apply to Champagne and Port)   DELIVERY Free within 25-mile radius of
Rotherham and Oswaldkirk (min 1 case); elsewhere at cost; mail order
available within 25-mile radius only   GLASS HIRE Free with 1-case order
TASTINGS AND TALKS 3 major tastings annually; to groups on request (20–
40 people)   CELLARAGE £2.50 per case per year

Extensions to the range of Australian wines, Ports, Chablis and
Champagne mark the most recent changes to the list from this
dual wine merchant. The two parts operate in tandem, with the
Patrick Toone outlet dealing in case sales only, while Bin Ends
have a retail licence for single bottle sales. They also have
separate fine wine list which contains Burgundy, claret and Port
for laying down.

The Australian wines certainly form a good introduction to
the list. There are wines from Rosemount, De Bortoli, Berri
Estates and Brown Brothers (look for the Brown Brothers
Liqueur Muscat at £11.95 for a truly liquorous treat). California
has some of the inexpensive wines from Gallo, while from Chile
come Torres Santa Digna Cabernet Sauvignon (1984 vintage at
£5.25), and wines from Concha y Toro.

When we arrive in France, we find Alsace wine from Dopff au
Moulin, and Beaujolais from the négociant house of Paul Sapin.
Claret is on the pricy side – as is Burgundy (with nothing under
£7 on the current list), but there is a good range of Chablis
(from Domaine Laroche, William Fèvre, Pascal Bouchard and
Domaine Servin). Bin Ends now sell the Champagnes of
Beaumet as well as their own house Champagne of De Meric
(Brut NV at £9.99). The Loire has Muscadet from Ch de
Chasseloir, but the Rhône is a bit of a disaster area.

From other parts of Europe, the stars are a very wide range of
Sherries from Garvey and Barbadillo, Madeira from Henriques
and Henriques, and Ports mainly from Fonseca, with a side
interest in Kopke. Look, too, for the Sicilian wines of Regaleali
and Riojas from CVNE and Berberana.

Best buys

Principe Manzanilla Amontillada, Barbadillo, £9.25
Chablis 1987, William Fèvre, £7.95
Muscadet sur lie 1987, Chasseloir Chêr Neuf, £6.95
Ch la Chapelle-Despagnet 1985, St-En.ilion Grand Cru, £6.65

Blayneys Wine Merchants

HEAD OFFICE
Riverside Road, Sunderland, Tyne &   TEL 091–548 4488
Wear SR5 3JW
156 branches and 15 Liquor Markets in the North

OPEN Generally Mon–Sat 10–10; Sun, public holidays 12–2, 7–10
CLOSED Chr Day   CREDIT CARDS Access, Visa   DISCOUNTS 5% on 1 case
DELIVERY Free from selected branches only   GLASS HIRE Free with any
case order   TASTINGS AND TALKS Occasional in-store tastings in certain
branches; to groups on request   CELLARAGE Not available

Blayneys have continued to expand. Last year, they purchased
Dickens Wine Warehouses and some branches of Agnews. This
year, they have taken over the branches of Morris's to give them
a foothold in the West Midlands. The quality of their wine list
continues to improve as well.

While some of their finer wines are only available at a few
branches (ring the head office for details), the range on general
release includes plenty of good things, for instance Beaujolais
and Mâconnais wines from Loron, Alsace wines from Kuehn,
and some good country wines (go for the Corbières Ch de
Cabriac at £2.79 and Ch de Fonscolombe from Provence at
£3.29). Germany is a mix of too many branded wines but also
some good estate wines. The same is true of Italy, where you
could avoid the Campelli range by going instead for the Barolo
Fontanafredda, the Chianti Classico Riserva Fizzano from Rocca
delle Macie at £7.85, or, somewhat less expensively, the
Teroldego red from the Trentino at £2.99. Spain brings us Riojas
from Faustino Martinez, and there's the usual good value from
Bulgaria.

Elsewhere, look for Gallo's good value from California, Cooks
wines from New Zealand, Brown Brothers and Jacob's Creek
from Australia, while avoiding the British 'wines'. As
compensation for those, there is a good line in Lustau Sherries
as well as Sandeman Ports.

Best buys

Señor Burgues Rioja, £2.99
Viña Carmen Cabernet Sauvignon 1986, Chile, £4.55

Domaine Langlois Château, Saumur 1987, £3.95
Côtes du Rhône 1987, Domaine de Grangeneuve, £2.99

Booths

HEAD OFFICE
4–6 Fishergate, Preston, Lancashire   TEL (0772) 51701
PR1 3LJ
21 branches in Cumbria and Lancashire
OPEN Mon–Fri 9–5.30; Sat 9–5   CLOSED Sun, public holidays
CREDIT CARDS Access, Visa   DISCOUNTS Not available   DELIVERY Free on
UK mainland (min 5 cases); mail order available   GLASS HIRE Free
TASTINGS AND TALKS Occasional in-store tastings; to groups on request
(maximum 50 people)   CELLARAGE Not available

A family-owned group of supermarkets which has been quietly
expanding its range of wines, so that it now stocks over 600.
While some of these are on a fine wine list (on order at the
stores, but not stocked), a sizeable range is readily available at
the stores.

In a recent tasting we enjoyed the Alsace Pinot Blanc of
Hartenberger (£3.15), Booths' own-label Kabinett at £2.43, the
Classic Rumanian Pinot Noir 1984 at £2.35, Booths' Rioja (which
comes from Bodegas Domecq) at £2.65 for the 1983 vintage, the
Montepulciano d'Abruzzo of Illuminati (1987 vintage at £3.75),
the Glen Ellen range from California, Booths' own crusted Port
1984 (from Smith Woodhouse) at £8.19, and their house
Champagne at £8.99.

On their fine wine list, there is plenty of interest from the
classic areas, especially Bordeaux (with vintages back to 1970),
from Burgundy (with a good mix of négociant and domaine-
bottled wines), from Alsace (with Schlumberger wines), a good
selection of German estate wines, a growing range of Italians
(look for the Morellino di Scansano Riserva Le Pupille 1983 at
£6.59), and Brown Brothers wines from Australia. Vintage Ports
from 1985, 1977 and 1980 abound.

Best buys

Booths Champagne, £8.99
Classic Rumanian Pinot Noir 1984, Dealul Mare, £2.35
Beaujolais Villages 1987, Raymond Mathelin, £3.49
Booths Fine Crusted Port 1984, Smith Woodhouse, £8.19
Wehlener Sonnenuhr Riesling Kabinett 1986, S A Prum, £5.99

Send us your views on the report forms at the back of the book.

Bordeaux Direct ☆

MAIL ORDER
New Aquitaine House, Paddock Road,   TEL (0734) 471144
Reading, Berkshire RG4 0JY
Retail arm through Taste Shops

OPEN 7 days a week (answering service outside office hours)
CLOSED 24 Dec-1 Jan   CREDIT CARDS All accepted; business accounts
DISCOUNTS Available   DELIVERY Free nationally (min £50 order); mail
order available   GLASS HIRE Not available   TASTINGS AND TALKS Regular
tastings in retail outlet; to large groups on request   CELLARAGE £2 per
case per year

Bordeaux Direct is a wine club, also known as the Sunday
Times Wine Club, but operating independently from that
newspaper. It doesn't have a specific list, but makes regular
offers – rather like a book club – often of wines which are
unusual, almost invariably of wines which are otherwise
unavailable in this country.

A recent list (arranged by wine style rather than country) had
wines from the Alpi Juliani, an area in Yugoslavia which makes
wines from vineyards which were once part of Italian Friuli.
Then there were wines from the Côtes du Forez, near the source
of the Loire in France, and plenty of interest from the South of
France (a happy hunting ground for Bordeaux Direct),
intermingled with a Beaujolais, a Valpolicella and a wine from
Ribera del Duero in Spain.

There are clarets here, and Burgundies, but, such is the nature
of Bordeaux Direct's approach to wine, they are treated as 'full
reds' rather than 'very special wines from classic areas' – a
healthy view of wine in many ways, when used sensibly as
here, and when balanced with other offers which include a
special case of German wines and even a mystery case for those
with a sense of adventure.

Best buys

Vin de Pays des Côtes de Pérignan, Cave de St-Exupéry 1987,
£3.33
Cabernet Sauvignon 1985, Los Vascos, Chile, £3.91
Rüdesheimer Bischofsberg Riesling Halbtrocken 1986, Von
Mumm, £5.87
Les Astes 1988, Gaillac, £3.80

If you disagree with us, please tell us why. You will find report forms at
the back of the book.

Borg Castel

Samlesbury Mill, Goosefoot Lane,
Samlesbury Bottoms, Preston,
Lancashire PR5 0RN

TEL (025 485) 2128

OPEN Mon–Wed, Fri 10–5; Thur 7–9.30; Sat possible; 1st Sun of each
month 12–4   CLOSED Sun except as above, some public holidays, 3rd and
4th week in January, 4th week in July   CREDIT CARDS None accepted
DISCOUNTS Available   DELIVERY Free within 30-mile radius (min 1 case);
elsewhere at cost; mail order available   GLASS HIRE Free with case order
TASTINGS AND TALKS Two annual tastings by invitation; tastings for new
wines by invitation; to groups on request on premises only (30–50
people)   CELLARAGE 75p per case per year

Two lists continue to operate at this merchant. One is a
constantly changing range of fine wines, with limited stocks
available on a cash and collection basis only.

The other is a retail list which ranges widely if not in any
great depth. Areas to look for are a useful set of mid-priced
clarets, Alsace wines from the Turckheim co-operative, Côtes du
Rhône from the Rasteau co-operative (which also supplies some
of the unusual sweet red Rasteau at £5.48), and a muddled if
potentially good range of German wines (such as those from
Deinhard). The rest of the world effectively does not exist, apart
from Ports from Ramos Pinto, and a couple of wines from
Orlando in Australia.

Best buys

Costières du Gard, Domaine de Beauregard, £2.94
Ch de Belcier 1983, Côtes de Castillon, £4.41
Côtes du Rhône 1988, Cuvée du Maître des Chais de Rasteau,
£3.71
Serriger Würzburg Weissburgunder Trocken 1986, Bert Simon,
£3.81
Quinta da Urtiga Vintage Character Port, Ramos Pinto, £8.50

The Wine Standards Board is the trade's disciplinary department and
wine watchdog. Their inspectors are responsible for rooting out any
malpractices – but they are concerned largely with labelling
irregularities. If you have genuine reason to suspect that the wine in a
bottle is not what the label claims it is, contact the Board at: 68½ Upper
Thames Street, London EC4V 3BJ; TEL 01-236 9512; or contact your local
Trading Standards Officer.

Bottle and Basket

15 Highgate High Street, London
N6 5JT

TEL 01–341 7018

OPEN Mon–Fri 11–3, 5–9; Sat 11–9; Sun 12–3, 7–9   CLOSED Chr Day
CREDIT CARDS Access, Visa   DISCOUNTS 5% on 1 case (may be mixed)
DELIVERY Free locally (min 1 mixed case); elsewhere not available
GLASS HIRE Free with reasonable order   TASTINGS AND TALKS Regular
Saturday tastings of selected wines   CELLARAGE Not available

There's plenty from Bordeaux and Burgundy at this small shop in North London's Highgate Village, but the most interesting area is Spain.

We find a range of Riojas going up from the basic, but very decent, Señor Burgues at £2.66, through a range of Reservas, to a stunning set of Gran Reservas dating back to the early 1970s (Muga 1973 at £10.93 is a bargain). Other Spanish areas do well too: look for Torres wines (including the 1981 Black Label at £15.68), Señorio de los Llanos Gran Reserva 1978 at £3.57, whites and reds from Mont Plané in Navarra, and a range of Don Zoilo Sherries.

Italy doesn't do too badly, either. We find plenty of Ruffino Chiantis (Aziano Chianti Classico 1986 is £3.99), and there are less familiar wines such as the white Luna de Feldi from Trentino/Alto Adige at £5.23, or Antinori's Vin Santo at £6.65. Australia seems to be dominated by wines from Wolf Blass, Brown Brothers, Hardy's and Tyrrells, and there are Stoneleigh Vineyards wines from New Zealand (Sauvignon Blanc 1987 at £5.51).

In France, the high spots are a neat range of clarets, Alsace wines from Dopff au Moulin, and a plethora of Champagnes, including – apart from the grande marque wines – Boizel and Louis Kremer.

Best buys

Ribera Duero 1983, Peñafiel Co-operative, £3.19
Rioja 1981, Samaniego, £3.57
Chianti Classico Aziano 1986, Ruffino, £3.99
Freixenet Carta Nevada, Cava, £4.61

Most wine merchants will hire out glasses free of charge, provided they are collected and returned clean, and that you are buying enough wine to fill them! In most cases, it's first come, first served, so get your order in early to ensure supply.

Bottoms Up

HEAD OFFICE
Astra House, Edinburgh Way, Harlow,   TEL (0279) 453408
Essex CM20 2BE
55 branches nationwide

OPEN Mon–Sat 10–10; Sun, public holidays 12–2, 7–10 (excluding
Scotland)   CLOSED Sun (Scotland only), Chr Day, 1 Jan
CREDIT CARDS Access, Grand Metropolitan Shareholders Card, Visa;
personal and business accounts   DISCOUNTS 5% on 1 mixed case
DELIVERY Free in general area of stores (min 1 case)   GLASS HIRE Free with
suitable quantity purchased from store   TASTINGS AND TALKS Tastings
held in-store from time-to-time; to groups on request   CELLARAGE Not
available

Changes are afoot at this chain of wine shops. A major
development programme is underway, we are told. The plan is
for Bottoms Up, which has been working with an expanded
version of the Peter Dominic list (see separate entry), to – as the
marketing phrase has it – stand alone, which means that they
will be operating more independently in the future. As we went
to press, though, more details were not yet available.

The Broad Street Wine Co

The Holloway, Market Place, Warwick,   TEL (0926) 493951
Warwickshire CV34 4SJ

CASE SALES ONLY   OPEN Mon–Fri 9–6; Sat 9–1   CLOSED Sun, public
holidays   CREDIT CARDS Access, Visa; personal and business accounts
DISCOUNTS Not available   DELIVERY Free in UK (min 6 cases); mail order
available   GLASS HIRE Free with £100+ order (locally only)
TASTINGS AND TALKS Participate in Edgbaston Wine Society, Solihull Wine
Society, Bradford & Leeds Wine Society, Warwick Wine Society; to
groups on request   CELLARAGE Not available

Apart from its wines, this is the place to come for early landed
vintage Cognacs and vintage Armagnacs and Calvados, which
are available in vintages back to 1908 for Larressingle Armagnac
or 1914 for Hine Cognac.

    As far as the wines are concerned, this is almost entirely a
French list; with just a few departures in the shape of
Australian wines from Cape Mentelle and Rouge Homme and
New Zealand wines from Cloudy Bay, plus the much-acclaimed
Pesquera wines from Ribera del Duero in Spain and the latest
wine country to hit us, Peru, with its Tacma red and white at
£4.88.

    In France, look mainly to Burgundy for wines from Joseph
Drouhin and Georges Blanc, as well as Alsace wines from the

Cave Vinicole de Turckheim and oddities such as the Madiran of Ch Peyros and the sweet Jurançon of Domaine Cauhapé (1985 vintage at £9.03).

Best buys

Pouilly-Fuissé 1987, Georges Blanc, £8.41
Tokay Pinot Gris 1987, Cave Vinicole de Turckheim, £4
Ch Pichon 1985, Haut-Médoc, £8.91
Rosada Cabernet 1988, Miguel Torres, Chile, £4.31

G E Bromley

London Street, Leicester, Leicestershire LE5 3RH	TEL (0533) 768471
271 Leicester Road, Wigston Fields, Leicester, Leicestershire LE8 1JW	TEL (0533) 882057
J H Measures & Sons, The Crescent, Spalding, Lincolnshire PE11 1AF	TEL (0775) 2676

OPEN (Leicester) Mon–Thur 8.30–1, 2.15–5.15; Fri 8.30–5.15, Sat 8.30–12; (Wigston) Mon–Sat 10–1, 5–10; Sun 12–1.30, 7–10; (Spalding) Mon–Sat 9–6   CLOSED Sun (Leicester and Spalding); most public holidays
CREDIT CARDS Access, Visa; personal and business accounts
DISCOUNTS 2.5% on 5 cases, 5% on 12+ cases   DELIVERY Free in Lincoln, Boston, Holbeach, Peterborough, Wellingborough, Rugby, Nuneaton, Ashby, Derby, Nottingham and Newark (min 3 cases); otherwise 1 case £3.45, 2 cases £2.50; elsewhere at cost; mail order available
GLASS HIRE Free with 1-case order   TASTINGS AND TALKS Major autumn tasting; to groups on request (minimum 20 people)   CELLARAGE £2.40 per case per year (in advance)

There are some familiar names – many of high quality – in this range, which sticks to the classic areas. So we find producers like Chanson in Burgundy, along with domaines such as Jean Germain, Paul Bocuse (the second label of Duboeuf) in Beaujolais, Jaboulet Aîné in the northern Rhône and Cellier de Marrenon and Domaine du Vieux Télégraphe for Châteauneuf, the Vacqueyras of Roger Combe at Domaine de la Fourmone and the Anjou Blanc of Moulin Touchais (the 1964 vintage at £14.99). There's a representative range of clarets as well.

Outside France, things are good in Germany (with plenty of estate wines), reasonable in Italy (with wines from Ruffino in Tuscany), interesting in Portugal (with plenty from J M da Fonseca), and devoted to Torres and CVNE Riojas in Spain. Australia provides wines from Hill-Smith, Brown Brothers, Tisdall and Berri Estates, while New Zealand has wine from Babich as well as Montana and Nobilo. There are still rather too many dull, branded wines, but a good few vintage Ports.

Best buys

Forster Jesuitengarten Riesling Kabinett 1982, £5.42
Gran Colegiata 1985, Bodegas Farina, Toro (Spain), £4.49
Colares Reserva 1980, Casal da Azenha, Portugal, £5.17
Valpolicella Classico Superiore Vigneti di Jago, Bolla, £4.89
Côtes du Rhône 1987, Ch du Grand Moulas, £3.39

Burlington Wines

46 Burlington Road, Ipswich, Suffolk   TEL (0473) 50242
IP1 2HS
ASSOCIATED OUTLET
Wines of Interest (see separate entry)

CASE SALES ONLY   OPEN Mon–Fri 9–6; Sat 9–1   CLOSED Sun, public
holidays   CREDIT CARDS None accepted; personal and business accounts
DISCOUNTS 5% on orders of £200   DELIVERY Free in City of London and
central Ipswich and Norwich; otherwise London £1.50 per case and
elsewhere £1.95 per case (min £5); mail order available   GLASS HIRE Free
with wine purchase (through Wines of Interest)
TASTINGS AND TALKS Through Wines of Interest   CELLARAGE £1.75 per case
per year

A short list, but one which has – as the firm's other name
(Wines of Interest) suggests – nuggets of pleasure in many
areas.

In Bordeaux, for example, there is a good cross-section from a
basic house claret from Louis Eschenauer at £2.89, up to Ch Cos
d'Estournel 1983 at £16.50. There's very little from Burgundy –
they argue that prices are too high (on the whole we would
agree, but look for the Mâcon Igé, Domaine des Roches 1987 at
£5.50) – but there are a few points of interest on the Rhône and
Alsace wines from Rolly Gassmann. Italy and Spain are briefly
represented.

Australia and Chile do best in the New World; with some
well-priced wines (try the Wyndham Estate Cabernet Sauvignon
at £4.40, or the RF Chardonnay of Orlando 1987 at £4.15, or the
Mystic Park Red at £2.85).

There are a few Champagnes (a rarity is the Le Mesnil of
François Billion at £12.75, grown a stone's throw away from
Krug's much pricier wine). Look also for Madeiras from Cossart
Gordon, Churchill Ports, and the Santos 1970 vintage Port.

Best buys

Cabernet Sauvignon Reserve 1983, Oriahovitza (Bulgaria), £2.75
Blanquette de Limoux 1983, Aimery, £5.45
Mystic Park Red and White, Australia, £2.85
Don Suero Tinto 1981, León, £4.89

The Butlers Wine Cellar

247 Queens Park Road, Brighton, East
Sussex BN2 2XJ
TEL (0273) 698724

OPEN Tue–Fri 9–5.30; Sat 9–1   CLOSED Mon, Sun, public holidays
CREDIT CARDS Visa; personal and business accounts   DISCOUNTS Not
available   DELIVERY Free within 15-mile radius (min 1 case); elsewhere at
cost (3+ cases free); mail order available   GLASS HIRE Free with 1-case
order   TASTINGS AND TALKS, CELLARAGE Not available

Regular lists come to us from Geoffrey Butler, full of fascinating
selections of bin-ends he has purchased. The most recent we
had received as we went to press included a number of English-
bottled clarets from 1970 (at prices markedly below those of the
château bottling, for very little difference in quality), red
Burgundy back to the 1959 vintage, some mature Côte Rôtie
(1976 vintage of Jaboulet Aîné), some old Cahors, and some of
the stupendous 1976 sweet wines from Germany. Apart from
these great wines, Geoffrey Butler keeps more everyday
selections, such as the Chardonnay Vin de Pays du Jardin de la
France at £3.50, or the 1985 Minervois Ch Fabas at £3.29.

Best buys

Bin-ends

Anthony Byrne Fine Wines

88 High Street, Ramsey,
Cambridgeshire PE17 1BS
TEL (0487) 814555

OPEN Mon–Sat 9–5.30;   CLOSED Sun, public holidays
CREDIT CARDS Access, Visa; personal and business accounts
DISCOUNTS 5% on mixed cases, 10% on unmixed cases   DELIVERY Free in
UK (min 2 cases); otherwise £2.50 within 150-mile radius of Ramsey and
£6.50 beyond (for orders under 2 cases); mail order available
GLASS HIRE Free with 1-case order   TASTINGS AND TALKS Wines regularly
available in-store; to groups on request   CELLARAGE £1.95 per case per
year or part year

When Anthony Byrne decides to cover a vinous area, he does so
very thoroughly indeed. That's why there are, for example, over
four pages of Beaujolais in his most recent list – and we lost
count adding up the pages of Burgundy.

There is an interesting contrast between the two
neighbouring areas on this list. Beaujolais is dominated
exclusively by Georges Duboeuf, but in a bewildering variety of
different cuvées, so that, for instance, there are ten different
wines from Chénas on the list, and 17 from Fleurie (including

half-bottles and magnums). On the other hand, Burgundy is full of wines from an enormous range of domaines. We find Domaine de l'Hermitage in Rully, Bernard Bachelet in Chassagne Montrachet and Santenay, Dubriel Fontaine in Corton, Gagnard Delagrange in Volnay, Domaine Arnoux in Chorey-lès-Beaune, Georges Clerget in Vougeot – and so the list goes on. Anybody who is anybody, it seems, is here.

The other two areas of France which Mr Byrne concentrates on are Alsace (with a big range of wines from Zind Humbrecht) and the Loire (where names featured include Sauvion in Muscadet, Lucien Crochet in Sancerre and Didier Dagueneau in Pouilly Fumé). On the Rhône, there are treats from Guigal, Clos St-Jean and Domaine les Silex in Châteauneuf and Domaine des Entrefaux in Crozes-Hermitage.

Beyond France, things are somewhat less intense. But attractive areas are the Delatite and Brown Brothers wines from Australia, Cuvaison wines from California, the Vinattieri wines from Italy (including the Chardonnay Portico de Leoni which we found so stunning in a *Which? Wine Monthly* tasting last year – 1985 vintage at £8.28) and Berberana Riojas. There are some German estate wines, vintage Ports back to 1963 and Sherries from Don Zoilo.

Best buys

Chianti Corfecciano Urbana 1988, Parri, £3.19
Coteaux du Lyonnais 1988, Duboeuf, £3.38
Bourgogne Passetoutgrain 1985, Domaine Arnoux, £4.30
Riesling Clos Hauserer 1986, Zind Humbrecht, £5.99
Chablis Vigne de la Reine 1987, £7.02
Bernkasteler Bratenhof Kabinett 1982, Reichsgraf von Kesselstatt, £4.95

D Byrne & Co

12 King Street, Clitheroe, Lancashire BB7 2EP   TEL (0200) 23152

OPEN Mon, Wed, Sat 9–6 Thur, Fri 9–8   CLOSED Sun, Easter holidays
CREDIT CARDS None accepted; personal and business accounts
DISCOUNTS £1 on mixed case, £1.20 on unmixed case, 5% on orders over £250   DELIVERY Free within 50-mile radius of Clitheroe; otherwise £4 for 1 case, £3.50 per case for 2 cases, 3 cases free; mail order available
GLASS HIRE Free with 1-case order   TASTINGS AND TALKS One week annual tasting, normally in September   CELLARAGE Limited

---

A spectacularly wide-ranging collection of wines, full of interest, in a rather slung together presentation which makes it more fun – if a little confusing – for customers.

The list moves from a big selection of clarets to an equally big range from Burgundy, which highlights many fine estate wines (plus plenty of Chablis). There's equal depth in the Rhône (especially Châteauneuf) and even five different rosés from that region (a record?). The Loire suffers only by comparison, but Alsace surfaces with a huge display of wines from top merchants (Hugel, Dopff et Irion, Trimbach). The French country wines section seems to mop up the rest of the country very satisfactorily.

The German section stars a fascinating collection of estate wines (including older vintages and sweeter wines); the Mosel fares especially well. Italy is similarly rich, with wines from numerous producers, many of them top names, in most of the major areas – Chianti particularly. The Spanish list is stuffed with Riojas, there's a serious showing from Australia, and California boasts plenty of big names as well. The Sherry selection is stunning, but Port – by contrast – disappointing.

Best buys

Cousiño Macul Antiguas Reservas Cabernet Sauvignon 1982, Chile, £4.29
Osborne Fino Quinta Red Label Sherry, £4.05
Orlando St Hugo Cabernet Sauvignon 1984, Australia, £6.89
Ch Haut Marbuzet 1985, St-Estèphe, £10.49
Ch des Coulinats 1983, Ste-Croix du Mont, £4.69

Cachet Wines

Lysander Close, North York Trading   TEL (0904) 690090
Estate, Clifton, York, North Yorkshire
YO3 8XB

CASE SALES ONLY OPEN Mon–Fri 9–6; Sat 10–4 CLOSED Sun, public holidays CREDIT CARDS None accepted; business accounts DISCOUNTS 5% on 1 unmixed case DELIVERY Free in Yorkshire (min 1 mixed case); elsewhere at cost GLASS HIRE Free with appropriate order TASTINGS AND TALKS Monthly wine tastings at local wine bar; to groups on request CELLARAGE £3 per case per year

A merger with another local company and an expansion of the range of directly imported French wines are the major changes at this merchant over the past year.

It's a range which is solidly based in France. Strengths include the Loire (the Touraine wines of the Confrérie des Vignerons de Oisly-et-Thésée and Sancerre from Domaine Thomas), Alsace wines from Willy Gisselbrecht (and including the sparkling Crémant d'Alsace at £5.99), a newly expanded range of wines from the South (look for Vin de Pays de l'Hérault of Domaine de la Fadèze and St-Chinian of Domaine du Guiraud-Boyer, Cuvée Spéciale 1986 red at £4.75), and wines from the Perrin family in the Rhône Valley (Beaucastel in Châteauneuf and La Vieille Ferme). In Bordeaux, there is a short *tour d'horizon* of recent vintages, while Burgundy has a short but interesting collection of domaine wines.

Outside France, we come to tiny sections for the rest of Europe, more of interest in California (Trefethen Eshcol Red at £4.99), New Zealand (Delegats wines) and Australia (mainly Orlando and Rosemount). Other countries put in fleeting appearances.

Best buys

Côtes du Rhône 1983, Cuvée Personnelle, £3.99
Vin de Pays des Côtes de Thongue, Cabernet Sauvignon 1988, £2.95
Côtes de St-Mont Rouge 1986, Producteurs Plaimont, £2.69
Ch Coucheroy 1987, Graves Blanc, £3.99
Mâcon-Lugny Les Charmes 1987, £4.75

Cadwgan Fine Wine Merchants

152A Ashley Road, Hale, Altrincham, Cheshire WA15 9SA   TEL 061–928 0357
55 Spring Gardens, Manchester M2 2BZ   TEL 061–236 6547

OPEN Mon–Fri 11–8; Sat 9–8   CLOSED Sun, public holidays
CREDIT CARDS Access, Visa; personal and business accounts
DISCOUNTS 5% on 1 case; quantity discounts by negotiation
DELIVERY Free within 10-mile radius (min 1 case); elsewhere at cost; mail order available   GLASS HIRE Free within 1-case order
TASTINGS AND TALKS Regular in-store tastings after hours, regular monthly dinners; to groups on request   CELLARAGE Negotiable

---

Expansion is afoot at this merchant. A Manchester city centre store has been opened in the past year, and more shops are promised in the next 12 months – good news, because Cadwgan have an interesting range. It's very much French-based, with sidelong peeps into Spain and Italy. In Champagne, featured producers are de Castellane, Pol Roger, Louis Roederer, Bollinger, Bricout, Alfred Gratien (and the house Champagne from Aubry – NV Brut at £9.41). Alsace is widely represented with wines from the Turckheim co-operative and Dopff et Irion.

There's plenty from the Loire to please: Muscadet from Ch des Gautronnières, Sancerre from Lucien Thomas, Savennières from Jean Baumard, Vouvray from Gaston Huet and a big clutch of Anjou Blanc from Moulin Touchais, with vintages back to 1949. There is a mixed bag of Burgundies, combining négociant and domaine wines, Bordeaux vintages in some depth from 1978 onwards and at all price levels, and a much smaller collection from the Rhône.

Spain has interest from Rioja – CVNE, Marqués de Murrieta – from Torres wines in Penedés and the Pesquera wines from Ribera del Duero. Italy is full of excitements, with star wines like the Soave of Pieropan, the Montepulciano d'Abruzzo of Tollo and Carema White Label, as well as Vernaccia di San Gimignano of Strozzi and Recioto della Valpolicella of Allegrini. Those with an interest in German wines will find plenty of estate wines from Deinhard. Look, too, for Garvey Sherries.

Best buys

Champagne Brut NV, L Aubry, £9.95
Ch Belcier 1983, Côtes de Castillon, £4.65
Savennières Clos du Papillon 1986, Jean Baumard, £6.29
Vintages of Moulin Touchais
Domaine de la Vallongue 1985, Coteaux des Baux en Provence, £4.25
Castillo Jumilla 1984, £3.20
Bianco di Custoza 1987, Portalupi, £3.85

Cairns & Hickey

17 Blenheim Terrace, Woodhouse Lane,   TEL (0532) 459501
Leeds, West Yorkshire LS2 9HN

OPEN Mon–Fri 9–6; Sat 9–4   CLOSED Sun, public holidays
CREDIT CARDS Access; personal and business accounts   DISCOUNTS 5% on wine only (min 1 case)   DELIVERY Free in West Yorkshire; elsewhere at cost; mail order available   GLASS HIRE Free with suitable wine order
TASTINGS AND TALKS 2 annual tastings (November and Spring); to groups on request   CELLARAGE £2.30 per case per year

This is a sound if unexciting range of wines, strong on the classic areas of France, rather dull elsewhere.

Come here to find plenty of mature claret (vintages back in quantity into the '60s), although we would have liked to see more wines in the lower and mid-price brackets. Come here, too, for a traditional range of Burgundy (many négociants, few domaines). But there's less to interest in other areas of France – rather dull Beaujolais, a few southern French wines (try the Ch la Coste Coteaux d'Aix-en-Provence at £2.95), only a few treats on the Loire (the Quarts de Chaume 1986 of Jean Baumard is a bargain at £7.35 but needs years to develop).

Outside France, the story is similarly patchy: a few good Riojas, a comparative disaster area in Italy, not much in Germany – and odd titbits from the rest of the world

(Stoneleigh Vineyards in New Zealand, Orlando in California are among the best morsels). Sherries from Valdespino, Gonzalez Byass and Harvey are more in this firm's traditional mould.

Best buys

Ch la Coste Rouge, Coteaux d'Aix-en-Provence, £2.95
Rioja Gran Reserva 1978, Campo Viejo, £5.55
Ch de Glana 1961, St-Julien, £30
Inocente Fino, Valdespino, £5.50

Cantina Augusto

91–95 Clerkenwell Road, London EC1R 5BX TEL 01–242 3246

OPEN Mon–Thur 9–6; Fri 9–6.30; Sat mornings in Dec CLOSED Sat (except as above), Sun, public holidays CREDIT CARDS Access, Visa; personal and business accounts DISCOUNTS Approximately 10% on 1 case
DELIVERY Free in London (min £100 order), £2 charge for orders under £100; elsewhere at cost; mail order available if requested
GLASS HIRE Free with order (deposit required)
TASTINGS AND TALKS Regular promotional tastings; to groups on request
CELLARAGE Not available

Italian wines were the reason for this firm's inclusion in the Guide. But now in their recently remodernised shop (gone is the chaos and the pleasant old-fashioned smell) they have more space for a wide-ranging list which delves quite seriously into France. So alongside some Italian delights, we find wines such as the Muscadet of Ch de la Ragotière, and a special offer of Rhône wines from négociants such as Louis Musset and Pascal. Another non-Italian point of interest is Portugal – try the Garrafeira Particular 1978 of Borlido at £5.70. To the heart of the list: there are Chiantis from the co-operative Le Chiantigiane at a bargain £2.25, Trebbiano di Romagna from Conavi at £2.20 and Chardonnay from Niedermayer in the Südtirol. Look, too, for the more serious Barolo of Prunotto and La Loggia Chianti Classico.

Best buys

Gewürztraminer 1987, Niedermayer, £4.10
Chianti Classico Riserva 1983, Fattoria La Loggia, £5.10
Pinot Grigio Isonzo 1987, Angoris, £3.80
Sangiovese di Romagna Conavi, £2.20

Caves de la Madeleine

82 Wandsworth Bridge Road, London   TEL 01–736 6145
SW6 2TF

OPEN Mon–Sat 9.30–8.30   CLOSED Sun, public holidays
CREDIT CARDS Access, American Express, Visa; personal and business
accounts   DISCOUNTS 5% on 1 case   DELIVERY Free in central London
(min 1 case); elsewhere at cost; mail order available   GLASS HIRE Free
with 1-case order   TASTINGS AND TALKS Monthly tastings (usually held in
the evening); to groups on request   CELLARAGE £3 per case per year

After dropping out of the Guide last year while they moved
from Fulham Road, Caves de la Madeleine are now firmly
ensconced in the Wandsworth Bridge Road, where they can
conveniently cater for Fulham from less expensive premises.

To suit local tastes, there are plenty of Champagnes, but for
quieter drinking, a good selection of French country wines is on
offer (try the unusual dry white Domaine de Mairan Vin de
Pays de l'Hérault, produced from a side clone of the
Chardonnay, at £3.75; or the Coteaux du Languedoc Abbaye de
Valmagne red 1986 at £3.85). Then we come to a smallish
selection of clarets, but a much grander range of Burgundy (look
for wines from Chartron et Trebuchet, Confuron and Fontaine
Gagnard, and Chablis from Christian Adine). There's less on the
Loire (but try the Quincy of Mardon – 1988 vintage at £6.65 or
the Pouilly Fumé of Ch de Tracy – 1987 at £8.80). The Rhône
offers the good-value Côtes du Rhône of Nick Thompson (1987
vintage at £3.20) and there are Alsace wines from Willy
Gisselbrecht. Plenty of half-bottles, too.

Best buys

Cuvée des Templiers, Vin de Pays de la Principauté d'Orange
1988, £3.20
Pinot Noir 1986, Bourgogne Grand Ordinaire, Robert Gibourg,
£4.45
Jolly Good Claret, £3.25
Ch St-Martins Berlans, Bordeaux, £4.45

Special awards

🐷 is for bargain prices   🚩 is for a very good range of
wines

✳ is for high quality wines   🏳 is for exceptional service

C C Enterprises

See The Wine Schoppen.

The Celtic Vintner

73 Derwen Fawr Road, Sketty, Swansea,   TEL (0792) 206661
West Glamorgan SA2 8DR

CASE SALES ONLY   OPEN Mon–Fri 8.30–6; other times by arrangement
(also 24-hour answering machine)   CLOSED Sat, Sun, public holidays
(except as above)   CREDIT CARDS Access; personal and business
accounts   DISCOUNTS Negotiable for quantity discounts   DELIVERY Free in
South and West Wales (min 1 case if on regular delivery run, otherwise
5 cases); elsewhere at cost   GLASS HIRE Available with suitable wine
order   TASTINGS AND TALKS Large annual tasting; to groups on request
CELLARAGE Possible

A newcomer to the Guide, the Celtic Vintner has brought
together a range of wines which is strongest in France, but does
hold pockets of interest elsewhere. The notes in the list make
compulsive reading.

To those pockets first. Italy has a good range of wines from
Frescobaldi in Tuscany, while Spain deals mainly in Riojas from
some well-known names and Penedés wines from René Barbier.
There are Chilean wines from Torres, a few Californians from
Robert Mondavi, and a much larger collection of Australian
wines which range the country widely – from de Bortoli in New
South Wales to Cape Mentelle in Western Australia. And there's
an enormous and excellent-value range of Bulgarian wines.

This must be one of the only merchants in the country not to
stock at least one Alsace wine. But they do have plenty of useful
French country wines (Domaine de Baudare 1986, Vin de Pays
de Comté de Tolosan, a Gamay-based wine at £2.82 is
recommended, as is the Corbières 1986 of Ch de Lastours at
£3.80). The Celtic Vintner also keeps some attractively mature
claret (Ch Lamothe Bergeron 1979, Haut-Médoc, is £7.19), as well
as some Sauternes.

The Fleurie co-operative provides Beaujolais, Burgundy has a
shortish but interesting set of domaine wines, there is Côtes du
Rhône from the highly regarded Rasteau co-operative, and, on
the Loire, look for the Sauvignon de Touraine of Domaine des
Haies Doûlins at £3.45 as well as the Sancerre Clos le Chêne
Marchand of Merlin-Cherrier at £6.61. There are useful half-
bottles especially of sweet wines.

Best buys

Bulgarian wines
Corbières Ch de Lastours 1986, £3.80
Ch la Pilar Blanc, Côtes de Duras, £2.76
Côtes du Rhône Villages 1987, Cuvée Royale, Celliers des
Dauphins, £3.34
Chianti Rufina Remole 1987, Frescobaldi, £3.62

Champagne and Caviar Shop

18 Leadenhall Market, London   TEL 01–626 4912
EC3V 1LR

OPEN Mon–Fri 9–6   CLOSED Sat, Sun, public holidays
CREDIT CARDS Access, American Express, Visa; personal and business
accounts   DISCOUNTS 5–10% (min 1 case)   DELIVERY Free in the City (min
£50 order) and West End (min £100 order); otherwise at cost; mail order
available   GLASS HIRE Free with bottle order   TASTINGS AND TALKS Regular
tastings held for customers   CELLARAGE Free for Champagne bought
from premises

It's the world's favourite fizz all the way here – along, that is,
with the caviar. It's a serious list, mainly of grande marque
houses (although there are alternatives such as Canard-Duchêne
and Joseph Perrier). Most producers are represented by a good
range of wines from the basic NV up to the de luxe cuvée.
Prices are rather high, certainly compared with last year, but
then look at the address, or try the half-bottles (magnums also
available).

Best buys

Canard-Duchêne Brut NV, £13
Joseph Perrier Cuvée Royale, £15
Lanson Black Label, £14.50

Champagne de Villages

9 Fore Street, Ipswich, Suffolk IP4 1JW   TEL (0473) 256922

OPEN Mon–Sat 9–5.30   CLOSED Sun, public holidays
CREDIT CARDS Access, Visa; personal and business accounts
DISCOUNTS Available   DELIVERY Free within 20-mile radius of Ipswich
(min 1 case) and outside the area (min 5 cases); otherwise £7 per case;
mail order available   GLASS HIRE Free with 1-case order
TASTINGS AND TALKS Wines always available in-store; comparative tastings
held every Saturday; to groups on request   CELLARAGE £3 per case per
year

This is fine wine territory, all French, with nothing at the lower
price levels. But given those parameters, there is plenty of

interest, and a new shop has helped customers develop that interest.

First, of course, Champagnes. These come from grower producers rather than the big Champagne houses. While prices have risen alarmingly in the past year (up £2 or £3 a bottle in most cases), it is worth considering wines such as the Brut Grand Cuvée of Georges Lilbert at £11.04 or Pierre Arnould's Brut Sélection Grand Cru to get some idea of the quality that small growers can produce.

Champagne de Villages doesn't just sell Champagne, however, despite its name. They import many wines direct; such as Ch de Caillou, a second growth in Barsac which makes both sweet and dry wines, the Fronsac estate of Ch Perron, and more famous names such as Chx Laville Haut Brion and Larrivet Haut Brion, both in the Graves.

There are Burgundy wines from Delaunay, and the good-value Hautes Côtes de Nuits wines of Domaine Val de Vergy, or the pricier Puligny Montrachet wines of Jean Pascal. The Loire has wines from Michel Bahuaud in Muscadet and Masson-Blondelet in Sancerre and Pouilly Fumé. Other treats include the Cahors wines of Pelvillain and the Reuilly of Domaine Chassiot.

Best buys

Sancerre 1988, Thauvenay, Masson-Blondelet, £6.44
Pierre Arnould Rosé Champagne NV, £13.51
Quincy 1988, P et J Mardon, £4.88
Georges Lilbert Brut Grand Cru, £11.04

The Champagne House

15 Dawson Place, London W2 4TH   TEL 01–221 5538

CASE SALES ONLY   OPEN Mon–Thur 9.30–6   CLOSED Fri, Sat, Sun, public holidays   CREDIT CARDS None accepted   DISCOUNTS Negotiable (min 3 cases)   DELIVERY Free in Kensington, Chelsea, Westminster, City of London (min 1 case); elsewhere at cost; mail order available
GLASS HIRE Free with 1-case order if collected
TASTINGS AND TALKS Tutored tastings for established customers
CELLARAGE Not available

This firm may not have the longest list of Champagnes in the Guide, but it certainly has one of the most fascinating. The combination of Champagnes from a select band of some of the top names in the region, and some smaller, high quality producers, gives us the chance to find out what fine Champagne is all about.

So alongside the great names of Krug, Perrier-Jouët, Roederer, Ruinart and Bollinger, we find the good-value wines of Albert

Le Brun, the bone dry Champagne of Robert Driant, the highly esteemed rosé of Roland Fliniaux and wines from the up-and-coming co-operative of Paul Goerg. A full range of styles is represented, including still red and white Coteaux Champenois. If the choice is difficult, consider buying a tasting case.

Best buys

Albert Le Brun Carte Blanche NV, £8.75
Robert Billion Blanc de Blancs 1982, £13.98
Goerg Blanc de Blancs, £11.66

Chaplin & Son

35 Rowlands Road, Worthing, West   TEL (0903) 35888
Sussex BN11 3JJ

OPEN Mon–Thur, Sat 8.45–1.15, 2.15–5.30; Fri 8.45–6   CLOSED Sun, public holidays   CREDIT CARDS Access, Visa; business accounts   DISCOUNTS 5% on 1 mixed case   DELIVERY Free within 7-mile radius (min 1 mixed case); elsewhere at cost; mail order available   GLASS HIRE Free with appropriate order   TASTINGS AND TALKS Occasional in-store tastings; to groups on request   CELLARAGE Only for large quantities under bond

This is a useful range of wines that does well by France and the New World, but seems to have missed out on many of the more exciting developments in Europe.

However, it starts well in France, with a sensible collection of clarets, plenty of them in the lower price bracket (try Ch de Gardegan 1986, Côtes de Castillon at £4.06), and stays satisfactorily around the £5 mark for some time. Burgundy's selection is based on a number of négociants – Antonin Rodet, Labouré-Roi, Chanson (and with Loron in Beaujolais). The Rhône is much less extensive and rather dull, and the Loire is disappointing.

Things look up again with the Champagnes, with plenty of grande marque names (and their house Champagne, Charles Balachat, at £8.99). Elsewhere in France, we find the Listel wines from the South and Trimbach wines from Alsace.

However, the rest of Europe has a terribly old-fashioned look. There are mainly branded wines from Germany, a sad list from Italy (only enlivened by wines such as the Soave of Masi or the Barolo of Oddero), and if there is more interest from Spain, that is because of the Torres wines and the single vineyard Contino Rioja.

Things perk up again in the New World. Look for a fine range of Penfolds wines from Australia (Kalimna Bin 28 red at £5.67 or the Cabernet/Shiraz blend of Koonunga Hill at £4.74, up to Grange Bin 95 at 1978 at £27.61). There are also Australia's contributions to fortified wines in the shape of Liqueur Muscats. From New Zealand come Montana and Cooks wines, and from California Paul Masson wines. Fortified wines are enlivened by the Madeiras of Cossart Gordon, Sherries under the Tio Carlos brand and treats like the Duque de Bragança 20-year-old tawny Port from Ferreira at £17.85.

Best buys

Médoc, Nathaniel Johnston, £3.87
Le Bourgogne Chardonnay de Rodet 1986, Antonin Rodet, £5.33
Domaine de Villeroy 1986, Blanc de Blancs, Listel, £3.69
Viña Real 1985, Rioja, CVNE, £3.73
Penfolds Dalwood Shiraz/Cabernet 1984, Australia, £3.93

Châteaux Wines

(NOT A SHOP)
11 Church Street, Bishop's Lydeard,   TEL (0454) 613959
Taunton, Somerset TA4 3AT

CASE SALES ONLY   OPEN Mon–Fri 9–5.30; Sat most mornings until 12.30
CLOSED Sun, public holidays   CREDIT CARDS Access, Visa; personal and business accounts   DISCOUNTS Negotiable   DELIVERY Free on UK mainland (min 1 case); elsewhere at cost; mail order available
GLASS HIRE Not available   TASTINGS AND TALKS Regional tastings; to groups on request   CELLARAGE £4 per case or part-case per year for wines purchased from premises

Châteaux Wines' list is bigger than last year's with particular expansion in Bordeaux: now there's a small but useful range of wines which includes familiar names such as Ch St-Bonnet in the Médoc (1981 vintage at £4.75) as well as pricier offerings such as Ch Gloria, St-Julien 1979 at £14.04.

Burgundy is still a well-served area. The proprietor's reserve red and white from Pothier-Rieusset is good value for £6.98 (the white) and £5.94 (the red), and there are also plenty of estate wines. Grande marque Champagnes are exclusively from Laurent-Perrier.

Despite the name, there's interest outside France as well: Ch Musar from the Lebanon, from Australia Rosemount wines, and from California, Clos du Val.

Best buys

Côte de Brouilly 1987, L'Ecluse, L & R Verger, £4.99
Ch Musar 1981, Lebanon, £5.21
Champagne H Blin & Co NV, £9.47
Ch des Agnéras, Bordeaux 1985, £3.99

Chesterford Vintners   ☞

The Old Greyhound, Great Chesterford,   TEL (0799) 30088
Saffron Walden, Essex CB10 1NY
Tempest Slinger & Co, Town and
Country Vintners, (address as above)

OPEN Mon–Wed 9.30–5.30; Thur–Fri 9.30–7.30; Sat 9–5   CLOSED Sun,
public holidays   CREDIT CARDS Access, Visa; personal and business
accounts   DISCOUNTS Available (min 1 case)   DELIVERY Free within 25-
mile radius of Great Chesterford and within central London (min 2
cases) and UK mainland (min 10 cases); otherwise single bottles-1 case
£4.80 per consignment, 2–4 cases £2.80 per case, 5–9 cases £1.20 per case;
mail order available   GLASS HIRE Free with order   TASTINGS AND TALKS In-
store tastings 2–4 times per year; to groups on request
CELLARAGE Occasionally; £5 per case per year

A mainly French-based range of wines, which offers
considerable interest outside the classic areas of Bordeaux and
Burgundy, and takes brief glances at what is happening in the
rest of the world. Many of the French wines are imported
directly from small estates, and this makes a welcome departure
from the sort of list which merely contains the great and the
good.

We start with sparkling wines. A smallish collection of
Champagnes includes the Grand Cru Mesnil Champagne of
Alex de St-Ives, which is the house Champagne at £9.80, plus a
few grande marque wines. There are also curiosities like a still
red Coteaux Champenois at £7.38.

Chesterford Vintners' view of Bordeaux is best summed up
when we see that it is linked with the rest of South-West
France – so we find a Madiran between two clarets (what would
the proud Bordelais say?). In Burgundy, we find some excellent
domaine wines – look for the wines of Bader-Mimeur at the Ch
de Chassagne-Montrachet, and more familiar names such as
Armand Rousseau and Jacques Prieur, plus a good range of
estate Beaujolais.

The Loire is the star area as far as we are concerned, with
wines from many growers who only sell to Chesterford in this
country, such as François and Bernard Cazin in Cheverny (try
the bone dry Romorantin at £3.78) or the Muscadet of
Bouchereau Frères. Other wines worth considering are the
Ménétou-Salon of Jean-Max Roger or the Chinon of Pierre
Manzagol. The Rhône, too, has good things to offer: from the
inexpensive Vin de Pays des Coteaux de l'Ardèche Cabernet
Sauvignon at £2.71 up to the Côte Rôtie of Domaine Jamet.
Smaller offerings come from Alsace (Trimbach), Savoie,
Provence (Ch la Coste) and the South.

Outside France, look for Chianti from Badia a Coltibuono in Italy, Torres wines from Spain, Andrew Quady's sweet Essensia Orange Muscat from California, and Rosemount from Australia. Sherries include a range from Delgado Zulueta and Domecq.

Best buys

Beaujolais Rosé 1988, Domaine des Sables d'Or, £3.98
Aligoté de Châtillon-en-Diois 1988, Cellier Hannibal, £3.72
Côtes du Vivarais Blanc, Vignerons Ardéchois 1988, £2.72
Côtes du Rhône Rouge 1988, Domaine des Causses, £3.79
Chinon 1987, Domaine de la Noblaie, £4.98

Chiswick Wine Cellar

84 Chiswick High Road, London   TEL 01–994 7989
W4 1SY

OPEN Mon–Sat 10–10; Sun 12–3   CLOSED Public holidays
CREDIT CARDS None accepted; personal and business accounts
DISCOUNTS Available   DELIVERY Free locally (min 1 case)   GLASS HIRE Free with case order   TASTINGS AND TALKS In-store tastings every two weeks (Friday or Saturday)   CELLARAGE Not available

A wide-ranging selection of wines which continues to be particularly strong in Italy, but has wines from most areas of the world. Wine lists seem to be unavailable here – you will just have to ask.

Best buys

Pinot Grigio 1988, Kettmeir, £4.99
Vino Nobile di Montepulciano 1986, Grifi, Avignonesi, £12.89
Cabernet Sauvignon Concha y Toro, Chile, £2.99

Christchurch Fine Wine Co

1–3 Vine Lane, High Street,   TEL (0202) 473255
Christchurch, Dorset BH23 1AE

OPEN Mon–Sat 10–5   CLOSED Sun, public holidays (except Good Friday)
CREDIT CARDS Visa; personal and business accounts   DISCOUNTS 5% on 1 case (unless Christchurch Fine Wine Club member)   DELIVERY Free in Bournemouth area (min 1 case); otherwise at cost; mail order available
GLASS HIRE Free with 1-case order   TASTINGS AND TALKS Club tastings held regularly; to groups on request   CELLARAGE £3 per case per year

In the coming year, customers who currently have to beat a narrow path to the wine shop door will find that a splendid avenue will link the attractive 18th-century building to the High Street.

The range of wines reflects a firmly traditional taste: Champagne (look for the Jacquesson Blanc de Blancs at £12.25), plenty of top-notch claret (but not much in the lower price bracket), a mouth-watering selection of sweet white Bordeaux to go with the puds, and plenty to drool about in Burgundy (wines from Prosper Maufoux, Marcel Amance, and many cuvées purchased from the Hospices de Beaune and the Hospices de Nuits). White Burgundy comes mainly from Louis Latour.

On the Loire, there are a few curiosities such as the Jasnières of Caves aux Tuffières at £6.90, or the medium dry Thouarsais wine of Michel Gigon at £4.45 – plus more familiar things as well. On the Rhône, the star turn is played by Chapoutier, but look also for vintages of Ch Grillet – or, less expensively, the Condrieu of Ch du Rozay at £19.65.

The only other areas covered are Alsace with wines from Kuentz-Bas, Germany with estate wines, many from Deinhard, and Ports from Taylor and Fonseca.

Best buys

Gigondas 1985, Domaine du Grapillon d'Or, £5.20
Ch Breuil 1982, Haut-Médoc, £5.30
Winkeler Hasensprung Riesling Kabinett 1983, Deinhard, £6.55
St-Amour, Clos du Chapitre, Aujoux 1987, £5.45

Christopher & Co

See Les Amis du Vin.

City Wines

ADMINISTRATION AND WAREHOUSE
35 St Benedicts Street, Norwich, Norfolk NR2 4PF — TEL (0603) 617967/ 619246
SHOPS
305 Aylsham Road, Norwich, Norfolk NR3 2RY — TEL (0603) 405705
221 Queens Road, Norwich, Norfolk NR1 3AE — TEL (0603) 660741

OPEN Mon, Tue 12–3, 4–9; Wed–Sat (Aylsham Road) 10–10, (Queens Road and St Benedicts Street) 9–9; Sun and public holidays 12–2, 7–9
CREDIT CARDS Access, Visa; personal and business accounts
DISCOUNTS 5% on 1 case (not on spirits or fortified wine) DELIVERY Free in Norwich (min 1 case); elsewhere at cost; mail order available
GLASS HIRE Free with case order TASTINGS AND TALKS Annual Wine Fair; regular end of week tastings in-store; to groups on request
CELLARAGE Not available

Newcomers to the Guide, who have already established a considerable reputation in the two years in which they have been in operation. City Wines run three shops in Norwich – a city which has long needed a good wine merchant, and are involved in local arts sponsorship. We hope that the recent departure of the wine buyer who built up their list will not change their direction too much.

They have built up an impressive list which seems to be well balanced among many areas. There are obvious enthusiasms, though. For example, Portugal is extremely well served – table wines include some of the excellent reds which are coming from the centre of the country (Redondo Reserva 1983 at £2.99, or Quinta dos Plantos 1985 at £3.59 are both terrific bargains): among Ports are a good selection of aged tawnies and Dow's Crusted Port at £8.49.

Another enthusiasm is Australia – City Wines ran a fascinating vertical tasting of the wines of Yarra Yering vineyard in the Yarra Valley, so they have a number of wines from this top estate. Other producers include Ch Reynella, Ch Tahbilk (look for their unusual, rich white Marsanne as well as their reds), Penfolds, Passing Clouds, Mount Ida and Rosemount.

Other areas worth watching are the French regions (wines from Ch La Jaubertie in Bergerac, or Ch Cahuzac Côtes de Frontonnais red at £2.99), Beaujolais from Jacques Dépagneux, a well-balanced set of clarets, a mixed bag of Italians, much more interest from Spain (particularly Sherries from Barbadillo and Garvey), and a good number of top wines from New Zealand.

Best buys

Paço dos Infantes 1985, Alentejo, Portugal, £4.19
Franciacorta Rosso 1986, Contessa Martinoni, £3.49
Ch du Croix 1987, Blanc de Sauvignon, £3.99
Drayton's Shiraz 1986, Hunter Valley, Australia, £4.99
Plaire Cabernet Sauvignon, Vin de Pays d'Oc, £2.39
La Jalousie, Cépage Ugni Blanc, Grassa, £2.69

Claridge Fine Wines ☞

WHOLESALE
Boarden Farm, Hawkenbury, nr   TEL (0580) 893303/
Staplehurst, Kent TN12 0EB   893292
RETAIL
Perfect Partners, Wine & Cheese Shop,   TEL (0580) 712633
7 Stone Street, Cranbrook, Kent
TN17 3HF

OPEN Mon, Tue, Thur–Sat 9–5; Wed 9–1   CLOSED Sun, most public
holidays   CREDIT CARDS None accepted; personal and business accounts
DISCOUNTS Quantity discounts available   DELIVERY Free in Kent, Surrey,
Sussex, Essex borders and London (min 3 cases); elsewhere £4.60 per
case; mail order available   GLASS HIRE Free with case order
TASTINGS AND TALKS Pre-Christmas tasting at local venue; to groups on
request   CELLARAGE £3.45 per case per year

A sign of the times is the way Claridge Fine Wines are finding
difficulty replacing their Australian stock – after all, they
describe themselves as Australian specialists – at prices that are
still affordable, and in quantities which are not ludicrously
small. It has meant a return to big, sound names such as
Rosemount (with many of their top wines), and a diminution of
smaller estates, but still look for Pirramimma in McLaren Vale,
Balgownie – and for liqueur Muscats and Tokays from
Rutherglen – to go with Brown Brothers, Mildara, Seppelts and
Peter Lehmann.

Other areas in this range which attract interest are a useful set
of French regional wines – Domaine de l'Arjolle in the Côtes de
Thongue in the South-West, or the white Bergerac Ch La Tour
des Gendres – the highlighted Bordeaux château of Ch Clarke in
Listrac, Dépagneux Beaujolais, a new selection of Saumur still
wines from Hardouin-Bougouin (Saumur Blanc 1988 at £3.60), a
number of wines from Ch Val-Joanis in the Côtes du Lubéron,
and from Lamberhurst vineyard in Kent. New to the list are the
wines of Jane Hunter in New Zealand (Sauvignon Blanc 1988 at
£6.80), and good-value Californians in the shape of R H Phillips
in Yolo County (Semillon Reserve 1987 at £4.90). There are good
Sherries from Garvey, and Riojas from Tondonia.

Best buys

Semillon Reserve 1987, Bird Label, R H Phillips, Yolo County
(California), £4.90
Ch Val-Joanis Rouge 1987, Côtes du Lubéron, £3.50
Saumur Blanc 1988, Hardouin-Bougouin, £3.60
Domaine de l'Arjolle Rouge 1988, Côtes de Thongue

Classic Wine Warehouses

Unit A2, Stadium Industrial Estate,   TEL (0244) 390444
Sealand Road, Chester, Cheshire
CH1 4LU

OPEN Mon–Fri 8–6; Sat 9–5   CLOSED Sun, public holidays
CREDIT CARDS All accepted; personal and business accounts
DISCOUNTS Negotiable   DELIVERY Free in the North of England (min 1
case); elsewhere £4 per case (larger quantities by negotiation); mail
order available   GLASS HIRE Free   TASTINGS AND TALKS Monthly in-store
tastings on Saturdays   CELLARAGE Available; charges subject to
negotiation

While Classic Wine Warehouses still stock too many branded
wines, and rather dull versions of great names (especially in
countries like Italy), they also offer some good value –
particularly in France.

Go for the decent range of petit château wines (but watch the
fact that prices on the list do not include VAT), or for the
Drouhin Burgundies. On the Loire, try the Sancerre of Alphonse
Mellot, or, in Alsace, a range of Hugel wines. There are odd
treats from southern France (Bergerac from Ch La Jaubertie, for
example), and a vast quantity of Champagne.

Outside France, there are a few wines from good German
estates, CVNE Riojas from Spain, Umani Ronchi Rosso Cònero
and Chianti from Rocca delle Macie from Italy, Lindemans and
Rosemount from Australia, and Valdespino Sherries.

Best buys

Claret Louis XIV, Nathaniel Johnston, £2.99
Ch la Joye 1982, Bordeaux Supérieur, £5.49
Champagne Massé NV Brut, £7.99
Valdespino Sherries, £4.19

Classic Wines

181 High Road, Chigwell, Essex   TEL 01–500 7614
IG7 6NU

CASE SALES ONLY   OPEN Mon–Fri 9–6   CLOSED Sat, Sun, public holidays
CREDIT CARDS None accepted; personal and business accounts
DISCOUNTS Negotiable   DELIVERY Free on UK mainland (min 5 cases);
mail order available   GLASS HIRE Not available
TASTINGS AND TALKS Occasional in-store tastings; to groups on request
CELLARAGE £5 per case per year

Fine wines are what this firm is all about. There is a changing
list of small parcels of wines from great years and great estates

in Bordeaux and Burgundy, not forgetting sweet white Bordeaux, featuring Ch d'Yquem, plus vintage Ports. Occasional rarities such as Tokay or the Mondavi/Rothschild Opus One also crop up.

Best buys
Fine clarets and Burgundies

Classic Wines (near Halifax)

See the Wine Schoppen.

Cliffe Cellars

See Ellis Son & Vidler.

College Cellar

See La Réserve. This is their fine wine arm, specialising in fine clarets, Burgundies and vintage Ports – and also look for their range of fine Sauternes.

Colombier Vins Fins

Ryder Close, Cadeley Hill Industrial Estate, Swadlincote, Burton on Trent, Derbyshire DE11 9EU

TEL (0530) 412350 (telephone number at new premises unavailable as we went to press)

CASE SALES ONLY   OPEN Mon–Fri 8.30–5; Sat by appointment
CLOSED Sun, public holidays   CREDIT CARDS None accepted; personal and business accounts   DISCOUNTS Quantity discounts for 10+ cases
DELIVERY Free in Leicester, Birmingham, Nottingham and Derby (min 2 cases); elsewhere at cost   GLASS HIRE Free with case order
TASTINGS AND TALKS To groups on request   CELLARAGE May be arranged

To the clarets (serious and pricy) and the Burgundies (plenty of domaine wines, including Colombier's own domaine in Mâcon, plus good Chablis), we must now add as areas of interest some Alsace wines from Willy Gisselbrecht, Châteauneuf from Paul Avril at Clos des Papes, and Champagnes from Leclerc Briant (Blanc de Noirs is £9.77 – the list does not include VAT but we have added it here).

Italy, too, is looking up. There is a new range from the Colli Orientali in Friuli, Brunello di Montalcino from Casanova di Neri (1983 vintage at £10.29), the Lugana of Villa Flora and

Lambrusco from Giacobazzi. Cavas Hill supply wines from the Penedés in Spain. Colombier also give a tiny nod in the direction of the New World.

Best buys

Pinot Grigio 1988 Colli Orientali di Friuli, Rubini, £4.54
Mâcon Supérieur Rouge 1988, Vallière, £3.62
Bourgogne Aligoté 1987, Moreteaux, £5.15

Copyhold Farm Shop

See Goedhuis & Co.

Corney & Barrow   ✿ ☞ ☆

12 Helmet Row, London EC1V 3QJ	TEL 01–251 4051
118 Moorgate, London EC2M 6UR	TEL 01–628 2898
44–45 Cannon Street, London EC4N 6JJ	TEL 01–248 1700
194 Kensington Park Road, London W11 2ES	TEL 01–221 5122

OPEN Mon–Fri 9–7 (City), 10.30–8.30 (Kensington); Sat 10.30–8.30 (Kensington)   CLOSED Sat (City), Sun, Chr Day, bank holidays
CREDIT CARDS Access, Visa; personal and business accounts
DISCOUNTS Negotiable   DELIVERY Free in central London (min 2 cases) and UK mainland (min 3 cases); otherwise £6.33 per case in London and £6.90 per case on UK mainland; mail order available   GLASS HIRE Free with case order   TASTINGS AND TALKS Tastings every 2 months at Kensington branch; organise wine courses organised for customers; tastings and talks to existing customers on request   CELLARAGE £4.60 per case per year

If we say that this is the wine merchant that gives us Ch Pétrus, and other fine wines from the firm of J P Moueix, who virtually created the current fame of Pomerol, this might suggest that Corney & Barrow's only concern is with very fine, very rare claret. It would certainly be a wrong impression: the claret list is long and very good, certainly, but there are wines at much less exalted levels than great Pomerols.

For instance, take the wines from Fronsac, just to the west of Pomerol, where value is still (just) good. Look, for instance, for Ch St-Nicolas 1985, a Fronsac estate bottled by Moueix, at £5.29; and Ch Richotey 1986, also Fronsac at £4.83. And there are wines from the St-Emilion satellites, such as Montagne St-Emilion and St-Georges St-Emilion which also offer good value. But then there are the stars as well, the vintages of these finest clarets going back to the great 1961 vintage.

In Burgundy, we are in the realm of fine domaines, such as that of Marquis d'Angerville, of Dujac, of Domaine Leflaive (and also the family négociant firm of Olivier Leflaive Frères). It's a fine role call of the good and great of the region.

Other French areas are somewhat pale, but even so we see Loire wines from the Oisly-et-Thésée group, Rhône wines from Jaboulet Aîné, and Alsace wines from Cattin and Heydt. We like the look of the range of French country wines such as a Ch de Parc 1986 from Corbières at £3.45 (a reflection on the changed quality of these wines – a few years ago a firm like Corney & Barrow would never have considered stocking wines such as these). Outside France, there are the Marqués de Griñon Cabernet Sauvignon wines from Spain, Antinori and Lungarotti wines from Italy, a fine clutch of estate bottles from Germany, Australian wines from Hungerford Hill, California wines from Simi (and the new Mouiex wine, Dominus); also Sherries from Garvey and a fine array of vintage ports.

Look for en primeur and special offers which supplement the main list.

Best buys

Pokolbin Chardonnay, Hunter Valley 1987, Australia, £6.09
Ch Richotey 1986, Fronsac, £4.83
Vin de Pays de l'Aude 1986, Domaine du Puget Cabernet Sauvignon, £2.99
Morgon, Cave Manin 1987, Marc Dudet, £5.63

Restaurant Croque-en-Bouche

221 Wells Road, Malvern Wells,   TEL (06845) 65612
Hereford and Worcester WR14 4HF

CASE SALES ONLY   OPEN Any reasonable time, by arrangement
CREDIT CARDS Access, Visa DISCOUNTS 5% on 4+ cases, cash & collect
DELIVERY Free locally; elsewhere at cost; mail order available GLASS HIRE, TASTINGS AND TALKS Not available CELLARAGE Short term only, which is free

---

While proprietor Robin Jones produces what he calls a retail wine list, don't be misled into thinking that this is all you can buy if you are not eating at the restaurant itself – it is perfectly possible to take away any one of the 900 wines on the restaurant wine list, at £3 less than the restaurant price.

What the restaurant list offers is a remarkable collection of fine wines, mainly, but not exclusively French, and with particular treats in the Rhône: five different Gigondas, ten different Châteauneufs (and the Cru de Coudoulet of Beaucastel which is a first rate Côtes du Rhône at nearly half the price of its big brother – £6.40 against £12.50). There's even more choice with Côte Rôtie, which Mr Jones regards as his favourite appellation – look for wines from Guigal, Jaboulet Aîné, de Vallouit and Vidal-Fleury. There's Crozes-Hermitage Thalabert and Hermitage La Chapelle, both from Jaboulet, and Cornas (try the 1980 of Jaboulet at £2.60 for a half-bottle).

The other good areas on this list are the Loire – with the biggest range of Savennières outside the region itself and plenty of Chinon and Bourgueil (excellent value as well). In Alsace, there are wines from Klipfel, Trimbach, Dopff et Irion and other famous names. There are plenty of pudding wines, and the clarets start inexpensively but soon move up in price smartly (but there are old vintages as well).

The rest of the world is not neglected, either. There are good ranges from Australia, California and New Zealand, Italy provides some very serious wines from Tuscany (at rather serious prices), Spain has Marqués de Cáceres Riojas, there are vintages of Ch Musar from the Lebanon – even the Crimea Ruby from the USSR, but, surprisingly, no fortified wines.

Best buys

Savennières, Ch du Chamboreau 1985, £6.60
Sauvignon Blanc 1988, Stoneleigh Vineyard, New Zealand, £6.40
Côtes de Buzet 1983, Ch de Geysze, £4.30
Côtes du Rhône 1984, Guigal, £5.60
Ch Patache d'Aux 1983, Médoc, £7.50

Cumbrian Cellar

1 St Andrew's Square, Penrith, Cumbria   TEL (0768) 63664
CA11 7AN

OPEN Mon–Sat 9–5.30; public holidays 9.30–5.30   CLOSED Sun, Chr Day, Boxing Day, Good Friday, May Day   CREDIT CARDS Access, American Express, Visa; personal and business accounts   DISCOUNTS 5% on 1 case   DELIVERY Free in Cumbria (min 1 case); elsewhere at cost; mail order available   GLASS HIRE Free with 1-case order
TASTINGS AND TALKS Occasional in-store tastings; to groups on request
CELLARAGE £3 per case per year

Mr Gear, of Cumbrian Cellar, is obviously a man of discernment: 'I will not sell a wine that I would not like to drink myself,' he writes, quite properly – but then adds 'possibly excepting retsina'. Instantly, we checked to find that there is indeed a retsina on the list (from Kourtaki at £3.05); but if that is the only bottle he won't drink, he is still going to be occupied interestingly for quite a while.

There are certain specialities, of course. One is, in fact, Greece, with the top wines of Ch Carras, the beefy red from Boutari, as well as the more familiar attractions of Demestica. Another is Sherry, with wines from Valdespino, Duke of Wellington, Findlaters and Williams & Humbert. The New World has attracted some big names: Lindemans, Rosemount, Tisdall and Orlando from Australia; Cooks and Babich from New Zealand; Concha y Toro and Santa Helena from Chile; but virtually nothing from California.

In Europe, Italy offers some good value with wines such as the Chianti of Rocca delle Macie, the Trebbiano d'Abruzzo of Illuminati and Cerasuolo, also from the Abruzzo. There are some of the fine Riojas of La Rioja Alta, and some estate German wines from Deinhard. In France, the listings are somewhat briefer: a few clarets (rather too many examples of basic wines from Calvet), some good Beaujolais (but virtually no other Burgundies), very little on the Loire, and rather pricy Champagnes.

Best buys

Ch Carras 1979, Côtes de Meliton Rouge, Greece, £4.90
Krondorf Rhine Riesling 1986, Eden Valley, Australia, £4.20
Duke of Wellington Sherries
Domaine de Baudare 1985, Côtes de Frontonnais, £4.99
Ch de Castéra 1985, Médoc, £6.05

D'Arcy's

Princes Square (off Buchanan Street),   TEL 041–226 4309
Glasgow G1 3SX

OPEN Mon–Sat 10–7; Sun, public holidays 11–5   CLOSED Chr Day, 1 Jan
CREDIT CARDS Access, Diners Club, American Express, Visa; personal and business accounts   DISCOUNTS 10% on 1 case   DELIVERY Free within 5-mile radius (min 1 case); elsewhere negotiable   GLASS HIRE Free
TASTINGS AND TALKS To groups on request   CELLARAGE Not available

A welcome addition to the few recommendable Glasgow wine merchants, D'Arcy's is also a cheesemonger and wine and food bar. The wine shop list is quite short and has stuck mainly with France, but contains some well-chosen wines to go with the British cheeses. There could be more wines in the lower price ranges to advantage.

A few clarets, ranging from Ch Latour Séguy 1985 at £4.90 to Ch Latour itself at £50 for the 1976 vintage, appear alongside some domaine Burgundies, Beaujolais from Ferraud, some beefy Rhône reds (including Côte Rôtie 1984 from Guigal at £12.90), and some Alsace wines from Victor Preiss to go with the softer cheeses.

Outside France, most interest centres on the good Chianti Classico of Ripanera, and Australian wines from Brown Brothers. There is a rather sad little collection of Ports to go with the Stilton.

Best buys

Jacob's Creek Dry Red, South Australia, £3.50
Quinta da Camarate 1984, J M da Fonseca, £4.50
Rioja Tinto 1985, CVNE, £3.50
Alsace Riesling 1986, Victor Preiss, £4.90

Davisons Wine Merchants   ☞ ☆

7 Aberdeen Road, Croydon, Surrey   TEL 01–681 3222
CR0 1EQ
75 Off-Licences in the South-East

OPEN Mon–Sat 10–2, 5–10; Sun 12–2, 7–9   CLOSED A few branches close one morning per week   CREDIT CARDS Access, Visa; personal and business accounts   DISCOUNTS 8.5% on 1 case   DELIVERY Free within reasonable radius of shop (min 1 case); elsewhere at cost; mail order available   GLASS HIRE Free with order   TASTINGS AND TALKS Selected tastings in certain shops   CELLARAGE Not available

The accountants at the multi-national-owned off-licence groups would blanch at the delighted claim of Davisons that they now have stocks of 60,000 cases of claret (that's 800 cases per shop) and 6,000 cases of vintage Port quietly maturing in their cellars in Croydon. What it is to be a family-owned company.

That depth of the range of clarets is reflected in the standard shop list (although there are plenty more finer wines and Ports available on order or at the Master Cellar Wine Warehouse – see separate entry). The list moves from inexpensive wines such as the popular Ch Timberlay 1985 at £3.95, through plenty of wines in the £6 area, up to Ch Mouton Rothschild 1966 at £96.50 a bottle. Some vintage Ports go back to the 1963 vintage, and some of the larger branches outside London carry stocks of some of these.

Nothing quite equals those two sections of the list – how could they? But there are good things from Burgundy with domaine wines (and Beaujolais from Georges Duboeuf), from Alsace with Hugel wines, odd treats from the South of France (Minervois Domaine de Ste-Eulalie at £2.99 is good value), and the house Champagne Ellner at £9.25.

Davisons have spread further beyond France than they used to. Italy has gained with white Veneto wines from Zenato and

Chianti Machiavelli, and Spain has Torres wines, Marqués de
Cáceres and Berberana Riojas. Bulgaria offers its usual good
value. The New World has gained, too – more from Australia
(Jacob's Creek and other Orlando wines are the best value) and
New Zealand (Cooks and Montana), but still very little from
California.

Best buys

Gewürztraminer Minosegi Bor, Hungary, £1.99
Ch Timberlay 1985, Médoc, £3.95
Ch Meyney 1981, St-Estèphe, £8.95
Rioja 1986, Laturce, £3.25
Taylors 1960 Vintage Port, £32.50
Tocai di San Martino 1988, Zenato, £3.99

Davys of London

151 Borough High Street, London   TEL 01–407 1484
SE1 1HR

OPEN Mon–Fri 10–6   CLOSED Sat, Sun, public holidays
CREDIT CARDS Access, Davys of London, American Express, Visa; personal
and business accounts   DISCOUNTS 5% on 1 case; 10% with Davys Card
DELIVERY Free in central London (min 2 cases); otherwise £3.50 per 6
bottles; mail order available   GLASS HIRE Free with reasonable wine
order   TASTINGS AND TALKS Occasional tastings in Davys wine bars
CELLARAGE Not available

This is one of the two retail outlets of the wine bar group
operated by Davys of London (which includes such bars –
familiar to Londoners – as Skinkers, the Chopper Lump and
City Flogger – and wine bars in Exeter and Hythe in Kent). For
their other outlet, see the separate entry for Wines Galore.
    Davys of London operate from the same list as the wine bars,
but sell the wines at retail rather than restaurant prices. Look for
their clarets, Burgundies and vintage Ports, and for Champagne
(Veuve Clicquot is the house Champagne at £13.95). The only
concession to the world outside France is Davys' Rioja at £4.35.

Best buys

Champagne Veuve Clicquot NV, £13.95
Davys' Claret NV, £3.50
Davys' Rioja, £4.35

Most wine merchants will supply wine for parties on a sale or return
basis.

Del Monico's

23 South Street, St Austell, Cornwall   TEL (0726) 73593
PL25 5BH

OPEN Mon–Sat 9–6; Sun (summer only) 12–2   CLOSED Some public
holidays   CREDIT CARDS Access, Visa   DISCOUNTS Negotiable
DELIVERY Free within 20-mile radius of St Austell (min 1 case)
GLASS HIRE Free   TASTINGS AND TALKS Occasional in-store tastings
CELLARAGE Free

Good for David del Monico, eponymous owner of Del Monico's.
'I have destocked all branded wines, I don't even look at stuff
like Malibu, and I'm slowly killing Martini and the like. There's
no beer, no cider, and no aggro.'

When he comes to what he does sell, though, his list becomes
rather circumspect – Corbières, it says, without a producer's
name; even worse, Volnay – no producer, no vintage. We
suspect there are some good wines lurking here, but we would
like confirmation.

Things get a little better when we move away from areas
which need producers' names. In Bordeaux it's easy – the
château name tells all – and we can appreciate a well-priced
collection of wines. But when we move out of France, we suffer
again in Germany, in Italy and even in poor old Greece. Why
should it be left to the New World to tell us who makes the
wines (Penfolds and Hill-Smith in Australia, Stoneleigh
Vineyards in New Zealand) and the years that they were made?

There is also a Cellar Selection list, which contains treats like
Don Zoilo Sherries, Churchill Ports, Délas Rhône wines and
Gaillac wines from Jean Cros.

Best buys

Beaujolais Blanc 1988, Paquet, £4.45
Ch Larroze Rouge de Garde, Gaillac 1986, £3.89
Regaleali Bianco 1987, £3.85
Apostoles Oloroso Abocado Sherry, Gonzalez Byass, £8.75

Cellarage is generally provided at the rates quoted only when the wines
have been bought from the merchant concerned.

If your favourite wine merchant is not in this section, write and tell us
about him or her. There are report forms at the back of the book.

The Delicatessen (North Berwick)

See J E Hogg.

Demijohn Wines

151 Penn Street, nr Amersham,   TEL (0494) 715376
Buckinghamshire HP7 0PX
(Minimum sale 6 bottles)

OPEN Tue, Wed, Fri 12–6; Sat 11–6   CLOSED Mon, Thur, Sun, public
holidays   CREDIT CARDS Access, Visa; personal and business accounts
DISCOUNTS 2.5% on 1 unmixed case, 7.5% on 5+ cases   DELIVERY Free
within 5-mile radius (min 1 case); elsewhere at cost; mail order
available   GLASS HIRE Free with 1-case order   TASTINGS AND TALKS 8-bottle
tastings every other Saturday Sept-Oct; to groups on request (Italian
tastings)   CELLARAGE Not available

Owner Gordon Medcalf made an environmentally attractive
offer to his customers this year: people driving up bearing lead-
free petrol stickers on their cars could get one bottle of organic
wine free if they bought a case of wine, two if they bought 15
bottles.

Four of the five organic wines were Italian, reflecting the bent
of the Demijohn list. There are French wines, but nothing that
can't be bought elsewhere, often at better prices.

But with Italy we are on firm ground. Barolo and Chianti are
the strong points: Chiantis from Badia a Coltibuono, the Riecine
of John Dunkley, Castel San Polo in Rosso, Ruffino; and for
Barolos we would recommend the San Guiseppe Riserva of
Cavallotto at £7.22. In the Veneto, look for the organic wines of
Guerrieri-Rizzardi, while further south, there are the Orvietos of
Antinori, wines from Lungarotti in Umbria (Rubesco di
Torgiano 1982 at £5.66), Merlot del Colle from Aquileia and Cirò
from Calabria. A few Australian and New Zealand wines have
strayed on to this strongly Italophile list.

Best buys

Cirò 1985, Librandi, £3.45
Montepulciano d'Abruzzo 1987, Barone Cornacchia, £3.79
Brunello di Montalcino 1980, Lisini, £8.98
Settesoli Bianco and Rosso, £2.78
Vin Santo della Toscana 1981, Lucignano, £6.82

Why not club together with friends to enjoy volume discounts and free
delivery?

Dennhöfer Wines

47 Bath Lane, Newcastle upon Tyne,   TEL 091–232 7342
Tyne & Wear NE4 5SP

OPEN Mon–Fri 9–5.30; Sat 9–1 CLOSED Sun, public holidays
CREDIT CARDS All accepted; personal and business accounts DISCOUNTS 5–
10% (min 1 case) DELIVERY Free in North-East (min 1 case); elsewhere
at cost GLASS HIRE Free with 1-case order TASTINGS AND TALKS May be
arranged in-store; occasional tastings with meal held at Blackgate
Restaurant; to groups on request CELLARAGE Free

A gently expanding range of wines (as they describe it) has
strengths in Germany, in Burgundy, with smaller successes in
Bordeaux and a nod in the direction of the New World.

Germany, though, retains the lion's share of interest. There
are estate wines from most areas, some from familiar names
(Plettenberg in the Nahe, Von Schorlemer in the Mosel, the
Baden co-operative, the State domaine in the Rheingau). Prices
are very competitive throughout the range, which is mainly of
QbA and Kabinett quality wines.

In France, Burgundy is covered by wines from a number of
négociants – Labouré-Roi, Charles Viénot and Henri Laroche in
Chablis, Pierre Dupond in Beaujolais. There are a few clarets
(good value are the 1984 Ch Respide at £5.58 or Ch Castéra 1985
at £6.82 – prices on the list do not include VAT, but we have
added it here); also Alsace wines from Ringenbach Moser
(Silvaner 1985 at £4.48), and a big range from the house
Champagne supplier H Blin (NV Brut at £10.29). The New
World gets a look in with wines from Wyndham Estate in the
Hunter Valley.

Best buys

Munsterer Schlosskapelle Kabinett 1986, Reichsgräflich von
Plettenberg, £4.02
Bickensohler Steinfelsen Ruländer 1986, Winzergenossenschaft
Bickensohl im Kaiserstuhl, £4.54
Chardonnay 1987, Bin 222, Wyndham Estate, Australia, £5.24
Ch Rousset 1983, Côtes de Bourg, £5.18

☆ celebrates the uninterrupted inclusion of this merchant in all ten
editions of *Which? Wine Guide*.

Rodney Densem Wines

OFFICE
Stapeley Bank, London Road, Nantwich,   TEL (0270) 623665
Cheshire CW5 7JW

RETAIL
4 Pillory Street, Nantwich, Cheshire   TEL as above
CW5 5BB

OPEN Mon–Tue 10–6; Wed 9–1; Thur–Fri 9–6; Sat 9–5.30   CLOSED Sun,
public holidays   CREDIT CARDS Access, Visa; personal and business
accounts   DISCOUNTS 5% on 1 case   DELIVERY Free within 25-mile radius
(min 1 case); elsewhere approximately £5 per single case; mail order
available   GLASS HIRE Free with 1-case order
TASTINGS AND TALKS Approximately 6 tastings annually; to groups on
request   CELLARAGE Not available

While the printed list has some areas of interest, the 100 or so
bin-ends that regularly fill the premises of Rodney Densem
Wines provide even more justification for a Guide entry. The
only way to check on these is to ask, since there are normally no
more than three cases of any wine.

On the standard list, areas worth considering include
Champagne (house Champagne is £9.19 – prices on the list do
not include VAT, but we have added it here). A useful range of
clarets stars Ch de la Rivière in Fronsac (1982 vintage is £10.11).
Burgundies rely on the firm of Drouhin to a considerable extent,
with Moillard second in command. There is little to detain us on
the Loire, but Alsace offers Hugel, and the Rhône has wines
from the négociant firm of Musset.

Outside France, Germany is depressing; Spain highlights
wines from Torres, and Italy has a few nuggets (Pomino from
Frescobaldi and Chianti from Rocca delle Macie). Australia has
wines from Lindemans and Rosemount as well as Brown
Brothers. and there are a few smatterings from the rest of the
world.

Best buys

Coronas 1985, Torres, Spain, £3.84
Prince de la Rivière 1982, Fronsac, £4.93
Pinot Blanc d'Alsace 1986, Hartenberger, £3.37

Prices were current in summer 1989 to the best of our knowledge but
can only be a rough indication of prices throughout 1990.

Desborough & Brown Fine Wines

21 George Street, St Albans,   TEL (0727) 44449
Hertfordshire AL3 4ES

CASE SALES ONLY   OPEN Tue–Fri 10–6; Sat 9–6   CLOSED Mon, Sun, public holidays   CREDIT CARDS All accepted; personal and business accounts DISCOUNTS 5% on 3 cases   DELIVERY Free within 40-mile radius of St Albans (min 2 cases); elsewhere at cost; mail order available
GLASS HIRE Free with 3-case order   TASTINGS AND TALKS Bottles available in-store on Saturdays; tastings twice a month by invitation only; to professional groups on request   CELLARAGE Not available

The list, with one exception, is entirely French. That is the newly acquired range of wines from Wyndham Estate in Australia, for which Desborough & Brown are now the main importers – look for the unusual Verdelho-based wines for which Wyndham are well known, as well as the Hunter Shiraz and Chardonnays.

In France, it is the regions which fare particularly well. In the South-West, interesting bottles come from Henry Ryman at Ch La Jaubertie, Producteurs Plaimont (Madiran, and Vin de Pays des Côtes de Gascogne), Côtes de Duras and Buzet. Midi wines are from the négociant firm of Bernard Jean-Jean.

Another négociant – Brotte – dominates the wines from the Rhône, and there's more interest in wines from Willy Gisselbrecht in Alsace, or the varietal Vin de Pays de l'Ardèche. There's a small selection of Bordeaux, a pretty dull range from Burgundy, and Champagne from the Mailly co-operative.

Best buys

Fitou 1982, Domaine de la Boulière, £3.75
Coteaux du Layon 1980, Ch Beaulieu, £4.85
Domaine de Savignettes 1988, Côtes de Duras Blanc, £3.15
Sancerre 1988, Jean-Max Roger, £6.50

Special awards

🐷 means bargain prices (good *value* may be obtained from merchants without this symbol, of course, if you wish to pay for service)

✸ means that the wines stocked are of consistently high quality

▱ means that the merchant stocks an above-average range

☞ means that extra-special service is offered; helpful advice, information lists and newsletters, tastings etc.

Direct Wine Shipments

5/7 Corporation Square, Belfast, Co   TEL (0232) 238700/
Antrim BT1 3AJ   243906
ASSOCIATED OUTLET
Duncairn Wines, 555 Antrim Road,   TEL (0232) 370694
Belfast, Co Antrim BT15 3BU

OPEN Mon–Fri 9.30–6; Sat 10–5   CLOSED Sun, public holidays
CREDIT CARDS Access, Visa; personal and business accounts
DISCOUNTS 5% on 1 unmixed case   DELIVERY Free in Greater Belfast or £2
per case anywhere in Northern Ireland   GLASS HIRE Not available
TASTINGS AND TALKS Tastings held in lecture room on premises; regular
6-week course held twice a year; to groups on request, in own lecture
room   CELLARAGE Free if purchased through en primeur offers

The solidly based range of wines from the only northern Ireland
merchant in the Guide has been expanded this year by the
introduction of a large range of Faiveley Burgundies, wines from
Dr Bürklin-Wolf in the Rheinpfalz of Germany and a splendid
set of mature vintages of Vega Sicilia in Spain (where the 1962
vintage is £44).

Clarets start well with some wines at very competitive prices
(Ch Lagrange 1986, Lussac St-Emilion at £5.25, for instance), and
then the list progresses magisterially on to a 1959 Cos
d'Estournel for £65 – a good price, in fact. More up to date,
Direct Wine Shipments made a 1988 en primeur offer.

Burgundy is dominated by négociants such as Faiveley, Louis
Latour, Chanson Père, Loron in Beaujolais and Domaine
Laroche in Chablis. The Rhône wines come from the very
traditional house of Chapoutier, and small points of interest can
be found in the South of France. Laporte Sancerres on the Loire
(1988 vintage at £6.75), and a large clutch of Hugel wines from
Alsace round off the French section.

Bürklin-Wolf is the only German star among a crowd of rather
basic wines, while in Italy, the wines of Antinori redeem a
bleak scene. Over in Iberia, Torres conquers from Penedés,
Marqués de Cáceres Riojas, and those Vega Sicilia wines...

Much further east are competitively priced Bulgarian wines,
while further south, we find Brown Brothers Australian wines.
Champagnes are from Pannier (Carte Noire is £9.95), Madeiras
from Cossart Gordon, Sherries from Lustau, and aged tawny
Ports from Noval.

Best buys

Bourgogne Rouge 1985, Faiveley, £4.85
Sangredetoro 1986, Torres, £3.15
Ch Fourcas Hosten 1986, Listrac, £6.60

Galestro 1987, Antinori, £3.99
Bulgarian wines

Domaine Direct

29 Wilmington Square, London   TEL 01–837 3521/1142
WC1X 0EG

CASE SALES ONLY   OPEN Mon–Fri 9–6   CLOSED Sat, Sun, public holidays
CREDIT CARDS None accepted; personal and business accounts
DISCOUNTS Not available   DELIVERY Free in central London (min 1 case)
and UK mainland (min 3 cases); otherwise 1 case £5.75, 2 cases £8.05;
mail order available   GLASS HIRE Free   TASTINGS AND TALKS 6 theme
tastings annually through Les Jeudis de Domaine Direct club; 2 tastings
a year of wines from catalogue for private customers; to groups on
request   CELLARAGE £5.75 per case per year

This is certainly one of the finest – if not the finest – Burgundy
lists in this Guide. It's also an exclusively Burgundy list,
concentrating, as the firm's name suggests, on domaine wines.

Lest you reach for your bank manager's phone number before
you buy, Domaine Direct's list contains some everyday
Burgundies as well. So if we start with Domaine Direct's own
Bourgogne Passetoutgrain 1986 at £5.17 (prices on the list do not
include VAT, but we have added it here) we can breathe before
we tackle the heights.

And what a galaxy of names are there. Just a few will suffice
to give the general idea: Simon Bize, Domaine de la Pousse
d'Or, Tollot-Beaut, Comte Armand, Alain Michelot, Armand
Rousseau, Domaine Corsin, Domaine Vincent, Etienne Sauzet.
Even here – as with the basic wines – there are good-value
pockets tucked away, often from lesser villages, such as Givry
1986 of J P Ragot at £6.73, or Monthélie 1983 of René Thévenin
at £8.62, before we get to the really great (and pricy) wines. In
Chablis, Jean Durup and René Dauvissat provide most of the
wines.

There are also a few Beaujolais – very much as an
afterthought. A tasting case helps set the scene for future
pleasures. And the Domaine Direct Cellar Account helps you
buy young Burgundy for laying down.

Best buys

Bourgogne Passetoutgrain 1986, Domaine Direct, £5.17
Mâcon Viré 1987, Bonhomme, £6.61
Montagny Premier Cru Coères 1987, Bernard Michel, £7.19
Savigny-lès-Beaune 1985, Jean-Marc Pavelot, £9.49

Peter Dominic ☆

HEAD OFFICE
Astra House, Edinburgh Way, Harlow,   TEL (0279) 626801
Essex CM20 2BE
ASSOCIATED OUTLET
Bottoms Up
Approx 650 outlets nationwide

OPEN Varies from store to store; majority open 7 days a week, Mon–
Sat 9–6; Sun, public holidays 12–2, 7–10 (excluding Scotland)
CLOSED Chr Day, 1 Jan   CREDIT CARDS Access, Diners Club, American
Express, Grand Metropolitan Shareholders Card, Visa; personal and
business accounts   DISCOUNTS 5% (min 1 mixed case)   DELIVERY Free
locally to store (min 1 case); mail order available   GLASS HIRE Free with
1-case order   TASTINGS AND TALKS Tastings held in most branches on a
weekly basis; to groups on request to the branch manager
CELLARAGE Not available

With recent management changes and a promise of a complete
overhaul of the organisation of these shops, we await with
trepidation changes to one of the few High Street off-licence
groups which has had a reputation for the quality of its wines.
The Bottoms Up chain (see separate entry), which is under the
same ownership, looks like being the home of the Peter
Dominic hopes for the future.

Drinksmart

Bull Head Street, Wigston, Leicester,   TEL (0533) 881122
Leicestershire LE8 1PA

OPEN Mon–Thur 10–8; Fri, Sat 9–8; public holidays 10–6   CLOSED Sun,
Chr Day, Boxing Day, 1 Jan, Good Friday   DISCOUNTS Available
DELIVERY Not available   GLASS HIRE Free   TASTINGS AND TALKS Tasting in-
store available daily; to groups on request   CELLARAGE Not available

New to the Guide, Drinksmart has been in operation since 1988.
It's described as 'the UK's largest drinks superstore' – not
necessarily a point in its favour, we feel, but it does mean that
there's an awful lot of wine on sale.

While much is good, there are some less successful areas –
Germany, for example, and Italy (redeemed by the wines of
Rocca delle Macie in Tuscany), and Burgundies without
producers' names. But the good points include a well-priced and
varied selection of clarets, some sound wines from the South of
France (Fitou Cave Pilote 1986 at £2.49 is typical good value
here), interesting bottles from Spain (Torres is there, as are
Domecq Riojas), Rosemount and McWilliams wines from
Australia, Coteaux de Kefraya wines from the Lebanon (another

producer besides Ch Musar?) which could be just a curiosity but might be more, and several fairly priced sparkling wines (Marqués de Monistrol Cava at £3.99) and Champagnes (house Champagne is Aubert Brut at £7.49 as we went to press – probably a little more now).

Best buys

Champagne Aubert, £7.49
Ch Montaigne 1986, Bordeaux Supérieur, £3.29
Côtes de Beaune Villages 1983, Labouré-Roi, £4.99
Plovdiv Cabernet Sauvignon 1984, Bulgaria, £2.39
Fitou 1986, Cave Pilote, £2.49

Drunken Mouse

195–7 Lower Richmond Road, London SW15 1HJ   TEL 01–785 2939

OPEN Mon–Sat 10.30–9; Sun 12–2   CLOSED Chr, 1 Jan
CREDIT CARDS Access, Diners Club, Visa; personal and business accounts   DISCOUNTS Available   DELIVERY Free in Greater London (min 1 case); elsewhere 1 case £3.50, 2 cases free; mail order available through Australian Wine Club   GLASS HIRE Free with 1-case order   TASTINGS AND TALKS In-store tastings every weekend   CELLARAGE Not available

Although Australia is the highlight of this list, other things of interest in this cheery, open shop in Putney are some good Chiantis (Remole from Frescobaldi), Chanson Burgundies, Torres wines from Spain, Robert Mondavi and Julius Wile wines from California, and a representative range from New Zealand.

But by far the largest space is devoted to Australia. Look for a plethora of wines from many top producers (Orlando, Penfolds, Rosemount, Wynns, Lindemans, Tyrrells) as well as smaller estates (Mount Hurtle, Leeuwin Estate, Vasse Felix, Petersons) – and remember that what is on the printed list is only a part of the full range. Good value is be had at the lower end with wines like Jacob's Creek or Mastersons Barossa Valley wines (at £3.69), and at the top end there are classics like Wynns John Riddoch Cabernet Sauvignon at £14.99 or Pipers Brook Chardonnay at £12.99.

Best buys

Orlando Jacob's Creek white Semillon/Chardonnay 1988, Australia, £3.19
Orlando RF Cabernet Sauvignon 1986, Australia, £4.39
Yalumba Angas Brut Sparkling, Australia, £4.99
Rioja 1984, Siglo Saco, £3.99

Duncairn Wines

See Direct Wine Shipments.

Duras Direct

61 Elmleigh, Midhurst, West Sussex   TEL (073 081) 4150
GU29 9HA

CASE SALES ONLY   OPEN Mon–Fri 9–6; Sat, Sun, public holidays 9–1
CLOSED Chr Day   CREDIT CARDS None accepted; personal and business
accounts   DISCOUNTS Negotiable   DELIVERY Free within 10-mile radius of
Midhurst (min 1 case); otherwise charges negotiable; mail order
available   GLASS HIRE Free   TASTINGS AND TALKS To invited guests and to
groups on request   CELLARAGE Not available

This remains a short list which specialises in the wines of
south-west France. Duras is there, of course, in the form of three
estate wines, but there are also wines from Cahors, St-Emilion
(Ch Labattut – good value at £4.31) and, at a complete tangent,
wines from Sancerre, Pouilly Fumé and Muscadet to provide the
white relief.

Best buys

Côtes de Duras 1985, Domaine de Ferrant, £4.07
Cahors 1986, Domaine de Fages, £4.07

George Dutton & Son

See Willoughbys.

Eaton Elliot Winebrokers

15 London Road, Alderley Edge,   TEL (0625) 582354
Cheshire SK9 7JT

OPEN Mon–Fri 9–6; Sat 9–5   CLOSED Sun, public holidays
CREDIT CARDS All accepted; personal and business accounts
DISCOUNTS 5% on 1 mixed case   DELIVERY Free within 30-mile radius of
Alderley Edge (min 1 case); elsewhere £6.50 for 1 case; mail order
available   GLASS HIRE Free with 1-case order   TASTINGS AND TALKS 2
annual tastings by invitation only; to groups on request   CELLARAGE Not
available

Many of the wines on the list from this firm are direct imports.
These include two famous names in Italy – Castello di Volpaia
Chianti, Duca d'Asti Barbaresco and Barolo – as well as wines
from the small Heathcote winery in Australia and from Schug
Cellars in California.

These are in addition to the interesting French range which has many areas of interest well away from the classic regions, including the largest set of Jura wines in the country (from the top estate of Ch d'Arlay), and comes up trumps with plenty of French country wines. Look for areas such as the Jurançon of Domaine Cauhapé, the Savoie wines of Pierre Boniface in Apremont, the Fronton wines of Ch Cahuzac and the Madiran of Ch Peyros.

In Burgundy, good wines come from Pierre Bourre, while there's much on offer from the Loire (Bourgueil from Caslot-Galbrun, organic Muscadet from Guy Bossard, Sancerre from Vacheron, Pouilly Fumé from Michel Bailly). Look, too, for Champagne from Nicolas Feuillatte and Alsace from the Turckheim co-operative.

Best buys

Ch Peyros 1983, Madiran, £4.35
Domaine de Rieux 1988, Vin de Pays des Côtes de
Gascogne, £2.95
Fronton 1986, Ch Cahuzac, £3.35
Christopher Tatham Monopole, La Chablisienne, £4.80

C C G Edwards

MAIL ORDER ONLY
Burlton, Shillingstone, Dorset DT11 0SP   TEL (0258) 860641
CREDIT CARDS None accepted   DISCOUNTS Not available   DELIVERY Free on UK mainland (min 1 mixed case)   GLASS HIRE Free
TASTINGS AND TALKS To groups on request   CELLARAGE Not available

A short list of organically produced wines of which only one or two are shipped each year. Currently the wine is Ch La Croix Simon, a Bordeaux (both from the 1987 vintage, red at £4.60, white at £4.20).

Eldridge Pope

HEAD OFFICE
Weymouth Avenue, Dorchester, Dorset   TEL (0305) 251251
DT1 1QT
8 branches (Dorchester, Shaftesbury, Sherborne, Wareham,
Westbourne, Weymouth, Wincanton and Winchester) and 3
Reynier Wine Libraries (London, Exeter and Bristol)
ASSOCIATED OUTLET
Godrich & Petman (see separate details)

OPEN Generally Mon–Sat 9–1, 2–5.30 (varying half-days); (Reynier in
London and Exeter) Mon–Fri 11–6.30,   CLOSED Sat (Reynier, London),
Sun, public holidays   CREDIT CARDS Access, Visa; personal and business
accounts   DISCOUNTS 5% on mixed or full case   DELIVERY Free locally for
orders of £20+ and on UK mainland for orders of 4+ cases (or £100);
otherwise at cost; mail order available   GLASS HIRE Available with order
TASTINGS AND TALKS Occasional in-store tastings; regular tutored tastings
at Wine Libraries; to groups on request   CELLARAGE £2 per case per year

This is one of the benchmark lists in the Guide. Big,
comprehensive and full of good things, it proves that it is
possible for a brewer to show a civilised interest in wine
(something too many of the major brewers seem determined to
disprove).

Over the past year, Eldridge Pope have opened two more
Reynier Wine Libraries – one in London EC3, one in Bristol –
and there's talk of a large development at their home base in
Dorchester. They have expanded their list as well, particularly
the carefully chosen Chairman's Range (individual wines from
classic areas) with a new Red Burgundy at £4.66.

But one new wine is a drop in the ocean at Eldridge Pope.
The list of clarets alone runs for 16 pages, and starts with wines
from 1928 and 1947 before moving sedately through the years to
the present day. While the earlier wines are predictably pricy,
by the time the 1980s are reached, there is a good cross-section
of wines, from petits châteaux to the classed growths.

Burgundy comes in for similar treatment. There are good
Beaujolais before we plunge into the region proper – reds here
start with 1970, whites much more modestly with 1984. There
are domaine wines aplenty. By contrast the Rhône is only
briefly covered, but once we reach the Loire, expansion sets in
again, featuring the wines of Jean Baumard in Coteaux du
Layon and Savennières and vintage after vintage of wines from
Moulin Touchais. Alsace comes from Dopff et Irion, and the
range offered includes some of the rich Vendanges Tardives and
Sélections de Grains Nobles.

After such luxuries, it is good to see that Eldridge Pope also have a sound collection of country wines, from vins de pays up to the southern appellations Corbières and Minervois, as well as the good-value wines from the co-operative of Haut-Poitou (Sauvignon is £3.46).

Then we move from France to the splendid range of German estate wines which features Schloss Vollrads in profusion (Eldridge Pope are the importers of wines from this famous estate), and other estates in more modest quantities. From Italy there is less of interest, apart from treats like the wines of Capezzana in Tuscany (Barco Reale 1986 at £4.66) and the good-value Cellaro wines from Sicily. Further north, the Luxembourg wines of Bernard Massard are featured, but other than a large range of Ports and Madeiras of note Spain and Portugal barely make an appearance.

In the New World, there are a few offerings – Grgich Hills and Gundlach Bundschu in California, and Montrose wines from Australia.

Best buys

Abbaye de Valmagne 1986 Rouge, Coteaux de Languedoc, £3.51
Ménétou-Salon 1987, Jean-Max Roger, £4.89
Schloss Vollrads Halbtrocken Kabinett 1985, Rheingau, £6.88
Côtes du Rhône 1987, Domaine de la Renjardière, £2.88
The Chairman's Late Bottled Port, £6.96
Gewürztraminer Les Sorcières 1986, Dopff et Irion, £6.24
Ch Tourtirac 1985, Côtes de Castillon, £3.86

Elite Wines

421 New Kings Road, London SW6 4RN   TEL 01–731 3131

CASE SALES ONLY   OPEN Normal office hours   CREDIT CARDS None accepted; personal and business accounts DISCOUNTS Quantity discounts DELIVERY Free for 3 cases otherwise at cost; mail order available GLASS HIRE, TASTINGS AND TALKS, CELLARAGE Not available

The fine wine arm of Majestic Wine Warehouses (see separate entry), specialising in fine claret, Burgundy and vintage Port.

Best buys

Fine clarets and Burgundies

> Please write to tell us about any ideas for features you would like to see in next year's edition or in *Which? Wine Monthly*.

Ben Ellis and Associates

The Harvesters, Lawrence Lane,   TEL (073 784) 4866/2160
Buckland, Betchworth, Surrey RH3 7BE   (answering machine)

CASE SALES ONLY   OPEN 'All hours' – 24-hour answering machine
CREDIT CARDS None accepted; personal and business accounts
DISCOUNTS Not available DELIVERY Free in Surrey and central London
(min 1 case) and elsewhere (min 5 cases); otherwise at cost; mail order
available GLASS HIRE Free with 2-case order TASTINGS AND TALKS Two
regular 3-day tastings in spring and summer; to groups on request
CELLARAGE £3 per case per year

This continues to be a strongly French list, with Bordeaux the
heart of the matter. There are plenty of clarets for laying down,
and older vintages for drinking now, but here – as elsewhere in
the range – plenty of attention has been paid to less expensive
wines for everyday drinking. So while there may be classed
growths, they do not outnumber such wines as Ch Ferrasses
1982, Côtes de Castillon at £3.68.

The interest in less expensive wines is also apparent in the
French regional wines, which include the Vin de Pays de
l'Ardèche, Cahors of Domaine Pelvillain, and Faugères from the
Val d'Orbieu producers. That interest – inevitably – is missing
in the Burgundy selection (good though this is, including
special vintage offers), but crops up again with wines such as
La Vieille Ferme Côtes du Lubéron from the Rhône Valley.

Beyond France, look for more value from wines like the
Cellaro Rosso and Bianco from Sicily (at £2.89), from
inexpensive Rioja from Campillo and the Chilean wines of Viña
Linderos. Small New World selections include Jekel wines from
California.

Best buys

Ch Haut Queyron 1982, Bordeaux, £3.51
Syrah Vin de Pays des Coteaux de Bessille, Vins Ronance, £2.50
Muscadet de Sèvres-et-Maine sur Lie 1987, Ch La Berrière, £3.49

Special awards

🐷 means bargain prices (good *value* may be obtained from
merchants without this symbol, of course, if you wish to pay for
service)

✵ means that the wines stocked are of consistently high quality

🏷 means that the merchant stocks an above-average range

☞ means that extra-special service is offered; helpful advice,
information lists and newsletters, tastings etc.

Ellis Son & Vidler ☆

Warnford Court, 29 Throgmorton Street, London EC2N 2AT	TEL 01–628 1855
Cliffe Cellars, 12/13 Cliffe Estate, Lewes, East Sussex BN8 6JL	TEL (0273) 480235

CASE SALES ONLY   OPEN Mon–Fri 9–5.30   CLOSED Sat, Sun, public holidays   CREDIT CARDS Access, Visa; personal and business accounts DISCOUNTS 5% on 10 cases   DELIVERY Free on UK mainland (min 5 cases); mail order available   GLASS HIRE Free with 5-case order
TASTINGS AND TALKS Bi-annual tastings in Sussex and London; to groups on request   CELLARAGE £4.50 per case per year

Management changes in the past year have focused attention on a new London office, although the Cliffe Cellars address continues to operate as before and is the main cellars for the company.

It is still very much a French-based list. There is plenty of interest in Bordeaux, with many wines at prices around the £6 mark, a few under; little is older than 1982. Burgundy comes from a good variety of domaines – no surprises in good value here, but plenty to choose from. The Rhône offers some good Côtes du Rhône (such as that from Ch St-Estève 1988 at £4.17). There are offerings from the Bourgeois family in Sancerre. The other regions are touched upon – look especially for the Coteaux Varois wines of Domaine de St-Jean de Villecroze.

Outside France, interest lessens. Italy is strangely almost lacking, Germany has a few of the fine wines of Max Ferdinand Richter, and Spain has Torres: there are a few Mondavi wines from California and Orlando wines from Australia. A few Sherries and many more Ports round off the range.

Best buys

La Cuvée Spéciale de St-Jean, Coteaux Varois 1986, £4.26
Ch du Tertre 1985, Bordeaux, £4.03
Chianti Rufina Banda Blu 1986, Grati, £3.35
Cabernet Sauvignon 1984, Concha y Toro, Chile, £3.22
Reichensteiner 1988, Carr Taylor, England, £5.19

Prices were correct to the best of our knowledge as we went to press. They, and ranges of wines stocked, are likely to change during the course of 1990 and are intended only as rough indication of an establishment's range and prices.

English Wine Centre

Drusilla's Corner, Alfriston, East Sussex   TEL (0323) 870532
BN26 5QS

OPEN Mon–Sat 10.30–5   CLOSED Sun   CREDIT CARDS Visa; personal and
business accounts   DISCOUNTS Trade only   DELIVERY Free within 20-mile
radius; elsewhere at cost; 5 cases £3.12 per case, 6–10 cases £2.12 per
case; mail order available   GLASS HIRE Free with 2-case order
TASTINGS AND TALKS Regular wine tours and tastings of English or
Continental wines; winter wine education courses; to groups around
southern England on request   CELLARAGE Limited

A good roll call of some well-established English vineyards are
represented here. Look for Lamberhurst, Carr Taylor, Breaky
Bottom, Nutbourne Manor, Hambledon and Biddenden. Start
with some of the best buys we list below.

Best buys

Sussex County 1988, £4.75
Wealden English Table Wine 1985, £4.35
Breaky Bottom Seyval Blanc 1986, £5.55
Penshurst Müller-Thurgau 1985, £4.35

English Wine Shop

3 Harcourt Street, London W1H 1DS   TEL 01–724 5009
HEAD OFFICE
Heywood Wines, 9 Montenotte Road,   TEL 01–340 9635
London N8 8RL

OPEN Tue–Fri 11.30–6.30; Sat 10–3   CLOSED Sun, Mon, public holidays
CREDIT CARDS Access; business accounts   DISCOUNTS Approx 10% on 1
case   DELIVERY Free in central London (min 3 cases); elsewhere by
quotation; mail order available   GLASS HIRE Free with 1-case order
TASTINGS AND TALKS In-store tastings held approx. every six weeks; to
groups on request   CELLARAGE Not available

A wide-ranging selection of English wines, taking in the wines
of nearly 20 vineyards. Most were from the 1985 and 1986
vintages as we went to press – English wine does mature over
this length of time very satisfactorily. Look for wines from New
Hall, Pilton Manor, Hambledon (the home of the modern revival
of English wine) and the popular wines from Carr Taylor.

Best buys

Headcorn 1987, £4.65
Stocks 1983, £4.05
New Hall Müller-Thurgau 1986, £4.15

Esprit du Vin

51a Upper Berkeley Street, London W1H 7PH	TEL 01–723 1713
88 High Street, London, SW19 5EG	TEL 01–946 7239

See Thresher; part of that chain, but with a separate, finer, range of wines.

Philip Eyres Wine Merchant

The Cellars, Coleshill, Amersham, Buckinghamshire HP7 0LW	TEL (0494) 433823 (enquiries)
	TEL (0494) 432402 (The Cellars)

CASE SALES ONLY   OPEN Personal callers by appointment; otherwise office hours   CREDIT CARDS None accepted; personal and business accounts   DISCOUNTS Not available   DELIVERY Free within 10-mile radius of Amersham, central London and other parts of London by mutual arrangement (min 1 case); on UK mainland 1–3 cases £5, 4+ cases free; mail order available   GLASS HIRE Free with case order
TASTINGS AND TALKS Occasional tastings; to groups on request
CELLARAGE Not available

A new wine merchant with a name that will be familiar to customers of Henry Townsend, the wine merchant that is now part of Findlater Mackie Todd (see entry), because Philip Eyres started Henry Townsend back in 1963 and ran that company until 1986. He runs this new company in association with Gregory Bowden and Florence Pike.

His new list contains many familiar names as well. It is sound in many areas, especially with a good set of ready-to-drink 1985 petit château clarets, while in areas such as the Rhône (with wines from Guigal and Florentin) or in Alsace (Rolly Gassmann), or in Spain (Torres), the great and the good feature strongly.

The German estate wines also present a forceful front (encouraging that a new merchant should think of listing these hard-to-sell wines), as do the domaine Burgundies, the wines from Montrose and Rouge Homme in Australia, Babich wines from New Zealand, and rarities such as the Salishan Pinot Noir from Washington State (£7.34 for the 1985 vintage), and the good-value Vila Regia Tinto from the Douro Valley in Portugal (£3.06 for the 1987 vintage). Look also for Sherries from Hidaigo, Chilean wines from Concha y Toro and some star French regional wines such as Le Guilleret Rouge of Sylvain Fessy at £3.10.

Best buys

Le Guilleret Rouge, Vin de Table, Sylvain Fessy, £3.10
Beaujolais Villages 1988, Domaine du Grand Chêne, £3.82
Salishan Pinot Noir Reserve 1985, Washington State, USA, £7.34
Manzanilla La Gitana, Hidalgo, £4.12

Farr Vintners

19 Sussex Street, London SW1V 4RR   TEL 01–630 5348

CASE SALES ONLY   OPEN Mon–Fri 9–6 (no personal callers)   CLOSED Sat,
Sun, public holidays   CREDIT CARDS None accepted; personal and
business accounts   DISCOUNTS Variable (min 10 cases)   DELIVERY At cost;
mail order available   GLASS HIRE Not available   TASTINGS AND TALKS Two
major wine tastings per annum; to groups on request   CELLARAGE £2.88
per case per year

A serious list of old and not so old clarets, of fine Burgundies,
Rhône wines and vintage Champagnes. These classics of wine
have now been joined by Opus One, the Mondavi/Rothschild
co-production, and by vintages of Sassicaia from Tuscany.

Best buys

Large bottles of claret

Farthinghoe Fine Wine and Food

The Old Rectory, Farthinghoe, Brackley,   TEL (0295) 710018
Northamptonshire NN13 5NZ

OPEN Mon–Fri 9–1, 2–5; Sat, Sun by arrangement   CLOSED Public
holidays   CREDIT CARDS None accepted; personal and business accounts
DISCOUNTS Quantity discounts (min 2 cases)   DELIVERY Free on UK
mainland (min 1 case); mail order available   GLASS HIRE Available
TASTINGS AND TALKS Regular tastings; to groups on request
CELLARAGE £3.25 per case per year (in bond only)

The double act of Simon and Nicola Cox – he running the wine
side of the business, she the cookery school – continues to
thrive in the Old Rectory of Farthinghoe. There is a shop which
sells cookery equipment, and a cookery demonstration theatre
just across the courtyard from the house.

The wine list has continued to expand. There are more
Champagnes (look for those of Georges Gardet, such as Brut
Spécial NV at £10.12), but for anyone looking for an alternative
there are Freixenet Cavas at a more modest £5.67. Interest in
Alsace is considerable, with wines from Rolly Gassmann, Louis
Gisselbrecht, Trimbach, Hugel and Beyer. And while French

areas like the Loire are only treated to a short list, there is always something of interest (try the Pouilly Fumé of André Dezat or the good-value Saumur Blanc of Ch de Villeneuve).

The largest French selection comes from Bordeaux, with some finer wines for laying down as well as some good everyday drinking. On the Rhône, wines are mainly from Jaboulet Aîné. There's little from other European countries, a smattering of Brown Brothers wines from Australia, but a much more solid selection of good estate wines from California. Look, too, for Garvey Sherries and Cossart Gordon Madeiras.

Best buys

Gewürztraminer 1987, Louis Gisselbrecht, £4.95
Champagne Georges Gardet 1979, £15.80
Saumur Blanc 1988, Ch de Villeneuve, £4.52
Ch Martouret 1987, Bordeaux Supérieur, £4.15
Finest Old Malmsey, Five Year Reserve Madeira,
Cossart Gordon, £8.50

Ferrers le Mesurier ☆

Turnsloe, North Street, Titchmarsh,   TEL (08012) 2660
Kettering, Northamptonshire
NN14 3DH

CASE SALES ONLY   OPEN Mon–Fri 8–6; Sat 9–1 (but best to telephone before calling)   CREDIT CARDS None accepted; personal and business accounts   DISCOUNTS By arrangement (min 1 case)   DELIVERY Free in London, Cambridge and within 50-mile radius of Titchmarsh (min 1 case); also by arrangement outside these areas; otherwise at cost GLASS HIRE Not available   TASTINGS AND TALKS Annual Cambridge college tasting; other tastings by arrangement   CELLARAGE Free if wine purchased from premises

When we first included Ferrers le Mesurier in the Guide, his list was almost exclusively Burgundy. Last year, he commented that he was cutting down on purchases of these wines because of high prices. It is perhaps a reflection of the way prices seesaw in that region that he now offers new red Burgundies, some at very acceptable prices.

An addition worth looking at is the Marsannay 1986 of Charlopin Parizot at £5.86; as is the Bourgogne Pinot 1986 of Confuron-Cotetidot at £6.90. There is also a new surge of interest in white Burgundy, with a good value Mâcon-Lugny les Charmes from the local co-operative at £4.60. These are the least expensive in a range which gets pretty serious at the top end.

Burgundy is now part of a wider list; so we have some Loire wines (try the Reuilly 1988 of Lafond at £4.89), a small amount

of Bordeaux at good prices (Ch Tour Blanche 1985 is £3.33),
Beaujolais from Colonge, Champagne from George Goulet and
even Warre's 1985 vintage Port (hard to find elsewhere at the
moment).

Best buys

Bergerac Blanc Ch la Tour des Gendres 1988, £3.27
Reuilly 1988, Comte Lafond, £4.89
Marsanny 1986, Charlopin-Parizot, £5.86
Beaujolais Villages 1988, Colonge, £4.31

Alex Findlater

SHOP
Vauxhall Cellars, 72 Goding Street,   TEL 01–587 1644
London SE11 5AW
OFFICE
Heveningham High House, Halesworth,   TEL (0986 83) 274
Suffolk IP19 0EA

CASE SALES ONLY OPEN Mon–Fri 10–1, 2–9; Sat 10–9 CLOSED Sun, public
holidays CREDIT CARDS Access, Visa; personal and business accounts
DISCOUNTS 5% on 1 case DELIVERY Free in central London and local to
Heveningham (min 1 case); otherwise 1 case £5.18, 2 cases £8.05; mail
order available GLASS HIRE Free with appropriate case order
TASTINGS AND TALKS Tastings by arrangement CELLARAGE £5.18 per case
per year

A massive collection of fine wines and, as always, one of the
foremost lists in this Guide. For those approaching it for the
first time and perhaps finding it a bit overwhelming in its depth
and range, it is worth looking at the major strengths.

There are a number. By far the most obvious, because it
warrants its own special list, is Australasia. This is one of the
most comprehensive listings that one could hope to see of wines
from both Australia and New Zealand, with many of the major
estates as well as plenty of smaller ones. Some estates are
available only from Alex Findlater.

The second strength is Germany. Alex Findlater is a strong
advocate of German wines, supporting his belief with an
encyclopedia of estate wines, including many of the new-style
Trocken and Halbtrocken wines which go well with food.

In Italy, it is the estate wines which shine, but there are also
some less expensive everyday wines as well as top producers'
wines (look especially at Tuscany). Then to yet another
impressive area, this time Sherry, covering many less usual
styles such as Palo Cortado and dry oloroso, as well as the more
familiar fino and sweet styles.

No mention of France yet. But that country is not neglected, either: plenty of claret, good country wines for less expensive purchases, a strong showing of pudding wines from Sauternes, smaller amounts from Burgundy and the Loire, Rhône wines from Jaboulet Aîné, and much to attract from Alsace.

Best buys

Ch Larroze Rouge 1986, Domaine Jean Cros, Gaillac, £4.45
Schloss Westerhaus Riesling Trocken 1986, Rheinhessen, £4.53
Barco Reale 1986, Villa di Capezzana, £5
Taltarni Shiraz 1982, Pyrenees, Victoria, Australia, £4.79
Solear Manzanilla Pasada, Barbadillo, £5.02

Findlater Mackie Todd   🖙 ☆

Findlater House, 22 Great Queen Street,   TEL 01–831 7701
London WC2B 5BB

OPEN Mon–Fri 9–6.30; Sat only during December   CLOSED Sun, public holidays   CREDIT CARDS All accepted; personal and business accounts DISCOUNTS Available   DELIVERY Free on UK mainland (min 1 case); Northern Ireland and offshore (excluding Isle of Wight) £3.50 per case; mail order available   GLASS HIRE Available   TASTINGS AND TALKS To groups on request   CELLARAGE Available

Findlater Mackie Todd now incorporates Henry Townsend (one of our award-winning merchants in last year's Guide), and both firms operate from the same list. What this has meant is that the combined firm has taken on aspects of both the old companies – and Findlater Mackie Todd's list has been considerably boosted. There continue to be regular special offers and mailings, including, in 1988, an en primeur claret and Sauternes offer, and the fine wine Inner Cellar list still operates.

The list is long and compendious, paricularly in France, with areas like Bordeaux taking on a considerable range of wines – including vintages back to 1976. Burgundy, too, is extensively covered, with plenty of domaine wines (Voarick, Lequin-Roussot, J-M Morey) and négociant wines from Louis Latour and Moillard. On the Rhône, there are the inevitable Jaboulet wines, but also bottles from Guigal, Paul Avril in Châteauneuf and Chapoutier in Hermitage. Alsace is a strong area, the Loire less so. There's a useful range of French regional wines, and Champagnes are present in plenty.

Germany – a former mainstay of the Henry Townsend range – plays an important role in the combined list, with many estate wines from all the major regions of the country. Italy is a growing area, with familiar names. Other countries whose contribution is important include Australia (Tyrrells,

Dalwhinnie, Basedow, Middlebrook are some of the names here – a good mix of the large and the small), and quite a few small New Zealand firms are represented as well. Sherries, of course, are Findlater's own (Dry Fly, a medium amontillado, is £4.75).

Best buys

Ch Thieuley 1985, Bordeaux, £4.97
Châteauneuf-du-Pape 1986, Chante-Cigale, £7.43
St-Chinian 1987, Roc-Prestige, £3.88
Marius Reserva 1982, Bodegas Piqueras, Almansa, £4.98
Semillon 1988, Willunga Hill, Australia, £5.45

Fine English Wine Company

Ashfield Grange, 2 Station Road,   TEL (0904) 706386
Copmanthorpe, York, North Yorkshire
YO2 3SX

CASE SALES ONLY   OPEN Mon–Sat 9–5 (other times by appointment)
CREDIT CARDS None accepted; personal and business accounts
DISCOUNTS Available   DELIVERY Free within 20-mile radius of York (min 1 case); otherwise £5 in Yorkshire and £8.50 on UK mainland; mail order available   GLASS HIRE Not available   TASTINGS AND TALKS To groups on request   CELLARAGE Not available

A new company, based in North Yorkshire away from England's vineyards, but already amassing a good list of English estate wines: familiar names such as Breaky Bottom and Carr Taylor as well as newer estates such as Saxon Valley. It is a pity that vintage information is not supplied, since this means we cannot recommend specific wines.

Fine Vintage Wines

3/5 Hythe Bridge, Oxford, Oxfordshire   TEL (0865) 791313/
OX1 2EW   724866
ASSOCIATED OUTLET
Grape Ideas Fine Vintage Wine   TEL 01–328 7317
Warehouse, 2a Canfield Gardens,
London NW6 3BS

OPEN Mon–Sat 11–7; Sun 11–2   CLOSED Public holidays
CREDIT CARDS Access, Visa; personal and business accounts
DISCOUNTS Large orders negotiable   DELIVERY Free locally (min 1 case); elsewhere negotiable; mail order available   GLASS HIRE Free with 1-case order   TASTINGS AND TALKS Regular tutored tastings; large annual tasting; to groups on request   CELLARAGE £5 per case per year

Fine Vintage Wines operates from the same premises as one of the branches of Grape Ideas Wine Warehouse (see separate entry), and is run by the same people. But, as its name suggests, this is fine wine territory, the most recent list featuring plenty of clarets, starting with recent vintages but moving back to the last century, and with famous names in abundance.

The same is true in Burgundy, where it is red Burgundy which takes the lion's share (plenty of domaine-bottled wines from the 1983 vintage which should be excellent drinking from now on). Smaller selections have been picked to represent the Rhône (mainly Jaboulet Aîné and Chapoutier). Outside France, there is an interesting short burst from Italy, with an unusual concentration on the Sardinian wines of Sella e Mosca (Nuraghe Majore 1986 at £3.95 is a good beefy bargain). There are Australian wines from Katnook estate, and plenty of older vintage Ports.

Best buys

Fine clarets and domaine-bottled Burgundies

Fortnum & Mason ☆

181 Piccadilly, London W1A 1ER   TEL 01–734 8040

OPEN Mon–Fri 9–5.30   CLOSED Sun, public holidays   CREDIT CARDS All accepted; personal and business accounts   DISCOUNTS 5–10% (min 1 case)   DELIVERY Free in Greater London (min £10 order); otherwise at cost; mail order available   GLASS HIRE Not available
TASTINGS AND TALKS Occasional promotional tastings
CELLARAGE £3 per case per year

You probably wouldn't expect to buy wines for everyday drinking at Fortnum & Mason, and you would be right. It's certainly one of the pricier wine merchants in the Guide.

But what it does offer is a splendid range of Champagnes, clarets (including wines from pre-war vintages), some good domaine Beaujolais, Alsace wines from some top houses and some famous names in Sancerre, Pouilly Fumé and Anjou.

Outside France, the Italian range has been enhanced by wines such as those of Jermann in Friuli, some of the Tuscan super vini da tavola and organic wines made by Guerrieri-Rizzardi in the Veneto. Germany has a modest but interesting collection of estate wines, Spain has Raimat wines, and there is a special line in Hungarian vintage Tokays.

Fortnums have rounded up top wines from all the major New World countries, with California the winner since some of the wines are not available elsewhere in Britain. Go, too, for vintage Ports, almacenista Sherries and a splendid trove of Madeiras.

Best buys

Tokay Aszu 5 Puttonyos 1979, Hungary, £8.15
Fortnum & Mason own-label wines
Clos des Litanies 1982, Pomerol, £12.75

Friarwood

26 New Kings Road, London SW6 4ST   TEL 01–736 2628

CASE SALES ONLY   OPEN Mon–Sat 9–6.30   CLOSED Sun, public holidays
CREDIT CARDS All accepted; personal and business accounts
DISCOUNTS Not available   DELIVERY Free in UK (min 5 cases); otherwise
at cost; mail order available   GLASS HIRE Free
TASTINGS AND TALKS Available upon request; to groups on request
CELLARAGE 8p per case per week (inc insurance)

Friarwood Fine Wine, they call themselves on their list, but this
doesn't mean just top claret and Burgundy: alongside the clarets
that go back to 1970 in profusion and the mainly domaine-
bottled red and white Burgundies, there are Loire wines
(especially from Sancerre – look for wines of André Leger), a
few Rhône wines (the Domaine Ste-Anne Côtes du Rhône at
£5.34 is worth considering – prices on the list do not include
VAT but we have added it here), and basic house white from
the Chablis region. Ports and Champagnes take us back to the
realm of fine wines proper.

Best buys

Clarets from the 1983 vintage

The Fulham Road Wine Centre

899/901 Fulham Road, London   TEL 01–736 7009
SW6 5HU   (retail shop)
                                        TEL 01–384 2588
                                               (offices)

OPEN Mon–Sat 10–8; Sun lunchtime   CLOSED Public holidays
CREDIT CARDS Access, Visa   DISCOUNTS 5% on 1 case   DELIVERY Free
locally; otherwise at cost to anywhere on UK mainland; mail order
available   GLASS HIRE Free with 1-case order   TASTINGS AND TALKS Wine
school in purpose-built tasting room; to groups on request
CELLARAGE Not available, but will make arrangements for customers with
a bond

A new shop which has already revealed very serious intent with
its range of wines, tastings and lecture programmes and its
high-powered management. The shop is spaciously laid out,
with enticing displays of wines and wine accessories.

Downstairs is a large lecture and tasting room, where the Fulham Road Wine School operates.

The range of wines reveals a wide-ranging taste, in similar vein to the Barnes Wine Shop, whose owner is a partner in this new venture. In addition, there is a constantly changing collection of fine wines. Countries or regions which are particularly well served in the main list are Australia, New Zealand, California and Italy.

In Australia, wines from a number of top estates – Rosemount, Taltarni, Blue Pyrenees, Wynns, Rouge Homme, Delatite and Tarrawarra in the Yarra Valley are out in force. New Zealand has Sauvignon from Montana, Villa Maria, Delegats, Selaks and Nautilus, Chardonnay from Cloudy Bay and Cabernet from Matua Valley. California looks good, with Mark West, Edna Valley, Château St Jean, Sanford and Robert Mondavi, with the less expensive Glen Ellen (Merlot 1986 at £4.99) to widen the price range.

In Europe, Italy offers wines from Ca' Donini in the Trivento (Chardonnay at £3.35), Rosso Cònero of Umani Ronchi, and Chianti Peppoli of Antinori. Spain has plenty of treats, too – Raimat wines from Catalonia (Cabernet Sauvignon at £6.50), Marqués de Griñon Cabernet Sauvignon from Rueda at £8.75 for the 1984 vintage, and Riojas from La Rioja Alta.

French wines are on the pricy side but some useful regional wines can be found (the Domaine de Limbardie Merlot is a deliciously fruity vin de pays): clarets hover around the middle price range, and other parts of this balanced set are Rhône wines from familiar names and Alsace bottles from the Turckheim co-operative. Pudding wines from around the world are a star section of the list.

Best buys

Domaine de San de Guilhem, Vin de Pays des Côtes de Gascogne 1988, £2.99
Ch Grand Caumont 1986, Corbières, £3.55
Mauro 1984, Tudela del Duero, £7.95
Verdelho 6-year-old, Bleasdale, Australia, £7.50
Raimat Chardonnay Brut, Cava, £6.95

We have tried to make the *1990 Which? Wine Guide* as comprehensive as possible, but we should love to hear from you about any other wine merchants you feel deserve an entry, or your comments on existing entries. Write to us either by letter or using the report forms supplied at the back of the book.

Fullers (Fuller, Smith & Turner)

HEAD OFFICE
Griffin Brewery, London W4 2QB   TEL 01–994 3691
59 shops in West London and Thames Valley

OPEN (Usually) Mon–Sat 10–2, 4–9; Sun 12–2, 7–9   CREDIT CARDS Access,
Visa; personal and business accounts   DISCOUNTS Up to 10% (min 1
case)   DELIVERY Free within reasonable radius of shop (min 1 case);
otherwise £2 per case   GLASS HIRE Free with reasonable order
TASTINGS AND TALKS 2 major tastings at Griffin Brewery annually; 20
shops hold regular tastings for customers; to groups on request (min 25
people)   CELLARAGE Not available

A chain of shops whose wine list has improved considerably
over the past few years and which now offers some interesting
wines at good prices. The layout of the shops still tends to give
the impression that cigarettes take precedence, but most
branches have good selections from the full range of wines.

The policy of sensible pricing is apparent in areas like petits
châteaux, the Alsace wines from Ste-Odile, the excellent clutch
of French country wines (including the Listel range from the
South of France, various vins de pays from the Ardèche, Ch La
Coste from Provence and Vin de Pays des Côtes de Gascogne).

Outside France, while Germany can offer only a few wines
from Rudolf Müller to go alongside the branded Liebfraumilchs,
and Italy still slumbers (apart from a few wines from Antinori),
interest awakens in Spain (wines from Torres, Navarra wines
from Cenalsa, and Riojas from Berberana and Domecq).
Australia offers Rosemount and Berri Estates wines, while New
Zealand has Cooks. There are a few Bulgarian wines, William
Wheeler wines from California, and a number of familiar names
among the Sherries.

Best buys

Ch des Vergnes 1988, Bordeaux Sauvignon, £2.95
Ch de Paraza, Cuvée Spéciale, Minervois, £3.25
Ch Le Gardéra 1985, Bordeaux Supérieur, £3.99
Castillo de Almansa Gran Reserva 1981, Almansa, £4.99

Wine in bag-in-box ages and spoils quicker than in bottle. If you buy
boxes, buy and drink up one box before you buy the next. Boxes in the
storecupboard will lose their freshness. Used or unopened, a wine box
will keep better if you store it tap downwards, keeping wine, not air, in
the valve.

Gardner Martens Fine Wines

87 Jermyn Street, London SW1Y 6JD · TEL 01–839 1171/ 930 3801

CASE SALES ONLY · OPEN Mon–Fri 9.30–5.30 · CLOSED Sat, Sun, public holidays · CREDIT CARDS None accepted; personal and business accounts · DISCOUNTS Quantity discounts available · DELIVERY Free in central London (min 1 case); elsewhere at cost · GLASS HIRE Free with 1-case order · TASTINGS AND TALKS By invitation; annual tasting in April; to groups on request · CELLARAGE Available through Smith and Taylor, Battersea

A new firm to the Guide, started in late 1988 with a policy of shipping wines not previously available in this country direct from France, and, in 1990, from Spain.

What we have at the moment, therefore, is a short list, containing many names new to us (plus some old familiar faces), but which promises a range of French estate wines. The Loire is a strong area: Anjou wines from Domaine des Forges, and varietal Touraine wines from Domaine de la Charmoise – the Sauvignon at £5.47 is worth considering, even at that price (list prices do not include VAT but we have added it here). There's also fine Chinon from Charles Joguet and Guy Jamet.

Elsewhere are to be found estate wines from Burgundy (stronger in white than red), good vins de pays from the Rhône (Vin de Pays de Vaucluse 1988, Bernard Chamfort is the firm's house red). In Bordeaux, wines seem mainly to come from St-Emilion, and there is Champagne from Léon Launois, who has vineyards in the Côte des Blancs (the Réserve Blanc de Blancs is £12.49).

Best buys

St-Emilion 1986, Héritiers Fourcaud-Laussac, £11.49
Sauvignon de Touraine, Domaine de la Charmoise, £5.47
Chinon 1987, Vieilles Vignes, Guy Jamet, £7.22

Gare du Vin ▱

HEAD OFFICE
Brook House, Chertsey Road, Woking,   TEL (04862) 5066
Surrey GU21 5BE
23 Old Brompton Road, London   TEL 01–589 1795
SW7 3HZ
123 Kings Road, London SW3 4PL   TEL 01–352 2255
68 Cross Street, Manchester, M2 4JO   TEL 061–832 8456
62 High Street, Tunbridge Wells, Kent   TEL (0892) 30711
TH1 1XF

OPEN Mon–Fri 10–8; Sat 10–7   CLOSED Sun   CREDIT CARDS All accepted;
personal and business accounts   DISCOUNTS 3% on 6 bottles; 5% on 1
case; larger orders negotiable   DELIVERY Free in SW3 area; mail order
occasionally available   GLASS HIRE Free with 1-case order
TASTINGS AND TALKS Occasional evening tastings   CELLARAGE Not
available

Although part of the same group as Victoria Wine Company,
Gare du Vin operates from a separate list. Originally just one
branch in South Kensington, London, there are now four –
another in London (formerly called South of the Bordeaux), one
in Kent and one in Manchester – and more are planned.

The list is long and impressive, a contrast to that of its parent
company. It's strong in traditional areas such as Bordeaux (with
wines back to the 1975 vintage), Burgundy (where the mainly
négociant wines come from Moillard, Louis Jadot, Bouchard
Père, with southern Burgundy and Beaujolais wines from
Georges Duboeuf), Alsace (where wines come from the estates
of Schlumberger) and the Rhône (Jaboulet Aîné).

But France doesn't dominate the list unduly. Good Italian
names include Antinori and Lungarotti, CaSal di Serra
Verdicchio, the varietal wines from Ca' Donini in Trentino,
Venegazzù from Gasparini in the Veneto. In Spain, look for the
Raimat wines as offering particularly good value. There are
estate wines from Germany, and a few, rather pricy, offerings
from Bulgaria.

Australia is a star area: plenty attracts (especially in the reds)
with wines from Penfolds, Wynns, Hill Smith and Rothbury
Estate. New Zealand has the wines of Villa Maria, Cloudy Bay
and Montana. Look, too for Mondavi, Trefethen, Firestone and
other names from California. There are Concha y Toro Chilean
wines, and a very serious range of Champagnes and sparkling
wines (probably due to the location of the London shops). Ports
are from Cockburn, Sherries from Harvey (including the
superior 1796 range).

Best buys

Cabernet Malbec 1987, Hill Smith, Barossa Valley,
Australia, £3.59
Bourgogne Pinot La Vignée 1985, Bouchard Père et Fils, £5.49
Teroldego Rotaliano 1986, Ca' Donini, £3.15
Chardonnay 1987, Raimat, Spain, £4.79
Sauvignon Blanc 1986, Gallo, California, £2.99

Garrards Wine Merchants

Mayo House, 49 Main Street,   TEL (0900) 823592
Cockermouth, Cumbria CA13 9JS

OPEN Mon 9.45–5.45; Tue, Wed 9.45–8; Thur 9.45–1, 6–8; Fri, Sat 9.30–
8.30; Sun 7–8; open Mon until 8 and all day Thur during July, Aug and
Sept   CLOSED Public holidays   CREDIT CARDS Access, Visa; personal and
business accounts   DISCOUNTS 5% on 1 case   DELIVERY Free within 20-
mile radius (min £20 order); elsewhere charges negotiable
GLASS HIRE Free with reasonable order   TASTINGS AND TALKS Occasional
tastings for invited customers; to groups on request   CELLARAGE Not
available

Not a vast range of wines, maybe, but well-chosen bottles from
most parts of the world provide a balanced list. If the occasional
branded wine (particularly from Bordeaux) could quietly
disappear, it would be even better.

The claret selection is short, and tends to move too quickly
from the branded wines to pricy classed growths. Burgundy is
better, with wines from some familiar négociant names – Louis
Latour, Chanson, Prosper Maufoux – and Beaujolais from
Georges Duboeuf. There is a small selection of French regional
wines.

Outside France, sensible choices include the German wines
from Deinhard, a recently expanded range of Italian wines,
Torres wines from Spain, and an excellent set of Sherries. New
World wines, numbering Orlando and Wolf Blass from
Australia, Babich from New Zealand and a small group of
California wines, are also due for expansion, say Garrards.

Best buys

White Cloud, Nobilo, Gisbourne, New Zealand, £3.80
Berri Estates Cabernet/Shiraz 1983, Australia, £4.35
Rioja 1985, Banda Azul, Paternina, £4.20

Which? Wine Guide does not accept payment for inclusion, and there is
no sponsorship or advertising.

M & W Gilbey

Eton Wine Bar, 82/83 High Street, Eton,   TEL (0753) 854921/
Windsor, Berkshire SL4 6AF   855182

CASE SALES ONLY   OPEN 7 days a week (wine bar hours)
CREDIT CARDS None accepted; personal and business accounts
DISCOUNTS Not available   DELIVERY £5.75 per delivery (min 1 unmixed
case); mail order available   GLASS HIRE, TASTINGS AND TALKS,
CELLARAGE Not available

This is an almost entirely French list, strong in Burgundy and
the Loire, shorter in Bordeaux, but with some very well priced
wines.

Beaujolais involves wines from Chanut Frères, with good
things from the cru villages' excellent 1988 vintage. Chablis is
well represented, and there's a small amount of white
Burgundy, much more of red. The Loire offers treats such as the
Pouilly Fumé of J C Dagueneau, and red and rosé from St-
Nicolas de Bourgueil. A few wines from the Rhône, three clarets
and the Bergerac of Ch Le Fage, plus house Champagne
Magenta at £9.50, complete the list (apart from two German
house wines which seem to have strayed in).

Best buys

Ch La Fage Sauvignon Blanc Sec 1988, £3.25
Saumur Blanc, Cave Coopérative de Saumur 1988, £3.25
Regnié 1988, Chanut Frères, £4.15

Matthew Gloag & Son

Bordeaux House, 33 Kinnoull Street,   TEL (0738) 21101
Perth, Perthshire PH1 5EU

OPEN Mon–Fri 9–5   CLOSED Sat, Sun, some public holidays
CREDIT CARDS Access; personal and business accounts
DISCOUNTS Available for Club members only   DELIVERY Free on mainland
Scotland (min 1 case); otherwise £3.45 per case; mail order available
GLASS HIRE Free   TASTINGS AND TALKS Gloag's Fine Wines Club holds a
large tasting twice a year, free to Club members and guests; occasionally
to groups on request   CELLARAGE £3.45 per case or part-case per year

A traditional list both in appearance (helped by Victorian
cartoons) and in content. Prices tend to be high. There is great
emphasis on Bordeaux, with a selection of wines from most
recent vintages (and a few wines of the 1970s). Burgundy relies
mainly on négociant wines from such firms as Louis Latour and
Thomas Bassot. The Loire and Alsace sections are short and

rather dull. Of the familiar names on the Rhône look for the good-value wines of Ch Val-Joanis.

In Spain, the most interest centres on Riojas from Montecillo and La Rioja Alta, while in Italy it is the wines of Frescobaldi which star. A few wines from Deinhard account for the German selection.

Outside Europe, there are some familiar names in Australia (Hill-Smith is a main supplier), while Selaks, Kumeu and Matua Valley make up a small but attractive New Zealand section. In the United States, look for Ch St Jean from California and Texas Vineyards. Sherries from Barbadillo and Ports in plenty (good mature vintage wines and aged tawnies) round off the Gloag collection.

Best buys

Ch Val-Joanis Blanc and Rouge, £4.50
Ch Tour du Mirail 1983, Haut Médoc, £9.55
Dow's Boardroom Tawny, £13.95

G M Vintners

OFFICE

7 Wellington Terrace, George Street, Truro, Cornwall TR1 3JA	TEL (0872) 79680
M R Vintners Wine Warehouse, 3 Alphinbrook Road, Marsh Barton, Exeter, Devon EX2 8RG	TEL (0392) 218186
Market Wine Stores, 5–7 Lemon Hall Market, Lemon Street Market, Truro, Cornwall TR1 2PN	TEL (0872) 41446

OPEN Mon–Sat 9–5 (Market Wines); Mon–Fri 9-late, Sat mornings (M R Vintners) CLOSED Sun, public holidays CREDIT CARDS Access, Visa; personal and business accounts DISCOUNTS Negotiable DELIVERY Free within Cornwall, Devon, Somerset, Avon and part of Dorset (min 1 case) and elsewhere for 6+ cases; otherwise at cost GLASS HIRE Free with order TASTINGS AND TALKS Tastings by appointment; to groups on request CELLARAGE £3 per case per year

G M Vintners operates two shops, the Market Wine Stores in Truro and M R Vintners in Exeter, which run with the same list. There is also a wholesale business operating from the G M Vintners address.

It's a wide-ranging list, with no particular strengths, but with pockets of interest in most areas. In Alsace we find good value in the wines from the Pfaffenheim co-operative, while in Bordeaux there are plenty of petit château wines before prices rise into the area of classed growths. Burgundy is a good mix of estate and négociant wines, and Clos des Roches 1987 of Vacheron at £6.49 in the Sancerre selection should be delicious.

The Rhône as a region is well treated: look for wines such as the white Côtes du Rhône of Ch St-Estève d'Uchaux (1988 vintage at £3.69) or the Châteauneuf of Ch de Beaucastel (1986 vintage – certainly not ready to drink – at £8.75). There are organic wines from Listel in the South of France. Sauvignon from the co-operative of Haut Poitou 1987 is a good-value £2.99.

Beyond France, look to Italy for Veneto wines from Bolla, Chianti from Melini and Regaleali Rosso from Sicily. Spain has Marqués de Cáceres Riojas and Torres wines, while in Australia, Penfolds reds form a star attraction (Koonunga Hill Shiraz/Cabernet 1987 at £4.59).

Best buys

Mondétour Bordeaux 1987, £2.99
Côtes du Rhône Tradition 1987, Ch St-Estève d'Uchaux, £3.45
Côtes de Buzet 1984, Cuvée Napoléon, £3.99
Listel Blanc de Blancs sur Lie 1987, £2.89
Chianti Classico 1987, Terrarossa, Melini, £3.99

Godrich & Petman

9A Parchment Street, Winchester,   TEL (0962) 53081
Hampshire SO23 8AT
ASSOCIATED WITH
Eldridge Pope, Weymouth Avenue,   TEL (0305) 251251
Dorchester, Dorset DT1 1QT

OPEN Mon–Fri 9–5.30; Sat 9–5   CLOSED Sun, public holidays
CREDIT CARDS Access, Visa; personal and business accounts
DISCOUNTS 5% on mixed and unmixed cases   DELIVERY Free in Andover, Basingstoke, Southampton and Winchester (min £20 order); elsewhere 1 case £3.45, 2–3 cases £5.75, 4+ cases (or orders of over £100) free
GLASS HIRE Free with reasonable order   TASTINGS AND TALKS In-store tastings approximately every 2 months (max 20 people); to groups on request   CELLARAGE Free

See Eldridge Pope.

Special awards

🐷 is for bargain prices   🏳 is for a very good range of wines

✻ is for high quality wines   👉 is for exceptional service

Goedhuis & Co

101 Albert Bridge Road, London   TEL 01–223 6057
SW11 4PF

CASE SALES ONLY   OPEN Mon–Fri 9.30–6   CLOSED Sat, Sun, public
holidays   CREDIT CARDS Access, Visa; personal and business accounts
DISCOUNTS Not available   DELIVERY Free in central London (min 3 cases)
and UK (min 5 cases); otherwise at cost; mail order available
GLASS HIRE Free with 1-case order   TASTINGS AND TALKS Two major annual
tastings in spring and autumn for customers; to groups on request
CELLARAGE £3.45 per case per year

A carefully chosen list which, while not long, has plenty of
high-class wines from the major areas of France, plus a few
offerings from Spain.

The most important area is certainly Bordeaux. Goedhuis deal
in small parcels of finer wines as well as having an encouraging
range of petits châteaux, regular en primeur offers (depending
on the vintages) and quantities of crus bourgeois from vintages
of the 1980s.

In Burgundy, a similar situation prevails: many wines from
some excellent producers (Domaine de la Pousse d'Or, Domaine
Pernin Rossin, Domaine Mongeard-Mugnaret, Domaine Ponsot),
the reds better than the whites. On the Rhône, there are fewer
wines, but again some famous names – Guigal, Chave, Ch de
Beaucastel, and here, as Goedhuis themselves comment, prices
now have to reflect the current craze for Rhône wines in the
United States.

Other areas receive more cursory treatment – we would
recommend the Alsace wines of Rolly Gassmann, the house
Champagne of Jeanmaire (Brut NV at £11.25), the Sancerre of
Vacheron, the Ménétou-Salon of Henri Pellé and the Sauvignon
de Touraine of Domaine Michaud at £3.75. Outside France,
Spain offers a few delights, alongside Australian wines from
Cape Mentelle, Hollick and Penfolds and New Zealand wines
from Cloudy Bay and Matua Valley.

Best buys

Sauvignon de Touraine Les Martinières, Domaine
Michaud, £3.75
Ch Grand Juan 1985, Bordeaux, £3.75
Mâcon-Prissé 1987, Cave Coopérative de Prissé, £4.75
Champagne Daniel Adam Brut, £10
Côtes du Rhône Cru de Coudoulet 1986, £5.50

Send us your views on the report forms at the back of the book.

Andrew Gordon Wines

Glebelands, Vincent Lane, Dorking, Surrey RH4 3YZ

TEL (0306) 885711 (24-hour answering service)
TEL (0306) 885686/888161 (orders/queries)

CASE SALES ONLY   OPEN Mon–Fri 9–6; Sat 9–4   CLOSED Sun, public holidays   CREDIT CARDS Access; business accounts   DISCOUNTS Not available   DELIVERY Free in central London and south to Horsham (min 1 case); elsewhere minimum charge £7.50 or £1.50 per case; mail order available   GLASS HIRE Free with 1-case order   TASTINGS AND TALKS Three general annual tastings; tutored tastings organised at cellars; to groups on request (for customers only)   CELLARAGE £2.50 per case per year

A good all-round list with plenty to entice from most areas of the world. And if you have ever felt like owning your own vineyard, this is the merchant who can sell you a row of vines in the Côtes de Duras with a guaranteed 30 cases of wine every year.

But if drinking Duras all year does not appeal, there's plenty more. In Bordeaux, for instance, you will find a solid phalanx from 1985, 1986 and 1983, and further vintages back to 1962. Burgundy offers good domaine wines and an interesting concentration on whites from the Mâconnais, which offer the best value in Burgundy (there are good Chablis as well), while reds come from some of the less familiar villages as a result of Andrew Gordon's searches for reasonable value.

The Loire has a few attractions, such as the Sauvignon de Touraine of Donatien Bahuaud, the Muscadet producer (1988 vintage is £2.95), while inexplicably on an otherwise informative list we are told nothing about the producers of wines from the Rhône, Germany or Portugal.

More treats appear in Italy: the Franciacorta Rosso 1986 at £3.60, or the Chianti Classico of top estate Isole e Olena (1987 vintage at £4.60); and in Australia – Hardy and Lindemans from South Australia and Yarra Yering from Victoria; also Montana wines from New Zealand. There are Sherries from Barbadillo, the Ramos Pinto Quinta da Ervamoira 10-year-old tawny Port at £8.20 (a bargain) and house Champagne Serge Mathieu at £8.35 (probably higher by now).

Best buys

Domaine de Montmarin 1988, Vin de Pays des Côtes de Thongue, £2.49
Cabardès 1986, Domaine St-Roch, £2.30
Ch des Annereaux 1985, Lalande de Pomerol, £5.75

Sauvignon de Touraine 1988, Donatien Bahuaud, £2.95
Quinta do Roêda 1980, Croft, £10

Richard Granger

West Jesmond Station, Lyndhurst TEL 091–281 5000
Avenue, Newcastle upon Tyne, Tyne &
Wear NE2 3HH

CASE SALES ONLY OPEN Mon–Fri 8.30–6.30; Sat 8.30–1 CLOSED Sun,
public holidays CREDIT CARDS Access, Visa; personal and business
accounts DISCOUNTS Not available DELIVERY Free within 20-mile radius;
otherwise negotiable; mail order available GLASS HIRE Available with
charge (69p/dozen) TASTINGS AND TALKS New wines shown to
customers; to groups on request CELLARAGE Limited

Richard Granger's is a short list, but dropping in on most areas
of the world. Prices continue to be good.

Bordeaux is probably the most attractive area, with a good
mix of wines in the middle price range (Ch La Gardéra 1985 is
£4.50). Burgundy, on the other hand, is brief – a reflection of
high prices, no doubt (though Beaujolais from Georges Duboeuf
is a bonus). In the Loire, we find an unusual Saumur
Champigny from Bouvet Ladubay (1986 vintage at £4.60), while
in Alsace, Hugel and Trimbach are the two featured producers.

In other European countries, Italy offers Chianti from Castello
di Lucignano (1986 vintage at £3.55), Spain has Torres wines,
and Germany has the new range of Deinhard Heritage Selection
dry wines (the Deidesheim 1986 at £4.65 is one of the best).
Offerings from Australia, New Zealand and Ch Musar from the
Lebanon complete the list.

Best buys

Ch Musar 1979, Hochar, Lebanon, £5.34
Langlois Château, Crémant, Saumur, £5.95
Ch St-Paulin 1985, Bordeaux, £3.35
Riesling Dry 1986, Deinhard, £3.60

If you disagree with us, please tell us why. You will find report forms at
the back of the book.

Find the best new wine bargains all year round with our newsletter,
Which? Wine Monthly, available for just £19 a year from: Dept WG90,
Consumers' Association, FREEPOST, Hertford SG14 1YB – no stamp is
needed if posted within the UK.

Grape Ideas Wine Warehouse 🐷

3/5 Hythe Bridge Street, Oxford, TEL (0865) 722137
Oxfordshire OX1 2EW
ASSOCIATED OUTLET
2A Canfield Gardens, Swiss Cottage, TEL 01–328 7317
London NW6 3BS

OPEN Mon–Sat 10–7; Sun 11–2 CLOSED Public holidays
CREDIT CARDS Access, Visa; personal and business accounts
DISCOUNTS Quantity discounts up to 5% DELIVERY Free locally (min 1
case); elsewhere at cost; mail order available GLASS HIRE Free with 1-
case order TASTINGS AND TALKS Monthly tastings; to groups on request
CELLARAGE 5p per case per week

Grape Ideas operates from the same Oxford address and is under the same ownership as Fine Vintage Wines (see separate entry). While Fine Vintage Wines emphasises its first word, the Grape Ideas range is more for everyday drinking – although in pretty wide terms.

For instance, the Grape Ideas range of clarets almost stops at crus bourgeois at which point Fine Vintage Wines picks up. At Grape Ideas, bargains are to be had in mid-priced clarets (Prieur de Meyney 1985, St-Estèphe at £5.95; Ch Trinité Valrose, Bordeaux 1986 at £3.95). In Burgundy, there is pricier stuff (such as some good domaine wines in reds) but also some Mâconnais wines at fair prices, while Champagne definitely has the grande marque bug, but coupled with good-value house Champagne at £9.45.

The eastern Loire – Sancerre and Pouilly Fumé – fares better than the western end of Muscadet, for instance featuring Touraine wines from Domaines Girault Artois in Touraine Mesland, while the Rhône enjoys wares from Jaboulet Aîné, Guigal and Chapoutier (good-value Côtes du Rhône Villages 1988 from Noémie Vernaux at £3.75). Look, too, for Alsace wines from Ziegler. French country wines are strong on Côtes de Duras and Madiran.

Other European countries well served on the list are Spain (Campo Viejo Riojas and Torres wines) and Italy (wines from Frescobaldi, Chianti from Isole e Olena, Südtirol wines from Lageder and Bianco di Custoza from Santa Sofia). Australia has Wyndhams and Leasingham wines, while from South America comes the largest selection of Argentine wines in this country (mainly from Andean Vineyards) and a smaller run from Chile (Linderos, Concha y Toro and Viña Carmen). Sherries are from De Soto, Madeiras from Blandy.

Best buys

Castillo de Tiebas Reserva 1975, Navarra, Spain, £3.95
Sauvignon de Touraine 1988, Guy Saget, £2.99
Cabernet Sauvignon 1983, Andean Vineyards, Argentina, £3.95
Campo Viejo Gran Reserva 1975, Rioja, £5.65
Bairrada 1985, Terra Franca Tinto, Portugal, £2.99

Grapehop

See La Reserva.

Great Northern Wine Company   ✉

The Dark Arches, Leeds Canal Basin,   TEL (0532) 461200/
Leeds, West Yorkshire LS1 4BR   461209

OPEN Mon–Fri 9–6.30; Sat, public holidays 10–5.30   CLOSED Sun, 25 & 26
Dec, 1 Jan   CREDIT CARDS Access, Visa; personal and business accounts
DISCOUNTS Variable (min 1 case)   DELIVERY Free within 30-mile radius of
Leeds (min 1 case); otherwise at cost; mail order available
GLASS HIRE Free   TASTINGS AND TALKS Monthly tastings to customers;
major annual tasting; to groups on request   CELLARAGE £2.75 per case
per year

There's interest from many areas on the Great Northern list.
What makes it different is that those areas are not necessarily
the obvious ones.

So claret for once takes a back seat behind the French
regions – wines worth looking out for include the Bergeracs of
Henry Ryman and the red Bonchalaz of Henri Maire in the
Jura – at £2.95 a real bargain. Similarly, there's more interest in
the range of Beaujolais from Jacques Dépagneux than there is
from Burgundy proper. Other good bottles are Alsace wines
from the co-operative of Turckheim, an enticing line-up in
Côtes du Rhône, and Champagne from Charbaut at £11.15.

Still more than half the list to go: Germany rejoices in some
good estate wines (a pity, as so often, we are not told who
makes many of them), Spain offers a good line in Riojas from
producers such as CVNE, Berberana and Muga as well as wines
from Torres and white Rioja from Marqués de Murrieta. Good
things from Italy, too (Chianti from Castello Vicchiomaggio,
Lungarotti wines, Barolo from Contratto).

And then, after a short burst through Selaks wines in New
Zealand, we find a big Australian pool of Lindemans, Brown
Brothers, Wyndham Estate and Montrose among producers in a
long and memorable selection. Look for Sherries from Don Zoilo
and Champagne from Laurent Perrier.

WHERE TO BUY

Best buys

Gamay 1988, Domaine Jean Cros, Gaillac, £3.89
Baileys Shiraz 1985, Glenrowan, Australia, £6.45
Corbières 1986, Ch de Lastours, £3.99
Cabernet Sauvignon 1986, Viña Carmen, Chile, £4.59
Vin de Pays des Côtes de Gascogne 1988, Domaine de
Perras, £2.75

Peter Green

37a/b Warrender Park Road, Edinburgh   TEL 031–229 5925
EH9 1HJ

OPEN Mon–Fri 9.30–6.30; Sat 9.30–7   CLOSED Sun, public holidays
CREDIT CARDS None accepted; personal and business accounts
DISCOUNTS 5% on unmixed cases   DELIVERY 50p per trip in Edinburgh;
mail order available   GLASS HIRE Free   TASTINGS AND TALKS Annual tasting
in October/November by invitation; to groups on request
CELLARAGE Not available

Other merchants may have longer lists of, say, Bordeaux or
Burgundy, but what is so attractive about Peter Green's is that it
gives due weight to all wine areas – and that, in each area, the
wines are thoroughly well chosen, with a good balance between
inexpensive and pricier offerings.

With a list as comprehensive as this, one could home in on
any area for commendation, but we pick out the French regional
wines, Alsace, the Loire (particularly the wines from Chinon,
Savennières and Quarts de Chaume), the Rhône for its range of
Hermitage wines from Chapoutier, and Champagnes – just for
the pleasure of contemplating the span.

There is plenty from Germany – a pleasure to see in these
days when German lists are being run down – with many
famous estates featured. Italy positively oozes with top names
(Borgogno Barolo, Brunello from Castelgiocondo, vintages of
Tignanello from Antinori, Lungarotti, the Moscato Passito Tanit
from Pantelleria (an ultra-sweet dessert wine made from sun-
dried grapes), and a small but notable selection of Amarone
Recioto della Valpolicella, plus well-priced offerings for more
everyday drinking occasions.

When we move to Iberia, the treasures continue to abound.
Good Riojas, including a number of Gran Reservas, vintages of
Valbuean (the second, more approachable wine of Vega Sicilia),
good value from Jumilla, rarities from Galicia. Portugal has
wines from J M da Fonseca, from Champalimaud in the Douro
(Quinta do Cotto), and dry Casalinho Vinho Verde (at £2.99).
There are good Madeiras and a huge range of Sherries but (by
contrast) disappointing Ports.

Australia comes up with another roll-call of names (and, again, some good value with Jacob's Creek from Orlando at £3.25 and other Orlando reds at good prices), New Zealand has a smaller, but equally interesting selection, there are wines from Argentina and Chile, Algeria and Greece, vintages of Ch Musar from the Lebanon – even the USSR and Zimbabwe are here. Don't forget the half-bottles. Phew!

Best buys

Andean Vineyards Monte Blanco NV, Argentina, £2.99
Pinot Blanc 1986, Schlumberger, Alsace, £4.60
Ribera del Duero 1985, Bodegas Ribera Duero, Spain, £4.99
Bergerac Sec Blanc 1983, Domaine de Grandchamp, £3.99
Bonarda Oltrepò Pavese 1986, Luzzano, £3.89
Trittenheimer Apotheke Riesling Kabinett 1986, Clüsserath-Weiler, Mosel, £5.20
Bourgogne Blanc Chardonnay, Cuvée du Muguet 1987, Patrick Javillier, £4.99

Green's   ☞ ☆

47–51 Great Suffolk Street, London   TEL 01–633 0936
SE1 0BS

CASE SALES ONLY   OPEN Mon–Fri 9–6   CLOSED Sat, Sun, public holidays
CREDIT CARDS Access, Visa; personal and business accounts
DISCOUNTS 2.5% for 2–5 cases, 5% for 6–11 cases; 7.5% for 12+ cases
DELIVERY Free in London postal district and within 30-mile radius of Oxford and Cambridge (min 1 case) and on UK mainland (min 6 cases); otherwise 1–5 cases £5.90 per consignment; mail order available
GLASS HIRE Free with reasonable order   TASTINGS AND TALKS To groups on request   CELLARAGE £5.75 per case per year

---

It seems that the constant changes at Green's may have come to an end, with the purchase of the company by the owners of Kurtz and Chan and a close connection with Oxford and Cambridge Fine Wine (see separate entries for both). Green's have moved temporarily from their offices in the City's Royal Exchange while renovation work takes place.

The new list gives some idea of the direction the new set-up is taking – quite a traditional view, with the emphasis on France, and on Bordeaux in particular. However, it is worth noting the small but useful bunch of French country wines (such as the Minervois Ch de Paraza at £3.95), the interesting Loire wines (such as the Ménétou-Salon of Jacky Rat and the red Saumur Champigny of Claude Daheuiller), and the Alsace wines of the Turckheim co-operative, before getting down to the meaty range of clarets and some good domaine Burgundies. The Rhône, too, is an area to watch.

Outside France, there is less of interest: a few offerings from Germany, Italy and Spain, a mere three wines from Australia (but good – the Shiraz of Basedows at £5.80 would be enjoyable). And then there are a number (but not a vast number) of Champagnes (house Champagne is Floquet at £10.45), Sherries from Barbadillo, Madeiras from Cossart Gordon and a range of vintage Ports.

Best buys

Minervois 1988, Ch de Paraza, £3.95
Ch La Valière 1986, Médoc, £5.75
Côtes du Rhône Villages, Caves des Vignerons de Rasteau 1986, £3.80
Ch Haut-Tuquet 1985, Côtes de Castillon, £4.65

Greenwood & Co

See Nickolls & Perks.

Hadleigh Wine Cellars

Unit A, Autopark, Eastgate Street, Bury   TEL (0284) 750988
St Edmunds, Suffolk IP33 1YQ

OPEN Mon–Fri 9.30–6; Sat 9.30–5   CLOSED Sun, public holidays
CREDIT CARDS Access, Visa; personal and business accounts
DISCOUNTS 5% on 1 case; larger quantities negotiable   DELIVERY Free
locally (min 1 mixed case); elsewhere at cost; mail order available
GLASS HIRE Free with order   TASTINGS AND TALKS In-store tastings in
spring and autumn; tastings arranged for customers; to groups on
request   CELLARAGE Restricted by limited space (usually available to en
primeur buyers)

'After months of looking', this merchant has moved to new premises which will give the extra space an expanded list needed. That list seems to offer most in Bordeaux, Burgundy and the French regions, but other areas all get walk-on parts in this comprehensive range.

Bordeaux certainly does well. There's plenty – at good prices, as well – from the 1985 and 1986 vintages, as well as 1983. Occasional magnums are from well-chosen châteaux. In Burgundy, there's less, much of it from négociants, while Loron supplies Beaujolais. The Rhône has wines from Jaboulet Aîné, including five different vintages of Hermitage La Chapelle (1979 is £25.07). In the French regions, look for the varietal wines of the Vin de Pays de l'Ardèche at £2.68 for excellent value.

While Germany is passed over quickly, and Italy almost does not exist, Australia is strong on interest with wines from smaller estates like Basedow and Sutherland as well as a variety from Orlando. Other highlights include Delegats and Cloudy Bay wines from New Zealand, the Gran Colegiata wines of Toro in Spain, Andrew Quady's Orange Muscat Essensia from California, and Sherries from Barbadillo.

Best buys

Champagne Rasselet Brut NV, £8.96
Gran Colegiata 1986, Bodegas Farina, Toro, Spain, £4.01
Syrah 1987, Vin de Pays de l'Ardèche, Les Caves de la Cévennes, £2.68
Ch Trinité-Valrose 1986, Bordeaux Supérieur, £3.86

Hampden Wine Company

Jordan's Courtyard, 8 Upper High Street, Thame, Oxfordshire OX9 3ER   TEL (084 421) 3251

OPEN Mon, Tue, Thur, Fri 9.30–5.30; Wed 9.30–1; Sat 9–5   CLOSED Sun, public holidays   CREDIT CARDS Access, Visa; personal and business accounts   DISCOUNTS 5% on 1 case; quantity discounts negotiable DELIVERY Free in Thame, Oxford and district (min 1 cases); elsewhere at cost; mail order available   GLASS HIRE Free with order
TASTINGS AND TALKS Bottles always open on Saturdays; to groups on request   CELLARAGE Free for customers only

A pretty little building on Thame's market square houses the Hampden Wine Company, now two years old and with organised tastings (and more promised) behind them. It is linked with a delicatessen (in fact you have to go through the one to get to the other), and they join forces in their wine and food hampers.

The wine list itself is growing, in areas old (Bordeaux) and new (Washington State). But the country that particularly interests us is Portugal: they have put together quite an attractive selection of wines, mainly from private estates – look for the Quinta do Carmo 1985 of Julio Bastos at £5.50, and the Bairrada of Luis Pato at £5.60 for the 1985, as well as wines from J M da Fonseca.

In France, we find Alsace wines from Rolly Gassmann, the organic Muscadet of Guy Bossard, a rather pricy lot of clarets, Burgundy from Henri Jayer (the Bourgogne Passetoutgrains 1986 at £6.45 is good value), and the Côte Rôtie of Gentaz-Dervieux, who makes tiny quantities of wine on his half-hectare.

There are familiar names from Spain and Italy (CVNE Riojas, Castello Vicchiomaggio Chianti). Australia chips in with Rouge

Homme and Cape Mentelle as well as Hardys, New Zealand
with Gisborne wines. There are Sherries from Hidalgo and
Garvey, Madeiras from Cossart Gordon.

Best buys

Cooks Cabernet Sauvignon 1986, Hawkes Bay,
New Zealand, £4.85
Reguengos de Monsarraz Tinto, Adega Cooperativa 1987,
Portugal, £2.90
Muscadet de Sèvre-et-Maine 1987, Guy Bossard, £3.95

Gerard Harris ☆

2 Green End Street, Aston Clinton,   TEL (0296) 631041
Buckinghamshire HP22 5HP

OPEN Mon–Sat 9.30–8   CLOSED Sun, public holidays
CREDIT CARDS Access, Visa; personal and business accounts
DISCOUNTS 10% for 1 case (does not apply to fine Clarets, Ports etc in
limited stock)   DELIVERY Free locally (min 1 case); otherwise at cost (min
£5.75); mail order available   GLASS HIRE Free with 1-case order
TASTINGS AND TALKS Four major tastings annually; to groups on request
CELLARAGE Not available

A change in management at Gerard Harris seems, so far, to have
changed the high quality of the list very little. The high points
of previous lists – the range of German wines, the quantities of
mature claret and Sauternes and the domaine-bottled
Burgundies – are still there. What is perhaps missing, indeed, is
any sign of movement – but then we must reserve judgement
on that until the new management has had a chance to settle.

The current state of play is very good. The German section
especially contains wines from the excellent 1983 and 1985
vintages from many major estates (even with a few wines from
the 1976 vintage). In Bordeaux, the best represented vintages are
1982, 1981 and 1979, but wines are available back to 1961. Look,
too, for vintages of Sauternes, some from the early 1970s.
Burgundy has wines from the great and the good – at great (but
perhaps not so good) prices.

Other parts of France are much less strongly represented.
There are some good Loire wines (Sancerre of Paul Millérioux,
Chinon of Raymond Desbourdes), small amounts of Rhône wine
(but the magnum of Chave's Hermitage 1984 at £33.25 looks
interesting), and interest from the lesser appellations (Coteaux
du Tricastin 1986, Domaine du Vieux Micocoulier at £3.85) as
well as the wines from Coteaux des Baux en Provence.

From other countries, look for a few wines from Tuscany
(Castello di Volpaia Chianti at £5.44), CVNE Riojas, Ch Tahbilk

from Australia and Trefethen wines from California. Don Zoilo Sherries are joined by a few aged tawny Ports and Madeiras from Blandy and Cossart Gordon.

Best buys

Kaseler Kehrnagel Riesling Auslese 1983, Reichsgraf von Kesselstatt, £7.72
Coteaux du Tricastin 1986, Domaine du Vieux Micocoulier, £3.85
Ch Tahbilk Shiraz 1985, Victoria, Australia, £5.40
Ch Haut-Sociondo 1983, Côtes de Blaye, £4.90

Roger Harris

Loke Farm, Weston Longville, Norfolk   TEL (0603) 880171
NR9 5LG

CASE SALES ONLY   OPEN Mon–Fri 9–5   CLOSED Sat, Sun, public holidays
CREDIT CARDS All accepted; personal and business accounts   DISCOUNTS
2 cases £1 per case, 5 cases £2 per case   DELIVERY Free in UK mainland
(min 1 case); otherwise at cost; mail order available   GLASS HIRE Not
available   TASTINGS AND TALKS To groups on request   CELLARAGE Free;
available for limited time only

Roger Harris is Mr Beaujolais. Apart from a brief foray into the Mâconnais (and some Champagne) he lists nothing else but the stuff. The enthusiasm for the region shines through all 48 pages, which are filled with information about the area, lists of restaurants and hotels, pictures and maps, quite apart from the wines.

All parts of Beaujolais are embraced, from simple Beaujolais through the Villages wines up to the great crus. Mr Harris buys from a wealth of producers – from small growers to the large co-operatives, but not, it seems, from the négociants. Every cru – even the new one of Régnié – is represented, and there is also Beaujolais Blanc, newly discovered here, and pink Beaujolais. And, if you are thinking about Beaujolais for Nouveau Day in November, Mr Harris can supply that as well.

Best buys

Beaujolais St-Vérand 1988, £4.40
Juliénas 1987, François Condémine, £6.00
Chiroubles 1987, La Maison des Vignerons, £5.70
Chénas 1987, Jean Benon, £5.90

Harrods ☆

Knightsbridge, London SW1X 7XL   TEL 01–730 1234

OPEN Mon, Tue, Thur–Sat 9–6; Wed 9.30–7; open most public holidays
CLOSED Sun   CREDIT CARDS All accepted; personal and business accounts
DISCOUNTS Available on full cases (on most wines) – 12 bottles for price
of 11   DELIVERY Free in inner London and within 25-mile radius (min
£30 order); otherwise at cost; mail order available   GLASS HIRE Not
available   TASTINGS AND TALKS Regular in-store tastings   CELLARAGE Not
available

This is an extensive and well-chosen list that suffers principally
because others charge less for the same wines. If you are
prepared to pay the extra, however, there is much of interest –
and not just from the classic areas.

For instance, there are good German estate wines, some pretty
serious Italians (with a strong emphasis on Tuscany), an
impressive range of Riojas, of Penedés wines (including those of
Jean León and Juve y Camps), and a big selection of Mondavi
wines from California. Ports are a splendid group (including
some fine aged tawnies).

In France, grande marque Champagnes in considerable
profusion are the stars (although here the prices seem especially
high – house Champagne at £13.25 is the cheapest). There are
clarets – at a price – from recent vintages, together with some
more mature wines back to 1970, and an enticing range of
Sauternes and other sweet white Bordeaux. Burgundy is rather
dull, Beaujolais better, the Rhône and Loire sections short but
with some good things. Wines from the French regions show
most excitement in Provence.

Best buys

Juve y Camps Brut Natural Reserva de la Familia, £10.35
Muscadet Métaireau (Harrods) 1986/7, £5.95
Pont de Chevalier Pinot Blanc de Blancs 1985, Hugel, £5.65

Special awards

🐷 means bargain prices (good *value* may be obtained from
merchants without this symbol, of course, if you wish to pay for
service)

✸ means that the wines stocked are of consistently high quality

▱ means that the merchant stocks an above-average range

☞ means that extra-special service is offered; helpful advice,
information lists and newsletters, tastings etc.

John Harvey & Sons ☞ ☆

HEAD OFFICE
12 Denmark Street, Bristol, Avon   TEL (0272) 253253
BS1 5DQ
SHOP AND OFFICES
31 Denmark Street, Bristol, Avon   TEL (0272) 273759
BS1 5DQ
27 Pall Mall, London SW1Y 4HJ   TEL 01–839 4695
16 The Hard, Portsmouth, Hampshire   TEL (0705) 825567
PO1 3DT

OPEN Mon–Fri 9.30–5.30   CLOSED Sat, Sun, public holidays
CREDIT CARDS All accepted; personal and business accounts   DISCOUNTS 5–
9 cases £1 per case; 10 cases £1.50 per case   DELIVERY Free on UK
mainland (min 2 case); elsewhere £5 per delivery; mail order available
GLASS HIRE Free with case order   TASTINGS AND TALKS Regular in-store
tastings; major tastings organised annually by each office; to groups on
request   CELLARAGE £4.37 per case per year

An aim to re-establish themselves as fine wine merchants has
led to a considerably expanded range and much more of interest
than we have seen in recent years.

Expansion has still to happen in some areas – witness the
paucity of Italian wines at present – but in other areas, such as
the New World, Spain and, gradually, Portugal, there is now a
satisfyingly balanced (not necessarily long) range of wines.
Cockburn Ports and the Harvey Sherries in the 1796 range (plus
those from Palomino y Vergara) are well priced.

The strongest areas are still France and Germany. In France,
the star remains Ch Latour, of which Harvey's parent company,
Allied-Lyons, are owners. From this hub there radiates a good
range of clarets, especially more mature wines (but also en
primeur offers as the vintage warrants), and good sweet white
Bordeaux from some famous names. In Burgundy, too, are some
fine domaine bottles, and the Beaujolais section is particularly
attractive. The Rhône is strongest in the southern vineyards,
with some good-value Côtes du Rhône (and look for the
excellent value of the St-Joseph of Guyot at £3.80). Don't ignore
the French regions – Ch Val-Joanis in Côtes du Lubéron, Ch des
Tuileries Vin de Pays de la Haute Vallée de l'Aude or Sauvignon
Bergerac from Ch Le Raz – all are well priced.

Best buys

Ch Jouanin 1985, Côtes de Castillon, £4.28
Ch Le Raz 1987 Sauvignon Blanc, Bergerac, £3.81
Bourgogne Passetoutgrains 1986, Domaine de Millefleurs, £4.37
Palo Cortado Sherry 1796, £8

Haughton Fine Wines ✉

Row's Ground, Chorley Green Lane,   TEL (0270) 74 537
Chorley, Nantwich, Cheshire CW5 8JR

CASE SALES ONLY   OPEN Mon–Fri 9.5.30; Sat 9–12.30; Sun, public holidays
by appointment   CLOSED Chr Day   CREDIT CARDS Access; personal and
business accounts   DISCOUNTS 3% for 10+ cases; 6% for 20+ cases
DELIVERY Free in North-West England, Wales and Midlands (min 1 mixed
case) and on UK mainland (min 6 cases); mail order available
GLASS HIRE Free with case order   TASTINGS AND TALKS Provide monthly
tastings; to groups on request   CELLARAGE Available

Although we haven't counted, the claim by Haughton Fine
Wines to be the country's biggest shipper of organic wines
looks very possibly justified. They have rounded them up from
all over the world, many from France, but also from Australia,
New Zealand, Italy – they've even found organic Cognac.
However, a further wealth of wines produced by conventional
methods is also to be found.

The list starts in Australia, with the organic wines of
Botolobar in Mudgee. A host of smaller wineries right round the
south-eastern corner of the country, from Yarra Valley to Barossa
to Coonawarra to Hunter, are assembled, including one of the
newest wine areas in the country, the Mornington Peninsula in
Victoria.

Another area given serious – but not organic – treatment is
Oregon in the United States: vineyards such as Lange, Bethel
Heights, Adelsheim and Ponzi. New Zealand also has much to
offer – with wines, again, from vineyards in small areas such as
Martinborough which have not sent anything to the UK before.

Nearer to home, strong areas in France include the South-
West (with considerable listings from many of the smaller
appellations); the regions of the Midi (organic wines here from
St-Jean d'Aumières in Coteaux du Languedoc, Domaine des
Soulié in St-Chinian and Mas de Daumas Gassac Vin de Pays de
l'Hérault); Provence (with wines from the almost entirely
organic region of Baux en Provence); the Loire (look for wines
from Savennières, Saumur and Bourgueil); and the Alsace wines
of Eugène Meyer. The Bordeaux and Burgundy sections reveal
plenty of organic wines in nicely balanced proportion with
conventional wines to create useful ranges. There's even an
organic Champagne (from André and Jacques Beaufort).

Best buys

Coteaux des Baux en Provence 1986, Mas de Gourgonnier, £4.66
Gaillac Blanc 1986, Les Graviers du Ch Lastours, £3.39

Muscadet de Sèvre-et-Maine sur Lie, Domaine de la Haute Fevrié, £3.75
Gigondas 1986, Domaine du Clos des Cazeaux, £5.97
Montlouis Demi-Sec, Domaine de la Bigarrière NV, Méthode Champenoise, £5.53

Haynes Hanson & Clark

HEAD OFFICE & WHOLESALE WAREHOUSE
17 Lettice Street, London SW6 4EH   TEL 01–736 7878
RETAIL
36 Kensington Church Street, London   TEL 01–937 4650
W8 4BX

OPEN Mon–Fri 9.15–7 (SW6); Mon–Sat 9.30–7 (W8)   CLOSED Sat (SW6), Sun, public holidays   CREDIT CARDS None accepted; personal and business accounts   DISCOUNTS 10% on 1 unmixed case   DELIVERY Free in central London and on regular van-delivery runs (Thames Valley and East Anglia) (min 1 case); elsewhere 1 case £4, 2 cases £2.90 per case, 3–4 cases £1.30 per case, 5+ cases free on UK mainland; mail order available   GLASS HIRE Free with 1-case order   TASTINGS AND TALKS Regular in-store tastings for customers; to groups on request   CELLARAGE Can arrange on customers' behalf

---

The link with Burgundy remains perhaps the strongest element of this fine range of wines. The list is impressively chock-a-block with domaine wines, not surprisingly, since one of the firm's directors, Anthony Hanson, is author of a definitive book on the region.

We find wines from domaines such as Gagnard-Delagrange, Simon Bize, André Mussy, Michel Lafarge, Jean Grivot. There is a major emphasis on wines from the new négociant firm of Olivier Leflaive Frères (the same family as Domaine Leflaive), as well as wines from some of the more established négociants.

At the same time, much is on offer from Bordeaux: classy bottles, mainly at prices that reflect the quality, but there are also less expensive wines to set the ball rolling (Ch Cayla 1986, Premières Côtes de Bordeaux at £3.98). Special offers for both Burgundy and claret are made regularly.

While these are the two most important sections of the list, other areas are not neglected. Worth looking at are a variety of interesting wines from the Loire, the Pierre Vaudon Champagne Blanc de Noirs, a very select range of top California wines (including the wines from Saintsbury Winery in Carneros) and various Australian wines, particularly from Western Australia.

Best buys

Ch Pessan 1983, Graves, £5.60
Mercurey 1986, Jean-Pierre Meulien, £7.68
Montagny Premier Cru 1987, Olivier Leflaive Frères, £7.90
Pinot Noir 1987, Carneros, Saintsbury Winery, California, £8.55
Champagne Pierre Vaudon Brut, £10.90

Hedley Wright

The Country Wine Cellars, Twyford   TEL (0279) 506512
Centre, London Road, Bishop's
Stortford, Hertfordshire CM23 3YT

CASE SALES ONLY   OPEN Mon–Wed 9–6; Thur, Fri 9–8; Sat 10–6
CLOSED Sun, public holidays   CREDIT CARDS Access, Visa; personal and
business accounts   DISCOUNTS Available for large orders   DELIVERY Free
within 20-mile radius of cellars and central London (min 1 case);
elsewhere at cost; mail order available   GLASS HIRE Free with 1-case
order   TASTINGS AND TALKS Two major annual tastings held for
customers; programme of tutored tastings; to groups on request
CELLARAGE £3.95 per case per year

If the quantity of communications we have had from these
merchants is anything to go by, their customers must be
hearing from them pretty frequently, with special offers, en
primeur offers and information about wine tastings. The list
itself is informative, the commentary showing evidence of
careful buying.

It is a range of wines which has good representation from all
over the world: not a vast array, but always something of
interest. It says something for the firm's interest in value for
money that they highlight wines under £4.50 in a separate
section.

Quite a few of those wines come from Chile, a definite
strength, with wines from Santa Helena and a number of
smaller estates. It looks more substantial than the other southern
hemisphere sections, interesting though these wines are: –
Australian wines from Victoria Gardens Estate and Renmano as
well as Leo Buring, and New Zealand wines from Montana,
Mission and Redwood.

In Europe, sections to give particular attention are Beaujolais
from Domaine Geoffray, Rhône wines with particular interest in
Côtes du Rhône and Châteauneuf, Campo Viejo Riojas and
Sherries from Manuel de Argueso, a small almacenista firm (try
the superb Palo Cortado del Carrascal at £7.15).

> Send us your views on the report forms at the back of the book.

Best buys

Blanc de Blancs Le Ragot NV, Ch de la Ragotière, £3.30
Côtes de Ventoux 1988, La Vieille Ferme, £3.80
Chardonnay 1988, Oak Aged, Santa Helena, Chile, £3.95
Domaine de Mirabeau 1987, Vin de Pays des Collines de la
Moure, £3.05

Douglas Henn-Macrae

81 Mackenders Lane, Eccles, Maidstone,   TEL (0622) 710952
Kent ME20 7JA
(Not a shop)

CASE SALES ONLY   OPEN Mon–Sat (personal callers by appointment only
up to 11pm) CLOSED Sun, Chr & Easter CREDIT CARDS Access, Visa
DISCOUNTS Occasionally available DELIVERY Free on UK mainland (min 5
cases); otherwise £5.75 per order; mail order available GLASS HIRE Not
available TASTINGS AND TALKS To groups on request CELLARAGE Not
available

Great Britain's most unusual list? Not our thought, but that of
Mr Henn-Macrae himself, in the introduction to his most recent
list. Certainly, if you are looking for a balanced list with wines
from most countries, this is not the place to come. But if, as he
says, you want wines from many of the smaller regions of
Germany (including what some would regard as a contradiction
in terms, German red wine), from Texas and the Pacific North-
West – then this is the wine merchant for you. His list reads
well – the unusual tasting notes are strewn with exclamation
marks (the better the wine the more liberal he is with them).

Taking the United States first, we find Adelsheim Vineyard
and Elk Cove Vineyards in Oregon and Covey Run in
Washington State; and Texas Vineyards, Fall Creek Vineyard,
Sanchez Creek and Llano Estacado in Texas.

In Germany, look for some serious Nahe wines from Berthold
Pleitz, Karlheinz Keber and Josef Höfer, with wines from the co-
operative in the Hessische Bergstrasse (probably the only source
in this country of wines from this small region), from Mosel and
Rheinpfalz estates and red wines from Württemberg.

Best buys

Grossgartacher Grafenberg Lemberger 1984, Heuchelberg
Kellerei, £4.39
Dorsheimer Beerenauslese 1971, Weingut Dr Josef Höfer, £5.59
(Half Bottle)
Gewürztraminer 1986, Texas Vineyards, Texas, £2.49

Charles Hennings

London House, Pulborough, West Sussex RH20 2BW	TEL (079 82) 2485/3909
10 Jenger's Mead, Billingshurst, West Sussex RH14 9TB	TEL (040 381) 3187
Golden Square, Petworth, West Sussex GU28 0AP	TEL (0798) 43021

OPEN Mon–Thur 9–6; Fri 9–7.30; Sat 8.30–6   CLOSED Sun, public holidays   CREDIT CARDS Access, Visa; personal and business accounts DISCOUNTS 5% on 1 case   DELIVERY Free in West Sussex (min 2 cases subject to distance); otherwise at cost; mail order available GLASS HIRE Free with 1-case order   TASTINGS AND TALKS In-store tastings on Saturdays; Christmas wine tasting in early December and midsummer tasting   CELLARAGE Not available

While there are still too many branded wines on this list, there are wines of greater interest, spread round the world, not just in classic areas of France.

Probably the strongest section of the list is the Spanish, with Riojas from Contino, Marqués de Cáceres, Faustino and CVNE, with Torres wines, Raimat Abadía and Ochoa Navarra wines to widen the range. And while Italy is still neglected, there's a good range of Penfolds Australian wines, and English bottles from Nutbourne Manor (try the Schönburger 1987 at £4.29).

In France, areas worth considering include a good range of Loire wines, Beaujolais from Loron, the house claret from Nathaniel Johnston and country wines like the Bergerac from Ch La Jaubertie.

Best buys

Médoc NV, Nathaniel Johnston, £3.89
Rioja Faustino V Tinto Reserva 1985, £5.29
Seaview Brut, Australia, £5.19

There is no connection between *Which? Wine Guide* and *The Good Wine Guide*, which is published by the Sunday Telegraph.

☆ celebrates the uninterrupted inclusion of this merchant in all ten editions of *Which? Wine Guide*.

Hicks & Don   🐷 ✳ 👓 ☆

HEAD OFFICE
Park House, North Elmham, Dereham,   TEL (036 281) 571
Norfolk NR20 5JY
ORDER OFFICE
4 The Market Place, Westbury, Wiltshire   TEL (0373) 864723
BA13 3EA
Mainly mail order

OPEN Mon–Fri 9–5.30; Sat by appointment   CLOSED Sun, public
holidays   CREDIT CARDS Access, Visa; personal and business accounts
DISCOUNTS Available on certain items   DELIVERY Free on UK mainland
and Isle of Wight (min 3 cases); charges to off-shore islands are
negotiable   GLASS HIRE Free (provided glasses collected and returned
clean)   TASTINGS AND TALKS To groups on request   CELLARAGE Available

This is one of those ranges in the Guide which is strong in
virtually every area of the world. There may not necessarily be
vast quantities of wines in each section, but what is there is of
high quality. Much, too, is reasonably priced.

France is a mainstay of the list: plenty of claret, for instance –
petit château wines as well as bottles for laying down (Hicks &
Don are one of the few merchants to offer petit château wines
en primeur as well as classed growths). Burgundy brings in
some good-value Beaujolais as well as some pricier domaine
wines from Burgundy proper. While the Loire contains
marginally less of interest, there's plenty of serious stuff from
the northern Rhône (as well as well-priced wines such as the
Côtes du Rhône of Ch de l'Estagnol). The French regions are
well served such as Domaine de Ravennes 1985, Vin de Pays des
Coteaux de Murviel at £4.12.

From other European countries, there are German estate
wines from the 1983 and 1985 vintages; and a small but
attractive section of Italian wines (the Vinattieri Rosso 1983 at
£7.25 is a blend of Montalcino and Chianti). Spain has Torres
wines and Olarra Riojas as stars as well as Barbadillo Sherries.
And, from England, Hicks & Don have their own wine from
Elmham Park in Norfolk.

Across the continents, Australia has a small band of offerings
(look for the wines of Mountadam in South Australia), and
while California is rather uninspired, New Zealand goes in for
wines from Nobilo, Stoneleigh Vineyard and Delegats.

Best buys

Ch Vertheuil 1983, Bordeaux, £4
Castillo de San Diego Palomino Blanco 1987, Barbadillo, £3.04
Vinattieri Bianco 1986, £4.58
Elmham Park Dry 1983, R S Don, England, £4.50

High Breck Vintners   ⌂ ⌂ ☆

Spats Lane, Headley, nr Bordon, Hampshire GU35 8SY	TEL (0428) 713689

ASSOCIATED OUTLETS

Nalders Wine Agency, Street House, The Street, Mortimer, Berkshire RG7 3NR	TEL (0734) 332312
Harbottle Wines, 27 Perrymead Street, London SW6 3SN	TEL 01–731 1972
Sir Ronald Preston, Beeston Hall Cellars, Beeston St Lawrence, nr Norwich, Norfolk NR12 8YS	TEL (0692) 630771
A G Barnett, 17 Windsor Road, Worthing, West Sussex BN11 2LU	TEL (0903) 32629
Col G P Pease, Milverton Cottage, Whitchurch, Pangbourne, Berkshire RG8 7HA	TEL (07357) 2624
J Dudley, Dukes Cottage, Rudgwick, Horsham, West Sussex RH12 3DF	TEL (040372) 2357

CASE SALES ONLY   OPEN Mon–Fri 9.30–6; Sat 9.30–12 noon; Sun, public holidays by arrangement   CLOSED Chr Day   CREDIT CARDS None accepted   DISCOUNTS By arrangement   DELIVERY Free on UK mainland and Isle of Wight (min 1 case locally, 3 cases nationally); elsewhere at cost; mail order available   GLASS HIRE Free with case order   TASTINGS AND TALKS 5 tastings annually at High Breck and 2 at each agent; to groups on request   CELLARAGE Not available

Not a long list and one which hardly strays from France, but which offers interest from a number of areas. One such is the Loire, where the wines of Gitton in Sancerre and Pouilly Fumé and those of Coteaux du Layon Chaume from Jean-Paul Tijou are highlights. Another is the Alsace wines of Wiederhirn, a small producer based in Riquewihr, and yet another the Beaujolais of l'Eventail des Vignerons Producteurs. Burgundy and Bordeaux are muted by comparison.

Other areas worth watching out for are the Sherries of Lustau (including some of the Landed Age Sherries, wines stored in cask in England before bottling) and Bergerac wines of Henry Ryman.

Best buys

Coteaux du Layon Chaume 1985, Jean-Paul Tijou, £4.60
Riesling d'Alsace Schoenenbourg 1985 Grand Cru Reserve Personnelle, Wiederhirn, £6.32
Sancerre 1984, Les Galinots, Gitton Père et Fils, £6.32
Ch de Chénas 1986, Un Eventail des Vignerons Producteurs, £4.89

Hilbre Wine Company

Gibraltar Row, Pierhead, Liverpool L3 7HJ   TEL 051–236 8800

OPEN Mon–Fri 8.30–5.45, Sat 9.30–12.30   CLOSED Sun, public holidays
CREDIT CARDS None accepted; personal and business accounts
DISCOUNTS Available   DELIVERY Free within Cumbria, Clwyd, Greater
Manchester, Lancashire, Manchester, Merseyside and north Staffordshire
(min 1 case); elsewhere at cost; mail order available   GLASS HIRE Free
with 1-case order   TASTINGS AND TALKS Regular in-store tastings; to
groups on request   CELLARAGE By arrangement (at the Liverpool
Warehousing Co)

Continuing expansion from a traditional base adds to the
interest all the time. This year, for example, we see a new range
of Mondavi wines from California, bottles from Washington
State and Chile, more from Australia and much more from Italy
and Spain.

Despite these new horizons, the list starts firmly with claret,
of which there is a fine range above the £6 mark, but little
under. Cordier is a featured supplier, alongside Domaines Baron
de Rothschild and Ch Loudenne. And while the Rhône
continues to be neglected, Burgundy offers a wide choice of
mainly négociant wines. The Loire has wines from Langlois
Château, while Alsace wines come from Dopff et Irion. House
Champagne is Lambert (at £9.04).

Germany is very possibly quite interesting although there is a
strange reluctance in some cases to tell us about producers. Italy
now contributes wines from Frescobaldi in Tuscany as well as
Capezzana wines in Carmignano and Fontanafredda Barolo.
Look in Spain for Torres wines as well as Rioja from Campo
Viejo and Marqués de Riscal.

Across the continents, Australia is offering Orlando wines,
New Zealand Montana wines, while California has Clos du Bois
and Inglenook as well as Mondavi. Washington State wines
come from Cascade Crest (Semillon Blanc 1987 at £4.19) and
Chilean wines from Santa Helena. There are also some of the
fine Valdespino Sherries.

Best buys
Ch Plagnac 1980, Médoc, £4.86
Côtes du Marmandais 1985, Cave de Beaupuy, £3.40
Campo Viejo Blanco 1987, Navarra, £3.43
California Red, Geoffrey Roberts, £3.01

Why not club together with friends to enjoy volume discounts and free
delivery?

George Hill of Loughborough

59 Wards End, Loughborough,   TEL (0509) 212717
Leicestershire LE11 3HB

OPEN Mon–Sat 9–6   CLOSED Sun, public holidays   CREDIT CARDS All
accepted; personal and business accounts   DISCOUNTS Approximately
10% on 1 case   DELIVERY Free within 30-mile radius (min 1 case);
otherwise dependent on area and quantity required; mail order
available   GLASS HIRE Free with 1-case order   TASTINGS AND TALKS In-store
promotions for new wines in stock; to groups on request
CELLARAGE £2.50–£3 per case per year

A useful list which has seen expansion in areas such as
Germany (good for them), as well as in the regions of France
and in Italy.

Germany now has plenty of estate wines from the 1983 and
1985 vintages, and they are sensibly arranged by category of
wine rather than by region – all the Auslesen, all the Kabinett
wines together. In the French regions, look for unusual wines
such as the Muscat Cuvée José Sala, a sweet Muscat de
Frontignan, or the wines of Domaine des Terres Blanches from
Coteaux des Baux en Provence. Italy now offers wines from top
producers such as Antinori in Tuscany, Lungarotti in Umbria
and Mastroberardino in Campania.

Other areas to show well here include Spain (with Riojas from
Bodegas Montecillo); a new range of Loire wines from smaller
producers in areas such as Quincy (Domaine de la Maison
Blanche), Domaine Bablut, producer of Sauvignon Blanc Vin de
Pays du Jardin de la France and Muscadet from Jules Olivier;
and Beaujolais from Benoit-Lafon.

Best buys

Cabardès 1986, Domaine St-Roch, £2.90
Nackenheimer Rothenberg Riesling Kabinett 1985, Louis
Guntrum, £4.72
Baileys Show Tokay, Glenrowan, Victoria, Australia, £9.18
Valdespino Fino Sherry, £3.69

The Wine Standards Board is the trade's disciplinary department and
wine watchdog. Their inspectors are responsible for rooting out any
malpractices – but they are concerned largely with labelling
irregularities. If you have genuine reason to suspect that the wine in a
bottle is not what the label claims it is, contact the Board at: 68½ Upper
Thames Street, London EC4V 3BJ; TEL 01-236 9512; or contact your local
Trading Standards Officer.

J E Hogg

61 Cumberland Street, Edinburgh   TEL 031–556 4025
EH3 6RA

OPEN Mon, Tue, Thur, Fri 9–1, 2.30–6; Wed, Sat 9–1   CLOSED Sun, local
public holidays   CREDIT CARDS None accepted   DISCOUNTS Not available
DELIVERY Free in Edinburgh (min 6 bottles); otherwise £3.80 per case;
mail order available   GLASS HIRE Free with order   TASTINGS AND TALKS To
groups on request   CELLARAGE Not available

James Hogg's tiny, old-fashioned, wood-floored shop is stacked
high with wines, and yet there just doesn't seem room for
everything that's on the equally tightly packed list. There's a
strong feeling that all the wines are personal choices, picked
from all over the world and with prices offering terrific value.

Certain areas are particularly strong. In France, we find
Alsace, with wines from Schlumberger, Dopff et Irion and
Trimbach. We would also recommend the Rhône section,
including many wines from Jaboulet Aîné (look for the Domaine
de Thalabert Crozes-Hermitage 1985 vintage at £5.70). There are
plenty of everyday drinking clarets around the £3 to £4 mark,
offering very good value, as well as classier wines.

The two other star areas are Italy and Germany. Look in Italy
for a big range, strong on meaty reds from Piedmont,
Montalcino and Chianti (but with an interesting sideline in
sweet Orvieto). In Germany, the best of the estate wines come
from the Mosel.

Then turn to fortified wines. There are good Sherries, with an
emphasis on the heavier style (Scottish taste?), Madeiras from
Blandy and Rutherford, and some good aged and blended
tawnies.

Best buys

Tokay Pinot Gris 1985, Dopff et Irion, £3.77
Ch Beauséjour 1983, Fronsac, £3.79
Côtes du Rhône 1986, Parallèle 45, Jaboulet Aîné, £3.15
Rosso di Montalcino 1985, Villa Banfi, £3.88
Dalwood Cabernet/Shiraz Penfolds, Australia, £3.79

Most wine merchants will hire out glasses free of charge, provided they
are collected and returned clean, and that you are buying enough wine
to fill them! In most cases, it's first come, first served, so get your order
in early to ensure supply.

Hopton Wines

Hopton Court, Cleobury Mortimer,   TEL (0299) 270482
Kidderminster, Hereford & Worcester
DY14 0HH

OPEN Mon–Fri 9–5.30   CLOSED Sat, Sun, public holidays
CREDIT CARDS None accepted; personal and business accounts
DISCOUNTS Available   DELIVERY Free within 35-mile radius of Cleobury
Mortimer (min 1 case); elsewhere 1 case £9.20, 2 cases £8.05 per case, 3+
cases free; mail order available   GLASS HIRE Free with 1-case order
TASTINGS AND TALKS Regular tastings at Hopton Court; to groups on
request   CELLARAGE Available; charges negotiable

A concise collection of wines, which remains firmly in France
for much of the time, but which has forays elsewhere to provide
other nuggets of interest.

Those nuggets include Chiantis from Fattoria la Casaccia,
Torres wines from Spain, a big selection of Cooks and
Stoneleigh Vineyard wines from New Zealand, Mondavi wines
from California and a shortish list from Australia.

Back in France, clarets are strong (a good range of older
vintages as well as petit château wines of the 1985 vintage).
There's good value (in Burgundian terms, that is) with some of
the basic Burgundies on offer (Bourgogne Rouge Christian de
Marjan at £5.11), some good value from the southern Rhône and
Alsace wines from Schlumberger. Look for the house
Champagne Faniel at £8.25 (plus a nice line in magnums) and a
few mid-priced country wines.

Best buys

Domaine du Bosc 1985, Corbières, £3.60
Champagne Faniel NV, £8.25
Ch Haut Rosset 1983, Côtes du Bourg, £5.16
Bourgogne Rouge, Christian de Marjan, £5.11

Hornsea Wine Market

See J Townend & Sons.

House of Townend

See J Townend & Sons.

Prices are only a rough indication, and were current in summer 1989.

Ian G Howe

35 Appleton Gate, Newark,   TEL (0636) 704366
Nottinghamshire NG24 1JR

OPEN Mon–Sat 9.30–7; Good Friday 12–2, 7–9   CLOSED Sun, public
holidays except Good Friday   CREDIT CARDS Access, Visa; personal and
business accounts   DISCOUNTS 2.5% for 1 case (may be mixed), 3.5% for
3 cases   DELIVERY Free locally (min 1 case) and within 20-mile radius
(min 2 cases); elsewhere by arrangement   GLASS HIRE Free with 1-case
order   TASTINGS AND TALKS In-store tastings on Saturdays; approximately
4 regional/vintage tastings annually; to groups on request
CELLARAGE By arrangement

'We have a passion for French wines', we are told by Mr Howe,
and that is very apparent in his list, dominated as it is (apart
from a short stab in the direction of Germany) by the wines of
France.

We start in Beaujolais with wines in profusion from Sylvain
Fessy, mainly of cru wines (special offers are often made when
these wines are released). Another prolific area is the Loire,
which has a good line in sweet wines such as Quarts de
Chaume, varietal wines from the Haut-Poitou co-operative and
a number of red Saumur-Champigny wines (look for those from
Filliatreau). The third strong area is French country wines, such
as Fitou Domaine de Courtal (1985 vintage at £3.95), or vintages
of Cahors from Domaine des Acacias (1985 at £4.45), or, from
Provence, the rare white Cassis Clos Ste-Magdeleine (1986
vintage at £5.85).

Look, too, for a good variety of Côtes du Rhône and petit
château clarets.

Best buys

Vin de Pays Catalan Cabernet, Mas Chichet (Midi), £4.75
Chardonnay 1985, Arbois, Jean Germain (Jura), £4.65
Fiefs Vendéens 1985, Domaine de la Chaignée, £3.65
Ch Thieuley 1985, Bordeaux, £4.75

Cellarage is generally provided at the rates quoted only when the wines
have been bought from the merchant concerned.

Prices were correct to the best of our knowledge as we went to press.
They, and ranges of wines stocked, are likely to change during the
course of 1990 and are intended only as rough indication of an
establishment's range and prices.

Victor Hugo Wines

HEAD OFFICE

Tregear House, Longueville, St Saviour, Jersey	TEL (0534) 78173 (order office)
The Stables, Belmont Place, St Helier, Jersey	TEL (0534) 78173
8B Quennevais Precinct, St Brelade, Jersey	TEL (0534) 44519
3 Stopford Road, St Helier, Jersey	TEL (0534) 23421
Bath Street Wine Cellar, 15 Bath Street, St Helier, Jersey	TEL (0534) 20237

OPEN Mon–Fri 8–6; Sat 9–5.30   CLOSED Sun, public holidays
CREDIT CARDS All accepted; personal and business accounts
DISCOUNTS Available   DELIVERY Free in Jersey (min 1 case)
GLASS HIRE Free with 5-case order   TASTINGS AND TALKS Various in-house promotions; to groups on request   CELLARAGE Free

Expansion into a cash and carry warehouse is promised this year, which brings the outlets of Jersey's only merchant in the Guide up to five.

They carry a good all-round range of wines, with particular strengths which seem designed to reflect the ideal life on Jersey: the big range of Champagnes, Loire wines (to go with the fish and shellfish), claret in profusion and plenty of mature wines.

But there is more to this list than that, even if some of it is tucked away. Look for sections such as Alsace, with its selection from top merchant Dopff et Irion; or for the selection of wines from Ch Val-Joanis in Côtes du Lubéron (as well as other French country wines). Outside France, while Italy is a disappointment, Germany offers a good range of wines from Louis Guntrum, and there is more from California than from Australia. Good aged tawny Ports as well as vintage wines, and Rutherford and Miles Madeiras, round off the list.

Prices in the best buys below reflect the fact that Jersey's taxes are lower than in mainland Britain.

Best buys

Prestige de Raoul Clerget, £1.76
Régnié Hospices de Beaune 1988, Robert Sarrau, £3.96
Ch Val-Joanis Rouge 1986, Côtes du Lubéron, £2.68
Apremont Blanc, Jean Cavaille, £2.65

Most wine merchants will supply wine for parties on a sale or return basis.

Hungerford Wine Company

HEAD OFFICE
Unit 3, Station Yard, Hungerford,   TEL (0488) 83238
Berkshire RG17 0DY
24 High Street, Hungerford, Berkshire   TEL as above
RG17 0NF

OPEN Mon–Fri 9–5.30; Sat 9.30–5   CLOSED Sun, public holidays
CREDIT CARDS All accepted; personal and business accounts
DISCOUNTS 5% on 1 case (approximately); larger quantities negotiable
DELIVERY Free within 15-mile radius of Hungerford (min 1 case) and on
UK mainland (min 5 cases); otherwise £7 per consignment; mail order
available   GLASS HIRE Free with 1-case order   TASTINGS AND TALKS Regular
tastings on Monday evenings at The Galloping Crayfish Wine Bar; to
groups on request   CELLARAGE £3.91 per case per year (including
insurance)

Apart from anything else, Hungerford Wine is one of the largest
suppliers of en primeur claret in the country, and certainly the
one that provides the most help in making up your mind. Each
year Nicholas Davies sends out innumerable listings and
information about the most recent vintage including copious
tasting notes, and in 1989, set up a helpline containing bang-up-
to-date information. Obviously it's designed to sell more wine,
but it's also good service.

Claret is the mainstay of this list. There are large-scale listings
of wines from recent vintages, but older wines are available too
(and there is a deeply impressive list of imperials – eight bottles
in one – for those with a large party or considerable thirst).

Although Bordeaux is the mainstay, there is now much more
from Burgundy, some of it good value, some of it awesome and
pricy. Most of the wines come from well-known domaines.
Champagnes, too, bristle with well-known names, and the
house Champagne at £9.50 is good value.

While other areas of France are not so generously endowed
(although Rhône wines include some fine wines from Jaboulet
Aîné, and there's a good line in wines from Listel and from the
South-West), Spain has been given a boost (look for Marqués de
Griñon Cabernet Sauvignon, Bodegas de los Llanos Gran
Reserva from Valdepeñas and white Monopole Seco from
CVNE). A small selection from California is the only nod
towards the New World. But there are plenty of vintage Ports.

Best buys

Monopole Seco Blanco, Rioja 1985, CVNE, £4.50
Crozes-Hermitage 1986, Domaine Thalabert, Jaboulet Aîné, £5.60
1987 clarets

Hurt & Daniel

10 Catherine Road, Surbiton, Surrey
KT6 4HA

TEL 01–399 7179

CASE SALES ONLY   OPEN Mon–Fri 9–5   CLOSED Sat, Sun, public holidays
CREDIT CARDS None accepted; personal and business accounts
DISCOUNTS 5% on 5 cases   DELIVERY Free in central London and Surbiton/
Kingston area (min 3 cases); mail order available   GLASS HIRE Not
available   TASTINGS AND TALKS To groups on request
CELLARAGE Available

There are some good-value wines in this merchant's middle
price range, especially from the French regions. So look, for
instance, for Ch La Baronne in Corbières (1986 red at £2.93 –
prices on the list do not contain VAT, but we have added it
here) or the organic Côtes de Provence wine, St-André de
Figuière at £4.41.

There are small selections from the more classic areas, such as
the Domaine Chante Perdrix wines in Châteauneuf, wines from
Roux Père et Fils in St-Aubin in Burgundy, some useful Anjou
Rouge (plus Chinon from Pierre Druet), and a small range of
clarets. From further afield comes the unusual Marsanne of Ch
Tahbilk in Victoria.

Best buys

Ch La Baronne 1986, Corbières, £2.93
Côtes de Provence, Domaine St-André de Figuière 1985, £4.41
Ch La Rose du Pin 1985, Bordeaux, £3.31

G Hush

235 Morningside Road, Edinburgh
EH10 4QT

TEL 031–447 4539

OPEN Mon–Thur 10–1, 2.30–7.30 Fri 10–1, 2.30–9.30 Sat 9–9.30
CLOSED Sun, public holidays   CREDIT CARDS None accepted; business
accounts   DISCOUNTS 5% on unmixed cases   DELIVERY Free within 3-mile
radius for reasonable order; otherwise at cost   GLASS HIRE Free with case
order   CELLARAGE Not available

We are told that extensive changes are under way at this
merchant. Watch this space next year.

Find the best new wine bargains all year round with our newsletter,
Which? Wine Monthly, available for just £19 a year from: Dept WG90,
Consumers' Association, FREEPOST, Hertford SG14 1YB – no stamp is
needed if posted within the UK.

Ingletons Wines

Station Road, Maldon, Essex CM9 7LF

TEL (0621) 852431
(office)
TEL (0621) 852433
(cash & carry)

OPEN (Cash & Carry) Mon–Fri 9–5; Sat 9–4.30   CLOSED Sun, public holidays   CREDIT CARDS None accepted; personal and business accounts   DISCOUNTS Not available   DELIVERY Free within 150-mile radius of Maldon (min 6 cases); elsewhere charges on request; mail order available   GLASS HIRE Available   TASTINGS AND TALKS To groups on request   CELLARAGE Not available

This is one of the longest listings of Burgundies in the Guide, and the quality is high, too.

The net has been spread wide, and has caught some good value in Burgundian terms. But there are also featured villages, such as Chassagne-Montrachet and Puligny-Montrachet in whites, Corton and Echézeaux in reds. Names to conjure with include Louis Trappet, Mongeard-Mugneret, René Monnier, Daniel Senard, Marc Colin, Etienne Sauzet. You don't have to look far for plenty of interest from Beaujolais either.

In other parts of the wine world are good things from the Loire (the Sancerre of Brochard), from Alsace (wines from the Hunawihr co-operative), and a good range of clarets from recent vintages. Further afield there are German estate wines, a small amount of dull Italian wine (what's it doing in a list like this?) and Australian wines from McWilliams.

Best buys

Chardonnay Bourgogne Blanc La Chablisienne 1987, £4.03
Pouilly Fumé Les Berthiers 1988, J-C Dagueneau, £5.64
Côtes de Malapère 1986, Domaine de Fournery, £2.30

Irvine Robertson Wines

10/11 North Leith Sands, Edinburgh
EH6 4ER

TEL 031–553 3521

ASSOCIATED OUTLET
Graham MacHarg Fine Wines,
Fowberry Tower, Wooler,
Northumberland NE71 6ER

TEL (06685) 274

CASE SALES ONLY   OPEN Mon–Fri 9–5.30   CLOSED Sat, Sun, Chr and New Year   CREDIT CARDS None accepted; personal and business accounts   DISCOUNTS Available (min 5 cases)   DELIVERY Free throughout the UK (min 3 cases except local deliveries); otherwise £4.02 per consignment; mail order available   GLASS HIRE Free with case order   TASTINGS AND TALKS To groups on request   CELLARAGE Not available

Up to date details from this merchant were unavailable as we went to press. However, we would recommend you look for their good-value clarets (house claret from Nathaniel Johnston), wines from the Loire and the Rhône, and good ranges from the New World.

Jacqueline's Wines

12a Florence Road, Sutton Coldfield,   TEL 021–373 5949
West Midlands B73 5NG

CASE SALES ONLY   OPEN Mon–Fri 9–6   CLOSED Sat, Sun, public holidays (answering machine outside normal hours)   CREDIT CARDS None accepted; personal and business accounts   DISCOUNTS 5% on 5 cases   DELIVERY Free in Birmingham and within 30-mile radius of Sutton Coldfield (min 1 case); elsewhere £9.50 per case; mail order available   GLASS HIRE Free with 1-case order   TASTINGS AND TALKS To groups on request   CELLARAGE £1.30 per case per year

A short list, but with some attractive components. Our choices would be Loron and Duboeuf Beaujolais, Riojas from Domecq and CVNE, the Châteauneuf of Les Cailloux, good-value Burgundy from the Hautes Côtes de Nuits, some German estate wines, Orlando wines from Australia, and Broadfield Court, Herefordshire English wines. Alsace wines are from the Turckheim co-operative, and the house Champagne is Maxim's.

Best buys

Rioja Tinto 1983, CVNE, £4.37
Ch Lamothe 1985, Premières Côtes de Bordeaux, £5.15
Riesling d'Alsace 1987, Cave Vinicole de Turckheim, £4.28

Jeroboams

24 Bute Street, London SW7 3EX   TEL 01–225 2232
51 Elizabeth Street, London SW1W 9PP   TEL 01–823 5623

OPEN Mon–Fri 9–7; Sat 9–6   CLOSED Sun, public holidays   CREDIT CARDS Access, American Express, Visa; personal and business accounts   DISCOUNTS 5% on 1 case   DELIVERY Free locally (min 1 case); elsewhere charges on application; mail order available   GLASS HIRE Free with 1-case order   TASTINGS AND TALKS Regular wine and cheese tastings in shops   CELLARAGE Not available

A branch of Jeroboams opened in Elizabeth Street, SW1 during the year with a more limited range than at Bute Street, and more shops are planned, so there must be enough customers for unpasteurised and rare soft French cheeses still around, food scares or no, to keep Jeroboams flourishing.

Despite the name of the shop, the wine side is not all Champagne. Of course, there is plenty of choice of bubbly, with Georges Vesselle the star producer, but you can take a useful trip round the rest of France, and pop over into a few other wine countries. Areas worth considering are some good mature clarets, wines from Henri Maire in the Jura, Morton Estate Sauvignon from New Zealand, some interesting 1986 white Burgundy and some crusted Ports (Warres, bottled 1981 at £11.95). There's an excellent range of half-bottles as well, strong on pudding wines.

Best buys

Champagne Georges Vesselle Brut NV, £12.99
Bourgueil 1987, Guy Saget, £4.85
Ch des Annereaux 1983, Lalande de Pomerol, £7.35

S H Jones   ❀ ▱ ☞ ☆

SHOP
27 High Street, Banbury, Oxfordshire   TEL (0295) 251178
OX16 8EW
WHOLESALE WAREHOUSE/CASH & CARRY
Unit 1, Tramway Road Industrial Estate,   TEL (0295) 251177
Banbury, Oxfordshire OX16 8TD

OPEN Mon–Fri 8.30–5.30; Sat 9–5   CLOSED Sun, public holidays
CREDIT CARDS Access, Visa; personal and business accounts
DISCOUNTS 5% on 1 case, 7.5% on 10+ cases, 10% on 20+ cases
DELIVERY Free in Banbury and district and along main wholesale delivery routes inc Oxford City (min 2 cases); elsewhere orders over £75 free, otherwise at cost; mail order available   GLASS HIRE Free
TASTINGS AND TALKS In-store promotional tastings; annual wine tasting (Nov); to groups on request   CELLARAGE £3.25 per case per year

An excellent all-round list, still firm in France and Germany, but with well-chosen selections from most countries of the world.

The two classic wine areas of France – Bordeaux and Burgundy – are very well treated. There are strong showings of vintages back to the early 1960s, in sweet white Bordeaux, too (including a useful selection of half-bottles). In Burgundy, we are firmly in domaine wine territory (names such as Jean Germain, Lequin-Roussot, Georges Lignier are well to the fore), followed by an attractive collection of domaine-bottled Beaujolais.

The Rhône is a major area, with wines from Guigal, Roger Combe Domaine de la Fourmone, a range of vintages of Domaine du Vieux Télégraphe Châteauneuf, and the excellent

Côtes du Rhône of Ch du Grand Moulas. Neither the Loire nor Alsace has quite the same star touch.

Outside France, German estate wines are prominent and in profusion, Italy is given a good showing (Frescobaldi in Tuscany, Venegazzù in the Veneto), while Spain has the Riojas of Olarra. Other choices could be a good range of Bulgarian wines, Tyrrells' Australian wines, Mondavi and Buena Vista in California, Santa Helena in Chile and Ch Musar in the Lebanon. Good Champagne (including some large bottles), vintage Ports and Sherries from Hidalgo round off this comprehensive list.

Best buys

Cabernet Sauvignon/Malbec 1987, Santa Helena, Chile, £3.40
Bourgogne Rouge Cuvée Spéciale 1986, Caves de Mancey, £5.40
Ch des Tours 1985, Ste-Croix du Mont, £5.20
Ch Tahbilk Shiraz 1985, Victoria, Australia, £5.55
Mâcon Chardonnay 1987, J Talmard, £5.05

Justerini & Brooks

61 St James's Street, London SW1A 1LZ   TEL 01–493 8721
39 George Street, Edinburgh, EH2 2HN   TEL 031–226 4202

OPEN (London) Mon–Fri 9–5.30 (6 in Edinburgh); Sat 9.30–1 (Edinburgh only)   CLOSED Sun, public holidays   CREDIT CARDS All accepted; personal and business accounts   DISCOUNTS 2–4 cases £1 per case; 5–7 cases £2 per case; 8+ cases £3 per case   DELIVERY Free in London and Edinburgh (min 2 cases) and elsewhere (min 5 cases); otherwise at cost
GLASS HIRE Free   TASTINGS AND TALKS To groups on request
CELLARAGE £3.75 per case per year (including insurance)

From their two smart shops – the one in St James's Street has been completely refurbished and now stocks more of the range – Justerini & Brooks offer a serious collection of wines, plus extras such as the Cellar Plan, en primeur offers, regular tastings for customers and something of the atmosphere of a gentleman's club.

Their list is replete with good things: large numbers of fine clarets, domaine-bottled Burgundies (and a new range of wines from négociant Faiveley), an excellent showing from the Rhône (especially the great vineyards of the north), less from the Loire, but some mature vintages of Mas de Daumas Gassac (the Cabernet Sauvignon super-star vin de pays from the Hérault), Alsace wines from Kuentz-Bas and Schlumberger, and piles of Champagnes.

Beyond France the same high quality is apparent in the fine range of German estate wines, in wines such as Vega Sicilia and Pesquera from Ribera del Duero, in the good – if short – listing of Tuscan wines from Italy (including some of the super vini da tavola) and in the Australian selection (which includes wines from Wynns, Penfolds, Rothbury Estate and the new top wines from Lindemans).

Worth considering as well are the almacenista Sherries, a large range of vintage Ports and the Madeiras of Cossart Gordon.

Best buys

Ch La Fleur Bonnet 1986, St-Emilion, £6.50
Côtes du Rhône Cuvée Capucines, Domaine du Vieux Chêne, £3.90
Mâcon Uchizy 1986, Domaine Talmard, £5.50
La Corte, Castello di Querceto 1981, £8.05
Erbacher Honigberg Riesling Kabinett 1983, Schloss Reinhartshausen, £5.20

J C Karn

Cheltenham Cellars, 7 Lansdown Place,   TEL (0242) 513265
Cheltenham, Gloucestershire GL50 2HU

OPEN Mon–Fri 9–6; Sat 9.30–1.30   CLOSED Sun, public holidays
CREDIT CARDS None accepted; personal and business accounts
DISCOUNTS 5% on 1 case   DELIVERY Free within Gloucestershire (quantity negotiable); elsewhere charges negotiable; mail order available
GLASS HIRE Free with 1-case order   TASTINGS AND TALKS To groups on request   CELLARAGE Charges negotiable

'We have the largest range of New Zealand wines in the northern hemisphere', is the boast. Well, we lost count, but certainly the list is very impressive, and many top names are here – Cooks and Montana of course, but also Babich, Selaks, Matua Valley, Villa Maria, Delegats and smaller producers such as C J Pask, Ngatarawa, The Mission, Roys Hill. Prices range around the £6 to £7 mark.

In other areas, J C Karn can't quite repeat their success in New Zealand. There are good petit château clarets, but only small areas of interest from the rest of France. In other European countries, Germany is still loitering in the old Liebfraumilch days, but there are a few delights such as Borgogno Barolo from Italy, Torres wines from Spain, and wines from Mitchelton and Plantagenet Vineyard in Western Australia.

Best buys

Montana Sauvignon Blanc 1988, Marlborough, £4.99
Babich Pinot Noir 1986, New Zealand, £5.99
Ch Roc St-Bernard 1982, Fronsac, £4.99

Richard Kihl

164 Regent's Park Road, London   TEL 01–586 5911
NW1 8XN

CASE SALES ONLY   OPEN Tue–Fri 9–5.30; Sat 11–5 (Wine Accessories
Shop)   CLOSED Mon, Sun, public holidays, Sats in August
CREDIT CARDS All accepted; personal and business accounts
DISCOUNTS Negotiable   DELIVERY Free in London (min 1 case); elsewhere
at cost; mail order available   GLASS HIRE, TASTINGS AND TALKS Not
available   CELLARAGE £4 per case per year

Wines go with wine accessories at Richard Kihl. The wines are
fine wines, parcels large or small of old clarets (many from
vintages of the 1960s and 1970s), red and white Burgundy and
vintage Ports.

The wine accessories range from antiques through to the most
practical tasting equipment – spittoons.

Best buys

Fine clarets, Burgundies and vintage Ports

Kiwifruits

25 Bedfordbury, Covent Garden,   TEL 01–240 1423
London WC2N 4BL
(mail order only)

OPEN Mon–Fri 10–6.30; Sat 10–6   CLOSED Sun, public holidays
CREDIT CARDS All accepted   DISCOUNTS Not available   DELIVERY Free in
London (min 6 cases); otherwise £9 per case   GLASS HIRE,
TASTINGS AND TALKS, CELLARAGE Not available

A short list entirely devoted to the wines from smaller estates in
New Zealand. Here you can find wines such as the
Martinborough Pinot Noir from the south of North Island,
wines from C J Pask, from Brookfields (no, not the Archers'
farm), from Matua Valley, Delegats, The Mission and
Ngatarawa. You could start with the two house wines, a
medium white and a dry white (Bakers Creek Crackling).

Best buys

Bakers Creek Crackling, New Zealand, £6.25
Matua Valley Sauvignon Blanc 1988, New Zealand, £6.35
C J Pask Cabernet Sauvignon/Merlot/Cabernet Franc 1988, New
Zealand, £6.50

Kurtz & Chan Wines

47–51 Great Suffolk Street, London SE1 0BS   TEL 01–928 9985

CASE SALES ONLY   OPEN Mon–Fri 8.30–7   CLOSED Sat, Sun, public
holidays   CREDIT CARDS None accepted; personal and business accounts
DISCOUNTS Available   DELIVERY Free in London postal area (min 5 cases);
otherwise at cost; mail order available   GLASS HIRE Free with 5-case
order   TASTINGS AND TALKS Tastings held regularly; to groups on
request   CELLARAGE £5 per year depending on quantity

Although Kurtz and Chan are now the owners of Green's, and
the same management also runs the Oxford and Cambridge Fine
Wine (see separate entries for both), each company runs its own
list.

Go to Kurtz & Chan for small parcels of fine wines – clarets,
Burgundies and Rhônes. On a recent list, you could have found
one bottle of 1948 Ch d'Yquem at £240 or a magnum of 1971 La
Tâche from Domaine de la Romanée-Conti at £1,600. Mature
vintages of Hermitage and Côte Rôtie or vintage Ports back to
1924 were also available, but the choice has no certainty or
pattern because of the nature of the wines.

Best buys
Old and rare wines

Lamb Wine Company

P O Box 38, Wallingford, Oxfordshire   TEL (0491) 35842
OX10 0UZ

CASE SALES ONLY   OPEN 7 days a week (24-hour answering machine)
CREDIT CARDS None accepted; personal and business accounts
DISCOUNTS 5% on 3 cases   DELIVERY Free within 15-mile radius of
Wallingford (min 1 case); otherwise at cost; mail order available
GLASS HIRE Free with 1-case order   TASTINGS AND TALKS To groups on
request   CELLARAGE Not available

A short list of carefully chosen wines, many of them from
France: Beaujolais from Chanut Frères, Bergerac from Ch La
Fage, a trio of clarets, Chablis from Domaine de l'Eglantière and
Laurent Perrier Champagne, and organically produced wines
from Terres Blanches in Coteaux des Baux en Provence. From
other countries, there are two Chilean wines from Viña Carmen,
Señorio de Sarria Navarra wines and Ramos Pinto Ports.

Please write to tell us about any ideas for features you would like to see
in next year's edition or in *Which? Wine Monthly*.

Best buys

Quinta Ervamoira 10-year-old tawny, Ramos Pinto, £10
Côtes du Rhône 1985, Domaine Martin, £3.96
Monbazillac 1982, Ch Le Fage, £5.12

Lay & Wheeler

✻ ⊏⊐ ☞ ☆

HEAD OFFICE AND WINE SHOP
Culver Street West, Colchester, Essex
CO1 1JA   TEL (0206) 764446
Wine Market, Gosbecks Road,   TEL as above
Colchester, Essex CO2 9JT

OPEN (Wine Shop) Mon–Sat 8.30–5.30; (Wine Market) Mon–Sat 8–8
CLOSED Sun, public holidays CREDIT CARDS Access, Visa; personal and
business accounts DISCOUNTS 1.5% on 4–12 cases, 3% on 12+ cases
DELIVERY Free in Essex and south Suffolk (min 1 case) and on UK
mainland (min 2) cases); otherwise £3.97 per delivery; mail order
available GLASS HIRE Free with order TASTINGS AND TALKS Regular
tastings held (all customers invited); 4–5 Wine Workshops held monthly
at Wine Market; major tutored Workshops held quarterly; to private
parties on request CELLARAGE £3.31 per case per year

By any yardstick this is one of the foremost lists in the Guide.
Just a glance at the number of times Lay & Wheeler appear as a
specialist stockist in our WHAT TO BUY section shows that they
are specialists in every major wine area of the world – which
means that their coverage is more than usually deep, in quality
as well as quantity.

Of course, with a list as comprehensive as this, the
importance of guidance and service is vital. The quality of the
Lay & Wheeler's list is high – and always makes fascinating
reading. Moreover, reports that we have on Lay & Wheeler
service are almost always complimentary.

Their range is huge, but certain areas stand out as being
particularly well served. These include the classic wines –
Bordeaux (including an en primeur offer as and when they feel
the vintage warrants it), Burgundy (plenty of domaine wines
here), Beaujolais (a very good selection of domaine wines),
Alsace (wines from Blanck). There is now a good and
encouraging set of wines from the South of France, and we can
recommend the house Champagne among the collection of
grande marque wines on their list. The Rhône comprises
another fine range of wines, from both the northern and
southern vineyards.

Outside France, Germany offers a superb spectrum of high
quality estate wines, with a special emphasis on bottles from
the Mosel–Saar–Ruwer. In Italy, Barolos vie with Chiantis and

Brunellos for pride of place on a list, which, by comparison with other countries, is short and somewhat predictable. Spain is dominated by Riojas from CVNE – and some excellent Sherries. Few Portuguese wines, but plenty of Ports.

Overseas, Australia really shines, with wines from many small boutique estates (look for Basedow, Bowen Estate, Woodstock, Henschke, Rothbury, Château Xanadu). By contrast, California's offering is short (although the Simi wines are highly regarded).

Regular customers are sent frequent special offers, a newsletter and en primeur offers as well as the splendid list.

Best buys

Sonoma White, Pedroncelli NV, California, £4.05
Chardonnay 1986, Lake's Folly, Hunter Valley, Australia, £12.90
Riesling 1987, Henschke, Adelaide Hills, Australia, £5.25
Ch Lacoste Borie 1985, Pauillac, £7.80
Côtes du Rhône Ch du Grand Moulas 1986, £4.05
Lay & Wheeler Extra Quality Brut Champagne, £10.65

Laymont & Shaw

The Old Chapel, Millpool, Truro, Cornwall TR1 1EX — TEL (0872) 70545

CASE SALES ONLY   OPEN Mon–Fri 9–5   CLOSED Sat, Sun, public holidays
CREDIT CARDS None accepted; personal and business accounts
DISCOUNTS Available   DELIVERY Free on UK mainland (min 2 cases); mail order available   GLASS HIRE Free   TASTINGS AND TALKS To groups on request   CELLARAGE Available

A fascinating diversity of wines from all the major regions of Spain. While many names will be familiar from other merchants' lists – Vega Sicilia, La Rioja Alta, Masía Bach, Scholtz Hermanos Málaga – this is the firm that actually imports them. (And many others are on sale.)

Their list makes fascinating reading – and not just for the lucid explanations offered by owner John Hawes. The range of wines in areas like the Penedés (wines from Jean León, Masía Bach and Torres are joined by the Cavas of Juve y Camps), or Rioja (La Rioja Alta, López de Heredia, Murrieta, Riscal, Beronia and other famous names are complemented by wines from lesser areas such as Toro (Gran Colegiata), Jumilla (a new find – a Bordeaux-style wine called Altos de Pío at £3.37) or Cariñena (Don Mendo Especial Tinto at £3.11).

There are two other star areas: Ribera del Duero, rightly now seen as a rival to Rioja among Spain's red wines, with wines from the two most famous bodegas of the region, Vega Sicilia

and Pesquera, as well as the improving local co-operative of
Bodegas Ribera Duero; and Sherry, where we find a highly
impressive range from a number of top names – Lustau, Diez
Hermanos, Barbadillo and Laymont & Shaw's own-label range.

Best buys

Señorio de los Llanos Reserva 1981, £3.29
Peñafiel 1983, 5th year, Bodegas Ribera del Duero, £9.54
Altos de Pío 1987, Jumilla, £3.37
Cava Juve y Camps Reserva de la Familia, £8.30

Laytons   ✿ ☞ ☆

20 Midland Road, London NW1 2AD	TEL 01–388 5081
ASSOCIATED OUTLETS	
André Simon Shops, 14 Davies Street, London W1Y 1LJ	TEL 01–499 9144
André Simon Shops, 50/52 Elizabeth Street, London SW1W 9PB	TEL 01–730 8108
André Simon Shops, 21 Motcomb Street, London SW1X 8LB	TEL 01–235 3723

OPEN Mon–Sat 9–7   CLOSED Sun, public holidays   CREDIT CARDS All
accepted; personal and business accounts   DISCOUNTS Not available
DELIVERY Free on UK mainland (min £100 order); mail order available
GLASS HIRE Free with 5-case order   TASTINGS AND TALKS Monthly tastings
at André Simon Shops; to groups by special arrangement
CELLARAGE £3.45–£5.75 per case per year depending on quantity; wines
are insured by Laytons

A classic list, strong on Bordeaux and Burgundy. The firm also
owns the André Simon shops – see the separate entry.

The clarets march in serried ranks back to fine old vintages
such as the 1966. There is plenty currently from the 1983
vintage, a good balance of prices, starting with Ch de Prieuré
Premières Côtes de Bordeaux at £4.12 and moving up through a
good range of crus bourgeois to Ch Latour at £41.68. The same
is true of 1982 – and there is excellent value from the 1981s.

Burgundy, though, is obviously first love for this merchant.
There is a deeply impressive range of wines. One of their
specialist suppliers is the exciting négociant firm of Chartron et
Trébuchet based at Puligny-Montrachet. Certain villages seem
well favoured – Volnay and Pommard, Gevrey Chambertin and
Meursault. There are some great (and therefore expensive) wines
here, but there's also good value with wines from the
Mâconnais and villages like Monthélie and Rully.

Beyond, look also for the wines of Newton Vineyard in California, Deutz Champagnes, good Côtes du Rhône Villages and Robertsons wood Ports.

Best buys

Mâcon Charnay 1987, Domaine Manciat Poncet, £5.65
Pinot Noir 1986, Bourgogne Grand Ordinaire, Robert Gibourg, £3.73
Ch de Cabriac 1987, Corbières, £3.16
Sancerre 1987, Chavignol, Jean Delaporte, £5.70
Deutz Late Disgorged Champagne 1976, £20.13

O W Loeb

64 Southwark Bridge Road, London   TEL 01–928 7750
SE1 0AS

OPEN Mon–Fri 9–5.30   CLOSED Sat, Sun, public holidays
CREDIT CARDS None accepted; personal and business accounts
DISCOUNTS 5% on 1–5 cases, 10% on 6–10 cases, wholesale prices on 10+
cases   DELIVERY Free in central London (min 1 case); otherwise 1–2 cases
£11.50 per consignment, 3–5 cases £3.45 per consignment, 6+ cases free;
mail order available   GLASS HIRE Not available   TASTINGS AND TALKS To
groups on request   CELLARAGE £4 per case per year or part year (only
available under bond)

Loeb's list has expanded in the last year to take on a famous range of Alsace wines, and it continues to be a fine listing of great estate wines from Germany and Burgundy.

O W Loeb is mainly a shipping company, acting as sole British importer for a number of famous names. This is the firm that brings the whole British wine trade Jaboulet Aîné wines from the Rhône. It is also now the firm that imports Hugel wines from Alsace (as well as those of Théo Faller Domaine Weinbach). And with their German links, they are importers of one of the most extensive ranges of German estate wines to be found anywhere.

That, of course, is only part of the Loeb list. They have a fine collection of clarets, with vintages going back to 1978, but with more recent vintages in considerable profusion. They have a range of Jura wines from Jean Bourdy which includes Ch Chalon Vin Jaune as well as red and white table wines. From the Loire, look for the wines of Foureau in Clos Naudin. And from the New World come Australian wines from Tolley in Hope Valley in South Australia, Matua Valley in New Zealand and Anderson Vineyard in California. Sherries are from M Hidalgo and there are a few vintage Ports.

Best buys

German estate wines
Beaujolais from Jacques Dépagneux

London Wine Co

Chelsea Wharf, 15 Lots Road, London   TEL 01–351 6856
SW10 0QF

CASE SALES ONLY   OPEN Mon–Fri 9.30–9; Sat, public holidays 10–7;
Sun 10.30–5.30   CLOSED Bank holiday Mondays   CREDIT CARDS All
accepted; personal and business accounts   DISCOUNTS Not available
DELIVERY Free in SW1, SW3, SW5–8, SW10–11 (min 1 case); elsewhere at
cost; mail order available   GLASS HIRE Free with 1-case order
TASTINGS AND TALKS Regular tastings held; to groups on request
CELLARAGE Available

Back in the Guide after two years' absence, London Wine has
dramatically expanded the range of wines it offers. There are
now two sides to the business – a fine wine side, which offers
small parcels of fine wines, and the keenly priced everyday
drinking side, whose list we consider here.

In a competent list certain regions and countries show up
particularly well: the French country wines, many well under £3
a bottle, Alsace wines from the Turckheim co-operative,
Beaujolais from Duboeuf, a well-priced range of everyday
drinking clarets (plus some more serious crus bourgeois),
excellent value CAVIT wines from the Trentino region of Italy,
well-priced Torres wines.

Overseas, look to Australia for Hill-Smith wines and the
superb Beresford Chardonnay (1987 vintage at £6.99), Montana
New Zealand wines, and a range of California wines which
includes inexpensive Gallo and pricier Washington State wines
from Ch Ste Michelle. There are Duke of Wellington Sherries
and Gould Campbell Ports.

Best buys

Quatro Vicariati 1985, CAVIT, £2.99
Côtes du Rhône 1983, Pascal, £3.49
Bourgogne Pinot Noir 1985, Caves Lugny, £3.75
Chardonnay 1987, Beresford, McLaren Vale, Australia, £6.99

If your favourite wine merchant is not in this section, write and tell us
about him or her. There are report forms at the back of the book.

Lorne House Vintners   🐷 ☆

Unit 5, Hewitts Industrial Estate,   TEL (0483) 271445
Elmbridge Road, Cranleigh, Surrey
GU6 8LW

CASE SALES ONLY   OPEN Mon–Fri 9–5; Sat 9–1   CLOSED Sun, public
holidays   CREDIT CARDS None accepted; personal and business accounts
DISCOUNTS Available   DELIVERY Free within 25-mile radius of Cranleigh
(min 2 cases) and UK mainland (min 7) cases); otherwise £5 per
consignment; mail order available   GLASS HIRE Free with 1-case order
TASTINGS AND TALKS Last weekend of each month in-store; to groups on
request   CELLARAGE Not available

From its original roots in the Loire, Lorne House Vintners have
now branched out to many of the other regions, as well as
Germany and Italy. Prices remain good.

The list still starts in the Loire where, as for many years,
Muscadets of Ch de Chasseloir feature strongly, but look also for
Vouvray – still and sparkling – from Serge Tellier and Quarts de
Chaume of Jean Baumard. Then we move to Bordeaux and a
strong showing of mid-priced wines (try those from Bourg and
Blaye) as well as recent vintages of the classed growths.
Burgundy has some domaine wines (and some domaine
Beaujolais), while on the Rhône Lirac wines from Domaine
Maby are featured. New varietal wines from the South (Vin de
Pays de Thongue Chasan at £2.90) are on show. House
Champagne is Alexander Bonnet (NV Brut Prestige at £9.10).

The German estate selection has undergone great
development – wines from Paul Anheuser in the Nahe,
Friedrich Wilhelm Gymnasium in the Mosel – while Italy's star
is Chianti from Viticcio (1986 vintage at £3.90). The familiar
Gran Colegiata from Toro is there in the Spanish section (along
with Garvey's Sherries), and we are told of future expansion in
the New World pages.

Best buys

Sauvignon de Touraine 1988, Domaine Guenault, £2.95
Chasan Vin de Pays des Côtes de Thongue (Midi), £2.90
Chianti Classico Viticcio Riserva 1985, £5.35
Jaume Serra Tinto and Blanco, £2.95

☆ celebrates the uninterrupted inclusion of this merchant in all ten
editions of *Which? Wine Guide.*

Luigi's Delicatessen

349 Fulham Road, London SW10 9TW   TEL 01–352 7739

OPEN Mon–Fri 9–10; Sat 9–7   CLOSED Sun, public holidays
CREDIT CARDS None accepted   DISCOUNTS 10% on 1 case   DELIVERY,
GLASS HIRE, TASTINGS AND TALKS, CELLARAGE Not available

A name new to the Guide, but whose food and wine shops are
familiar to many west Londoners.

The list is entirely Italian and contains some wines not easily
available elsewhere. Be prepared for considerable lack of interest
from the staff who are more concerned with slicing salami than
discussing wine.

If you persevere, you will find plenty of interest. White wines
include Galestros from Frescobaldi and Cantina Geografico;
wines from Antinori: less familiar wines such as the Libaio of
Ruffino, Arneis from Ceretto in Piedmont, Gavi di Gavi la
Scolca. Among reds, there is plenty to please from Tuscany
(good Vino Nobile di Montepulciano), Barolos from Oddero, the
splendidly named Inferno from the Valtellina. Look, too, for
Brunello from Fattoria dei Barbi and Biondi-Santi, the Prima
Vigna Riserva of Castello Vicchiomaggio, and Peppoli of
Antinori. There's a good range of sparkling wines (Asti
Spumante from Gancia and Fontanafredda) and a small
collection of Vin Santo (the dessert wine of Tuscany).

Best buys

Locorotondo Bianco, Leone de Castris (Puglia), £3.45
Franciacorta Bellavista (Lombardy), £5.95
Chianti Remole 1986, Frescobaldi (Tuscany), £4.75
Selvatico Rosso (Sardinia), £3.50

Luxembourg Wine Company

80 Northend, Batheaston, Bath, Avon   TEL (0225) 858375
BA1 7ES

CASE SALES ONLY   OPEN Mon–Sun 8–8   CREDIT CARDS None accepted;
personal and business accounts   DISCOUNTS Negotiable   DELIVERY Free
on UK mainland (min 4 cases); mail order available
GLASS HIRE Available if necessary   TASTINGS AND TALKS To groups on
request   CELLARAGE Not available

A small selection of wines from the Mosel vineyards in
Luxembourg. Wines come from the co-operative of
Wormeldange in the main vineyard area. The current selection
includes Rivaner, Elbling, Pinot Gris, Riesling and
Gewürztraminer varietal wines; sparkling wines and a rosé

wine made from Pinot Noir. Prices for some of the wines are very good (Rivaner 1985 at £2.70), rising to £4.55 for the top Riesling and Gewürztraminer.

Best buys

Rivaner 1985, Cave Coopérative de Wormeldange, Luxembourg, £2.70
Le Comte de Wormeldange, Vin Mousseux, Luxembourg, £5.25

Graham MacHarg

See Irvine Robertson.

Majestic Wine Warehouses

HEAD OFFICE
421 New Kings Road, London SW6 4RN   TEL 01–731 3131
32 branches in London, Birmingham, Bristol, Cambridge, Gloucester, Guildford, Ipswich, Leeds, Norwich, Oxford, Poole, Salisbury and Swindon

CASE SALES ONLY   OPEN (Generally) Mon–Sat 10–8; Sun 10–6   CLOSED Chr Day, Boxing Day, 1 Jan   CREDIT CARDS Access, Diners Club, American Express, Majestic Wine Charge Card, Visa; personal and business accounts   DISCOUNTS Not available   DELIVERY Free locally to branch (min 1 case) and for 10+ cases mail order; mail order available
GLASS HIRE Free with 1-case order   TASTINGS AND TALKS Monthly organised tastings in all branches; to groups on request to local manager or Head Office   CELLARAGE Not available

This innovative chain of wine warehouses has continued to expand at a prodigious rate – eight warehouses last year, another dozen this. They are gradually creeping north (Leeds was one of the lucky places last year). A spot of turbulence when they bought up a large group of American wine shops and sold them again seems to have had only marginal effect on the UK warehouses (apart from seeing an increase – and then a fall – in American wines).

What they offer is a huge variety of wines, many at unbeatable prices. There are still occasional hiccoughs in the quality (areas that could be improved include Beaujolais and Burgundy), but also plenty of 'finds', an area in which Majestic have always specialised.

One such is Hugh Ryman, son of Henry of Ch de la Jaubertie, who is now making wine in his own right in South-West France (try Domaine Le Pûts, a dry white wine from the Côtes de Gascogne). Another is the range of commune wines from the

209

Médoc (St-Julien NV at £4.99 is the latest) which are blended wines from some top estates.

Bordeaux, in fact, comes up with some star wines, such as the perennial favourite Ch Méaume (1986 vintage at £3.95) and wines from J-P Moueix, producer of Ch Pétrus and also more affordable wines from Fronsac and St-Emilion.

Other areas of France which do well are the Loire (with a vast range of Muscadet), the regions (especially the South and South-West) and Alsace. Outside France, the best places are Australia (they still manage to find some bargains here, such as the Coromandel Rhine Riesling at £2.99 or Chardonnay at £3.29, both made by Glenloth). Best value from California is the Canterbury range (Chardonnay 1987 at £4.49). And there's a full range of Bulgarian wines. (See also Elite Wines, the fine wine arm.)

Best buys

Hollydene Chardonnay 1987, Australia, £3.99
Champagne de Telmont Réserve NV, £8.95
Domaine le Pûts, Vin de Pays des Côtes de Gascogne, Hugh Ryman, £2.49
Ch Méaume 1986, Bordeaux Supérieur, £3.95
St-Nicolas de Bourgueil 1987, Les Gravières, £4.75

Market Wine Stores

See G M Vintners; these are the retail shops.

Marks & Spencer

Michael House, 47–67 Baker Street, London W1A 1DN
264 licensed branches nationwide

TEL 01–935 4422

OPEN Varies from store to store but generally 9–5.30 (most stores also have late night shopping once a week) CLOSED Sun, public holidays (some stores) CREDIT CARDS Marks & Spencer Chargecard DISCOUNTS 12 bottles for the price of 11 DELIVERY £2.95 per order; mail order available GLASS HIRE, TASTINGS AND TALKS, CELLARAGE Not available

By comparison with other stores with numerous branches, the Marks & Spencer list is not long. But it is a very coherent one which has followed a consistent policy (as with their foods) of not necessarily going in for the cheapest, but of offering good value in the middle price range.

This is most apparent in the French selection, by far the largest part of the list. There you will find a strong showing in white Burgundy and Chablis (of which M&S claim to sell more than anyone else in the country) and of claret (they have developed a good line in generic commune wines, many from top estates such as Léoville-Barton – for the St-Julien – or Pichon Longueville – for the Pauillac). A connoisseur's range specialises in the second wines from major Bordeaux châteaux and wines from Burgundy.

Outside those two classic areas, M&S do well on the Rhône and have a very popular Blanc de Blancs Champagne from the Union Champagne (at £9.99). Outside France, their Rioja is very good, as is the Chianti Classico of Villa Cafaggio (1985 vintage at £4.99), and then – moving further afield – we find a highly successful range of Australian wines under the St Michael label (try the Semillon at £4.50 or the Shiraz Cabernet at £3.99). New in 1989 was a set of California wines (mainly from Christian Brothers), but the launch of bottles containing two glasses of wine – an innovation – was spoilt by the quality of some of the contents.

Best buys

Muscadelle, Lauderaut, Bordeaux, £2.75
St-Julien 1985, Léoville-Barton, £7.99
California Sauvignon Blanc 1987, Buena Vista, £5.99
Shiraz Cabernet, Penfolds, Australia, £3.99

Marske Mill House

London Road, Sunninghill, Ascot,   TEL (0990) 22790
Berkshire SL5 0PN

CASE SALES ONLY   OPEN Telephone enquiries or orders 7 days per week – open all hours   CREDIT CARDS None accepted; personal and business accounts   DISCOUNTS Available   DELIVERY Free on UK mainland (min 3 cases); otherwise 1 case £3, 2 cases £1 per case; mail order available   GLASS HIRE Not available   TASTINGS AND TALKS To groups on request   CELLARAGE Not available

An unusual list of Italian wines – unusual because it specialises in wines from central Italy, particularly Umbria and in estates whose wines are not otherwise found here.

This is the place to come if you want Lamborghini wines from the shores of Lake Trasimene or those of Carlo Polidori in northern Umbria in the Colli Altotiberini, or of Arnaldo Caprai in Montefalco (Sagrantino di Montefalco 1985 at £6.56 is a rich, deep, opulent red wine).

Supplementary lists, aimed mainly at trade customers (although some wines can be supplied to private customers from stock), include the inexpensive wines from the Cantina

Sociale del Trasimeno, and occasional wines from Piedmont (Barolos from Elio Grasso and Palladino).

Best buys

Rosso di Montefalco 1986, Caprai (Umbria), £4.52
Rubino Riserva 1983, Polidori (Umbria), £4.71

Martinez Fine Wine

36 The Grove, Ilkley, West Yorkshire
LS29 9EE
TEL (0943) 603241

Corn Exchange Cellars, The Ginnel, off
Parliament Street, Harrogate, North
Yorkshire HG3 4JS
TEL (0423) 501783

OPEN Mon–Fri 9–6.30/7; Sat 9–6; Bank Holiday Mondays 10–5
CLOSED Sun, Good Friday, Chr Day, Boxing Day, 1 Jan
CREDIT CARDS Access, American Express, Visa; personal and business
accounts   DISCOUNTS 5% on 1 mixed case, 7.5% on 1 full case
DELIVERY Free in north and west Yorkshire (min 1 case) and elsewhere
(min 10 cases); otherwise 1–4 cases £2.50 per case, 5–9 cases £1.75 per
case; mail order available   GLASS HIRE Free with 1-case order
TASTINGS AND TALKS 3/4 tastings per year; monthly tastings and annual
dinner through Martinez Wine Club; to groups on request
CELLARAGE £3 per case per year

'Over 400 wines on the list, over 600 in our shops,' Mr
Martinez-Perez tells us. Certainly, customers are well served in
many wine areas, in Spain – as they have been for many years
here – but also France and, increasingly, the New World.

Starting with France, we find that Bordeaux is the star section,
not so much for its length (other merchants' claret ranges are
much longer) but for the good value it offers (with plenty of
wines under £5, including the cru bourgeois Ch Lestage 1985 at
£5.95 or Ch Puy-Castéra 1986 at £4.85). Other parts of France
that are treated well include Burgundy (with wines from
négociants Jaffelin) and Alsace (Willy Gisselbrecht). French
country wines offer good value, too.

Spain remains splendid. This is the firm that was among the
first to sell the excellent-value red and white Castillo de
Alhambra (now £2.65 for red, £2.45 for white). But if you're after
a classier bottle look at the splendid collection of Gran Reserva
Riojas, Torres and René Barbier wines, and the Protos Gran
Reserva Ribera del Duero at £13.25.

Other sections worth investigating for occasional treats are
Italy, J M da Fonseca wines from Portugal, Brown Brothers
wines from Australia and Montana from New Zealand, not
forgetting the good quality Santa Rita wines from Chile, Garvey

and Lustau Sherries and Martinez Gassiot Ports (the name is coincidental).

Best buys

Castillo de Alhambra Tinto 1988, £2.65
Imperial Reserva Rioja 1981, CVNE, £7.30
Madiran 1985, Domaine de Fauron, £4.75
Ch Puy Castéra 1985, Cru Bourgeois, £4.85

Master Cellar Wine Warehouse

5 Aberdeen Road, Croydon, Surrey   TEL 01–686 9989
CR0 1EQ
Associated with Davisons Wine Merchants

CASE SALES ONLY   OPEN Tue–Fri 10–8; Sat 10–6; Sun 10–2   CLOSED Mon,
public holidays   CREDIT CARDS Access, Visa   DISCOUNTS 2.5% on 10
cases   DELIVERY Free locally; elsewhere 1–9 cases by arrangement, 10+
cases free; mail order available   GLASS HIRE Free with order
TASTINGS AND TALKS Tutored tastings in-store and to wine clubs on
request   CELLARAGE Not available

This wine warehouse, associated with Davisons shops (see separate entry) builds upon Davisons' strengths in Bordeaux and vintage Port, and ventures into areas where the shops less often go.

So, of course, you will find a mouthwatering hoard of mature clarets stretching in vintage back to 1970 (Ch Lafite at £184 for a magnum). Many of these wines offer excellent value, especially the classed growths from the 1978 vintage. While the outlook is less impressive in Burgundy, there are some fine domaine wines and some mature reds, again at good prices.

Other areas of France provoke less excitement, but it's worth considering Duboeuf Beaujolais, some good wines from the southern Rhône and the Sancerre of Jean-Max Roger. Germany has some estate wines, Italy is a trifle uninspired, but Spain thrives with a fine array of wines from Ribera del Duero (Tudela, Bodegas Mauro 1983 at £6.65). Bulgaria and Portugal come up with a handful of nice bottles, while, beyond Europe, look to Australia for a range which includes Orlando, Moss Wood, Rosemount and Brown Brothers, all at good prices.

On to the array of mature vintage Ports at some excellent prices, as with the clarets.

Best buys

Ch Talbot 1976, St-Julien, £15.80
Domaine de Limbardie 1988, Vin de Pays des Coteaux de
Murviel (Midi), £2.60
Ch Beaumont 1985, Haut-Médoc, £6.15
Quinta de Vargellas 1978, Taylor's, £14.80
Champagne Ellner Brut NV, £7.95

Mayor Sworder & Co

21 Duke Street Hill, London SE1 2SW   TEL 01–407 5111

OPEN Mon–Fri 9–5   CLOSED Sat, Sun, public holidays   CREDIT CARDS None
accepted; personal and business accounts   DISCOUNTS Negotiable
DELIVERY Free in London postal district and Home Counties; elsewhere
at cost; mail order available   GLASS HIRE Free
TASTINGS AND TALKS Annual tasting in June for customers; to groups on
request   CELLARAGE £3.25 per case per year

A varied diet of wines from this City Wine merchant but one
which always seems to end up back with the classic areas of
France.

So, although you will find interest in Australia (with Idyll
Vineyard and Wirra Wirra), German estate wines, Italian wines
like the Soave of Pieropan or the Chianti of Volpaia, or Riojas
from CVNE, by far the widest variety is found in France.

There is a useful range of clarets back to 1978 but mainly of
more recent vintages, and interest in both red and white
Burgundies. In Alsace, the wines of J Becker attract, while in the
Rhône it is Châteauneuf from Ch la Nerthe and good Côtes du
Rhône from Domaine de Signac that are appealing. The Loire is
especially strong in Sancerre and Pouilly Fumé. French regional
wines include the white Côtes de Gascogne Domaine de Rieux
and the red Domaine de St-Marthe Vin de Pays de l'Hérault.

Regular customers will know that the list is only part of
what's on offer and regular promotions expand the range much
further. (Prices on the list do not include VAT, but we have
added it to the Best Buys below.)

Best buys

Domaine de St-Marthe, Vin de Pays de l'Hérault 1985, £3.28
Domaine de Rieux, Vin de Pays des Côtes de Gascogne, £3.45
Idyll Vineyard Cabernet Shiraz 1985, Geelong, Australia, £6.32
St-Nicolas de Bourgueil 1986, Claude Bureau, £4.60

Andrew Mead Wines

Shovelstrode, Presteigne, Powys
LD8 2NP
TEL (05476) 268

CASE SALES ONLY   OPEN By appointment only (and limited to known clients)   CREDIT CARDS None accepted   DISCOUNTS Not available
DELIVERY Free on regular delivery routes (throughout England & Wales) (min 3 cases); £4 for smaller orders on delivery routes; otherwise at cost   GLASS HIRE Free for regular customers   TASTINGS AND TALKS, CELLARAGE Only exceptionally

A husband and wife team run this business from their mid-Wales home in a very personal way, which is is reflected in the tasting notes contained in the list, in the direct contact Mr Mead has with his producers, and in their operation of a personalised delivery system, touring the country to supply customers.

The list is very French-based, with probably as much interest in the smaller areas as in the major areas. For example, they offer a fine selection of Alsace wines from Rolly Gassmann, wines from Ch Larroze in Gaillac and plenty of other regional bottles from the South and South-West of France.

In Bordeaux, there are some well-priced petit château wines, plus classed growths back to 1970 (but in small quantities). Some fine estate wines from Burgundy are joined by comparatively inexpensive whites (Mâcon-Lugny Les Charmes at £4.65, for instance). The Loire offers good Vouvrays from Gaston Huet and St-Pourçain wines (including a rare red) from Jean and François Ray, while on the Rhône, Guigal is the star.

Outside France, the offerings come from Germany (with a new list of estate wines), a few Riojas, one Chianti and a good selection of vintage Ports.

Best buys

St-Pourçain Blanc 1988, Ray, £3.55
Philippe Hérard Brut Blanc de Blancs, £4.45
Côtes de Duras 1988, Ch de Conti, £3.05
Trittenheimer Apotheke Riesling Spätlese 1985,
Stefan Bollig, £4.65

The Wine Development Board is a small organisation with the responsibility of encouraging more people to drink wine. They may be able to supply literature and general promotional material. Contact them at: Five Kings House, Kennet Wharf Lane, Upper Thames Street, London EC4V 3BH; TEL 01-248 5835.

J H Measures & Sons

The Crescent, Spalding, Lincolnshire
PE11 1AF
TEL (0775) 2676

G E Bromley & Sons, London Street,
Leicester, Leicestershire LE5 3RH
TEL (0533) 768471

OPEN Mon–Sat 9–6 CLOSED Sun, public holidays CREDIT CARDS Access,
Visa; personal and business accounts DISCOUNTS Approx 5% on 1 case
DELIVERY Free in south Lincolnshire and East Midlands (min 1 case);
elsewhere at cost; mail order available GLASS HIRE Free with case order
TASTINGS AND TALKS Bottles open in-store most weeks; major annual
tasting in October; to groups on request CELLARAGE Not available

See G E Bromley & Sons.

Michael Menzel

297/299 Ecclesall Road, Sheffield, South
Yorkshire S11 8NX
TEL (0742) 683557

OPEN Mon–Sat 10–9; Sun 12–2, 7–9 CLOSED Public holidays
CREDIT CARDS All accepted; personal and business accounts
DISCOUNTS Available (min 1 case) DELIVERY Free in Sheffield (min 1 case)
and surrounding area (min 5 cases); elsewhere at cost GLASS HIRE Free
with case order TASTINGS AND TALKS, CELLARAGE Not available

Mr Menzel has now established some order on last year's list
and he has plenty to offer of interest from many areas. His
prices do not include VAT but we have added it in this report.

One of the strongest areas is Burgundy, where the wines of
Joseph Drouhin take centre stage, supported by Faiveley,
Bouchard Père and Louis Jadot. Drouhin also supplies the
Beaujolais. On the Rhône, it is Jaboulet Aîné and Chapoutier
who are the mainstays, while in Alsace it is Hugel.

There is serious stuff from Bordeaux, but it starts
inexpensively enough with Ch Belingard at £3.43 before rising
through some good crus bourgeois to classed growths.
Champagnes are extensive.

Moving beyond France, Italy is well served with good things
from Masi in the Veneto, Borgogno in Piedmont, Col d'Orcia
Brunello, less expensive Spanna and Gattinara from Brugo, and
whites such as Pomino from Frescobaldi and Gavi from Pio
Cesare. Other hot spots are Gran Reserva Riojas, wines from
Brown Brothers and Lindemans, Californian Mondavi and, new
to the list, Chilean wines from Santa Helena.

If you disagree with us, please tell us why. You will find report forms at
the back of the book.

Best buys

Pol Roger NV Champagne, £12.64
Domaine Ch Mandelot 1985, Hautes Côtes de Beaune, Bouchard
Père et Fils, £6.89
Soave Classico 1988, Guerrieri-Rizzardi, £3.43

Mi Casa Wines

77 West Road, Buxton, Derbyshire   TEL (0298) 3952
SK17 6HQ

OPEN Mon–Fri 3–10; Sat 11–10; Sun, Good Friday 12–2, 7–10; Chr Day
12–1 (other public holidays as normal days) CREDIT CARDS None
accepted; business accounts DISCOUNTS 5% on 1 case DELIVERY Free
within 10-mile radius of Buxton (min 1 case) GLASS HIRE Free with 1-
case order TASTINGS AND TALKS To groups on request CELLARAGE Not
available

Although a couple of clarets, Stanley Leasingham wines from
Australia and a 1975 German Auslese offered some interest on a
recent list, the essence of Mi Casa's business is Spanish wines.
    A well-balanced range of Riojas includes Reservas and Gran
Reservas from producers such as Campo Viejo, Viña Real,
Faustino, Marqués de Murrieta and La Rioja Alta's Reserva 904.
From Penedés, there is René Barbier and Torres. Cavas are those
of Freixenet and Conde de Caralt as well as Faustino (Brut
Reserve at £7.75). Sherries come from Penmartin, De Soto and
Cabrera, and wines from smaller areas such as Priorato and
Tarragona are also stocked.

Best buys

Rioja 1985, Campo Viejo, £3.60
Cava Carta Nevada, Freixenet, £5.30
Viña Valduero, Foux & Read 1985 (Ribera del Duero), £5.95

Millevini   ✉

3 Middlewood Road, High Lane,   TEL (0663) 64366
Stockport, Cheshire SK6 8AU

CASE SALES ONLY OPEN Mon–Fri 9–3 (answering service after 3 pm on
weekdays and all day Sat and Sun) CREDIT CARDS None accepted;
business accounts DISCOUNTS 4% on 3 cases DELIVERY Free within 20-
mile radius of shop (min 1 case) and elsewhere (min 4 cases); otherwise
£5.50; mail order only GLASS HIRE Free TASTINGS AND TALKS To groups
on request CELLARAGE Not available

It's Italy, Italy all the way with this merchant. The list is full of
great names, fine wines – and everything is cheaper than it was

last year because they have decided to do away with quantity discounts and go instead for competitive bottle prices.

As an interesting contrast with most Italian lists, which emphasise the north and neglect the south, this range has quite a lot of interest in the Mezzogiorno south of Rome. There's the fine Torre Ercolana of Colacicchi (1981 vintage at £10.25), Trebbiano and Cerasuolo d'Abruzzo from Valentini, Torre Quarto, the Malbec-based wine from Puglia, Salice Salentino 1981 Riserva from the heel of Italy, Cirò from Calabria, vintages of Aglianico di Vulture from d'Angelo in Basilicata, not forgetting wines from Sella e Mosca in Sardinia.

But the north is hardly ignored: classic Trentino wines of Fedrigotti, Südtirol wines of Tiefenbrunner, Valpolicella from Tedeschi, Barbaresco from Castello di Neive, Bonarda Oltrepò Pavese from the Fugazza sisters, Chiantis from Pagliarese, varietal Friuli wines from Collavini. And much more...

Best buys

Barbaresco 1983, Arione (Piedmont), £4.95
Valcalepio Rosso 1985, Tenuta Castellodi Grumello (Lombardy), £3.70
Montepulciano d'Abruzzo 1985, Barone Cornacchia (Abruzzo and Molise), £3.35
Cirò Classico Rosso 1985, Librandi (Calabria), £3.67
Galestro 1986, Rocca delle Macie (Tuscany), £3.77

Mitchell & Son

21 Kildare Street, Dublin 2, Republic of Ireland   TEL (0001) 760766
Associated with John Henchy & Sons, Cork

OPEN Mon–Fri 10.30–5.30; Sat 10.30–1   CLOSED Sun, public holidays
CREDIT CARDS All accepted; personal and business accounts
DISCOUNTS 5% on 1 case   DELIVERY Free within 45-mile radius of Dublin city (min 2 cases); otherwise 1 case £3.80, 2 cases £4.20, 3 cases £5.40, 4 cases £6.80; 5+ cases free; mail order available   GLASS HIRE Free with 2-case order   TASTINGS AND TALKS Tastings of new wines for customers; to groups on request   CELLARAGE Not available

The Republic of Ireland's only entry in the Guide, Mitchells offers a full range of wines covering most wine areas even if, in some cases, only sparsely. Comparison of prices will show United Kingdom readers how lucky they are compared with wine drinkers in Ireland.

The most interest lies in France and in the classic areas. There's a good range of claret at fair prices (for Ireland), mainly of recent vintages and including some top classed growths. In

Burgundy, the majority of wines come from Mommessin who also supply the Rhône wines. The Loire is a disappointment, but Alsace wines from Dopff au Moulin are a compensation.

Outside France, consider the German estate wines, many from Deinhard. Tiny points of interest occur in Italy (Chianti from Castello Vicchiomaggio, for example), but there's plenty from Hardy's in Australia and wines from J M da Fonseca in Portugal. Ports are from Fonseca, Sherries from Lustau and house Champagne is Laurent Perrier.

Best buys

Garrafeira 1980, J M da Fonseca, £IR7
Faugères 1986, Domaine de Pierre Cauvy, £IR5.25
Ch Rausan-Ségla 1985, Margaux, £IR25
Deinmoselle, Deinhard, £IR5

Moffat Wine Shop

8 Well Street, Moffat, Dumfries & TEL (0683) 20554
Galloway DG10 9DP

OPEN Mon–Sat 9–5.30   CLOSED Sun, Wed pm in Jan and Feb
CREDIT CARDS Visa   DISCOUNTS 5% on 1 case   DELIVERY Free in
Dumfriesshire (min 1 case); elsewhere at cost; mail order available
GLASS HIRE Free   TASTINGS AND TALKS Monthly tastings at Well View
Hotel, Moffat from September to April; to groups on request
CELLARAGE Free

A move across the street to larger premises has meant more room for the varied stock the Moffat Wine Shop list, including their huge collection of malt whiskies.

It's a wide-ranging list, even if it does not go particularly deep. So, for instance, jostling for attention are small ranges of clarets and Burgundies, Loire wines including Vouvray from Marc Brédif, regional wines such as Gaillac from Jean Gros.

While Germany is equally briefly treated, there is more on offer in Italy – Masi Valpolicella, Chianti Machiavelli, Dolcetto from Pio Cesare and the splendid table wines of Donnafugata in Sicily. Spain has Torres wines and Rioja from Berberana and Muga, and Portugal wines from J M da Fonseca and Aveleda Vinho Verde. In Australia, we find bottles from Hill-Smith, and from New Zealand wines from Stoneleigh Vineyard. Chilean wines come from Torres and Santa Helena. Moffat Wine Shop also carries almacenista Sherries and an interesting collection of single quinta vintage Ports.

Best buys

Refosco Calunghetta 1986 (Friuli–Venezia–Giulia), £2.99
Fumé Blanc Santa Helena 1988, Chile, £3.99
Ch Larroze 1985, Gaillac, £4.85

Moreno Wines

11 Marylands Road, London W9 2DU   TEL 01–286 0678
2 Norfolk Place, London W2 1QN   TEL 01–723 6897 and
724 3813

OPEN Mon–Fri 9–9 (W9), 9.30–8 (W2); Sat 10–9 (W9), 10–8 (W2); Sun 12–2
(W9) CLOSED Sun (W2), public holidays CREDIT CARDS Access, Visa
DISCOUNTS 5% on 1 case; larger quantities negotiable DELIVERY Free in
West London (min 1 case); otherwise 1 case £5, 2 cases £5; 3+ cases
free; mail order available GLASS HIRE Free with wine
TASTINGS AND TALKS Moreno Wine Club meets last Friday every month at
Canning House, 2 Belgrave Square; to groups on request
CELLARAGE Not available

A Spanish-speaking list, the lion's share consisting of wines
from Spain, but boosted by interest in Chile.

Moreno Wines imports a considerable range of wines from
Spain as well as listing other producers' wines already available
in this country. They have a powerful list of Riojas – Bodegas
Alavesas, Bodegas Navajas, Faustino Martinez, Riscal, Murrieta,
Lopez de Heredia (Tondonia), Bodegas Riojanas, Bodegas Muga,
Berberana – and more. Especially impressive is the Gran
Reserva range, even if much of it is in short supply.

Other areas of Spain are not neglected. Look for Conde de
Caralt wines from Penedés, Raimat (including the Chardonnay
1986 at £4.65), and Navarra's Bodegas Carricas (the wines of
Mont-Plané). New to the list are the wines of Fermoselle in Toro
(Banda de Plata Tinto Reserva 1981 at £5.99); then wines from
Jumilla, from León, from Ribera del Duero (in quantity from the
Bodegas Ribera Duero, the local co-operative) and plenty of
Cavas. There are even some of the crisp Albarinho wines from
Galicia.

Chile weighs in with wines from the Santa Rita bodega, as
well as Torres and Concha y Toro. And there is a big showing
of Sherries from firms like Bobadilla, Barbadillo and Don Zoilo.

Best buys

Condestable Tinto 1986, Señorio de Condestable, Jumilla, £2.49
Conde de Caralt Cava Brut NV, £4.35
Vega de Toro Tinto Reserva 1981, Luis Mateos, £4.55
Ribera Duero Crianza Tinto 1985, Bodegas Ribera Duero, £4.75

Morris & Verdin

28 Churton Street, London SW1V 2LP   TEL 01–630 8888

CASE SALES ONLY   OPEN Mon–Fri 9–5.30; Sat 10–3   CLOSED Sun, public
holidays   CREDIT CARDS None accepted; personal and business accounts
DISCOUNTS Available   DELIVERY Free in central London and Oxford (min 1
case); otherwise £8.50 per consignment; mail order available
GLASS HIRE Free with case order   TASTINGS AND TALKS To groups on
request   CELLARAGE £4.60 per case per year (inc insurance)

This is a range of wines whose heart is Burgundy. There is an
impressive array of domaine wines, from producers like Comte
Lafon, Etienne Sauzet, Monthélie-Douhairet, Domaine Daniel
Rion, Denis Bachelet; and smaller growers such as Pierre Amiot,
Paul Chapelle in Puligny-Montrachet and François Jobard in
Meursault.

If only by contrast the Bordeaux range is much narrower but
even here there are good things from areas such as St-Emilion
and Pomerol, and a goodly number of sweet white wines. Other
French areas do well too: Alsace with the wines of Ostertag (the
firm with the paschal lamb on its label – their name means
Easter), the organic wines from St-André de Figuière in Côtes
de Provence, Rhône wines from Ch de Beaucastel in
Châteauneuf and Emile Florentin Clos de l'Arbalastier in St-
Joseph.

There are now a few New World wines: watch for Tarra
Warra in the Yarra Valley (Chardonnay 1987 at £14.20 a match
for any Burgundy) and Au Bon Climat in California (makers of
fine Pinot Noir).

Best buys

Hautes Côtes de Beaune 1986, Domaine Mazilly, £6.30
Pinot Blanc 1987, Domaine Ostertag d'Alsace, £4.30
Beaujolais Villages 1987, Jacky Janodet, £4.90

Special awards

means bargain prices (good *value* may be obtained from
merchants without this symbol, of course, if you wish to pay for
service)

means that the wines stocked are of consistently high quality

means that the merchant stocks an above-average range

means that extra-special service is offered; helpful advice,
information lists and newsletters, tastings etc.

Morrisons

OFFICES/WAREHOUSE
Wakefield 41 Industrial Estate,   TEL (0924) 822996
Wakefield, West Yorkshire WF2 0XF
46 branches in Cumbria, Derbyshire, Lancashire, Lincolnshire,
Staffordshire, Teesside and Yorkshire

OPEN (Generally) Mon, Tue, Wed, Sat 8.30–6; Thur, Fri 8.30–8
CLOSED Sun, some public holidays   CREDIT CARDS Access, Visa
DISCOUNTS, DELIVERY Not available   GLASS HIRE Available in selected
stores   TASTINGS AND TALKS Regular in-store tastings   CELLARAGE Not
available

This group of supermarkets continues to offer excellent value in
its range of wines. Like most supermarket groups, Morrisons
run two lists, one of standard wines carried by all stores, the
other of fine wines available only in larger branches.

There has been expansion all round this year, and customers
can expect to see new introductions from Chile, Australia,
California, even Greece. This means that the range, always
strong in areas such as French vins de pays, petit château clarets
and Italian wines, is now more broadly based.

Special offers and regular promotions make this competitive
range even more attractive.

Best buys

La Vieille Ferme, Côtes du Ventoux 1987, £2.99
Bin 444 Cabernet Sauvignon, Wyndham Estate, Hunter Valley,
Australia, £3.49
Beaujolais Regnié 1988, Georges Duboeuf, £3.99
Pouilly Fuissé 1986, Maurice Chenu, £5.99

M R Vintners

See G M Vintners.

The Wine & Spirit Education Trust is the body in charge of educating
those in and on the fringes of the wine trade. They offer a series of
courses right up to Master of Wine level, the more basic of which are
open to non-trade members who can convince the Trust of their
intention to enter the wine trade. Contact them at: Five Kings House,
Kennet Wharf Lane, Upper Thames Street, London EC4V 3AJ; TEL 01-
236 3551.

Le Nez Rouge

See Berkmann Wine Cellars.

Nickolls & Perks

37 High Street, Stourbridge, West
Midlands DY8 1TA
ASSOCIATED COMPANY
Greenwood & Co, 178 High Street, Lye,
Stourbridge, West Midlands DY9 8LH

TEL (0384) 394518/
377211

TEL (038 482) 2217

OPEN Mon–Sat 9–10; Sun 12–2, 7–10   CREDIT CARDS Access, American
Express, Visa; personal and business accounts   DISCOUNTS 5–10% on
1 case   DELIVERY Free locally; elsewhere at cost; mail order available
GLASS HIRE Free with order   TASTINGS AND TALKS Events through
Stourbridge Wine Society; to groups on request possible
CELLARAGE Available

This is mainly a fine wine merchant, specialising in clarets, red
Burgundy and vintage Ports. But within those areas there are
concessions to those with less capacious pockets, with some
mature wines at good prices (Ch Cos Labory 1978 at £10.95, for
example, or some inexpensive 1981s). The list goes on into an
impressive collection of 1985s.

In Burgundy, there is again a mix between fine wines from
estates like Romanée-Conti and inexpensive Beaujolais. With
Champagne, featured producers are Mumm, Veuve Clicquot,
Lanson and Moët & Chandon. Rather too many Liebfraumilchs
for such august surroundings (plus some German estate wines)
and some branded sparkling wines – again seeming out of
place.

Best buys

Grahams 1975 Vintage Port, £18
Ch Senailhac Cru Bourgeois 1985, Médoc, £5.95

We have tried to make the *1990 Which? Wine Guide* as comprehensive as
possible, but we should love to hear from you about any other wine
merchants you feel deserve an entry, or your comments on existing
entries. Write to us either by letter or using the report forms supplied
at the back of the book.

Nicolas

157 Great Portland Street, London W1N 5FB	TEL 01–580 1622
98 Holland Park Avenue, London W11 3RB	TEL 01–727 5148
6 Fulham Road, London SW3 6HG	TEL 01–584 1450
282 Old Brompton Road, London SW5 9HR	TEL 01–370 4402
71 Abingdon Road, London W8 6AW	TEL 01–937 3996

OPEN (W1) Mon–Fri 10–7; Mon–Sat 11–8   CLOSED Sun, public holidays
CREDIT CARDS Access, Visa; personal and business accounts
DISCOUNTS 5% on 1 full case   DELIVERY Free local to store; otherwise at
cost; mail order available   GLASS HIRE Free with appropriate case order
TASTINGS AND TALKS Promotional tastings generally held every two
months; to groups on request   CELLARAGE Charges negotiable

Buckinghams have been taken over by the French wine
merchant Nicolas – famous in France not so much for the
branded wine but for its wine shops – and the shops have been
re-named in honour of the new owners. Plans are afoot for more
shops.

As we went to press, the stock was changing, and the promise
was of many more French wines as part of a general expansion.

The Nobody Inn

Doddiscombsleigh, nr Exeter, Devon EX6 7PS	TEL (0647) 52394

OPEN Mon–Sat 11–11; Sun 12–10.30   CLOSED Chr Day evening
CREDIT CARDS Access, Visa; personal and business accounts
DISCOUNTS 5% for 1 case   DELIVERY Free within 10-mile radius
(min 1 case); otherwise at cost; mail order available   GLASS HIRE Free
with 1-case order   TASTINGS AND TALKS Tastings organised from time
to time   CELLARAGE Not available

If this huge list, packed with quality and interesting wines,
sometimes seems to get out of hand, the reason is probably a
commendable over-enthusiasm.

Certain areas are particularly strong: since Nobody Inn is also
a restaurant, we are delighted to see so many half-bottles and
pudding wines. But there is also an immense range of clarets,
starting with 1961 and moving on to 1985. They are informative
about which wines are ready to drink.

Burgundy and the Rhône get sound – if somewhat less
extensive – treatment, and there's a good line in Alsace wines
(ideal, of course, for restaurants). The Loire is noteworthy,

mainly for its delicious sweet white wines, but for a few dry wines as well.

Outside France, turn to Germany rather than Italy for estate wines and to Spain for good Riojas and Torres wines in profusion. The New World has increased by leaps and bounds in the past two years. Look for Heitz, Mondavi, Carmenet, Ridge, Conn Creek from California; Lindemans, Huntingdon, Tisdall, Taltarni, Ch Tahbilk from Australia, not forgetting the liqueur Muscats; and wines from smaller New Zealand estates. All three areas offer enormous choice.

If the fortified wine section seems short by comparison, despite the Sherries, it would be worth turning to the pages of malt whiskies for rewarding compensation.

Best buys

Basedows Shiraz 1985, Barossa Valley, Australia, £4.45
Ch Segonzac 1985, Premières Côtes de Blaye, £5.52
Penfolds Grange 1976, South Australia, £39.54
Concha y Toro Merlot 1985, Chile, £2.99
Quarts de Chaume 1983, Domaine Baumard, £8.64

Rex Norris

50 Queens Road, Haywards Heath,   TEL (0444) 454756
West Sussex RH16 1EE

OPEN Mon, Tue, Thur 9–5.30; Wed 9–1; Fri 9–7.30; Sat 9–4.30
CLOSED Sun, public holidays   CREDIT CARDS Access, Visa; personal and business accounts   DISCOUNTS 10% on 1 case   DELIVERY Free in mid-Sussex   GLASS HIRE Free with 1-case order   TASTINGS AND TALKS Very occasionally   CELLARAGE Not available

Although Rex Norris produces no list, it's worth visiting this shop to find out what's in stock. At any one time there could be 20 different Australian wines, the same number from Spain and Italy, sweet German wines, Nobilo wines from New Zealand, some 1983 red Burgundies or wines from Jean Cros in Gaillac.

Best buys

Sauvignon Blanc, E & J Gallo, California, £2.99
Campo Viejo Gran Reserva 1978, Rioja, £6.09
Wyndham Estate Shiraz, Hunter Valley, Australia, £4.99

Please write to tell us about any ideas for features you would like to see in next year's edition or in *Which? Wine Monthly*.

Oddbins

HEAD OFFICE

31–33 Weir Road, London SW19 8UG   TEL 01–879 1199

145 branches

OPEN (Generally) Mon–Sat 9–9; Sun, public holidays 12–2, 7–9.30 (not all shops open on Sun)   CLOSED Chr Day   CREDIT CARDS Access, American Express, Oddbins Credit Card, Visa; personal and business accounts DISCOUNTS 5% on unmixed cases; 'seven for the price of six' on almost all Champagne   DELIVERY Free within locality of shop (min 1 case) GLASS HIRE Free   TASTINGS AND TALKS Regular in-store tastings on Saturdays; regular customer tastings in Scotland; to groups on request CELLARAGE Not available

Signs of Oddbins' success are that everybody else in the wine trade is jealous of them; that their wines are always being recommended by wine writers; and that, from reports we receive, they are often out of stock.

We hope that they can get their stocking policy right, because what Oddbins has to offer is by far the best range from any of the major multiple wine retailers. Because of its consistent quality and willingness to be experimental, the list remains one of the top ones in this Guide.

Don't come to Oddbins if you want an in-depth range of clarets or Burgundies – that is best left to more traditional merchants, although they had a splendid offer of 1986 wines during the summer of 1989 at prices lower than the original en primeur offers. You will, however, find a stunning range of Champagnes (and they were still offering seven bottles for the price of six as we went to press), a big range of Rhône wines, and very good value from both the South and South-West of France.

Outside France, Italy and Portugal perform better than Spain and Germany (although Sherries come in plenty of styles and producers). Australia continues to be a major star area, with Penfolds wines under all their many names (Seaview, Wynns, Kaiser Stuhl, as well as Penfolds itself), Barossa Valley Estates wines which are currently the least expensive on the market, Orlando, Brown Brothers... And now America has provided Oddbins with the best value range in our shops, some, from the Glen Ellen winery, at under £4, many more at under £5. Washington State, too, has come in with surprising value from Kiona and Columbia Crest.

And, if this wasn't enough, Oddbins continue to debunk wine with the cartoons of Ralph Steadman which adorn their lists.

Best buys

Mailly Grand Cru Champagne NV, £8.99
Corbières 1985, Dame Adelaide, £2.99
Seaview Cabernet/Shiraz 1986, South Australia, £3.69
Glen Ellen Merlot 1986, Sonoma, California, £3.99
Josephine Doré, De Bartoli, Sicily, £4.49
Quinta da Abrigada 1984, Portugal, £3.49

Old Street Wine Company

309 Old Street, London EC1V 6LE   TEL 01–729 1768

OPEN Mon–Fri 10–7; Sat 11–3   CLOSED Sun, public holidays
CREDIT CARDS Access, Visa; personal and business accounts
DISCOUNTS 5% on 1 case   DELIVERY Free in EC1 and EC2 (min 2 cases);
rest of London negotiable; elsewhere at cost; mail order available
GLASS HIRE Free with order   TASTINGS AND TALKS Tastings available
through the Private Wine Club; to groups on request   CELLARAGE Not
available

Expansion is in the air at this merchant, with a new shop
planned for the West End of London. Loire wines continue to
be highlighted, especially (unusually) the reds (Bourgueil
Vieilles Vignes 1987 of Domaine Richou at £4.95). The company
often has small parcels of wines not featured on the main list.

For other French areas, look for some mature clarets,
Burgundies from Charles Viénot (including some older
vintages), special offers from areas such as the northern Rhône,
Alsace wines from Willy Gisselbrecht, small offerings from
Spain and Italy and wines from Hardy's in Australia.

There are always small parcels of vintage Port, and often of
old vintage Madeira.

Best buys

Anglesey Estate Chardonnay, Australia, £4.59
Touraine Tradition Rouge 1988, Hubert Sinson, £4.29

Special awards

🐷 means bargain prices (good *value* may be obtained from
merchants without this symbol, of course, if you wish to pay for
service)

🏵 means that the wines stocked are of consistently high quality

🍷 means that the merchant stocks an above-average range

☞ means that extra-special service is offered; helpful advice,
information lists and newsletters, tastings etc.

Organic Wine Company

P O Box 81, High Wycombe,   TEL (0494) 446557
Buckinghamshire HP13 5QN
ASSOCIATED OUTLET
Lincolnshire Wine Company, Chapel
Lane, Ludborough, nr Grimsby,
Lincolnshire DN36 5SJ

CASE SALES ONLY   OPEN Mon–Sat 9–6; Sun, public holidays by
arrangement   CLOSED Chr Day, Boxing Day   CREDIT CARDS Access, Visa;
business accounts   DISCOUNTS Available   DELIVERY Free within 10-mile
radius of High Wycombe (min 1 case); otherwise £3.70 within 40-mile
radius of High Wycombe and all London postal districts; elsewhere £5
for 1 case, £6 for 2–3 cases; mail order available   GLASS HIRE Free with 3-
case order   TASTINGS AND TALKS In-store tastings by arrangement at retail
premises; company-run tastings at various regional centres throughout
the year; tastings and tutored tastings by arrangement   CELLARAGE £3.75
per case per year

The name says it all: this is a range of nearly 150 organically
produced wines from France and Germany, often at very good
prices.

There are wines from most French regions: from Bordeaux
(look for Ch du Puy, a Bordeaux Supérieur, in vintages back to
1970), from Burgundy (from Alain Verdet in the Hautes Côtes de
Nuits) and from Alsace (wines from André Stentz), not
forgetting the Baux en Provence wines of Mas de Gourgonnier
and the Côtes du Rhône of Domaine St-Apollinaire (1983
vintage at £3.70).

Germany offers a wide range from Konrad Knodel in the
Nahe, a young grower who produces wines in what the list
describes as a light dry style (and there are also wines from
Rheingau and Franconia). For some sparkle, try the Champagne
of Poirrier and Clairette de Die of Achard-Vincent.

Best buys

Muscadet de Sèvre-et-Maine sur lie 1987, Guy Bossard, £3.75
Windesheimer Rosenberg Riesling Trocken 1987, Konrad
Knodel, £3.95
Ch du Puy 1976, Bordeaux Supérieur, £9.75
Mas de Gourgonnier 1986, Réserve du Mas, Nicolas Cartier,
£4.35

There is no connection between *Which? Wine Guide* and *The Good Wine Guide*, which is published by the Sunday Telegraph.

Oxford & Cambridge Fine Wine

48 Clifton Road, Cambridge,
Cambridgeshire CB1 4FQ

TEL (0223) 215274

OPEN Mon–Fri 9–6   CLOSED Sat, Sun, public holidays
CREDIT CARDS Access, Visa; personal and business accounts
DISCOUNTS 3% on 1 case, 5% on 5–9 cases, 7.5% on 9+ cases
DELIVERY Free within 30-mile radius of Oxford and Cambridge and
London postal districts (min 1 case); elsewhere £1.50 per case (minimum
charge £6), 5+ cases free; mail order available   GLASS HIRE Free with 1-
case order   TASTINGS AND TALKS To groups on request   CELLARAGE £3.50
per case per year

A fairly conventional list, obviously aimed at Oxbridge colleges,
with plenty of claret (including their own house claret, College
Claret, at £3.18 – prices on the list do not include VAT, but we
have added it here), smaller amounts of Burgundy from some
good domaines, brief but well-chosen selections from the Loire
and the Rhône, and Alsace wines from the Turckheim co-
operative. Italy's offering is pretty dull, but Spain's is better
(Riojas from CVNE), and there is some New World interest from
producers like Basedow in the Barossa Valley and Montana in
New Zealand. Still in tune with the clientèle, Oxford and
Cambridge Fine Wine stock a big range of vintage Port.

The managing director of this company now also manages
Green's (see separate entry), and the companies may merge
during the coming year.

Best buys

College Claret NV, Bordeaux, £3.18
Corbières, Ch Les Ollieux, £3.54
Semillon 1987, Basedow, Barossa Valley, Australia, £5.82

Pallant Wines

Apuldram Manor Farm, Appledram
Lane, Chichester, West Sussex
PO20 7PE

TEL (0243) 788475

CASE SALES ONLY   OPEN Mon–Sat 9.30–5; Sun, public holidays 10.30–1
CLOSED Chr Day, Boxing Day, 1 Jan   CREDIT CARDS Access, Visa; personal
and business accounts   DISCOUNTS Available   DELIVERY Free within 15-
mile radius of Chichester (min 3 cases normally); elsewhere by
arrangement   GLASS HIRE Free with 1-case order
TASTINGS AND TALKS Saturday tastings throughout summer season; to
groups on request   CELLARAGE Not available

A welcome return to the Guide for Pallant Wines for the first time since 1986, largely on the strength of a greatly increased range of wines, including some organic wines.

We find a well-priced stock of petit château clarets, Côtes du Rhône from the Cellier des Templiers, Alsace wines from Cattin and some good Beaujolais. While Italy seems fairly ordinary, Spain fares better (Marqués de Murrieta and Faustino Riojas and Torres wines). There are mainly Rosemount wines from Australia, and Cooks and Stoneleigh Vineyard wines from New Zealand. A small choice of sparkling wines includes an unusual red Burgundy from Prosper Maufoux.

Best buys

Ch Les Bedats Boismontets 1985, Bordeaux Supérieur, £3.99
Juliénas 1987, La Bottière, £4.87
Cabernet d'Anjou 1988, Domaine de Dreuille, £3.71

Pavilion Wine Company

Finsbury Circus Gardens, Finsbury   TEL 01–628 8224
Circus, London EC2M 7AB

CASE SALES ONLY   OPEN Mon–Fri 9–8   CLOSED Sat, Sun, public holidays
CREDIT CARDS Access, American Express, Visa; personal and business
accounts   DISCOUNTS 2% for 6 cases; 3.25% for 12–25 cases
DELIVERY Free on UK mainland (min 3 cases); mail order available
GLASS HIRE Free with reasonable case order   TASTINGS AND TALKS Not
available   CELLARAGE £5.75 per case per year (inc insurance)

We like this range of wines. It's not long, but it has been carefully thought out. Thus, in Bordeaux, there is a nice balance between a few petit château clarets and classed growths for laying down. In Champagne, the house Champagne is offset by some rather classy numbers. The Burgundy listing – longer than that of Bordeaux – is almost entirely of domaine-bottled wines, but many of them are from lesser communes and therefore can be had for reasonable prices.

In the Loire, interest centres around the wines of Yves Soulez in Savennières, but there's also a rather good Muscadet from Domaine Beau Soleil (at £3.41 – prices on the list do not include VAT but we have added it here). Rhône wines come from Guigal, Jaboulet Aîné and Domaine du Vieux Télégraphe (who also supply a deliciously rich white). All three styles – white, red and rosé – are mustered from Mas de Daumas Gassac in the Hérault.

Outside France, the list shortens, but the same care has been taken in assembling the collection: Balgownie wines from

Australia, a few Spanish and Italian wines, and a small selection of fortified wines.

Best buys

Alsace Marée 1986, Zind-Humbrecht, £3.64
Côtes du Ventoux 1985, Domaine des Anges, £2.87
Manzanilla La Gitana, Hidalgo, £3.45
Ménétou-Salon 1988, Domaine de Châtenoy, £4.73

Thos Peatling

HEAD OFFICE
Westgate House, Bury St Edmunds,   TEL (0284) 755948
Suffolk IP33 1QS
33 branches throughout East Anglia

OPEN Hours vary from branch to branch   CREDIT CARDS Access, American Express, Visa; personal and business accounts   DISCOUNTS 5% on 1 case   DELIVERY Free in East Anglia (min 1 bottle); elsewhere 1 case £3.80, 2 cases £7.60, 3 cases £11, 4 cases £14.50, 5+ cases free; mail order available   GLASS HIRE Free with appropriate case order
TASTINGS AND TALKS Occasional in-store tastings (varies from branch to branch); to groups on request   CELLARAGE Free

We rather envy the people of East Anglia for the quality of their wine merchants. In the company of firms such as Lay & Wheeler and Adnams, Thos Peatling fit very comfortably. Their shops, now in the process of being revamped, contrast strongly and to advantage with other national brewery-owned multiples, showing that it *is* possible for brewers to run a top-class wine merchant.

The list can best be described as traditional with modern additions. That means that it starts with a fine range of clarets back to the 1960s – although, sadly, fewer of those wines this year than last. Peatling's own bottlings are often very good value. Moving across France, there is a good span from Beaujolais, and then we get an in-depth range of Burgundies (better, as so often, on the reds) from a mix of négociants and domaines.

Neither the Rhône nor the Loire quite lives up to these other two areas (although there are goodies in both – vintages of St-Joseph La Grande Pompée, for example, on the Rhône; or Sancerre Clos de la Poussie of Cordier on the Loire). But moving past the Alsace wines from the Bennwihr co-op, we cross the Rhine to a fine range of German estate wines (many from the 1983 and 1985 vintages).

Italy offers more than it used to – look for wines such as Corvo from Sicily, or less expensive wines such as the Chianti

Classico La Colombaia at £3.99. From Spain, consider the Gran Colegiata from Toro or Riojas from Beronia and La Rioja Alta. The full complement of Bulgarian wines is present.

Outside Europe, Australia offers the best choice: certainly try Peatling's own Australian white and red at £3.99, but also consider wines from smaller vineyards such as Wirra Wirra or St Leonards, or Capel Vale in Western Australia. Smaller ranges are forthcoming from New Zealand and California, and there's a solid showing of vintage Port. Plenty of half-bottles, too.

Best buys

Vin de Pays des Côtes de Gascogne, Domaine de Rieux, £2.99
Ch Le Monge 1985, Médoc, £3.99
Ch Haut-Sociondo 1982, Premières Côtes de Blaye, £3.99
Peatling's Australian Red and White, £3.99

Pennine Wines

5/11 Station Street, Huddersfield, West   TEL (0484) 425747
Yorkshire HD1 1LS
ASSOCIATED OUTLET
Wine Schoppen, 1 Abbeydale Road,   TEL (0742) 365684
Sheffield, South Yorkshire S7 2QL

OPEN Mon–Sat 9.30–5 (closed Wed pm)   CLOSED Sun, public holidays
CREDIT CARDS All accepted; personal and business accounts
DISCOUNTS 5% on 1 case   DELIVERY Free in Huddersfield (min 2 cases); elsewhere at cost   GLASS HIRE, TASTINGS AND TALKS, CELLARAGE Not available

This shop offers the same list as the Wine Schoppen (see entry).

Pennyloaf Wines

96 Station Road, Odsey, Ashwell,   TEL (046 274) 2725
Hertfordshire SG7 5RR

CASE SALES ONLY   OPEN Most of the time; advisable to telephone before calling   CREDIT CARDS None accepted; personal and business accounts
DISCOUNTS Available   DELIVERY Free within 15-mile radius (min 1 case); elsewhere negotiable   GLASS HIRE Free with 1-case order
TASTINGS AND TALKS Usually five 3-day tastings annually; to groups on request   CELLARAGE £1.75 per case per year

A short list whose interest lies principally on the Loire and in South-West France. On the Loire, we find a good selection of wines from producers such as Gaston Huet in Vouvray and Berger Frères, offering a rare chance to taste the wines of Montlouis: Sancerre is that of Pierre Prieur and reds are from

Chauveau in Chinon and Ch de Chaintres in Saumur-Champigny. The South-West offers interest with Cahors of Ch Cayrou, the Buzet Cuvée Napoléon, Gaillac from Domaine Jean Cros and Madiran of Ch Montus.

The other main stars of this list are the Georges Duboeuf Beaujolais, and wines from Jacques Parent in Pommard.

Best buys

Touraine Rouge Cabernet Franc 1986, Domaine des Liards, £4.05
Pécharmant 1986, Domaine des Bertranoux, £5
Coteaux du Layon Rochefort 1976, André Sorin, £6.73

Le Picoleur

See La Réserve.

Pimlico Dozen

46 Tachbrook Street, London SW1V 2LX   TEL 01–834 3647

CASE SALES ONLY   OPEN Mon–Fri 10.30–7.30; Sat 10–6   CLOSED Sun, public holidays   CREDIT CARDS Access, Visa; personal and business accounts   DISCOUNTS Not available   DELIVERY Free in some London postal districts (min 1 case); elsewhere depending on size; mail order available   GLASS HIRE Free with 1-case order   TASTINGS AND TALKS Held 2–3 times annually; to groups on request   CELLARAGE £4 per case per year (min £12)

The Pimlico Dozen collection is an interesting balance of fine clarets and more everyday wines from Italy and Spain.

The clarets themselves contain a mix – from petit château wines of recent vintages to top-notch classed growths of vintages well back into the '60s. There are also half-bottles and magnums.

Burgundy is less impressive, but again there are some fine domaine wines from the major communes as well as some more basic appellations. Among French regional wines look for the Côtes de Provence wines of Ch Lacoste as well as the varietal wines from the Ardèche.

Chianti from Fattoria dell'Ugo, Barolo from Borgogno and Vernaccia di San Gimignano of San Quirico are among the good Italian bottles on offer. The list from Spain includes Campo Viejo Riojas. Portugal, England and even Switzerland come up with a few suggestions.

Prices were current in summer 1989 to the best of our knowledge but can only be a rough indication of prices throughout 1990.

Best buys

Chianti 1987, Fattoria dell'Ugo, £2.95
Campo Viejo 1978, Gran Reserva Rioja, £5.75
Ch Pontet Canet 1984, Pauillac, £10.50

Christopher Piper Wines

1 Silver Street, Ottery St Mary, Devon
EX11 1DB

TEL (0404) 814139/
812197

OPEN Mon–Fri 8.30–6; Sat 9–1, 2.30–5.30   CLOSED Sun, public holidays
CREDIT CARDS Access, Visa; personal and business accounts
DISCOUNTS 5% on 1 mixed case, 10% on 3 mixed cases   DELIVERY Free in
South-West (min 4 cases) and rest of UK (min 6 cases); otherwise £6.90
per consignment; mail order available   GLASS HIRE Free
TASTINGS AND TALKS In-store tastings every fortnight; three major tastings
annually; to groups on request   CELLARAGE £3.60 per case per year

We got it a little wrong last year when we described owner
Christopher Piper as the owner of a Beaujolais vineyard. In fact,
he makes the wine at Ch des Tours in Brouilly – and very good
he is at it – because his 1988 wine came top in the *Which? Wine
Monthly* tasting of Beaujolais crus in the summer of 1989.

From this, it will also be obvious that the range of Beaujolais
on this list is rather good. Apart from Ch des Tours, it
concentrates on wines from Georges Duboeuf, many of them
single estate wines and including the special Duboeuf 25th
anniversary wine in a crystal bottle. Neighbouring Burgundy is
the other main star area on the list, with good domaine wines
and including some less expensive whites from the Côte
Chalonnaise.

Moving to Bordeaux, there is a fair selection of petit château
wines, but the main emphasis is on bourgeois crus at around £7
a bottle – still good value, compared with Burgundy. Those
seeking out less pricy wines could dip into a nice listing of
French regional bottles – from the Maîtres Vignerons in St-
Tropez (Côtes de Provence) or from Cahors (Ch d'Eugénie and
Clos la Coutale). Both Rhône and Loire lists have been
expanded this year.

Outside France, the best sections are Frescobaldi wines from
Italy (as well as Masí Veneto wines), Brown Brothers wines from
Australia and Mondavi wines from California.

Don't forget the top flight range of half-bottles – probably the
longest in the Guide.

Best buys

Côtes du Rhône 1986, Ch de St-Georges, £3.60
Bordeaux Blanc Sauvignon 1988, Ch des Roches, £3.93
Cahors, Clos la Coutale 1986, £5.15
Brouilly 1988, Ch des Tours, £5.97

Pond Farm Wines

120 High Street, Cottenham,   TEL (0954) 51314
Cambridge, Cambridgeshire CB4 4RX
ASSOCIATED OUTLET
Wines of Argentina (at same address)

OPEN Mon–Sat 9.30–7 (until dusk in summers); Sun 12–3 (advisable to
telephone before calling) CLOSED Some public holidays
CREDIT CARDS None accepted; personal and business accounts
DISCOUNTS 1–4 cases 2.5%, 5–9 cases 5%, 10+ cases 7.5% DELIVERY Free
locally (approx 10-mile radius); elsewhere by arrangement
GLASS HIRE Free with 1-case order TASTINGS AND TALKS To groups on
request CELLARAGE Not available

The most interesting bottles on this short list are the Argentine
wines from Goyenechea (which Pond Farm imports) – try the
Syrah at £3.09 or the Cabernet Sauvignon at £3.35.
    Other areas to explore are the Beaujolais of Thomas la
Chevalière, Riojas imported directly from the co-operative of
Cenicero (using the brand name of Valdemontán); Ports from
Ramos Pinto; Chilean wines from Concha y Toro; and excellent
Sherries from Lustau (try the dry Oloroso Old East India at
£6.34).

Best buys

Cabernet Sauvignon 1983, Goyenechea, Argentina, £3.35
Valdemontán Tinto 1981, Rioja, £3.50

Premier Wine Warehouse

3 Heathmans Road, London SW6 4TJ   TEL 01–736 9073
CASE SALES ONLY OPEN Mon–Fri 11–8; Sat 10–7; Sun 11–4 CLOSED Public
holidays CREDIT CARDS Access, Visa; personal and business accounts
DISCOUNTS Not available DELIVERY Free within 2-mile radius (min 1
case); elsewhere at cost; mail order available GLASS HIRE Free
TASTINGS AND TALKS 5–6 tastings annually by invitation; to groups on
request CELLARAGE Not available

There's plenty of good value at this wine warehouse, especially
from the French regions. The style is casual and the range has

been pitched very well for everyday drinking among the young things of Fulham.

The printed list places the wines in price order, starting (in France) with a Touraine Blanc 1987 Comte d'Ormont from Guy Saget at £2.59 and progressing through much more interesting bottles such as Sauvignon de St-Bris 1987 of Luc Sorin at £4.49, or the excellent value 1982 claret of Ch Lagarosse-Rochas at £3.75, up to more serious considerations like the Côte Rôtie of Domaine Gerin 1979 at £9.95.

There's some good value in Spain, too: Colegiata Tinto from Toro, Torres wines, Riojas from Tondonia and even some Vega Sicilia Valbuena (1982 vintage at £18 is probably a bargain). Lastly it's the turn of Australia – Rosemount, Ch Tahbilk, Cape Mentelle, Geoff Merrill – and with some good prices yet again.

Best buys

Ch Lagarosse-Rochas 1982, Premières Côtes de Bordeaux, £3.75
Gris de Gris Vin de Pays des Sables du Golfe de Lion, Listel, £2.99
Monte Ory 1978, Reserva Navarra, £3.25
Conde de Caralt Brut Cava, £4.25

Premier Wines

The APL Centre, Stevenston Industrial Estate, Stevenston, Ayrshire   TEL (0294) 602409

CASE SALES ONLY   OPEN Mon–Fri 9–5   CLOSED Sat, Sun, public holidays
CREDIT CARDS All accepted; personal and business accounts
DISCOUNTS Available   DELIVERY Free in Scotland (min 3 cases); mail order available   GLASS HIRE Free with 5-case order   TASTINGS AND TALKS To groups on request   CELLARAGE Not available

---

A curiously unbalanced list, which lurches from some rather dull Burgundy and a dozen different varieties of basic German plonk to some rather unusual and interesting specialisations.

We were particularly attracted to the fortified wines – especially the Madeiras but also the Niepoort Colheita vintage tawnies (1975 at £11.35) which make a delicious alternative to heavier vintage Ports. (Prices on the list do not include VAT, but we have added it here.) Then there are two rare corners – Israeli wines from the Golan Heights, and Austrian wines from a number of producers (giving Premier Wines by far the longest listing of Austrian wines in the Guide).

They also get quite serious about Bulgarian wines, with virtually everything that's imported to the UK on the list. In Italy, the dull and the good are apparent again, so seek out the

Ceretto wines from Piedmont, or the Donnafugata wines of
Sicily, or the Südtirol wines from Schreckbihl, or the Veneto
wines of Guerrieri-Rizzardi, and pass by the less than
interesting Lambrusco.

Best buys

Niepoort Colheita 1975, £11.35
Bulgarian wines
Roter Husar 1987, Sepp Hold, Austria, £4.59

Prestige Vintners

TEL 01–485 5895

CASE SALES ONLY   OPEN By appointment only   CREDIT CARDS None
accepted; personal and business accounts   DISCOUNTS Not available
DELIVERY Free in central London (min 1 case) and elsewhere (min 5+
cases); otherwise at cost   GLASS HIRE Free with 1-case order
TASTINGS AND TALKS To groups on request   CELLARAGE Not available

A move of premises was in progress for this merchant as we
went to press, and no details of stock were available.

Pugsons Food and Wine

Cliff House, 6 Terrace Road, Buxton,   TEL (0298) 77696
Derbyshire SK17 6DR

OPEN Mon–Sat 9–5.30; Sun 11–5; public holidays 10–5.30   CLOSED Chr
Day, Boxing Day   CREDIT CARDS Access, Visa; personal and business
accounts   DISCOUNTS 5% on 1 case   DELIVERY Free locally (min 1 case or
with groceries); otherwise £5.75 per case, £3.50 for 5+ cases; mail order
available   GLASS HIRE Free with 1-case order   TASTINGS AND TALKS Annual
tasting; to groups on request   CELLARAGE £3.50 per case per year

When Peter Pugson's business was last in the Guide, he was
based in London. Now he is dispensing the same mix of cheese
and wine from the Peak District of Derbyshire.
    The wine list has obviously been put together by a
Francophile who nevertheless feels the need for bursts in other
countries as well: Torres wines from Spain, Badia a Coltibuono
Chianti from Italy, a couple of Hill-Smith wines from Australia,
and some good Sherries from Manuel de Argueso.
    At the hub of the list we find some good red vins de pays
(Domaine de Mirabeau from the Collines de la Maure is typical),
some second wines from top Bordeaux châteaux, small amounts
of Beaujolais from Gerard Brisson and Loire wines mainly from
Guy Saget. On the Rhône, look for the old-fashioned rich
Châteauneuf of Elisabeth Chambellan.

Best buys

Domaine de Mirabeau, Vin de Pays des Collines de la
Maure, £3.05
Rivarey Tinto, Marqués de Cáceres, Rioja, £3.48
Côtes de Provence Rouge, Sélection Roger Vergé, £3.95

Queens Club Wines

2 Charleville Road, London W14 9JZ   TEL 01–385 3582

OPEN Mon–Sat 10.30–10.30; Sun 12–2, 7–9   CREDIT CARDS None accepted;
personal and business accounts   DISCOUNTS 5% on unmixed cases
DELIVERY Free locally (min 1 case); otherwise at cost   GLASS HIRE Not
available   TASTINGS AND TALKS Occasional tastings on Sunday mornings
(8 per year)   CELLARAGE Not available

There's no formal list here, but locals will approve of the
constantly changing range of wines. Look for Germany, the New
World, Portugal and Spain as the best bets.

Arthur Rackhams

HEAD OFFICE AND CELLARS
Winefare House, 5 High Road, Byfleet,   TEL (09323) 51585
Surrey KT14 7QF
The Vintner, 66 Kensington Church   TEL 01–229 2629
Street, London W8 4BY
Le Viticulteur, 391 King's Road, London   TEL 01–352 6340
SW10 0LP
12 branches in London and Surrey

OPEN Some outlets Mon–Sat 10–8; Sun, public holidays 12–2; other
outlets Mon–Sat 10–10; Sun, public holidays 7–9   CREDIT CARDS All
accepted; personal and business accounts   DISCOUNTS Members' Club
discount (The Vintner Wine Club)   DELIVERY Free on UK mainland (min
3 cases); mail order available   GLASS HIRE Free
TASTINGS AND TALKS Tastings in-store every weekend; tutored tastings; to
groups on request   CELLARAGE Available through Wine Club only

If all the names above have confused you, join the club! It
seems that Arthur Rackhams outlets come in three guises – 12
Arthur Rackhams by name, one Viticulteur, and one Vintner. All
have wines in common, but each also has wines of its own. Is
that clear?

To take the Arthur Rackhams shops first. They stock wines
from all the producers who supply Le Viticulteur, but range
more widely beyond France, into Italy, for instance (with wines
from Zenato in Lugana and Soave, Castello Vicchiomaggio in
Chianti and the super vini da tavola of Monte Vertine in

Tuscany). They have a good range of Riojas and Raimat wines from Spain, Bulgarian wines, Australian wines from Wyndham Estate, Lindemans and Leeuwin Estate and Californian wines from Hawk's Crest, Stag's Leap and Gallo. And don't forget the superb range of Champagnes, or the classed growth clarets from the early 1980s.

Le Viticulteur is all French. The range brings together many smaller producers, for whom Le Viticulteur is the sole outlet in Britain. Personalities are the thing here, and each producer – described quaintly as Viticulteur or Viticultrice – is given a good billing. Most names are unknowns in this country, and Viticulteur is certainly to be praised for bringing this range and this quality of wine into our shops. Wines come from the Loire, Bordeaux (with wines from St-Emilion and Pomerol), Bergerac, Corbières (wines from Ch Les Ollieux), Minervois, Côtes de Provence, the Rhône (the Côtes du Rhône of Didier Charavin), Beaujolais (a very good range here) Burgundy (some well-priced wines), Jura, Alsace and Champagne. Of these, we would pick the Loire and Beaujolais as star areas.

To the third element – the Vintner. This is the name of Arthur Rackham's Wine Club (which operates from the same list as the main shops, but at lower prices), and also the name of a fine wine shop in Kensington, which was the original shop in the group, and which now sells a range of fine clarets, Burgundies and Ports.

Best buys

Ch Maison-Neuve 1985, Montagne St-Emilion, £4.99
Domaine Charpentier Brut NV, £9.69
St-Véran 1987, Thierry Guerrin, £5.75
Fiefs Vendéens Blanc and Rouge de Brem, Patrice Michon et Fils (Loire), £2.99

Raeburn Fine Wines and Foods

23 Comely Bank Road, Edinburgh   TEL 031–332 5166
EH4 1DS

OPEN Mon–Sat 9–7; Sun 10–6 (not open for alcoholic drinks on Sun)
CREDIT CARDS None accepted; business accounts   DISCOUNTS 5% on unmixed cases, 2.5% on mixed cases; large quantities negotiable
DELIVERY Free in Edinburgh (min 1 case); elsewhere negotiable; mail order available   GLASS HIRE Free with wine order   TASTINGS AND TALKS To groups on request   CELLARAGE £2.95 per case per year (under bond)

Here is a range of wines designed to take your breath away, all run from the back of a small grocery shop. More and more, it is a list of wines which Raeburn import themselves from Europe, from some of the best (but not necessarily the most expensive) estates in each region.

Great names fall out of the list like confetti. With such a plethora of wines, we can only point out some highlights. From the French South-West, look for the wines of Guy Kreusch in Pécharmant, while from Bordeaux an interesting approach is to feature certain châteaux – Ch Sociando-Mallet, Ch Pavie, Vieux Château Certan – in addition to a wide range of other middle-ranking estates. In Burgundy domaine names abound, and there is plenty of interest in all the communes. The Rhône, while shorter, offers some good producers from the northern vineyards, while the Loire stars are mature vintages of Vouvray from Gaston Huet and of Coteaux du Layon from different producers. Alsace weighs in with the wines of Rolly Gassmann.

Outside France, a few top German estates make a serious showing. There is a comparatively less exciting range of Spanish wines, but a star-studded collection from Italy (Quintarelli in the Veneto, Monsanto in Chianti, Bruno Giacosa in Piedmont).

Australia majors in wines from top small estates such as Cape Mentelle and Redgate in Western Australia, Seville Estate in the Yarra and Balgownie in Bendigo, and California offers Ridge Vineyards.

Look for the en primeur offers when relevant, and don't forget the half-bottles.

Best buys

Sylvaner 1987, Rolly Gassmann (Alsace), £3.95
Gros Plant Blanc de Blancs, Guy Bossard (Loire), £2.99
Bourgogne Passetoutgrains 1986, Jayer, £5.30
Rioja Reserva 1981, Beronia, £3.99

Ravensbourne Wine Co

49 Greenwich High Road, London SE10 8JL   TEL 01–692 9655

CASE SALES ONLY   OPEN Mon–Fri 9–5; Sat 10–2   CLOSED Sun, public holidays   CREDIT CARDS None accepted; business accounts DISCOUNTS Variable   DELIVERY Free in Greater London (min 1 case); elsewhere charges negotiable; mail order available   GLASS HIRE Free with 1-case order   TASTINGS AND TALKS Spring/summer tasting by invitation to launch new list; to groups on request   CELLARAGE Not available

A newcomer to the Guide – one of the pioneers of organic wines and offering a good range of wines from many wine-producing areas.

The strongest areas on a rather messy list (they promise a proper printed one for 1990) are Bordeaux, Burgundy and Italy, with a big range of Bulgarian wines and more than just a single English wine.

Beaujolais and Burgundy both offer reasonable value – with Beaujolais from Henri Fessy and some decent enough basic Burgundy. From Bordeaux comes a good collection of petit château wines. Other French areas offer Quincy from Domaine de la Maison Blanche, Muscadet from Domaine des Dorices and a well-priced regional collection.

In Italy, try the Guerrieri-Rizzardi organic wines from the Veneto, Chiantis from the Geografico co-operative, Corvo wines from Sicily. Spain has good-value Rioja from Olarra, and the popular Señorio de los Llanos from Valdepeñas. Of the small ranges from the New World, the most interesting are from New Zealand – Mission and Delegats. Organic wines pop up throughout and are also listed separately.

Best buys

Côtes de Provence 1987, Domaine du Jas d'Esclans, £3.89
Wake Court Bacchus/Reichensteiner 1984, Dorset, £4.35
Bardolino Chiaretto Classico 1986 (rosé), Portalupi, £3.39

Redpath and Thackray Wines

WAREHOUSE AND OFFICE
Thurland Castle, Tunstall, via Carnforth,   TEL (046 834) 360
Lancashire LA6 2QR
ASSOCIATED OUTLET
Vessel du Vin (address as above)

CASE SALES ONLY   OPEN Office hours Mon–Fri 9–5   CREDIT CARDS None accepted; personal and business accounts   DISCOUNTS Available (min 11 cases)   DELIVERY Free on mainland UK (min 5 cases); mail order available   GLASS HIRE Not available   TASTINGS AND TALKS Tastings by invitation from time to time; to groups on request   CELLARAGE £3.60 per case per year

Redpath and Thackray now operate from a rather splendid castle near Carnforth, acting as the retail arm for the wine-importing offshoot of Vessel du Vin.

The approach has been to restrict the areas they cover. In France they have gone for Bordeaux, with some good middle-priced wines from the outlying petit château areas, as well as smarter things like Les Forts de Latour 1979, at £14.20 (prices on the Vessel du Vin list do not include VAT, but we have added it here). But the two star areas are the southern Rhône, where we find some excellent-value Côtes du Rhône Villages (try the Cairanne Domaine de l'Oratoire de St-Martin 1985 at £4.37) as well as Gigondas and Châteauneuf; and Provence, where wines come from basic Côtes de Provence up to the rare wines of Ch Simone in Palette. Worth looking out for here are Commanderie de la Bargémone Coteaux d'Aix-en-Provence 1987 at £3.91 and the rosé Ch de Crémant from Bellet 1987 at £7.24, the wine they drink in Nice.

Then it's on to the other featured country, Italy. Look here for good Barolo and the Barbaresco of the Produttori dei Barbaresco, the top quality local co-operative, and Soave from the equivalent co-op there, the Cantina Sociale di Soave.

Best buys

Côtes du Rhône Villages Cairanne 1985, Domaine de l'Oratoire de St-Martin, £4.37
Côtes du Bourg 1978, Ch Rousset, £4.71
Chianti Villa Petraia 1987, Cantina Sociale di Cortona, £3.33

Reid Wines

The Mill, Marsh Lane, Hallatrow,   TEL (0761) 52645
Nr Bristol, Avon BS18 5EB
Reid Wines Warehouse, Unit 2, Block 3,   TEL (0732) 458533
Vestry Trading Estate, Otford, Kent
TN14 5EL

OPEN (Hallatrow) Mon–Fri 9.30–5.30; Sat by arrangement; (Warehouse) Mon–Fri 10–6; Sat 10–1   CLOSED Sun and public holidays (Sevenoaks)
CREDIT CARDS None accepted; personal and business accounts
DISCOUNTS Not available   DELIVERY Free in central London and within 25 miles of Hallatrow and Otford (min 1 case); elsewhere at cost; mail order available   GLASS HIRE Free   TASTINGS AND TALKS Monthly tastings at Otford; to groups on request   CELLARAGE £6.50 per case per year

There has been considerable expansion of the range on offer at this merchant. While extravagant collections of mature and rare claret and Burgundy continue as the core business, Reid Wines have made striking inroads into Italy and have also increased their range within the other areas of France.

Of the mature vintages of both claret and Burgundy on the most recent list, the oldest claret was from the 1919 vintage – a bottle of Ch Montrose at £82.50; in red Burgundies, 1926 was the starting point. Another fine listing is of sweet white Bordeaux, again with plenty of mature wines.

Other French areas offering much of interest are the northern Rhône (more mature wines, this time back to 1961) and a concentration of top producers such as Guigal and Jaboulet Aîné, but also with Ch Grillet (the rare white single-vineyard appellation wine). Look in Alsace, too, for mature wines from top producers. New to the list is a small collection of French country wines, and there's plenty of vintage Champagne.

Outside France, in addition to a few deliciously mature German estate wines, the star attraction is Italy, especially Tuscany. Sadly, we don't get the mature wines here, but there is plenty from major producers, such as Maculan in Breganze in the Veneto, Antinori in Tuscany (plus a big range of super vini da tavola), Lungarotti in Umbria and Di Angelo in Basilicata.

The final areas of interest are California and Australia, from where Reid Wines import Clos du Val wines and those of its Australian sister company, Taltarni. Also look for good serious Sherries, vintage Ports and some old vintage Madeira.

Best buys

Gigondas 1985, Pierre Amadieu, £5.17
Champagne Paul Goerg Brut Tradition, £9.50
Taltarni Moonambel Red 1984, Australia, £4.60
Old vintages of claret

La Reserva Wines ✉

Unit 6, Spring Grove Mills, Manchester Road, Linthwaite, Huddersfield, West Yorkshire HD7 5QG	TEL (0484) 846732
ASSOCIATED OUTLET	
Grapehop, 17 Imperial Arcade, Huddersfield, West Yorkshire HD1 2BR	TEL (0484) 533509

OPEN Mon–Sat 9–5.30   CLOSED Sun, Chr and New Year
CREDIT CARDS Access, Visa; personal and business accounts
DISCOUNTS 10% on 1 mixed case   DELIVERY Free within 25-mile radius (min 1 case locally, 3 cases over 5 miles); elsewhere 3–5 cases £4.50; mail order available   GLASS HIRE Free with 1-case order
TASTINGS AND TALKS Regular tastings by invitation; to groups on request
CELLARAGE Not available

An enormous and impressive list of Spanish wines shouldn't be allowed to hide the wealth of other treats here.

For example, Australia offers wines from Redgate and Plantagenet in Western Australia, Lindemans, Brown Brothers, Rosemount, Geoff Merrill, Krondorf and Mildara; while New Zealand has a similar run of wines from the smaller producers. Chile, too, is served by Concha y Toro, Cousiño Macul and Viña Santa Rita. There's even a good range of wines from Israel, and what for many merchants would be a sound collection of French wines, even if they stocked nothing else. The Italian complement has expanded over the past year as well, while the selection from Portugal offers a much bigger range than is available elsewhere.

But then we turn to Spain, the most comprehensive list of Spanish wines in the Guide. It's adorned, certainly, with Riojas from most of the major and many of the minor producers, but the list not only goes beyond this classic area, into Navarra, Rueda, and of course Penedés, but also into more obscure places such as Galicia, Ribera del Duero, La Mancha and Valdepeñas. And what is so good about this list is that there's very often more than one bodega from an area which we normally look on as a one-bodega region – Jumilla, for example. There are plenty of cavas as well, and a very fine display of Sherries from many of the major producers.

Best buys

Palácio de León Tinto, Vinos de León, £2.79
Valpaços 1980 Reserva, £4.20
Ochoa Tinto Reserva 1978, Bodegas Ochoa, Navarra, £5.60
Puerto Fino Superior Dry, John William Burdon, £5.38
Vinho Verde, Quinta do Tamariz, £3.77

La Réserve   🖾 ☆

56 Walton Street, London SW3 1RB	TEL 01–589 2020
Le Picoleur, 47 Kendal Street, London W2 2BU	TEL 01–402 6920
Le Sac à Vin, 203 Munster Road, London SW6 6BX	TEL 01–381 6930

OPEN Mon–Fri (SW3) 9.30–8, (W2) 10.30–8, (SW6) 10.30–2.30, 4.30–9.30; Sat (SW3) 9.30–6, (W2) 10–6, (SW6) 10–9.30; Sun (SW6) 12–2, 7–9 CLOSED Sun (SW3,W2), public holidays CREDIT CARDS Access, Visa; personal and business accounts DISCOUNTS 5% on 1 case DELIVERY Free in central London; otherwise £6 per case; mail order available GLASS HIRE Free with 1-case order TASTINGS AND TALKS Regular programme of tastings – all held at The Ski Club of Great Britain, SW1; to groups on request CELLARAGE £6 per case per year (inc insurance)

A change of ownership at La Réserve (and its associated shops Le Picoleur and Le Sac à Vin) has meant a restructuring of the list and a change in pricing policy. The owners say that the emphasis will continue to be on a large range of fine, old and rare wines, but that they will add a wider range of wines from the New World, especially New Zealand, as well as more wines under £4.

The Sac à Vin shop specialises in wines between £3 and £8, while Le Picoleur already has a big collection of New World wines on top of its French bottles. All three shops offer the

Cellar Planning service, which is particularly aimed at Burgundy purchases.

Best buys

Henriot Blanc de Blancs Champagne Crémant, £14.95
Beaune Hautes Côtes Chardonnay Tastevin 1986, Thévenot le Brun, £7.70
Savennières 1987, Clos St-Yves, Jean Baumard, £5.95
Ch Mercier 1986, Côtes de Bourg, £5.25

Reynier Wine Library

See Eldridge Pope.

Richmond Wine Warehouse

138C Lower Mortlake Road, Richmond,   TEL 01–948 4196
Surrey TW9 2JZ

CASE SALES ONLY   OPEN Mon–Sat 10–7   CLOSED Sun, public holidays
CREDIT CARDS Access, Visa   DISCOUNTS Negotiable   DELIVERY Free locally
(min 1 case); otherwise at cost   GLASS HIRE Free with 1-case order
TASTINGS AND TALKS Every Saturday in-store   CELLARAGE Not available

A range of wines which is good in patches. Best areas are Bordeaux, with a good selection from recent vintages (and en primeur offers if they feel the vintage warrants it), Alsace wines from Pierre Sparr, lots of Chanson Burgundies, a number of large bottles of Champagne, an increasingly interesting Italian selection (Bolla wines from the Veneto, San Felice Chianti), Australian wines from Ch Reynella and Lindemans, and Ports from the small house of De Souza.

Best buys

Wood Port 1978, De Souza, £8.90
Bourgogne Rouge 1987, Chanson, £3.95
Ch La Coste Rouge, Coteaux d'Aix-en-Provence, £3.15

Special awards

is for bargain prices   is for a very good range of wines

is for high quality wines   is for exceptional service

Howard Ripley

35 Eversley Crescent, London N21 1EL TEL 01–360 8904
Mainly mail order

CASE SALES ONLY   OPEN Mon–Sat 9–10; Sun, public holidays 9–12
CREDIT CARDS None accepted; business accounts   DISCOUNTS Not
available   DELIVERY Free in London postal districts (min 4 cases);
otherwise at cost; mail order available   GLASS HIRE Free with 4-case
order   TASTINGS AND TALKS Every Wednesday lunchtime (by invitation
only); to groups on request   CELLARAGE Not available

What is it that makes dentists turn to wine? Here is a follower
in the trail blazed by Robin Yapp of Yapp Brothers, and with a
similar enthusiasm. Mr Ripley's obsession with Burgundy is
revealed in a splendid list of wines from top domaines right
through the region.

His reds are stronger than his whites (which simply reflects
the greater importance of red wine in the region anyway). But
in both colours of wine you will find major names: Bonneau du
Martray, Pierre Morey, Domaine Michelot, Simon Bize, Domaine
l'Arlot, Dujac, Jacqueline Jayer. All the wines are direct imports
and, for the quality and generally high prices of Burgundy, Mr
Ripley's prices are good (the advantage, perhaps, of a one-man
band).

There are also smaller selections of Sauternes, claret and
Beaujolais.

Best buys

Beaune Premier Cru Grèves 1987, Domaine Baptault, £9.89
Les Perrières 1985, Simon Bize, £6.90
Hautes Côtes de Beaune 1986, Domaine Cornu, £6.67

C A Rookes

Unit 7, Western Road Industrial Estate, TEL (0789) 297777
Stratford-upon-Avon, Warwickshire
CV37 0AH

OPEN Mon–Sat 9–6   CLOSED Sun, public holidays   CREDIT CARDS Access,
Visa; personal and business accounts   DISCOUNTS Not available
DELIVERY Free within Stratford upon Avon and district; elsewhere at
cost; mail order available   GLASS HIRE Free with order to regular
customers   TASTINGS AND TALKS Regular monthly tutored tastings through
C A Rookes Wine Club; to groups on request   CELLARAGE £3.45 per case
per year (inc handling, transport and insurance)

Missing from last year's Guide while moving premises, this merchant can now be welcomed back, with a larger warehouse and the possibility of further expansion during the year.

The list is attractively balanced, with interesting things from most parts of the world. It starts firmly enough in France: wines from the Listel vineyards in the South, a small but useful range of clarets featuring Ch de la Rivière in Fronsac, Ch Lamothe in Premières Côtes de Bordeaux and Ch Fombrauge in St-Emilion. Burgundy comes from Moillard and Charles Gruber. The highlight from France, though, has to be the big collection of Champagnes (Ellner, Pierre Gimmonet, Gosset, Krug, Laurent-Perrier, Heidsieck Monopole).

Outside France, look for estate wines from Germany (S A Prum, Louis Guntrum, von Buhl). Look in Italy for the wines of Rocca delle Macie in Chianti, and in Spain for CVNE Riojas.

Australia brings in a small range of estate wines from producers such as Taltarni, Krondorf, and Lindeman's, and there's Clos du Val from California.

Best buys

C A Rookes Finest Hunting Port, £6.90
Seppelt Moyston Red Shiraz Cabernet 1985, Barossa Valley, Australia, £4.10
Ch Lamothe Blanc Première Cuvée 1985, £6

The Rose Tree Wine Co

| 15 Suffolk Parade, Cheltenham, | TEL (0242) 583732 |
| Gloucestershire GL50 2AE | FAX (0242) 222159 |

OPEN Mon–Fri 9–7; Sat 9–6   CLOSED Sun, public holidays
CREDIT CARDS Access, Visa; personal and business accounts
DISCOUNTS 5% on 1 case   DELIVERY Free within 30-mile radius – M4 corridor to London and south Devon (min 1 case); otherwise 2–5 cases £2.50 per case, 1 case £5; mail order available   GLASS HIRE Free
TASTINGS AND TALKS Monthly in-store tastings; 4 major tastings in London and Cheltenham (spring and Christmas); to groups on request
CELLARAGE £1.65 per case per year

Steady growth is the order of the day at this wine merchant. There has been no great expansion, although we are promised more clarets in the near future, and we are pleased to see already more Italian wines.

The list starts with French regional wines, which include the attractive Ch Petite Borie from Bergerac at £3.74 (prices on the list do not include VAT, but we have added it here), also in white and rosé styles. The clarets are primarily at the cru bourgeois level, but some classed growths and small parcels of older wines are also available. Note also the nice line in château second wines.

Burgundy, too, is well chosen with some decent estate wines, and Beaujolais has wines from Sarrau, alongside treats from the Loire and the Rhône. Look for the Alsace wines from the Turckheim co-operative, and a strong turnout of Champagnes.

Other European countries' pages now include German estate wines from Prinz von Metternich, Berberana Riojas and, new to the list, the excellent Soave of Anselmi, as well as Chianti from Felsina Berardenga and Barolo from Giacomo Ascheri. In the New World, it is New Zealand with Montana wines and California with Dry Creek and Parsons Creek, which come off best. Look for Santa Rita wines from Chile and Don Zoilo and Garvey Sherries.

Best buys

Ch Petite Borie 1987, Bergerac, £3.74
Minervois 1985, Ch de Vergel, £3.95
Cellaro Bianco 1987 and Rosso 1987, Cantina Sociale di Sambuca (Sicily), £3.25

William Rush

Tecklewood, Uplands Close, Gerrards Cross, Buckinghamshire SL9 7JH   TEL (0753) 882659

CASE SALES ONLY   OPEN Daily 9.30–7.30 and by arrangement
CREDIT CARDS Access; business accounts   DISCOUNTS 5% on unmixed cases (cash payment)   DELIVERY Free within 10-mile radius of Gerrards Cross (min 1 case); otherwise at cost; mail order available
GLASS HIRE Free with minimum case order
TASTINGS AND TALKS Occasional tastings at premises by invitation; to groups on request   CELLARAGE Not available

One of the aims of David Rush, proprietor of William Rush, is 'not to be boring or tendentious'. There seems to be little chance of this, what with the comments on his informative list and his defence of the smaller wine merchant against the multiples in the columns of the wine press.

His range of wines is well balanced and well priced. It comes mainly from France, and starts in Burgundy, which Mr Rush regards as 'the greatest wine in the world'. He manages to find some good value in this pricy region (look for the St-Aubin Rouge 1985 of Guy Larue at £7.35, for example). With clarets there is a similar good value (Ch Tanesse 1984, Premières Côtes de Bordeaux at £4.75). Other interest in France centres on Champagne from André Drappier, Pouilly Fumé of J C Dagueneau, and a few country wines.

Apart from France, look to Italy to find Chianti from San Felice, to Spain to find a CVNE Rioja and to England for Chalkhill Bacchus, a good-value dry white. Ports are Churchill, Sherries are Pemartin.

Best buys

Côtes de Gascogne 1987, San de Guilhem, £3.05
Ch Tanesse 1984, Premières Côtes de Bordeaux, £4.75
Bourgogne St-Bris 1987, André Sorin, £5.50

Russell & McIver ☆

OFFICE
The Rectory, St Mary-at-Hill, London   TEL 01–283 3575
EC3R 8EE
CELLARS
Arch 73, St Thomas Street, London   TEL 01–403 2240
SE1 3QX
Customers may collect wine from the office if they telephone in advance

OPEN Mon–Fri 9–5.30   CLOSED Sat, Sun, public holidays
CREDIT CARDS None accepted; personal and business accounts
DISCOUNTS Negotiable   DELIVERY Free on UK mainland (min 1 case in London, 5 cases elsewhere); otherwise £4.60 per consignment; mail order available   GLASS HIRE Free with 1-case order
TASTINGS AND TALKS Tastings organised around the country, particularly for private customers; tastings held in office by invitation; to groups on request   CELLARAGE £3.45 per case per year

There's an attractive family feel to this City wine merchant, perhaps prompted by the photographs in the list of the wine-buying team on its trips, perhaps by the enjoyable and entertaining comments on the wines, perhaps by the popular range of own-label wines.

There is also, as befits the location of this merchant, quite a traditional feel to this range, which is strong in areas such as Bordeaux, Burgundy and Ports. But it also veers off down some fascinating byways as well, such as the Madeiras of Lomelino, or the wines of Ch Ste Michelle in Washington State.

Even in the classic areas, things are not too obvious – plenty of petit château wines for instance, as well as pricier classed growths, and in Burgundy, wines from some less well known villages (Cheilly les Maranges in the Côte de Beaune, for instance; or Mâcon-Solutré in the Mâconnais). The Rhône offers Lirac Les Queyrades as well as the popular Côtes du Rhône from the Rasteau co-operative. And there's a good range of country wines.

In Germany, look for the wines of Max Ferd Richter, but bother less about Spain and Italy (although don't overlook the Chianti of Rocca delle Macie or the Barolo of Ascheri). In the New World, pounce on Jekel and Inglenook in California, Babich in New Zealand and Seppelts and Brown Brothers in Australia.

Quite properly for a City merchant, there are, in addition to the Madeiras, plenty of Ports and Sherries.

Best buys

Dr Richter's Riesling 1986, Max Ferd Richter, Halbtrocken, £4.31
Ch de France 1983, Pessac-Léognan, £5.75
Vin de Pays des Collines Rhodaniennes 1986, Domaine de Vallouit Cépage Syrah, £3.34
Russell & McIver's Finest Crusted Port bottled 1986, £8.63

Le Sac à Vin

See La Réserve.

Safeway

HEAD OFFICE
Argyll House, Millington Road, Hayes,   TEL 01–848 8744
Middlesex UB3 4HY
Approximately 250 branches

OPEN Varies from store to store, generally Mon–Fri 8–8; Sat 8–6
CLOSED Sun, public holidays CREDIT CARDS All accepted DISCOUNTS, DELIVERY, GLASS HIRE Not available TASTINGS AND TALKS Occasional consumer educational tastings CELLARAGE Not available

Since we last reported on Safeway's wines in the 1988 edition, a tremendous reorganisation has taken place at this supermarket group (which now incorporates the former Presto shops), with the result that it has steamed towards (even if it has not quite reached) the top league of supermarket wine departments.

Recent tastings of new wines (which means the vast majority of the stock) have shown considerable interest in many areas. One star buy at the end of 1988 was of Burgundies from Labouré-Roi, many of them reds from the 1983 vintage. The wine buyers have also put together some attractive wines from the Rhône – the varietal wines of the Ardèche at £1.95 and the Châteauneuf of Ch St-André at £5.65. In other parts of France, look for the sweet Ch de Berbec Premières Côtes de Bordeaux at a bargain £3.95, or the Quincy, Domaine de la Maison Blanche at £3.95.

Away from France is a good-value range from the Italian Triveneto (including a surprisingly good Lambrusco dell'Emilia at £1.95). The German shelves are disappointing, despite a number of introductions. Outside Europe, look for the Australian wines from Seaview (Shiraz 1985 at £3.49) and some Californian goodies such as the Petite Sirah 1980 at £2.89.

Best buys

Safeway Pinot Grigio 1987 del Triveneto, GIV, £2.69
Safeway Australian Padthaway Riesling, £2.89
Bourgogne Pinot Noir 1985, André Ropiteau, £3.99
Ch de Berbec 1983, Premières Côtes de Bordeaux, £3.95

J Sainsbury   ▢ ▭ ☆

HEAD OFFICE
Stamford House, Stamford Street,   TEL 01–921 6000
London SE1 9LL
280 licensed branches; 7 licensed SavaCentres

OPEN Generally Mon–Sat 8.30–6 (late night trading Thur/Fri until 9)
CLOSED Sun, public holidays (except Good Friday)   CREDIT CARDS None
accepted   DISCOUNTS Available (min 3 bottles)   DELIVERY, GLASS HIRE,
TASTINGS AND TALKS, CELLARAGE Not available

Lots of new wines have been added to the already extensive range at this, the nation's largest wine retailer. They've flowed in from Germany, Spain, California, Chile, Washington State and, of course, France. Most have been good, some less interesting, but they have illustrated the commendable way in which Sainsbury's see the need to keep the excitement going if they are to remain number one.

Sainsbury's achievements at offering a great variety of wines, at good prices, to a wide public, are enhanced by the Vintage Selection – smaller parcels of finer wines (in selected stores) that would otherwise be available only through specialist wine merchants.

So, while at one end of, say, Bordeaux, you have the familiar and reliable Sainsbury's Claret (at £2.29), at the other end you can find Pavillon Rouge du Ch Margaux 1982 at £16.75 or Les Forts de Latour 1979 at £13.95, both in the Vintage Selection racks. The same is true of Burgundy – Mâcon Rouge at £2.85 or Nuits St-Georges Clos de Thorey 1985, Moillard at £15.45.

France is certainly a strong area, but there are plenty of others – Italy, Portugal, Germany (with some estate wines as well as more basic wines) and, increasingly, the New World, with Chile offering Sauvignon Blanc at £2.75 and Columbia

Crest Sauvignon Blanc at £3.95. California hasn't quite reached its full potential, unlike Australia.

Fortified wines contain some delicious Sherries in half-bottles, and specialities like Dow's Crusted Port, as well as more standard lines. And there's a whole rash of sparkling wines, from Portugal, from Australia, from Germany – and, of course, France.

Best buys

Sainsbury's Prosecco (Veneto), £3.65
Chianti Classico Riserva 1982, Castello di San Polo in Rosso, £4.45
Ch Mirefleurs 1986, Bordeaux Supérieur, £3.65
Sainsbury's Baden Dry, Badischer Winzerkeller, £2.45

Sapsford Wines

33 Musley Lane, Ware, Hertfordshire   TEL (0920) 467040
SG12 7EW

CASE SALES ONLY   OPEN 'All hours'   CLOSED Easter, Chr
CREDIT CARDS None accepted   DISCOUNTS 5% on 5 cases collected
DELIVERY Free within 10-mile radius of Ware (min 1 case) and elsewhere
(min 5 cases); otherwise £3.50 per case; mail order available
GLASS HIRE Free with 2-case order   TASTINGS AND TALKS 6–8 tastings
annually in Ware; to groups on request   CELLARAGE £3 per case per year

'Loire Valley specialists' is how Sapsford Wines describe themselves. Small sections from Bordeaux, Burgundy, Italy and Australia (and Sherries from De Soto) make a token presence, but everything really revolves around the Loire.

It's a fascinating collection. The Muscadet region has spawned surprisingly little, but once into Anjou, you can find the sweet wines of the Coteaux du Layon and Quarts de Chaume, and Saumur from Floch-Ernoult. In Touraine – by far the biggest section – there's wine from Montlouis, from Cheverny (including sparkling wine), from Vouvray and reds from Bourgueil and Chinon, as well as the varietal wines of the basic Touraine appellation. Further up river still are a few nice bottles from Sancerre and Pouilly Fumé.

Best buys

Domaine de la Renaudie 1981, Gamay de Touraine, £3.95
Cheverny Romorantin Sec 1985, Gendrier, £3.39
Blanc de Blancs, Vin de Table, Guy Bossard, £3.70

SavaCentre

See J Sainsbury.

Ashley Scott

P O Box 28, The Highway, Hawarden,　　　TEL (0244) 520655
Deeside, Clwyd CH5 3RY

CASE SALES ONLY　　OPEN Mon–Sat 8.30–6 (customers may phone at any
reasonable time; 24-hour anwering service available at other times)
CREDIT CARDS None accepted; personal and business accounts
DISCOUNTS 5% on 1 unmixed case　　DELIVERY Free in North Wales,
Cheshire, Merseyside, Lancashire (min 1 case); elsewhere at cost; mail
order available　　GLASS HIRE Free with 1-case order
TASTINGS AND TALKS Annual tasting in November by invitation (available
on request); talks and tastings provided for local organisations
CELLARAGE Not available

While French wines form the bulk of the list, it's worth looking
beyond that country for some of the greatest interest for
example, to the Navarra wines of Julián Chivite, and the
Bairrada Reservas from Caves Aliança in Portugal (plus Madeira
from Antonio Eduardo Henriques and Port from Taylors and
Churchill). The fortified possibilities also include Sherries from
Delgado Zuleta. Interestingly, Luxembourg puts in an
appearance with wines from Vinmoselle.

In France, the Alsace wines of Muré, Burgundies from Charles
Viénot, and some good-value petit château clarets offer the most
scope for exploration.

Best buys

Domaine de Grezan 1988, Vin de Pays des Coteaux de
Murviel, £2.60
Ch Buisson Redon 1985, Bordeaux, £3.35
Bairrada Reserva 1982, Caves Aliança, Portugal, £3.50
Rivaner 1987, Vinsmoselle, Luxembourg, £2.97

We have tried to make the *1990 Which? Wine Guide* as comprehensive as
possible, but we should love to hear from you about any other wine
merchants you feel deserve an entry, or your comments on existing
entries. Write to us either by letter or using the report forms supplied
at the back of the book.

Sebastopol Wines

Sebastopol Barn, London Road,   TEL (0235) 850471
Blewbury, Oxfordshire OX11 9HB

CASE SALES ONLY   OPEN Tue–Sat 10.30–5.30   CLOSED Sun, Mon
CREDIT CARDS Access, Visa; business accounts   DISCOUNTS 5% on 1
unmixed case; collection discount of £1 on unmixed case   DELIVERY Free
within 10-mile radius from Blewbury (min 1 case); elsewhere 1 case
£5.50, 2 cases £5 per case, 3 cases £4.50 per case, 4+ cases free; mail
order available   GLASS HIRE Free with 1-case order
TASTINGS AND TALKS At least once a month on Saturdays   CELLARAGE Not
available

The past year has been one of consolidation at Sebastopol
Barn – prices have been kept steady and pleasurable bottles
continue to attract in most wine areas (except – as last year –
Italy and Germany, which seem to be totally ignored).

France does best. The French regions cover a wide span, from
the top Mas de Daumas Gassac at £10.45 for the 1986 vintage, to
a fresh red from the Var at £2.87. In other parts of the list are a
short but well-balanced set from the Loire, Jaboulet Aîné wines
from the northern Rhône, and La Vieille Ferme and Ch de
Beaucastel from the south, a rather pricy list of clarets and some
estate wines from Burgundy.

Outside France, we would go for the Rioja of Muga and
Contino, the Jean León wines from Penedés, and the wines from
J M da Fonseca in Portugal (Tinto Velho 1983, Reguengos de
Monsaraz at £5.10). The New World stars wines from Penfolds
in Australia, including two vintages of the world-class Grange.
Sherries are from Lustau, Ports from Churchill.

Best buys

Madiran 1985, Collection Plaimont, £4.10
Sauvignon de Touraine 1988, Domaine de la Presle, £3.88
Côtes du Rhône 1986, La Vieille Ferme, £3.85

Seckford Wines   ✉

2 Betts Avenue, Martlesham Heath,   TEL (0473) 626072
Ipswich, Suffolk IP5 7RH

CASE SALES ONLY   OPEN Mon–Sat 10–6   CLOSED Sun, public holidays
CREDIT CARDS Access, Visa; personal and business accounts
DISCOUNTS Negotiable   DELIVERY Free within 25-mile radius (min 1 case);
elsewhere negotiable; mail order available   GLASS HIRE Free with 1-case
order   TASTINGS AND TALKS 4–5 weekend tastings annually by invitation;
tastings and talks by arrangement   CELLARAGE Available

The star area of this merchant's list continues to be Australia. Many of the major firms are out in force – Orlando, Brown Brothers, Rosemount, De Bortoli and, new this year, a good range of wines from Seppelt – but plenty of small wineries, like Oakwood Estate in the Hunter Valley, Pipers Brook in Tasmania and Ch Tahbilk and Yarra Yering in Victoria, are also worthy of attention. House wines from the Water Wheel vineyard continue to offer good value considering the rise in prices from Australia (Shiraz Bin 50, 1985 at £4.25).

France offers pleasures from the Loire, estate wines from Burgundy, a balanced claret list, excellent bottles from the Rhône (Guigal, and Côtes du Rhône from Domaine les Goubert), and Champagnes from Charbaut.

Italy has some classy wines such as the Veneto wines of Tedeschi, Chianti from Fattoria dell'Ugo and the Spanna of Agostino Brugo, while the main Spanish attraction is the Cabernet Sauvignon/Merlot Viña Magana from Navarra (1980 vintage a bargain at £5.95).

Best buys

Water Wheel Shiraz Bin 50, 1985, Australia, £4.25
Ch Le Raz 1986, Bergerac Rouge, £3.49
Mâcon La Roche Vineuse 1987, Domaine du Vieux St-Sorlin, £5.79

Selfridges

400 Oxford Street, London W1A 1AB   TEL 01–629 1234

OPEN Mon–Wed, Fri, Sat 9.30–6; Thur 9.30–8   CLOSED Sun, some public holidays   CREDIT CARDS All accepted, Sears Gold Card; personal and business accounts   DISCOUNTS Available on full cases   DELIVERY Free in central London and within M25 (min £25 order); mail order available GLASS HIRE Not available   TASTINGS AND TALKS In-store promotional tastings most weekends   CELLARAGE Not available

---

A mammoth list, packed with delectables, almost, perhaps, too much to digest. In some countries – Australia, the USA, Italy, Portugal and Spain, as well as France – virtually anybody who is anybody is represented. And, although this is a London department store, prices remain reasonable.

Australia offers wines from all the states. Of particular interest are those from Coldstream Hills in the Yarra Valley, the wines of Stephen Henschke in South Australia, the liqueur Muscats from Rutherglen, the Chardonnay of Tarra Warra and wines from Western Australia.

Moving to America, we find a similar array – Buena Vista, Carneros Creek, Cuvaison, Iron Horse, Simi and Ridge are just a few. New Zealand, too, comes up with stars from many important wineries.

Back in Europe, Italy offers a treasure trove, from the Barolos of Pio Cesare and Mascarello through the Chiantis of Pagliarese, Selvapiana, Antinori and then on to Brunello di Montalcino, Veneto wines, wines from the Südtirol... Spain contributes a serious line up of Riojas and Sherries, while Portugal does the same for Ports.

In France, we are overwhelmed by the clarets, the domaine Burgundies, the Beaujolais, and, certainly, by the Champagnes. Quite a marathon.

Best buys

Rosewood Vineyards Liqueur Muscat, Rutherglen, Victoria, £8.35
Ch Beaumont 1985, Haut Médoc, £7.75
Sancerre 1987, Masson-Blondelet, £7.50
Montana Sauvignon Blanc/Chenin 1987, New Zealand, £4.25

Edward Sheldon

New Street, Shipston-on-Stour,   TEL (0608) 61409/61639/
Warwickshire CV36 4EN   62210

OPEN Mon–Fri 8.30–1, 2–5.30 Sat 8.30–1   CLOSED Sun, public holidays
CREDIT CARDS All accepted; personal and business accounts
DISCOUNTS 5% on 1 case, 10% on 6 cases   DELIVERY Free within 50-mile radius (min 1 case); otherwise 1 case £6, 2–5 cases £3 per case, 6–10 cases £2 per case, 11+ cases free; mail order available
GLASS HIRE Available   TASTINGS AND TALKS Annual spring and autumn tastings; tastings through Wine Coaster Wine Club; to groups on request   CELLARAGE Not available

---

This is a high-class list, brimming with claret and Burgundy, but not forgetting the wine world outside France.

The classic French areas are the focus: the array of clarets has an interesting sideline in second wines of the top châteaux, and also shows off some mature wines back to the 1960s (although most wines are from 1985, 1983 and 1982). In Burgundy, it's the turn of some of the major domaine names. In both cases, there are magnums as well as bottles.

The other two most prominent areas on the list fit into this classy scenario: Champagne, with a good balance between non-vintage, vintage and de luxe cuvées (and again some large bottles); and vintage Port, of which there is a fine selection.

Elsewhere in France, the Rhône offers bottles worth acquiring, especially from the northern vineyards; while Alsace has wines from Kuentz-Bas.

In other areas, the choice is somewhat less wide, but still offers a good collection of Riojas from La Rioja Alta, some estate wines from Germany and New World wines, of which Mondavi in California is the pinnacle.

Best buys

Coteaux du Layon Chaume 1987, Ch de Suronde, £5.09
Ch Mayne-Vieil 1985, Fronsac, £5.55
Côtes du Rhône 1988, Edward Sheldon, £3.29

Sherborne Vintners

The Old Vicarage, Leigh, Sherborne,	TEL (0935) 873033
Dorset DT9 6HL	TEL (0935) 872222
	(orders)

CASE SALES ONLY OPEN Mon–Fri 9–9; Sat 9–5; Sun 9–1 CLOSED Some public holidays CREDIT CARDS None accepted; personal and business accounts DISCOUNTS 6–10 cases £1 per case, 11+ cases £2 per case DELIVERY Free within 20-mile radius of Sherborne (min 1 case) and UK mainland (min 2 cases); elsewhere £4 per case; mail order available GLASS HIRE Free with 1-case order (locally) TASTINGS AND TALKS 3–4 tastings a year for up to 100 people; to groups on request CELLARAGE £3 per case per month

While this list remains strong in Spain, other wine areas are also very much up and coming. Sherborne Vintners have adopted an interesting buying policy of listing wines which receive awards in blind tastings run by the wine press – does this cut out the costs of all those buying trips abroad, we wonder?

In Spain, look for the Gran Reserva Riojas back to the 1960s, the wines of Navarra, of Valdepeñas, La Mancha and Ribera del Duero. Cavas from Penedés are other attractions, as are the wines of Torres, and those from Extremadura in the extreme west of the country (Lar de Barros Tinto 1983 Reserva at £3.53).

Australian wines from Leasingham, Hardy's and Geoff Merrill are other winners. There's plenty from Italy, a small number of clarets and some interesting fortified wines such as Setúbal 20-year-old from J M da Fonseca in Portugal and Málaga from Scholtz Hermanos.

Best buys

Domaine du Tariquet 1987, Grassa, £2.95
Campo Viejo Rioja 1982, £3.45
Ch La Gurgue 1985, Bordeaux, £7.49
Rioja Reserva 1978, Bodegas Sierra Cantabria, £4.90

André Simon ☆

50/52 Elizabeth Street, London   TEL 01–730 8108
SW1W 9PB
21 Motcomb Street, London SW1X 8LB   TEL 01–235 3723
14 Davies Street, London W1Y 1LJ   TEL 01–499 9144

OPEN Mon–Fri 9.30–7, (Elizabeth St) 9.30–8.30; Sat (Davies St) 9.30–1,
(Motcomb St) 9.30–6, (Elizabeth St) 9.30–7.30   CLOSED Sun, public
holidays   CREDIT CARDS Access, Visa; personal and business accounts
DISCOUNTS 5% on 1 case   DELIVERY Free in central London (min 1 case);
elsewhere at cost   GLASS HIRE Free with 1-case order
TASTINGS AND TALKS Occasional in-store promotional tastings; to groups
on request   CELLARAGE Available on a small scale

Since this group of three shops is part of the same company as
Laytons (see separate entry), it is hardly surprising that many of
the wines will be familiar to customers of that company. This
means, of course, that it is a Francophile's list, full of lovely
Burgundies (the reds, especially, at good prices for this region),
some mature clarets as well as some everyday claret and wines
for laying down, and a good range of Champagnes (look for
those from Deutz).

Other areas are not neglected. In France, the Sancerre of Jean
Delaporte is recommended, as are the Rhône wines of Delas
Frères, and the Alsace wines of Zind-Humbrecht. A few treats
pop up from Italy (wines from Antinori and Brunello from
Altesino), while other pockets of interest are the Olarra Riojas
from Spain, and wines from the English-owned Newton
Vineyards in California.

Best buys

Ch Clairfont 1985, Margaux, £9.25
Ch de Cabriac 1987, Corbières, £3.65
Mâcon Charnay 1987, Domaine Manciat Poncet, £6.95

Smedley Vintners

Rectory Cottage, Lilley, Luton,   TEL (046 276) 214
Bedfordshire LU2 8LU

CASE SALES ONLY   OPEN Mon–Fri 8.30–9; Sat, public holidays 9–5;
Sun 10–5   CREDIT CARDS None accepted; personal and business
accounts   DISCOUNTS Available   DELIVERY Free within 50-mile radius of
Lilley (min 1 case); otherwise £7.50 per delivery; mail order available
GLASS HIRE Free   TASTINGS AND TALKS 2 main tastings annually; occasional
tutored tastings; to groups on request   CELLARAGE Not available

An attractive list, with many familiar names (but few surprises) gathered together in a well-balanced whole.

The area of the list that deserves the greatest applause is that of the French country wines. There's plenty to choose from here – from Minervois, Côtes du Roussillon, Fitou, as well as westwards in Bergerac and Gaillac and eastwards in Côtes de Provence. Prices are good, with most wines under £4.

The Loire and the Rhône make a brief impact, but the other French area to do well is Bordeaux, although prices here tend to rise from the less expensive levels pretty fast.

Italian wines come from top names: Antinori, Lungarotti, Bertani, as well as Ceretto in Piedmont. Look in Spain for Torres wines and those of Jaume Serra (El Padruell Tinto 1984 from the Penedés is £3.20). As far as the New World is concerned, Montana wines come from New Zealand, and Firestone and Trefethen from California, joined by a good showing of Western Australian wines. Chilean wines are from Santa Helena.

Best buys

Vin de Pays des Côtes de Gascogne, Domaine des Landes 1988, £2.84
Minervois 1986, Ch Fabas, £3.36
Chianti Classico 1987, Santa Cristina, Antinori, £3.46
Fumé Blanc 1988, Santa Helena, Chile, £3.30

Snipe Wine Cellars

87 High Street, Needham Market, Suffolk IP6 8DQ	TEL (0449) 721943
34 North Station Road, Colchester, Essex CO1 1RQ	TEL (0206) 578171
WAREHOUSE A93 Cowdray Centre, Cowdray Avenue, Colchester, Essex CO1 1BG	TEL (0206) 67670

OPEN Mon 4.30–9; Tue–Fri 10–2, 3–9; Sat 10–9; Sun, public holidays 12–2
CREDIT CARDS Access, Visa; personal and business accounts
DISCOUNTS Available   DELIVERY Free in Essex, Suffolk and south Norfolk (min 6 bottles)   GLASS HIRE Free with 1-case order
TASTINGS AND TALKS Regular in-store tastings (3–4 wines); to groups on request   CELLARAGE Not available

The Kings Lynn branch of this merchant has closed in the past year, but the Needham Market and Colchester branches have grown.

The Snipe Wine Cellars list remains a good-value collection, but you need to probe a bit to find out about the maker and the vintage. That said, the French regional wines and Bordeaux are

worth exploring for interest and value. Other ports of call could be Beaujolais from Sarrau, Alsace from the Ribeauvillé co-op and, in the New World McWilliams Australian wines, a new Chilean intake and even English wines from local vineyards.

Sookias and Bertaut

The Cottage, Cambalt Road, Putney Hill, London SW15 6EW   TEL 01–788 4193

CASE SALES ONLY   OPEN Tue–Fri 10–6; Sat 10–1   CLOSED Mon, Sun, public holidays, 2 weeks in August   CREDIT CARDS Access, Visa
DISCOUNTS 2.5% for 1 unmixed case   DELIVERY Free within central London (min 1 case); otherwise at cost; mail order available
GLASS HIRE Free locally with order   TASTINGS AND TALKS To groups on request   CELLARAGE Not available

This remains the touchstone list for the South-West of France. What began as a holiday love affair with the region has now become a fully fledged, firmly established business which marshals wines from many top estates, as well as from appellations that other merchants' lists hardly reach.

Stars on a strong list include Ch Court-les-Mûts in Bergerac (the Rouge 1986 is £5.20), Domaine de Gaudou in Cahors, Domaine de Labarthe in Gaillac and Ch Flotis in Fronton. But there are also wines from lesser appellations, such as Pacherenc du Vic-Bilh, the VDQS area of Tursan, and the white wines from Entraygues et du Fel. Sparkling wine is from Jean Cros in Gaillac, and the Blanquette de Limoux of Tournié (but – a bit of a cheat, this – Champagne, too).

Best buys

Ch Flotis 1988, Côtes du Frontonnais, £3.90
Domaine de Labarthe Blanc Sec 1988, Gaillac, £4.00
Domaine de la Pineraie 1986, Cahors, £5.20

Frank E Stainton

3 Berry's Yard, Finkle Street, Kendal,   TEL (0539) 731886
Cumbria LA9 4AB

OPEN Mon–Sat 8.30–6   CLOSED Sun, public holidays
CREDIT CARDS Access; personal and business accounts   DISCOUNTS 5% on
1 case (mixed)   DELIVERY Free in south Cumbria and north Lancashire
(min 1 mixed case); otherwise 1 case £7, 2 cases £9, 3 cases £12; mail
order available   GLASS HIRE Free with 1-case order
TASTINGS AND TALKS Tasting room on premises available for tastings/
lectures; talks given to local clubs and organisations   CELLARAGE Not
available

No surprises here, but a well-balanced list that has a little of everything, and generally shows a good choice of wines.

The longest section is of clarets, with some decent wines at decent prices as well as more expensive offerings. Burgundy has wines from Prosper Maufoux, Joseph Drouhin and Chanson Père as well as Beaujolais from Georges Duboeuf in quantity. The Loire comes up with less of interest, but the Alsace wines of Kuentz-Bas are to be recommended, as are the Rhône wines of Benoît-Lafont.

In Germany, Louis Guntrum is the supplier on the Rhine, with Deinhard on the Mosel – all good quality wines. Italy provides pleasure with the Orvietos of Bigi and the Chianti of Rocca delle Macie, while Spain – apart from the ubiquitous Torres range – has wines from CVNE and the Navarra wines from Ochoa. Sherries are from Garvey.

The New World gives us Mondavi from California, Hill Smith and Brown Brothers from Australia and Matua Valley and Delegats from New Zealand.

Best buys

Ochoa Reserva 1978, Navarra, £5.35
Ch de l'Ile 1986, Corbières, £3.65
Dry Old Oloroso, Garvey, £6.50

Stapylton Fletcher

3 Haslemere, Sutton Road, Maidstone,   TEL (0622) 691188
Kent ME15 9NE

CASE SALES ONLY   OPEN Mon–Fri 8–6; Sat 8.30–5   CLOSED Sun, public
holidays   CREDIT CARDS Access, Diners Club, Visa; personal and business
accounts   DISCOUNTS £1.15 per case on 6+ cases   DELIVERY Flat rate of
£1.15 for any quantity anywhere in the UK; mail order available
GLASS HIRE Free   TASTINGS AND TALKS First 2 Saturdays in June;
programme of tutored tastings in May; spring and autumn tastings in
Kent by invitation; to groups on request   CELLARAGE £4.60 per case per
year

Good value continues to be the hallmark of this list, which
brings together a very satisfying array of wines from round the
world. Rather than concentrating on the great wines, the
emphasis is on wines for pleasurable drinking.

So, in Bordeaux, at the start of the list, we find good value at
around £3 (Ch du Pic 1986, £3) and plenty more under £5. In
Burgundy, inevitably, prices are higher, but even here wines
such as the Mâcon-Lugny of Domaine du Prieuré 1987 at £4.95
are good value. There's plenty of Beaujolais, a nice line in Loire
wines (look for Saumur Réserve Blanc 1987 of Couly-Dutheil at
£3.75), and excellent examples from the Rhône (St-Joseph 1987,
de Vallouit at £4.75). Stapylton Fletcher have always been good
at French regional wines.

In other parts of Europe, the Italian selection has grown (such
as the Chianti from Castello di Rampolla and wines from the
Puglian firm of Rivera); Spain has received a boost in the form
of Penedés wines of Jaume Serra (Reserva 1982 at £4.60).
Portugal offers the Douro red and white from Tuella.

New to the list are the Chilean wines of Santa Helena, and
the Australian wines of Orlando. Set against smaller selections
from New Zealand and California are the wines of Staton Hills
winery in Washington State. Look, too, for English wines from
Penshurst and Chiddingstone, Sherry from Hidalgo and a range
of Ports from Martinez Gassiot.

Best buys

Ch Fabas Rosé 1988, Minervois, £2.90
Côtes du Luberon Cuvée Réserve 1988, Cellier du
Marrenon, £2.50
10-year-old Tawny Port, Martinez Gassiot, £7.90
Ch du Puy 1985, Montagne St-Emilion, £4.45

> Why not club together with friends to enjoy volume discounts and free
> delivery?

Stones of Belgravia

6 Pont Street, London SW1R 9EL   TEL 01–235 1612
Stones of Chelsea Harbour, Unit M29,   TEL 01–823 3720
Chelsea Garden Market, Chelsea
Harbour, London SW10 0XJ

OPEN Mon–Fri (SW1) 9.30–8.30, (SW10) 10–6; Sat (SW1) 10–8, (SW10) 12–6   CLOSED Sun, public holidays   CREDIT CARDS Access, American Express, Visa; personal and business accounts   DISCOUNTS 5% on 1 case
DELIVERY Free in London with suitable order; elsewhere at cost; mail order available   GLASS HIRE Free with 1-case order
TASTINGS AND TALKS Tastings usually in spring and early summer; to groups on request   CELLARAGE Not available

This remains a distinctly up-market portfolio of wines, with plenty of Champagnes, fine clarets and Burgundies and perhaps less at the less expensive end. To those who know them, it will come as no surprise to learn that a second branch has opened in London's priciest new development at Chelsea Harbour.

By using the word 'up-market' we certainly do not mean to be pejorative. We admire the quality of Stone's Champagne range, and the span of clarets in magnum (vintages go back to 1961). While Burgundy is not so ambitious, there is still plenty of mature wine to enjoy. On the Rhône, the list drips with Hermitage from Chave, Cornas from Clape and Côte Rôtie from Jasmin, while Alsace boasts a similarly top name, Hugel. Top estates in Provence are not to be overlooked.

Outside France, a full range of the organic wines of Guerrieri-Rizzardi in the Veneto has been mustered. Spain has more familiar names (Torres and Marqués de Murrieta), while the luscious Muscat wines of Quady in California (Essencia Orange Muscat at £10.95) and selections from Brown Brothers in New Australia and Nobilo in New Zealand are New World favourites. Plenty of vintage Ports, too.

Best buys

Stones Cava, Freixenet, £4.25
St-Joseph 1984, J-L Grippat, £9.25
Réserve Mirabelle de Ch la Jaubertie 1986, Bordeaux Blanc Sec, £10.75

Most wine merchants will hire out glasses free of charge, provided they are collected and returned clean, and that you are buying enough wine to fill them! In most cases, it's first come, first served, so get your order in early to ensure supply.

Summerlee Wines

Summerlee Wine Centre, 64 High
Street, Earls Barton, Northamptonshire
NN6 0JG

TEL (0604) 810488

ASSOCIATED REPRESENTATIVE
Freddy Price, 48 Castlebar Road,
London W5 2DD

TEL 01–997 7889

OPEN Mon–Fri 9–6 CLOSED Sat, Sun, public holidays CREDIT CARDS None accepted; personal and business accounts DISCOUNTS Not available DELIVERY Free locally, London postal districts, Oxford and Cambridge (min 2 cases); otherwise £5.75 per consignment; mail order available GLASS HIRE Free with 2-case order TASTINGS AND TALKS Occasional in-store tastings (every 6 months approximately); monthly tastings held by Freddy Price through The Winetasters wine society; to groups on request CELLARAGE By arrangement

This is not a long list, but it does contain some very fine wines. In 1989, Summerlee Wines made an en primeur offer for clarets, and continue to offer wines from other vintages, particularly 1985, but with some mature vintages as well. Burgundies are mainly from domaines and concentrate on some of the top wines from the region.

The Rhône is less ambitious, but you can find wines here (such as those of Aujoux in Crozes-Hermitage) that are not widely available elsewhere. On the Loire, the star wines are those from Bailland-Chapuis in Sancerre.

Over to Germany and another important section, with wines from the top estates of Max Ferd Richter in the Mosel, and Ebert in the Saar. Other countries' lists are shorter, but quality can be found in the Lindeman's wines from Australia, the Soaves of Roberto Anselmi and the Sherries of Rodriguez. The house Champagne is Ivernel (Brut at £9.53).

Best buys

Marignan Brut Champagne, Ivernel, £9.53
Doktor Richter Riesling Halbtrocken 1987, £3.79
Soave Classico Superiore 1987, Anselmi, £3.89
Irancy 1986, León Bienvenue, £5.97

Prices were correct to the best of our knowledge as we went to press. They, and ranges of wines stocked, are likely to change during the course of 1990 and are intended only as rough indication of an establishment's range and prices.

Supergrape

81 Replingham Road, Southfields,   TEL 01–874 5963
London SW18 5LU

OPEN Mon–Fri 10–2, 5–9.30; Sat 10–9.30; Sun, public holidays 12–2, 7–9
CREDIT CARDS Access, Visa DISCOUNTS 5% on 1 case DELIVERY Free
locally (min 1 case) GLASS HIRE Free with case order
TASTINGS AND TALKS Tastings available through Supergrape Wine Club; to
groups on request CELLARAGE Not available

Very much in the tradition of the jolly, laid-back breed of wine
merchants, describing itself as 'the best little wine shop on the
south side', Supergrape offers some excellent value both in
inexpensive wines and in pricier products.

The range is strongest in clarets, many mature, many at good
prices (Ch Pontet Canet 1970 at £21, or, at the other extreme, Ch
Bel Air 1986, Bordeaux Supérieur at £4.50). Burgundy is a bit
more scrappy, but good value can be found in the Rhône, the
French regions, and in Champagne (house Champagne from
Georges Gardet, plus a good range of grandes marques).

Outside France, Australia and New Zealand do well – New
Zealand particularly – while Mondavi dominates the California
listing. Finally, we have good Reserva Riojas, but somewhat less
interest from Italy.

Best buys

Bergerac Blanc 1987, Le Raz, £3.95
Ch Prieur de Meyney 1983, St-Estèphe, £7.50
Stoneleigh Vineyard Sauvignon Blanc 1987, Marlborough, New
Zealand, £5.95

Tanners Wines

26 Wyle Cop, Shrewsbury, Shropshire
SY1 1XD

TEL (0743) 232400
TEL (0743) 232007
(sales order office)

72 Mardol, Shrewsbury, Shropshire
SY1 1PZ

TEL (0743) 66389

39 Mytton Oak Road, Shrewsbury,
Shropshire SY3 8UG

TEL (0743) 66387

36 High Street, Bridgnorth, Shropshire
WV6 4DB

TEL (07462) 3148

4 St Peter's Square, Hereford, Hereford
& Worcester HR1 2PG

TEL (0432) 272044

The Old Brewery, Brook Street,
Welshpool, Powys SY21 7LF

TEL (0938) 2542

OPEN Mon–Sat 9–5.30 CLOSED Sun, public holidays
CREDIT CARDS Access, American Express, Visa; personal and business
accounts DISCOUNTS Available DELIVERY Free on UK mainland (min £75
order); mail order available GLASS HIRE Free if wine purchased from
shop TASTINGS AND TALKS Regular tasting evenings held at Wyle Cop
CELLARAGE Not available

Anyone with any acquaintance of Tanners would put them at or
near the top of a list of best wine merchants. Their wines seem
able to satisfy all customers, from those who want everyday
drinking to those who are looking for the very finest. Don't be
fooled by the old-fashioned appearance of premises like their
Wine Market: in their way they are as go-ahead as any more
modern-looking merchant.

Their list ranges widely, and in every area, the quality of their
buying is tip-top across the cross-section of choices.

Starting with France, there is a fine showing of regional wines
from most parts of the Midi, from Gaillac and Bergerac, from
Cahors and Madiran. On the Loire, there is a good range of
wines from Sancerre and Pouilly Fumé and a strong presence
from Alsace in the form of wines from Blanck and Gassmann.
But it is Bordeaux and Burgundy, both wide and deep and
including mature wines, which are the major sections. House
Champagne is £9.33, and there are good large bottles as well as
half-bottles.

Of the other European countries, the list is strongest in Italy,
with wines from Tiefenbrunner in the Alto Adige, Frescobaldi
in Tuscany, Borgogno in Piedmont and rarities like the Moscato
Passito from Pantelleria at £6.42. Spain comes up with some
good-value reds as well as some more serious offerings from
Ribera del Duero and Rioja, while Portugal has Douro wines as
well as those of J M da Fonseca. The fortified wines of both

countries (especially the best house Sherries we have come across) are very enjoyable ranges.

Tanners' Australian range covers a wide cross-section of wineries, both large and small; they obviously have an affection for the Liqueur Muscats of Rutherglen. California wines come from Ridge and Mondavi.

Best buys

Tanners Claret NV, £3.40
Tanners Champagne Brut, £9.33
Tanners Crusted Port, bottled 1985, £9.90
Mariscal Manzanilla Sherry, £4.16
Tanners Bordeaux Sauvignon, £3.32

Tempest, Slinger & Co

See Chesterford Vintners.

Tesco

HEAD OFFICE
New Tesco House, P O Box 18,   TEL (0992) 32222
Delamare Road, Cheshunt,
Hertfordshire EN8 9SL
For wine enquiries write to: HEAD   TEL as above
OFFICE Bentley House, Pegs Lane,
Hertford, Hertfordshire SG13 8EG
350 licensed branches

OPEN Varies from branch to branch CREDIT CARDS Access, Visa
DISCOUNTS, DELIVERY, GLASS HIRE Not available
TASTINGS AND TALKS Occasional in-store tastings CELLARAGE Not available

Tesco continues to offer an ever-widening range of wines, some stars, some which disappoint, but all of which show a willingness to experiment and broaden the horizons of customers in a very satisfactory way.

France takes something of a back seat in comparison to some other supermarkets' lists. To be sure, there is plenty on offer, especially in the way of petit château clarets and regional wines. But, in fact, the star French area is Champagne, where the shelves are packed with a range of grande marque and other brands, as well as own-label Champagnes.

Italy and Portugal are two countries where Tesco has obviously made sterling efforts. Look, for instance, for the Chianti Rufina Selvapiana at £3.49, or Tiefenbrunner Südtirol wines, or, the Tinto Velho Reguengos de Monsaraz 1983 at

267

£3.79. Germany offers a few estate wines mingled with the inevitable Liebfraumilchs.

Overseas, look for the Fetzer California wines, Cooks and Montana from New Zealand, and Rosemount from Australia. In fortified wines, the own-label Sherries are to be recommended as are the Montillas and the aged tawny Ports.

Best buys

Tesco Malmsey Madeira, £5.29
Tinto Velho Reguengos de Monsaraz 1983, £3.79
Fetzer Californian Zinfandel 1985, £3.59
Domaine des Baumelles 1987, Côtes du Lubéron, £2.69
Domaine d'Escoubes 1986, Vin de Pays des Côtes de Gascogne, £2.29

Thresher ⊏⊐ ☆

HEAD OFFICE
Sefton House, 42 Church Road, Welwyn   TEL (0707) 328244
Garden City, Hertfordshire AL8 6PJ
ASSOCIATED OUTLET
Esprit du Vin, 51A Upper Berkeley   TEL 01–723 1713
Street, London W1H 7PN
Approximately 1,000 branches nationwide

OPEN Hours vary from branch to branch but generally Mon–Sat 10–10; Sun 12–2, 7–9   CREDIT CARDS Access, Visa; personal and business accounts   DISCOUNTS Available   DELIVERY Free locally   GLASS HIRE Free TASTINGS AND TALKS, CELLARAGE Not available

Of all the national High Street multiples, it is Thresher which has shown the greatest improvements over the past year. Stores are now either Wine Shops or Wine Merchants, the latter offering a wider range of wines. Two first-class shops, Esprit du Vin and Wine Rack (see separate entry), have also emerged.

Just as important, the quality and range of wines have improved considerably. One hundred new wines have been added over the past year, with more to come. What we now have is some excellent quality. Strong areas include the good-value petit château clarets at around £5, some good French regional wines (Minervois Domaine Ste-Eulalie at £2.99), interest from Beaujolais with Georges Duboeuf wines and a few Gustave Lorentz Alsace wines.

In other countries, look for the Italian range, with wines from Antinori, Portuguese wines (Thresher are the only stockists in this country of that country's top red, Barca Velha from Ferreira – the 1981 vintage is £17.95), including Ports, and Raimat wines from Spain.

Outside Europe, Australia now holds its head up (house white is Piggott Hill Semillon at £3.99), with plenty of reds from Penfolds and Brown Brothers, and there are smaller – but good quality – selections from California and New Zealand as well.

Best buys

Penfolds Kalimna Bin 28 Shiraz 1986, Barossa Valley, Australia, £4.99
Domaine de Tariquet 1987, Cuvée Bois, Grassa, £3.99
Minervois Domaine Ste-Eulalie 1987, £2.99
Bourgogne Chardonnay 1987, Domaine Ste-Claire, £4.99

Touchstone Wines

ORDER OFFICE
14 Vine Street, Kidderminster, Hereford   TEL (0562) 746978
& Worcester DY10 2TS

CASE SALES ONLY   OPEN Mon–Fri 9.30–6.30   CLOSED Sat, Sun, public holidays   CREDIT CARDS None accepted; personal and business accounts DISCOUNTS 5% on 5+ cases   DELIVERY Free within 50-mile radius of Birmingham (min 1 case); elsewhere 1–4 cases at cost, 5+ cases free; mail order available   GLASS HIRE Free with 1-case order within 50-mile radius   TASTINGS AND TALKS Monthly tastings at Brockencote Hall, nr Kidderminster and Stafford; to groups on request   CELLARAGE Not available

This is not a long list, but it has plenty to attract from some of the classic areas – and one speciality where Touchstone beats all comers.

That speciality is Rumania, from where Touchstone bring in such rarities as the Pietroasele-Tamiioasa, a lusciously sweet white tongue-twister which comes in half-bottles at £2.75. Alternatively, you could go for Simburesti Fetească Neagra, a rich red from a viticultural research station at £2.49; or the dry white Blaj Fetească Regala at £2.79. Wines from neighbouring Bulgaria are also available here.

More conventional choices would be some attractive French regional wines, wines from Cahors, Alsace and the Loire. But, back with the unusual, Touchstone offer wines from the Franche-Comté – a Chardonnay and a Pinot Noir – and wines from Worcestershire and Somerset as the English contingent.

Most wine merchants will supply wine for parties on a sale or return basis.

Best buys

Pietroasele-Tamiioasa Romanească 1979, Rumania, £2.75 (half-bottle)

Fitou 1985, Domaine de Balansa, £3.25

Wootton Müller-Thurgau 1986, £4.35

J Townend & Sons

HEAD OFFICE

Red Duster House, 101 York Street,   TEL (0482) 26891
Hull, Humberside HU2 0QX

The Wine Cellars, Oxford Street, Hull,   TEL as above
Humberside HU2 0QX

Willerby Manor Wine Market, Well   TEL (0482) 656475
Lane, Willerby, Humberside HU10 6ER

8 branches (House of Townend) and 5 branches (Wine Markets) in Humberside and Yorkshire

OPEN (Winecellars, Oxford Street) Mon–Fri 9–5.30; Sat am during December; other branches vary but generally Mon–Sat 10–10; Sun 12–2, 7–10 CLOSED Sun (Winecellars, Oxford Street), public holidays
CREDIT CARDS Access, Visa; personal and business accounts
DISCOUNTS Available DELIVERY Free within 60-mile radius of Hull (min 2 cases); elsewhere at cost; mail order available GLASS HIRE Available
TASTINGS AND TALKS Tastings and promotions held during specific months; Wine Market Wine Club; to groups on request
CELLARAGE £3.10 per case per year

There are 15 different outlets at J Townend: the Wine Cellars in Hull and the Willerby Manor Wine Market, the Hornsea Wine Market and two wine centres (at Cottingham and Driffield), all of which carry most of the wines on the list. The remaining branches, called House of Townend, operate from a shorter version of the list but can obtain the other wines.

If all that sounds a little confusing, the contents of the list are not. It is a traditional one, many areas offering a reasonable choice and some of which are covered in depth.

Bordeaux is one of the latter, with wines in quantity back to 1970. The same is true of Beaujolais, where wines from the two Duboeuf labels, Paul Bocuse and Georges Duboeuf, are present in profusion. Ditto the southern Rhône, with good things from Châteauneuf and the Côtes du Rhône, and also Germany, with a splendid range of estate wines.

Those are the stars, but don't ignore the French regional wines, Champagnes, good things from the Tuscan vineyards, Brown Brothers and Rosemount from Australia, a strong range of Sherries (Wisdom & Warter) and plenty of vintage Ports.

Best buys

Vinho Verde Solar, Portugal, £2.38
Ch de Brondeau 1985, Bordeaux Supérieur, £3.77
Beaujolais Villages 1987, Georges Duboeuf, £3.93
Frascati Superiore 1987, Villa Catone, £3.90

Madeleine Trehearne Partners

20 New End Square, London NW3 1LN   TEL 01–435 6310

CASE SALES ONLY   OPEN '24 hours, 7 days a week'   CREDIT CARDS None
accepted; personal and business accounts   DISCOUNTS 5% on 5 cases
DELIVERY Free in North London (min 1 case); elsewhere by arrangement;
mail order available   GLASS HIRE Free with 1-case order
TASTINGS AND TALKS 4 tastings a year for mailing list; to groups on
request   CELLARAGE £3 per case per year

Still short, still well chosen, this range concentrates on wines
from the Loire with small selections from other French areas.
There are wines from Bernard Clément in Ménétou-Salon, and
from Quincy, along with reds from Chinon and St-Nicolas de
Bourgueil. Other areas of France offer Champagne from Jean-
Jacques Cartier, a few clarets and Burgundies and Alsace eaux-
de-vie, as well as a Vendange Tardive wine from the Leiber
family.

Best buys

Chinon 1986, Raymond Desbourdes, £5.75
Ménétou-Salon 1988, Bernard Clément, £5.55

Turville Valley Wines

The Firs, Potter Row, Great Missenden,   TEL (02406) 8818
Buckinghamshire HP16 9LT

CASE SALES ONLY   OPEN Mon–Fri 9–5   CLOSED Sat, Sun, public holidays
CREDIT CARDS None accepted; personal and business accounts
DISCOUNTS Available occasionally   DELIVERY Free in London (min 5
cases); elsewhere at cost; mail order available   GLASS HIRE,
TASTINGS AND TALKS Not available   CELLARAGE £4.03 per case per year

A fine and rare wine list, specialising in clarets, Burgundy,
Rhône wines and Champagne, with a nice sideline in Madeira
and Port.
    A recent list offered claret back to 1914, with plenty of large
bottles. There are sweet white Sauternes and Barsac (including
vintages of Ch Gilette as well as of Yquem). In Burgundy, the
story is similar, with red Burgundy vintages back to 1911 and
plenty of top names. Mature wines on the Rhône include

Guigal's Côte Rôtie from 1952, and vintage Ports start with the famous 1927 vintage. And to celebrate an incredibly special occasion in two years' time you could turn to the 1792 Blandy's Bual Madeira.

Best buys

Fine and rare wines

T & W Wines

51 King Street, Thetford, Norfolk
IP24 2AU

TEL (0842) 765646

OPEN Mon–Fri 9.30–5.30; Sat 9.30–2.30   CLOSED Sun, public holidays
CREDIT CARDS All accepted; personal and business accounts
DISCOUNTS Not available   DELIVERY Free within 15-mile radius of
Thetford (min 1 case) and elsewhere (min 4 cases); otherwise 1–3 cases
£8.50, 3–4 cases £7.50; mail order available   GLASS HIRE Free with 1-case
order   TASTINGS AND TALKS In-store tastings; tastings organised in hotels
and restaurants; to groups on request   CELLARAGE £3.75 per case per
year

'Purveyors of fine wines' is how T & W Wines, operating from a pretty shop in Thetford, describe themselves.

The range is a splendid one, all the better for its enormous choice of half-bottles. It starts with a bang in clarets, with old wines such as a 1919 Ch Lafite (at £402.50 – prices on the list do not include VAT, but we have added it here), and makes stately progress through noble wines and great vintages up to the present day. There are good things in Sauternes, too – look for old vintages of Ch Gilette.

Burgundy, too, kicks off in splendour, the wines from the Domaine de la Romanée-Conti in pride of place, and then moves on to a super collection of domaine and négociant wines, many mature wines among them. A similar pattern applies to the Rhône and Champagne.

As a contrast, T & W import a number of California wines from wineries which are not otherwise seen here – Flora Springs, Dunn Vineyards, Far Niente, Silver Oak Cellars and Duckhorn Vineyards, all boutique producers making top quality wine. And, if that wasn't enough, T & W have the largest hoard of Hungarian Tokays of any merchant in this Guide.

Best buys

Rully 1986, Domaine Guyot, £7.99
Bourgogne Pinot Noir 1985, Domaine Bertrand, £6.84
Margaux Private Reserve 1985, £7.99

Ubiquitous Chip Wine Shop 📧

12 Ashton Lane, Glasgow G12 8SJ   TEL 041–334 7109

OPEN Mon–Fri 12–10; Sat 10–10   CLOSED Sun   CREDIT CARDS Diners Club, American Express, Visa; personal and business accounts   DISCOUNTS 5% on 1 case   DELIVERY Free in greater Glasgow (min 3 cases); mail order available   GLASS HIRE Free with 1-case order
TASTINGS AND TALKS Occasional Sunday tastings for customers in restaurant; to groups on request   CELLARAGE Not available

The emphasis of this list has completely changed. Where before France, and especially Bordeaux, were the dominant sections, now there is an excellent balance between most wine-producing countries. The minus side of this, of course, is that you lose out on the excitement that an in-depth study of one area gives you.

However, clarets from more recent vintages, many at good prices, still form one of the most satisfying sections. In Burgundy, there is less choice, but the Rhône offers some good value from the southern vineyards and Alsace has wines from Dopff et Irion and Rolly Gassmann. Star names from the Loire include Jean Baumard and René Couly.

Fizz is all the rage at Ubiquitous Chip, it seems – plenty of Champagnes, Cavas and other French sparklers, too. If good value is what you're after, explore the range of French country wines.

Italy has some serious things, such as Veneto wines of Quintarelli, Barolos from Pio Cesare and Chianti from Ripanera; while in Spain, the Gran Reserva Riojas, and, in Portugal, wines from Champalimaud and Piementel (both in the Douro), catch the eye. Rumania, too, offers a wide choice.

Beyond Europe, try the Sanford Winery wines from California (Sauvignon Blanc 1986 at £6.75), while Australian and New Zealand wines come from a number of famous names, all already familiar to Ubiquitous Chip customers.

Best buys

Pinot Blanc d'Alsace 1987, Rolly Gassmann, £4.20
Vin de Pays de l'Hérault, Domaine de Clairac, £3.25
Rumanian Classic Pinot Noir 1984, £2.20
Sanford Sauvignon Blanc 1987, California, £6.75

Special awards

🐷 is for bargain prices

📧 is for a very good range of wines

✳ is for high quality wines

👉 is for exceptional service

Unwins Wine Merchants

HEAD OFFICE
Birchwood House, Victoria Road,   TEL (0322) 72711
Dartford, Kent DA1 5AJ
300 branches in South-East England

OPEN Mon–Sat 10–2, 4–10; Sun, public holidays 12–2, 7–9.30
CREDIT CARDS All accepted; personal and business accounts
DISCOUNTS 10% on case lots   DELIVERY Free in South-East England (min
case lots); mail order available   GLASS HIRE Free with 1-case order
TASTINGS AND TALKS Occasional tastings; to groups on request (contact
Head Office)   CELLARAGE Not available

This continues to be a firmly traditional range, with the best
value to be found in the finer wines, but for everyday drinking
you are likely to be disappointed.

Fine if you want to study the range of clarets, many of them
mature, most of them classed growths and priced accordingly.
Fine for vintages of Sauternes (most have to be ordered). Yet,
when it comes to things such as Muscadet or Sancerre, what is
on offer is either rather pricy or unappealing.

As you go through the list, the problem seems to be
compounded by a strange mix of the good and the rather
indifferent – Ruffino Chianti or Campo ai Sassi Rosso di
Montalcino alongside a thousand and one versions of
Lambrusco, for example. Spain gets a generally better deal than
Italy with plenty of good Riojas.

Back on the rails with the good ranges of Port and Sherry, and
the splendid set of Champagnes and other sparkling wines.

Best buys

Riesling d'Alsace 1987, Cave Vinicole de Turckheim, £3.39
French Colombard 1986, E & J Gallo, California, £2.99
Garrafeira 1974, Paula da Silva, Portugal, £4.99

The Upper Crust

3–4 Bishopsmead Parade, East Horsley,   TEL (04865) 3280
Surrey KT24 6RT

OPEN Mon–Sat 9–9; Sun 12–2, 7–9; public holidays 10–1, 6–8   CLOSED Chr
Day   CREDIT CARDS Access, Visa; personal and business accounts
DISCOUNTS 5% for 1 case   DELIVERY Free within 25-mile radius (min 1
case); elsewhere at cost; mail order available   GLASS HIRE Free
TASTINGS AND TALKS Regular tutored evenings; to groups on request
CELLARAGE £3 per case per year

The Upper Crust team must enjoy travelling, because they have put together a splendid list, much of which could only have come about after tasting on the spot rather than masterminding it from home.

With such a fine assembly, all we can do is pick out the star areas. Starting at the beginning of the alphabet (Alsace), we find wines from Trimbach, Schlumberger, Cave Vinicole de Turckheim and Willm. Both Beaujolais and Burgundy offer a fine range, with domaine wines from both areas and some heady names in Burgundy, balanced well by some less expensive bottles. In clarets, the list goes back to 1905, but hovers mainly around the late '70s and early '80s, with some good value in the younger wines.

The Loire displays the full variety to be found along the river, with Touraine wines strong, Coteaux du Layon sweet wines and some interesting choices from Sancerre and Pouilly Fumé. The South-West has wines from the Domaine de Circofoul in Cahors, while the Rhône has a surfeit of Châteauneuf. And the Champagne list bubbles with excitement.

Highlights outside France include Italy (especially in Piedmont, but also in Tuscany), while Torres dominates the Penedés in Spain and Marqués de Murrieta in Rioja. For followers of Ch Musar in the Lebanon, here is the chance to taste the 1964 vintage at £28 as well as more recent wines, while further afield than that, look for Mondavi wines from California, Columbia Crest from Washington State, some treats from New Zealand and a huge range from Australia. And that's not forgetting English wine from Lamberhurst.

Best buys

Sauvignon de St-Bris 1988, Goiset, £4.95
Chianti Rufina Remole 1987, Frescobaldi, £3.85
Ch Ramuage La Batisse 1985, Haut Médoc, £7.95
Touraine Gamay 1987, Domaine des Acacias, £4.25
Chardonnay 1986, Firestone Vineyard, California, £5.95

Valvona & Crolla

19 Elm Row, Edinburgh EH7 4AA   TEL 031–556 6066

OPEN Mon–Sat 8.30–6   CLOSED Sun, 1–7 January   CREDIT CARDS Access, Visa; business accounts   DISCOUNTS 5% on 1 case   DELIVERY Free on UK mainland (min £60 order); otherwise £3.90 carriage charge; mail order available   GLASS HIRE Free with £50 case order
TASTINGS AND TALKS Regular in-store tastings planned for the end of 1990; 2–3 large tastings annually; to groups on request   CELLARAGE Not available

You need to come to this shop just to experience the full glories of a proper Italian delicatessen. The shelves lining the walls are piled high with foodstuffs as well as wine, and the noise and the delicious smells of cheeses, coffee, pasta and salamis defy you not to spend madly.

The abundance of wines from all over the country has much the same effect on an Italophile. Highlights are the Gaja Barbarescos from Piedmont, the Jermann wines from Friuli, Tiefenbrunner from the Südtirol, various Amarone Recioto della Valpolicella, the dark, rich red made from semi-dried grapes, Biondi-Santi Brunello di Montalcino back to 1945 (just ready to drink), Chianti from Villa Vetrice and Ruffino, wines from Fattoria Paradiso in Emilia-Romagna, Mastroberardino wines from Campania, Vin Santo from a number of Tuscan producers and de Bartoli Marsala.

It's also probably the only place (although we would be happy to be corrected) where you can find Sagrantino, a sweet red from Adanti in Umbria; the powerful red Patrioglione Rosso Brindisi from Puglia; or the red Falerno of Villa Matilde (the favourite wine of the Romans) from Campania.

Best buys

Settesoli Rosso 1987 (Sicily), £1.99
Montepulciano d'Abruzzo 1987, Bianchi, £2.79
Montefalco Rosso 1985, Adanti (Umbria), £3.99
Ser Gioveto 1986, Rocca delle Macie (Tuscany), £5.99
Pinot Grigio Ca' Donini (Veneto), £2.99

Helen Verdcourt Wines

Spring Cottage, Kimbers Lane,
Maidenhead, Berkshire SL6 2QP

TEL (0628) 25577

CASE SALES ONLY   OPEN 24-hour answering machine   CREDIT CARDS None accepted; personal and business accounts   DISCOUNTS 5% for order of more than 12 cases   DELIVERY Free in central London and most of south-east England by arrangement (min 1 case)   GLASS HIRE Free with 1-case order   TASTINGS AND TALKS Tastings through various clubs; to groups on request   CELLARAGE Available (limited space)

In an amazing show of versatility, this one-woman business organises tours and tastings, buys wine and continues to offer a good all-round list of wines for sale.

It is all-round, certainly, but there are obvious enthusiasms. One of these most definitely is the Rhône, where in both northern and southern vineyards fine bottles are on offer, from Terres Brunes Vin de Pays d'Oc of Vallouit at £2.60 right up to Châteauneuf from a whole clutch of top producers, or from

Crozes-Hermitage of Jaboulet Aîné to Hermitage 1985 of Vallouit.

The list offers other treats: for example, three vintages of Mas de Daumas Gassac, the Cabernet-Sauvignon-based Vin de Pays de l'Hérault: also a select range of 1985 and 1983 clarets, and Alsace wines from the Cave Vinicole de Turckheim.

From outside France, Helen Verdcourt has rounded up Torres wines from Spain, Guerrieri-Rizzardi wines from the Italian Veneto, a very good posse of Australian wines (Taltarni, Wynns, Yarra Yering, Mildara), and Hunter's Vineyard wines from New Zealand.

Best buys

Leziria 1987 Tinto, Almeirim, Portugal, £2.50
Châteauneuf-du-Pape, Ch de Beaucastel 1986, £7.85
Terres Brunes Vin de Pays d'Oc, Vallouit, £2.80
Sauvignon de Touraine 1988, Domaine du Pré Baron, £3.50

Victoria Wine Company

HEAD OFFICE
Brook House, Chertsey Road, Woking,   TEL (04862) 5066
Surrey GU21 5BE
Over 1,000 branches nationwide

OPEN Hours vary from branch to branch   CREDIT CARDS All accepted;
personal and business accounts   DISCOUNTS 5% on 1 case of wine, 3% on any 5 bottles of wine   DELIVERY Mail order available
GLASS HIRE Free   TASTINGS AND TALKS Promotional tastings in-store from time to time; to groups on request (apply to Head Office)
CELLARAGE Not available

Have Victoria Wine finally turned the corner back towards being a wine merchant? It seems so, judging from the expansion of their Gare du Vin shops (see separate entry) and the improvements in their own range.

They have divided their enormous number of shops into four categories, and have designated certain ones primarily as wine shops, which will stock at least 300 wines, according to local demand. Other shops, we must assume, will remain more for beer and fags than wine, but at least this is a move in the right direction.

Moreover, 50 new wines were introduced in the months before we went to press. These include a whole clutch of good-value petit château and classier clarets from the 1985 vintage, a welcome expansion of the Italian section, vintage Ports from the great 1985 vintage, and occasional goodies elsewhere.

Overall, the range has improved beyond these additions. Strengths include Bordeaux and Burgundy (with wines from Moillard and Louis Jadot), the Rhône (wines from Jaboulet Aîné as well as an excellent own-label Châteauneuf) and a fine range of Champagnes. The smaller French regions continue to defeat them, however.

Outside France, the Italian selection is now improved immeasurably (especially in Tuscany), while Spain benefits from the Raimat wines from Catalonia as well as well-priced Marqués de Murrieta Rioja. Australia is an excellent source now, with wines from Wynns, Hill Smith, Rosemount, Hardy's; while Chile shows off the wines of Concha y Toro and Erraruriz Panquehue. Gallo and Beringer are the producers of the Californian selection.

Best buys

Ch La France 1985, Graves, £6.99
Raimat Abadía 1986, Lerida, £4.99
Victoria Wine Riesling d'Alsace 1987, £3.99
Zinfandel 1982, Inglenook, California, £4.50

La Vigneronne

105 Old Brompton Road, London SW7 3LE TEL 01–589 6113

OPEN Mon–Sat 10–9; Sun 12–2 CLOSED Some public holidays, Chr Day, Boxing Day, Easter Day CREDIT CARDS All accepted DISCOUNTS 5% on 1 case (may be mixed) DELIVERY Free locally (min 1 case) and nationally (min 3 cases); otherwise £3.50 per delivery in England and Wales and £7.50 per case to Scotland and Northern Ireland; mail order available GLASS HIRE Not available TASTINGS AND TALKS Regular tutored tastings CELLARAGE £6 per case per year (inc insurance)

This is serious wine territory, spanning the world and picking out wine-producers who are doing interesting things, great things, startling things, often unique things. Never is the list dull, and it puts La Vigneronne among the top merchants in the Guide.

If you are looking for the out-of-the-ordinary, try the vintages of Vega Sicilia, Spain's most renowned wine (1960 is £75), or try vintages of Ch Simone, the main estate in the tiny Provençal appellation of Palette; or a number of examples of the sweet red fortified wine from Banyuls.

And that's just the unusual. When you come to more classic wines, what you find is in-depth collections: clarets back to 1934, splendid sweet white Bordeaux, seriously serious domaine Burgundies, Alsace wines in glorious profusion, top producers from the northern Rhône vineyards, vintages of Mas de Daumas Gassac and of Lebanese Ch Musar back to 1960, a galaxy of Gran Reserva Riojas, a huge portfolio from Italy.

Overseas collections are in the same vein, whether in California or Australia (including the newly released top single vineyard wines from Lindemans); New Zealand is smaller but still interesting, and lastly we are treated to some superb old solera Madeiras and vintage Ports back to 1922.

Best buys

Ch Musar 1978, Serge Hochar, Lebanon, £8.95
Balgownie Chardonnay 1987, Australia, £5.99
Grande Escola, Quinta do Cotto 1985, Portugal, £7.85
Coteaux des Baux en Provence 1985, Terres Blanches Rouge, Cuvée Aurélia, £6.95
Ch Lousteau Vieil 1985, Ste-Croix du Mont, £5.95

Villandry

89 Marylebone High Street, London W1M 3DE   TEL 01–487 3816

OPEN Mon–Fri 9.30–7; Sat 9.30–6   CLOSED Sun, public holidays
CREDIT CARDS Access, Visa   DISCOUNTS 5% on 1 case   DELIVERY Mail order available   GLASS HIRE Free   TASTINGS AND TALKS, CELLARAGE Not available

Villandry, a new entry to these pages, describes itself as a Paris shopping street in miniature. What that means is that cheeses, salads, breads are all under one roof – and wines, all French, of course. Prices are not cheap, but then the address is good.

It's not a long list, but there are attractions in most areas: for example, the Burgundy wines of Jayer-Gilles or J-J Confuron, Ménétou-Salon of Henri Pellé, some good Vin de Pays d'Oc Domaine d'Ormesson in all three colours; also a small selection of clarets, Champagnes from Legrand and Crémant de Bourgogne from the same source.

Best buys

Ménétou-Salon Blanc 1987, Henri Pellé, £6.80
Coteaux du Languedoc 1986, Abbaye de Valmagne, £4.90
Blanc de Blanc Vin de Pays d'Oc, Domaine d'Ormesson, £4.80

If your favourite wine merchant is not in this section, write and tell us about him or her. There are report forms at the back of the book.

Villeneuve Wines

27 Northgate, Peebles, Borders EH45 8RX	TEL (0721) 22500
116 High Street, Biggar, Strathclyde ML12 6BH	TEL (0899) 20999

OPEN Mon–Wed 10–1, 2–6; Thur 10–1, 2–8; Fri 10–1, 2–10; Sat 9–10
CLOSED Sun, public holidays   CREDIT CARDS Access, Visa; personal and
business accounts   DISCOUNTS 5% on 1 case   DELIVERY Free in
Edinburgh, Borders/Lanarkshire area (min 1 case); otherwise at cost;
mail order available   GLASS HIRE Free   TASTINGS AND TALKS 2 annual
tastings for private customers; to groups on request   CELLARAGE Not
available

A small grouping of shops, new to the Guide, which is planning
to grow in an area of the country which certainly needs more
wine merchants.

Villeneuve Wines offer a sensible range, not too ambitious. In
some areas, there is evidence of lazy buying – as on the Loire
where they rely principally on wines from one négociant. But
elsewhere, Alsace offers the wines of the top co-operative of
Ribeauvillé, the Rhône has good-value Côtes du Ventoux as well
as more serious things, Burgundy shows off wines from
Faiveley, as well as other producers, and there are Bergerac
wines from Ch La Jaubertie.

On the whole, clarets are on the pricy side, but a few petit
château wines compensate. Provence offers wines from two fine
estates – Domaines Ott and Domaine de Trévallon, and there's a
good line in French country wines. Plenty of Champagnes, too.

From other countries, highlights include a bunch of Barolos
from Borgogno (back to the 1947 vintage), and some good
Reserva Riojas. From California come the inexpensive wines of
Gallo, while from Australia there's Wolf Blass and Lindeman's,
and from New Zealand Montana and Stoneleigh Vineyard.
Bulgarian bottles and a lone Russian wine offer some eastern
promise.

Best buys

Beaujolais Villages 1988, A Gauthier, £3.99
Chardonnay 1987, Viña Carmen, Chile, £4.49
Ch La Jaubertie Rosé 1987, Bergerac, £3.99

Vinature

16 Cotton Lane, Moseley, Birmingham   TEL 021–449 1781/7472
B13 9SA

OPEN Mon–Fri 9–6; Sat 10–4; Sun if necessary (24-hour answering
machine) CREDIT CARDS None accepted; personal and business
accounts DISCOUNTS Available DELIVERY Free in Greater Birmingham;
elsewhere 1–4 cases £3.95 per case, 5+ cases free GLASS HIRE Free
TASTINGS AND TALKS Tutored tastings on organic wines in-store; to groups
on request CELLARAGE Not available

Vinature, new to the Guide, deal in organic wines, mainly from
France, but with excursions to familiar names such as Guerrieri-
Rizzardi in the Italian Veneto and Botobolar in Australia.

It is in France that the major discoveries are to be made.
These include a range of Gaillac wines from Domaine de
Matens, Coteaux Varois from Domaine St-Cyriaque, Loire wines
such as the Bourgueil of Christian Georget, a small but
interesting clutch of clarets and Burgundy from Chaumont. Look
also for the excellent Crozes-Hermitage 1985 of Bégot at £5.76,
and the Muscat de Rivesaltes of Coronat, typically luscious and
honeyed.

Best buys

Budgee Budgee 1989, Botobolar, Mudgee, Australia, £4.79
St-Chinian 1986, Domaine des Soulie, £3.38
Gaillac Brut, Domaine de Matens, £5.71

Vinceremos Wines

Beechwood Centre, Elmete Lane, Leeds,   TEL (0532) 734056
West Yorkshire LS8 2LQ

CASE SALES ONLY OPEN Mon–Fri 9–5.30; Sat 10–4 CLOSED Sun, public
holidays CREDIT CARDS Access; personal and business accounts
DISCOUNTS Available DELIVERY Free in Yorkshire (min 1 case) and on UK
mainland (min 5 cases); otherwise £5.75 per order; mail order available
GLASS HIRE Free TASTINGS AND TALKS Bi-annual tastings held on premises;
offers through World Wine Club; to groups on request CELLARAGE Not
available

Here you can find the unusual and the organic – not necessarily
at the same time.

To take the unusual first: Vinceremos is the merchant who
brought us the Flame Lily wines from Zimbabwe; now they are
offering a Russian sparkling wine, Indian table wines as well as
the more familiar Omar Khayyam sparkling, as well as (for those
whose constitution is up to it) a range of Soviet vodkas.

Then the organic: they come mainly from France – plenty from the Midi, but also some reasonably priced clarets, some Rhône wines, sweet wines from Coteaux du Layon and Bordeaux, Alsace from Pierre Frick and Champagne Carte d'Or from José Ardinat. Outside France, look for the Tuscan wines of Roberto Drighi (including a Vin Santo) and Penedés wines (including a Cava) from Albet i Noya.

Best buys

Chianti San Vito 1987, £3.25
Domaine de Clairac-Joubio, Vin de Pays de l'Hérault, £2.91
Coteaux du Layon 1973, Gérard Leroux, £5.95

Vintage Roots

25 Manchester Road, Reading, Berkshire   TEL (0734) 662569
RG1 3QE

CASE SALES ONLY   OPEN Mon–Fri 9–6; Sat 10–6; Sun, public holidays answering machine; callers by appointment only   CLOSED Chr Day CREDIT CARDS None accepted; personal and business accounts DISCOUNTS Available   DELIVERY Free within 30-mile radius of Reading (min 1 case); elsewhere at cost; mail order available   GLASS HIRE Not available   TASTINGS AND TALKS 2 annual London tastings; to groups on request in-store only   CELLARAGE Not available

Organic and nothing but organic is the recipe at this shop, covering France principally, but also looking at Germany, Italy, Australia and England.

France offers good things from many areas – for example, the Côtes du Rhône of Domaine St-Apollinaire, the Muscadets of Guy Bossard, the white Vin de Pays de l'Aude made from the Mauzac grape, or, from the tiny Vin de Pays area of Coteaux de Cèze, a light fruity wine, Lou Pas d'Estrech.

Outside France, new names join the more familiar organic producers: a good line in Italian reds (the Tuscan red vino da tavola Massaciuccoli, and the great Barolos of Clerico). Botobolar represents Australia and wines from the Frey Vineyards are California's contribution. Champagne is from Serge Faust, and other sparklers include a sweet, honeyed Clairette de Die.

Best buys

Clairette de Die Tradition, Achard Vincent, £5.99
Vino Rosso di Massaciuccoli 1987, Seidler (Tuscany), £3.20
Cabernet d'Anjou 1987, Domaine de Dreuille, £3.42

The Vintner/Viticulteur

See Arthur Rackhams.

A L Vose

Town House, Main Street, Grange-over-Sands, Cumbria LA11 6DY   TEL (05395) 33328
OFFICE
92 Kentsford Road, Grange-over-Sands, Cumbria LA11 7BB

OPEN Mon–Sat 9–6   CLOSED Sun   CREDIT CARDS Access; personal and business accounts   DISCOUNTS 10% on 1 case   DELIVERY Free in Cumbria (min 1 case); elsewhere at cost; mail order available   GLASS HIRE Free TASTINGS AND TALKS Monthly tastings through tasting club; to groups on request   CELLARAGE £1.50 per case per year

Although these Lakeland vintners carry many of the wines that are also available at the Wine Schoppen (see separate entry), they also import some wines themselves, and are among the few merchants in the UK to have a serious range of Austrian, or indeed Brazilian, wines.

The Austrian wines come from Winzer Krems in the Danube Valley: Grüner Veltliner Kremser Schmidt and the Rhine Riesling Kremser Rosengarten, or wines in the Kellermeister Privat top quality range would make interesting choices. Look, too, for the sparkling wines.

Brazil's vineyards, south of São Paulo, produce varietal wines, based on the familiar international grape varieties. Best are the Cabernet Sauvignon and the Chardonnay.

Best buys

Brazilian wines from Palomas
Kremser Rosengarten 1983, Winzer Krems, Austria, £3.45
Graf Bubna-Litic 1987, Kabinett, Austria, £5.28

The Wine & Spirit Education Trust is the body in charge of educating those in and on the fringes of the wine trade. They offer a series of courses right up to Master of Wine level, the more basic of which are open to non-trade members who can convince the Trust of their intention to enter the wine trade. Contact them at: Five Kings House, Kennet Wharf Lane, Upper Thames Street, London EC4V 3AJ; TEL 01-236 3551.

Waitrose ☐☐☆

HEAD OFFICE
Doncastle Road, Southern Industrial   TEL (0344) 424680
Area, Bracknell, Berkshire RG12 4YA
90 licensed branches in London, Midlands and the Home
Counties

OPEN Varies from store to store but generally Mon, Tue 9–6; Wed 9–8;
Thur 8.30–9; Fri 8.30–9; Sat 8.30–5.30   CLOSED Sun, public holidays
CREDIT CARDS None accepted   DISCOUNTS 5% on £100 expenditure
DELIVERY Not available   GLASS HIRE Free   TASTINGS AND TALKS Occasional
evening tastings for customers   CELLARAGE Not available

This remains by far the most individual and interesting range of
supermarket wines: Waitrose is a small group which can
therefore buy in smaller quantities than the major supermarkets,
and its shops are all in the prosperous South-East.

The wines are displayed informatively and attractively in
wine shops that are separate from the main body of the
branches. We have few changes to report since the previous
edition, but the list was already well balanced. It is particularly
strong in Italy and the French regions, and makes a speciality of
good-value Burgundy and sparkling wines.

From a wide choice, we would recommend the Dom Ferraz
Vinho Verde at £2.25, the Beaujolais Blanc 1988 at £3.95, the
Madiran from the Co-operative du Vic-Bilh at £2.85, the top
quality Montepulciano d'Abruzzo of Illuminati at £3.75 and the
Lindeman's Shiraz Bin 50, 1985 from Australia at £4.95. Other
best buys are listed below.

Best buys

Vin de Pays de l'Aude 1987, Domaine du Puget Merlot, £2.35
Ch de Rochemorin 1986, Pessac-Léognan, £4.75
Ch Reynella Ten-Year-Old Tawny, Australia, £6.95
Rioja Blanco 1984, Marqués de Murrieta, £5.55

Peter Watts Wines

Wisdom's Barn, Colne Road,   TEL (0376) 61130
Coggeshall, Essex CO6 1TD

CASE SALES ONLY   OPEN Mon–Fri 9–1, 2–5.30; Sat 9–1   CLOSED Sun, public
holidays   CREDIT CARDS Access, Visa; personal and business accounts
DISCOUNTS By arrangement (min 1 case)   DELIVERY Free in England and
Wales (min 2 cases); otherwise at cost; mail order available
GLASS HIRE Free with 1-case order   TASTINGS AND TALKS Tastings held 2/3
times annually at local venues   CELLARAGE 5p per week

Come to this merchant for many wines from small growers that are otherwise unavailable in the UK.

In France, Burgundy and Beaujolais do well, while in Bordeaux, Peter Watts has winkled out a number of small estates from which he is offering the 1983 vintage. On the Loire, look for the St-Pourçain wines of Jutier and Serra Frères, and the varietal Touraine wines from Gérald Angier. Over in Alsace Domaine Siffert is the name to go for.

There's a greatly expanded range of German estate wines – new this year are examples from Freiherr von Zwierlein in the Rheingau – and expansion is in the air, too, in Italy – try the Barolos from Livio Pavese or Soave from Santa Sofia. Portugal has wines from Alenquer (the Quinta de Pancas Reserva 1986 at £4.35 is a red made from a blend including Cabernet Sauvignon), while in Australia, the featured producer is the small Scarpantoni Estate in McLaren Vale.

Good fortified wines include Ports from De Souza, Madeira from Cossart Gordon and Sherry from Valdespino.

Best buys

Chardonnay St-Pourçain 1987, Jutier and Serra Frères, £3.85
Ch Puit du Parre 1985, Bordeaux Supérieur, £3.75
Shiraz 1981, Scarpantoni Estate, McLaren Vale, Australia, £5.80

Weatherbury Vintners

5 Trinity Street, Dorchester, Dorset   TEL (0305) 65586/66246
DT1 1TU

OPEN Mon–Sat 9.30–6   CLOSED Sun, public holidays
CREDIT CARDS Access, Visa; personal and business accounts
DISCOUNTS Available for large quantities   DELIVERY Free within 40-mile radius (min 1 case) and elsewhere (min 6 cases); elsewhere £3.45 per case; mail order available   GLASS HIRE Free with order
TASTINGS AND TALKS To groups on request   CELLARAGE 5p per week

There should be a new look to this Dorchester vintners' shop this year, as a new front is added and the inside is redesigned. What isn't due to change is the wide-ranging list: it covers most areas of the world, with a few areas that are particular strengths.

France offers the greatest interest: a range of cru bourgeois and cru classé clarets (but with little at a lower level); good Champagnes, Burgundies from Moillard and Chablis from Jeanne-Paule Filippi, and a few wines from Bergerac and Cahors.

Other countries are treated more briefly, but there is interest in Spain with Berberana Riojas, in wines from Adolph Huesgen in Germany, in Mildara wines from Australia and in Gould Campbell Ports.

Best buys

Ch Bel-Air 1986, Bordeaux Supérieur, £3.96
Sauvignon Blanc/Chenin Blanc 1987, Montana, New Zealand, £3.95
Côtes du Roussillon Villages 1987, Duc d'Orcatel, £2.75

Welbeck Wine

3 Montrose Road, Dukes Park,   TEL (0245) 461210
Springfield, Chelmsford, Essex CM2 6TE

CASE SALES ONLY   OPEN Mon 9–5; Tue–Thur 9–6; Fri 9–7; Sat 9.30–6 CLOSED Sun, public holidays   CREDIT CARDS Access, Visa; personal and business accounts   DISCOUNTS Negotiable   DELIVERY Free in Essex (min 2 cases) and UK mainland (min 5 cases); elsewhere by negotiation; mail order available   GLASS HIRE Free with suitable wine order
TASTINGS AND TALKS Regular weekly tastings (Sat) at the warehouse; large annual tasting in October; to groups on request   CELLARAGE Not available

A short list (accompanied by a fine wine list), which stays mainly in France but also slips over to Italy, California and Australia.

The starting point is Bordeaux, with some good value under £4 (but also greater things on the fine wine list and some attractive sweet white wines). The wines of Delaunay in Beaujolais are to be recommended, as are those of Faiveley and André Delorme in Burgundy. The Loire has wines from Domaine Saget, while Zind-Humbrecht is the name in Alsace. There's plenty of Champagne, too.

Italy's stars are Chianti from Fattoria di Felsina Berardenga and Fattoria dell'Ugo, plus Veneto wines from Boscaini and Barolo from Borgogno. The New World offers competition in the shape of Orlando and Rosemount in Australia, Firestone and Edna Valley in California.

Best buys

Ch Tarreyro 1986, Côtes de Castillon, £3.49
Beaujolais Villages 1987, Delaunay, £3.39
Tokay Pinot Gris 1987, Vieilles Vignes, Zind-Humbrecht, Alsace, £7.19

Wessex Wines

197 St Andrews Road, Bridport, Dorset   TEL (0308) 23400
DT6 3BT

CASE SALES ONLY   OPEN Mon–Sun 8.30–9   CLOSED Occasional holidays
CREDIT CARDS None accepted; personal and business accounts
DISCOUNTS 5% on minimum of 6 bottles (unmixed)   DELIVERY Free within
20-mile radius of Bridport (min 1 case); elsewhere at cost; mail order
available   GLASS HIRE Free with 1-case order   TASTINGS AND TALKS Large
general tastings in November; to groups on request   CELLARAGE Not
available

Good value is the keynote of this list, with the majority of
wines under £5 and almost all under £6. And the range is
spread wide, from the lesser areas of France to the wider
regions of Australia.

Inevitably, in France, it is the country wines which shine:
Cahors and Bergerac and the Midi. The Loire offers wines from
Touchais (also well known for their sweet white Anjou), while
on the Rhône, the co-operative of Tulette in Côtes du Rhône is
the supplier. Clarets cover the smaller appellations, while not
surprisingly it is Burgundy which breaks the £6 price barrier.

Italian wines from Guerrieri-Rizzardi in the Veneto star
alongside Chianti from Rocca delle Macie and Franciacorta from
Martinoni. There's a small but useful choice of Spanish wines
(including the familiar Señorio de los Llanos Reserva 1981 at
£3.39), plus plenty of Bulgarian wines and small pickings from
round the world – look for vintages of Ch Musar from the
Lebanon and wines from Argentina and Chile.

Best buys

Tolaga Bay Dry Red, Cooks, New Zealand, £3.45
Pinot Blanc d'Alsace 1987, Cave Vinicole de Turckheim, £3.60
Sauvignon Blanc 1986, Gallo, California, £3.23
Ch du Basty Beaujolais Villages 1988, Perroud, £4.84

Cellarage is generally provided at the rates quoted only when the wines
have been bought from the merchant concerned.

Wine in bag-in-box ages and spoils quicker than in bottle. If you buy
boxes, buy and drink up one box before you buy the next. Boxes in the
storecupboard will lose their freshness. Used or unopened, a wine box
will keep better if you store it tap downwards, keeping wine, not air, in
the valve.

West Heath Wine

West Heath, Pirbright, Surrey   TEL (04867) 6464
GU24 0QE

CASE SALES ONLY   OPEN Mon–Fri 9–6; Sat 9–1   CLOSED Sun, public
holidays   CREDIT CARDS None accepted; personal and business accounts
DISCOUNTS 5% on 5 cases   DELIVERY Free (min 5 cases); otherwise 1 case
£3.75, 2 cases £6, 3 cases £7.50, 4 cases £8; mail order available
GLASS HIRE Free with 2-case order   TASTINGS AND TALKS Tastings arranged
through the various stores supplied; quarterly tastings at various
London venues; to groups on request   CELLARAGE Not available

Here is a range of organically produced wines that bring
together a number of familiar names as well as some discoveries
that are unique to West Heath.

So, for instance, in Italy the widely available wines of
Guerrieri-Rizzardi sit alongside Chianti from Villa Angiolina
and Barbera from Clerico. The only Australian organic producer,
Botobolar, is represented and Austrian wines come from Schloss
Gobelsberg.

In France, wines from the Jura and the Coteaux du Languedoc
demand just as much attention as a good range of clarets (try
the Ch de Prade 1985, Bordeaux Supérieur, at £4.23) and a sound
mix of Burgundies (one star is the Puligny-Montrachet 1986 of
J-C Rateau at £11.80). Champagne is from André Beaufort.

In Germany, there are some good estate wines from the
Mosel, Rheingau and Rheinhessen (look for the Mosel wines of
Dr Loosen).

Best buys

Lorcher Pfaffenwies Riesling Kabinett Trocken, Graf von
Kanitz, £5.07
Chardonnay 1987, Hautes Côtes de Nuits, A Verdet, £6.75
Ch Chavrignac 1987, Bordeaux, £3.61

Whighams of Ayr

8 Academy Street, Ayr, Ayrshire   TEL (0292) 267000
KA7 1HT
Whighams Young & Saunders at   TEL 031–225 2442
Jenners, 48 Princes Street, Edinburgh
EH2 2YJ

OPEN Mon–Sat 9.30–5.30 CLOSED Sun, public holidays
CREDIT CARDS American Express, Visa; personal and business accounts
DISCOUNTS 15% on 1 case DELIVERY Free in Scotland (min 3 cases)
GLASS HIRE Free with 1-case order TASTINGS AND TALKS Couple of major
tastings annually; to groups on request CELLARAGE £3.45 per case per
year

If you've ever fancied drinking a claret with your golfing friends
called Le Birdie, this is the place to buy it. You can also buy Le
Drive, an AC Médoc, or Le Bogie, a Bordeaux Blanc.

But if golf isn't your bag, there are plenty more conventionally
labelled clarets, with some good mature classed growths. In
Burgundy, the main suppliers are Chanson and Albert Bichot,
with smaller ranges from the Loire and the Rhône (look there
for Gigondas Domaine Raspail 1986). Alsace wines are from
Dopff au Moulin.

Who could resist the selection from the splendidly named
Reichsgraf und Marquis zu Hönsbröch in Baden? But other
highly promising choices would be Chianti Classico from
Castell' in Villa, and Pirramimma wines from Australia, backed
up by a good line in aged tawnies from Fonseca and numerous
grande marque Champagnes.

Prices tend to the high side throughout the range.

Best buys

Whighams Claret, Barrière Frères NV, £3.99
Chianti Classico 1983, Castell' in Villa, £4.75

Prices were correct to the best of our knowledge as we went to press.
They, and ranges of wines stocked, are likely to change during the
course of 1990 and are intended only as rough indication of an
establishment's range and prices.

White Hart Vaults

See Wines Galore.

Whiteside's of Clitheroe

Shawbridge Street, Clitheroe, TEL (0200) 22281
Lancashire BB7 1NA

OPEN Mon–Sat 9–6 CLOSED Sun, public holidays CREDIT CARDS Access,
Visa; personal and business accounts DISCOUNTS 5% on 1 case unmixed
table wine; quantity discounts negotiable DELIVERY Free locally (min 1
case); elsewhere 3% per delivery; mail order available GLASS HIRE Free
with any case order TASTINGS AND TALKS Grand tasting twice annually;
quarterly wine club tastings with buffet; to groups on request
CELLARAGE Free on own premises; in bond at cost

The past year has witnessed a further welcome increase in the
range of mid-priced wines available from this merchant while in
the coming year we are promised a change of name – to
Whiteside's Wines (poor old Clitheroe) – and more bottles at the
pricier end.

In France, the senior partner is definitely Bordeaux, where the
mid-priced wines come into their own, with plenty of good-
value clarets as well as more serious wines and maturer
vintages. Burgundy is dominated by négociants such as Rodet,
Chandesais and Labouré-Roi, while Beaujolais is from Duboeuf;
there's plenty of Chablis. Look on the Rhône for Ch de
Beaucastel Châteauneuf-du-Pape and wines from Jaboulet Aîné,
while on the Loire, try the Ménétou-Salon and Sancerre of Jean-
Max Roger and the organic Muscadet of Guy Bossard. In the
French regions, star buys are the wines of Val-Joanis in Côtes
du Lubéron, and the well-appointed Champagnes.

German wines seem to be somewhat stuck in the
Liebfraumilch era, but the Italian section has flashes of interest
in Chianti from Ruffino and Tiefenbrunner Südtirol wines.
Reserva and Gran Reserva Riojas are welcome choices from
Spain.

Australia boasts a huge and splendid collection of wines from
many of the top names such as Penfolds, Lindeman's and
Orlando, Seppelts and Rosemount, Brown Brothers and Hardy's
and – very impressive – the largest collection of Liqueur
Muscats we've seen. New Zealand and California also do well.

Best buys

Brown Brothers Chenin Blanc 1986, Milawa, Australia, £4.15
Faugères 1987, Les Crus Faugères (Midi), £2.79
Vacqueyras 1985, Jaboulet Aîné (Rhône), £4.55

Baileys Founders Award Liqueur Muscat, Glenrowan,
Australia, £8.59

Whittalls Wines

Darlaston Road, Walsall, West Midlands   TEL (0922) 36161
WS2 9SQ

CASE SALES ONLY   OPEN Mon–Fri 9–5.30   CLOSED Sat, Sun, public
holidays   CREDIT CARDS None accepted; personal and business accounts
DISCOUNTS Not available   DELIVERY Free delivery (min 5 cases); otherwise
1–3 cases £3, 3–5 cases £5; mail order available   GLASS HIRE Available
TASTINGS AND TALKS Regular tastings in-store; to groups on request (25–50
people required)   CELLARAGE £1 per case per year

Although this is essentially a fine wine list, it does not just
contain wines for which you would need your bank manager's
approval to buy, but some wines for everyday drinking, too.

But it does stick to classic areas in France – Bordeaux (with a
good choice from the vintages of the early 1980s and smaller
quantities back to 1926), Burgundy (with a predominance of
wines from Rodet and Chandesais, but with domaine wines as
well), the Rhône (wines from Guigal and Jaboulet Aîné). Alsace
and the Loire are also given attention.

The reliance on one producer in Germany is disappointing,
and Italy too is less than exciting. But in Spain pleasure is to be
had from the Muga Riojas, while the reliable wines of J M da
Fonseca make up the Portuguese section. There are a few
Australian and New Zealand wines, and the list ends on a high
note with its Champagnes and vintage Ports.

Best buys

Côte Rôtie 1986, Levet, £9.89
Ch Timberlay 1986, Bordeaux, £3.68
Adler Fells Fumé Blanc 1987, California, £6.44

Special awards

🐷 means bargain prices (good *value* may be obtained from
merchants without this symbol, of course, if you wish to pay for
service)

✸ means that the wines stocked are of consistently high quality

▱ means that the merchant stocks an above-average range

☞ means that extra-special service is offered; helpful advice,
information lists and newsletters, tastings etc.

Willerby Wine Market

See J Townend & Sons.

Willoughbys ☞

53 Cross Street, Manchester M2 4JP	TEL 061–834 6850
98–100 Broadway, Chadderton, Oldham,	TEL 061–620 1374
Greater Manchester OL9 0AA	
1 Springfield House, Water Lane,	TEL (0625) 533068
Wilmslow, Cheshire SK9 5AE	

ASSOCIATED OUTLETS

George Dutton & Son, Godstall Lane,	TEL (0244) 321488
Stowerburgh Street, Chester, Cheshire	
CH1 1LN	
Thomas Baty & Sons, 37–41 North John	TEL 051–236 1601
Street, Liverpool L2 6SN	

OPEN Mon–Fri 9–5.30; Sat–9–1   CLOSED Sun, public holidays
CREDIT CARDS Access, Visa; personal and business accounts
DISCOUNTS 5% on 1 case, 10% on 10 cases   DELIVERY Free within 10-mile
radius of store (min 1 case); Mail order available at Christmas
GLASS HIRE Free with charge for breakages   TASTINGS AND TALKS To groups
on request   CELLARAGE £2.08 per case per year.

A list that is strong and exciting in French classic wines and many French regions, but is still rather unadventurous when it comes to wines from other countries.

To start positively, Willoughbys have one of the finest Champagne lists in the guide – full of grandes marques in all shapes, sizes and styles. There follows a serious look at Bordeaux, with wines from vintages back to 1970, and with a good mix of inexpensive petit château wines as well as grands vins. In Burgundy, the emphasis is on négociant wines with, again, a wide range from the comparatively inexpensive to the very pricy indeed.

The rest of France is made up of Hugel wines from Alsace, the full range of Haut Poitou wines, curiosity corners in Corsica and the Jura, and a wide selection of wines from the South and South-West.

After that, the sails are trimmed somewhat. There are German wines from Louis Guntrum, some interest in Italy with wines from Tiefenbrunner in the Südtirol, and Venegazzù in the Veneto, plus Brunello from Villa Banfi and Biondi-Santi. Riojas come in mainly standard styles from a number of producers. Willoughbys take a patriotic view of English wine. After that, the high spots are Buena Vista and Hamilton and

Tuttle in California and Brown Brothers in Australia (plus some Liqueur Muscats).

Don't forget the excellent Madeiras and the huge range of malt whiskies.

Best buys

Bonchalaz Rouge, Henri Maire, Jura, £2.95
Willoughbys Cava, £4.59
Minervois 1986, Ch Villerambert, £3.19
Selaks Sauvignon/Semillon 1987, New Zealand, £7.05

Windrush Wines

WHOLESALE OUTLET
The Barracks, Cecily Hill, Cirencester,   TEL (0285) 650466
Gloucestershire GL7 2EF
RETAIL OUTLET
3 Market Place, Cirencester,   TEL (0285) 657807
Gloucestershire GL7 2PE

CASE SALES ONLY   OPEN Mon–Sat 9–6; Sat (Barracks) 10–2   CLOSED Sun, public holidays   CREDIT CARDS None accepted; personal and business accounts   DISCOUNTS By arrangement for large quantities   DELIVERY Free on mainland UK (min 1 case); mail order available   GLASS HIRE Free with 1-case order   TASTINGS AND TALKS 2–3 annual tastings; to groups on request   CELLARAGE £4.60 per case per year (min 5 cases)

Certainly producer of one of the best written lists in this Guide, Windrush offers fascinating information about the producers who supply the wines, and, in doing so, gives an insight into the way those wines were chosen. Individuals are obviously important to Mark Savage, who runs Windrush: individuals and their philosophy of winemaking, which combine to steer the whole list away from the obvious and into many new and exciting pastures.

That is true even if the ground has been well trod, as in France. In Bordeaux, for example, there are certainly some top châteaux, but the flavour of this list is really supplied by the featured estates, such as the St-Emilion Grand Cru of Le Tertre Rôteboeuf or the Côtes de Castillon estate of Ch Haut Bardoulet, where the winemakers put so much of themselves into the winemaking.

The same is true in the fascinating Italian range, which visits classic areas, but then looks at producers like Livio Sassetti in Montalcino (pictured in the list with his cows rather than his vines) who relies on tradition, or lists the wines of San Giusto a Rentennano in Gaiole in Chianti rather than one of the more familiar names.

It was probably in the same spirit that Windrush became the best source of wines from the Pacific North-West of the United States (and despite increased interest still ships from more wineries than any other merchant). Here you can find wines from the Eyrie Vineyards, Tualatin and Alpine Vineyards in Oregon; Columbia, Arbor Crest and Chinook in Washington State (plus Salishan and the unpronounceable Snoqualmie), and Rose Creek and Covey Rise from Idaho.

All this, of course, doesn't mean we should forget the wide-ranging Californian selection, the wines of Zind-Humbrecht in Alsace, the Burgundies and Chablis or the Champagnes of Billecart-Salmon.

Customers who live locally or are visiting Cirencester will be glad to know that there is now a retail shop in the town's Market Place.

Best buys

Chardonnay Covey Rise 1986, Idaho, £7.19
Clos la Coutale 1986, Cahors, £4.74
Chianti Classico 1986, San Giusto a Rentennano, £5.03

The Wine Club

MAIL ORDER WINE CLUB
New Aquitaine House, Paddock Road,   TEL (0734) 481713
Reading, Berkshire RG4 0JY   (enquiries)
    TEL (0734) 472288
    (orders)

OPEN 24 hours, 7 days a week (answering service) CLOSED Christmas CREDIT CARDS AA DISCOUNTS Available DELIVERY Free nationwide (min £50 order); otherwise £3.75 per delivery GLASS HIRE Not available TASTINGS AND TALKS Regular tastings throughout the year all over the country; range of wine tours offered CELLARAGE Available

For details see Bordeaux Direct.

Most wine merchants will supply wine for parties on a sale or return basis.

Find the best new wine bargains all year round with our newsletter, *Which? Wine Monthly*, available for just £19 a year from: Dept WG90, Consumers' Association, FREEPOST, Hertford SG14 1YB – no stamp is needed if posted within the UK.

The Wine Emporium

7 Devon Place, Edinburgh EH12 5HJ   TEL 031–346 1113

CASE SALES ONLY   OPEN Mon–Fri 10–8; Sat 10–7; Sun 11–5   CLOSED Chr
Day, 1 Jan   CREDIT CARDS Access, Visa; personal and business accounts
DISCOUNTS Available on large quantities only   DELIVERY Free in
Edinburgh and Glasgow (min 1 case); elsewhere £1.50–£4 per case; mail
order available   GLASS HIRE Free with 1-case order
TASTINGS AND TALKS Monthly tastings in-store; tastings through Wine
Emporium Cellar Club; to groups on request   CELLARAGE £2 per case per
year

The Glasgow branch of this merchant unfortunately closed
during the year, but the Edinburgh branch is left to flourish in a
large warehouse in the Haymarket end of the city.

It's not a long list, but it contains plenty of good value – from
some inexpensive clarets and French regional wines (look for
the Minervois 1987, Ch Millegrand at £2.69 and the wines of
Listel), through good-value Alsace from the Ribeauvillé co-
operative to various wines from La Vieille Ferme in the Rhône.

Other countries offer some nice bottles, too: Italy's Trentino
wines of Ca' Donini, the Colares Beira Mar from Portugal (1979
vintage at £4.29), Riojas from Campo Viejo, and Australian
wines from Wyndham Estate and Brown Brothers. New Zealand
wines from Nobilo and Californian from Buena Vista and
Mondavi complete the list.

Best buys

Corbières 1987, Ch de Capendu (Midi), £2.79
Spanna 1986, Dessilani (Piedmont), £3.59
Côtes du Rhône 1986, Cru du Coudoulet, £4.99

Wine Growers Association

MAIL ORDER ONLY
430 High Road, Willesden, London   TEL 01–451 0981/1135
NW10 2HA
OR
Freepost, London NW10 1YA

CREDIT CARDS Access, Diners Club, American Express, THF Goldcard,
Visa; business accounts   DISCOUNTS Possible   DELIVERY Free on UK
mainland (min 6 cases)   GLASS HIRE, TASTINGS AND TALKS Not available
CELLARAGE £3 per unmixed case per year for wines bought from the
Association

While this wine merchant (who operates on a mail order basis only) is best known for its extraordinary range of Italian wines, other areas of interest can also be recommended.

One such is Bordeaux, with a good collection from recent vintages, both top wines and bottles for everyday drinking. There's also a most attractive list of sweet white wines. Burgundy is dominated by wines from La Reine Pédauque, while in Provence the wines from the large estate of Ch de Beaulieu are prominent. Champagnes are from Ayala.

But then we turn to Italy. There are wines from virtually every region of the country (we didn't spot one from the Val d'Aosta, but that will probably arrive at any minute), many from top producers already familiar from other merchants, but here in greater profusion, since Wine Growers Association is part of the group that imports the wines in the first place. The strongest regions are Piedmont (Barolos from Borgogno, Barbaresco from Marchesi di Gresy, Spanna from Brugo); Tuscany (Chianti from Pagliarese and Castellare, Brunello di Montalcino from Caparzo, Vino Nobile di Montepulciano from Cerro), and the Veneto (Tedeschi and Boscaini). But we musn't ignore wines from the Alto Adige, from Friuli (Collavini is the supplier here), Frascati (Villa di Catone), the wines of Sella e Mosca in Sardinia, or rarities such as the Aglianico del Vulture from d'Angelo in Basilicata, the Campania wines of the Ocone family, or Torre Ercolana from Lazio.

A new interest this year is a range from California, featuring producers such as Mondavi, Heitz, Firestone and the sparkling wines of Schramsberg.

Best buys

Spanna del Piemonte 1987, Brugo, £3.25
Chardonnay di Appiano 1988, Cantina Sociale di Appiano (Alto Adige), £4.30
Chianti Classico Pigiatello 1988, Pagliarese, £4.15
Cirò Classico Rosso, Librandi (Calabria), £3.50

The Wine House

10 Stafford Road, Wallington, Surrey
SM6 9AD
TEL 01–669 6661

OPEN Tue–Sat 10–6; Sun 12–2; public holidays variable   CLOSED Mon
CREDIT CARDS Access, Visa; personal and business accounts
DISCOUNTS To members of Wine Circle only   DELIVERY Free within 5-mile radius (min 1 case); elsewhere at cost; mail order available
GLASS HIRE Free   TASTINGS AND TALKS 6–10 annual tastings by ticket only; to groups on request   CELLARAGE Not available

---

It's amazing what can happen in two years. Then the Wine House was part of a franchise operation which specialised in Spanish wines. Now, it's independent, an award-winner as Young Wine Merchant of the Year, and wielding a list that manages to be comprehensive in about every wine region.

What's more – as we discovered when we visited these enthusiastic premises – everything's in stock somewhere in the friendly clutter.

In such a wealth of wines, we are hard put to single out any one area as deserving of more praise than any other. However, we are probably most impressed by the range of Spanish wines – an enormous display of Riojas, especially Reservas, but also wines from most other regions, and plenty of Cavas and Sherries as well. Italy, too, offers good things, again, from every region, with perhaps the Veneto and Tuscany coming out best.

New this year are many of the German estate wines. The same is true of the Yugoslav wines, giving a wider selection in seven bottles than virtually any other merchant. There's a good choice from Portugal, with welcome additions to the familiar names. And, well overseas, the Australian range is exciting, adventurous and full of wines from smaller wineries.

If France seems to take second place (as we suggested last year), it is only by comparison with everything else on the list. But we are impressed by the range of clarets, the high quality of the Loire wines, the choice from the Rhône, and the wines from Provence as well as those from the Midi and the South-West – a range that would be enough on its own for many other wine merchants.

Best buys

Givry 1986, Baron Thénard, £8.40
Piesporter Michelsberg Riesling 1987, Hans Reh, £2.84
Bardolino Classico Superiore 1987, Guerrieri-Rizzardi (Veneto), £3.38
Rioja Gran Reserva 1980, Montecillo Viña Monty, £4.82
Beresford Chardonnay 1987, Southern Vales, Australia, £6.62

Wine Rack

108 Pitshanger Lane, London W5 1QP	TEL 01–997 4666
71 Abbeville Road, London SW4 9JW	TEL 01–673 1421

OPEN Hours may vary from store to store   CREDIT CARDS Access, American Express, Visa; personal and business accounts
DISCOUNTS Quantity discounts   DELIVERY Free locally   GLASS HIRE Free
TASTINGS AND TALKS Plans for weekly in-store tastings   CELLARAGE Not available

A group of shops under the same management as Thresher (see separate entry), but which has a wider range of fine wines. As we went to press, two shops were announced, with three more to come, and the promise of more in the future. The aim, we are told, is to move away from the atmosphere of a High Street off-licence and present wines more in the way of a traditional wine merchant. For the moment we will suspend judgement.

The range is certainly classier than is to be found in an ordinary branch of Thresher, improved though these are. Clarets embrace some 1982 and 1983 vintages of classed growths, and Burgundies include some domaine wines as well as wines from Louis Jadot and Beaujolais from Duboeuf. The Rhône selection is disappointing, but some good things pop up in the small Loire selection (look for the Muscadet of Donatien Bahuaud). Among the French regional wines are some treats once you get past the boring branded wines.

Italy is a star area, with wines from Antinori in Tuscany and Zenato in the Veneto, plus a few wines from Lungarotti. Spain has Raimat and Torres wines, plus the good-value Castillo di Alhambra red and white at £2.49. The Bulgarian wines are rather pricy. Germany contributes little but branded wines.

Outside Europe, go for Penfolds and Rosemount wines from Australia, Mondavi and Julius Wile wines from California, Cooks and Montana from New Zealand and a litany of famous names in the realms of fortified wines.

Best buys

L'Ermitage de Chasse Spleen 1986, Haut Médoc, £6.39
Ch de Lastours 1986, Corbières (Midi), £4.15
Penfolds Bin 2 Shiraz 1985, Australia, £3.99
Champagne Charles Heidsieck 1982, £12.99

The Wine Schoppen

1 Abbeydale Road South, Sheffield, South Yorkshire S7 2QL	TEL (0742) 365684/ 368617
ASSOCIATED OUTLETS	
Wine Schoppen (Kidderminster), 131 Stourbridge Road, Broadwaters, Kidderminster, Hereford & Worcester DY10 2UH	TEL (0562) 823060
A L Vose & Co, Barnton, Kentsford Road, Grange-over-Sands, Cumbria LA11 7BB	TEL (05395) 33328
Wine Warehouse, Holme Leigh, East Lane, Stainforth, Nr Doncaster, South Yorkshire DN7 5DT	TEL (0302) 841254
Pennine Wines, 5/7 Station Street, Huddersfield, South Yorkshire HD1 1LS	TEL (0484) 25747
R T Wines, Unit 11a, The Springboard Centre, Manth Lane, Coalville, Leicestershire LE6 4DR	TEL (0530) 39531 Ext 235
Classic Wines, 12 Wadehouse Road, Shelf, Halifax, West Yorkshire HX3 7PB	TEL (0274) 691053

OPEN Mon–Fri 9.30–6 Sat 9–5   CLOSED Sun, public holidays
CREDIT CARDS Access, Visa; personal and business accounts
DISCOUNTS 2·5% for 3–5 cases, 5% for 6–9 cases, 7·5% for 10–15 cases, 10% for 16–25 cases   DELIVERY Free within 15-mile radius of Sheffield, Kidderminster and of all associated companies (min 1 case); elsewhere £3.95 per consignment; mail order available   GLASS HIRE Free with 1-case order   TASTINGS AND TALKS In-store tastings held every first Saturday of the month; tastings by invitation 4 times per year; wines always available for tasting in-store; to groups on request   CELLARAGE £2.50 per case per year

The Wine Schoppen heads up a buying group which includes some merchants who stock the same range, and others who operate with part of the list, buying their other wines independently.

Germany and Austria are the focus: look here for the plentiful German estate wines (try the Niersteiners of Weingut Sandel and Weingut Schneider, or the Franconian wines from Ernst Gebhardt). In Austria, the wines from Winzer Krems on the Danube would be rewarding.

Elsewhere, things are less interesting, but it would be worth considering the range of good-value clarets, the Alsace wines of Joseph Cattin, wines from the Châteauneuf estate of Mont-Redon, or, further afield, Australian wines from Basedow and Bleasdale. And there's a bright spot with a big range of Calem Ports.

WHERE TO BUY

Best buys

Minervois 1986, Domaine du Pech d'André (Midi), £3.25
Gau Odernheimer Herrgottspfad Riesling Kabinett 1986, Grode
Erben, £3.65
Calem 10-year-old tawny Port, £9.55

The Wine Society   ❀ ▭ ☞ ☆

REGISTERED OFFICE (MAIL ORDER ONLY)
Gunnels Wood Road, Stevenage,   TEL (0438) 741177
Hertfordshire SG1 2BG   (enquiries)
                                              TEL (0438) 740222
                                    (24-hour answering service)

OPEN Mon–Fri 9–5; Sat 9–12 noon at Christmas for collections
CREDIT CARDS Access, Visa; personal and business accounts
DISCOUNTS £1.20 on 1 unmixed case   DELIVERY Free in UK (min 1 case);
otherwise at cost   GLASS HIRE Free   TASTINGS AND TALKS Regular ticketed
tastings in venues around the country; local tasting groups; to groups
on request   CELLARAGE £3.60 per case per year (including insurance)

The oldest and biggest of the wine clubs, the International
Exhibition Co-operative Wine Society, has a dauntingly
impressive list of fine wines, but it also manages to offer its
members a good haul for everyday drinking, on the whole well
chosen and – with greatly enlarged premises – well cellared.
Introduced last year was a scheme under which the Society will
choose your wines for you – and deliver them regularly.

The Wine Society orders its list in a way of which we
approve – by wine style rather than just by country. A useful
range of sampler cases includes the Half Bottle Case and a Tour
du Monde, which moves from England to Hungary to New
Zealand to California to France to Chile (among other countries)
for £50.

If we say that a major part of the list is from the classic wine
areas, that is not to suggest a particularly traditional outlook.
But the Society is certainly generous with clarets (and makes
regular en primeur offers as the vintage warrants). Plenty of
domaine Burgundies (both red and white) and a wide range of
Champagnes are additional adornments.

Within France, the Rhône section is strong, and the French
country wines, Alsace contributions and sweet Loires also look
good. In Germany, there are some classic estate names from
most of the regions. The Italian range is short but to the point

---

Please write to tell us about any ideas for features you would like to see
in next year's edition or in *Which? Wine Monthly.*

---

with, for example Barolos of Renato Ratti, Antinori's Tignanello and Chianti from Castello Vicchiomaggio. In Spain, Remelluri single vineyard Rioja and Mauro from Tudela del Duero are worth more than just a cursory glance.

In the New World, it is Australia that fares best: look for wines from Ch Tahbilk, Wirra Wirra, the superb Pyrus from Lindeman's and Cape Clairault Cabernet Sauvignon. Fortified wines are a great strength: a very good range of fino and manzanilla Sherries and an equally good showing of aged tawny Ports.

Best buys

The Society's Chianti Classico, £3.65
Beaujolais Villages Ch de Lacarelle 1988, £4.35
Marsanne Vin de Pays de l'Hérault, Domaine de la Gardie 1988 (Midi), £3.35
Ch Pitray 1985, Bordeaux Supérieur, £4.20

Wine Warehouse (Stainforth)

See The Wine Schoppen.

Winecellars

153/155 Wandsworth High Street,   TEL 01–871 2668
London SW18 4JB
ASSOCIATED OUTLET
The Market, 213 Upper Street, London   TEL 01–359 5386
N1 1RL

OPEN Mon–Fri 10.30–8.30; Sat 10–8.30; Sun, public holidays 10.30–6
CLOSED Chr Day, Boxing Day   CREDIT CARDS Access, Visa; personal and business accounts   DISCOUNTS Approximately 10% on 1 case
DELIVERY Free on UK mainland (min 1 case within M25, 2 cases outside); mail order available   GLASS HIRE Free   TASTINGS AND TALKS Regular series of tutored tastings covering autumn, winter and spring; to groups on request   CELLARAGE Not available

This merchant sold all but one of its supermarkets, the Market on Islington's Upper Street, during 1989, to concentrate their energies, as they put it, on the wine side of the business. Their reputation is certainly as one of the top Italian wine specialists in the UK.

But it would be wrong to think of this South London warehouse as packed only with Italian goodies. They also have a strong French showing – you might choose to explore their French country wines (Cabardès 1986, Domaine St-Roch at £2.70, or Côtes du Roussillon Villages Fûts de Chêne Mas Camo 1985 at £4.50), their sensibly priced Burgundies, Rhône wines from Ch de Beaucastel, Vouvray Ch de Moncontour or good petit château clarets. Other European countries offer a slimmer choice, but wines from various small wineries in Australia and California make for interesting deliberations.

But Italy remains the heart of the list. Every important region is represented (as well as many of the lesser areas), in many cases with wines which Winecellars import direct. The strongest areas are Piedmont and Tuscany – Cavallotto and Conterno Barolos and Moscato d'Asti of Ascheri in Piedmont; Selvapiana Chianti Rufina, Brunello di Montalcino from Altesino, Carmignano from Capezzana, Frascati from Colli di Catone from Latium. But look also for the good-value Cellaro wines from Sicily, Sardinian wines from Dolianova, Soaves from Anselmi and Pieropan, Friuli wines from Jermann, or the wines of De Bartoli in Pantelleria and Marsala. Once you've tried those, there are plenty more – or, if confusion sets in, sampler cases to set things straight.

Best buys

Cellaro Bianco (Sicily), £2.94
Ronco di Mompiano 1985, Pasolini (Lombardy), £4.84
Barbaresco 1984, Pasquero (Piedmont), £4.84
Cabardès 1986, Domaine St-Roch (Midi), £2.70
Bukkuram Moscato Passito di Pantelleria, De Bartoli (Sicily), £10.94 (also halves)

Winelines

7 Baronsfield Road, St Margarets,   TEL 01–744 1711
Twickenham TW1 2QT

CASE SALES ONLY   OPEN Enquiries by telephone at any reasonable hour
CREDIT CARDS None accepted   DISCOUNTS Not available   DELIVERY Free within 10-mile radius of Richmond/Twickenham; elsewhere £4 per case; mail order available   GLASS HIRE Free with order
TASTINGS AND TALKS Two 10-week intermediate wine tasting courses held annually; to groups on request   CELLARAGE Not available

Winelines is a new company whose short but useful list shows an obvious shine to Bulgarian wines (with prices that are not always competitive), but also offers good selections from Portugal and the Loire, and is enchanced by a nice line in Joseph Perrier Champagne.

Other areas in which there is interest are clarets (including some second wines from estates like Ch Meyney and Ch Cantemerle), Ports (go for the Dow's Crusted Bottled 1985 at £9.50 for a taste of what vintage Port is like) and curiosities like

the Greek Ch Carras 1979 (£4.49) or the Portuguese Almeirim
Branco white 1987 at a good-value £2.39.

Best buys

Almeirim Branco 1987, Portugal, £2.39
Oriahovitza Reserve 1981, Bulgaria, £2.99
Ch des Coulinats 1982, Ste-Croix du Mont, £4.50

Wines from Paris   ⊨

The Vaults, 4 Giles Street, Leith,   TEL 031–554 2652
Edinburgh EH6 6DJ

CASE SALES ONLY   OPEN Mon–Sat 10–6   CLOSED Sun, Chr Day, Boxing
Day, 1–2 Jan, Easter   CREDIT CARDS Access, Visa; personal and business
accounts   DISCOUNTS Available; £1 off per case collected   DELIVERY Free
on mainland Scotland; otherwise £2.50 per case; mail order available
GLASS HIRE Free   TASTINGS AND TALKS Monthly (approx) tastings usually
tutored; wines always available in tasting room; to groups on request
CELLARAGE Not available

Judith Paris still talks of turning part of her 12th-century vaulted
cellars into a wine bar, but over the past year she has been
concentrating on increasing her stock. It's still a well-balanced
list, with many wines that are imported direct, as well as some
more familiar names.

Strong areas include the French regions, particularly wines
from Ch La Jaubertie in Bergerac, the Cahors of St-Didier
Parnac, and the stunning wines from Mas de Daumas Gassac.
The Rhône has good things from Ch de Beaucastel (and the
related Cru du Coudoulet Côtes du Rhône), while in Alsace,
Domaine Ostertag contributes a full range. The Loire continues
to be a weaker section, but the good thing about the Burgundies
is that many of the wines offer reasonable value (plus plenty of
Chablis from Jean Durup). Look, too, for Beaujolais from Pierre
Ferraud.

From beyond France come the Veneto wines of Guerrieri-
Rizzardi, and Lageder wines from the Südtirol (plus Chianti
from Isole e Olena). Germany offers a smattering of estate
wines, while the Spanish delegation is made up of Torres in
Penedés as well as Montecillo Riojas. From much further east is
an interesting assembly of Tokays from Hungary.

The other strong area is Australia, with wines from smaller
outfits such as Peel Estate in Margaret River and Leo Buring in
the Barossa. In sparkling wines, look for Pommery Champagne,
and in fortifieds try the Ramos Pinto Ports.

Best buys

Petit Chablis 1987, Jean Durup, £5.99
Ch La Jaubertie Cépage Sauvignon 1988, Bergerac, £4.85
Rockford Shiraz 1986, Barossa Valley, Australia, £8.85

Wines Galore

161–165 Greenwich High Road, London   TEL 01–858 6014
SE10 8JA

OPEN Mon–Fri 10–7; Sat 10–5   CLOSED Sun, public holidays
CREDIT CARDS All accepted, Davys of London   DISCOUNTS Approx 10% per
case   DELIVERY At cost   GLASS HIRE Free with appropriate case order
TASTINGS AND TALKS Monthly tastings in wine bar; to groups on request
CELLARAGE Not available

Wine Galore operate from a similar list to that of Davys of
London (see separate entry), with its emphasis on several good
clarets, a limited range of Burgundies, Rhône wines from Ch de
Beaucastel and La Vieille Ferme and Alsace wines from Louis
Gisselbrecht. Look for regional wines such as Bergerac from Ch
Bélingard, Provence rosé from Commanderie de Bargemone,
Spanish wines which include the single vineyard Rioja,
Conterno, and a few Italian wines (we would recommend the
Chianti Rufina Castello di Nipozzano of Frescobaldi 1982 at
£5.85).

Australian wines from Seppelts and New Zealand wines from
Stoneleigh Vineyard have joined the list, along with a few
Bulgarian wines and some estate-bottled German wines. In
fortified wines, look for the Australian Liqueur Muscats, the
house Sherries and a range of vintage Ports.

Best buys

Davy's Rioja 1985, £4.15
House Claret NV, £3.25
Beaune Vignes St-Jacques NV, Coron, £7.80

☆ celebrates the uninterrupted inclusion of this merchant in all ten
editions of *Which? Wine Guide*.

Prices were correct to the best of our knowledge as we went to press.
They, and ranges of wines stocked, are likely to change during the
course of 1990 and are intended only as rough indication of an
establishment's range and prices.

Wines of Argentina

See Pond Farm Wines.

Wines of Interest

46 Burlington Road, Ipswich, Suffolk   TEL (0473) 215752
IP1 2HS

OPEN Mon–Fri 9–6; Sat 9–1   CLOSED Sun, public holidays
CREDIT CARDS None accepted; personal and business accounts
DISCOUNTS Available for large quantities   DELIVERY Free in City of
London and central Ipswich and Norwich (min 1 case); otherwise at
cost; mail order available   GLASS HIRE Free   TASTINGS AND TALKS To
groups on request   CELLARAGE £1.75 per case per year

See Burlington Wines.

Wines of Westhorpe   ☆

Field House Cottage, Birch Cross,   TEL (0283) 820285
Marchington, Staffordshire ST14 8NX

CASE SALES ONLY   OPEN (Warehouse) Mon–Fri 8–4.45; Sat 8.30- 12 (office
only)   CLOSED (Warehouse) Sat, Sun, public holidays
CREDIT CARDS None accepted; personal and business accounts
DISCOUNTS Available   DELIVERY Free on UK mainland (min 1 case); mail
order available   GLASS HIRE Not available
TASTINGS AND TALKS Occasionally to groups on request   CELLARAGE Not
available

France on this list is sewn up in 15 wines, and one rapidy
realises that this merchant remains almost single-mindedly
concerned with wines from Hungary and Bulgaria. The full
range of Bulgarian wines available in this country is stocked
here, at prices which are distinctly competitive. The story is
much the same with Hungary, where the range contains a good
few of the famous sweet Tokays from the east of the country.
Tasting cases are available.

Best buys

Villany Merlot, Hungary, £1.92
Villany Chardonnay, Hungary, £1.92
Svichtov Cabernet Sauvignon 1985, Bulgaria, £3
Asenovgrad Mavrud 1983, Bulgaria, £3

If you disagree with us, please tell us why. You will find report forms at
the back of the book.

Wizard Wine Warehouses

HEAD OFFICE
6 Theobold Court, Theobold Street,   TEL 01–207 4455
Borehamwood, Hertfordshire WD6 4RN
10 outlets in London, Surrey, Buckinghamshire, Berkshire and
Kent

OPEN Long hours, 7 days a week (may vary from branch to branch)
CLOSED Sun (Surbiton and Bletchley stores only)   CREDIT CARDS Access,
Visa, Wizard and Bejam Chargecard; business accounts   DISCOUNTS 5%
for 10 cases   DELIVERY Free within 20-mile radius of each warehouse
(min £100 order); otherwise at cost; mail order available
GLASS HIRE Free   TASTINGS AND TALKS Weekly tastings; some warehouse
managers organise their own wine clubs; to groups on request
CELLARAGE Not available

Value remains good at this group of wine warehouses. But value
doesn't just mean inexpensive wines, as their well-chosen range
of clarets proves (plenty of wines under £5, yes, but good choice
in the classed growths, too). In Burgundy, they have pursued
the value-for-money policy by going for lesser communes rather
than the big names – we particularly like their choice of white
Burgundies.

But it is outside the classic areas that you find the very best
value. The Quincy Domaine de la Maison Blanche at £3.89 is
just one of the good things from the Loire, while from the
Rhône, there is interest in the southern vineyards (try the
Gigondas 1985 of Domaine de la Daysse at £4.39). Wizard's
range of French regional wines continues to expand, offering
masses of choice under £3.

The Italian range continues to be very strong: look for
curiosities such as the Sauvignon from Puglia at £3.49, or more
familiar names such as Chianti Classico of Rocca delle Macie,
wines from Umani Ronchi in the Rosso Cònero region and
Barolo from Fontanafredda. Spain features Torres wines, while
the small Portuguese contingent is supplied courtesy of J M da
Fonseca.

After dropping in on Bulgaria, head for the New World:
Orlando wines from Australia, Montana from New Zealand and
an increasingly impressive range from California.

Best buys

Rioja Muga 1984, Crianza, £3.99
Beaujolais 1987, Cave Coopérative de Bully, £2.59
Ch Thieuley 1987 Sauvignon, Bordeaux, £3.49
Domaine de la Source Chardonnay, Vin de Pays de
l'Hérault, £2.99

Wright Wine Co

The Old Smithy, Raikes Road, Skipton,   TEL (0756) 794175
North Yorkshire BD23 1NP

OPEN Mon–Sat 9–6   CLOSED Sun, some public holidays
CREDIT CARDS None accepted; personal and business accounts
DISCOUNTS 5% on mixed cases, 8–9% on unsplit cases   DELIVERY Free
within 35-mile radius of Skipton; elsewhere at cost   GLASS HIRE Free
with purchase   TASTINGS AND TALKS To groups on request
CELLARAGE Not available

'We wish to continue to be a traditional wine merchant', writes
the Wright Wine Co, new to the Guide, but not to Skipton.
Their list shows that they have achieved exactly that: it is firmly
based in traditional areas, but shows an awareness of what is
happening in the wider world, expecially the New World.

The kick-off takes place in France, with plenty of Champagnes
and a smaller range of other sparklers. On to Bordeaux, with
some mature clarets as well as larger selections of more recent
vintages, where petit château wines balance the classed
growths. There is plenty of Beaujolais from Loron, and a mix of
domaine and négociant wines from Burgundy (look for the
excellent range of Chablis). On the Loire, look for the Sancerre
of Alphonse Mellot, and the Pouilly Fumé of Jean Claude
Dagueneau.

Outside France, an estate-bottled range from Germany is
followed by an impressive Italian line-up, and Riojas from
Olarra and Campo Viejo, J M da Fonseca Portuguese wines
follow hot on the heels of a few Greek wines. Then it's off to the
New World, with wines from smaller producers such as
Montrose in Mudgee as well as larger producers such as Brown
Brothers.

Best buys

Madiran Domaine de Margalide 1987, £3.53
Bairrada 1980, Caves São João, Portugal, £3.94
Vin de Pays Charentais Cabernet/Merlot 1988, Sornin, £3.23

Special awards

   is for bargain prices   is for a very good range of
                                           wines

   is for high quality wines   is for exceptional service

Peter Wylie Fine Wines

Plymtree Manor, Plymtree, Cullompton, TEL (088 47) 555
Devon EX15 2LE

OPEN Mon–Fri 9–6; Sat 9–3 CLOSED Sun, public holidays
CREDIT CARDS None accepted; personal and business accounts
DISCOUNTS Quantity discounts DELIVERY Free in central London (min 3
cases); otherwise at cost; mail order available GLASS HIRE,
TASTINGS AND TALKS Not available CELLARAGE £4.60 per case per year

This stunning range of fine claret, Burgundy, Champagne and
vintage Port would make any wine lover get very excited
indeed. Peter Wylie specialises in small parcels of fine, rare and
mature wines and the list changes as wines arrive or are sold.

One recent list offered delights such as a pre-1860 claret (Ch
Bel Air Marquis d'Aligré), the first-growth clarets from most of
the best vintages of this century, and an increasingly
comprehensive selection of other clarets from about 1928
onwards, with plenty of magnums to add to the fun.

There's a similar range in sweet white Bordeaux (and not just
Ch d'Yquem, although that's here as well), while in red
Burgundy, you could start off with Grands-Echézeaux of 1948
and move onwards.

Look, too, for vintage Champagnes, right back to 1928, and
vintage Port from the turn of the century.

Best buys

Fine and rare wines

Yapp Brothers

The Old Brewery, Mere, Wiltshire TEL (0747) 860423/
BA12 6DY 860017

OPEN Mon–Fri 9–5; Sat 9–1 CLOSED Sun, public holidays
CREDIT CARDS Access, Visa; personal and business accounts
DISCOUNTS Case discounts DELIVERY Free on UK mainland (min 2 cases);
mail order available GLASS HIRE Free with 1-case order
TASTINGS AND TALKS Some wines open daily; regular organised tastings
and lunches; to groups on request CELLARAGE £2.50 per case per year or
part-year

They had a big party at Mere last summer to celebrate 20 years
of shipping wines from the Rhône and the Loire. Some famous
composers wrote songs celebrating the Yapps (the business is
run by a husband-and-wife team) and their achievements in
bringing to the nation's attention the wines of these two rivers.

Certainly 20 years ago it would have been foolish to predict how important those areas would become to wine drinkers right round the world. And if we now take them for granted we shouldn't overlook the fact that it is because of a very few merchants, including Yapp Brothers, that we can now enjoy the wines as part of the natural course of events.

To the Rhône and Loire the Yapps have added a third speciality – Provence. There seems almost to be a challenge to find appellations or areas in any of these regions which nobody else has ever heard of – Thouarsais on the Loire, Bellet in Provence, Brézème on the Rhône – and often to unearth the only producer left in that particular appellation. But they have also rounded up famous names from famous areas: on the Rhône Auguste Clape in Cornas, Chave in Hermitage, Jasmin in Côte Rôtie (alongside other producers from the same appellation). Condrieu and Ch Grillet to show the wonders of the Viognier vine, and they don't neglect good Villages Côtes du Rhône.

In Provence, the story is the same – Ch Simone in Palette, Domaine de Trévallon in Coteaux des Baux en Provence, Mas de la Rouvière in Bandol. On the Loire, we would go for Sancerre of Jean Vatan or Pouilly Fumé of Jean-Claude Guyot, or, further west, the Montlouis of Berger Frères, Bourgueil of Pierre-Jacques Druet, or Savennières of Soulez and Nicolas Joly at Coulée de Serrant.

Best buys

Sancerre Clos les Perriers 1988, Jean Vatan (Loire), £6.50
Vin de Thouarsais Sec 1988, Michel Gigon (Loire), £3.75
Gigondas 1985, Domaine St-Gayan, Meffre (Rhône), £6.50
Coteaux du Tricastin 1987, Domaine de Grangeneuve (Rhône), £4.15

Yorkshire Fine Wine Company

Sweethills, Nun Monkton, York, North   TEL (0423) 330131
Yorkshire YO5 8ET

CASE SALES ONLY   OPEN Mon–Fri 9.30–5.30   CLOSED Sat, Sun, public holidays   CREDIT CARDS Access, Visa; personal and business accounts DISCOUNTS 4% for 7-day settlement   DELIVERY Free in north of England; elsewhere at cost; mail order available   GLASS HIRE Free TASTINGS AND TALKS In-store tastings and to groups on request CELLARAGE £5.75 per case per year

If you held a competition for the most discreet cover of any wine list in this Guide, Yorkshire Fine Wines – with its white embossed lettering on white – would win hands down. Inside, modesty gives way to an expanded range of wines, which is certainly fine, but which no longer sticks just to the classic areas.

One is left in no doubt of a firm commitment to Champagne – piles of it with lots of top cuvées as well as non-vintage wines, and a speciality in Krug. Then we move to a splendid list from Burgundy, ranging wide and covering domaines as well as négociants in profusion. The Rhône is interestingly strong in the southern vineyards, less strong further north.

Then we move to Bordeaux, and here again the wines march in, representing vintages back to the 1960s and with an emphasis on classed growths. Other French points of interest are Alsace wines from Domaine Marcel Deiss, various bottles from Sancerre and Pouilly Fumé, and a few regional wines.

Beyond France, look for a useful rather than exciting range of German estate wines, and a splendidly updated and increased range from Tuscany (Chianti from Castello di San Polo in Rosso, and Barolos from Ceretto and Mascarello). Some top names resound in California, plus wines from Washington State, Idaho and Oregon: the best wines are from Western Australia and a few smaller wineries in New Zealand. Finally, vintage Ports are an impressive range, with an emphasis on Fonseca.

Best buys

Touraine Sauvignon 1988, Domaine Octavie (Loire), £4.71
Ch Bel-Air Fonroque 1986, Bordeaux, £4.23
Hautes Côtes de Nuits 1987, Jayer Gilles, £11.85
Vacqueyras 1985, Bérard Père et Fils (Rhône), £5.26

Wine at auction

Why buy at auction?

Buying wine at auction is a recognised part of the way in which both the wine trade and private buyers stock up their cellars. Purchases may be a few bottles of rare old wines, or several cases of newer wines. But the buyers go to the auction house rather than to a wine merchant either because the wine merchant is unable to supply a particular wine, or because the buyers believe they can get better bargains at auction.

Both reasons can be justified. Certainly more rare wines go through auction houses than are found on the lists of all but the most specialised merchants (who probably bought much of their stock at auction anyway). And certainly it is possible to pick up some amazing bargains, as well as wines at useful prices, by buying at auction.

But, of course, as with all auctions, the principle of *caveat emptor* applies. That means that you take the risk that the goods may not be in good condition: it is up to you to check on the quality. Normally, of course, it is possible to do this physically, by looking at a painting or a piece of furniture before the auction.

With wine, though, pre-sale tastings occur only rarely. So buyers have to take the advice of the auctioneers as to the quality of the wine and where it has been stored (a vital piece of information – the quality of the cellaring will affect the quality of the wine). Indications in auction catalogues about the quality of the labels (if they are damaged it could mean the wine was stored in damp, and therefore unsatisfactory, conditions), the level of wine in the bottle and the condition of the corks (old wines evaporate unless topped up professionally and then re-corked) – all these are important in deciding whether it is worth taking the risk and bidding for a wine.

What to buy in 1990

The big story in the auction rooms during 1989 was the one that didn't happen. For months, everyone had been predicting that wine bought as part of the Business Expansion Schemes in the mid-1980s would be dumped on to the auction market as the schemes expired, causing an immediate depression in prices.

But nothing happened. The period of comparative stagnation that has seen auction prices of wine remain fairly steady since 1985 has continued. Much of this has been due to the considerable quantities of young claret (the main constituent of auctions) which are available on the open market, reducing the need for private or wine trade buyers to go to auction houses for supplies.

Claret and vintage Port take the main parts in wine auctions, with red Burgundy, vintage Champagne and sweet white Bordeaux having smaller walk-on parts. Occasionally, German wines, rarities like old Madeira or old Cognac, Italian wine, individual estate Riojas, even New World wines, appear – but in general, auctions are not the place to go for these.

Over the year 1988/89, prices for claret remained relatively steady. There was an overall 5 per cent increase in prices from July 1988 to July 1989 in the price index issued by *Decanter* magazine, with the greatest interest in years before 1980. Of more recent vintages, 1981 and 1983 seem to be good value, 1982 is highly priced but static, and more recent vintages are only just appearing at auction.

With vintage Port, the rise in the *Decanter* index was similar at 6 per cent. Here the vintage (great as it is) to avoid is 1977 which has seen a spectacular rise of 27 per cent over a year, while vintages of the early 1980s (1980 especially, but also 1983) are good value for buying to lay down. Buying vintage Port – certainly of earlier vintages – at auction is often the only way to find the wine you want. Port from Portuguese-named houses will be cheaper than wine from British-named houses (but will also be less long-lasting).

Preparing for the sale

Sales dates *Decanter* magazine gives dates and times of forthcoming sales, and both Christie's and Sotheby's advertise their sales in the national press. You can also put yourself on an auction house's mailing list, which, for a fee, will provide you with pre-sale tastings. Catalogues are normally sent out three weeks before a sale. If you are not a subscriber, you can buy catalogues individually, by post, or call in to collect one.

Bidding by post Postal bidding forms arrive with the catalogue: most auction houses provide a free postal bidding service. You merely need to indicate the maximum you are prepared to pay for a particular lot. The auctioneer will secure the lot for you at a lower price if possible. The estimates in the catalogue will be based on prices fetched for the same or similar wine at recent auctions, and on the reserve price the vendor has placed on his wine, so it's rare to find a successful bid going below the minimum of the estimate.

Pre-sale tasting These are normally held the day before the auction (the catalogue will tell you when and where). Don't expect to taste 1905 Ch Mouton-Rothschild if it happens to be in the sale, but most wines tend to be available for tasting. If you have a particular wine in mind, telephone in advance to see if the wine will be available for tasting, or ask advice. Arrive early and remember that catalogue subscribers are allowed in first.

What's in the catalogue

The estimated price against a wine is only the beginning of what you will have to pay at auction. It pays to read the small print at the front of the catalogue carefully, but here are some pointers.

Duty paid Wines marked 'duty paid' (normally in the second section of the auction) will have been cleared by Customs and Excise, so the estimated price will include duty. Foreign buyers prefer to buy wines 'in bond' (see below) so you will more likely be bidding against British buyers in this section of the sale.

In bond No excise duty has yet been paid. When you have secured the lot, the auctioneers will sort out the Customs paperwork for a small fee. Whatever the price of the wine, you pay a flat rate per bottle.

Duty paid available in bond For British buyers, duty is already paid. For foreign buyers, duty will be subtracted after the auction.

VAT The estimates do not include VAT. VAT is charged only if the wine is being sold by a merchant registered for VAT. Wines being sold by private individuals do not attract VAT. Remember, VAT is payable as a percentage of the final price, and not, as with duty, as a flat rate, so higher-priced bottles attract more VAT than cheaper ones.

FOB Free on Board is the term used to describe the wine that is being sold while still overseas. You will have to pay a proportion of the shipping costs, plus duty, VAT and customs clearance charges, which can be arranged by the auction house.

Ex cellar This means that the wine is still in the cellar of the estate where it was made. It's a guarantee that the wine will have been kept in the best possible condition.

How to bid

You are bidding for a numbered lot. The lot can either consist of one wine (generally in one case or multiples of cases) or what is called a mixed lot – a ragbag of wines which have been lumped together because they are old bottles. If you want only one particular wine in a mixed lot you will have to buy everything else as well. Occasionally special bottles will be auctioned separately.

Bid steps The catalogue sets out in the front the steps in which bidding is conducted. These vary according to the price reached – lower prices in the bidding will rise by small steps, higher prices by larger steps, for example, by single pounds up to £30, say, then, by £2 a time up to £100, £5 a time up to £200 and so on.

Bidding Just raise your hand when you want to make a bid, and preferably wave your catalogue. The auctioneers have eagle eyes, and once your first bid is noted, they'll keep an eye on you until that lot is sold. Once the hammer has fallen, the wine is legally yours. If you make a mistake, such as bidding for the wrong lot, tell the staff at once, before the end of the sale, and it will normally be re-auctioned.

Options The buyer of the first lot may be offered the option to buy the remaining lots of the same wine at the same price. This practice will be announced at the beginning of the sale, and is designed to help trade customers who need to buy large quantities of one particular wine. So if you really want a wine, make sure you bid for the first lot.

Paying for the wine

Once the hammer has fallen, the auction house staff will take your name and address. Invoices are posted after the sale, and you will then be told where the wine can be collected from. If it is actually on the sale room premises, you can pay for it and take it away - but that's less common because it is normal practice not to move the wine too much. Delivery can usually be arranged.

You may have to pay the buyer's premium (see the details for each auction house), normally 10 per cent of the sale price. You will also have to pay VAT on the premium. Vendors have to pay a commission to the auction house, at a percentage depending on the wine and the volume involved.

If the wine is faulty, tell the auction house. They are not responsible since they are acting as middlemen between you and the vendor, but they will normally help in negotiations.

London auction houses

Christie's

8 King Street, London SW1Y 6QT TEL 01-839 9060
85 Old Brompton Road, London SW7 3LD TEL 01-581 7611
56-60 Gresham Street, London EC2V 7BB TEL 01-588 4424
164-166 Bath Street, Glasgow G2 4TB TEL 041-332 8134

Christie's run the largest number of auctions. The King Street
auctions are of finer wines; Old Brompton Road sells everyday
wine as well as finer wines and bin-ends; and the City branch
tends to deal in Port, Burgundy and claret. Catalogue
subscriptions cost: (King Street) £40 a year for fine wine other
than claret, £30 a year for claret; (Old Brompton Road) £30;
(Glasgow) £7. Pre-sale tastings take place between 11 am and
noon the day before the sale at King Street and on the day of
the sale at Old Brompton Road and in the City. Advice on the
market in general and on whether to sell in particular is
available. Delivery from the South Kensington branch to
elsewhere in the UK is charged at £4 plus VAT per case or part
case, and insurance is the responsibility of the purchaser.
Insurance is included in the price and delivery is free from the
other two addresses if the wine is paid for within 21 days.
There is a 10 per cent buyer's premium. Two sales a year are
held in Glasgow or Edinburgh.

Sotheby's

34-35 New Bond Street, London W1A 2AA TEL 01-493 8080
Summers Place, Billingshurst, West Sussex RH14 9AD
TEL (040 381) 3933
Unit 5, Albion Wharf, London SW11 4AN TEL 01-924 3287

Sotheby's hold fewer auctions than Christie's. The auctions at
the New Bond Street address correspond to the auctions in
Christie's King Street rooms, with fine wines dominating. A
wider range is sold in Sussex. Sotheby's have set up a
computer-linked bidding service. Subscription to the catalogues
is £31 (London) and £12 (Sussex). Delivery is free, including
insurance, within the UK. There is a 10 per cent buyer's
premium.

International Wine Auctions

40 Victoria Way, London SE7 7QS TEL 01-293 4992

This auction house attracts the top end of the wine market, and
is aimed very much at the international wine-buying
connoisseur. They hold six auctions a year. Catalogues are £5,
and there is no buyer's premium. Delivery is free during
working hours. Insurance is the responsibility of the purchaser
after 5.30pm on the day of the sale.

Country auctioneers

While all the country auctioneers deal principally in goods other
than wine, those below do hold a few wine auctions a year.
Since international buyers tend not to come to these auctions,
you can often find amazing bargains, but prices can also go sky-
high for no apparent reason.

Bigwood Auctioneers Ltd

The Old School, Tiddington, Stratford-upon-Avon,
Warwickshire CV37 7AW TEL (0789) 69415

Sales take place on Thursday evening, quarterly. There is a pre-
sale tasting that afternoon. Subscription to the mailing list is
£10. There is a buyer's premium of 10 per cent (plus VAT), and
the vendor's commission is negotiable. Wines must generally be
collected, although delivery can be arranged.

Lacy Scott

10 Risbygate Street, Bury St Edmunds, Suffolk IP33 3AA
TEL (0284) 763531

One sale a year. Subscription to the catalogue is free; wines
must be collected. There is no buyer's premium, but vendors
pay a 12½ per cent commission. Insurance is the responsibility of
the buyer.

Lithgow, Sons & Partners

The Auction House, Station Road, Stokesley, Middlesbrough,
Cleveland TEL (0642) 710158

Two sales a year in December and June. Sales are advertised
locally and sometimes in *Decanter* and the *Daily Telegraph*, but
you can be put on their list to be sent catalogues (30p each).
Wines must be collected. Insurance is the responsibility of the
buyer.

Phillips, Son & Neil

39 Park End Street, Oxford OX1 1JD TEL (0865) 723524

The largest of the country auctioneers. There are four sales a
year, held on Tuesdays, with a pre-sale tasting on the day of the
sale. You can subscribe to the mailing list for £13 per year.
There is a 10 per cent buyer's premium, and a vendor's
commission. Wines must be collected from the saleroom within
two weeks of the sale. Insurance costs 1 per cent and is the
responsibility of the buyer.

Buying wine en primeur

The Bordeaux vintage of 1987 was the one when everybody said that the idea of buying en primeur was dead. The vintage was no good, it was too expensive, it wasn't worth tying up your money in wine that wouldn't appreciate in value.

Up to a point that was quite true. The vintage was not a great wine although it certainly did not deserve the write-off that it received from some wine writers. And it was certainly true that there was little interest in en primeur buying of 1987 claret – a few merchants made opening offers, and those few had a very restricted list.

But then came 1988, and suddenly en primeur wasn't dead after all. Offers flooded out, and although the wines were mixed, some were very good, we were told. If you don't buy now, the merchants said, the Americans and the Japanese and even the French will – so buy now or never see the wines again.

It's obviously in the interest of merchants to hype up these things – they have wine to sell and en primeur is a useful way of getting money in fast. But what happened with the 1988 vintage proved the point that en primeur buying is with us to stay, provided we are selective about which vintage to buy, and which vintage we ignore.

How it works

So what is en primeur? Essentially, it is the purchase of young claret (and other wines, too, but mainly claret) in the spring and summer following the vintage, while the wine is still in cask in Bordeaux. You pay for the wine itself now, but pay shipping, duty and VAT only when the wine is ready for shipment. Normally you can expect to see the wine in your cellar three and a half years after the vintage.

The advocates of en primeur buying claim as advantages the fact that you will never be able to by the wine so cheaply again (even if it is available) and that because it moves pretty well direct from the château to your cellar (or the wine merchant's cellar) you know the condition in which it is being kept. That is something you cannot know if you buy the wine some years later either at auction or from a wine merchant, and with a wine that needs some years to mature, it is an important consideration.

While it is too late to buy 1988 en primeur, now is the time to start thinking about 1989 claret. Since we went to press before the harvest, we cannot comment on the vintage, but our advice to potential en primeur buyers is to read the wine press carefully when it reports on it in April 1990.

If it is reckoned to be a good vintage, start sending off for en primeur information from any of the merchants we list below (or ask your local specialist wine merchant). By reading between the lines, and comparing a number of en primeur brochures, you should be able to come up with an idea of which part of Bordeaux the best wines come from, and which châteaux have made good wines.

Next comes the question of price. Compare prices from the different wine merchants – one may be cheaper for one château, one for another. You need only buy one case from each, so buy selectively, making sure – and this is vital – you keep all the paperwork and notes of what you have bought in a safe place. When you receive invoices, keep a note of all payments: you may hear nothing for three years, so you need to have everything written down. And if you move house in the interim, don't forget to tell the wine merchant where you have gone.

When the wine is eventually delivered, be patient. Store it carefully and wait. The pleasure will come a few years later when you break open the wooden case and try the first bottle.

Is it worth buying as an investment?

The short answer is that it all depends on the year and the wine. A Ch Pétrus or a Ch Lafite might bring you return on your money. If you buy Ch Petit X down in the Graves, your money would be better off in a building society. Buying wine for investment – like any form of speculation – is a risky business.

However, it is quite possible to buy wine en primeur to sell later to finance further wine purchases. There are those who claim that they can finance all their wine buying with sales of surplus claret which they have bought en primeur. Provided you don't expect to make a profit on the transaction – or a great return on investment – this is perfectly practicable. Take your wine merchant's advice.

Outside Bordeaux

Beyond the heady confines of Bordeaux, the idea of en primeur buying is spreading. For the first time this year we have seen opening offers for 1988 Burgundy, and even 1988 Beaujolais (not a wine for laying down too long, we feel).

The only other area where a form of en primeur selling takes place is Port. 1987 saw the release of the 1985 vintage, and at the time of writing it looks definite that neither the 1986 nor the 1987 vintages will be declared as a general vintage year; nobody has made up their minds about 1988. Port shippers wait until they are ready to bottle their vintage Port before declaring a vintage and opening it up for sale.

The following merchants have made en primeur offers for 1988 vintage wines (for claret unless indicated otherwise):

Averys (for Burgundy)
Nigel Baring
Bibendum
Corney & Barrow
Findlater Mackie Todd
Hicks & Don (and for Beaujolais)
Hungerford Wine Company
Justerini & Brooks
Lay & Wheeler
Laytons (and for northern Rhône)
London Wine
Morris & Verdin
Raeburn Fine Wines & Foods
Russell & McIver
Summerlee Wines
Tanners
The Wine Society

Part II

What to buy

Argentina

Watch this space

Early in 1989, a large group of Masters of Wine – the British wine trade's equivalent of graduates of Harvard Business School – went to Argentina (and Chile) to see what was afoot. Now if anything is calculated to bring about a complete change in our buying pattern of Argentine wines (for the last few years, we have perhaps not surprisingly bought almost none), then this visit by the people with an awful lot of wine-buying power was it. As we write, it is still too early to say what will happen – except that we can be sure to hear more from this, one of the world's top five producers of wine.

Most Argentine wine is of the immediately enjoyable, quaffing sort. They seem to be a thirsty lot, so the scope for exports is limited. But there is an attractive range of wines from the largest producer in the country (see below), and at very competitive prices.

The Italian influence is strong, with Nebbiolo, Barbera and Sangiovese grapes all adding sophistication to wines made generally from Malbec and Criolla (reds) and Palomino and Torrontes (whites). But noble French varieties – Chardonnay, Sylvaner (called Riesling), Chenin Blanc (called Pinot Blanc) and lesser varieties like Ugni Blanc – are now being added to the whites. Cabernet Sauvignon, Merlot, Syrah and Pinot Noir are also putting in an appearance.

The vineyard area is spread widely over the northern two-thirds of the country, but the biggest concentration is in the Mendoza area, on the eastern side of the Andes mountains from the main Chilean vineyards. This is principally red wine country, although recent reports suggest that modern-style white wines are now being made as well. But it has been suggested that the Rio Negro area, much further south, is more suited to premium grape growing than the hot, almost desert-like conditions of Mendoza.

Who's who in Argentina

Peñaflor The largest producer in Argentina. Wines are sold under the Andean brand name.
Cachet Wines; Continental Wine Warehouses; Grape Ideas; David Scatchard

Specialist stockists
Grape Ideas Wine Warehouse; Peter Green; Pond Farm Wines

Australia

Dominating the headlines

Australia has continued to dominate wine headlines over the past year. The Bicentenary helped, of course – it did seem to be the longest party in history. Enthusiasm and general interest came from a widening cross-section of the wine-drinking public. But, above all, the quality of the wines has continued to demand attention.

However, it would be only right to put all this excitement and interest into perspective. By the end of the 1987/88 marketing campaign (that is the period ending with the harvest of 1988), Australia was sending Britain 7.5 million litres of wine – that's an increase of 226 per cent over the previous year. Since then, figures have continued to leap up.

But that still represents only 1.5 per cent of all our wine imports. Australia has only just migrated out of the 'other countries' category in wine statistics.

Running out of wine

Drinking Australian bottles has been a little harder this past year. The 'out of stock' signs have been going up all over the place, as importers have struggled to get wines out of a country where demand was rapidly outstripping supply. The plenty of two years ago – when there was a small but useful Australian wine lake – has changed dramatically.

There are a number of reasons for this, but two are worth particular mention. One is a crazy 'vine-pull' scheme, in which the South Australian government (South Australia produces 60 per cent of Australian wine) paid farmers to pull up their vines – merely because of the small lake. There immediately followed two small harvests – the 1988 depleted because of frost and hail; and the 1989 reduced because of a heat wave. Who said Australia had a reliable climate?

And, despite that wine lake, Australia really doesn't produce much wine – certainly when compared with France or even California. She is well down the league table of wine-producing nations. So although the vine-pull programme has been put into rapid reverse, and more land is now being planted (especially with Chardonnay, the grape variety which has been in the greatest demand and the shortest supply), we will need to wait two or three years before the country can produce more to quench our thirst.

In the meantime, prices have risen from the vineyard onwards. Chardonnay has been the worst affected: prices of grapes went up by 50 per cent between the 1987 harvest and the 1988, but smaller price rises for other grapes – especially Cabernet Sauvignon – were also recorded.

The net result for us has been that the days of the super-cheapies from Australia are over – at least temporarily (the strengthening of the Australian dollar hasn't helped either). But we can still get some supermarket Australians for under £3 that would put wines from any other part of the world at that price to shame. And we can still get some superb top-class wines at under £10 a bottle that knock spots off anything in the most prestigious areas of Europe.

In the middle, things are a little more difficult. It's getting harder to find Australian wine at around £5 a bottle that is quite as good as it seemed to be a few years ago. Tasters at the annual Australia Day tasting at Lord's cricket ground this year were heard to complain about the Australians' excessive use of citric acid to give their white wines acidity. Some of the wines which had once overwhelmed with their combination of rich oak and equally stunning fruit this time seemed more muted – overcropping was suggested as a possible reason for this.

But these are quibbles about what is still a picture of high quality wine-making – Australian wine technology is second to none in the world – and a country which continues to show its ability to produce some of the most drinkable wines anywhere.

Getting colder

Although the bulk of Australia's wine is produced in a semi-circle of land in the south-eastern corner of the country, there is a surprisingly wide variety of micro-climates in what is often seen as a land of perpetual sunshine. The weather in Melbourne, capital of Victoria, they say, can pass through all four seasons in one day, and that variability of climate is what makes some of the areas of Victoria – such as the Yarra Valley and the coastal regions of Geelong – such high quality vineyards for cool-climate wines. In addition, Victoria has the highest vineyard in Australia (at Whitlands near Milawa in the north-east of the state), and the potential of this for Pinot Noir and Riesling – both vines which like cooler weather – is enormous. At the other extreme, areas like Mildura on the Murray River and Rutherglen – only an hour's drive from the

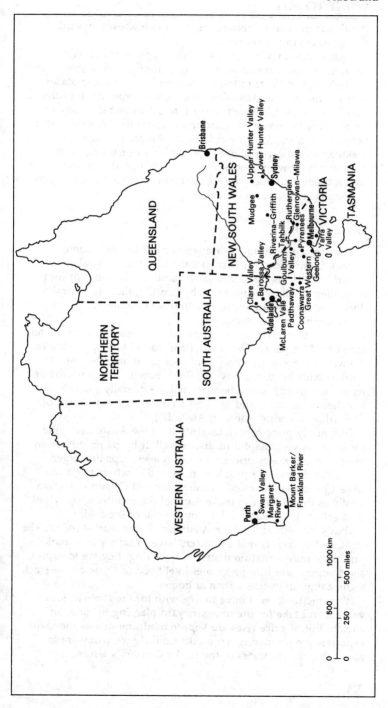

Australia

Whitlands vineyard – record some of the highest vineyard temperatures in the country.

What is true in Victoria is also true in other states. Western Australia has just the same extremes – from the cool vineyards of the Margaret River to the hot flat lands of the Swan Valley.

While the bulk of Australia's wine comes from the traditional, warmer areas, there is increasing interest among the pioneers for planting their vines higher up or nearer the Southern Ocean (with its cold winds straight from the Antarctic). They are seeking the greater subtleties and delicacy of fruit that come from wines grown in cooler climes – although it is unlikely that any of them will forget the strident almost over-the-top quality that made Australian wine so popular.

Good drinkers

Australian wine producers are well served by their home market. If anybody still harbours the idea that Australians regard wine drinking as a namby-pamby activity not fit for real men, they should be disabused by learning that an Australian's thirst is slaked by an average of 20 litres of wine every year – about double our consumption.

Much of that is cheap and cheerful and comes in boxes, often called bladder packs. The Australians don't hype up a wine in the way the Americans do – if it costs too much, they don't think it must be good, they just don't buy it. Which is why any wine store in any Australian city will be liberally stocked with top-class wine at around $5 or $6 a bottle – the equivalent of £2.50 (duty on wine is low in Australia).

This firmly price-conscious attitude of the Australian wine consumer is very helpful for us, as well. It keeps producers on their toes and keeps prices down. If it also helps the larger firms, that is less of a problem in Australia, where the three largest producers (Penfolds, Lindemans and Orlando - known locally as the PLO), also make some of the country's top wines (and set the good value prices for the rest of the trade).

That's the plus side of the Australian home market for us. The minus, of course, is that producers have to satisfy that market first. That means that no matter how willing they are to export, short supply will bring a greater likelihood of those out-of-stock signs going up overseas than at home.

It's something we'll have to live with for the three or four years it will take for the new vineyard planting to come on stream. But, if price rises are kept to a minimum – as the main exporters are promising – then it's unlikely we will want to forget the vibrant tastes of the Lucky Country's wines.

What's what in Australia

Australian wines are named after the grape variety from which they are made. If there is only a single variety on the label, the wine must contain 85 per cent of that variety. Many wines are a blend of two or more grapes, and these will be indicated on the label, with the predominant grape first.

Nearly a hundred grape varieties are planted in Australia. Most are used in branded blends for the domestic market while others are grown only in tiny quantities. Here we give the ones we come across in Britain.

WHITE GRAPES

Chardonnay This was the grape which started the fashion for Australia. Larger than life, full of fruit and the taste of new wood, wines made from the Chardonnay were almost over the top. But they worked. When softened with a year or so in bottle, the balance of ripe fruit and oak was a fine combination. It has also been the grape most hit by shortages, so expect Chardonnay-based wines to be the priciest from Australia.

Best areas: most Australian vineyard areas seem to produce good examples, but Coonawarra, Southern Vales and Clare seem best in South Australia; the Upper Hunter and Mudgee in New South Wales; Margaret River in Western Australia and almost anywhere in Victoria and Tasmania.

Gewürztraminer This is normally known simply as Traminer and tends to make rather over-blown wines which suffer from the grape's predisposition to lack acidity. However, in parts of Victoria, some good examples can be found.

Marsanne The white grape of the Rhône Valley in France is grown in the Goulburn area of Victoria, producing rather big, fat wines that lack definition unless they are given some wood ageing.

Muscadelle The grape used in what in Australia are called liqueur Tokays. Like the Muscats below, these are intensely liquorous dessert wines, often of great age. There's nothing quite like them outside Australia. The best Muscadelle wines come from Rutherglen (Victoria) and nearby Milawa.

Muscat This makes rich, sweet fortified wines, especially in Victoria. They are deliciously luscious and taste of orange marmalade. Some Dry Muscat styles are also available. Best areas: Rutherglen and Milawa/Glenrowan (Victoria).

Rhine Riesling This grape makes full, dry, medium dry and sometimes sweet wines, this last in a special Australian style which we hope will gain wider acceptance. Don't confuse Australian Rhine Rieslings with German wines in any way, although there has been a tendency to sweeten some Rhine Rieslings for the export market. Not to be confused with so-called Hunter Valley Riesling, which is in fact Semillon. Best areas: Barossa Valley, Clare and Eden Valleys (South Australia).

Sauvignon Blanc This variety works best in cooler areas of the country. Some Australian wine producers bring in wine from New Zealand to give their Sauvignon Blanc wines the herbaceous character which their own warmer climate cannot provide. Best areas: Margaret River (Western Australia), Pyrenees (Victoria), King Valley (Victoria).

Semillon The grape of Sauternes in France here makes really fine dry wines, with or without oak, and with some ageing potential. Australia has realised the Semillon's potential to produce dry wines in a way that France never has, and good examples are well worth seeking out. It's also blended with Chardonnay and occasionally Chenin Blanc. Best areas: Hunter Valley (New South Wales), Southern Vales and Barossa Valley (South Australia), but other areas make some good examples as well.

RED GRAPES

Cabernet Sauvignon The major varietal in red wines. Wood is an important element of the style, as with Chardonnay. The wines tend to develop fast – faster than they ever do in France, so that three- and four-year-old Australian Cabernets are very drinkable. Moreover, they don't necessarily fade – ten year old wines can still be very good.
   Best areas: Most areas produce good examples, but Coonawarra (South Australia), Tasmania, Margaret River (Western Australia), Geelong and Yarra Valley (Victoria), Langhorne Creek and McLaren Vale (South Australia) stand out.

Shiraz This is the other widely grown red variety, and is used to make a distinctively Australian style of wine. It has a direct relationship with the Syrah of the northern Rhône, but in Australia it makes much more of a hot country wine than it does in France. It produces rich, soft, rounded, peppery wines, often more approachable than the more tannic Cabernet Sauvignons, with which it is often successfully blended.
   Best areas: Hunter Valley (New South Wales), and Barossa Valley, Southern Vales and Coonawarra (South Australia).

Pinot Noir The hardest red vine of all to grow outside Europe. At last it seems that the Australians are getting it right, with some soft, mellow wines with good colour and a typically vegetal taste. Areas to watch are Yarra Valley and King Valley (Victoria), Upper Hunter Valley (New South Wales), Tasmania, Margaret River (Western Australia).

Cabernet Franc, Merlot and Malbec are also planted in many areas, but are rarely seen unblended.

Australian wine regions

SOUTH AUSTRALIA

The biggest wine-producing state, producing 60 per cent of the country's total. Much of this comes from the high-yielding **Riverlands** area (where South Australia, New South Wales and Victoria meet) source of most of the boxed wines.

Higher quality areas are:

Barossa Valley Originally best known for its Rhine Riesling wines, but increasingly for its Chardonnay and Cabernet Sauvignon as well as Shiraz. Home of the biggest Australian wine producers. Higher vineyards associated with Barossa are the nearby Eden Valley and Pewsey Vale.

Clare Smaller area, generally considered to be making very high quality wines. Good for Rhine Riesling, but also Cabernet Sauvignon, Malbec and Shiraz, with smaller amounts of Semillon.

Coonawarra Generally agreed to be one of the best quality producing areas in Australia. Its finest wines are red, especially Cabernet Sauvignon, but increasingly whites – Sauvignon Blanc, Chardonnay and Gewürztraminer – are being planted.

Padthaway An increasingly important area, north of Coonawarra but with some of the same soil, now providing grapes for blending. Reds are the most important wines.

Southern Vales Small wineries abound in this area just outside Adelaide. McLaren Vale and Reynella are part of Southern Vales, and the Adelaide Hills, a new vineyard area, is close by. Cabernet Sauvignon, Chardonnay, Shiraz all do well.

NEW SOUTH WALES

The original home of vines in Australia. The vineyards now consist of two areas in the Hunter River Valley, close to the coast, and two inland areas.

Hunter Valley First planted as early as 1828, this is now a small area, the furthest north (and therefore one of the hottest) of the quality wine-producing areas. The heat is tempered by summer rains and the ocean. The classic grapes are Shiraz (once called Hermitage) and Semillon, but Chardonnay is also cultivated.

Upper Hunter Valley A new area, on higher and cooler land than the Hunter Valley proper. Chardonnay is the success story here, as well as Semillon and Cabernet Sauvignon.

Mudgee A small area on the west of the Great Dividing Range, which produces high quality Chardonnay as well as Cabernet Sauvignon.

Riverina Based on the huge Murrumbidgee Irrigation Area, producing 60 per cent of the State's grapes, and making mostly soft, inexpensive wines.

VICTORIA

The vineyard area in this state was once much larger, but the phylloxera louse sniffed it out (it never even discovered South Australia). The vineyards have never fully recovered in size: growers seem to have planted where it suits them; so the areas are now scattered. Some commentators reckon that Victoria's potential for great wine-making is only just being rediscovered.

Geelong Area to the south-west of Melbourne, suited to cool-climate whites and Cabernet Sauvignon.

Goulburn Dominated by three estates, Ch Tahbilk, Mitchelton and Tisdall. Cabernet Sauvignon and Marsanne are the specialities.

Milawa/Glenrowan An amorphous area which includes the cool-climate King Valley vineyards, plus the hotter Ovens River Valley.

Pyrenees A cooler area, north of Ballarat, which produces some good Cabernet Sauvignon.

Rutherglen Best known for its Liqueur Muscats and Liqueur Tokays (Muscadelles), sweet dessert wines. Also some fine Tawny Port-style wines, made from the Shiraz, Grenache and (to a lesser but increasing extent Portuguese grape varieties. See the section on Fortified wines (page 664).

Yarra Virtually every grape variety – including the notoriously difficult Pinot Noir – seems to work in this small area just outside Melbourne. High prices are charged for top wines from the boutique wineries here.

WESTERN AUSTRALIA

The newest wine state, and one of the most interesting. The best vineyards are clustered in the cool south-western corner of the State, where the Southern Ocean meets the Indian.

Margaret River Cool-climate area which produces wines that are full of flavour. Estates include the Leeuwin Estates, backed by Californian Robert Mondavi. Most grapes seem to work here.

Mount Barker/Frankland River Whites seem to work best here, especially Rieslings.

Swan River The original vineyard area of Western Australia, just outside Perth. Its hot summers make it more suitable for fortified and dessert wines than table wines, and enable it to be the first wine-producing region to send en primeur wines.

TASMANIA

The southernmost Australian state reproduces northern European growing conditions. White wines and cool-climate reds like Pinot Noir work best here, although in good years, Cabernet Sauvignon can be very fine too.

Australian vintages – they do matter

1989 Heatwaves in South Australia reduced yields and cut quality, while in Victoria heavy rain affected the quality of the white wines. In New South Wales quality of both white and red is average.

1988 A good quality vintage in many regions, but quantities were down, especially in South Australia which was badly hit by frost and hail.

1987 A mixed bag of a vintage, with low yields and poor weather affecting South Australia and Victoria. Western Australia and New South Wales were better off.

1986 Average crop but exceptional quality. Whites have benefited from cooler weather.

1985 Another cool year, giving flavoursome wines with high natural acidity.

1984 A cloudy period during the harvest has made high-class whites and elegant reds.

1983 A much warmer year producing some great red wines and rather fuller whites.

1982 Some of the best red wines for many years, with quality good to very good.

Please write to tell us about any ideas for features you would like to see in next year's edition or in *Which? Wine Monthly*.

Who's who in Australia

Tim Adams (Clare, South Australia) Small operation with extremely careful wine-making. Wines: Rhine Riesling, Cabernet Franc, Shiraz, Tawny.
Bibendum; Alex Findlater; Lay & Wheeler; Tanners

All Saints (Rutherglen, Victoria) Old family wine company making some interesting Liqueur Muscats.
Thomas Baty; D Byrne & Co; Claridge Fine Wines; George Dutton & Son; Hicks & Don; Nobody Inn; Willoughbys; Wine Emporium

Allandale (Hunter Valley, New South Wales) Makes single vineyard wines from grapes bought in from individual farmers. Wines: Semillon, Chardonnay, Shiraz, Cabernet Sauvignon.
Majestic

Balgownie (Bendigo, Victoria) Well-balanced wines from one of the coolest areas of Victoria. Wines: Chardonnay, Cabernet Sauvignon, Pinot Noir.
D Byrne & Co; Pavilion Wine Co; Raeburn Fine Wines & Foods; La Vigneronne

Bannockburn (Geelong, Victoria) Good reds, including a Pinot Noir, from cool southern vineyards. Wines: Chardonnay, Pinot Noir, Shiraz, Cabernet Sauvignon.
Les Amis du Vin; D Byrne & Co; Raeburn Fine Wines & Foods; Winecellars

Jim Barry (Clare, South Australia) One of the best producers of Rhine Riesling. Wines: Chardonnay, Cabernet Sauvignon, Rhine Riesling.
Cumbrian Cellar; Tanners

Beresford (McLaren Vales, South Australia). Small winery making a good Sauvignon Blanc. Wines: Sauvignon Blanc, Chardonnay.
D Byrne & Co; London Wine

Berri Estates/Renmano (Riverland, South Australia). Major co-operative selling wine in boxes and finer wine in bottle, some very good value. Wines: Chardonnay, Fumé Blanc, Rhine Riesling, Traminer/Riesling, Cabernet Sauvignon, Merlot, Cabernet/Shiraz.
Widely available

De Bortoli (Bilbul, New South Wales). Specialises in sweet dessert whites from botrytised grapes. Other wines are more run-of-the-mill. Wines: Traminer, Riesling, Fumé Blanc, Chardonnay, Cabernet Sauvignon, Botrytised Semillon, Merlot.

Barnes Wine Shop; D Byrne & Co; Peter Green; J E Hogg; Master Cellar Wine Warehouse; Nobody Inn; La Vigneronne

Bowen Estate (Coonawarra, South Australia). Premium estate making excellent Cabernet Sauvignon. Wines: Cabernet Sauvignon, Shiraz.
Adnams; Alex Findlater

Brown Brothers (Milawa, Victoria) High quality family winery, with a full range of whites and reds and excellent dry Muscat. Wines: Dry Muscat, Late Picked Muscat, Estate Chardonnay, Estate Shiraz, Cabernet Sauvignon (from cool vineyards at Koombahla).
Widely available

Campbells of Rutherglen (Rutherglen, Victoria) One of the oldest Rutherglen producers. Wines: Liqueur Muscat, Old Rutherglen Liqueur Muscat.
Asda (some stores); D Byrne & Co; Alex Findlater; Fortnum & Mason; Majestic; La Réserve; Upper Crust

W H Chambers (Rutherglen, Victoria) One of the top two Rutherglen Muscat producers. Wines: Liqueur Muscat, Special Liqueur Muscat, Old Liqueur Muscat.
Adnams; Averys; Barnes Wine Shop; Claridge Fine Wines; George Dutton; Hicks & Don; Raeburn Fine Wines & Foods; Selfridges; Tanners; Whitesides of Clitheroe; Yorkshire Fine Wines

Conti-Forest Hill (Mount Barker, Western Australia) First vineyard in this cool-climate area. Best known for Rhine Riesling and Cabernet Sauvignon. Wines: Rhine Riesling, Cabernet Sauvignon, Traminer, Chardonnay.
Alex Findlater

Coriole (McLaren Vale, South Australia) Australian wines, with good Chenin Blanc. Wines: Chenin Blanc, Sangiovese, Cabernet Sauvignon.
Bibendum; Tanners

Delatite (Mansfield, Victoria) Small family winery producing a highly rated range of wines. Wines: Rhine Riesling, Pinot Noir, Cabernet Sauvignon/Merlot.
Anthony Byrne Fine Wines; Michael Gooding, 31 Church Gate Street, Bury St Edmunds, Suffolk; Nectar Wines, 8 Sussex Street, Cambridge

Evans & Tate (Swan Valley, Western Australia) High reputation for good well-made reds. Wines: Semillon, Gnangara Shiraz, Redbrook Cabernet Sauvignon, Redbrook Hermitage.
Alex Findlater; Lay & Wheeler

Jeffrey Grosset (Clare, South Australia) Small, high quality boutique winery. Wines: Chardonnay, Rhine Riesling, Cabernet Sauvignon.
Alex Findlater; Lay & Wheeler

Hardy's (based in Adelaide, South Australia) Large company making big wines and a range of lighter, more European-style wines. Wines: Cabernet Sauvignon, Chenin Blanc, Fumé Blanc, Chardonnay, Rhine Riesling, Keppoch Cabernet Sauvignon, Keppoch Cabernet/Shiraz, McLaren Vale Shiraz, Ch Reynella Cabernet Sauvignon and Chardonnay.
H Allen Smith; D Byrne & Co; Alex Findlater; G M Vintners; S H Jones; Majestic; Queens Club Wines; Wizard Wine Warehouses

Henschke (Adelaide Hills, South Australia) Traditional rich wines, many made from old vines. Wines: Mount Edelstone Shiraz Cabernet, Hill of Grace Shiraz, Cabernet Sauvignon, Riesling, Semillon.
Lay & Wheeler

Hill Smith Estate (Barossa Valley, South Australia) Family firm making premium varietal wines largely from their own vineyards. Wines: Old Triangle Vineyard Rhine Riesling, Estate Semillon, Estate Chardonnay, Old Triangle Shiraz/Malbec, Estate Shiraz, Estate Cabernet Sauvignon, Botrytised Semillon, own Barossa Valley Estates brand and Yalumba (see below). Plain Hill Smith wines (without the estate appellation) are less expensive.
David Baillie Vintners; D Byrne & Co; Rodney Densem Wines; Drunken Mouse; Alex Findlater; Grape Ideas; Peter Green; Great Northern Wine Company; Harrods; Michael Menzel; Upper Crust

Houghton (Swan River, Western Australia) One of the first commercial vineyards of Western Australia, now part of Hardy's. Wines: Chardonnay, Cabernet Sauvignon, Blue Stripe Supreme (blend of Chenin Blanc and Verdelho), Rhine Riesling, Frankland River Cabernet Sauvignon.
H Allen Smith; Alex Findlater; Waitrose

Hungerford Hill Wines (Lower Hunter Valley, New South Wales) Producer owning vineyards in the Hunter and Coonawarra (and sometimes blending the grapes). Results are good. Wines: Semillon/Sauvignon Blanc, Chardonnay. Rhine Riesling, Pinot Noir, Cabernet/Merlot.
Corney & Barrow

Idyll Vineyard (Geelong, Victoria) Cool-climate vineyards making elegant wines. Wines: Gewürztraminer, Shiraz Rosé, Cabernet/Shiraz.
Mayor Sworder & Co

Tim Knappstein (Clare Valley, South Australia) The first person to make Sauvignon Fumé Blanc wines in Australia. Wines: Chardonnay, Sauvignon, Cabernet Sauvignon, Cabernet/Merlot. *Averys; D Byrne & Co*

Lake's Folly (Hunter Valley, New South Wales) Only two wines are made here, but they are among the best. Max Lake, who runs the vineyard, is one of the great gurus of Australian wine. Wines: Chardonnay, Cabernet Sauvignon. *D Byrne & Co; Alex Findlater; Lay & Wheeler; Raeburn Fine Wines & Foods*

Leeuwin Estate (Margaret River, Western Australia) Highly priced wines established with help from Mondavi of California. Wines: Cabernet Sauvignon, Chardonnay, Pinot Noir. *D Byrne & Co; Alex Findlater; Fortnum & Mason; Lay & Wheeler; La Vigneronne*

Lindemans (Hunter Valley, New South Wales) A large firm, one of the top three in Australia, with vineyards in most regions. Their recently introduced estate wines (from Coonawarra) are aimed at the top. Wines: Padthaway Chardonnay, St George Cabernet Sauvignon, Rhine Riesling. Estate wines: St George Cabernet Sauvignon, Limestone Ridge Cabernet Sauvignon/ Shiraz, Pyrus (a blend of Cabernet Sauvignon, Cabernet Franc, Malbec and Merlot). *Widely available*

McWilliams (Hunter Valley, New South Wales) Estate wines are a welcome addition to a rather dull range of old-style wines. Wines: Hanwood Estate Chardonnay, Fumé Blanc, Rhine Riesling, Cabernet Sauvignon, Shiraz, Beelbangera Semillon, Traminer Riesling, Yenda Cabernet Sauvignon, Hermitage, Pinot Noir, Mount Pleasant Estate. *Barnes Wine Shop; Berry Bros & Rudd; Davisons; Peter Dominic; Alex Findlater; Peter Green; Oddbins; Ubiquitous Chip*

Geoff Merrill (McLaren Vale, South Australia) The winemaker at Hardy's (see above) also makes two very fine wines from his own Mount Hurtle vineyards. Wines: Cabernet Sauvignon, Semillon. *Ad Hoc Wine Warehouse; H Allen Smith; D Byrne & Co; Hungerford Wine Company; La Reserva Wines; Upper Crust*

Mildara (Coonawarra, South Australia and Mildara, Victoria) The best wines, improving all the time, come from Coonawarra vineyards rather than the firm's original Mildura vineyards. Wines: Coonawarra Chardonnay, Sauvignon, Cabernet

Sauvignon, Fumé Blanc, Traminer Riesling, Shiraz, Cabernet/
Merlot, Church Hill Chardonnay, sparkling wines.
*Cumbrian Cellar; Alex Findlater; Fortnum & Mason; Peter Green;
Victoria Wine Cellar*

Mitchell (Clare Valley, South Australia) Fine producer of Rhine
Riesling. Wines: Watervale Rhine Riesling, Shiraz.
D Byrne & Co; Alex Findlater; Lay & Wheeler

Mitchelton (Goulburn, Victoria) Commercial vineyard making
rather straightforward unexciting wines. Wines: Mitchelton
Rhine Riesling, Marsanne (white), Cabernet Sauvignon.
*D Byrne & Co; Alex Findlater; Hedley Wright; Richmond Wine
Warehouse; J Sainsbury; Tesco; Waitrose*

Montrose (Mudgee, New South Wales) Award-winning wines,
including a top Chardonnay. Wines: Chardonnay, Show Reserve
Chardonnay, Fumé Blanc, Pinot Noir, Cabernet Sauvignon,
Special Reserve Shiraz.
*D Byrne & Co; Eldridge Pope; Alex Findlater; Fortnum & Mason;
Yorkshire Fine Wines*

Moorilla Estate (Tasmania) Fine claret-style wines from cool
climate vineyards. Wines: Cabernet Sauvignon.
D Byrne & Co

Morris (Rutherglen, Victoria) Morris of Rutherglen makes some
of the top Liqueur Muscats in an area renowned for that style.
Wines: Liqueur Muscat, Liqueur Tokay, Durif (red table wine).
Part of Orlando (see below).
*D Byrne & Co; Alex Findlater; Hadleigh Wine Cellars; Oddbins;
Winecellars*

Moss Wood Estate (Margaret River, Western Australia) Its high
quality Cabernet Sauvignon gave the winery its reputation.
Wines: Semillon, Chardonnay, Pinot Noir, Cabernet Sauvignon.
*Adnams; Barnes Wine Shop; D Byrne & Co; Restaurant Croque-en-
Bouche; Drunken Mouse; Alex Findlater; Fortnum & Mason; Gerard
Harris; Great Northern Wine Company; Haynes Hanson & Clark;
Master Cellar Wine Warehouse; Mitchells Wine Bin; Morris &
Verdin; Seckford Wines; Yorkshire Fine Wines*

Orlando (Barossa Valley, South Australia) Commercial wines
made on a large scale but with good quality, plus some estate
wines which are up with the best. Wines: Jacob's Creek brand,
RF brand, Rhine Riesling, Chardonnay, Shiraz/Cabernet, St
Hilary Chardonnay, St Hugo Cabernet Sauvignon.
*David Baillie Vintners; D Byrne & Co; Cumbrian Cellars; Davisons;
Alex Findlater; Hadleigh Wine Cellars; Master Cellar Wine
Warehouse; Oddbins; Safeway; J Sainsbury; Tanners; Tesco*

Peel Estate (Mandurah, Western Australia) Single estate wines from south of Perth. Wines: Shiraz, Chenin Blanc, Cabernet Sauvignon.
Alex Findlater

Penfolds (Barossa, Coonawarra, Clare, Morgan in South Australia) Largest wine producer in Australia. Very high quality in both whites and reds. Wines: Chardonnay, Traminer Riesling, Grange Hermitage, St Henri Cabernet/Shiraz, Dalwood Shiraz/Cabernet, Kalimna Bin, selected Bin wines, Koonunga Hill, Magill Estate, Seaview, Kaiserstuhl, Grandfather Tawny.
Adnams; Berry Bros & Rudd; D Byrne & Co; Chaplin & Son; Davisons; Alex Findlater; Fortnum & Mason; J E Hogg; Majestic; Oddbins; La Vigneronne; Yorkshire Fine Wines

Petaluma (Adelaide Hills, South Australia) Some of the country's most prestigious wines, made by Brian Croser, a driving force in Australian wines. Wines: Rhine Riesling, Chardonnay, Coonawarra Cabernet Sauvignon.
Les Amis du Vin; D Byrne & Co; Alex Findlater; Fortnum & Mason; J E Hogg; Majestic; Ostlers; La Vigneronne

Peterson (Hunter Valley, New South Wales) Small estate making very fine Chardonnay. Wines: Chardonnay, Semillon, Shiraz.
D Byrne & Co; Drunken Mouse; Hungerford Wine Company; Lay & Wheeler; Tanners

Pipers Brook (Tasmania) Not only fine wines, but beautiful labels as well. Wines; Chardonnay, Pinot Noir.
D Byrne & Co; Alex Findlater

Rosemount Estate (Hunter Valley, New South Wales) The firm that was in on the beginning of the current enthusiasm for Australia. More recently, the standard Diamond Label range has slipped and now seems rather thin, as do the Rosemount Estate wines, but look for the better Show Reserve and Roxburgh ranges. Wines: Traminer, Sauvignon Blanc, Fumé Blanc, Chardonnay, Shiraz, Cabernet/Malbec, Cabernet Sauvignon, Show Reserve Chardonnay, Gewürztraminer, Cabernet Sauvignon, sparkling wine.
Adnams; Les Amis du Vin; D Byrne & Co; Alex Findlater; Fortnum & Mason; J E Hogg; Majestic; La Vigneronne

Rothbury Estate (Hunter Valley, New South Wales) Top quality wines made by Len Evans, one of the heroes of Australian wine-making. Wines: Chardonnay, Shiraz, Pinot Noir, Semillon.
H Allen Smith; Les Amis du Vin; Barnes Wine Shop; D Byrne & Co; Alex Findlater; Fortnum & Mason; J E Hogg; Lay & Wheeler; La Réserve; La Vigneronne

Rouge Homme (Coonawarra, South Australia) Part of Lindemans (see above) but wines are sold under their own name, which is a play on words (the founders were called Redman). Wines: Chardonnay, Shiraz/Cabernet, Cabernet Sauvignon.
Asda; Averys; Barnes Wine Shop; Bibendum; G E Bromley; D Byrne & Co; Davisons; Drunken Mouse; Restaurant Croque-en-Bouche; Peter Green; Hampden Wine Company; Harrods; Lay & Wheeler; Stapylton Fletcher; Upper Crust; La Vigneronne

Saltram (Barossa Valley, South Australia) Large producer of good quality wines. Part of Seagrams. Wines: Mamre Brook Chardonnay, Metala Shiraz.
Oddbins

Seppelt (Barossa Valley, South Australia) Large-scale commercial producer. Their fortified wines are the best. Wines: Rhine Riesling, Chardonnay, Shiraz, Cabernet Sauvignon. Mount Rufus Finest Tawny, Rutherglen Liqueur Muscat.
D Byrne & Co; George Dutton; Alex Findlater; Gerard Harris; Oddbins; Tanners; Thresher; Victoria Wine Company; Willoughbys

Stanley (Clare, South Australia) The Leasingham range is the best of this firm's wines. Wines: Leasingham Rhine Riesling, Bin 56 Cabernet/Malbec, Cabernet Sauvignon, Coonawarra Shiraz/Cabernet.
D Byrne & Co; Grape Ideas; Richard Granger; J E Hogg; David Scatchard; Vintage House

Stanton and Killeen (Rutherglen, Victoria) Another of the high quality lighter Muscat producers of Rutherglen.
Averys; D Byrne & Co; Claridge Fine Wines; Davys of London; George Dutton; Alex Findlater; Fortnum & Mason; Majestic; Raeburn Fine Wines & Foods; La Vigneronne; Willoughbys

Château Tahbilk (Goulburn, Victoria) Very traditional producer, making stupendous, long-lived wines. Wines: Marsanne, Cabernet Sauvignon, Shiraz.
David Alexander; D Byrne & Co; Chiswick Cellars; S H Jones; The Wine Society

Taltarni (Moonambel, Victoria) Cool-climate vineyard, mainly planted with red varieties. Wines: Cabernet Sauvignon, Shiraz.
David Alexander; David Baillie Vintners; Alex Findlater; D Byrne & Co; Nobody Inn; Oddbins; Ubiquitous Chip; Upper Crust

Tisdall (Goulburn Valley, Victoria) Pricy but good Chardonnay is the star from this winery. Wines: Traminer Riesling, Mount Helen Chardonnay, Pinot Noir, Cabernet Sauvignon.
G E Bromley; Claridge Fine Wines; Alex Findlater; Hicks & Don;

Master Cellar Wine Warehouse; Mitchells of Lancaster; Arthur Rackhams; Wine Schoppen

Tollana (Barossa Valley, South Australia) Sound, commercial wines but nothing exciting. Part of Penfolds (see above). Wines: Langhorne Creek Chenin Blanc, Barossa Valley Shiraz.
D Byrne & Co; Oddbins

Tyrrells (Hunter Valley, New South Wales) Interesting and traditional blends. Reds are better than whites. Good fortifieds as too. Wines: Long Flat White, Vat 1 Semillon, Vat 47 Chardonnay, Long Flat Red, Pinot Noir, Shiraz.
Adnams; H Allen Smith; Berkmann Wine Cellars; D Byrne & Co; Alex Findlater; S H Jones; Lay & Wheeler; J Sainsbury; Tanners; Wizard Wine Warehouses; La Vigneronne

Vasse Felix (Margaret River, Western Australia) Small winery producing very fine complex wines. Wines: Riesling, Cabernet Sauvignon, Hermitage.
Alex Findlater; Lay & Wheeler; La Vigneronne

Wirra Wirra (McLaren Vale, South Australia) Top quality, small-scale winery. Wines: Rhine Riesling, Sauvignon Blanc, Pinot Noir, Church Block Cabernet/Shiraz/Merlot.
Alex Findlater; The Wine Society

Wolf Blass (Barossa Valley, South Australia) One of the showmen of Australian wine, Wolf Blass specialises in top quality blended wines, but owns few vineyards. Wines: Classic Dry White, Cabernet/Shiraz, Yellow Label Cabernet Sauvignon, President's Selection Cabernet Sauvignon.
Averys; Augustus Barnett; D Byrne & Co; Davisons; Alex Findlater; Peter Green; Oddbins; Reid Wines; Raeburn Fine Wines & Foods

Woodstock (McLaren Vale, South Australia) Smallish family winery run by one of Australia's leading winemakers, Scott Collett. Wines: Cabernet Sauvignon, Sauvignon Blanc, Chardonnay.
Lay & Wheeler

Wyndham Estate (Hunter Valley, New South Wales) The oldest continuously operating winery in Australia, started in 1828. Their wines are good, middle-of-the-road quality, with the white dry Verdelho a speciality. Wines: Oak Cask Chardonnay, Bin TR2 Gewürztraminer Riesling, Bin 444 Cabernet Sauvignon, Bin 555 Shiraz, Verdelho, Pinot Noir.
Alex Findlater; Grape Ideas; Majestic; Morrisons; J Sainsbury; David Scatchard; Whitesides of Clitheroe

Wynns (Coonawarra, South Australia) Large firm making sound reds and excellent whites. Part of Penfolds (see above). Wines: Coonawarra Chardonnay, Rhine Riesling, Shiraz, Cabernet Sauvignon, Ovens Valley Shiraz.
Berry Bros & Rudd; D Byrne & Co; Alex Findlater; Majestic; J Sainsbury; Tanners; Victoria Wine Company; Wizard Wine Warehouses

Château Xanadu (Margaret River, Western Australia) Carefully made wines, the whites the best. Wines: Semillon, Chardonnay.
Lay & Wheeler

Yalumba (Barossa Valley, South Australia) Owned by the Hill Smith family, this winery makes a wide range of good quality wines. Wines: Semillon, Sauvignon Blanc, Signature Series Chardonnay and Cabernet Shiraz, Galway Pipe Tawny.
Adnams; Les Amis du Vin; Berry Bros & Rudd; D Byrne & Co; Peter Dominic; Fortnum & Mason; Tesco; Yorkshire Fine Wines

Yarra Burn (Yarra Valley, South Australia) Small boutique winery in a beautiful setting at the head of the Yarra Valley. Wines: Cabernet, Pinot Noir, Chardonnay.
Adnams; Barnes Wine Shop; D Byrne & Co; Alex Findlater; Fortnum & Mason; Tanners

Yarra Yering (Yarra Valley, Victoria) Leading winery in a small, exciting area. Wines: Pinot Noir, Chardonnay, Dry Red No 1, Dry Red No 2.
Adnams; Barnes Wine Shop; D Byrne & Co; Alex Findlater; Fortnum & Mason; Tanners

Best buys from Australia

See also Fortified wines on page 664 and Sparkling wines on page 634.

WHITE

Yalumba Semillon 1987, Barossa Valley (*Addison Avenue Wine Shop*)
Tyrrells Long Flat White 1987, Hunter Valley (*Bentalls of Kingston*)
Semillon 1988, Willunga Hill (*Findlater Mackie Todd*)
Jacob's Creek Dry White, Orlando (*widely available*)
Hardys Premium Classic White, South Australia (*H Allen Smith*)
Pewsey Vale Rhine Riesling 1985, Barossa Valley (*Les Amis du Vin*)
Hollydene Chardonnay 1987, South Australia (*Majestic*)
Safeway Australian Padthaway Rhine Riesling (*Safeway*)
Brown Brothers Chenin Blanc 1986, Victoria (*Whiteside's*)

RED

Ch Tahbilk Shiraz 1985, Victoria (*David Alexander; Gerard Harris; S H Jones*)

St Michael Shiraz Cabernet, Penfolds (*Marks & Spencer*)

Rouge Homme Shiraz Cabernet 1984, Coonawarra (*Averys of Bristol*)

Jacob's Creek Dry Red, Orlando (*widely available*)

Bin 444 1985 Wyndham Estate, Hunter Valley (*Abbey Cellars; Morrisons*)

Orlando RF Cabernet Sauvignon 1986, Barossa Valley (*Drunken Mouse*)

Taltarni Shiraz 1982, Pyrenees, Victoria (*Alex Findlater; Reid Wines*)

Penfolds Dalwood Shiraz/Cabernet 1984, Barossa Valley (*Chaplin & Sons; J E Hogg; Oddbins*)

Water Wheel Shiraz Bin 50 1985, South Australia (*Seckford Wines*)

Seaview Cabernet/Shiraz, South Australia (*Oddbins*)

Peatlings Australian Red (*Thos Peatling*)

Penfolds Kalimna Bin 28 Shiraz 1986, Barossa Valley (*Thresher*)

Cabernet Malbec 1987, Hill Smith (*Gare du Vin*)

Specialist stockists

Adnams; David Alexander; Les Amis du Vin; Averys of Bristol; B H Wines; Bibendum; Bin Ends; D Byrne & Co; City Wines; Claridge Fine Wines; Drunken Mouse; Alex Findlater; Great Northern Wine Company; Haughton Fine Wines; Nobody Inn; Oddbins; Raeburn Fine Wines and Foods; La Reserva Wines; Seckford Wines; Selfridges; Tanners Wines; Upper Crust; La Vigneronne; Whiteside's of Clitheroe; Wine House

Austria

If coverage in the wine press is anything to go by, the tide could well be turning for Austria. From a virtual silence a couple of years ago, there has been a flurry of articles from journalists who have visited the vineyards and tasted what Austrian wine is about now.

There has certainly been a change of emphasis in the way Austrian producers – and their British importers – would like us to perceive their wines. Gone are the days when they were trying to compete with Germany for the cheap and cheerful market. Germany won that contest hands down – and the Austrians can now see what harm it has done to the German quality image.

They are currently very busy pointing out the differences between their wines and those of Germany. In many ways, even the use of some of the same grapes simply shows how differently an Austrian producer will treat them. The difference is as great – and in many ways similar to – the difference between Alsace and Germany (and we are now, at last, beginning to appreciate that one).

The main difference between the two countries is that Austrian wines are dry, and not with the thin dryness that some German Trocken wines have, but with a full, ripe dryness that comes from a much warmer climate and a longer growing season. And although some of the grapes used are the same – Rhine Riesling, for example, and Gewürztraminer – the main Austrian grape, the Grüner Veltliner, is unique to that country. And Austria, unlike Germany, has the ability to produce regular quantities of lusciously sweet, botrytis-affected wines, as a counterbalance to the essentially dry character of most of her white wines. Austrian red wines, too, although not as familiar here as her whites, are certainly properly full-bodied (after all, Hungary, whose hearty reds we know well, is only an hour's drive from Vienna).

The 1988 harvest in Austria may also help to mark a change in Austria's attitude to exporting. Ever since the diethylene glycol wine scandal, when Austria's exports virtually dried up, a succession of small harvests has hampered even the most dedicated exporter to show off his wares to the rest of the world. There was only just enough to go round Austria, prices were high, the Austrian Schilling remained resolutely one of the strongest currencies in Europe and the bureaucrats of Vienna, anxious to avoid another wine scandal, made it very difficult (and expensive) to get the right permissions to export wine.

1988 has changed the supply situation, at least. While recent harvests have been good on quality, but very low on quantity, 1988 is tops on both. For the first time since the 1984 harvest, frost was not a problem in the spring of 1988, and the result has been a good average harvest of 3.2 million hectolitres (to put that in perspective, only a third of the average harvest in Germany – Austria should never be considered a volume producer).

The taste of Austria

Austria is a white wine country. About 80 per cent of her wines are white, and the reds, while refreshingly light and fruity, are quite expensive for what they are. Most of the whites are dry, apart from the luscious stickies from the Burgenland. But because the best grape varieties are the very floral, fruit-flavoured ones such as Rhine Riesling and Grüner Veltliner, they tend to have much more attractive perfumed fruit flavours than do French dry white wines. There are also wines based on the Pinot Blanc (or Weissburgunder), but these are less exciting.

To get the true flavour of Austria, go for the Grüner Veltliner. It has quite high acidity and a slightly peppery taste, but is crisply refreshing. It's not a wine style for ageing: look now for 1985, 1986 wines or younger.

The other taste of Austria is its sweet wines. Despite price rises, any of the sweet dessert wines from the Burgenland are still bargains compared to their German equivalents. They are rather more obviously sweet than the German wines, and lack some of that stunning acidity which balances the cloyingness of the sweetness, but at maybe a third of the price it's difficult to complain.

Some of the reds, soft and not quite dry, with a vanilla touch, are light and easy to drink, fuller than Germany's pale efforts, but in the same style. Blauer Portugieser and Blaufrankisch (similar to Gamay) are the popular grape varieties here. Reds up to two or three years old are good now, but tend to dry out if left for much longer.

Austrian grapes

Most Austrian wines now carry the name of the grape variety on their label. The latest fashion is to name the grapes in French, so we have included French equivalents which the Austrian producers may use.

WHITE GRAPES

Gewürztraminer Typically spicy grape variety, used in Austria also to make sweet wines.

Grüner Veltliner Austria's own white grape variety, producing slightly spicy dry wines, with a hint of steeliness. Best drunk young, except for some better Prädikat wines. Definitely no French equivalent for this.

Muscat Sylvaner (Sauvignon Blanc) Makes steely dry wines, but with rather more aroma than you might find on the Loire.

Muskat Ottonel An aromatic grape variety, producing slightly honeyed wines. Used in many sweet wines.

Rheinriesling The familiar German grape variety, here making dry white wines, especially in the Wachau.

Ruländer (Pinot Gris) Ripe, full wines that tend to lack acidity are made from this grape in the Burgenland region.

Spätrot-Rotgipfler Blend of two grape varieties from which much Gumpoldskirchener wine is made.

Weissburgunder (Chardonnay) The Pinot Blanc of Alsace and the Pinot Bianco of Italy. It makes fresh, dry white wines.

Welschriesling Also known as the Italian or Laski or Olasz Riesling (depending on which part of central or eastern Europe you're in). Its acidity in Austria makes it a good base for sparkling wines. Also used for some sweet wines in Burgenland.

RED GRAPES

There is a growing interest in red wines among Austrian producers. Cabernet Sauvignon, Cabernet Franc and Merlot have all been spotted in the vineyards even if they are not used commercially.

Blauer Portugieser Popular grape variety making wines for early drinking.

Blaufrankisch Similar to the Gamay but not related.

St Laurent Produces deep, plum-coloured wines with a distinctive flavour.

Spätburgunder (Pinot Noir) Makes light, slightly vegetal red wines for early drinking.

What's what in Austria

Following the introduction of new wine laws, Austria is now divided into four main wine regions, (Weinbauregionen) picked out in bold type, with their sub-divisions (Weinbaugebieten) in brackets. They are: **Niederösterreich** (Wachau; Kamptal-Donauland; Donauland-Carnutum; Thermenregion); **Burgenland** (Neusiedlersee; Neusiedlersee-Hugelland; Mittelburgenland; Sudburgenland). **Steiermark** (Weststeiermark; Sud-Oststeiermark; Sudsteiermark); and **Wien** (Vienna) which has no sub-divisions. The use of these names on a wine label indicates that the wine in the bottle is all from that area.

Other names that help us to locate an Austrian wine's origins, or give a clue to its taste, are:

Apetlon Village on the eastern shore of the Neusiedlersee, near the Austrian border. Famous for sweet wines.

Donnerskirchen Town in Burgenland famous for its Trockenbeerenauslese wines.

Durnstein Town on the Wachau (see below), home of the Wachau co-operative and the castle in which Richard Lionheart was imprisoned.

Falkenstein Village of Lower Austria, north-west of Vienna, producing easy-drinking wines from the Grüner Veltliner grape.

Gumpoldskirchen Village south of Vienna and source of modern-style, fresh white wines (especially those made at the local co-operative).

Heurigen Jug wines drawn from the barrel, associated especially with the suburbs of Vienna, where they are sold in bars also called Heurigen.

Klosterneuberg Government testing station, viticultural school and wine producer all share this green domed abbey complex just outside Vienna. The wines are straightforward, the red being very acceptable.

Krems/Langenlois Quality districts just east of the Wachau.

Rust Lakeside village in Burgenland famous for its sweet white wines. The surrounding area is called Rust-Neusiedlersee.

Voslau Red wine district just south of Gumpoldskirchen.

Wachau Top quality dry and medium dry white wine area based on vineyards lining the Danube gorge west of Vienna. Some wines are made from the Rheinriesling and some have keeping qualities rare for Austrian wines.

The Austrian wine law

The basis for the Austrian wine law is similar to Germany's and is based upon the degree of ripeness of the grapes as much as the geographical origin. All the categories are the same as in Germany (Kabinett through to Trockenbeerenauslese) but are based on different (usually higher) levels of natural sugar in the grape – because Austria is further south, the grapes have a chance to get riper than in Germany.

There is only one extra category of which examples are hardly ever seen in this country. This is Ausbruch, midway in sweetness between Beerenauslese and Trockenbeerenauslese.

Who's who in Austria

H Augustin Good quality wines, many based on the Grüner Veltliner grape.
H Augustin, 271/273 King Street, London, W6

Sepp Hold Burgenland producer of sweet wines.
H Augustin, 271/273 King Street, London, W6; Premier Wines (Ayr); A L Vose

Johann Kattus Lower Austria producer of some sparkling wines.
Fernley Vintners, 7 Fernley Road, London, SW12; for further information contact Caxton Tower, 239 Munster Road, London, SW6

Klosterneuberg A range of sound wines, including the branded Klosterdawn and Klostergarten.
Selected Co-op branches; for further information contact Kloster International (0280-822077)

Metternich Weinguter Princely family firm in Lower Austria who make very drinkable Grüner Veltliner.
For further information contact Direct Wines (0734-481711)

Lenz Moser The top quality producer of Austria. Still producing branded Blue Danube and Schluck as well as some fine estate wines.
Asda; Peter Dominic; Victoria Wine Company

Fritz Salomon Small firm near Krems, producing some of the best and most long-lasting dry whites.
Fernley Vintners, 7 Fernley Road, London, SW12; for further information contact Caxton Tower, 239 Munster Road, London, SW6

Schloss Gobelsburg Monastery-owned vineyard in Lower Austria (Niederösterreich), making a range of high quality

wines from Grüner Veltliner, Rheinriesling, Müller-Thurgau, Grüner Sylvaner, and red Blauburgunder.
Gallery 34, 34 Swadford Street, Skipton, N Yorks; Parkmill, Brougham Street, Skipton, N Yorks; for further information contact Caxton Tower, 239 Munster Road, London, SW6

Alexander Unger
Neville Cox Wines, 44 Hunts Hill, Glemsford, Suffolk

Winzergenossenschaft (Means co-operative.) The best are at Wachau and Krems.
Neville Cox Wines, 44 Hunts Hill, Glemsford, Suffolk; Morrisons; A L Vose

Best buys from Austria

WHITE

Kremser Rosengarten 1983, Winzer Krems (*A L Vose*)
St Lorenzi Grüner Veltliner, Co-op of Wachau (*Alba Wine Society*)

RED

Roter Husar, Sepp Hold 1987 (*Premier Wines*)

Specialist stockists
Alba Wine Society; Premier Wines; A L Vose

Brazil

There are 64,000 hectares of vines in Brazil – that's 100 square miles – which makes this country the third-largest producer in South America, after Argentina and Chile.

Moreover, Brazil's wine industry has a history, its oldest operational winery having been established in 1908. That winery is around São Paulo, Brazil's largest city, and most of the vineyards are south of that, down towards the Uruguayan border, where it's a little cooler, and the sea breezes keep temperatures down.

The newest vineyard plantation – at Palomas in Rio Grande do Sul province – is the source of the only wine we see in this country. They are making varietal wines: Pinot Noir, Cabernet Sauvignon, Chardonnay, Merlot and Chenin Blanc. They're probably not going to set the wine world on fire – but they should make an interesting talking point.

Best buys from Brazil

Palomas Cabernet Sauvignon
Palomas Chardonnay
(both available from George Dutton & Son; A L Vose; Willoughbys)

Bulgaria

Steaming ahead

The Bulgarian success story continues unabated. They are now the fourth largest exporters of wine in the world (it helps that they hardly drink any at home, preferring spirits). Their Cabernet Sauvignon is the largest-selling red wine in Britain. Their Chardonnay is steaming ahead in the white wine stakes. Some of the wines are even in short supply, so unquenchable has been our thirst for the Bulgarian bottle.

What more can they do? Well, for a start, they can do something about improving the reliability of the wine they sell. There's absolutely nothing wrong with the wine when it's good – let us get that clear straight away – but we seem to receive more complaints about the quality of individual bottles of Bulgarian wines than about wines from anywhere else. Obviously the fact that they sell a lot of wine means there are going to be some complaints. But even allowing for the volume of wine sold, there are still too many drinkers disappointed by Bulgarian inconsistency.

One explanation for the occasionally variable quality may be that there is probably still quite a bit of work to be done on what in the New World or many parts of Western Europe would be regarded as normal hygiene on the bottling line. But whatever the reason, we would expect the importers to institute a system of quality control to ensure that what we are getting is not affected by problems back on the Black Sea.

It would certainly be a pity if Bulgaria's reputation were to be affected in this way, because the wines have so many natural advantages. For a start, they are not plagued by a complex system of categorisation or labelling. Bulgaria went straight down the varietal path: although the cheapest brand, Mehana, is a blended wine of a number of local Bulgarian varieties, it is being phased out, and the most familiar wines are Cabernet Sauvignon, Rhine Riesling, Chardonnay, Merlot – names we recognise already.

Then there's the price. For wine of such good quality, Bulgarian wine is absurdly cheap. In the summer of 1989, the standard Suhindol Cabernet Sauvignon was still selling for well under £2.50. Even the next range of quality is less than £3 – and for that you are getting some sophisticated, quite complex wines. Nowhere else in the world is this price/quality ratio so favourable to the consumer. The role of a heavy state subsidy is irrelevant – the fact is that the wines are here, and they're good and inexpensive.

What's what in Bulgaria

The Bulgarian system of labelling is simple: most wines are sold under their varietal name. At the most basic level, blends of local grapes are sold either under the Mehana brand name or under a shop's own label.

Next come the Country Wines, blend of varietals (some international), selling at around £2. At present there are four of these, the reds offering the best quality.

Russe (white), a blend of Riesling and Misket
Varna (white), a blend of Aligoté and Ugni Blanc
Bourgas (white), a blend of Muscat and Ugni Blanc
Pavlikeni (reds), a blend of Cabernet Sauvignon and Merlot
Suhindol (reds), a blend of Merlot and Gamza.

The middle range consists of the varietal wines which first made Bulgaria famous. Most usual varietals to be seen here are Riesling and Chardonnay in whites, Cabernet Sauvignon and Merlot in reds. These are still the biggest sellers in the UK, along with Mehana blends.

Above this come the Reserve wines, which are from larger areas than the Controliran regions (see below) and which have stricter regulations than the standard varietal range. Wines in this category include Khan Krum Chardonnay, Oriahovitza Cabernet Sauvignon and Melnik Reserve (made from the Shiroka Melnishka Loza grape). Their production includes some wood-ageing in small barrels, and some bottle-ageing before release.

Over these again are the Controliran wines, specially designated regions like super appellation contrôlée areas. The Controliran wine areas are:

Asenovgrad: makes Cabernet Sauvignon, Merlot and Mavrud
Harsovo (Melnik): makes wine from local grapes
Juzhnyabryag: makes rosé styles
Kralevo and Preslav: make Riesling
Lozica: makes Cabernet Sauvignon
Novo Selo: makes Gamza
Oriahovitza: makes Cabernet Sauvignon and Merlot
Preslav: makes Chardonnay
Rozova Dolina: makes Misket – mainly white
Sakak: makes Merlot
Sakar: makes Cabernet Sauvignon

Stambolovo: makes Merlot
Svichtov: makes Cabernet Sauvignon
Varna: makes Chardonnay.
  More regions are expected to follow.

Best buys from Bulgaria

WHITES

Bulgarian Chardonnay, Bulgarian Riesling and Reserve Khan
Krum Chardonnay 1984 (*all widely available*)

REDS

Bulgarian Suhindol Cabernet Sauvignon (*widely available*)
Plovdiv Cabernet Sauvignon (*widely available*)
Damianitza Melnik Reserve 1983 (*Peter Dominic; Majestic; Arthur
Rackhams; Thresher; Wines from Paris; Wines of Westhorpe*)
Asenovgrad Mavrud 1983 (*Celtic Vintner; Peter Dominic; Majestic;
Thos Peatling; Wines of Westhorpe*)

Specialist stockists

*Celtic Vintners; Davisons; Direct Wine Shipments; Peter Dominic;
Majestic; Oddbins; Wines of Westhorpe*

Canada

In the past year, a quality control system for wines produced in Ontario province, and especially for wines from the Niagara Peninsula, has been set up. Niagara produces the only wine we know in Britain – Inniskillin.

It is a hopeful sign, certainly. But the fact that wines from hybrid vines (and not just the *Vitis vinifera* that makes all the wines we drink) are included in the scheme shows just how far the Canadian industry has to go before it achieves international recognition.

However, from the 1989 vintage, the *Vitis vinifera* wines from Inniskillin will come adorned with a special medallion and the guarantee that the wines contain only Ontario grapes. The wines themselves – from a winery that makes both *Vitis vinifera* and hybrid wines – are unlikely to change. They are interesting rather than sensational, and rather expensive for what they are.

Wines from the Inniskillin winery in Niagara Peninsula are available from:
Averys of Bristol; Mitchell's of Lancaster; David Scatchard; Stapylton Fletcher

Chile

Over the past two years, we have wondered if Chile would be the country to follow Australia and New Zealand as the 'buzz' place. Well, it still hasn't happened. And now we are waiting to see if a visit to Chile and Argentina by a large group of British Masters of Wine will speed up the process.

The reasons that Chile has not yet taken off are not hard to find. While she produces some superb, world-beating red wines, she makes much less white wine of the sort we can appreciate. Her whites (with some exceptions) have tended to remain in the era when oxidised wine was the norm, when freshness was unusual (and not necessarily wanted) and when long barrel-ageing was a sign of a great wine.

While we have no desire to stop the Chileans drinking that sort of white wine if the fancy (and tradition) takes them, it's not for us. As we have said in the past, there are exceptions, such as the fresh whites from Miguel Torres, the Spanish producer who has set up a winery in the Maule Valley, well to the south of the principal red wine-growing areas. And a handful of other producers make clean and characterful Chardonnay and Sauvignon Blanc wines.

But even if the influence of these enlightened producers is spreading, quantities are still small. Despite the 116,000 hectares of vines in Chile, the past decade has seen a fall in production, as land-owners have replanted with more profitable crops and as local demand has fallen. This cutback hasn't yet reduced the comparatively limited quantities of finer wines, but it has certainly affected the volumes of everyday wines.

At the moment, with a weak local currency, Chilean prices are highly advantageous to us. The best wines are normally available under £6, and much wine of good quality comes on to our shop shelves at £3 or £3.50. Cabernet Sauvignon at this price – and of this quality – is something that has almost entirely disappeared from other countries (except perhaps Bulgaria where the exchange rate is controlled).

All the luck

Chile starts out with all the advantages, viticulturally speaking. The Chilean vineyards are just across the Andes from the main Argentine vineyard areas. But the climb up to 17,000 feet and down again does wonders for the climate. Where Argentine vineyards are almost in desert, in Chile the rainfall is twice as high and the cool, moist winds blowing off the Pacific Ocean give a climate not unlike that of Bordeaux.

There's another link with Bordeaux in the well-drained soil sitting on a high water table which keeps the vines well watered but not sodden. Add to that the fact that Chile's vineyards are free from phylloxera (so the vines don't have to be grafted on to American root stock as they do in Europe and California), plus a low incidence of all the dreadful diseases that can strike vines, and it's not surprising that Chile has the potential to be one of the most exciting vineyard areas in the world.

Compromising integrity

We are now seeing some very good wines coming out of Chile. Some are made by traditional firms who have stayed firmly traditional, but have still taken advantage of new techniques to make their wines more acceptable on the international stage. Others are made by companies who have embraced wholeheartedly the modern school of wine-making: often their wines taste as though they come from Australia or California (another influence on Chile's wine producers).

All those wines are good in their different ways. But a number of producers are making cheap wine, at a low price, which is often sold under an own-label: not only is it cheap, it tastes cheap.

Chile can't afford to start devaluing its reputation before it is even established. Much better for her producers to concentrate on quality wines at what are often very reasonable prices rather than trying to beat the Europeans at a game they can play only too well.

What's what in Chile

There are two main growing regions in Chile. Both are in the central valley zone, around the capital of Santiago. The furthest north (and therefore warmest) is the Maipo Valley, on a level with Santiago. This has long been the traditional area for premium wine production. Further south, cooler climate areas have been planted more recently in the Lontué and Maule Valleys. Here the grapes – especially those for white wines – can take advantage of a longer ripening season to attain excellent fruit flavours.

Many Chilean wines are labelled varietally, in the manner of

New World wines. The main grape varieties likely to appear on UK wine shelves are:

Whites: Muscat, Semillon, Sauvignon, Riesling.

Reds: Cabernet Sauvignon, Merlot, Pinot Noir, Cot.

Other wines have fancy names as well as grape varieties. If a grape is specified on the label, the wine must contain 85 per cent of that grape. With two varieties, the predominant one will be mentioned first.

Categories of quality are also indicated on the label. The standard quality (**Courant**) will have no qualification, but a wine called **Special** will have been bottled after two years in tank or wood; **Reserva** after four years; **Gran Vino** after six years.

Another (voluntary) system used by the top producers is a series of five Categories. Wine from the top Category One will contain grapes from the Central Valley only (the north-south valley which contains all the main grape-growing areas) and will have spent some time ageing in oak. Category Two wines undergo less ageing. Category Three wines are basic table wines. Category Four describes young wines, while Category Five wines are the most basic and are unlikely to be seen outside Chile.

Who's who in Chile

All the top producers – as well as a few lesser ones – now send their wines to Britain.

Concha y Toro, Maipo Valley Chile's largest wine producer who turns out reliable wines at good prices. The top wines are getting better all the time. Wines: Cabernet Casillero del Diablo, Cabernet/Merlot blends. Cabernet Marqués de Casa Concha (worth keeping for six or seven years), white Sauvignon/Semillon blend (drink young); also good sparkling Brut and rosé.
Widely available

Cousiño Macul, Maipo Valley Source of Chile's best red wines – some of the Cabernet Sauvignons last for years. Also makes Chardonnay wines. Wines: Cousiño Macul Antiguas Reserva (will last 10 or 15 years), Chardonnay (drink it at two years).
Peter Dominic; Alex Findlater; Nobody Inn; Pond Farm Wines; Queen's Club Wines; Stapylton Fletcher; La Reserva Wines; Touchstone Wines; A L Vose; Thresher

Errauriz Panquehue Producer of Cabernet Sauvignon, Sauvignon Blanc and Semillon.
Thresher

Los Vascos, Colchagua Make superb Cabernet Sauvignon wines, full of fruit. Wines: Cabernet Sauvignon (drink now, but worth keeping for a couple of years).
The Wine Club

Linderos, Maipo Valley Top quality Cabernet Sauvignon with good ageing potential. Wines: Viña Linderos Cabernet Sauvignon.
Asda; Les Amis du Vin; Augustus Barnett; Berry Bros & Rudd; Peter Dominic; Fortnum & Mason; Peter Green; Grape Ideas; Majestic; Nobody Inn; David Scatchard; Selfridges

Santa Carolina, Maipo Valley Dull, commercial range. Wines: Chardonnay, Sauvignon Blanc, Cabernet Sauvignon, Merlot.
For further information contact Caxton Tower, 239 Munster Road, London, SW6

Santa Marta, Maipo Valley Modern-style wines, of good quality, which could come from any New World country, but are none the worse for that. Their prices are good as well. A name to watch. Wines: Sauvignon Blanc, Chardonnay, Merlot, Cabernet Sauvignon.
For further information contact Eldorobo Wines (01-740 4123)

Santa Rita, Maipo Valley One of the oldest wineries in Chile, started in the 1700s. Now makes an excellent, if pricy, range of varietal wines. Wines: Chardonnay, Sauvignon Blanc, Cabernet Sauvignon.
Bibendum; Moreno Wines; Victoria Wine Company; Wizard Wine Warehouses

Torres, Maule Valley The great innovator in Chile as in Spain. Whites and reds are in the modern style but have considerable character. Wines appear under the Santa Digna and Bellaterra names; also Cabernet Sauvignon, Sauvignon Blanc, rosé (made from Cabernet Sauvignon), Don Miguel (Riesling and Gewürztraminer).
Adnams; Bottoms Up; D Byrne & Co; Peter Dominic; Peter Green; Lay & Wheeler; Arthur Rackhams

Viña San Pedro, Lontué Valley A mixed bag. The best are called Llave de Oro and Castillo de Molina. Avoid the Gato de Oro range. Wines: Sauvignon Blanc, Chardonnay, Cabernet Sauvignon, Merlot.
Majestic; J Sainsbury; Wizard Wine Warehouses

Undurraga, Maipo Valley Old-established firm, specialising in reds, based in a fine colonial-style mansion in the Maipo Valley. Wines: Cabernet Sauvignon, Chardonnay, Sauvignon Blanc.
For further information contact Gama Wines (0734-583074)

Best buys from Chile

WHITE

Chardonnay, Viña Carmen 1987 (*Villeneuve Wines*)
Fumé Blanc 1988, Santa Helena (*Moffat Wine Shop; Smedley Vintners*)
Chardonnay 1988 Oak Aged, Santa Helena (*Hedley Wright*)

ROSÉ

Rosada Cabernet 1988, Miguel Torres (*Broad Street Wine Co*)

RED

Viña Carmen Cabernet Sauvignon 1986 (*Blayneys; Great Northern Wine Company*)
Viña Undurraga Cabernet Sauvignon 1987 (*Averys of Bristol*)
Concha y Toro Cabernet Sauvignon 1984 (*Balls Brothers; Chiswick Wine Cellar; Ellis Son & Vidler*)
Santa Rita Reserva Cabernet Sauvignon (*B H Wines*)
Cousiño Macul Antiguas Reservas Cabernet Sauvignon 1982 (*D Byrne & Co*)
Viña Linderos Cabernet Sauvignon 1983 (*Battersea Wine Company*)
Cabernet Sauvignon/Malbec 1987, Santa Helena (*S H Jones*)

Specialist stockists
Hedley Wright; Moreno Wines

China

First there was Great Wall, and then there was Dynasty. That, too, faltered because supply outstripped demand. Fortunately, for those who must have this white Chinese wine, some supplies are now available from a few specialised wine merchants (including Willoughbys).

Whether China is going to be a major force in wine is uncertain. French companies – chief among them Rémy Martin – have already developed wines like Dynasty, and others are dipping their toe into these waters. The soil in certain areas is right but the problem, apparently, is the climate. It's either too hot and wet or too hot and dry.

Cyprus

Forget the wine lake. As far as Cyprus is concerned, the problem is a grape mountain. The country has the highest production of grapes per capita in the world, and the problem is to know what to do with all that fruit, when demand for Cyprus wines is falling.

Much of it is sold as table grapes. An awful lot more is made into grape must, some of which ends up as British 'Sherry'. They distil it into a killer spirit, which locals consume in mind-boggling quantities. They even make grape jam.

But that still leaves around a third of the annual production of 200,000 tons of grapes to be made into wine. There was a time, only a year or so ago, when much of this wine went to quench the Soviet thirst. But Mr Gorbachev put a stop to that in his campaign against alcoholism (although wine exports may revive as an alternative to vodka). But, all in all, times are tough, with exports of wines down from 45 million litres in 1982 to 15 million in 1987 – and still falling.

Another major reason has been the disastrous decline in Cyprus 'Sherry' exports to Britain. While some of the dry Sherry-style wines to come from Cyprus are reasonably recognisable – even to the point of using flor imported from Jerez – tastes in Sherry in Britain have changed and the market has declined.

Which leaves table wines. Cyprus has been slow to enter the 1980s: for years, an experimental research station near Limassol has been developing wines in a modern style, using grapes other than the two native varieties (Mavro for the red wines, Xynisteri for the white), neither of which have much potential for great quality. Instead work has been done on a mixed bag which includes Syrah, Grenache, Carignan, Cabernet Franc in the reds; and Riesling Italico, Palomino, Sauvignon, Semillon and Malvasia Grossa in whites.

Only a few of these new-style wines – crisp, clean, fruity whites and smooth, not over-ripe reds – are being made commercially. Some have been available in Britain for a while (see below under Best Buys), but they are competing in a market saturated with modern wines.

Another move in Cypriot wine production may actually lead to greater things in the long term. This is the creation of village wineries which can process the grapes at the vineyard. Until

360

now, all grapes had to be transported in searing heat down to the four main wineries in Limassol – a process which could take 24 hours from the time of picking, with the obvious results on the wine. Everybody at the wineries was aware of the problem, but the conservatism of the growers was against them. Now the solution is to take the wineries to the growers – and results so far have been impressive, even if quantities are small.

The Cypriot contribution

Sadly, Cyprus's best wine, Commandaria of St John, a rich dessert wine made from grapes dried in the sun, and the island's contribution to the great wines of the world, has suffered along with other wines from Cyprus. Commandaria, if you can find it, has affinities to Malmsey Madeira and Moscato de Pantelleria from Italy, and is certainly in the same class. The wine dates from at least the times in the Middle Ages when the island was governed by the Knights Templar, although its origins are much older.

Best buys from Cyprus

Amathus The dry red partner to the Palomino, blending Carignan, Oellade and Mataro grapes.
Milia & Co, 200 St Ann's Road, London N15 and 11-13 Pratt Street, London NW1; other north London Cypriot off-licences

Bellapais Medium-sweet, slightly fizzy white wine, a good example of a modern-style white.
Cumbrian Cellars; Thresher (some branches); Victoria Wine Company; Wine Spot

Commandaria of St John (See above) The best two that are widely available are made by Keo (*Cumbrian Cellars; Wine Spot*) and Sodap – St Barnabas (*Michael's Vineyards, 5 Banister Road, London W10 – case sales only*).

Domaine d'Ahera A light, smooth red wine made from Carignan grapes.
Many north London Cypriot off-licences

Thisbe A medium dry white wine launched to compete with German-style wines.
Cumbrian Cellars; Wine Spot; many north London Cypriot off-licences

Palomino One of the two new dry whites.
Same stockists as for Amathus

England and Wales

Call for expansion

England must be one of the few wine-producing countries where the demand is to make more, not less. A small comparison may help to explain why: in 1987, the other countries of the EC produced 34 million more hectolitres of wine than they could sell (it was bought in and mainly distilled). In England and Wales the total production that year was a mere 5,000 hectolitres.

So it's a tiny industry in continental European terms, but one that is lively, surprisingly full of confidence (despite two lousy summers in 1987 and 1988), and expanding to fill the demand.

But it is also a cottage industry. Most of production – all of it in the case of smaller vineyards – is sold over the farm gate to visitors who call in to see a 'real' vineyard in operation and buy a bottle or two. Hardly grown-up stuff – no wonder the French can't really take it seriously (even though one producer actually sells their wine in top Paris stores).

It is only in the past year or so that supermarkets, for instance, have been able to buy sufficient quantities of English wines to make listing them a sensible proposition. Few wine merchants stock more than a couple (often including the wine from their local vineyard if they happen to be in the right part of the world).

There are those involved in the English wine trade who argue that it will never become more than an amateur business until marketing and selling are built into the equation along with producing. There are certainly some sturdy individualists around, both in terms of vineyard husbandry but also now in terms of self-promotion, something the English tend to frown on but which elsewhere is a very natural way of going about things. So you get people like Gay Biddlecombe of St George's Vineyard, who launches wines to coincide with every centenary there is (and supplies the House of Commons and sells in France and Japan); and Andy Vining of Wellow Vineyards, who sends out press releases on every conceivable occasion; and David Carr-Taylor, the sole standard-bearer of English wines at the Vinexpo exhibition in Bordeaux.

Good for them for shouting about English wine. Scoff and sneer as some will (although fewer than there used to be, especially if they've actually tasted the stuff), England and Wales can make wines with a character that sets them apart from any other wine-producing area, and with a reliability now (with the advent of professional winemakers and new equipment) that could be emulated by some other parts of the world.

The taste of England and Wales

Most vineyards make two styles of wine: a dry and a less dry version. In good years, the dry style is superb, making a crisp, clean-tasting wine which some have likened to the smell of an English country garden and which has piercing fruit and acidity.

In poor years, the producers are allowed to add some unfermented grape juice or sugar to raise the alcohol level and keep the acidity from overwhelming the unripe fruit. So – with exceptions – 1985 and 1986 wines are slightly better in a medium dry or off-dry style. The same is true of 1987, although not of 1988, when there was a reasonably warm autumn. Even then, though they may be made with German grape varieties, they don't taste the same – their acidity is keener and their steely quality sets them apart.

A few intrepid souls also make red wines, and some achieve surprisingly good results considering the way nature is stacked against them. But such wines should be approached with caution, and shouldn't be bought before tasting, simply because they are so unlike the red wines we are used to in their lightness and considerable acidity.

English v British

There are many wines around that describe themselves as British. For those who have never tasted them, we would point out that British 'wines' are not the same as English and Welsh wines which are the subject of this section. British 'wines' are made from concentrated grape must imported into this country, to which is added British water. Most wine drinkers would not be impressed by the result, although there is a healthy market based mainly on their cheapness.

Another category is made in this country, which derives from a long and honourable tradition. Called Country Wines, these are the commercial equivalent of home-made wines – damson, elderflower and the like. Some achieve high quality and shouldn't be dismissed as the source of instant headaches. Again, though, they should not be confused with wines made in this country from grapes grown here.

English and Welsh vintages

1988 The fourth wet spring in succession promised little in the way of succour to grape growers. The flowering in late June was followed by a damp July and August, but because harvesting did not take place until November, a comparatively warm September and October ensured decent sugar levels even if quantities were below average.

1987 The flowering, which took place in early July, was completely rained and blown off in East Anglia and Kent. Many vineyards produced hardly any grapes, let alone wine. Further west, while wine was made, it was quite acid stuff, and needed the addition of some sugar. Stick to the medium dry styles.

1986 After a wet, cold summer, sunshine in September and October did much to improve the final quality of wines, although quantity was down on 1985. The wines should not all be dismissed as too old.

1985 The first of the series of wet springs and cold summers. But, as often, the harvest was saved by a dry September and October. Although the quantity was down by a third on 1984, the wines from the good vineyards were excellent, crisp and full of summery acidity, as English wine should be. They should certainly be drunk now.

Not all English and Welsh wines carry a vintage indication, and may be a blend of two years – rarely more. They will probably be dominated by the most recent vintage, and so should be drunk accordingly.

The grapes

Nearly all English and Welsh vineyards are planted with strains of vine developed in Germany for northerly vineyards. Many actually produce better wine in Britain because the ripening season is long and slow and this brings out their flavours without a loss of acidity. A few French varieties are planted – Pinot Noir, Pinot Meunier, Sauvignon Blanc and Chardonnay – but they need very special microclimates to succeed.

WHITE GRAPES

Bacchus Can be very flowery and fragrant, but also rather sharp.

Ehrenfelser Adaptable, disease-resistant variety. Very useful, making wines that can mature.

Gutenborner Neutral-tasting grape giving fat wines.

Huxelrebe Can be honeyed and Muscat-like in good years.

Madeleine Angevine A hybrid grape, which has table grapes somewhere in its past and which has adapted to producing slightly honeyed wines.

Müller-Thurgau The German workhorse grape has been galloping around England as well. It's the most widely planted vine and makes medium-bodied wines of good acidity with a taste reminiscent of blackcurrants.

Ortega An early-ripening variety with a very perfumed flavour, often quite full, and quite successful in blends.

Reichensteiner A neutral grape variety, widely planted, with a hint of honey and ripe fruit.

Schönburger One of the most successful grapes produced in England. Gives a honeyed, fruity wine with good balancing acidity. Hints of Muscat and Gewürztraminer in the taste.

Seyval Blanc A hybrid vine well suited to northern vineyards because it is resistant to frost. Produces wines with acid fruit.

Siegerrebe Highly aromatic variety. A little goes a long way.

RED GRAPES

Triomphe d'Alsace A hybrid variety which originates – as its name suggests – in Alsace, but is now little seen there.

Wrotham Pinot A variation of Pinot Meunier which was developed in England.

Many English and Welsh wines will be blends of one or more of these grapes and will simply go under a brand name and a description of 'dry' or 'medium'. There is a trend towards blends, and away from single varietal wines: this helps to bring out the best characteristics of two or more grapes.

Who's who in England and Wales

Here we give a selection of vineyards with a reliable record and whose wines are distributed beyond the vineyard gate.

The English Vineyards Association publishes a list of its members vineyards open to the public (38 West Park, London SE9; telephone 01-857 0452; a stamped addressed envelope must be sent).

Adgestone Vineyard on the Isle of Wight making dryish wines from Müller-Thurgau, Reichensteiner and Huxelrebe.
Asda; Peter Dominic (local branches); Peter Green; Harrods

Barton Manor Another Isle of Wight producer, making medium dry and dry wines, usually blended. Grapes used are Müller-Thurgau, Seyval Blanc, Huxelrebe, Gewürztraminer, Riesling and Reichensteiner.
Harrods

Biddenden Kent vineyard producing wines from Müller-Thurgau, Reichensteiner and Ortega, plus a rosé.
Berry Bros & Rudd; English Wine Centre; Victoria Wine Company; Welbeck Wines

Bruisyard St Peter Suffolk vineyard making medium dry wines.
Berry Bros & Rudd; English Wine Centre; Willoughbys

Carr-Taylor The most export-oriented vineyard (in Sussex). Gutenborner, Huxelrebe, Kerner and Reichensteiner all go to make a blended wine. Also a successful Champagne method sparkling wine, using technical advice from Champagne.
Peter Dominic (local branches); Ellis Son & Vidler; English Wine Centre; Victoria Wine Co; Waitrose; Wine Growers Association

Chalkhill Müller-Thurgau in a dry style is a particularly successful wine from this Wiltshire vineyard. Wines also sold under the Chalke Valley name.
William Rush

Chilford Hundred Müller-Thurgau, Huxelrebe, Schönburger, Ortega, making a dry wine in Cambridgeshire.
Peter Dominic (local branches); Thos Peatling

Ditchling A Sussex vineyard making a pleasant Müller-Thurgau.
Berkmann Wine Cellars; English Wine Centre; Arthur Rackhams

Elmham Park Norfolk producer of dry blended wines which
need a little time to lose their acidity.
Hicks & Don; Thos Peatling

Felsted Innovative Essex vineyard that is also one of the longest
established (since 1966). Look for a Chardonnay and Seyval
Blanc blend, Felstar Müller-Thurgau.
The Vineyard, Crix Green, Felsted, Essex; (0245) 361504

Hambledon The first modern vineyard to be planted (in
Hampshire). Chardonnay, Pinot Noir and Seyval Blanc.
English Wine Centre

Ightham Müller-Thurgau, Reichensteiner, Huxelrebe,
Schönburger, and good Müller-Thurgau wine from this Kent
vineyard.
Ivy Hatch, Sevenoaks, Kent; (0732) 810348

Joyous Garde Berkshire vineyard making blended wines on the
dry side. Names used include Crazies and Henley Reserve.
Crazies Hill, Wargrave, Berkshire; (073 522) 2102

Lamberhurst The biggest vineyard (in Kent) and most widely
distributed. Always high quality. Now making a sparkling
Champagne method wine.
*Berry Bros & Rudd; Davisons; English Wine Centre; Grape Ideas;
Harrods; Victoria Wine Company; Welbeck Wines; Wine Growers
Association*

Pilton Manor Somerset vineyard producing Müller-Thurgau,
Huxelrebe and Seyval Blanc. Also a sparkling bottle-fermented
wine.
Averys

Pulham Magdalen Müller-Thurgau (or Rivaner as this Norfolk
producers calls it). Very good Chardonnay amongst some rich,
tropical fruit-tasting wines.
English Wine Centre

Saint Edmund A blended medium dry blend of Huxelrebe and
Müller-Thurgau, from the Highwaymans Vineyard in Suffolk.
Tesco

St George's This Sussex producer sells wines (Müller-Thurgau
and Gewürztraminer) to France, Japan and the House of
Commons. Produce rosé as well as white.
Waldron, Heathfield, East Sussex; (043 53) 2156

Staple St James Kent grower of medium dry wines from Müller-Thurgau.
English Wine Centre; Arthur Rackhams; Victoria Wine Company

Tenterden Another Kent vineyard. Wines include two Müller-Thurgaus, one called Tenterden, the other Spots Farm, as well as a Reserve wine aged in Limousin oak casks, a rosé from Pinot Noir and a red from Dunkenfelder.
Davisons; English Wine Centre; Victoria Wine Company

Three Choirs Large Gloucestershire vineyard planted with Müller-Thurgau and Reichensteiner.
Peter Dominic; English Wine Centre; Grape Ideas; Majestic; Christopher Piper Wines; Tanners; Thresher; Victoria Wine Company; Willoughbys; Wine Growers Association; Wizard Wine Warehouses

Wellow Vineyards An expansionist vineyard in Hampshire, first producing with the 1986 harvest and planning half a million bottles by 1990.
Merryhill Farm, Tanners Land, East Wellow, Romsey, Hampshire; (0794) 522860

Wootton Long-established (by English standards) Somerset producer of good quality Schönburger, Müller-Thurgau and Seyval Blanc.
English Wine Centre; Nobody Inn; Wine Society

Yearlstone Small Devon vineyard making one of the most convincing reds in England, which is aged in wood.
Chilverton, Coldridge, Crediton, Devon; (0363) 83302

Best buys from England and Wales

Wootton Müller-Thurgau 1986, Somerset (*Touchstone Wines*)
Elmham Park Dry 1983 (*Hicks & Don*)
Wines of England Pulham 1986 (*Waitrose*)
Adgestone 1986 (*Asda*)
Reichensteiner 1988, Carr Taylor (*Ellis Son & Vidler*)
New Hall Müller-Thurgau 1986 (*English Wine Shop*)
Wealden English Table Wine 1985 (*English Wine Centre*)

Specialist stockists
English Wine Centre; English Wine Shop; Fine English Wine; Selfridges

France

ALSACE

Wine for Francophiles

One of the comments made most often about Alsace wine is
that the British don't understand it. They think it's German –
after all, many of the producers' names have a Germanic ring to
them, and the wine comes in tall, green, Mosel-like bottles –
and we all know what most drinkers think about German wine:
it's sweet, inexpensive and innocuous.

Very occasionally those same people may open a bottle of
Alsace. What they will find is a revelation in its absolute
difference from anything that Germany makes. Alsace wines are
dry, often imbued with high alcohol and certainly with richness.
The spicy flavours of the Tokay Pinot Gris alternate with the
lychee tastes of the Gewürztraminer or the piercing steeliness of
the Riesling. This is the land of wines that taste of their fruit,
with no extras like wood to eclipse their direct tastes.

It does at last seem that more people are willing to try those
tastes. Maybe it's all those glasses of Pinot Blanc we've
consumed in wine bars, but in 1988 sales of Alsace wines in the
UK went up by 21 per cent over the previous year, to 2 million
bottles. It's still quite a pitiful amount compared with our
purchases of white Burgundy (seven times as much) from a
much smaller area.

Creating a hierarchy

Our resistance to things Alsatian may not just stem from the
fact that the wines are Germanic in feel if not in taste, but also
perhaps because it has been much more difficult to relate to a
sea of producers' names with no hierarchy. In Bordeaux there
are the first growths of the Médoc, and in Burgundy, the great
wine villages and their Grand Cru vineyards. But in Alsace
there has been no way of telling from the label the good but
fairly ordinary wines from the very finest examples.

So Alsace has felt the need to invent its own Grand Cru
system. The way it works is explained below, but essentially it
is based on certain good vineyards (named on the bottles).

There are a number of problems with such a scheme. First, the vineyard can be owned by a number of people, so you get good Grand Cru X as well as indifferent Grand Cru X depending on whether Producer A has old vines and low yields and Producer B has young vines and high yields (an old Burgundian problem).

The second problem returns us to the identity crisis of Alsace: Germanic names of producers, villages and even some of the grape varieties on the tall green bottles.

Third, to many people in Alsace, adding the complexity of the Grand Cru hierarchy undermines the system where the simplicity of the wines (100 per cent varietals) had been reflected on the label. That's the view of the négociants, the merchants who buy wine from all over the region and whose wines represent the most familiar names in Britain. The growers who happen to find themselves owning a Grand Cru vineyard and who see their prices shooting up very satisfactorily, thank you, inevitably take the opposite view.

Somewhere in the middle – because they not only represent growers but also sell wine – are the co-operatives, who make around 30 per cent of the region's wines. From Alsace co-operatives comes much of the wine sold by supermarkets and multiple retailers. And the standard of many co-operatives is higher here than in other regions of France. We list the good ones in the Who's who section for the first time.

The Alsace label

Alsace is the only region of France where the wine is labelled entirely varietally – that is, it is called after the name of the grape from which it is made.

There are two appellations for still wines, and one for sparkling, which cover the whole or parts of the region, from the German border in the north to the Swiss border in the south.

Alsace AC This is the basic appellation which covers 85 per cent of the vineyard area. All the grape varieties (see below), either singly or in blends, can be used in an Alsace AC wine.

Alsace Grand Cru A superior AC covering specific vineyards. If the wine comes from just one Grand Cru vineyard, this will be specified on the label. If it's a blend of Grand Cru wines, the label will simply say 'Alsace Grand Cru' without any vineyard name. Only the four noble varieties – Tokay Pinot Gris, Gewürztraminer, Riesling and Muscat – can go to make Alsace Grand Cru. All other grape varieties – even if grown on Grand Cru sites – are straight Alsace AC.

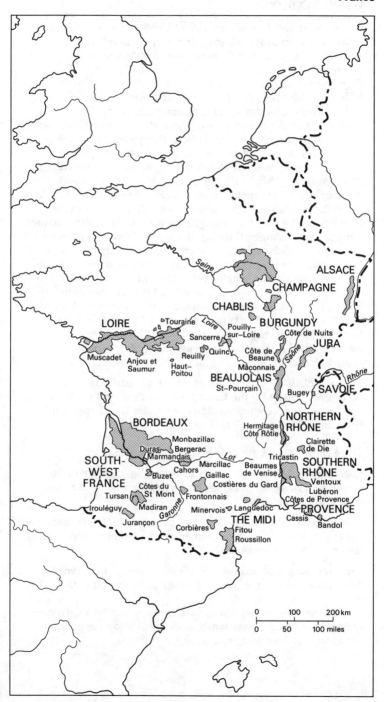

ALSACE

CHAMPAGNE

CHABLIS

LOIRE

BURGUNDY

Touraine

Pouilly-
sur-Loire

Sancerre

Côte de Nuits

JURA

Quincy

Côte de
Beaune

Muscadet

Reuilly

Anjou et
Saumur

Haut-
Poitou

Mâconnais

BEAUJOLAIS

St-Pourçain

Bugey

SAVOIE

NORTHERN
RHÔNE

BORDEAUX

Hermitage
Côte Rôtie

Monbazillac

Clairette
de Die

Duras

Bergerac

Tricastin

SOUTH-
WEST
FRANCE

Marmandais

Marcillac

Beaumes
de Venise

SOUTHERN
RHÔNE

Buzet

Cahors

Gaillac

Costières du Gard

Ventoux

Côtes du
St Mont

Lubéron
Côtes de Provence

Tursan

Frontonnais

PROVENCE

Irouléguy

Madiran

Minervois

Languedoc

Cassis

Bandol

Jurançon

THE MIDI

Corbières

Fitou
Roussillon

Seine

Loire

Saône

Rhône

Lot

Garonne

0	100	200 km
0	50	100 miles

Approved and provisional Grand Cru vineyards (with their village name in brackets) are: Altenberg de Bergbieten (Bergbieten); Altenberg de Bergheim (Bergheim); Altenberg de Wolxheim (Wolxheim); Brand (Turckheim); Eichberg (Eguisheim); Engelberg (Dahlenheim); Frankstein (Dambach-la-Ville); Froehn (Zellenberg); Furstentum (Kientzheim); Geisberg (Ribeauvillé); Gloeckelberg (St-Hippolyte); Goldert (Gueberschwihr); Hatschbourg (Hattstatt and Voegtlinshoffen); Hengst (Wintzenheim); Kanzlerberg (Bergheim); Kastelberg (Andlau); Kessler (Guebwiller); Kirchberg de Barr (Barr); Kirchberg de Ribeauvillé (Ribeauvillé); Kitterlé (Guebwiller); Mambourg (Sigolsheim); Mandelberg (Mittelwihr); Marckrain (Bennwihr); Moenchberg (Andlau and Eichhoffen); Muenchberg (Nothalten); Ollwiller (Wuenheim); Osterberg (Ribeauvillé); Pfersigberg (Eguisheim); Pfingstberg (Orschwihr); Praelatenberg (Orschwiller); Rangen (Thann); Rosacker (Hunawihr); Saering (Guebwiller); Schlossberg (Kaysersberg and Kientzheim); Schoenenbourg (Riquewihr); Sommerberg (Niedermorschwihr and Katzenthal); Sonnenglanz (Beblenheim); Spiegel (Bergholtz and Guebwiller); Sporen (Riquewihr); Steinert (Pfaffenheim); Steingrubler (Wettolsheim); Steinklotz (Marlenheim); Vorbourg (Rouffach and Westhalten); Wiebelsberg (Andlau) Wineck-Schlossberg (Katzenthal); Winzenberg (Blienschwiller); Zinnkoepflé (Westhalten and Soultzmatt); Zotzenberg (Mittelbergheim).

Crémant d'Alsace This is the name for all sparkling wine in Alsace. It is made by the Champagne method and much of it is very good. For recommendations see under the chapter on sparkling wine (page 636).

Three more specific terms can appear on the label:

Edelzwicker A relatively cheap blend of two or more of the permitted grape varieties (see below). More widely seen in Alsace than outside.

Vendange tardive Late-picked grapes with a high, concentrated sugar content. The resultant wines can be sweet or dry. Quality is good – and the price high.

Sélection de grains nobles An official category since 1983, describing sweet wine made using grapes infected with noble rot.

The terms Réserve spéciale, Sélection spéciale and Cuvée spéciale are fancy names which may mean a top cuvée from a producer – or just fancy prices.

The grapes of Alsace

Chardonnay This is grown specifically for Crémant d'Alsace and cannot be used in any Alsace still wines.

Gewürztraminer Heavily spicy, perfumed grape variety that made its name in Alsace before spreading elsewhere in the world. It can be a little cloying and unsubtle if made by the wrong hands, but is the easiest wine to identify with your eyes shut.

Muscat Two Muscats are grown in Alsace. The Muscat à Petits Grains makes delicate, honey-smelling wines. The Muscat Ottonel (more widely planted) makes rather heavier wines. Both are dry. Normally the two varieties are blended and the label on the bottle does not specify which is used.

Pinot Blanc Simple, fruity wines, with just a hint of Chardonnay in their flavour; to be drunk young. The vineyard area has increased, owing to greater demand.

Pinot Noir Some rosé or pale red wines are made in Alsace. Few leave the region (and most shouldn't), although a few producers (Hugel among them) are experimenting with wood-ageing with some success.

Riesling The finest wines in Alsace are made from this grape – full but elegant, often steely dry but always giving off perfumed fruit. Quality varies from not bad to very good indeed – prices indicate the range.

Sylvaner Rather neutral wines, but in cool years have pleasant, straightforward acidity. Often attractive with a slight prickle. Some villages (Beblenheim is one) have made a speciality of this grape.

Tokay Pinot Gris Used to be called Tokay d'Alsace (and still is unofficially) until the EC thought it would be confused with Tokay from Hungary. This underrated grape variety produces rich, dry, peppery wines, sometimes lacking in acidity, but making up for that in full body.

The Alsace vintages

1988 Described as 'a promising year'. It was an early vintage, which suggests good quality and average quantity. The wines will be quite heavy, low in acid and with some ageing ability.

1987 A good average vintage, with reasonable quantity. Ready to drink now.

1986 A lighter vintage than either 1983 or 1985 of easy-to-drink wines which we are drinking up fast.

1985 Widely acclaimed as an exceptional vintage. The wines are fine, excellently balanced, with richness but also elegance. The most successful varieties have been Gewürztraminer and Tokay Pinot Gris. Large quantities of vendange tardive and sélection de grains nobles were made. Apart from high quality, the crop was down by 20 per cent of a normal year.

1984 Not such a bad year as originally thought, but the wines should be drunk up now.

1983 Another great vintage, with very full wines, possibly lacking acidity but certainly not alcohol. Rieslings are delicious now but will keep for many years, while the Gewürztraminer is highly spiced, and the Tokay Pinot Gris rich and delicious. Top cuvées will last for a while yet.

1976 A few miraculous vendange tardive Rieslings will still keep. A few good examples of Riesling, Tokay Pinot Gris and Gewürztraminer to be drunk now.

Other vintages with top wines that are still worth considering are 1978 and 1981.

Who's who in Alsace

The Alsace wine trade is divided into growers, some of whom also bottle and export, but using only wines from their own vineyards; the merchants who, as in Burgundy, may own vineyards but also buy in wines; and co-operatives, some of a good standard, who are supplying much of the wine bought for supermarket brands.

THE GROWERS

Caves J Becker, Zellenberg Long-established firm, now run by a young brother and sister. One-third of production comes from their own land. Wines: Pinot Blanc, Riesling Hagenschlaff, Tokay Pinot Gris Sonnenglanz.
Berkmann Wine Cellars/Le Nez Rouge; Mayor Sworder & Co

Blanck, Kientzheim High quality grower making wines with good ageing potential.
Adnams; Balls Brothers; S H Jones; Lay & Wheeler; Tanners

Théo Faller, Kaysersberg One of the top growers making superb wines from the Clos de Capucins vineyard. Small production, high prices. Wines: Cuvée Théo (Riesling and Gewürztraminer), vendange tardive, Domaine Weinbach.
O W Loeb; La Vigneronne

Kientzler, Ribeauvillé Grower with land in Grand Cru
vineyards around Ribeauvillé. Wines: Grand Cru Geisberg,
Grand Cru Kirchberg de Ribeauvillé.
La Vigneronne

Domaine Klipfel, Barr One of the best domaines on the Bas-
Rhin (in the north of the region). Wines: Clos Zisser
Gewürztraminer, Kirchberg Riesling, Tokay Pinot Gris Freiberg.
Cadwgan Fine Wines; Restaurant Croque-en-Bouche

Charles Koehly, Rodern Good Tokay Pinot Gris, Riesling Grand
Cru Altenberg de Bergheim.
Haynes Hanson & Clark

Hubert Krick, Wintzenheim Good-value wines from a small
producer. Wines: Grand Cru Hengst.
Windrush Wines

Catherine Lacoste, Andlau Grower (married to Marc
Kreydenweiss – see below under merchants) in northern Alsace,
producing very good Tokay Pinot Gris. Wines: Tokay Pinot
Gris, Grand Cru Kastelberg.
La Vigneronne

Domaine Ostertag, Epfig Grower making Riesling and
Gewürztraminer. Since his name means 'Easter' his labels carry
a picture of a Paschal lamb. Wines: Tokay Pinot Gris, Riesling,
Gewürztraminer.
*H Allen Smith; Gare du Vin; Morris & Verdin; La Vigneronne;
Winecellars; Wines from Paris*

Rolly Gassmann, Rorschwihr Small estate (37 acres of land) in
Rorschwihr, Bergheim and Rodern making high quality wines
which are on the pricy side but which often emerge at the top
of tastings. Wines: Riesling Reserve, Gewürztraminer, Tokay
Pinot Gris.
*Bibendum; Findlater Mackie Todd; Andrew Mead Wines; Raeburn
Fine Wines & Foods; Tanners*

Schlumberger, Guebwiller The biggest domaine in Alsace,
based in the southern end of Alsace. Firm, concentrated wines
of high quality. Wines: Kitterlé vineyard; Gewürztraminer
Cuvée Christine Schlumberger.
*Les Amis du Vin; Booths; Alex Findlater; Gare du Vin; Peter Green;
Harrods; Justerini & Brooks; Lay & Wheeler; T & W Wines; Victoria
Wine Company; La Vigneronne*

René Schmidt, Riquewihr A 22-acre vineyard with some land in
Grand Cru Schoenenberg. The top range is Cuvée Exceptionelle.
Wines: Tokay Pinot Gris, Gewürztraminer.
Haynes Hanson & Clark

Sick-Dreyer, Ammerschwihr Clean, straightforward domaine wines for early drinking. Wines: Riesling and Gewürztraminer from Kaefferkopf vineyard.
La Vigneronne

Zind-Humbrecht Single vineyard wines made with painstaking care from Turckheim, Wintzenheim and Thann. Wines: Thann Clos St-Urbain (Riesling), Turckheim Brand (Riesling), Turckheim Herrenweg (Gewürztraminer).
Laytons; André Simon; La Vigneronne; Windrush Wines

THE CO-OPERATIVES

All the co-ops make a full range of varietal wines, sometimes under their own name, but more often under an own-label. Some also make top cuvées.

Cave Coopérative de Beblenheim et Environs (*David Baillie Vintners; Balls Brothers; Ellis Son & Vidler; Haynes Hanson & Clark*)
Caves de Bennwihr (*Thos Peatling*)
Wolfberger, Cave Vinicole d'Eguisheim, Eguisheim (*Asda; Peter Dominic; Wines from Paris*)
Les Producteurs Réunis de St-Hippolyte (*Majestic*)
Les Producteurs Réunis à Ingersheim (*Davisons; Master Cellar Wine Warehouse*)
Les Producteurs Réunis de Pfaffenheim (*Marks & Spencer*); also use the name Hartenberger (*Booths*)
Cave Coopérative de Ribeauvillé (*Averys; Augustus Barnett*)
Cave des Vignerons, Turckheim (*H Allen Smith; Cadwgan Fine Wines; Eaton Elliot Winebrokers; Safeway; Unwins; Upper Crust; Victoria Wine Company; Winecellars; The Wine Society*)
Coopérative de Bennwihr (*J Sainsbury*)
Coopérative d'Eguisheim (*Tesco*)

THE MERCHANTS

Léon Beyer, Eguisheim Merchant (who also owns vineyards) selling full-bodied, very dry wines, which can last for years. Specialises in Gewürztraminer. Wines: Riesling Cuvée des Ecaillers, Gewürztraminer Cuvée des Comtes.
Peter Green; Gerard Harris; Majestic; Selfridges; T & W Wines; La Vigneronne; The Wine Society

E Boeckel, Mittelbergheim Long-established grower and merchant making wines in a traditional style. Wines: Zotzenberg Sylvaner, Riesling and Gewürztraminer, Brandluft and Wibelsberg Rieslings, Ch d'Issembourg Gewürztraminer.
Wizard Wine Warehouses

Théo Cattin, Voegtlinshoffen Growers and négociants, making soft wines. Wines: Tokay Pinot Gris, Gewürztraminer Bollenberg, Grand Cru Hatschbourg.
Corney & Barrow

Dopff au Moulin, Riquewihr Merchant who also has a large vineyard holding in the best wine-growing area of central Alsace. Wines from Schoenenburg (Riesling) and Turckheim (Gewürztraminer) vineyards; Fruits de Mer blend; Crémant d'Alsace sparkling.
Matthew Gloag & Son; Peter Green; Gerard Harris; Harrods; La Vigneronne

Dopff et Irion, Riquewihr Growers and merchants who have been in business for three centuries, and were once linked to Dopff au Moulin. Wines: Riesling Les Murailles, Gewürztraminer Les Sorcières, Muscat Les Amandiers, Tokay Pinot Gris Les Maquisards, branded Crustacés and Crystal, Crémant d'Alsace.
Eldridge Pope/Reynier Wine Libraries; Peter Green; Hilbre Wine Company; Selfridges

Louis Gisselbrecht, Dambach-la-Ville Small vineyard holding and négociant business making some reliable wines. Best are the Rieslings. Wines: Riesling, Gewürztraminer, Pinot Blanc.
H Allen Smith; Hungerford Wine Company; Lay & Wheeler; Andrew Mead Wines; Thos Peatling; Christopher Piper Wines

Willy Gisselbrecht, Dambach-la-Ville Négociant and grower with large vineyard holding in Dambach-la-Ville.
Alex Findlater; Martinez Fine Wine; Old Street Wine Company; Waitrose

Hugel et Fils, Riquewihr Most famous (partly because of high quality, partly good publicity) grower and négociant in Alsace. Their wines tend to be rounder, less dry than others in Alsace. They developed the idea of vendange tardive wines. Wines: those from the Schoenenburg and Sporen vineyards; Cuvée Personnelle and vendange tardive are top wines; house brands are Flambeau d'Alsace, Fleur d'Alsace.
Widely available

Marc Kreydenweiss, Andlau High quality grower and négociant (married to Catherine Lacoste – see above under growers) in the northern Alsace vineyards, including the Domaine Fernand Gresser. Wines: Riesling, Grand Cru Moenchberg, Gewürztraminer, Muscat, Pinot Noir.
La Vigneronne

Kuentz-Bas, Husseren-les-Châteaux Small family house making excellent wines: Riesling, Gewürztraminer, Muscat, Pinot Blanc, Tokay Pinot Gris.
Alex Findlater; Harrods; Justerini & Brooks; Oddbins; The Wine Society

Michel Laugel, Marlenheim Négociant and grower in the most northerly of Alsace wine villages. Wines: Riesling de Wolxheim, Pinot Rosé de Marlenheim, Gewürztraminer de Wangen.
For more information, contact France Vin, 20 Perivale Industrial Park, Horsenden Lane South, Perivale, Middx

Gustave Lorentz, Bergheim Large firm of growers and négociants making very good Gewürztraminer. Wines: Altenberg, Kanzlerberg vineyards are top Crus.
Gare du Vin; Thresher; Victoria Wine Company

Jos Meyer, Wintzenheim Grower and négociant making Grand Cru and good Gewürztraminer and Riesling wines from local vineyards. Wines: Gewürztraminer Les Archenets, Riesling, Pinot Blanc, vendange tardive wines.
Augustus Barnett

A & O Muré, Rouffach Three-centuries-old firm making intense, smooth wines from a single vineyard. These are wines to keep. Wines: Clos St-Landelin.
Chaplin & Son; Alex Findlater

Jean Preiss-Zimmer, Riquewihr Top Rieslings and Gewürztraminers.
Victoria Wine Company

Pierre Sparr, Sigolsheim A large négociant house which also manages to produce some good wines from its own vineyards in Sigolsheim, Kaysersberg and Turckheim. Wines: Grands Crus Mambourg and Brand; Edelzwicker, Pinot Blanc, plus some vendange tardive wines.
Barwell & Jones

F E Trimbach, Ribeauvillé Family domaine and négociant founded in the 17th century. Fine wines in a light style but which nevertheless last. Wines: Riesling Clos-Ste-Hune, Réserve and Réserve Personnelle, Riesling and Gewürztraminer.
Les Amis du Vin; Balls Brothers; Chaplin & Sons; Alex Findlater; Gerard Harris; Harrods; Lay & Wheeler; T & W Wines; Upper Crust; La Vigneronne

Willm, Barr Best known for Gewürztraminer, but also makes good Riesling and Sylvaner. Wines: Grand Cru Gaensbroennel, Riesling Kirchberg de Barr.
Les Amis du Vin; Findlater Mackie Todd

Best buys from Alsace

Muscat d'Alsace, Louis Sipp (*William Addison*)
Tokay Pinot Gris 1987, Cave Vinicole de Turckheim (*Barnes Wine Shop; Broad Street Wine Co*)
Tokay Pinot Gris, Dopff et Irion 1985 (*J E Hogg*)
Victoria Wine Riesling d'Alsace (*Victoria Wine Company*)
Gewürztraminer 1987, Louis Gisselbrecht (*Farthinghoe Fine Wine and Food*)
Alsace Marée 1986, Zind-Humbrecht (*Pavilion Wine Company*)
Riesling d'Alsace Cave Vinicole de Turckheim (*widely available*)
Pinot Blanc d'Alsace, Hartenberger 1986 (*Rodney Densem Wines*)
Sylvaner 1987, Rolly Gassmann (*Raeburn Fine Wines and Foods*)

Specialist stockists

Anthony Byrne Fine Wines; D Byrne & Co; Restaurant Croque-en-Bouche; Eldridge Pope; Peter Green; High Breck Vintners; J E Hogg; Lay & Wheeler; O W Loeb; Morris & Verdin; Raeburn Fine Wines and Foods; Reid Wines; La Vigneronne

BEAUJOLAIS

End of the party?

Nearly all the Beaujolais Nouveau imported into Britain in 1988 was sold – hardly surprisingly, because imports were down on 1987, and those in turn were 60 per cent down on 1986. That makes 1986 the last year of the Nouveau boom.

So what about the party on Beaujolais Nouveau day 1989 and 1990? Are we, sophisticated wine drinkers that we are, going to turn away from such frivolity and order a bottle of claret instead?

We certainly won't be ordering a bottle of any other style of Beaujolais if we don't go for Nouveau. Alone among the major wine areas of France, Beaujolais sent less wine to the UK in 1988 than in 1987.

The Beaujolais themselves are perhaps less worried about the dwindling British market. They've discovered new markets for Nouveau – quantities were airfreighted to Japan last year (heaven knows what that cost per bottle when it got there), and so far only in Britain has there been a reaction against the hype of Nouveau.

Getting serious

However, the more serious producers in Beaujolais would like to do something to correct the image that all Beaujolais should be *'vendu, bu et pissé'* (purchased, consumed and consigned to the sanitary system) before Christmas. They feel that the time has come to put Nouveau in a niche separate from what they would regard as the real, serious Beaujolais.

Some producers are now even experimenting with ageing the wine in small wooden casks, the Bordeaux barriques, to give what they see as added complexity to the basic strawberry-fruit simplicity of the Gamay grape of the region.

Of course, you can go too far along such lines. Beaujolais, more than any other of the great wines, is not to be taken too seriously, nor, with certain exceptions, is it for ageing. We would certainly agree that most Beaujolais should be drunk in the year before the next harvest. But we would also like to see more Beaujolais drunk throughout the year (slightly chilled, it makes a delicious summer red), and not just in November.

White surge

While talking of summer wines, we mustn't forget Beaujolais Blanc. While Beaujolais Rouge suffered a decline in sales last year, Beaujolais Blanc surged ahead by an astonishing 32 per cent between 1987 and 1988. Most Beaujolais Blanc comes from vineyards whose wines may be called St-Véran in the Mâconnais – some producers have decided that the name Beaujolais sells more wine than St-Véran and have renamed their white wine accordingly. Beaujolais Blanc certainly makes a good partner to the red, with the same directness and simplicity of flavours.

That simplicity of flavours seems to have inspired some wine producers in Australia to call their wine 'Beaujolais', and to pretend that Beaujolais is a style rather than a geographical region of France. Mindful of what happened with Chablis, the Beaujolais producers have been quick to try and nip the idea in the bud before it spreads. We feel obliged to support them and suggest to the Australians that they would be better off thinking up their own names for their own wines.

Where's where in Beaujolais

Beaujolais classification is divided into three groupings. The basic wine is called simply **Beaujolais** and comes from the southern half of the region. This wine forms the basis of most

Beaujolais Nouveau and as such is drunk fairly fast. But try it slightly chilled in the summer of the following year for a deliciously fruity drink.

Beaujolais Villages Forty villages in the northern half of the region are entitled to this appellation. The wine is stronger, has greater depths than ordinary Beaujolais and keeps better. Some is sold as Beaujolais Nouveau, which is a bit of a waste.

Beaujolais Crus Ten villages are entitled to their own individual appellations. Their styles vary from quite light to serious wines with some ageing potential. All the villages regard themselves as having individual character:

Brouilly The lightest and fruitiest style among the crus. Needs to be drunk fairly young.
Chénas Less often seen than some of the crus, but full of flavour and worth keeping.
Chiroubles Another light style, which should be drunk within the year of the harvest. Full of fruit.
Côte-de-Brouilly Smallest of the crus, making strong wines with some keeping power. They tend to age gracefully.
Fleurie The most expensive of the cru wines (probably because the name is so attractive). They are wines which age, but not for long. They taste good but are not worth the money at the moment.
Juliénas Long-lasting wines with a more serious style than other crus.
Morgon Another long-lasting cru. These are the wines which as they age really take on some of the characteristics of Burgundian Pinot Noir.
Moulin-à-Vent The finest of the crus, the wine of this village will last well and is worth laying down.
Regnié The newest of the crus – it had been trying to join the others since 1936 and finally made it in 1988. The wines are light, not for ageing.
St-Amour Soft, easy-drinking wines – as the name might suggest. Like Fleurie, these wines have become too pricy for their own good.

White Beaujolais Made from the Chardonnay grape, this normally appears under the Burgundy appellation of St-Véran.

The vintages of Beaujolais

1988 A somewhat uneven year, with some wines tasting very soft and without much depth. But good producers have made some deliciously fruity wines which are not for long ageing.

1987 A good year for the more serious Beaujolais wines. Some of the better crus are ageing well and are certainly worth keeping.

1986 Drink up Beaujolais Villages and most cru wines.

1985 A very fine year, compared to 1976, with wines of considerable fruit. The best cru wines are still improving. Finish up others and Villages wines.

1983 Longer-lasting cru wines will still be worth keeping.

Older vintages 1981, 1978 and 1976 Moulin-à-Vent, Morgon, Juliénas and Côte de Brouilly are still interesting.

Who's who in Beaujolais

The growers

Merchants still tend to be more important than growers in Beaujolais. However, there is an increasing tendency for the better estates in the crus to bottle their own wine. In this list, some of the names below will be from individual growers, some from merchants who bottle individual estate wines with special labels (indicated here with the name of the merchant or group of growers).

Brouilly
Domaine André Ronzières, Un Eventail des Vignerons Producteurs (*Hicks & Don*)
Vignoble de l'Ecluse, Un Eventail des Vignerons Producteurs (*Welbeck Wines*)
André Large, Un Eventail des Vignerons Producteurs (*Winecellars*)
Ch de la Chaize (*Fortnum & Mason; Selfridges; Stapylton Fletcher*)
Grand Clos de Briante (*Averys; Hungerford Wine Company; Wright Wine Company*)

Chénas
Jean Benon (*Roger Harris Wines*)
Domaine Louis Champagnon (*Morris & Verdin*)
Ch de Chénas, Un Eventail des Vignerons Producteurs (*Eldridge Pope; Haynes Hanson & Clark; High Breck Vintners; Stapylton Fletcher; Winecellars*)
Manoir des Journets, Duboeuf (*Anthony Byrne Fine Wines*)
Henri Lespinasse (*Roger Harris Wines*)

Chiroubles

Domaine Desmeures Père et Fils, Duboeuf (*Anthony Byrne Fine Wines; Corney & Barrow; Christopher Piper Wines*)

Ch de Javernand, Duboeuf (*Anthony Byrne Fine Wines; D Byrne & Co*)

Domaine de la Grosse Pierre, Un Eventail des Vignerons Producteurs (*Eldridge Pope; Haynes Hanson & Clark; Hicks & Don; High Breck Vintners; Stapylton Fletcher; Winecellars*)

Ch de Raousset, Duboeuf (*Berkmann Wine Cellars/Le Nez Rouge; Anthony Byrne Fine Wines; Christopher Piper Wines*)

La Maison des Vignerons à Chiroubles (*Adnams; Fortnum & Mason; Roger Harris Wines*)

Côte de Brouilly

Domaine de Conroy, Dépagneux (*Hurt & Daniel; The Wine Society*)

Domaine André Large, Un Eventail des Vignerons Producteurs (*Haynes Hanson & Clark; High Breck Vintners; Lay & Wheeler; Stapylton Fletcher*)

Ch Thivin (*Asda; Peter Green; Roger Harris Wines; Lay & Wheeler*)

Ch du Grand Vernay (*Roger Harris Wines*)

Domaine de la Berthaudière, Cave Besson (*Victor Hugo Wines*)

Domaine Pierre Bleue (*Eldridge Pope; Oddbins*)

Fleurie

Cave Coopérative de Fleurie (*Peter Dominic; Roger Harris Wines; Harrods; Lay & Wheeler; Selfridges; Wright Wine Co*)

Ch de Fleurie, Loron (*Averys; Chaplin & Son; Eldridge Pope; Peter Green; Hungerford Wine Company; Thos Peatling*)

Domaine de Montgenas, Un Eventail des Vignerons Producteurs (*Haynes Hanson & Clark; High Breck Vintners; Majestic; Russell & McIver; Stapylton Fletcher; Welbeck Wines; Winecellars*)

Ch des Déduits, Duboeuf (*Anthony Byrne Fine Wines; Fortnum & Mason; Christopher Piper Wines*)

Domaine des Quatres Vents, Duboeuf (*Berkmann Wine Cellars/Le Nez Rouge; Anthony Byrne Fine Wines*)

Michel Chignard (*Caves de la Madeleine; Laytons; Morris & Verdin; Arthur Rackhams*)

Ch des Labourons (*Fulham Road Wine Centre; Roger Harris Wines; La Vigneronne*)

André Colonge (*Hicks & Don*)

Domaine de la Grand Cour (*H Allen Smith; Bibendum; D Byrne & Co; Gerard Harris; Hicks & Don; Hungerford Wine Company; Thos Peatling; Tanners*)

Juliénas
Les Capitans, Louis Tête (*Peter Green*)
Domaine Monnet, Un Eventail des Vignerons Producteurs
(*Haynes Hanson & Clark; High Breck Vintners; La Vigneronne*)
François Condemine (*Fortnum & Mason; Roger Harris Wines*)
Domaine André Pelletier, Un Eventail des Vignerons
Producteurs (*Russell & McIver; Winecellars*)
Domaine de la Seigneurie de Juliénas, Duboeuf (*Anthony Byrne
Fine Wines; D Byrne & Co*)
Ernest Aujas (*Roger Harris Wines*)
Jean Benon (*Roger Harris Wines*)
Trenel Fils (*Yorkshire Fine Wines*)
Domaine du Grand Cuvage, Duboeuf (*Davisons*)
Domaine de la Vieille Eglise (*Wright Wine Company*)

Morgon
Domaine Georges Brun, Un Eventail des Vignerons Producteurs
(*Gerard Harris; High Breck Vintners; Stapylton Fletcher; La
Vigneronne; Winecellars*)
Domaine Jean Descombes, Duboeuf (*Berkmann Wine Cellars/Le
Nez Rouge; Anthony Byrne Fine Wines; D Byrne & Co; Fortnum &
Mason; Christopher Piper Wine; Thresher; Victoria Wine Company;
Wright Wine Company*)
Domaine Lieven, Duboeuf (*Anthony Byrne Fine Wines*)
Domaine des Vieux Cèdres, Loron (*Chaplin & Son; Hungerford
Wine Company; Thos Peatling*)
Domaine de Lathevalle, Mommessin (*Les Amis du Vin; Yorkshire
Fine Wines*)
Ch Gaillard, Sarrau (*Victor Hugo Wines*)

Moulin-à-Vent
Domaine des Caves Famille Delore, Duboeuf (*Anthony Byrne
Fine Wines*)
Ch des Jacques, Thorin (*Asda; Findlater Mackie Todd; Harrods*)
Domaine Jacky Janodet (*H Allen Smith; D Byrne & Co; Morris &
Verdin; La Réserve*)
Ch du Moulin-à-Vent (*Roger Harris Wines*)
Pierre Bélicard, Un Eventail des Vignerons Producteurs (*Eldridge
Pope; Majestic*)
Jean Brugne, Un Eventail des Vignerons Producteurs (*Gerard
Harris; Stapylton Fletcher; La Vigneronne; Winecellars*)
Domaine Berrod (*Sebastopol Wines*)
Fernand Charvet (*Hicks & Don; Hungerford Wine Company*)
Cave du Château de Chénas (*Roger Harris Wines; Victoria Wine
Company*)
Jean Picolet (*Roger Harris Wines*)
Domaine des Rosiers, Duboeuf (*Les Amis du Vin; Berkmann Wine
Cellars/Le Nez Rouge; Selfridges*)

Domaine de la Tour du Bief, Duboeuf (*Berkmann Wine Cellars/Le Nez Rouge; D Byrne & Co; Davisons; Christopher Piper Wines; Thresher; Wright Wine Company*)

Regnié

Ch la Tour Bourdon, Georges Duboeuf (*Anthony Byrne Fine Wines; Christopher Piper Wines; Windrush Wines*)
Domaine du Laboureur, Un Eventail des Vignerons Producteurs (*Eldridge Pope*)
Domaine de la Ronze, Sornin (*Hicks & Don*)
Domaine des Braves, Paul Cinquin (*Caves de la Madeleine; Laytons*)

St-Amour

Domaine des Duc (*Fortnum & Mason; Anthony Byrne Fine Wines; D Byrne & Co; Roger Harris Wines*)
Domaine du Paradis, Duboeuf (*Berkmann Wine Cellars/Le Nez Rouge*)
Domaine Guy Pâtissier, Un Eventail des Vignerons Producteurs (*Thos Peatling; Winecellars*)
Domaine de Breuil, Sarrau (*Victor Hugo Wines; Rose Tree Wine Company*)
Ch de St-Amour, Chanut Frères (*David Alexander; M & W Gilbey*)

Beaujolais Villages

Ch la Tour Bourdon, Duboeuf (*Christopher Piper Wines*)
Ch du Grand Vernay (*Roger Harris Wines*)
Geny de Flammacourt (*Roger Harris Wines*)
Ch Lacapelle, Jacques Dépagneux (*Windrush Wines*)
Cuvée Pierre Soitel, Sylvain Fessy (*Windrush Wines*)
Ch Vierres, Duboeuf (*Davisons*)
Domaine de la Chapelle de Vatre, Sarrau (*Victor Hugo Wines*)
Domaine du Grand Chêne, Un Eventail des Vignerons Producteurs (*High Breck Vintners; Winecellars*)
Ch de la Roche, Loron (*Averys; Chaplin & Son; Hungerford Wine Company; Russell & McIver; Tanners; Wright Wine Company*)
Ch des Vergers (*Findlater Mackie Todd; J Sainsbury; Wright Wine Company*)

Co-operatives and growers' groups

Caves de Bully (for basic Beaujolais and some cru wines) (*Oddbins*)
Cave du Château du Chénas (for Chénas and Moulin-à-Vent) (*Roger Harris Wines; Selfridges*)
Cave Coopérative Fleurie (for Fleurie) (*Roger Harris Wines; Selfridges*)

Cave des Producteurs Juliénas (for Juliénas and Beaujolais Villages) (*Roger Harris Wines*)
Cave Beaujolais de Bois d'Oingt (*Roger Harris Wines*)

Un Eventail des Vignerons Producteurs A grouping of nearly 50 growers who have joined together for central bottling and marketing, although still making their own wine. A range of very good wines.
See under individual crus and Beaujolais Villages above for stockists

The merchants

Chanut Good quality range of Beaujolais and Beaujolais Villages.
David Alexander; M & W Gilbey

Joseph Drouhin One of the Beaune merchants to take Beaujolais seriously. His wines are quite heavy, almost Burgundian, but well made.
Willoughbys; Wright Wine Company; Yorkshire Fine Wines

Georges Duboeuf Top quality range, often from individual growers. One of the best and most reliable names. Also uses the Paul Bocuse label.
Widely available

Pierre Ferraud High quality reputation, making good Nouveau and Villages.
Willoughbys; Yorkshire Fine Wines

Sylvain Fessy A good range of wines at most quality levels.
Selfridges; Windrush Wines; The Wine Society

Loron Sound, fruity wines at all quality levels. Occasional estate cru wines aim higher.
Widely available

Mommessin Another Burgundy merchant with an interest in Beaujolais, making a rich style, and a few estate wines.
Les Amis du Vin; Averys; Majestic; Waitrose; Wizard Wine Warehouses; Yorkshire Fine Wines

Pasquier-Desvignes Light style of wines, but of good commercial quality. The St-Amour is the best cru.
Victor Hugo Wines

Piat Their best claim to fame is the attractive bottle. They are better at Beaujolais cru wines than basic Beaujolais. They also make the branded Piat d'Or which everybody thinks is a Beaujolais but is in fact a vin de table.
Bottoms Up; Peter Dominic; Victoria Wine Company

Sarrau Good quality crus and Villages. A go-ahead young firm.
Victor Hugo Wines; Rose Tree Wine Company; J Sainsbury;
Tanners; Yorkshire Fine Wines

Louis Tête Serious basic Beaujolais, as well as cru wines.
Fulham Road Wine Centre; Peter Green; Thos Peatling

Thorin Good wine from Moulin-à-Vent, Ch des Jacques and also
Beaujolais Blanc.
Berry Bros & Rudd; Findlater Mackie Todd; Thos Peatling;
J Sainsbury

Trenel Small firm making good Morgon.
Majestic; Selfridges; Tanners; La Vigneronne; Yorkshire Fine Wines

Beaujolais Blanc
Les Caves de Bully (*Tesco*); Chaintré (*Marks & Spencer*); Loron
(*Averys*); Domaine de Savy, Duboeuf (*Anthony Byrne Fine*
Wines).

Best buys from Beaujolais

WHITE

Beaujolais Blanc 1988, Paquet (*Del Monicos*)

ROSÉ

Beaujolais Rosé 1988, Domaine des Sables d'Or (*Chesterford*
Vintners)

RED

Coteaux du Lyonnais, Georges Duboeuf (*Anthony Byrne Fine*
Wines)
Chiroubles 1987, La Maison des Vignerons (*Roger Harris Wines*)
Beaujolais Villages 1987, Georges Duboeuf (*widely available*)
Beaujolais Regnié 1988, Georges Duboeuf (*Morrisons*)
Le Guilleret Rouge Vin de Table, Sylvain Fessy (*Philip Eyres*
Wine Merchant)
Beaujolais Cave Cooperative de Bully 1987 (*Wizard Wine*
Warehouses)
Brouilly 1988, Ch des Tours (*Christopher Piper Wines*)
Beaujolais Villages 1987, Delaunay (*Welbeck Wine*)
Chénas 1986, Ch de Chénas, Un Eventail des Vignerons
Producteurs (*High Breck Vintners*)

Specialist stockists

Anthony Byrne Fine Wines; Berkmann Wine Cellars/Le Nez Rouge;
Roger Harris Wines; Ian G Howe; Ingletons Wines; Lay & Wheeler;
Thos Peatling; Christopher Piper Wines; J Townend & Sons; Le
Viticulteur

BORDEAUX

In all the hurly-burly and excitement about the new wine areas of the world, we shouldn't forget that most of our wine still comes from France, and most of our red wine still comes from Bordeaux. So the amount of red Bordeaux (claret) that we drink is a pretty good indication of our wine-drinking habits. The latest figures show that not only has our consumption between 1987 and 1988 gone up by 16 per cent, but we have also been prepared to pay a whacking 52 per cent more for it.

But does that mean that we are buying more claret, and more expensive claret as well? Or does it just mean that there's extra money going into the coffers in Bordeaux, all ready to smarten up already plush offices and build extra cellars?

The answer to both questions is yes. We are prepared to pay more for good claret, but it is also true that prices have risen in Bordeaux for no other reason than that the château owners and négociants think the market can bear it. And, as we go to press, it seems that for the 1988 vintage, they are right. There has been a mad scramble for wines from the top châteaux, with rises of as much as 40 per cent as soon as wines leave the châteaux and reach the open market. And even the threat of scandal – re-labelling wines from neighbouring Bergerac as Bordeaux – has done nothing to lessen the clamour.

The situation has been made worse by the little game the châteaux owners have of only releasing small amounts of wine (called *tranches* of wine) at a time. Dealers scramble for what little is available, the price is pushed up, and next time round the château can offer its second *tranche* at the price that was finally reached with the first *tranche*. It's an art that has been perfected over the past few years.

The excitement with buying the 1988 vintage en primeur is a fascinating contrast with what was happening exactly a year before with the 1987 vintage. The silence, as they say, was almost deafening as nobody bought, while in Bordeaux there was a firm, arrogant refusal to lower prices for wines which, while not the greatest, were still enjoyable.

Review of the 1980s

At the threshold of the 1990s, it is worth looking back over the past decade at the way the Bordelais have come to determine the price of their wine in a way that might have been unimaginable back in 1979. It is also worth recalling that until

Bordeaux

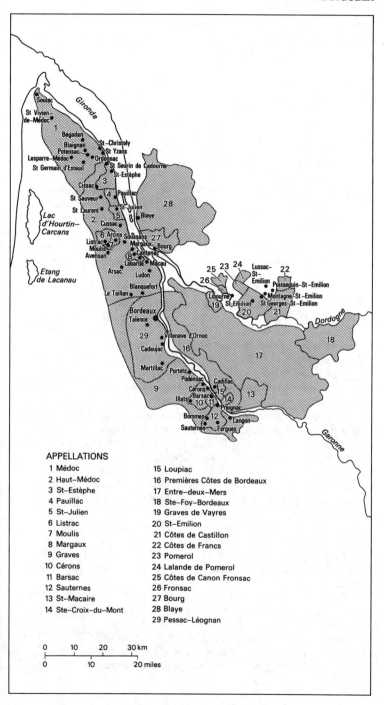

APPELLATIONS

1 Médoc
2 Haut–Médoc
3 St–Estèphe
4 Pauillac
5 St–Julien
6 Listrac
7 Moulis
8 Margaux
9 Graves
10 Cérons
11 Barsac
12 Sauternes
13 St–Macaire
14 Ste–Croix–du–Mont

15 Loupiac
16 Premières Côtes de Bordeaux
17 Entre–deux–Mers
18 Ste–Foy–Bordeaux
19 Graves de Vayres
20 St–Emilion
21 Côtes de Castillon
22 Côtes de Francs
23 Pomerol
24 Lalande de Pomerol
25 Côtes de Canon Fronsac
26 Fronsac
27 Bourg
28 Blaye
29 Pessac–Léognan

| 0 | 10 | 20 | 30 km |
| 0 | 10 | | 20 miles |

the late 1970s or even early 1980s, most Bordeaux châteaux weren't making any profit at all: it was only in the merchants' offices in Bordeaux that the figures were in the black rather than the red.

Things changed with the fabulous 1982 vintage. The greatest vintage since 1961, it was also probably the most talked about vintage of all time. It created the en primeur market – the market for futures in Bordeaux (see also page 318) – and it set in train a succession of fine vintages – 1983, 1985, 1986 and possibly 1988 – which were unique in the history of the region. Prices could rise, because the interest was there and because the wines were so good.

It is quite probable that 1987 will be seen not as a turning point in the inexorable rise in prices, but simply as a slowing down while the rest of world looked at its cellars over-flowing with fine wine, most of it still undrinkable. Certainly the interest from around the world in the top wines of Bordeaux has never been more intense, and certainly the châteaux owners can never have been in a better position.

As long, that is, as they aren't being bought up by big business. There has been a spate of takeovers of Bordeaux estates in the past few years. Many of the purchasers are wealthy French industrialists who like the idea of a vineyard-cum-château in the country which they can use for prestige entertaining as well as making wine. Others have been bought by Japanese, Italians, plenty of British. While many château owners may relish the idea of having money in the bank rather than tied up in the vineyard, the more serious people in the region are worried that as the current generation of owners dies, and their families pay the 40 per cent inheritance tax, they will be selling up to more insurance companies, and that in 20 years' time there may be no private estates left in Bordeaux.

So far, we have been talking about a tiny percentage of all the claret made. Most of the wine coming out of Bordeaux – itself the largest quality wine area in the world – is of the sort that ends up in bottles labelled simply Claret, AC Bordeaux. And here we enter very different territory: no headlines, but thousands of peasant farmers hoping to make a living and finding it pretty hard to do so. It is still very easy to buy plenty of their wine for under £3 a bottle, and for most of us this is what we think of as claret.

There's an awful lot of wine like this back in Bordeaux. While stocks have fallen slightly (owing to increased sales), they are still relatively higher than those for other areas of France, meaning that the demand-led pressure for these lesser wines of Bordeaux is unlikely to push prices up much, if at all. So we have in Bordeaux the widest range of prices imaginable - from

£2.50 a bottle at one end, to £30 or £40 at the other. No other wine region can match such a span.

Don't forget the white wines

Of course, while Bordeaux is mainly known for its red wines, we must not neglect the whites. Sweet white wines, Sauternes and Barsac in particular, have been enjoying considerable success recently, especially in France, with prices doubling in three years. That means that what were totally under-valued stars are now much more realistically priced in Bordeaux terms (which means we can't afford them).

Dry whites are the one style of Bordeaux wine which hasn't been caught up in the price spiral. A lot of that, of course, is to do with the quality of much that is made. But there are now some middle-ranking estates (especially in the Graves) and some blended wines from well-known merchant houses which, with their shot of grassy Sauvignon to give edge to the oily Sémillon, are worth seeking out. We list some of these later on in this section under 'Bordeaux names to watch'.

The taste of Bordeaux

THE REDS

Claret (red Bordeaux) is a blended wine, containing varying proportions of Cabernet Sauvignon, Cabernet Franc and Merlot. Two lesser varieties (in quantity but not in quality) that are planted increasingly rarely are Petit Verdot and Malbec.

Cabernet Sauvignon This is the major grape in the Médoc and Graves. It is also the most important quality red grape variety in the world. In Bordeaux, greatly influenced by the Atlantic Ocean, it makes long-lasting wines, full of blackcurrant fruit when young, but always heavily structured with tannin. With maturity, it mellows and a complex of tastes and flavours – spice, cedar, cigar-box – come in as the tannin softens. In Bordeaux, there is no such thing as a 100 per cent Cabernet Sauvignon wine, although some estates (especially in Pauillac) get quite close.

Cabernet Franc Lower tannin than the Cabernet Sauvignon, the Cabernet Franc gives a fresh, faster-maturing wine which, when blended, takes the hard edges off the Cabernet Sauvignon; it is used in many of the wines of St-Emilion and Pomerol.

Merlot The grape variety that comes into its own on the Right Bank of the River Dordogne, in St-Emilion and Pomerol. It makes wines with quite high initial acidity, but which soften and mellow faster than Cabernet Sauvignon. Jammy fruit is often the characteristic of these wines – plump, opulent and easier to appreciate than the more austere Cabernet Sauvignon wines of the Médoc.

THE WHITES

Sémillon Used for sweet wines, this grape, along with Sauvignon and Muscat, produces the luscious, honeyed style of Sauternes and Barsac, with great ageing ability derived from the noble rot. In dry whites, great care needs to be taken over its vinification, although the great dry whites of Bordeaux also rely on its ageing qualities.

Sauvignon The great white grape of the Loire. In Bordeaux, it makes wines which should have crispness and freshness when young, but which do not age well. A little Sauvignon in some of the sweet whites adds firmness.

The structure of the Bordeaux vineyard

There are various levels of appellation in Bordeaux. The most basic wines are labelled either Bordeaux or Bordeaux Supérieur (the latter has half a degree more alcohol than Bordeaux and is generally slightly better wine). These wines can come from anywhere in Bordeaux not covered by one of the more localised appellations, or are blends produced from young vines or vines which have given a higher yield than is allowed for a village or local AC.

Bordeaux and Bordeaux Supérieur represent bargain country – provided you can find the right wine.

REGIONAL APPELLATIONS

Above the basic appellation, there are a number of regional appellations.

Côtes de Bourg A large vineyard area on the north bank of the River Gironde making red wines. It is becoming a good source of what are called petit château wines (ie wines from small, lesser-known estates which are not classified according to one of the Bordeaux classifications). The best estates are on the river front, but properties away from the river do offer bargains.

Côtes de Castillon and **Côtes de Francs** Two small areas to the east of St-Emilion which make some delicious easy-drinking wines mainly from Merlot and Cabernet Franc. Try them if you come across them.

Entre-Deux-Mers A large region that forms the land between the two Rivers (or Mers) of Garonne and Dordogne. In the past it has been simply the source for over-sulphured medium sweet whites and a few reds, but now dry whites are assuming much greater importance. You won't find great quality, but you may come across good value.

Graves The huge stretch of vineyard south of Bordeaux. This was the original vineyard of the region before the Médoc was opened up. Both whites and reds are produced here. The finest wines come from the northern end in the suburbs of Bordeaux itself, some of which are in the new appellation of Pessac-Léognan (see below). The whole region has been seeing a renaissance in quality, not – at least not yet – followed by a commensurate increase in price. So, for both reds and whites, this is the area to watch at the moment.

Graves Supérieur A stronger version of a white Graves. Sometimes medium dry, so beware if you want a dry wine.

Médoc Geographically, this is the whole of the strip of land that runs north of Bordeaux out into the Atlantic at the mouth of the Gironde. But in appellation terms, AC Médoc is only the northern half from just above St-Estèphe, where the gravelly soil of the southern half peters out and becomes more clay. Occasional pockets of gravel give a clue to extra quality. This is an area, like the Graves, where prices have not yet caught up with increases in quality, and it can offer some good bargains.

Haut-Médoc This is the southern half of the Médoc, as far as the northern edge of the city of Bordeaux. Although the area covers all the land stretching away from the River Gironde, in wine terms, châteaux using this appellation will generally be further away from the river than the principal Médoc vineyards, which will be covered by the village appellations (see below). Villages without their own appellations include St-Seurin-de-Cadorne, Cissac, St-Saveur, St-Laurent, Ludon. But even in these villages there are classed growths and bourgeois growths which can now command high prices.

Premières Côtes de Blaye A small area attached to Côtes de Bourg. Somewhat more refined than the average Bourg wine, the red wines are also somewhat more expensive, but still acceptable value.

Premières Côtes de Bordeaux A narrow strip of vineyards on the north bank of the Garonne facing the Graves. Produces some good red wines as well as sweet whites.

Fronsac A couple of miles west of Pomerol, this area is producing some really exciting wines. Prices are rising, but they are still comparatively good value for money. They have something of the smoothness of St-Emilion and the intensity of Pomerol. There is also a smaller, slightly superior appellation of **Canon-Fronsac**. Both are worth looking for.

Margaux (Haut-Médoc) The perfumed bouquet of a good Margaux is the thing. Less concentrated than, for example, a Pauillac, the best wines have immense charm, finesse and breeding, although of all the Haut-Médoc villages this seems to have the most variable quality at the lower levels. The village of Cantenac is included in the Margaux appellation.

Moulis and **Listrac** Two smaller appellations in the hinterland of the Haut-Médoc. Only now becoming better known and therefore less expensive, they make more austere wines but also some wines with class. A number of good estates in Moulis especially are producing good wines at the moment.

Pauillac (Haut-Médoc) The most famous village appellation because it contains three of the five first growths (Lafite, Latour, Mouton-Rothschild – see below under Crus Classés). The wines are intense, full, firm and tannic with the greatest ageing potential. Words like 'blackcurrant' are used to describe the young wines; matured, they can be some of the greatest wine experiences anywhere – if you can afford them.

Pessac-Léognan New appellation at the northern end of the Graves, which takes in the best vineyard areas of the area. The châteaux include Haut-Brion, La Mission-Haut-Brion, Pape-Clément, La Louvière, Malartic-Lagravière and Domaine de Chevalier. This twin commune appellation is the source of the interest that the whole of the Graves is now beginning to generate, which means that prices (as well as quality) are higher.

Pomerol Next door to St-Emilion on the northern bank of the River Dordogne, but making wines with much greater intensity and strength. A tiny production from a small vineyard area ensures that even the least wines from this appellation are expensive, while Ch Pétrus, at the top, is the most expensive wine in the world, and almost certainly not worth the silly prices (for the same money at auction would you prefer one bottle of Pétrus 1961 or three of Lafite?). The satellite appellation of **Lalande de Pomerol** is less expensive (but not so top-class).

St-Emilion Vineyards surround the most attractive town in the Bordeaux region, built on a hill on the north bank of the River

Dordogne. There is a complex system of classification – at the top is Premier Grand Cru Classé, then Grand Cru Classé, then Grand Cru, then the basic level. This is an area where prices quite often don't justify the quality, especially at the middle range of estates.

On the edges of St-Emilion are the satellite villages of Montagne-St-Emilion, Puisseguin-St-Emilion, St-Georges-St-Emilion, Lussac-St-Emilion, Parsac-St-Emilion. The wines here are cheaper than Cru St-Emilion and often just as good as basic St-Emilion.

St-Estèphe The northernmost of the great Haut-Médoc villages, and probably making the least refined wines. They tend to be sturdier, darker in colour, more tannic than other Haut-Médoc wines.

St-Julien Haut-Médoc village making elegant, soft, round wines, which – for the Médoc – mature early. In many ways these are the classic clarets, mixing great fruit with elegance and restraint.

THE SWEET WHITE WINE AREAS

Sauternes and **Barsac** The two great dessert wine areas, carved out of the forests of the Landes, relying on the noble rot – 'pourriture noble' – to make intense, lusciously honeyed sweet wines. Under-valued for many years, their prices are now rising seriously, but the experience of drinking them makes it worth paying them (especially if you can find half-bottles).

Cadillac, (Côtes de Bordeaux, St-Macaire and Cérons Lesser sweet wines for drinking young and well chilled as aperitifs. Occasionally, some châteaux will spring surprises in terms of higher quality.

Loupiac and **Ste-Croix-du-Mont** Somewhere between the two previous groups in intensity and with some noble rot in good years. Generally best drunk young, but will keep in better years.

THE DRY WHITES OF BORDEAUX

The range in dry whites is as great as in the reds. Some of the top châteaux in the Graves produce a white wine, aged in oak, that matures well to deep, rich flavours (Haut-Brion Blanc, Laville-Haut-Brion, Domaine de Chevalier, Malartic-Lagravière, Rahoul, Carbonnieux).

At the bottom end of the scale, much dry white is downright dull, relieved only by flashes of the grassy acidity of Sauvignon. If the name of one of these wines includes 'Cépage Sauvignon' or an equivalent phrase, the latest vintage will be fresh, crisp and fruity, but the wines fade fast. While much basic white Bordeaux comes under the Bordeaux AC, look also for the small appellation of **Graves de Vayres**, which is a small area of Entre-Deux-Mers and for wines from **Bourg** and **Blaye**.

Recent tastings have shown that the quality of dry whites is improving considerably. Modern stainless steel equipment has cut down on the sulphur and boosted the fruit. But with a slow rise in price, many of the lesser white Bordeaux don't really represent value for money: there are better, more individualistic wines from elsewhere in the world.

What's on the Bordeaux label

Château The name which applies to an estate rather than a building, and signifies only that the wine in the bottle comes from a specified vineyard. The vineyard doesn't have to be in one piece of land, provided it is all in the same appellation area.

Crus Bourgeois A voluntary local classification of wines which are just under the formal Cru Classé status. Often good value wines at this level, although many names that are now commanding high prices are also Crus Bourgeois.

Crus Classés Most of the major Bordeaux areas are classified in one way or another. In the Médoc, the most famous classification of them all (which took place in 1855 and, with one adjustment, still stands) places the top estates in classes one (first growth, the top) to five (fifth growth). Contrary to popular misconception, the classification was not based on quality but on the prices the wines were fetching (with class one representing the most expensive wines). While many of the estates still justify their placing in terms of quality, others have disappeared or live on their classification rather than their wine.

In the Graves, there has also been a classification system, but this seems to have been swallowed up by the creation of the new appellation of Pessac-Léognan (see under village appellations). In St-Emilion, a complex system has three tiers of quality – from Premier Grand Cru Classé, through Grand Cru Classé to Grand Cru. Sauternes and Barsac have 22 classed growths which were also classified in 1855. Pomerol has no classification, but all its wines are expensive anyway.

Grand Vin Can be used for any wine from Bordeaux Supérieur upwards. It has no legal significance, but it helps sales.

Mis/Mise en bouteille au château/à la propriété Loose terms: propriété can mean a huge warehouse in Bordeaux owned by the owner of the vineyard or the négociant or it can mean a cellar on the estate. Bottled at the château may mean bottled on a bottling line hired for the occasion. The advantage of bottling at the estate is that the wine moves less between vat or wooden cask and bottle, but there are still British merchants who bottle some claret and this often represents terrific value for money.

Négociant Bordeaux merchant who buys wine to blend, as well as holding stocks of fine wines. The négociants control the sale of much of the wine even from the top estates. The line between merchants and vineyard owners is now very blurred, since most négociants also own châteaux.

SECOND WINES

Many of the top châteaux do not put all their wine from a vintage into the blend for their best wine. Some wine – good, but not the absolute best (sometimes because it comes from young vines) – is put aside and sold separately as a second wine. By any other standard, this is still very good wine. It's not cheap, but it's cheaper than the first wine and gives some idea of what all the fuss is about.

While nearly every self-respecting estate brings out a second wine (fashion is very important in Bordeaux), we give a list in the section on Bordeaux names to watch of those we reckon offer the best value. Other names you might come across are (with the main château in brackets):

Médoc de Marbuzet (Cos d'Estournel), Les Forts de Latour (Ch Latour), de l'Amiral (Ch Labégorce-Zédé), de Clairefont (Ch Prieuré-Lichine), La Dame de Montrose (Ch Montrose), Moulin-Riche (Ch Léoville-Poyferré), Amiral de Beychevelle (Ch Beychevelle), Domaine de Martiny (Ch Cissac), Ch Gallais-Bellevue (Ch Potensac), Ch La Tour d'Aspic (Ch Haut-Batailley), Moulin des Carruades (Ch Lafite), Marquis de Ségur (Ch Calon-Ségur), Pavillon Rouge (Ch Margaux), Segonnes (Ch Lascombes), Clos du Marquis, St-Julien (Ch Léoville Las Cases), Lacoste-Borie (Ch Grand-Puy-Lacoste), Réserve de la Comtesse (Ch Pichon-Lalande), Réserve du Général (Ch Palmer).

Graves Bahans Haut-Brion (Ch Haut-Brion), La Parde de Haut-Bailly (Ch Haut-Bailly), Coucherat (Ch Louvière), Petit Rahoul (Ch Rahoul), Hauts de Smith Haut-Lafitte (Ch Smith Haut-Lafitte), La Tour Léognan (Ch Carbonnieux).

Many other classified growths and Cru Bourgeois châteaux sell a second wine; it would be worth asking your merchant what he or she stocks.

Bordeaux vintages

We have already commented on the magnificent vintages of the 1980s. In the 1970s and 1960s, things were much more variable, partly because wine producers were unable to call upon the wonders of modern technology to help them out, but also because the weather has been particularly kind over the past ten years.

Modern technology also means that even in poor years, producers of any talent make reasonable wine which matures more quickly than wines from great vintages and can be very enjoyable if the price is right. One of the problems in Bordeaux in recent years, of course, is that all too often the price hasn't been right.

The great sweet white wines need the right climatic conditions much more than the reds, so there are fewer fine vintages, but even in lesser years the wines are better than they used to be.

1988 *Reds*: a mixed vintage, with fine wines and some near-disasters, depending on whether the grapes were Merlot/Cabernet Franc or Cabernet Sauvignon. Because Merlot is generally picked earlier than Cabernet Sauvignon, it avoided the early October rains. The Cabernet Sauvignon growers who did not panic but waited for the rain to go away have made some intense, fruity wines; those who picked during the rains will have wines suffering from unripe tannin. In general terms, St-Emilion and Pomerol (Merlot-based wines) are very ripe and rich, while Graves and Pauillac are the best of the Cabernet Sauvignon wines. *Sweet whites*: a great year, with almost perfect picking conditions that allowed growers to pick nobly rotten grapes right through to November. Superb wines will have been made.

1987 *Reds*: another vintage where rain played an important part, depending on whether the crop was picked before or after the rain. It won't develop into a great year, but some producers – especially in St-Emilion and Pomerol – will have made average quality wines, which will probably mature quickly. It was also a year when the best producers declassified much of their wine down to their second wines, so there are some bargains in this area. *Sweet whites*: a small crop of wines which will mature quickly.

1986 *Reds*: a large vintage. The Merlot regions on the right bank of St-Emilion and Pomerol suffered from high yields, and those producers who removed bunches during the summer to lessen the final yield will have made the best wines. In the Médoc and Graves, the wines are big and tannic after a long, hot September. They should last a long time. *Sweet whites*: it looks as though this has been a very great vintage, with good botrytis and plenty of fruit. Medium levels of acidity mean medium-term development.

1985 *Reds*: the largest vintage ever. Generally regarded as a very good year, although not hitting the heights of 1982. The finest wines have immense richness, depth of colour and concentration which presage a long, slow maturation. Wines from the Graves are developing fast, while those from the Médoc need a long time to soften up. St-Emilion and Pomerol wines are rich and concentrated. This is a vintage to buy if you can. *Sweet whites*: a middle quality vintage, with only the top estates producing really good wines. They will be ready to drink during 1990.

1984 *Reds*: generally lack fruit and also the roundness given by the Merlot, which failed to flower in the cold, damp spring. The wines will have a short life (three to ten years) but when made by a reputable château should give some austere pleasure. Prices were initially too high for the quality but are likely to fall. *Sweet whites*: soft, light, early-maturing wines. Drink now.

1983 *Reds*: elegant, structured wines which are just beginning to soften out and will then mature slowly. The Médoc wines are better than St-Emilion or Pomerol, but prices for all areas have remained good. Start drinking St-Emilion now. *Sweet whites*: a very great year indeed in Sauternes, with honeyed fruit but quite high acid levels which will give the wines a long life. Don't even touch them before the mid-1990s.

1982 *Reds*: the big ones – in price as well as quality. At the petit château level, some very fine wines were made, and there are some bargains to be had. At the higher levels, prices are high. The wines of St-Emilion and Pomerol will be drinkable this year, but others may not really mature until the turn of the century. *Sweet whites*: a quick-maturing vintage – drink up now.

1981 *Reds*: a bargain vintage. Lean, austere wines, often well structured. The best wines – from the Médoc in particular – will mature for another two or three years, but many are ready to drink now. St-Emilion, too, is ready to drink, but keep Pomerols. *Sweet whites*: variable vintage in which only the top estates made wines with any lasting power. These can survive till well into the 1990s, but drink the others now.

1980 *Reds*: wines to drink now. They are rather dry, but the prices are good. Most have already been drunk – check that any you have are not drying out, and taste before you buy. *Sweet whites*: medium quality vintage, quite light, but with some bargains. Ready to drink.

Please write to tell us about any ideas for features you would like to see in next year's edition or in *Which? Wine Monthly*.

1979 *Reds*: suddenly, everybody expects these wines to go on developing. The petits châteaux and St-Emilions are fading, but the best Médoc wines will go on for three or four years before reaching their peak. *Sweet whites*: a rather light vintage, but there is some pleasure in the top wines.

1978 *Reds*: slow-maturing wines, of which the best are only just opening up. Most petit château wines are for drinking now and over the next few years, but the top wines will go on and on. The Mêdoc and Graves wines will last the longest.

1976 *Reds*: ripe wines that can be slightly watery, but good wines are packed with slightly sweet fruit which tastes good now. Drink any of the wines now, especially Pomerols. *Sweet whites*: this is a great vintage to drink now – the wines are rich and oily. The best wines will keep, but are enjoyable now.

1975 *Reds*: a problem year. After great initial enthusiasm, because the power and tannin suggested a long life, nothing has happened. The wines are still very dry and tannic and don't have much underlying fruit. Only the best will open out; the rest will probably just get drier. Check on the colour – if it's brown, it needs drinking now. *Sweet whites*: lighter than 1976, with excellent balance of fruit and acidity. They are developing an attractive, mature taste, and are good for drinking now.

1970 *Reds*: this is a year with a great future still ahead of it. Although any petit château wines should be drunk, top wines will go on – enjoy them now and into the next century. *Sweet whites*: big, rich, almost over-the-top wines that may mature for even longer. Drink any of them now, although the top classed growths will last a while yet.

DRY WHITES

There are two levels of drinkability for dry whites. Most – especially if they have a high amount of Sauvignon – need to be consumed within two or three years of the harvest, so drink 1986 and 1988 this year, and taste 1987 before you buy. Wines aged in wood from some top estates (especially in the Graves) will go on for much longer – decades even. Consult the vintage guide for reds for these wines.

Drink now – or keep?

As a general rule, the higher up the classification scale, the longer a red Bordeaux will keep. (The same goes for sweet white Sauternes.) So ordinary Bordeaux appellation wine needs drinking first, basic St-Emilion next – and so on up the scale: the top classed growths of the Médoc seem to last decades.

Bordeaux names to watch

It is not possible to indicate stockists against Bordeaux châteaux since British merchants do not buy every vintage. In the Where to buy section, and under the Specialist stockists at the end of this section, we indicate those merchants who have large stocks of Bordeaux and specialise in buying direct from the area. Ask their advice as well as looking for some of the names we give below.

As a general rule, you will find better value in the Médoc and Graves than you will in St-Emilion and (certainly) Pomerol.

The reds

We have included in this section a list of branded and own-label wines that we can recommend. Some are non-vintage wines – not necessarily a bad thing when consistency of style is important. If they are vintage wines, look for the vintage and buy according to the vintage notes above. Wines from the 1985 and 1986 vintages will generally be better than 1987 vintage.

BRANDED AND OWN-LABEL CLARETS

Sandeman Claret (*Oddbins*)
Tanners Claret (*Tanners*)
Maître d'Estournel (*Laytons; André Simon*)
Ch Chauffepied (*Wizard Wine Warehouses*)
Chevalier de Védrines (*Wine Growers Association*)
Tesco Claret (*Tesco*)
Ch de Brondeau (*Balls Brothers*)
Willoughbys Sunday Claret (*Thomas Baty; George Dutton; Willoughbys*)
Sainsbury's Claret (*J Sainsbury*)
Beau Rivage, Borie Manou (*Davisons*)
St-Emilion, Sélection Jean-Pierre Moueix (*Adnams; Corney & Barrow*)
Sirius, Peter Sichel (*Berkmann Wine Cellars/Le Nez Rouge; Lay & Wheeler; Edward Sheldon*)
Peatling's Mature Claret (*Thos Peatling*)

THE CHÂTEAUX

Châteaux listed here are enjoying a high reputation at the moment. Additionally, their wines are good value for money.

Bordeaux and **Bordeaux Supérieur** Ch Méaume, Ch Mirefleurs, Ch Le Gardéra, Ch Thieuley, Ch Terrefort-Quancard, Ch Timberlay, Ch de Belcier, Ch Tour de Mirabeau, Ch Sables-Peytraud, Ch La Pierrière, Ch du Juge, Ch La Dominique Siegla, Ch de Brondeau, Ch Senailac, Ch Lalande.

Médoc Ch La Clare, Ch Patache d'Aux, Ch Blaignan, Ch Roquegrave, Ch du Castéra, Ch La Cardonne, Ch Haut-Canteloup, Ch Potensac, Ch de By, Ch La Tour de By, Ch Greysac, Ch Le Boscq, Ch Liversan, Ch Les Ormes-Sorbet.

Haut-Medoc Ch Hanteillan, Ch Maucamps, Ch de Camensac, Ch Cantemerle, Ch Bel-Orme-Tronquoy-de-Lalande, Ch Caronne-Ste-Gemme, Ch Cissac, Ch Lamothe-Cissac, Ch du Moulin-Rouge, Ch Citran, Ch Coufran, Ch Lamarque, Ch Malescasse, Ch Reysson, Ch Larose-Trintaudon, Ch Sociando-Mallet, Ch La Tour Carnet, Ch Villegeorge, Ch Barreyres, Ch Lanessan, Ch La Tour Carnet, Ch Soudars, Ch Beaumont, Ch Ramage La Batisse, Ch Barthez, Ch Lapiey, Ch Sénéjac, Ch Le Bourdieu, Ch de Lamarque, Ch La Tonnelle, Ch Victoria.

St-Estèphe Ch Beau-Site, Ch Haut-Marbuzet, Ch Tronquoy-Lalande, Ch Cos Labory, Ch Commanderie, Ch de Pez, Ch Lafon-Rochet, Ch Meyney, Ch Chambert-Marbuzet, Ch Les Ormes-de-Pez, Ch Houissant, Ch Laffitte-Carcasset, Ch Calon-Ségur.

Pauillac Ch Clerc-Milon, Ch Grand-Puy-Lacoste, Ch Haut-Bages-Libèral, Ch Haut-Batailley, Ch Pontet-Canet, Ch Fonbadet, Ch Pédesclaux, Ch Colombier-Monpelou.

St-Julien Ch Lagrange, Ch Léoville-Barton, Ch Langoa-Barton, Ch Talbot, Ch St-Pierre-Sevaistre, Ch Gloria, Ch Hortevie, Ch Branaire-Ducru, Ch du Glana.

Margaux Ch d'Angludet, Ch d'Issan, Ch Monbrison, Ch Pouget, Ch du Tertre, Ch La Gurgue, Ch Siran, Ch Dauzac, Ch Labégorce-Zédé, Ch Kirwan, Ch Rausan-Ségla, Ch Desmirail, Ch Tayac, Ch Prieuré-Lichine.

Moulis and **Listrac** Ch Brillette, Ch Chasse-Spleen, Ch Fourcas-Dupré, Ch Maucaillou, Ch Moulin-à-Vent, Ch Anthonic, Ch Dutruch-Grand-Poujeaux, Ch Fonréaud, Ch Fourcas-Hosten, Ch Clarke, Ch Lestage, Ch Ruat Petit Poujeaux, Ch Duplessis-Fabre.

Graves Ch Roquetaillade la Grange, Ch Rahoul, Ch Cabannieux, Ch Pouyanne, Ch Coucheroy, Ch Chicane, Domaine de Gaillat, Ch Chantegrive.

Pessac-Léognan Ch Carbonnieux, Ch Rochemorin, Ch de Fieuzal, Ch Haut-Bailly, Ch La Louvière, Ch de France, Ch Picque-Caillou, Ch Bouscaut, Ch Olivier.

St-Emilion Ch L'Arrosée, Ch Fombrauge, Ch Fonroque, Ch La Fleur, Ch Monbousquet, Ch Larmande, Ch Cadet-Piola, Ch La Dominique, Ch Ripeau, Ch Croque-Michotte, Ch Fonplégade, Ch Le Tertre Rôteboeuf, Ch Balestard-la-Tonnelle, Ch Cap-de-

Mourlin, Ch Haut-Sarpe, Ch La Tour-de-Pin-Figeac, Ch Bellefont-Belcier, Ch Cardinal-Villemaurine, Ch Montlabert, Ch La Serre, Vieux-Château Mazerat, Ch Franc-Mayne.

In the sub-appellations (Puisseguin-St-Emilion, Lussac-St-Emilion, Montagne-St-Emilion, St-Georges-St-Emilion, Parsac-St-Emilion) look for Ch Belair-Montaiguillon (St-Georges), Ch des Laurets (Puisseguin), Ch Maison-Blanche (Montagne), Ch Roudier (Montagne), Ch St-Georges (St-Georges), Ch Vieux-Bonneau (Montagne), Ch Haut Bernat (Puisseguin), Vieux-Château Guibeau (Puisseguin).

Pomerol Clos du Clocher, Clos René, Ch Latour-à-Pomerol, Ch Le Bon Pasteur, Ch Lafleur Gazin, Ch L'Eglise-Clinet, Ch La Grave (formerly La Grave-Trignant-de-Boisset), Ch Petit-Village.

Lalande de Pomerol Ch Belles-Graves, des Annereaux, Ch Bertineau St-Vincent, Les Hautes Tuileries.

Fronsac and Canon-Fronsac Ch Coustolle, Ch Pichelèbre, Ch La Rivière, Ch Mayne-Vieil, Ch Canon de Brem, Ch Mazeris, Ch Rouet, Ch La Dauphine.

Côtes de Bourg Ch La Croix de Millorit, Ch Lalibarde, Ch Mille-Secousses, Ch de Barbe, Ch Eyquem, Ch Tour-Séguy, Ch du Bousquet, Ch Mendoce, Ch Falfas.

Côtes de Blaye Ch Charron, Ch L'Escadre, Ch Segonzac, Ch Peyraud, Ch Les Moines, Ch Petits Arnauds, Ch Fontblanche, Ch Haut-Sociondo, Ch Perenne, Ch Cap-Martin.

Premières Côtes de Bordeaux Ch Gardéra, Ch Reynon, Ch Peyrat, Ch Lafitte, Ch Bel Air Montaigne, Ch Laroche, Ch Le Clyde.

Côtes de Castillon, Côtes de Francs Ch Montbadon, Ch de Clotte, Ch Moulin Rouge, Ch Pitray, Ch Laclaverie, Ch Puyguéraud, Ch de Belcier, Ch Les Douves de Francs, Ch du Palanquey, Ch Bois des Naud.

SECOND WINES

Here we give a selection of second wines from major estates that are good value. The main estate name is given in brackets.
Connétable Talbot, St-Julien (Ch Talbot)
Prieur de Meyney, St-Estèphe (Ch Meyney)
Sarget de Gruaud-Larose, St-Julien (Ch Gruaud-Larose)
Baron Villeneuve de Cantemerle, Haut-Médoc (Ch Cantemerle)
Ch Artigues Arnaud, Pauillac (Ch Grand-Puy-Ducasse)
Les Fiefs de Lagrange, St-Julien (Ch Lagrange)
Ch Abiet, Haut-Médoc (Ch Cissac)
Ch La Salle Poujeaux, Haut-Médoc (Ch Poujeaux)
Ch Lamouroux, Margaux (Ch Rausan-Ségla)

L'Ermitage de Chasse-Spleen (Ch Chasse-Spleen)
Ch de Candale (Ch d'Issan)
Marks & Spencer St-Julien (Ch Léoville-Barton)
Ch Haut-Bages Avérous (Ch Lynch-Bages)

The sweet whites

Sauternes and **Barsac** Ch Chartreuse, Ch Sigalas-Rabaud, Ch Broustet, Ch Doisy-Dubroca, Ch Doisy-Védrines, Ch Bastor-Lamontagne, Ch Guiteronde, Ch Liot, Ch St-Amand, Ch Cantegril (second wine of Ch Doisy-Daëne), Ch de Malle, Ch de Fargues, Ch Suduiraut, Ch Lafaurie-Peyraguey, Ch Raymond-Lafon.

Other sweet whites Ch Loubens, Ch des Coulinats, Ch de Tastes (both Ste-Croix-du-Mont), Ch Loupiac-Gaudiet (Loupiac), Ch de Berbec (Premières Côtes de Bordeaux).

The dry whites

Graves Ch Malartic-Lagravière, Ch La Tour-Martillac, Ch Montalivet, Ch Olivier, Ch Rahoul, Ch Roquetaillade la Grange, Ch d'Arricaud, Ch Coucheroy, Ch La Garance.

Entre-Deux-Mers Ch St-Florin, Ch Bonnet.

Bordeaux Sirius Blanc (Peter Sichel), Maître d'Estournel, Blanc de Sénéjac, Ch Thieuley.

Best buys from Bordeaux

DRY WHITE

Ch du Croix Sauvignon (*City Wines*)
Ch Thieuley Sauvignon, Bordeaux (*widely available*)
Sirius Blanc 1987, Peter Allan Sichel (*widely available*)
Ch des Vergnes 1988, Bordeaux Sauvignon (*Fullers*)
Ch Coucheroy 1987, Graves (*Cachet Wines*)
Ch de Rochemorin 1986, Pessac-Léognan (*Waitrose*)
Ch des Roches 1988, Bordeaux Blanc Sauvignon (*Christopher Piper Wines*)

SWEET WHITE

Ch des Coulinats 1982, Ste-Croix-du-Mont (*D Byrne & Co; Winelines*)
Ch des Berbec 1983, Premières Côtes de Bordeaux (*Safeway*)
Ch Lousteau Vieil 1985, Ste-Croix-du-Mont (*La Vigneronne*)
Ch Laurette 1986, Sauternes (*Barnes Wine Shop*)
Ch des Tours 1983, Ste-Croix-du-Mont (*Berry Bros & Rudd; S H Jones*)

RED

Ch Haut Sociondo 1983, Côtes de Blaye (*Gerard Harris; Thos Peatling*)

St-Julien 1985, Léoville-Barton (*Marks & Spencer*)

Le Fronsac, Jean-Pierre Moueix (*Berkmann Wine Cellars/Le Nez Rouge*)

Ch Timberlay 1986, Médoc (*Davisons; Whittalls Wines*)

Jolly Good Claret (*Caves de la Madeleine; Laytons*)

Ch Tourtirac 1985, Côtes de Castillon (*Eldridge Pope*)

Ch Le Gardéra 1985, Bordeaux Supérieur (*Fullers*)

Ch de Brondeau 1985, Bordeaux Supérieur (*Balls Brothers; J Townend & Sons*)

Ch Puy Castéra 1985, Cru Bourgeois (*Martinez Fine Wine*)

Ch Pitray 1986, Côtes de Castillon (*John Armit Wines; Wine Society*)

Prince de la Rivière 1982, Fronsac (*Rodney Densem Wines*)

Ch Trinité Valrose 1986, Bordeaux Supérieur (*Hadleigh Wine Cellars*)

Ch Méaume 1986, Bordeaux Supérieur (*Majestic*)

Ch Mirefleurs 1986, Bordeaux Supérieur (*J Sainsbury*)

Ch de France 1983, Pessac-Léognan (*Russell & McIver*)

Ch du Puy 1985, Montagne-St-Emilion (*Organic Wine Company; Stapylton Fletcher*)

Ch Respide 1981, Graves (*Berry Bros & Rudd*)

Ch La Chapelle-Despagnet 1985, St-Emilion Grand Cru (*Bin Ends*)

Ch Belcier 1983, Côtes de Castillon (*Borg Castel; Cadwgan Fine Wine Merchants*)

Ch Beauséjour 1983, Fronsac (*J E Hogg*)

L'Hermitage de Chasse-Spleen 1986, Haut Médoc (*Wine Rack*)

Specialist stockists

Adnams; John Armit Wines; Averys of Bristol; Ballantynes of Cowbridge; Nigel Baring; Berry Bros & Rudd; D Byrne & Co; Cairns & Hickey; Classic Wines; College Cellar; Corney & Barrow; Davisons; Eldridge Pope; Farr Vintners; Alex Findlater; Findlater Mackie Todd; Fine Vintage Wines; Friarwood; Goedhuis & Co; Andrew Gordon Wines; John Harvey & Sons; Haynes Hanson & Clark; Victor Hugo Wines; Hungerford Wine Company; S H Jones; Justerini & Brooks; Richard Kihl; Kurtz & Chan; Lay & Wheeler; Laytons; O W Loeb; Master Cellar Wine Warehouse; Nickolls & Perks; Nobody Inn; Thos Peatling; Pimlico Dozen; Raeburn Fine Wines and Foods; Reid Wines; La Réserve; Selfridges; Edward Sheldon; Stones of Belgravia; Supergrape; Tanners Wines; J Townend & Sons; Turville Valley Wines; T & W Wines; Upper Crust; La Vigneronne; Whittalls Wines; Willoughbys; Wine House

BURGUNDY

Waking up to the real world?

On 1 December 1988 an historic event took place in London – the first ever generic Burgundy tasting. And to those in the wine trade who have seen Burgundy's inertia in promoting itself, the event was significant indeed.

If Burgundy had decided to organise a tasting, it must have been because it felt the need to promote itself. That in itself is an unusual thought: of all the French regions, Burgundy is the one that had spent not a sou on marketing itself.

But now, it seems, Burgundy is willing to spend. The 1989 Vinexpo saw a huge Burgundian stand, members of the wine trade are receiving regular Burgundian newsletters (they don't tell you anything, but the thought is there), tastings are being laid on in the United States.

What is happening? Here is Burgundy which over the last few years has been able to sell most of what it produces (after all, it doesn't make very much in comparison with Bordeaux), and keeps on raising its prices, doing exactly what an up-and-coming region of the south of France might do. Why?

Well, even in Burgundy, that bastion of conservatism where working jointly with your vineyard neighbour used to be almost unheard of, things change. A new generation is taking charge in the négociant offices and the cellars. They see that they have

Burgundy

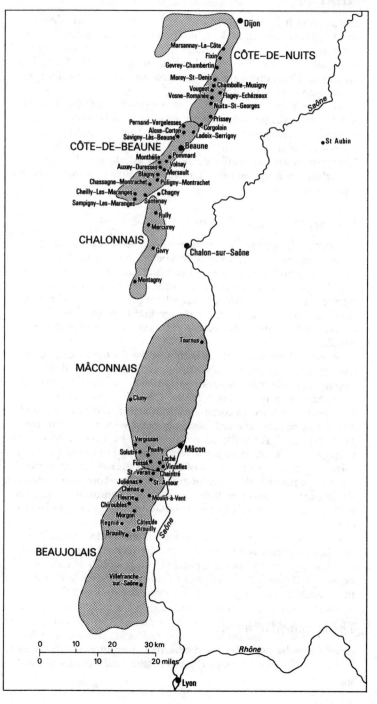

CÔTE-DE-NUITS

Dijon
Marsannay-La-Côte
Fixin
Gevrey-Chambertin
Morey-St-Denis
Vougeot
Chambolle-Musigny
Flagey-Echézeaux
Vosne-Romanée
Nuits-St-Georges
Prissey
Corgoloin
Pernand-Vergelesses
Aloxe-Corton
Ladoix-Serrigny
Savigny-Lès-Beaune

CÔTE-DE-BEAUNE

Beaune
St Aubin
Monthélie
Pommard
Auxey-Duresses
Volnay
Blagny
Mersault
Chassagne-Montrachet
Puligny-Montrachet
Cheilly-Les-Maranges
Chagny
Sampigny-Les-Maranges
Santenay
Rully
Mercurey

CHALONNAIS

Givry
Chalon-sur-Saône
Montagny

Saône

MÂCONNAIS

Tournus

Cluny

Vergisson
Solutré
Pouilly
Mâcon
Fuissé
Loché
Vinzelles
St-Véran
Chaintré
Juliénas
St-Amour
Chénas
Fleurie
Moulin-à-Vent
Chiroubles
Morgon
Régnié
Côtesde
Brouilly
Brouilly

BEAUJOLAIS

Villefranche-sur-Saône

Saône

| 0 | 10 | 20 | 30 km |
| 0 | 10 | | 20 miles |

Rhône

Lyon

competition from the rest of the world: Australia, New Zealand and California can all make Chardonnay as good as any but the greatest white Burgundy – and at a fraction of the price. They note that even the problems of producing great Pinot Noir outside red Burgundy are being overcome. And they realise the need to do something about it.

Their solution is to remind us of the smaller appellations, the less famous villages, where Burgundy is still relatively inexpensive (Burgundy is never cheap). They tell us about the virtues of Fixin, St-Aubin, St-Véran, Givry, Rully, Monthélie, Chorey-lès-Beaune, Pouilly Loché. They emphasise that not everything in Burgundy is Meursault and Vosne-Romanée at £50 a bottle or more.

Up the price, hype the wine

It's encouraging news for anyone who doesn't want to see a great wine area succumbing to the belief that the market will continue to take price rises and still buy. But by the look of the 1988 Hospices de Beaune auction - the benchmark for price-setting for each new vintage and where price rises of 35 per cent for reds were recorded – the message that Burgundy needs to get out and sell itself still has to get through to a great many people.

To most observers of that auction, it wasn't the price rise in itself that was interesting, but rather the reason behind it. Certainly, while the comparatively small production of white Burgundy (only two villages on the Côte d'Or make more white than red) continued to command high prices, those for red had stagnated, because the only really fine red wine vintage in the 1980s was 1985. A very good reason to hype up the 1988 vintage – and price rises are a very good way of doing that.

In Burgundy it's not a case of six bottles for the price of five, but five bottles for the price of six – an interesting way of going about business, and one that is calculated to infuriate those who realise that Burgundy's former reputation is not going to last for ever.

Whichever way you look at it, we come back to comparisons. Would you prefer New Zealand Chardonnay at £6 to £7 a bottle or white Burgundy from a reputable village at £20 or more – especially if you have to engage in considerable research into the reputation of the grower before you decide to buy?

The minefield of names

Apart from the price the main deterrent from buying Burgundy is the complexity of the appellation system and the number of individual growers. There are something like 5,000 growers in Burgundy and 150 négociants, and most of the growers and a good many négociants seem to share just a few surnames. No wonder a Mondavi Chardonnay or a Brown Brothers Australian Chardonnay seem safer bets.

But while this plethora of producers may be off-putting, it's also a sign of the great changes in Burgundy over the past 10 to 15 years. Gone are the days when the négociants controlled nearly all the trade in Burgundy. Now, the names to conjure with are not those of the négociants but of the younger generation of growers. They have been to university, to wine school (even to wine school in the United States), they talk to one another, they exchange ideas. And they are redefining what Burgundy is all about.

It is among these challengers to the old order that Burgundy will find a new place in the world of wine. It is never going to be an area of vast quantities at cheap prices – the vineyard area is too small. What it can do well is set yardsticks for quality, creating the epitome of Chardonnay, the epitome of Pinot Noir. Then we might not mind paying the high prices.

Burgundian whodunnit

Buying Burgundy is a question of detective work. We need to understand something of the appellation system in Burgundy. We need to know the name of the village it comes from and, even more important, the name of the grower or négociant who made the wine (or, as the French would say, did the élevage – raised it up). And, probably the most important of all, we need to know the name of good wine merchants in this country who have carefully built up a reputation for buying wine from the best people in Burgundy.

Where's where in Burgundy

The appellation system is the most complex in France, with five different levels, from the region-wide appellation to one that refers to a single vineyard.

General appellations A wine bearing an appellation such as Bourgogne or (even lower in quality) Bourgogne Grand Ordinaire can come from anywhere within the whole Burgundy region. The wine can be white or red: Bourgogne Rouge has to be made from Pinot Noir, while Bourgogne Grand Ordinaire can be made from Gamay. Other general appellations include Bourgogne Passetoutgrain (a blend of Pinot Noir and Gamay) and Bourgogne Aligoté (a white made from the Aligoté grape).

The success of the basic Burgundy wines depends on the grower or négociant. Some Bourgogne Rouge is very good at comparatively modest prices, but some can be a bit of a disaster, so although you shouldn't dismiss these wines, shop around at this level with care.

Regional appellations Terms like Côte de Nuits Villages, Côte de Beaune Villages, Hautes Côtes de Nuits fall into this category. Each covers more than one village and the wine will probably be a négociant's blend.

Village appellations Most Burgundian communes or villages are entitled to their own appellation and the vineyards covered by the appellation will be strictly defined. Any vineyards that fall outside the defined area go under one of the more general categories. Typical appellations would be Vosne-Romanée or Savigny-lès Beaune, Pommard or Nuits-St-Georges (see also below).

While these are supposed to be not so good as single vineyard wines, they are often every bit as good and much cheaper. Like the Burgundy-wide appellation wines, but to a lesser degree, they rely on judicious buying from a reasonable variety of vineyards. The smaller the area from which grapes can come, the greater the risks (from localised hail storms, for instance), but the greater the rewards as well.

Premier Cru appellations Confusingly, this is only the second rank of greatness. Certain single vineyards are designated Premier Cru and are entitled to their own appellation which is normally put on the label in conjunction with the village name, eg Meursault (the village)-Charmes (the vineyard). A wine that is a blend of wines from different Premier Cru vineyards in one appellation can be called simply Beaune Premier Cru, for example.

Grand Cru appellations These are the very top vineyards, and can appear on the label as appellations in their own right with no reference to the village eg Le Montrachet, La Tâche. At their best, they are the stars of Burgundy but, inevitably, their prices reflect their star quality.

The Burgundy villages

The main Burgundian vineyard faces east across the valley of the Saône from low slopes that mark the eastern edge of the Massif Central. The northern end is a low ridge, broken up by small side valleys. This is the Côte d'Or. Moving south from Dijon, the first section of the Côte d'Or is known as the Côte de Nuits, but as it nears Beaune it becomes the Côte de Beaune. In the hilly country behind this main slope is the lesser area of the Hautes Côtes – again divided into the Hautes Côtes de Nuits and the Hautes Côtes de Beaune.

South of Beaune, the slope breaks up and the Côte Chalonnaise starts. This leads into the Mâconnais, which in turn runs into the northern end of the Beaujolais hills.

Côte de Nuits From north to south, the main villages are: Marsannay, Fixin, Gevrey-Chambertin, Morey St-Denis, Chambolle-Musigny, Vougeot, Vosne-Romanée, Nuits St-Georges.

The villages in the Côte de Nuits to watch as offering better value for money than others are Fixin and Marsannay (red wines).

Côte de Beaune Continuing south, the villages are: Aloxe-Corton, Pernand-Vergelesses, Chorey-lès-Beaune, Savigny-lès-Beaune, Beaune, Pommard, Volnay, Monthélie, Auxey-Duresses, Meursault, Puligny-Montrachet, Chassagne-Montrachet, St-Aubin, St-Romain, Santenay.

Villages in the Côte de Beaune to watch as offering better value for money than others are: (*for reds*) Auxey-Duresses, Chorey-lès-Beaune, Savigny-lès-Beaune, Monthélie and Santenay; (*for red and whites*) St-Aubin; (*for whites*) St-Romain.

The Côte Chalonnaise The villages here are: Bouzeron, Rully, Mercurey, Givry, Montagny. Look for Bouzeron whites and Mercurey and Givry reds.

The Mâconnais The region is best for whites, especially for the over-priced Pouilly-Fuissé. However, look instead for St-Véran, Pouilly-Loché, Pouilly-Vinzelles, Mâcon-Prissé, Mâcon-Viré, Mâcon-Clessé, Mâcon-Lugny.

Vintages in Burgundy

Of all the great wine-producing areas in France, Burgundy suffers most from extreme climatic conditions. It can have harsh winters, and the quality of a summer cannot be guaranteed: it may be short and too hot, or wet and too cold. Probably in only three years each decade will the weather be absolutely right.

The other problem with Burgundy vintages is that when the weather is right for red wines it may not be right for white, and vice versa, a comment that is more appropriate to Burgundy than other wine-producing areas. Add to that the fact that Burgundian weather seems to operate in tiny areas – a terrible hailstorm may devastate one vineyard, while a couple of hundred yards down the road the sun is shining brilliantly – and it becomes obvious that great store cannot be put by generalised comments about Burgundian vintages.

1988 A slow spring followed by a wet July were not hopeful signs but from then until the end of September it was hot and dry, which reduced the crop but improved the quality. The harvest was earlier than usual. *Reds*: normal quantity, but mixed quality. This is not a Vintage of the Century (Burgundy claims them several times a decade), but rather an above average one. *Whites*: high yields – a perennial Burgundy problem – were the culprit, with low alcohol and plenty of chaptalisation (adding sugar to the must to increase the eventual alcohol). Not a great year at all.

1987 A year of small crops, following a wet spring. *Reds*: these are probably better than the whites, with every sign of a useful medium-term vintage of soft, fruity wines. Nothing exciting, though. *Whites*: acidity has softened in these wines, and they now seem to be wines to drink comparatively quickly – watch out for the hint of rot on some wines from lesser producers.

1986 A classic hit-and-miss vintage. *Reds*: better than whites, especially in the Côte de Beaune, but only producers can guarantee the quality. The wines will have a medium-term life, although Côte d'Or wines may last longer. *Whites*: much more impressive, and this could be the best white vintage of the 1980s (certainly if the prices are anything to go by).

1985 Some considered it impossible to make bad wine with the quality of the grapes at harvest time. *Reds*: quite firm with good, rounded tannin and decent acidity; definitely need to be kept for some time. This is by far the best red vintage of the 1980s (but watch for what happens in 1989). *Whites*: delicious now, somewhat like the 1983s in character but with lower alcohol, more fruit and more acidity. The best wines will age well, but some are quite ready for drinking now.

1984 *Reds*: light in colour and alcohol, most of these wines, with the exception of Premier Cru and Grand Cru, should be drunk now. *Whites*: should also be drunk young. They are light and a touch on the acid side (although that aspect has softened in the last year). Except for Grand Cru and Premier Cru, drink now.

1983 *Reds*: acclaimed as a fine year, with some of the wines expected to have a long life, although some others seem just too hard and tannic ever to give any pleasure. As always, avoid the wines that taste of rot. *Whites*: full, rich wines that are not typical of Burgundy and seem to have something of the New World in them. The top wines have good keeping potential.

1982 *Reds*: a difficult year. More than ever the quality of a wine depends on its producer. Much is thin and watery, although better producers made some delicious wines. Drink them now.

Drink any *whites* you have now and taste carefully before buying any more.

1981 *Reds*: a few fine wines are around in an otherwise mediocre vintage. *Whites*: buy carefully as most of these wines are way past their best.

1980 *Reds*: this vintage is turning out better than originally billed, and although most need drinking now, the occasional bottle especially in the Côte de Nuits – will survive for a year or two yet.

1979 *Reds*: while a few of these easy-to-drink wines will survive for a while yet, most should be drunk. *Whites*: only the top growths can still provide plenty of enjoyment.

1978 *Reds*: great wines with lots of life in them yet. Wines from the Côte de Nuits will last longer than those from the Côte de Beaune – but that is generally the case anyway.

Older vintages Approach with caution – in general the wines are not tremendously long-lived. On the other hand, the right bottle from the right wine merchant (see our list of specialist stockists) will provide a treasured experience.

Who's who in Burgundy

Here is a list of the firms and estates which we consider to be producing good Burgundy at the moment. Our advice in Burgundy is always to look for the producer's name. Where the wine was actually grown is often less important. Stockists are indicated, but the list cannot be exhaustive.

Burgundy growers

The strange and complex structure of the vineyard holdings in Burgundy means that a grower may have a couple of rows of vines in a number of different villages. He will produce small quantities of many wines. If he is any good, all his wines will achieve a standard, so look for the name of the grower first, then the name of the wine.

Domaine Pierre Amiot *Morris & Verdin*
Robert & Michel Ampeau *Lay & Wheeler; Howard Ripley*
Marquis d'Angerville *Peter Green; La Vigneronne*
Domaine l'Arlot *Howard Ripley*
Domaine Arnoux *Anthony Byrne Fine Wines; Fine Vintage Wines; Laytons*
Bernard Bachelet *Anthony Byrne Fine Wines*
Denis Bachelet *Morris & Verdin; Howard Ripley*

Jean-Claude Bachelet *Bibendum; Raeburn Fine Wines & Foods*
Domaine Bachelet-Ramonet *Howard Ripley*
Barthod-Noëllat *Bibendum*
Domaine Bertagna *Anthony Byrne Fine Wines*
Jean Berger *Bibendum*
Domaine Bitouzet-Prieur *La Vigneronne*
Simon Bize *Adnams; Domaine Direct; Haynes Hanson & Clark; Lay & Wheeler*
Blain Gagnard *Bibendum; Domaine Direct; Raeburn Fine Wines & Foods*
Domaine Boillot *Bibendum*
Bonneau de Martray *Domaine Direct; Lay & Wheeler; Laytons; Howard Ripley*
Luc Camus-Bruchon *Bibendum*
Carillon *Lay & Wheeler; Howard Ripley; La Vigneronne*
Paul Chapelle *Morris & Verdin*
Guy Chaumont *Vintage Roots*
Jean Chauvenet *Bibendum; Justerini & Brooks; La Vigneronne*
Daniel Chouet-Clivet *La Vigneronne*
Bruno Clair *Justerini & Brooks*
Henri Clerc *Averys; Eldridge Pope*
Georges Clerget *Anthony Byrne Fine Wines; Greens*
Michel Clerget *Justerini & Brooks*
Raoul Clerget *Peter Green; Yorkshire Fine Wines*
Alain Coche *Bibendum*
Jean-François Coche *Lay & Wheeler*
Domaine Coche Debord *Anthony Byrne Fine Wines*
P Cogny *Adnams; Majestic*
Domaine Colin *Ingletons Wines*
Domaine de la Combe, Mâcon Bray *Bibendum*
Domaines des Comtes Lafon *Domaine Direct; Morris & Verdin; Raeburn Fine Wines & Foods; Tanners*
Alain Constant *Hungerford Wine Company*
Domaine Corsin *Domaine Direct*
Henri Courtin *Mayor Sworder & Co*
J-J Confuron *Haynes Hanson & Clark; Laytons*
Domaine Demageot *Anthony Byrne Fine Wines*
Domaine Dubriel-Fontaine *Anthony Byrne Fine Wines*
Guy Dufouleur *Davisons*
Domaine Dujac *Adnams; Lay & Wheeler; Howard Ripley; The Wine Society*
Domaine Fleurot-Larose *Anthony Byrne Fine Wines*
Domaine de la Folie *Domaine Direct; Raeburn Fine Wines & Foods*
Jean-Noël Gagnard *Justerini & Brooks*
Domaine Gagnard-Delagrange *Anthony Byrne Fine Wines; Haynes Hanson & Clark; Laytons*
Domaine Garaudet *Laytons*

Domaine J-P Gauffroy *Laytons*
H Germain *Adnams; Tanners*
Jean Germain *Balls Brothers; Tanners; The Wine Society*
Vincent Girardin *Helen Verdcourt Wines*
Jean Grivot *Haynes Hanson & Clark; Lay & Wheeler; The Wine Society*
Robert Groffier *Laytons*
Guillemard-Pothier *Lay & Wheeler*
Domaine de l'Hermitage *Anthony Byrne Fine Wines*
Jean Javillier *Vintage Roots*
Patrick Javillier *Anthony Byrne Fine Wines; Davisons; Majestic*
Georges et Henri Jayer *Justerini & Brooks*
Jayer-Gilles *Adnams; Majestic; Yorkshire Fine Wines*
Henri Jayer *Bibendum; Raeburn Fine Wines & Foods*
Jacqueline Jayer *Haynes Hanson & Clark; Howard Ripley*
François Jobard *Haynes Hanson & Clark; Raeburn Fine Wines & Foods*
Domaine Michel Juillot *Domaine Direct*
Domaine Laborbe-Juillot *Haynes Hanson & Clark*
Michel Lafarge *Haynes Hanson & Clark; Christopher Piper Wines; Howard Ripley*
Laleure Piot *Ingletons Wines*
Hubert Lamy *Lay & Wheeler*
Domaine Latour-Giraud *Haynes Hanson & Clark*
Domaine Paul de Launay *Anthony Byrne Fine Wines*
Domaine Yves de Launay *Great Northern Wine Company; Tanners*
Domaine Vincent Leflaive *Adnams; Averys; Lay & Wheeler; Raeburn Fine Wines & Foods*
Lequin-Roussot *Anthony Byrne Fine Wines*
Domaine Chantal Lescure *Christopher Piper Wines; Willoughbys*
Georges Lignier *Bibendum; Justerini & Brooks; Raeburn Fine Wines & Foods*
Domaine Machard de Gramont *Adnams; Tanners*
Duc de Magenta *La Vigneronne*
Jean Maréchal *Haynes Hanson & Clark; Raeburn Fine Wines & Foods*
Domaine Pascal Massenot *Arthur Rackhams/Le Viticulteur*
Domaine Maume *Adnams*
Mazilly Père et Fils *Haynes Hanson & Clark*
Domaine Méo-Camuzet *Raeburn Fine Wines & Foods*
Alain Michelot *Domaine Direct; Christopher Piper Wines*
Bernard Michelot *Lay & Wheeler*
Millot-Battault *Averys; George Hill of Loughborough*
Mongeard-Mugneret *Adnams; Domaine Direct; Ingletons Wines*
René Monnier *Ingletons Wines*
Domaine Monthélie-Douhairet *Morris & Verdin*
Domaine de Montille *Domaine Direct*

Albert Morey *Christopher Piper Wines*
Bernard Morey *Anthony Byrne Fine Wines; Davisons; Greens*
Domaine Pierre Morey *Howard Ripley*
Gérard Mugneret *Hungerford Wine Company*
J-F Mugneret *Haynes Hanson & Clark*
André Mussy *Howard Ripley*
Domaine Newman *Peter Green*
André Nudant *Ingletons Wines*
Domaine Parent *George Hill of Loughborough; Christopher Piper Wines; Willoughbys; Wizard Wine Warehouses*
Domaine des Perrières *Haynes Hanson & Clark; Yorkshire Fine Wines*
Domaine Pitoiset Uréna *Morris & Verdin*
Domaine Ponsot *Morris & Verdin*
Domaine de la Pousse d'Or *Anthony Byrne Fine Wines; Domaine Direct; La Vigneronne; The Wine Society*
Domaine Prieur Brunet *Eldridge Pope*
Henri Prudhon *Adnams; Bibendum; Lay & Wheeler*
Michel Prunier *Justerini & Brooks*
Prunier-Brunet *Peter Green*
Domaine Charles Quillardet *Arthur Rackhams/Le Viticulteur*
Jean-Marie Raveneau *Haynes Hanson & Clark*
Henri Rebourseau *Laytons*
Domaine de la Renarde *Yorkshire Fine Wines*
Domaine Daniel Rion *Morris & Verdin; Yorkshire Fine Wines*
Rollin Père et Fils *Bibendum; Raeburn Fine Wines & Foods*
Domaine de la Romanée-Conti *Adnams; Domaine Direct; Gerard Harris; Hungerford Wine Company; Willoughbys*
Emmanuel Rouget *Bibendum; Justerini & Brooks*
Marc Rougeot *Adnams*
Domaine Guy Roulot *Domaine Direct*
Georges Roumier *Haynes Hanson & Clark; Tanners*
Domaine Armand Rousseau *Adnams; Domaine Direct; Lay & Wheeler; Tanners; The Wine Society*
Roux Père et Fils *Domaine Direct; Eldridge Pope; The Wine Society*
Etienne Sauzet *Adnams; Ingletons Wines; Lay & Wheeler; Morris & Verdin; Tanners; The Wine Society*
Daniel Senard *Ingletons Wines*
Domaine Baron Thénard *Laytons*
Jean Thévenet *Tanners; Yorkshire Fine Wines*
Thévenot le Brun *Ingletons Wines*
Thévenot Machal *Laytons*
Domaine Gérard Thomas *Arthur Rackhams/Le Viticulteur*
Domaine Tollot-Beaut *Anthony Byrne Fine Wines; Gerard Harris; Justerini & Brooks; Lay & Wheeler*
Domaine Louis Trapet *Anthony Byrne Fine Wines; Ingletons Wines; Christopher Piper Wines*

Domaine des Varoilles *Fine Vintage Wines; Tanners*
Vaudoisey-Mutin *Bibendum*
Domaine Charles Viénot *Anthony Byrne Fine Wines*
Aubert de Villaine *Adnams*
Domaine Vincent *Bibendum; Domaine Direct; Eldridge Pope;*
Raeburn Fine Wines & Foods; Tanners
Emile Voarick *Hungerford Wine Company*
Michel Voarick *Lay & Wheeler; Yorkshire Fine Wines*
Domaine Comte de Vogüé *Peter Green; Christopher Piper Wines*
Girard Vollot *Morris & Verdin*

Burgundy co-operatives

Despite the growth of domaine-bottling, much of Burgundy in
the lesser-known appellations is still handled through the co-
operatives. The biggest concentration is in the Mâconnais and
the Côte Chalonnaise, while there are relatively few in the Côte
d'Or.

Cave des Vignerons de Buxy Wines: Montagny, Bourgogne
Rouge and Blanc.
Matthew Gloag; Gerard Harris; J E Hogg; Majestic; Christopher
Piper Wines; Helen Verdcourt Wines

Groupement de Producteurs Lugny-St-Genoux-de-Scisse Wines:
Mâcon-Lugny, Mâcon Villages.
City Wines; Waitrose

Cave Coopérative de Viré Wines: Mâcon-Viré.
Wizard Wine Warehouses

Les Producteurs de Prissé Wines: St-Véran, Mâcon-Prissé.
Haynes Hanson & Clark

Burgundy merchants

Bouchard Père et Fils Wines: Beaune, Le Montrachet, Corton,
Volnay.
City Wines; Haynes Hanson & Clark; J E Hogg; Upper Crust

Brenot Père et Fils Wines: Mâcon, Meursault, Bâtard
Montrachet, Puligny Montrachet, Santenay.
Mayor Sworder & Co

Chandesais Wines: Beaune, Hospices de Beaune, Rully,
Savigny-lès-Beaune.
Eldridge Pope; Willoughbys

Chanson Père et Fils Wines: Beaune, Pernand-Vergelesses, Côte
de Beaune, Chambertin, Vosne-Romanée.
Balls Brothers; City Wines; Direct Wine Shipments; George Hill of
Loughborough; Laytons; Tanners; House of Townend

Chartron et Trébuchet Wines: Hospices de Nuits, Mercurey, Meursault, Le Montrachet, Puligny Montrachet.
Laytons

B et J-M Delaunay Wines: Savigny-lès-Beaune, Gevrey-Chambertin.
City Wines; Matthew Gloag

J Dépagneux Wines: Mâcon-Clessé, St-Véran, Pouilly-Fuissé.
Cadwgan Fine Wines

Doudet-Naudin Wines: Savigny, Beaune, Aloxe-Corton.
Berry Bros & Rudd

Joseph Drouhin Wines: Beaune, Puligny, Corton-Charlemagne, Corton-Bressandes, Volnay, Chambertin, Chambolle-Musigny, Echézeaux, Musigny.
Berry Bros & Rudd; Peter Green; Gerard Harris, Wizard Wine Warehouses

Georges Duboeuf Principally in Beaujolais but also in Mâcon and St-Véran.
Anthony Byrne Fine Wines; House of Townend (under the Paul Bocuse name); Wizard Wine Warehouses

Joseph Faiveley Wines: Nuits St-Georges, Mercurey, Rully, Corton, Clos de Bèze, Echézeaux, Gevrey-Chambertin, Chambolle-Musigny.
Balls Brothers; Claridge Fine Wines; Direct Wine Shipments; Gerard Harris; J E Hogg; Justerini & Brooks; Ubiquitous Chip

Geisweiler The négociant firm which opened up the Hautes Côtes de Nuits. Wines: Hautes Côtes de Nuits, Hautes Côtes de Beaune.
Balls Brothers; House of Townend

Hospices de Beaune The Beaune charity which also owns vineyards. Wines: Volnay, Beaune.
City Wines; Eldridge Pope; Yorkshire Fine Wines

Louis Jadot Own Domaine Clair-Daü. Wines: Corton, Beaune, Pernand-Vergelesses.
Fine Vintage Wines (for Clair-Daü); Gare du Vin; Peter Green; Justerini & Brooks

Jaffelin Wines: Gevrey-Chambertin, Hospices de Beaune, Pommard.
Hungerford Wine Company; Helen Verdcourt Wines

Labouré-Roi Wines: Meursault, Auxey-Duresses, Beaune, Pommard, Chassagne Montrachet.
Chaplin & Son; Great Northern Wine Company; Majestic; Christopher Piper Wines; Safeway; Willoughbys

Louis Latour Wines: Corton, Romanée-St-Vivant, Chambertin, Pommard, Beaune, Montagny.
Berry Bros & Rudd; Matthew Gloag; George Hill of Loughborough; Ubiquitous Chip; The Wine Society

Olivier Leflaive Frères Part of the Leflaive family at Puligny, but acting as négociant. Wines: Rully, Puligny Montrachet, Meursault Porusots, St-Aubin, Pernand-Vergelesses, Corton.
Adnams; Corney & Barrow; Lay & Wheeler; The Wine Society

Loron et Fils Wines: Mâconnais wines (plus Beaujolais – see under that section).
Chaplin & Son; Direct Wine Shipments

P de Marcilly Wines: Bourgogne Rouge, Bourgogne Réserve, Monthélie.
Matthew Gloag

Prosper Maufoux Wines: Santenay, Puligny Montrachet.
Berry Bros & Rudd; J E Hogg; Willoughbys

Moillard Wines: Large vineyard holdings on Côte de Nuits and Côte de Beaune.
Berry Bros & Rudd; Gare du Vin

Mommessin Owners of Clos du Tart. Wines: Chassagne Montrachet, Clos du Tart.
Balls Brothers; Willoughbys; Yorkshire Fine Wines

Remoissenet Wines: Le Montrachet, Beaune.
Averys; The Wine Society

Antonin Rodet Wines: Corton Charlemagne, Meursault, Le Montrachet.
Chaplin & Son; Great Northern Wine Company; Willoughbys

Best buys from Burgundy

WHITE

Rully 1986, Domaine Guyot (*T & W Wines*)
Rully 1987, Ch de Rully (*William Addison*)
Mâcon Bray 1988, Domaine de la Combe (*Bibendum*)
Mâcon Prissé 1987, Cave Coopérative de Prissé (*Goedhuis & Co*)
Pouilly Fuissé 1986, Maurice Chenu (*Morrisons*)
Mâcon la Roche Vineuse 1987, Domaine du Vieux St-Sorlin (*Seckford Wines*)
Bourgogne Blanc les Setilles 1987, Olivier Leflaive (*John Armit Wines*)
Bourgogne Blanc Chardonnay, Cuvée du Muguet 1987, Patrick Javillier (*Peter Green*)
Bourgogne Chardonnay 1987, Domaine Ste-Claire (*Thresher*)
Montagny Premier Cru Coères 1987, Bernard Michel (*Domaine Direct*)

RED

Bourgogne Passetoutgrains 1985, Domaine Arnoux (*Anthony Byrne Fine Wines*)

Bourgogne Pinot Noir 1985, Domaine Bertrand (*T & W Wines*)

Bourgogne Pinot Noir 1985, André Ropiteau (*Safeway*)

Bourgogne Passetoutgrains 1986, Jayer (*Raeburn Fine Wines and Foods*)

St-Véran 1987, Domaine des Deux Roches (*Adam Bancroft Associates*)

Hautes Côtes de Beaune 1986, Domaine Mazilly (*Morris & Verdin*)

Bourgogne Pinot la Vinée 1985, Bouchard Père et Fils (*Gare du Vin*)

Les Perrières 1985, Simon Bize (*Howard Ripley*)

Bourgogne Pinot Noir, Caves Lugny (*London Wine*)

Specialist stockists

Adnams; John Armit Wines; Averys of Bristol; Ballantynes of Cowbridge; Berkmann Wine Cellars/Le Nez Rouge; Berry Bros & Rudd; Bibendum; Anthony Byrne Fine Wines; D Byrne & Co; Caves de la Madeleine; Christchurch Fine Wine; College Cellar; Colombier Vins Fins; Corney & Barrow; Domaine Direct; Eldridge Pope; Farr Vintners; Goedhuis & Co; Haynes Hanson & Clark; Hungerford Wine Company; Ingletons Wines; S H Jones; Justerini & Brooks; Richard Kihl; Kurtz & Chan; Lay & Wheeler; Laytons; O W Loeb; Andrew Mead Wines; Michael Menzel; Morris & Verdin; Thos Peatling; Christopher Piper Wines; Raeburn Fine Wines and Foods; Reid Wines; La Réserve; Howard Ripley; Russell & McIver; Edward Sheldon; Tanners Wines; Turville Valley Wines; T & W Wines; La Vigneronne

CHABLIS

The great original

From just a small wine-producing area in the north of France, Chablis has become the epitome of today's taste worldwide: dry, fruity, not too soft, not too acid. Go to Australia or – until recently at least – to the United States and there would be locally produced 'Chablis' purporting to be in the style of the original, but which more often than not was vaguely soft, vaguely fruity and distinctly lacking in the true character of the French prototype.

But what is that character? In days not so long ago, it could be described by writers such as Hugh Johnson (*The World Atlas of Wine*) as 'hard but not harsh, reminds one of stones and minerals, but at the same time of green hay'. It is rare indeed today to find a Chablis that fits that description, that taste that set wine producers in other parts of the world scurrying to stick 'Chablis' on their bottles.

Today, the taste may be dramatically different, depending on the producer and the quality of the wine. It could be soft, possibly quite rich and certainly dry, perhaps like a good Burgundian Mâconnais, but equally likely bland and rather watery. Or it could taste of wood, like a lighter version of a wine from another area of Burgundy, the Côte d'Or.

But tart, steely or acid it is unlikely to be, because over the past 20 or 30 years, Chablis growers have discovered malolactic fermentation, that second fermentation of a wine which converts malic acid into softer lactic acid, stabilising the wine in the process and making it easier and more acceptable to a wider-drinking public. So great acidity is out, and the taste of fruit in the Chardonnay (with or without wood) is in.

Whether to use wood or not is a local controversy. Previously, any old container was used as long as it was watertight. Now, one school believes that using stainless steel and no wood brings out the best in the fruity character of the Chardonnay, and enables it to be drunk reasonably quickly. The minority, opposite, view is that Chardonnay needs an extra layer of complexity and a longer life from wood-ageing.

Good arguments

Controversy is good for a region because it keeps it on its toes. And despite the sleepy appearance of the tiny town of Chablis itself, the wine producers are in the middle of a boom era. Responding to demand (you do it with baked beans, so why not Chablis?), they have increased the area under vine by leaps and bounds since the 1950s. Production figures tell the tale: 10,000 hectolitres made 30 years ago, 60,000 hectolitres 10 years ago, 100,000 hectolitres today.

Is the wine as good as it was when its reputation was being made? It all depends on what category of wine you are talking about (see below for definitions). The top wines, the Grands Crus, are probably as good as they ever were, and more reliable because stainless steel is better for reliability than dirty old wooden barrels.

But come down a notch and things are different. Chablis Premier Cru vineyards have been increased enormously, and some would argue that the newer vineyards are not on the right

soil to make the right style of wine for Premier Cru. The same
has happened with straight Chablis, where new vineyards have
been planted and land that was previously making Petit
Chablis, the bottom rung of the ladder, has been promoted
(because the producers claimed that 'Petit' implied that their
wine was inferior – which of course it was).

At the same time, yields have been allowed to go up, even for
Grand Cru wines. And, as any student of wine knows, high
yields can easily lead to thin, bland, characterless wines.

So, what with quality and yields being affected by greed, and
the fact that people can now buy the Chablis taste at a less than
Chablis price, maybe we have learnt to put this archetypal dry
white wine in its proper place: a great original, yes, but now
often passed over in preference for its many better and less
expensive imitators.

Where's where in Chablis

The appellation system in Chablis is much simpler than that in
the rest of Burgundy. For a start, only white wine can be
Chablis: any red wines made in the area go under the
appellation of Bourgogne or of one of the small village names
(see below). All Chablis is made from Chardonnay grapes.

The Chablis vineyards are graded on a quality basis. At the
bottom, there is basic Petit Chablis. There's not much of this
around now because most of it has been upgraded to the next
quality level, Chablis, which covers the vast bulk of the Chablis
vineyard.

Above Chablis AC are the Premier Cru vineyards. These are
divided into 12 different groupings which consist of more than
one vineyard: They are: Beauroy, Côte de Léchet, Fourchaume,
Les Fourneaux, Mélinots, Montée de Tonnerre, Montmains,
Monts de Milieu, Vaillons, Vaucoupin, Vaudevey, Vosgros. If a
wine is a blend of more than one Premier Cru, it will simply be
called Chablis Premier Cru without a vineyard name.

At the top of the Chablis tree are the seven Grands Crus,
making the classic wines, at top prices: Blanchots, Bougros, Les
Clos, Grenouilles, Les Preuses, Valmur, Vaudésir.

Vintages in Chablis

1988 A large crop resulting in a lack of concentration,
underlining the problems of high yields. It should mean that
prices remain stable, though.

1987 Not prolific, with still smaller than average production of
Premiers and Grands Crus because of the 1985 frosts. But the

quality is good, even if acidity is low. More like any other white Burgundy.

1986 A small crop, not much bigger than 1985. It produced wines with some attractive acidity, which are therefore more typically Chablis in the old style. Basic Chablis is definitely ready to drink up, though better wines are worth keeping.

1985 A small crop of high quality – if quite full – wine, 35 per cent lower than in 1984 because of frost in January and February. The main problems with quantity were in the Grand Cru and Premier Cru vineyards. Quantities of Chablis and Petit Chablis were nearer normal. Start drinking the top wines, finish up any basic wines.

1984 Rot was the problem in the vineyards after a wet September and warm October. The wine has more acidity than immediately preceding vintages and is in a classic style. The better wines will last a while longer.

1983 Soft, full-bodied wines which lacked the edge that is the hallmark of a good Chablis vintage. They are now definitely on their way out.

1981 Some really good Chablis with intense flavours and a lovely tangy bite were made, but only the Grands Crus are worth keeping.

Few vintages before 1981 (apart from some Grand Cru 1978) are worth keeping now, and it's unlikely that there will be any to buy.

Drinking Chablis

Expect the wines made with some wood-ageing (as indicated in the Who's Who section) to last a little longer than those made entirely in stainless steel. Drink basic Chablis in three years – depending on the vintage. Premier Cru wines will last anything from three to eight years. Grand Cru wines are not really ready for six years after the vintage.

Who's who in Chablis

Apart from the divisions into classes of Cru (from Petit Chablis to Grand Cru) as an indication of quality, names of producers are as important in Chablis as in Burgundy. One problem in Chablis, however, is that the big co-op, La Chablisienne, sells wine under some of its members' names: so what might seem like a wine from an individual domaine will in fact have been made in the co-op. There's nothing necessarily wrong with these wines, but if you want to know where you are, check the small print carefully for the co-op's name as bottler.

THE GROWERS

Jean-Marc Brocard Makes big, mellow wines, often quite rich, using wood. Wines: Domaine Ste-Claire.
Adnams; Balls Brothers

René Dauvissat One of the well-established names of Chablis, with some complexity to his wines, which spend some time in oak. Grands Crus: Les Clos and Les Preuses; plus Premier Cru.
Domaine Direct; Majestic; Tanners; Waitrose

Bernard Defaix Modern wine-making without the use of wood; the wines tend to be fat and Burgundian in taste. Premiers Crus: Côte de Léchet, Vaillons.
Berry Bros & Rudd; Bibendum; Thos Peatling

Jean-Paul Droin Very fine Chablis using judicious amounts of oak-ageing. Grands Crus: Vaudésir, Les Clos, Grenouilles, Valmur; Premier Cru: mainly Vaillons.
Bibendum; Davisons; Domaine Direct; Tanners

Jean Durup Large holding of 140 acres makes him a major force in Chablis. Uses stainless steel in his wine-making, and achieves high standards. Wines: Durup, Domaine de l'Eglantière, Ch de Maligny, Domaine de la Paulière, Domaine de Valéry, Les Folles Pensées.
H Allen Smith; Anthony Byrne Fine Wines; Hedley Wright; Victor Hugo Wines; Wizard Wine Warehouses

William Fèvre A proponent of the use of new oak barrels for Chablis, making rich, rounded wines which age well. Grands Crus: Les Clos, Bougros, Les Preuses, Grenouilles, Vaudésir, Valmur; Premier Cru, Chablis.
Findlater Mackie Todd; Oddbins; Irvine Robertson Wines

Alain Geoffroy Elegant, light wines, made in stainless steel.
Victor Hugo Wines; Irvine Robertson Wines

J-P Grossot Young grower owning land in Chablis as well as having Premier Cru vineyards. Uses some wood. Premiers Crus: Vaucoupin, Mont de Milieu.
Lay & Wheeler

Louis Michel Modern, fruity wines that are ready to drink young. No wood is involved. Grands Crus: Vaudésir, Grenouilles, Les Clos; Premiers Crus: Montmains, Montée de Tonnerre. Domaine de la Tour Vaubourg is a second label.
Anthony Byrne Fine Wines; Gerard Harris; Justerini & Brooks; Lay & Wheeler; O W Loeb; Oddbins; The Wine Society; Yorkshire Fine Wines

Louis Pinson Traditional wines, aged in wood, and needing at least three years before drinking. Grand Cru: Les Clos; Premiers Crus: Montmains, La Forêt, Montée de Tonnerre.
Bibendum; Morrisons

François Raveneau Very traditional wines, intended for long ageing. Plenty of wood here. Grands Crus: Valmur, Les Clos, Blanchots; Premier Cru.
Haynes Hanson & Clark

Domaine Servin Traditional style of Chablis, which needs some bottle-ageing. Premier Cru: Montée de Tonnerre; Chablis.
Morris & Verdin

Philippe Testut The remains of an old estate, most of which was sold by the family. The wines are classic Chablis, with both wood and tank maturation. Wines: Grand Cru: Les Grenouilles; Premier Cru, Chablis.
Majestic

Robert Vocoret Ferments his wines in barrel, but ages them in stainless steel to keep some of the freshness. Grands Crus: Les Clos, Blanchots, Valmur; Premier Cru, Chablis.
Laytons; Reid Wines; Winecellars

Cave Co-opérative La Chablisienne Controls a quarter of all Chablis production, producing wines which may lack some of the depths of smaller producers. Wines: about 50 different labels, including La Chablisienne. Growers' individual cuvées (see above) include Domaine Jean Bourcey, Suzanne Tremblay, Rémy Lefort, Fèvre Frères, Jean-Claude Dauvissat, Michaut Frères.
The most widely available Chablis: look for the co-op's name as bottler on the label

THE MERCHANTS

Bacheroy-Josselin Successful and expanding Chablis merchant with vineyards divided between Domaine Laroche and Domaine de la Jouchère. The holding company is called Henri Laroche.
Justerini & Brooks

Albert Bichot Burgundy négociant with interests in Chablis. Also owns Domaine A Long-Depaquit in La Moutonne, whose wines are a better bet than their standard Chablis.
Unwins

Joseph Drouhin Another Burgundy merchant who now owns vineyards in Chablis, and uses lot of wood in his wines.
Rodney Densem Wines; Findlater Mackie Todd; Michael Menzel

Labouré-Roi Famous Burgundy négociant now taking an interest in Chablis. Premiers Crus: Montmains, Montée de Tonnerre.
Majestic; Willoughbys

Moreau The largest landowner and, after the co-op, the largest producer. The vineyards are still owned by M Moreau, but the cellars and production are now part of Hiram Walker, the British-owned drinks giant. The wines are good and reliable though with no great excitement, and are best drunk young. Moreau Blanc, the firm's branded wine, is not Chablis but Vin de Table. Wines: Domaine de Bieville Chablis; Premier Cru: Les Vaillons; Grand Cru: Les Clos.
Berry Bros & Rudd; Blayneys; Davisons; Findlater Mackie Todd; The Wine Society

Guy Mothe et ses Fils Small firm, also owning vineyards, including Domaine du Colombier.
Thos Peatling

A Regnard et Fils Firm of négociants who don't own any vineyards but buy in grapes from a wide range of properties. Now owned by de Ladoucette of Pouilly Fumé. Wines: Albert Pic, Michel Remon; Premier Cru:Fourchaume; Grands Crus: Valmur, Vaudésir.
Berry Bros & Rudd; John Harvey & Sons; Hungerford Wine Company; Lay & Wheeler; Victoria Wine Company

Simmonet-Febvre Small vineyard holding backed up by a large négociant business. Good source of wines from the smaller appellations around Chablis as well as Chablis itself. Grand Cru: Les Preuses; Premiers Crus: Monts de Milieu, Montée de Tonnerre, Fourchaume, Vaillons.
Les Amis du Vin

The other wines of the Chablis region

While Chablis itself covers a fairly small vineyard area, in the surrounding country of the Yonne are a handful of tiny, once mightier appellations. Some have almost disappeared, others are coming back to life, but all provide some interest.

Coulanges-la-Vineuse Strictly speaking, not an appellation; the red wine from this village is actually called Bourgogne (with the name of the village appearing as a second thought). The grape is the Pinot Noir, the style light and elegant.

Irancy Another red wine village, this time with its own appellation. Pinot Noir is again the grape, with a little César to give body. The wines can have surprising depth.

St-Bris-le-Vineux and **Chitry-le-Fort** The two villages combine to produce Sauvignon de St-Bris, now enjoying something of a cult following. The wines are not dissimilar to some Sancerre (not that far away) and have followed Sancerre in the way of huge price rises.(St-Bris-le-Vineux): *Les Amis du Vin*; (Sauvignon de St-Bris): *Peter Dominic; Lay & Wheeler; Upper Crust; La Vigneronne; Wine Growers Association*

Best buys from Chablis and the environs

Chablis AC, La Chablisienne (*Marks & Spencer*)
Chablis Vigne de la Reine 1987 (*Anthony Byrne Fine Wines*)
Chardonnay Bourgogne Blanc 1987, La Chablisienne (*Ingletons Wines*)
Petit Chablis 1987, Jean Durup (*Wines from Paris*)
Chablis 1987, William Fèvre (*Bin Ends*)
Chardonnay St-Pourçain 1987, Jutier and Serra Frères (*Peter Watts Wines*)

Specialist stockists

Bibendum; Bin Ends; D Byrne & Co; Domaine Direct; Ingletons Wines; Justerini & Brooks; Lay & Wheeler; O W Loeb; Marks & Spencer; Raeburn Fine Wines and Foods; Tanners Wines; Whiteside's of Clitheroe

CHAMPAGNE

Up go the prices

Last year the cost of grapes, the strength of the French franc and worldwide demand all conspired to make Champagne prices spiral resolutely upwards. No longer could Champagne be found at under £7.50: even the supermarkets were forced to go through that magic barrier and put an end to the price war which had kept their bubblies ridiculously cheap.

So what happened? Why, of course, we drank more Champagne than ever before: 20 million bottles, up 7 per cent, keeping us well ahead of every other export market. If there is one sector of the wine market that seems determined to break its own records every year, it's Champagne.

What we have been drinking has tasted better than for a couple of years as well. Certainly, the famous names are tasting as good as they ever did, but we are now drinking the fruits of a succession of good vintages in 1985 and 1986, even with the non-vintage blends now that they have gone through the thin 1984 vintage. (Despite the skills of the blenders in Champagne, a poor vintage shows up even in non-vintage wines, so the indifferent 1987 may similarly make a change in style as those wines filter into the blends.)

We want some age

However, demand has had an unfortunate side effect, even on the most famous names. The wines may be good, but, in many cases, they are too young. That doesn't mean too young according to the law, of course – regulations in Champagne are stricter than in any other French wine region – but too young according to taste: the wines need more bottle-ageing to taste their best.

The problem is compounded by the fact that in this country we don't buy Champagne (except vintage Champagne) to store away in the cellar, but to drink at a party, to celebrate that night. Some reputable wine merchants say that they give their own house Champagnes some bottle age, and certainly some of these have the right biscuity character. But they don't always do that with the famous names, and if you are paying a lot of money, there could be disappointments in store, with young, green-tasting wines instead of ones with some maturity.

If greenness is true of famous names, how much more true is it of supermarket and off-licence own-label Champagnes. We were recently tasting a range of these and the general impression was one of tartness and immaturity, relieved only when the 'dosage' (the final touch of sweetness added to a wine to stop it being relentlessly acid) had been upped a little to take the edge away. And although some wines were obviously never going to improve in the bottle, there were others which just needed a few months to soften and be much more enjoyable.

There is a theory that people drink Champagne not because they enjoy it, but because of the lifestyle it symbolises. But some of these cheap and cheerful Champagnes cannot truthfully be called a pleasant experience, and an alternative sparkler – from Australia, for example – would often be preferable.

Worries and upsets

In Champagne itself, there are worries and upsets. Basically, they are running out of space. Of the 35,000 hectares permitted for planting, only 6,000 are left – and there's no sign of a fall in demand. What are the Champenois going to do?

One school of thought argues that those 35,000 hectares are an artificial figure anyway, and there's no reason why more land couldn't be made available for planting – a third as much again has been suggested.

The other school accepts the limits, and has decided to go abroad to make sparkling wine in other regions of the world. So Champagne houses have gone to California, Australia, even India, exporting technology and know-how as well as investing in vineyards themselves. They can't call it Champagne under European rules, but the differences between Domaine Chandon (in California) and Moët et Chandon (in France), or Roederer Estate (California) and Roederer (in France) are close enough, we reckon, to confuse quite a few drinkers. They are certainly trading off the Champagne-linked cachet of their names.

The Champenois are upset because they have been caught out using a practice which, while perfectly legal, they would rather not have been seen doing. This is the practice of buying wine rather than grapes to make up their blends. It's called buying 'sur lattes' (literally, the narrow strips of wood on which bottles are stacked) and occurs when a Champagne producer is short of wine to meet demand. Nothing wrong, as we say, except that all these great and noble Champagne houses claim they don't do it, and try to give the impression that they press all the grapes themselves.

Technology comes into play

Champagne houses also like to give the impression that their practices are enshrined in tradition. They will show you the 'pupitres' – the racks where bottles are stored, neck down – a view familiar in every book or article on Champagne. But they won't show you the machines that do the job of the pupitres – getting the yeast into the neck of the bottle – in a fraction of the time.

They're equally cagey about a development which may make all this expensive processing unnecessary – or at least speed it up so that costs can come down. A new alginate bead has been developed which gathers the dead yeast cells to itself, and forms a lump which will fall to the bottom of the bottle quickly. This cuts out the 'riddling' of the bottles in the pupitres which takes on average three weeks of expensive time-consuming labour – and presumably cuts down on the costs of the machines which do the same job.

One of the reasons for their cageyness is that the technique is too new to tell if it makes any difference to the wines. But another reason may be that if new technology cuts down on costs, there is less reason to put up prices yet again – 15 per cent in early 1988 and more to come. After all, profit margins have to be protected, don't they?

White wine from black grapes

Champagne is made from three grape varieties – one white and two black. Because the juice of the black grapes is white (only the skins are black), it is possible with careful pressing of the grapes to extract the white juice completely uncoloured by the skins.

Chardonnay is the white grape, which may appear by itself in Blanc de Blancs. Pinot Meunier and Pinot Noir are the black grapes. Pinot Noir makes the better quality wine (and is occasionally seen by itself in Blanc de Noirs wines), but Pinot Meunier is an important constituent even of top blends.

What's what in Champagne

Most Champagne is sold under a brand name, whether it's from one of the great houses (Bollinger, Veuve Clicquot, Moët et Chandon, etc) or a smaller house or co-operative, a grower, or under a buyer's own label (Sainsbury's or Tanner's Champagne).

But it is also possible to find out from the label something about the type of producer and his status. At the bottom of the label are two letters followed by a series of numbers. The numbers are the code for a particular producer; the letters indicate what sort of company that producer is.

NM (négociant manipulant) means that the Champagne was made by a merchant or négociant who buys grapes and wine from anywhere in the region and then makes his own blend. All the major houses are merchants like this and those two letters are a good guarantee of quality.

RM (récoltant manipulant) indicates that the producer is a grower who is making the wine only from grapes grown in his vineyard. Often this wine can be very good indeed, but because the grower cannot buy in grapes from elsewhere, he is at the whim of weather and general crop failures – always a risk in vineyards so far north as Champagne. Look for growers who describe their wines as Grand or Premier Cru – the terms have a definite quality status in the highly regulated world of Champagne.

MA (marque d'acheteur) indicates that the brand is a buyer's own brand – a merchant or retail chain have put their own name on the label of Champagne which it has bought from a producer. The best guide to the quality of this Champagne is the quality of the merchant or shop.

CM (coopérative manipulant) indicates that the wine has been made by a co-operative. The reputation of the brand name is the best guide to quality here.

Two new codes were introduced in 1989:

RC (récoltant-coopérateur) is a grower who sells wine from his own grapes but which was made for him by a co-operative.

SR (Société de Récoltant) is a company created by members of the same family.

A new rule introduced at the same time says that the name of the producer must appear on all labels, either in one of the codes above or spelt out. If the name is in code, the distributor of the wine must give the name of the producer if requested. A better course would have been to insist that the producer's name appear on every label rather than to allow codes to remain, the key to which is not available to any consumers.

Another rule now says that own-label Champagne cannot be called simply Tesco Champagne or Asda Champagne, for instance. It must be called 'Champagne, specially selected by Asda (or Tesco)'. This is a move aimed at promoting the producers rather than the own-brand owners, and is obviously designed to help the Champagne famous names who will, of course, still be allowed to call their Champagne 'Dupont's Champagne' because they are producers. It would seem a short-sighted move when most of the Champagne we drink is own-label or house Champagne.

What else is on the label?

There are many other terms used to describe Champagne on the label. Here are the most commonly found ones.

Blanc de Blancs Champagne made only from the Chardonnay grape. Generally light, flowery, delicate.

Blanc de Noirs Champagne made only from black grapes (Pinot Noir and Pinot Meunier). Full, quite heavy and not often seen.

Bouzy Rouge Still red wine made from Pinot Noir grapes. Expensive and very light in style: an acquired taste.

Brut Very dry, the standard term used to describe most of the Champagne we drink. A few firms make extremely dry Champagne as well as their standard brut: this will be described as something like Ultra Brut (Laurent Perrier) or Brut Sauvage (Piper Heidsieck).

Coteaux Champenois Red, white or rosé still wines made from Champagne grapes grown in Champagne.

Crémant Fermented in the bottle to a lower pressure than Champagne so that the bubbles are creamier and less fizzy. This term – although not the technique – is being phased out.

Crus All the Champagne vineyards are graded on a quality scale. The best are graded at 100 per cent and are called Grands Crus; the next level – at 90 to 99 per cent – are Premiers Crus. Deuxième Crus run from 80 to 90 per cent. Some Champagnes will be made only from Grand Cru vineyards and can then describe themselves as such. But many of the finest Champagnes use lesser vineyards for their grapes because that's the way they can achieve the consistent blend: it's not necessarily a way of cutting corners.

De luxe or prestige cuvées On the theory that Champagne is like perfume (the more you charge for it, the more people want to buy it), Champagne houses have launched top-price blends which can be either vintage or non-vintage. They are often distinguished more by the flamboyance of the bottle than the quality of the wine, although some de luxe cuvées are very fine. Equal quality and certainly better value are to be found in straightforward vintage Champagne or the RD brands (see below).

Demi-sec A medium sweet Champagne, best drunk at the end of a meal.

Doux Sweet Champagne. Not much in demand in the UK, but very popular in South America.

Extra Dry Not as dry as brut but drier than sec.

Non-vintage The vast bulk of Champagne is a blended wine, using wines from different years to give continuity of style. The Champagnes reflect their house styles, and the master blenders (who may be putting 40 or 50 different wines in the blend) are highly regarded.

RD (Récemment Dégorgé) A few houses (Bollinger, Gratien, Bruno Paillard and Joseph Perrier) don't remove the yeasts from the wine as soon as the second fermentation in the bottle has finished, but leave the sediment in the wine for some time afterwards to give added richness to the Champagne. It's done only for a small proportion of the production which will be labelled accordingly and for which large sums of money will be charged. But for special occasions, these wines are very memorable – and certainly better value than many de luxe blends.

Riche The sweetest category of Champagne.

Rosé Champagne Normally made from adding red wine to white wine to give consistency of colour. The old method was to leave the red grape juice in contact with the skins after pressing to get its colour and then ferment the wine as a rosé. A few firms, such as Laurent Perrier, still do this.

Sec Medium dry, less dry than extra brut or brut.

Vintage Champagne A Champagne in which all the wine will be from one year. Vintage Champagne is made only in exceptional years which are 'declared', but not every producer will make a vintage each declared year. This was the way Champagne always used to be made until the Second World War. Vintage Champagne can represent very good value for money for a top-rate wine, but needs some time in bottle before drinking – at least six or seven years. There's no point in drinking vintage Champagne too young – you might as well buy the less expensive non-vintage.

Bottle sizes Apart from the standard 75cl Champagne bottle, Champagne comes in a whole range of other sizes of bottle. The larger the bottle size, the more slowly the wine will mature.

Halves and quarters Champagne matures very quickly in these small bottles – especially the quarter-bottles sometimes seen on aeroplanes. Be cautious with quarters - the quality of the wine tends to suffer.

Magnum Two ordinary bottles.

Jeroboam Four ordinary bottles.

Rehoboam Six ordinary bottles.

Methuselah Eight ordinary bottles.

Salmanazar Twelve ordinary bottles.

Balthazar Sixteen ordinary bottles.

Nebuchadnezzar Twenty ordinary bottles.

Champagne vintages

In Champagne – as in Port – not every year is a vintage year. In the lesser years, all the wine goes into the non-vintage blends. In certain top quality years, a small amount of wine is put aside for producing vintage wines.

1988 High quality and average quantity. Watch out for vintage releases in a few years' time.

1987 A big vintage of fairly average quality, so unlikely to be turned into vintage wines, but very useful for blending.

1986 Another useful vintage, probably better than 1987. It was the first big crop since 1983, producing good rather than great quality. Some houses may make vintage wines, but they would be better off using the wines for blending.

1985 Small crop because heavy frosts at the beginning of the year did immense damage to the vineyards. The quality, though, was high after a warm summer and autumn, and some vintage wines were announced. Wine held back from the bumper 1982 and 1983 vintages was used to augment the quantity.

1984 A pretty awful vintage, small in quantity and with rather thin, acid wines. No vintage wines were made.

1983 and 1982 Bumper years in Champagne, both for quality and quantity. Most producers declared vintages: the 1982 tastes delicious now, while the 1983 is just reaching maturity.

1981 The crop was small and the wines tend to be a little acid, so buy vintages with care. Most need drinking by now.

1979 An excellent vintage. Some stocks are still around and, although ageing, they are showing very well at the moment.

1976 Many of the lesser vintage wines from this year are past their best. Some of the top houses' wines, though, are still delicious.

1975 One of the great vintages of the past 15 years. If you see a bottle, buy it, just to see what mature Champagne can really taste like.

Older vintages: 1973, 1971, 1966, 1964, 1961 Generally only the top cuvées from the best producers are worth considering – although there can be surprises.

Who's who in Champagne

Here is a list of producers whose Champagnes are available in UK shops. We have not included own-label Champagnes, but since most wine merchants as well as supermarkets and wine warehouses have an own-label brand, we would recommend trying them for value for money.

Ayala Fair, reasonably enjoyable wines with consistent quality and some bottle age. Non-vintage, vintage and rosé are available.
Les Amis du Vin; Asda; Champagne & Caviar Shop; Peter Green; Majestic; Selfridges; Wine Growers Association

Barancourt Medium-sized family company, with extensive vineyard holdings. Cuvées are named after the villages in which the vines are. Bouzy Brut, Bouzy Rose, Cramant Brut, Réserve Brut, vintage.
Peter Green; Selfridges; Willoughbys

Besserat de Bellefon Lightish style, better at Crémant than straight Champagne. Non-vintage, vintage, crémant (to be re-christened Cuvée des Moines), Crémant Rosé (Cuvée des Moines Rosé), de luxe Cuvée B de B.
Champagne & Caviar Shop; Peter Green; Selfridges; Willoughbys

Billecart-Salmon Serious, traditional Champagne in a dry, austere style. Non-vintage, Blanc de Blancs, rosé, de luxe Cuvée Nicolas-François Billecart.
Champagne & Caviar Shop; Windrush Wines

Boizel Good value Champagne, without excitement but reliable. Non-vintage, vintage, rosé.
Augustus Barnett

Bollinger Full, rich Champagnes with a faithful following. There was a dip in quality a year ago, which we hope has now been restored. Non-vintage, vintage, rosé, RD, Vieilles Vignes Françaises.
Widely available

Bonnaire A small producer in the top quality village of Cramant. Makes a non-vintage and Blanc de Blancs Cuvée Anniversaire.
Willoughbys

Bonnet Small, family-owned house. Non-vintage, Blanc de Blancs, vintage.
Champagne de Villages; Martinez Fine Wine; Winecellars

de Castellane Soft wines with a hint of wood to give them character. Non-vintage and vintage.
Cadwgan Fine Wines; Arthur Rackhams; Willoughbys

Canard-Duchêne Easy-drinking Champagne offering good value. Non-vintage, rosé, de luxe Cuvée Charles VII.
Balls Brothers; Peter Dominic; Alex Findlater; Findlater Mackie Todd; Gare du Vin; Harrods; Selfridges; Thresher; La Vigneronne; Waitrose

Cattier Light, straightforward non-vintage and vintage wines, and a stylish Clos du Moulin non-vintage prestige brand.
Mail order from Patrick Grubb, Orchard Lee House, Steeple Aston, Oxfordshire

Charbaut Light, perfumed wine of good quality. Non-vintage, vintage, rosé, de luxe Certificat Blanc de Blancs.
Seckford Wines

Deutz Well-aged wines, full and soft. Non-vintage, vintage, rosé, de luxe Cuvée William Deutz.
Caves de la Madeleine; Champagne & Caviar Shop; Laytons; André Simon; La Vigneronne

Duval Leroy The suppliers of Sainsbury's and other buyers' own brands; also produce a Champagne available under their own name. Non-vintage, vintage, rosé, de luxe Cuvée des Roys.
Lay & Wheeler; J Sainsbury

Nicolas Feuillatte Light style of wines. Makes a rosé and a non-vintage.
Eaton Elliot Winebrokers; Harrods

Roland Fliniaux Small producer with only four hectares under vine. Non-vintage, vintage, rosé.
Champagne House

Michel Gonet Good value Blanc de Blancs.
Bottoms Up; Peter Dominic

Gosset The oldest house in Champagne, founded in 1584, producing quite rich wines with Pinot predominating. Non-vintage, vintage, rosé, de luxe Grand Millésime, Cuvée Quatrième Centenaire.
Les Amis du Vin; Champagne & Caviar Shop; Gare du Vin; Selfridges

George Goulet Mature wines on the lighter side. Non-vintage, vintage, rosé de luxe Cuvée de Centenaire.
H Allen Smith; Gare du Vin; M & W Gilbey; Thos Peatling; Christopher Piper Wines; Selfridges; Willoughbys

Granier Well-matured wines with a high proportion of Pinot. Non-vintage, vintage, rosé, de luxe Cuvée Réserve.
Willoughbys; Wines from Paris

Alfred Gratien Immensely old-world, traditional producers, who ferment their wines in wood. The wines are full and go well with food. Non-vintage, rosé, vintage.
Cadwgan Fine Wines; Oddbins; Arthur Rackhams; Selfridges; La Vigneronne; Willoughbys; Winecellars; The Wine Society

Heidsieck Light, commercial wines, but good value. Non-vintage, vintage, de luxe H de Heidsieck.
Morrisons; Thos Peatling

Charles Heidsieck Full-bodied wines which have seen a dramatic improvement in quality, and are now offering good value. Non-vintage, vintage, rosé, de luxe Champagne Charlie.
Widely available

Heidsieck Monopole Attractive, biscuity-yeasty wines, very dry. Non-vintage, vintage, rosé, de luxe Diamant Bleu.
Champagne & Caviar Shop; Peter Dominic; Morrisons; Oddbins; Selfridges; Victoria Wine Company; Willoughbys

Henriot One of the brands in the Moët/Clicquot conglomerate making wines under the Baron Philippe de Rothschild name as well as a non-vintage called Henriot.
Peter Dominic; Grape Ideas; Harrods; Justerini & Brooks; Oddbins; Selfridges; Willoughbys

Jacquart High quality wines from one of the Champagne co-operatives. Good bottle age. Vintage, non-vintage, rosé.
Booths; Findlater Mackie Todd; Hilbre Wine Company; Hungerford Wine Company; Morris & Verdin; Oddbins; Old Street Wine Company

Jacquesson Drinkable, soft, high quality. Non-vintage, vintage, rosé, de luxe Signature.
La Vigneronne; Wizard Wine Warehouses; Yapp Brothers

Jeanmaire A grower/producer owning 62 hectares of vineyard. Their non-vintage Brut has considerable bottle age. Non-vintage, vintage, Blanc de Blancs, Blanc de Noirs, Rosé.
H Allen Smith; Gare du Vin

Louis Kremer Full, fruity, quite heavy wines. Non-vintage, vintage, rosé.
George Hill of Loughborough (rosé); Willoughbys

Krug Great Champagnes that are (almost) worth the price. Very traditional techniques, with wood fermentation. Vintages last for years and the rosé is a great experience. Vintage, rosé, de luxe Grande Cuvée, Clos du Mesnil.
Widely available

Lanson Light, fresh wines with Chardonnay predominating. Non-vintage, vintage, rosé, de luxe Noble Cuvée.
Widely available

Laurent Perrier Lovely, traditional, very clean-tasting wines. Non-vintage, vintage, rosé, de luxe Cuvée Grande Siècle. The largest of the few remaining family-owned firms.
Widely available

Abel Lepitre Very high class Champagnes with good bottle age and maturity in the taste. Non-vintage, vintage, de luxe Prince A de Bourbon.
Clifton Cellars, 22 The Mall, Clifton, Bristol, Avon; Stogden Wine, 14A Chatham Row, Walcott Street, Bath, Avon

Mercier The second company in the Moët et Chandon group makes good, reliable Champagne which is also generally good value. Non-vintage, vintage, rosé.
Widely available

Moët et Chandon The biggest seller, often maligned, but actually of good, reliable quality. Quite full-bodied. Non-vintage, vintage, rosé, de luxe Dom Pérignon.
Very widely available

Mumm Slightly sweeter than most bruts, which gives a full, creamy taste. Non-vintage, vintage, rosé, de luxe René Lalou.
Widely available

Oudinot Light, undemanding wines. The top cuvée is called Gold Label.
Contact Giles de la Mare, The Old Dower House, Maiden Bradley, Warminster, Wilts

Bruno Paillard Delightful light, elegant, fruity Champagne from one of the most recently established private firms. Vintage, non-vintage, rosé.
Berkmann Wine Cellars/Le Nez Rouge; Bordeaux Direct; Findlater Mackie Todd; Harrods

Palmer Independent producers, owned by their grape growers. Non-vintage, Cuvée Rubis, Vintage, Blanc de Blancs, Cuvée Amazone.
Caves de la Madeleine

Pannier House whose vineyards and production are away from the main Champagne centres in Château-Thierry, on the way to Paris. Non-vintage, rosé.
Laytons

Joseph Perrier Ripe, rich, firm Champagne, which matures well. Non-vintage, vintage, rosé, de luxe Cuvée de Cent-Cinquantenaire.
Widely available

Perrier-Jouët Light, predominantly Chardonnay wines, with hints of lemon. Non-vintage, vintage, rosé Belle Epoque, de luxe Belle Epoque, Blason de France.
Widely available

Philipponnat Good value, very approachable Champagne. Non-vintage, vintage.
Grape Ideas; Oddbins

Piper Heidsieck Light, well-structured, flinty wines. Non-vintage, vintage, rosé, de luxe Champagne Rare (very dry).
Averys; Fullers; Gare du Vin; Harrods; Hilbre Wine Company; Justerini & Brooks; Morrisons; Oddbins; Arthur Rackhams; T & W Wines; La Vigneronne

Pol Roger Light, elegant, firm wines. Non-vintage, vintage, rosé, de luxe Cuvée Sir Winston Churchill.
Widely available

Pommery et Greno Just known as Pommery. Dry, light, balanced wines. Quality has improved after a dull patch. Non-vintage, vintage, rosé, de luxe Cuvée Louis Pommery.
Champagne & Caviar Shop; Gare du Vin; Peter Green; Harrods; Oddbins; Arthur Rackhams; Wines from Paris

Louis Roederer One of the great Champagne houses, producing fruity, rich, firm wines with lots of character. Pricy, but a great experience to drink. Non-vintage, vintage, rosé, de luxe Cristal.
Widely available

Alfred Rothschild Vintage and non-vintage wines of a pleasant, light quality.
Willoughbys

Ruinart Another Moët et Chandon company making soft, gentle wines of good quality. Vintage Blanc de Blancs, de luxe Dom Ruinart.
Les Amis du Vin; Champagne & Caviar Shop; Harrods; Hungerford Wine Company; Thos Peatling; Unwins; The Upper Crust; Willoughbys; Wine Growers Association

Salon Tiny production of superb 100 per cent Chardonnay wines made only in best years. Vintage Salon le Mesnil, de luxe Cuvée S.
Les Amis du Vin; Champagne & Caviar Shop; Oddbins; Selfridges; Willoughbys

Jacques Selosse Wines of character and depth which age well. Non-vintage, vintage, de luxe Special Club.
Bentalls of Kingston; Oldacre-Field, Hazel Road, Altrincham, Cheshire

Taittinger Attractive, lively, dry, gentle. Non-vintage, vintage, rosé Comtes de Champagne, de luxe Comtes de Champagne, Taittinger Collection.
Widely available

de Venoge Well balanced with elegance and some finesse. Non-vintage, vintage, rosé, de luxe Champagne des Princes.
Old Street Wine Company; Selfridges; Victoria Wine Company; Willoughbys

Veuve Clicquot Great quality and consistent style make this one of the most popular Champagnes. Non-vintage, vintage, rosé, de luxe La Grande Dame.
Widely available

Best buys in Champagne

LESS EXPENSIVE NON-VINTAGE

Waitrose Non-Vintage (*Waitrose*)
Asda Champagne Brut (*Asda*)
De Telmont Non-Vintage (*Majestic*)
Ellner Extra Brut (*Davisons; Lay & Wheeler; Master Cellar Wine Warehouse*)
Pierre Vaudon Non-Vintage (*Haynes Hanson & Clark*)
Lay & Wheeler Extra Quality Brut (*Lay & Wheeler*)
Tanners Brut Extra Reserve (*Tanners*)
Albert Beerens Reserve (*Bibendum*)
Booths Champagne Brut (*Booths*)
Champagne Blanc de Blancs (*Marks & Spencer*)

MORE EXPENSIVE NON-VINTAGE

Jacquesson Perfection (*Yapp Brothers*)
Alfred Gratien Cuvée de Réserve Brut (*Arthur Rackhams*)
Billecart-Salmon Non-Vintage Brut (*Windrush Wines*)
Henriot Brut Souverain (*Caves de la Madeleine; Champagne & Caviar Shop; Peter Dominic – some branches; Willoughbys*)
Laurent-Perrier Non-Vintage Brut (*widely available*)
Charles Heidsieck Non-Vintage Brut (*widely available*)
Bruno Paillard Non-Vintage Brut (*Berkmann Wine Cellars/Le Nez Rouge*)
Lanson Black Label Brut (*widely available*)
Moët et Chandon Première Cuvée Brut (*widely available*)

VINTAGE

(Vintages may have changed between going to press and publication. These producers or retailers seem to have a good vintage style for their wines.)

Sainsbury's Vintage Champagne 1983 (*J Sainsbury*)
Champagne St-Gall 1985 (*Marks & Spencer*)
Pol Roger 1982 (*H Allen Smith; Les Amis du Vin; Cadwgan Fine Wines; Peter Dominic; Peter Green; Harrods; Justerini & Brooks; Oddbins; Selfridges; Upper Crust*)
Taittinger 1983 (*Oddbins; Selfridges*)

Louis Roederer 1982 (*Averys; Bibendum; Cadwgan Fine Wines; Gare du Vin; Grape Ideas; Gerard Harris; Majestic; Upper Crust*)
Joseph Perrier 1982 (*Gerard Harris; Lay & Wheeler*)

DE LUXE AND SPECIAL CUVÉES

Heidsieck Dry Monopole Diamant Bleu (*Harrods; Oddbins; Selfridges*)
Laurent Perrier Cuvée Grande Siècle (*H Allen Smith; Les Amis du Vin; Eldridge Pope; Gerard Harris; Harrods; Oddbins; Selfridges*)
Deutz Cuvée William Deutz (*Laytons; André Simon; La Vigneronne*)
Bollinger RD (*widely available*)
ʼSalon Le Mesnil 1979 (*Les Amis du Vin; Oddbins; Selfridges*)

ROSÉ CHAMPAGNE

Landragin Non-Vintage (*Oddbins*)
Lanson Non-Vintage (*Augustus Barnett; Davisons; Peter Dominic; Lay & Wheeler; Morrisons; Oddbins; Thos Peatling; Arthur Rackhams; Selfridges; Unwins; Victoria Wine Company; Waitrose*)
Besserat de Bellefon Non-Vintage (*Peter Green; Selfridges*)
Sainsbury's Rosé Champagne Brut (*J Sainsbury*)
Mercier Non-Vintage (*Harrods; Unwins; Wizard Wine Warehouses*)
Krug Non-Vintage (*Booths; Cadwgan Fine Wines; Gerard Harris; Justerini & Brooks; André Simon; T & W Wines*)
Taittinger Comtes de Champagne (*Oddbins; Selfridges*)

Specialist stockists

William Addison (Newport); Bentalls of Kingston; Berry Bros & Rudd; Cadwgan Fine Wines; Champagne and Caviar Shop; Champagne de Villages; Champagne House; Classic Wine Warehouses; Findlater Mackie Todd; Fortnum & Mason; Peter Green; Harrods; Victor Hugo Wines; Oddbins; Arthur Rackhams; C A Rookes; Selfridges; Stones of Belgravia; Tesco; T & W Wines; Whiteside's of Clitheroe; Willoughbys

CORSICA

Vive la différence

Nielluccio, Sciacarello, Pagedebit, Montaccio – not names to trip off the tongue in any list of the world's most popular grape varieties. But this is Corsica – and Corsica is different from mainland France (*le continent*, they call it), and for many producers it is these grapes that preserve the individuality of Corsican wine.

Of course, Cabernet Sauvignon, Chardonnay and Syrah have turned up on the island as well, following in the footsteps of the lesser southern French varieties like Carignan and Cinsault, which were planted back in the 1960s by Algerians fleeing that country after independence. That experiment didn't work (yields were too low), and the graph of Corsican wine production forms a huge inverted U shape over 30 years or so – from 9,000 hectares in 1958, to 32,000 in 1973, back to 10,000 in 1987.

What we are left with is two schools of thought – but one sense of commitment. There are those who believe in the local grapes and make their wines under a number of appellation names. And there are those who have imported the international grape varieties to the island, but are allowed to call their wines only vins de pays.

Whether you think the local varieties do better than the international ones depends on your point of view: do you want safety in familiar tastes, or are you willing to experiment with the Italian tastes of Nielluccio (the Sangiovese of Tuscany) or Sciacarello (a peppery grape found nowhere else in the world)?

The major disadvantage of trying any of these wines is price. Transport (both of bottles and corks in one direction and of wines in the other) adds an extra to the costs that mainland French wines do not have to bear. At the moment, quality hasn't quite reached the level at which we can reconcile the sort of price being charged.

Where's where in Corsica

The two main AC regions are Patrimonio and Ajaccio. In Patrimonio, reds are made from the Nielluccio while whites come from the Malvoisie. In Ajaccio, Sciacarello provides the reds and the Vermentino the whites. Other AC areas are Coteaux du Cap Corse, Porto-Vecchio, Sartène and Calvi.

The picturesque-sounding Vin de Pays de l'Île de Beauté covers the island. Reds can be made from Syrah and Cabernet Sauvignon, whites from Chardonnay.

Who's who in Corsica

Domaine de Fontanella, Vin de Pays (*Waitrose*)
Domaine Comte Peraldi, Vin de Corse Ajaccio (*Bordeaux Direct*)
Domaine Discala, Vin de Corse (*Adnams*)
Vignerons des Pieve, the largest co-operative on the island, making wines using international grape varieties (of which the best is the Cabernet Sauvignon) as well as local grapes (*Cadwgan Fine Wines; Stones of Belgravia*)

Specialist stockist

Willoughbys

HAUT-POITOU

This is a region which has revived as the result of the wine-making and marketing efforts of the local co-operative of Neuville de Poitou. In the vineyard area north of Poitiers they produce a range of varietally labelled wines: an excellent aromatic Sauvignon similar to that made in Touraine; a light, fruity Gamay; and a soft Chardonnay. Drink the wines young.

What's what in Haut-Poitou

Sauvignon de Haut-Poitou (*Augustus Barnett; Eldridge Pope/ Reynier Wine Libraries; Grape Ideas; Peter Green; Lay & Wheeler; Majestic; Stapylton Fletcher; Waitrose; Willoughbys*)
Chardonnay de Haut-Poitou (*Eldridge Pope/Reynier Wine Libraries; Grape Ideas; Harrods; Lay & Wheeler; Majestic; Master Cellar Wine Warehouse; Sebastopol Wines; Stapylton Fletcher; Willoughbys*)
Gamay de Haut-Poitou (*Eldridge Pope/Reynier Wine Libraries; Lay & Wheeler; Stapylton Fletcher; Willoughbys*)

JURA

In the days of the much-travelled international grape varieties, the Chardonnays and Cabernet Sauvignons of the world, it is reassuring to find an area of France where the grapes are unknowns, where the most famous product is the only wine in Europe to grow a natural flor outside Jerez, and where the producers have no intention of changing their ways.

The region is the Jura, one of the most beautiful and unspoilt parts of France, where villages are so pretty that you need to see them to believe the pictures, and where the Savagnin, the Trousseau and the Poulsard grapes reign.

A full range of wine styles is produced in the Jura. Reds come from the Trousseau grape, with a small amount of the Pinot Noir of Burgundy, just down the road. Rosés are made from the Poulsard, which gives a pale coloured wine sometimes known as vin gris. Savagnin goes to make the white wines (with some Chardonnay).

Savagnin also turns up in the region's most famous – if rarely tasted – product, vin jaune. A strong, Sherry-like wine which grows a natural flor and which needs considerable ageing before it's drinkable, vin jaune is an acquired taste. But as one of the more unusual wine tastes of France it's well worth trying.

There's an even rarer wine than vin jaune. Vin de paille (straw wine) is a medium sweet wine made from grapes dried on straw mats and which, when the dried grapes are converted into wine, has high alcohol – another memorable experience.

The appellations of the Jura are: Arbois, Côtes de Jura, l'Etoile. Village names to look for are Ch Chalon, Poligny and Pupillin.

Who's who in the Jura

By far the biggest shipper of note from the Jura is Henri Maire who makes the full range of styles – try Cendre de NovembreVin Gris (*Fortnum & Mason; Harrods*). Jean Bourdy makes Ch Chalon and Vin Jaune (*Fortnum & Mason; Gerard Harris; O W Loeb; La Vigneronne; Wine Society*) while a third name to look for is the single vineyard Ch d'Arlay which produces red and white wines as well as vin jaune (*Eaton Elliot Winebrokers; Harrods; J Sainsbury; La Vigneronne*).

Specialist stockists
Eaton Elliot Winebrokers; O W Loeb; La Vigneronne; Willoughbys

THE LOIRE

River of variety

The Loire offers the widest variety of wine styles of any area in France, from the driest wines like Muscadet or Sancerre, through lightweight reds, Beaujolais-style wines and sparkling wines, finishing up with some luscious sweet wines.

But they all share one characteristic – a streak of piercingly clean acidity lurking somewhere in their make-up (even with the sweet wines), which gives them a light touch and a freshness, a refreshingness, that comes from the northerly position of the major Loire vineyards.

However, far too much wine that comes from the Loire seems to have taken this acidity to extremes, so that the wines are tart rather than fresh, and suffering from an over-enthusiastic use of sulphur in the wine-making. One is more likely to emerge from a tasting of Muscadet, for example, with tears streaming down from the reek of sulphur than with the palate refreshed by clean, simple, fruit tastes.

Why so much sulphur? Sulphur is used in wine-making to keep the fruit hygienic before fermentation starts and to preserve it when it has become wine (see the feature on additives at the beginning of the Guide). An excessive use suggests that the quality of the fruit was poor in the first place, which means that the growers were producing too much from their vines and that they weren't taking enough care over what they picked, which in turn means that they probably aren't being paid very much for their grapes.

That certainly seems to sum up the problem in two of the Loire's most popular wines – Muscadet and Anjou Rosé (which is now more often called Blush, because it has been shown to be a more successful marketing ploy). They are cheap, not so cheerful – and taste like it. Remember Liebfraumilch?

The fashionable wines

But at the other end of the spectrum the Loire also produces some of France's most fashionable wines in the shape of Sancerre and Pouilly Fumé. While, even here, the spectre of sulphur is not unknown, there are some fine producers (see under Who's who) making wines from the Sauvignon grape. Like any other star areas, there are pressures on prices, but in recent years they have remained comparatively static.

While producers in both Muscadet and Sancerre/Pouilly are producing tastes that everybody wants, there seems to be a big area in the middle reaches of the river where what is made is deeply unfashionable. This is the realm of the Chenin Blanc, the grape we love to hate. Thinly acid, it is often used to produce high-yielding, low quality wines without even the redeeming qualities of refreshingness that characterise the lesser offerings from Muscadet. Although things are changing, with the coming of a younger generation of wine-makers, the good producers are vastly outnumbered by the bad.

Yet, paradoxically, Chenin also makes the greatest wines on the river: from Vouvray, from Quarts de Chaume, from Bonnezeaux, from Savennières come great dessert and dry wines that yield their tastes only slowly - so that 20, 30 years are needed before they can be fully appreciated. Even here, though, the natural acidity is always evident, creating wines that are lighter in character than Sauternes, never cloying, always perfectly poised. The cool, northern location of the Loire is never lost.

We have divided the sections on Loire wines by style: dry whites, sweet whites, and reds and rosés.

Dry white wines – the epitome of the Loire

If any tastes epitomise the Loire, they are the herbaceousness of Sauvignon Blanc and the clean acidity of Muscadet. These are produced at the eastern and western extremities of the main Loire vineyard areas: the Sauvignon of Sancerre and Pouilly Fumé, far to the east, almost in Chablis; the Muscadet, the wine of Brittany, from the mouth of the river near Nantes.

In between, there are the excellent value Sauvignon Blanc wines of Touraine, and – as we've seen – the varied quality of the Chenin Blanc wines of Anjou.

Besides the appellation contrôlée wines of the Loire, there are a number of excellent vins de pays – from the basic – and romantic-sounding – regional Vin de Pays du Jardin de la France to smaller areas whose wines have hardly left the vineyard, let alone reached our shops. There are also some VDQS areas, of which the most interesting (for dry whites, that is) is away from the main river: St-Pourçain on the Allier.

Where's where in dry white Loire wines

Sancerre and Pouilly Fumé

The two towns of Sancerre and Pouilly-sur-Loire virtually face each other across the north-flowing Loire just before it turns west. Although reds and rosés are also made in Sancerre, the whites are the most important in terms of quality. Made from the Sauvignon grape, they have hints of blackcurrants and gooseberries and a slightly smoky flavour (not, however, the origin of Fumé in Pouilly Fumé, which refers instead to the smoky-grey bloom on the Sauvignon grape), and at their best are some of the most flavourful wines around. Pouilly Fumé tends to be more full-bodied than Sancerre, and needs just a little more time before it is ready to drink.

Certain villages in each area are reckoned to make exceptional wines: in Sancerre – Bué, Chavignol, Verdigny, St-Satur; in Pouilly – Les Loges, Les Berthiers, Tracy, Maltaverne. Look for the grower's address on the label.

Other appellation areas producing white wines of similar style but at lower prices than the fashionable Sancerre and Pouilly Fumé are Reuilly, Quincy and Ménétou-Salon. The appellation of Pouilly-sur-Loire uses the Chasselas grape to make unmemorable whites.

In most cases these wines don't improve with keeping, so you should be drinking 1987 or 1988 wines now. But there is a special character to a mature Sancerre or Pouilly Fumé which makes older wines worth seeking out. They certainly don't fade away but develop a mellow, slightly cheesy taste that is often less penetrating and more subtle than the taste of the younger wines.

Vouvray and Montlouis

The most important vineyards of Touraine in the central Loire are just to the west of the city of Tours. As with Sancerre and Pouilly-sur-Loire, another pair of towns – Vouvray and Montlouis – face each other across the river. Both Vouvray and Montlouis are made from the Chenin Blanc grape.

Considering their potential for quality, we've neglected these wines unfairly. The trouble is that many wines are bottled by négociants elsewhere on the Loire and are not very good. With a few exceptions, the best wines are those bottled in Vouvray or Montlouis ('mise en bouteille au château/domaine' or a Vouvray or Montlouis address will give a clue).

Vouvray wines range from bone dry to sweet and also include sparkling versions (see the Sparkling wines section). It's important to check the style and sweetness or dryness of the Vouvray you're buying. Good, still dry Vouvray can have considerable depth and richness, but the sweeter wines tend to aim higher. Montlouis is softer and more likely to be sweet.

Jasnières

This tiny area of dry white production is away to the north of the Loire on the River Loir (the Loire is La Loire, the Loir is Le Loir). The wine made in Jasnières is from the Chenin Blanc, which here achieves some quality in a dry, under-ripe sort of way.

Sauvignon de Touraine

A wide appellation which covers any wines made in Touraine from the Sauvignon grape. The value for money of these wines is good and the quality reliable, sometimes even good, so they make a good cheaper substitute for the Sancerre/Pouilly wines.

Saumur

This small town west of Angers is now best known in the UK for its sparkling wines made by the Champagne method using the often under-ripe wines based on the Chenin Blanc (see more in the Sparkling wines section).

Still dry white wines are produced here under the Saumur appellation, but few achieve greatness or even leave the area. More important still dry whites are made in Coteaux de Saumur but, again, few leave France.

Savennières

A minuscule appellation with a deservedly growing reputation.
The wines are some of the best dry wines made in the Loire
from the Chenin Blanc grape, with all the overtones of
sweetness in the honey and lemon bouquet and crisp, deep fruit
on the palate. They need some ageing – around five or six
years – to be at their best. Sadly, their reputation has forced up
the price of the small amount of wine made. Savennières-style
wines are also made in the single vineyard appellations of
Coulée de Serrant and La Roche aux Moines.

Anjou Blanc

This is the appellation which has suffered from the problem of
high acidity/high sulphur of the Chenin Blanc. Many of the
wines tend to be in a vaguely sweet style, while the dry wines
are often just sharp and acid. There does, though, seem to be a
general improvement in quality, so it might be worth
reconsidering this appellation.

Muscadet

Muscadet is one of France's major wine exports. Last year 26
million bottles left the vineyards at the mouth of the Loire, and
an awful lot of that came straight across the Channel. Muscadet
has become for us the most accessible and easily purchased dry
white wine.

The problem – as with all popular products – is that plenty of
that Muscadet is pretty nasty stuff. Sulphur sometimes seems to
play a more important part in the wine than fruit. Either that, or
the wine tastes of nothing at all because the grapes have been
over-cropped.

One of the problems lies in the curious classification system
in Muscadet (see below). The top category – Muscadet de Sèvre
et Maine – is also the largest, and not, as you would expect with
something implying quality, one of the smallest. So under a
supposed quality label march most of the dull wines as well as
the few good.

Those producers of good wine are getting fed up with
Muscadet's poor image. They are proposing a vineyard
classification scheme, so that single vineyard Muscadet can be
made which can proclaim its greater quality on the label. They
have also introduced a number of prestige blends – many with
English-sounding names like Le Master from Donatien Bahuaud
or One from Louis Métaireau, acknowledging Muscadet's
popularity in the UK.

Another change in Muscadet is away from the tart, appley
style that the local grape (called, not unsurprisingly, the

Muscadet) is prone to make. Some producers are going for a richer, more Burgundian style of wine that can age more than the 12 months' maximum that we would normally expect of Muscadet.

Whether this is all too serious for Britain's favourite white tipple is another matter. It might be better if Muscadet producers looked at cleaning up their cheaper wines if they are trying to promote the image of Muscadet as a top quality wine.

Here are some of the words to look out for on a Muscadet label.

Sèvre et Maine This is the name of the region at the heart of Muscadet production. The quality is higher than ordinary Muscadet, even though 85 per cent of all Muscadet carries this appellation.

Sur lie This indicates that the wine has been kept on its lees until it was bottled. In theory it should mean that the wine has been bottled at the estate where it was grown, but the regulations allow merchants to take the wine off to their huge bottling plants – where 'sur lie' becomes meaningless. So look for 'mise en bouteille au château' or 'au domaine' on the label.

Other styles of wine made in the Muscadet region are generally less worth buying. They are:

Muscadet AC The basic stuff – and it tends to taste like it.

Gros Plant A VDQS appellation for wine made using the Gros Plant grape. Very tart, acid stuff, all right as a thirst-quencher on a very hot day and not much cheaper than Muscadet. This can also be bottled sur lie.

In general, drink all wines from the Muscadet area as young as possible. The 1989 vintage will be in the shops by the late spring and by then it will be the only one to buy. Muscadet Primeur (a white copy of Beaujolais Nouveau) should arrive here by Christmas and will be a good quaffing wine over the Christmas period and into January.

Sweet white wines – microclimate is all

The sweet wines of the Loire are an excellent example of what a microclimate can achieve. While Anjou can be the source of some pretty venomous-tasting sweet wines, in the valleys of the Layon and Aubance, south of Angers, the Chenin Blanc grape suddenly becomes the source of some very fine nobly rotted sweet wines. The autumn mists here act in the same way as they do in Sauternes, causing a benign fungus on the grapes to shrivel them up, removing the water and just leaving the sweet essence of grape juice.

Four main appellations produce sweet wines. Two – Coteaux du Layon and Coteaux de l'Aubance (which seems to have disappeared, so little is made) – produce simple, sweet, fruity wines but without the added extra of noble rot. But Quarts de Chaume and Bonnezeaux are two tiny pockets of vineyard where the noble rot creates rich, intense, peach-and-apricot wines of great stature and immensely long life. These wines don't really come into their own for as much as 10 or 15 years, but the wait is worth while in great vintages (see below). Bonnezeaux is better value than Quarts de Chaume.

Back in the main Loire valley, Vouvray and Montlouis, source of dry whites and sparkling wines, also make some intense sweet wines with a honey-like consistency, again capable of long ageing but rarely with noble rot. They are less intense than Quarts de Chaume or Bonnezeaux, and tend to be more attractive when young, but age seemingly indefinitely, going through sweetness and out to dryness again with maturity.

Sweet white wines – vintages

1988 A very good year, with high sugars in the grapes and a good incidence of noble rot. This is being considered as the vintage of the decade. These are wines that will last many years.

1987 Not a particularly good year, with virtually no true noble rot wines made. Vouvray and Montlouis fared better than Bonnezeaux and Quarts de Chaume.

1986 On the whole soft, quick-maturing wines, but with plenty of attractive fruit. No classic sweet wines, though.

1985 An exceptionally fine year with a good deal of noble rot. The wines will need some years before they are ready to drink.

1984 Charming, agreeable wines of comparative lightness. Most will be drinkable within two or three years.

1983 Great depth and richness means that most of the sweet wines will last for anything from 15 to 25 years. Don't drink any yet.

1981 Just coming through a period of dumbness, these wines are beginning to be drinkable in a light sort of way.

1978 Slow-developing vintage that is beginning to show its potential as one for great richness. Worth keeping for some time yet.

1976 Very ripe fruit, full of flavours and complexity. This is a year where the lesser wines are ready to drink now but the greater wines need another five years before they begin to mature.

Older vintages 1969, 1964, 1961 and 1959 are the great long-term vintages of recent years. They're not cheap and are hard to find, but are worth buying for future drinking experience, even if not for the investment.

Red and rosé Loire wines – not such a light touch

While we've long been familiar with the mildly sweet Anjou Rosé (and more recently, Blush), this is a market which is making little headway. Even the dry rosés, of which there are a few (see below), are hardly best sellers in Britain (although they do well in smart Paris restaurants).

In the UK we seem to be much more interested in the reds of the Loire. Despite the northern location, some intense and long-lived reds are made in small pockets in the valley, and there are plenty more lighter, fresher wines which have some similarities to a Beaujolais-style wine.

Pinot Noir and Cabernet Franc are the two principal grape varities used to make both Loire reds and rosés, with Gamay an important third. If you are in Côtes du Forez on the Upper Loire, you will find wines from Gamay; further down river, in Sancerre or Coteaux du Giennois, they will be from Pinot Noir; in Touraine, Cabernet Franc and Gamay are the grapes; and in Chinon, Bourgueil or Anjou, Cabernet Franc.

While the Pinot Noir wines of Sancerre are highly fashionable at the moment, and the Gamay is gulpable (but with rather too much acidity in poor years and not quite the fruit flavours of Beaujolais), it is Cabernet Franc which provides the finest reds, those from Chinon and Bourgueil.

As we've suggested, most Loire reds are to be drunk young and quite possibly chilled. They have a northern taste, with high acidity and not too much colour. But in Chinon and Bourgueil, wines can become smooth, velvety, intense with age, smelling of violets and vanilla and tasting herbaceous and surprisingly complex. And at the moment prices are still good, too.

Where's where in Loire reds

Sancerre

The reds and rosés of Sancerre, made from the Pinot Noir grape, have in recent years been very fashionable in smart restaurants, particularly in Paris (and for a short time in London). Consequently, prices shot up. At the moment they don't represent good value at all, even though the recent vintages have turned out to be very good indeed. Reds from a few producers mature for a surprisingly long time.

Chinon and Bourgueil

The most serious Loire reds are made from the Cabernet Franc (with a little Cabernet Sauvignon) in these two towns near Saumur west of Tours. Chinon produces a softer wine but with some ageing potential in good years, while Bourgueil makes more austere wine that is not particularly attractive when young, and does need three or four years. St-Nicolas-de-Bourgueil makes a lighter version of Bourgueil.

Gamay de Touraine

The Gamay grape is used to produce very enjoyable light wine which goes under the Gamay de Touraine varietal name. The wines are lighter, slightly tart equivalents of Beaujolais. Those wines made from Cabernet Franc don't need much ageing either.

Saumur-Champigny

Light, fruity reds from the Cabernet make this tiny area around the town of Saumur a good source of wines. Like Sancerre, though, they have become fashionable and prices are not particularly cheap.

Anjou

The rosés of Anjou are the wines that have long been the staple production of the area. Slightly sweet wines are now being supplemented by somewhat better (and drier) rosés made from the Cabernet. Since the appellations are complex, here we give the major styles which appear in UK shops:

Cabernet d'Anjou Good quality rosés, generally slightly sweet but with some depth.

Rosé d'Anjou The principal appellation of sweet rosés made from the Gamay and other grapes. On the whole, a dull lot.

Rosé de la Loire An appellation for dry reds using the Cabernet grape. Not widely found but worth looking out for.

Anjou also produces good, standard reds from the Cabernet, under the Anjou Rouge appellation.

Other reds of the Loire

Small outposts of red production are dotted in and around the Loire valley. In the south, look for Côtes Roannaises and Côtes du Forez, which are Gamay wines made not far from Beaujolais. Coteaux Giennois produces some light wines from the Pinot Noir and Gamay, just north of Pouilly-sur-Loire. Near Saumur, apart from Saumur Rouge, small amounts of fresh Gamay wine are made under the VDQS of Thouarsais.

Red and rosé vintages

Rosé wines should be drunk young, but in certain years, reds are made which do mature and last.

1988 An excellent year for wines based on Gamay and Cabernet, with above average quality from the Pinot Noir wines of Sancerre. Chinon and Bourgueil both made wines which will keep for a long time.

1987 A cool, wet year, with consequent acidity – and a short life – for reds.

1986 A middle-weight vintage, with some acidity in the wines. The reds from Chinon and Bourgueil have good staying power.

1985 A fine vintage producing some ripe wines from all areas. The Chinon and Bourgueil wines will keep for a while, as will other reds, including Sancerre.

1984 Avoid.

1983 A good vintage with reds at their best. The top wines from all areas will last a while yet.

1982 Bourgueil and Chinon reds are still worth drinking, but others are beginning to fade.

Older vintages 1978 and 1976 are the two vintages of Bourgueil and Chinon still worth drinking.

Who's who on the Loire

DRY WHITES

Sancerre

Vacheron – also for reds (*Adnams; Averys; Fortnum & Mason; Grape Ideas; Majestic; Tesco; The Wine Society; Wines from Paris*)
André Vattan (*Yapp Brothers*)
Lucien Crochet Clos du Chêne Marchand (*Berkmann Wine Cellars/Le Nez Rouge; Peter Dominic; Michael Menzel Wines*)
Clos Beaujeu Vincent Delaporte (*Caves de la Madeleine*)
Paul Millérioux Clos du Roy (*Peter Green; Gerard Harris*)
Le Grand Chemarin, Jean Max Roger (*Cadwgan Fine Wines; Davisons; Master Cellar Wine Warehouse*)
Les Monts Damnés, Henri Bourgeois (*T & W Wines*)
Les Monts Damnés, Paul Prieur (*Stapylton Fletcher*)
Clos de la Crèle, Lucien Thomas (*Cadwgan Fine Wines; Eldridge Pope/Reynier Wine Libraries*)
Reverdy (*Harrods; Lay & Wheeler*)

Comte Lafond (*Peter Green; Tanners*)
Henri Natter (*Bibendum; Lay & Wheeler*)
François and Paul Cotat (*Adnams; Caves de la Madeleine*)
Alphonse Mellot (*Classic Wine Warehouses; Wright Wine Co*)
Jean Vatan (*Yapp Brothers*)

Pouilly Fumé

Jean-Claude Guyot (*Yapp Brothers*)
Ch de Tracy (*Adnams; Caves de la Madeleine; Hungerford Wine Company; Lay & Wheeler; Tanners*)
Didier Dagueneau (*Lay & Wheeler; Tanners; La Vigneronne*)
de Ladoucette, Ch de Nozet (*widely available*)
Domaine Saget (*Grape Ideas; Peter Green; Majestic; Marks & Spencer; Welbeck Wines; Wines from Paris; Wizard Wine Warehouse*)
Michel Bailly Les Griottes (*Asda; Tesco*)
Les Bascoins Domaine Masson-Blondelet (*Gerard Harris; Christopher Piper Wines*)
Les Champs la Croix, Roger Pabot (*Laytons*)
Les Chantalouettes, Gitton (*Cadwgan Fine Wines; J Sainsbury; Windrush Wines*)
Patrick Coulbois (*Majestic*)

Quincy, Ménétou-Salon, Reuilly, St-Pourçain

Quincy Pierre Mardon (*Adnams; Caves de la Madeleine*)
Quincy, Domaine de la Maison Blanche (*Ellis Son & Vidler; Oddbins; Safeway; Stapylton Fletcher; Waitrose; Winecellars; Wizard Wine Warehouses*)
Quincy, Jacques Rouze (*Majestic*)
Ménétou-Salon Henri Pelle (*Gerard Harris; Prestige Vintners; Willoughbys*)
Ménétou-Salon Morogues (*Asda; Eldridge Pope/Reynier Wine Libraries; Winecellars*)
Ménétou-Salon, Domaine Clément (*Nobody Inn*)
Ménétou-Salon Jean Teiller (*Yapp Brothers*)
Ménétou-Salon Domaine Montaloise (*Harrods; Tesco*)
Reuilly Didier Martin (*Majestic*)
Reuilly Claude Lafond (*Lay & Wheeler; Thos Peatling; Christopher Piper Wines; Tanners*)
St-Pourçain Cuvée Printanière, Union des Vignerons (*Averys; Nobody Inn; Christopher Piper Wines*)

Vins d'Orléanais

Clos de St-Fiacre (*Yapp Brothers*)

Vouvray/Montlouis

Most producers here make both sweet and dry wines. See under sweet wines below for list.

Jasnières

Joël Gigou (*Adnams*)
Jean-Baptiste Pinon (*Ian G Howe; Yapp Brothers*)

Sauvignon de Touraine

Confrèrie des Vignerons de Oisly-et-Thésée (*widely available*)
Domaine de la Chapinière (*Thos Peatling*)
Domaine Vincent Girault (*Berkmann Wine Cellars/Le Nez Rouge*)
Domaine Octavie (*Majestic*)
Domaine de la Charmoise (*Bibendum*)
Domaine des Corbillières (*Fortnum & Mason*)
Sainsbury's Sauvignon de Touraine (*J Sainsbury*)
Domaine des Acacias (*Oddbins*)

Saumur (still white)

Domaine Langlois-Chateau (*Blayneys; Cadwgan Fine Wines; Peter Green; Whighams*)
Domaine du Val Brun, Charruau (*Hedley Wright*)
Co-opérative de St-Cyr-en-Bourg (*Bordeaux Direct*)

Savennières

Domaine des Baumard (*Cadwgan Fine Wines; Caves de la Madeleine; Eldridge Pope/Reynier Wine Libraries; Fortnum & Mason; Peter Green; Mayor Sworder & Co; La Réserve; Tanners; Willoughbys*)
Mme Joly Coulée de Serrant and Roche aux Moines (*Hurt & Daniel; Oddbins*)
Yves Soulez Domaine de la Bizolière (*Cadwgan Fine Wines; Sebastopol Wines; La Vigneronne; Yapp Brothers*)
Ch de Chamboureau (*Asda; Peter Green; Lay & Wheeler; Old Street Wine Company; The Wine Society*)

Muscadet

Guy Bossard (*Winecellars*)
Ch de l'Oiselinière Chereau Carré (*The Wine Society*)
Ch de Chasseloir, Chereau Carré (*Caves de la Madeleine; Hungerford Wine Company; Lay & Wheeler; Majestic*)
Louis Métaireau (*Harrods*)
Domaine des Dorices Léon Boullault (*Barwell & Jones; Peter Green*)

Ch du Cléray Jean Sauvion (*Berkmann Wine Cellars/Le Nez Rouge; Nobody Inn; Christopher Piper Wines*)
Marquis de Goulaine (*Averys; Michael Menzel Wines*)
Ch de la Ragotière (*Augustus Barnett*)
Ch de la Berrière (*Welbeck Wines*)
Donatien Bahuaud (*Peter Dominic; Willoughbys*)
Ch la Noë (*Willoughbys*)
Domaine de la Haute Carrizière (*Majestic*)
Domaine de Hautes Noëlles (*Oddbins*)

Vin de Thouarsais (VDQS)

Michel Gigon, Cépage Chenin (*Yapp Brothers*)

SWEET WHITES

Vouvray Ch de Moncontour (*Berry Bros & Rudd; Fortnum & Mason; Oddbins; Tesco; Waitrose; Winecellars*)
Gaston Huet (*Adnams; Les Amis du Vin; Averys; Bibendum; Cadwgan Fine Wines; Hurt & Daniel; Nobody Inn; Old Street Wine Company; Prestige Vintners*)
Prince Poniatowski Clos Baudoin (*Sebastopol Wines; La Vigneronne*)
Marc Brédif (*Les Amis du Vin; Nobody Inn; Prestige Vintners; Sebastopol Wines; La Vigneronne*)
Foreau Clos Naudin (*Adnams; Gerard Harris; Nobody Inn; Old Street Wine Company*)
Jean-Pierre Laissement (*Lay & Wheeler; Nobody Inn*)
Ch des Bidaudières (*J Sainsbury*)

Montlouis

G Delétang Montlouis (*Adnams; The Wine Society*)
Berger Frères, Domaine des Liards (*Lay & Wheeler; Old Street Wine Company; Prestige Vintners; Yapp Brothers*)

Quarts de Chaume, Bonnezeaux, Coteaux du Layon

Domaine des Baumard Coteaux du Layon/Quarts de Chaume (*Les Amis du Vin; Cadwgan Fine Wines; Eldridge Pope/Reynier Wine Libraries; Fortnum & Mason; Peter Green; Nobody Inn; Thos Peatling; La Réserve; Sebastopol Wines*)
Quarts de Chaume Lalanne Ch de Belle-Rive (*Oddbins; Prestige Vintners; Willoughbys; The Wine Society*)
Quarts de Chaume Ch de Fesles (*Gerard Harris*)
Ch de Gauliers Mme Fourlinnie (*Nobody Inn; Yapp Brothers*)
Coteaux du Layon, Ch de Plaisance (*Sebastopol Wines; Willoughbys*)

Anjou Blanc

Les Vins Touchais are renowned for a rare collection of old vintages of sweet Anjou Blanc (*Adnams; Barwell & Jones; Fortnum & Mason; Fullers; Gerard Harris; Michael Menzel Wine; Nobody Inn; J Sainsbury; Waitrose*)

REDS AND ROSÉS

Sancerre

Sancerre Rosé and Rouge Vacheron (*Averys; Fortnum & Mason; Grape Ideas; Majestic; The Wine Society; Wines from Paris*)
Sancerre Rosé Michel Thomas (*Les Amis du Vin; Cadwgan Fine Wines; Majestic; Smedley Vintners*)
Sancerre Rouge Domaine Daulny (*Willoughbys*)
Bernard Bailly-Reverdy (*Lay & Wheeler*)
Ch de Maimbray (*Willoughbys*)

Bourgueil, St-Nicolas de Bourgueil and Chinon

Chinon Raymond Desbourdes (*Fortnum & Mason; Ian G Howe; Yapp Brothers*)
Chinon Domaine de la Chapellerie (*Bibendum; Thos Peatling*)
Chinon Olga Raffault (*Lay & Wheeler; The Wine Society*)
Chinon Charles Joguet (*Adnams; O W Loeb*)
Chinon Couly-Dutheil (*Berry Bros & Rudd; Eldridge Pope/Reynier Wine Libraries; Peter Green; Old Street Wine Company; Prestige Vintners; Sebastopol Wines; Stapylton Fletcher; T & W Wines; Welbeck Wines*)
Chinon Domaine de la Noblaie (*Chesterford Vintners*)
Pierre Ferrand (*Richard Harvey Wines*)
Bourgueil Maître et Viémont (*High Breck Vintners; O W Loeb*)
Bourgueil Caslot-Galbrun La Hurolaie (*Tesco*)
Domaine des Chesnaies (*Old Street Wine Company*)
Caslot-Jamet (*The Wine Society*)
Pierre-Jacques Druet (*Adnams; Hurt & Daniel; Nobody Inn; Yapp Brothers*)
Joël et Clarisse Taluau (*Hurt & Daniel; The Wine Society*)
St-Nicolas de Bourgueil, J-C Mabileau (*Peter Green; Majestic; Old Street Wine Company*)
Domaine du Fondis (*Tanners*)

Stockists given in *italic* type after wines in this section will be found in the WHERE TO BUY section earlier in the book.

Touraine

Confrèrie de Oisly et Thésée (*Windrush Wines*)
Ch du Petit Thouars (*Berry Bros & Rudd; Bibendum; Tanners*)
Touraine-Mesland Ch Gaillard (*Berkmann Wine Cellars/Le Nez Rouge*)

Saumur-Champigny

Paul Buisse (*Berkmann Wine Cellars/Le Nez Rouge*)
Domaine Filliatrieu (*Ian G Howe; Yapp Brothers*)
Caves des Vignerons de Saumur (*Wine House*)
Domaine de Nerleux (*Berkmann Wine Cellars/Le Nez Rouge*)
Ch de Targé (*Haynes Hanson & Clark; Lay & Wheeler; Old Street Wine Company*)

Anjou Rouge

Clos de Coulaine (*Adnams; Bibendum; Justerini & Brooks; Lay & Wheeler; Thos Peatling*)
Logis de la Giraudière (*Eldridge Pope/Reynier Wine Libraries*)
Anjou Villages Domaine Richou (*Old Street Wine Company; Prestige Vintners*)

Côtes du Forez

Les Vignerons Foréziens Gamay (*Bordeaux Direct*)

Vins de Pays

de Loire-Atlantique (*Waitrose*)
de Loire-Atlantique, Domaine du Cléray (*Berkmann Wine Cellars/ Le Nez Rouge*)
du Jardin de la France, Caves des Vignerons de Saumur (*H Allen Smith*)
du Jardin de la France, cépage Sauvignon (*H Allen Smith; Les Amis du Vin; Averys; Cadwgan Fine Wines; Ellis Son & Vidler; Hungerford Wine Company; Majestic; Welbeck Wines; Whighams of Ayr; Winecellars; Wines from Paris*)

Best buys from Loire

DRY WHITE

Domaine Langlois Château, Saumur (*Blayneys*)
Sancerre 1988, Masson-Blondelet (*Champagne de Villages; Selfridges*)
Muscadet de Sèvre et Maine 1988, Guy Bossard (*Asda; Hampden Wine Company*)

Pouilly Fumé Les Berthiers 1988, J-C Dagueneau (*Ingletons Wines*)
Sauvignon de Touraine 1988, Domaine du Pré Baron (*Helen Verdcourt Wines*)
Ménétou-Salon 1987, Jean-Max Roger (*Eldridge Pope*)
Sauvignon de Touraine 1988, Donatien Bahuaud (*Andrew Gordon Wines*)

Vin de Thouarsais Sec 1988, Michel Gigon (*Yapp Brothers*)
Sancerre Chavignol 1987, Jean Delaporte (*Laytons; André Simon*)
Savennières 1987, Clos St-Yves, Jean Baumard (*La Réserve*)
Ménétou-Salon 1987, Henri Pellé (*Villandry*)
Sauvignon de Touraine 1988, Domaine de la Presle (*Sebastopol Wines*)

SWEET WHITE

Coteaux du Layon 1980, Ch Beaulieu (*Desborough & Brown Fine Wines*)
Quarts de Chaume 1983, Domaine Baumard (*Nobody Inn*)
Coteaux du Layon Chaume 1987, Ch de Suronde (*Edward Sheldon*)
Ch de Moncontour Vouvray (*Winecellars*)

ROSÉ

Gris Fumé Vin de Pays du Jardin de la France (*Adnams*)

RED

Gamay de Touraine 1988, Henry Marionnet (*Bibendum*)
St-Nicolas-de-Bourgueil 1986, Claude Bureau (*Mayor Sworder & Co*)
Chinon 1987, Vieilles Vignes (*Gardner Martens Fine Wines*)
Chinon 1986, Raymond Desbourdes (*Madeleine Trehearne Partners*)
Chinon 1987, Domaine de la Noblaie (*Chesterford Vintners*)
St-Nicolas de Bourgueil 1987, Les Gravières (*Majestic*)
Touraine Gamay 1987, Domaine des Acacias (*Upper Crust*)

Specialist stockists

Adnams; Berkmann Wine Cellars/Le Nez Rouge; Bibendum; Anthony Byrne Fine Wines; Cadwgan Fine Wines; Chesterford Vintners; Restaurant Croque-en-Bouche; Eldridge Pope; Peter Green; High Breck Vintners; Ian G Howe; Lay & Wheeler; Majestic; Nobody Inn; Old Street Wine Company; Pennyloaf Wines; Sapsford Wines; Madeleine Trehearne Partners; Upper Crust; Le Viticulteur

THE MIDI

Rising up from the wine lake

Of those areas which regularly supply us with our everyday wine, the Midi has perhaps been the least reliable in the past. It has come up with some pretty dreadful stuff (after all, this is the home of the blue-overalled French workman's tipple, *le gros rouge*), and seemed, until recently, to be drowning in a wine lake of mediocrity.

Much has changed, though, in the last decade. One of the most important from the point of view of our glass of vin ordinaire was the creation of vin de pays. While there are vin de pays regions all over France, this is their spiritual home: their purpose was to recognise local traditions and at the same time to haul the quality of wine produced by those local traditions into the 20th century. It has been a brilliant piece of marketing – the instant creation of wine areas with the feel of having been around a long time coupled (essentially) with a dramatic improvement in quality.

That is one aspect of the qualitative change that has come about in the vinous heartlands of the South of France. There are certainly plenty of areas – especially on the flat plains of the Hérault and Gard départements – where wine lake material is still produced in vast quantity. But more and more British merchants are able to winkle out a bewildering variety of wines from the hills and backwaters of this vast region, stretching around the arc of the French Mediterranean coast from the mouths of the Rhône to the Spanish border.

Although most – probably 90 per cent – of wine in the region comes from co-operatives, it is the individual estates which have been setting the pace. However, the co-ops are not far behind – and much good value is now coming from supermarkets' or wine retailers' own-label wines which are adorned simply by a set of mysterious initials to indicate the name of the bottler.

Taking off at the top

If the quality of everyday wine has improved with the introduction of the vin de pays category, at the other end of the quality spectrum much has changed has well. More and more, single estate wines are showing that certain areas – Fitou, Faugères, St-Chinian, La Clape, Corbières and Roussillon in particular – can make very fine wines, even using the local grape varieties. In today's climate, where the solution to every quality problem seems to be to use Cabernet Sauvignon or Chardonnay in the blend, it is always encouraging to find growers who believe in their local grapes and work to bring out the best in them. In fact, the noble – but 'foreign' – varieties are actually banned under most appellation contrôlée regulations.

And growers are doing more than that. A fascinating combination of old and new techniques is being brought into play in the *chais*. Tradition has been that red wines in the Midi are stuck into these large wooden barrels which were probably in service at the turn of the century. Their only discernible effect was to make the wines oxidise and lose what little freshness they had.

Then along came stainless steel, and the freshness and fruit stayed, but any depths and complexity disappeared. Now we are finding go-ahead producers introducing two new elements: one is the use of small Bordeaux-style wood barriques (which are often purchased from a Bordeaux château after one year's use there). The other is the Beaujolais technique of macération carbonique, a technique which brings out the fruit in grapes like Carignan, the southern workhorse grape not normally known for its robust fruit flavours.

Combine the use of barriques and that of macération carbonique by treating some of the wine in one way and some in the other and then blending the two, and you end up with wines to which the terms 'elegance' or 'finesse' – not often used for southern French wines – can justifiably be applied.

Where's where in the Midi

In this survey of the Midi we move from east to south, looking at AC, VDQS and vin de pays wines. The section is divided by département.

LANGUEDOC (GARD)

Most of the AC and VDQS wines in this département are only just beginning to be other than dull. The vins de pays are better.

Clairette de Bellegarde White wines of an uninspired nature.

Costières du Gard VDQS area near Nîmes which is best for full-bodied reds of a reliable quality. Whites here are dull.

Vin de pays Vin de Pays du Gard, Côtes du Salavès and Uzège: all cheap and reasonably cheerful, especially the Gard wines. The very best vins de pays are from the Sables du Golfe du Lion (the home of the largest single vineyard in France, owned by Listel and planted on the sands by the sea).

LANGUEDOC (HÉRAULT)

This is the département which presents the greatest contrasts at the moment. There are still seas of vines producing cheap plonk on the flat plains, but up in the hills, or in small enclaves near the coast, quality in AC and vin de pays wines is now improving rapidly, offering excellent value.

Coteaux du Languedoc is the main AC appellation and its best wines are sturdy, simple reds. La Clape, the best of the 12 Coteaux du Languedoc Villages, makes good red, rosé and white on chalky soil. St-Saturnin, another sub-division, makes solid reds. Quatourze produces some heady reds and lighter whites.

Faugères Soft and full-bodied red AC wines that have suddenly became popular in France. That means that some prices are artifically inflated, but this is nevertheless an area to watch.

Picpoul de Pinet Dry whites made from Picpoul, Clairette and Terret Blanc. Drink them as young and fresh as possible – stick to 1988 or 1989.

St-Chinian Tough, spicy, tannic wines which are worth keeping a year or two. 1985 or 1986 would be ideal now.

Vins de pays
There are 28 vin de pays zones in the Hérault département. The largest production area is Vin de Pays de l'Hérault, which ranges in quality from the pretty ordinary to the superb Cabernet Sauvignon wines of Mas de Daumas Gassac. Other vins de pays in the Hérault that can be found in UK shops include Côtes de Thongue and Coteaux du Salagou.

LANGUEDOC (AUDE)

Languedoc is perhaps the area of the Midi where the greatest strides have been made – helped by the strong traditions of the hill wines which are now the main AC and VDQS areas.

Blanquette de Limoux Sparkling wine from near Carcassonne (see the Sparkling wines section on page 636).

Cabardès Red wines from just north of Carcassonne, which are best drunk young and fresh.

Corbières AC area that makes a large amount of reds by carbonic macération (which brings out plenty of fruit and colour but requires the wine to be drunk young). A few single estates are turning out wines of good quality.

Côtes de la Malapère An area which includes Cabernet Sauvignon and Cabernet Franc in its blend, with consequent high quality.

Fitou Carignan grapes make some well-aged wines in this AC area which will last for three to five years from vintage and are characterised by good ruby-coloured fruit.

Minervois A huge AC area using Carignan and Cinsault in its big, beefy reds. The wines are good value and one or two producers make something that much better (see under Who's who below). An area that represents good value.

Vins de pays
Vin de pays regions in the Aude département include Vin de Pays de l'Aude, Coteaux de la Cité de Carcassonne, Val d'Orbieu and the romantically named Vallée du Paradis. The two big French wine merchants, Nicolas and Chantovent, have made much of vins de pays from the Aude, and have certainly helped keep standards up.

ROUSSILLON (PYRÉNÉES-ORIENTALES)
There's an interesting cross-fertilisation with Spain in some of the grapes used in Roussillon, with the white Macabeo and Malvoisie in evidence. This is home, too, of the unusual red, sweet, Grenache-based Banyuls (see the section on Fortified wines on page 665).

Côtes du Roussillon and Côtes du Roussillon Villages
The main area, Côtes du Roussillon, makes good, soft, colourful reds from Carignan and Grenache. Interspersed are wines from the better sites of the Villages with slightly higher alcohol but also greater finesse. Collioure is a smaller area for some very good - if hugely beefy – reds.

Vins de pays
Best in Roussillon are Catalan and Pyrénées-Orientales making large quantities of reds and whites. The majority of the wines for the Vin de Pays d'Oc, which covers the whole of the Midi, come from the Pyrénées-Orientales.

Vintages in the Midi

It's rare for vintages to be much affected by the weather in this part of France. A general rule is that, except where indicated in the Where's where section above, most white wines are ready to drink when they reach the shops, while two or three years should be enough for reds.

Who's who in the Midi

While this section suggests wines which appear under château or estate names, many wine merchants and supermarkets offer own-label generic wines. Look at the Best buys below for our recommendations of these.

LANGUEDOC (GARD)

Costières du Gard Ch de la Tuilerie (*Averys*); Ch Roubaud (*Findlater Mackie Todd*); Ch de Nages (*Waitrose*); Domaine la Courbade (*Wizard*); Domaine de la Louis Perdrix (*Corney & Barrow*).

Vin de Pays des Sables du Golfe du Lion, Listel
White: Blanc de Blancs (*D Byrne & Co; Thos Peatling*); Domaine de Villeroy Blanc de Blancs (*Averys; D Byrne & Co; George Hill of Loughborough; Thresher*).
Rosé: Gris de Gris (*D Byrne & Co; Grape Ideas; George Hill of Loughborough; Thos Peatling; Thresher*); Domaine de Jarras Gris de Gris (*Grape Ideas; Willoughbys*);
Red: Domaine du Bosquet (*Averys; D Byrne & Co*); Listel Rubis (*D Byrne & Co; Thos Peatling*); Domaine de Bosquet-Canet (*Averys; Grape Ideas; Gerard Harris; Harrods; Oddbins*).

Vin de Pays du Gard Domaine de Valescure (*Bibendum*).

LANGUEDOC (HÉRAULT)

Coteaux du Languedoc Domaine de Lavabre (*Morris & Verdin; Tanners*); Ch de la Condamine Bertrand (*Stapylton Fletcher*); Domaine de l'Abbaye Valfernière (*Wizard*); St-Christol (*Majestic; La Vigneronne*); Ch Pech Céleyran (*Adnams; Fulham Road Wine Centre; Smedley Vintners*).

St-Chinian Rouanet (*High Breck Vintners; Waitrose*); Les Coteaux du Rieu-Berlou (*D Byrne & Co*); Clos Bagatelle (*Mayor Sworder*); Cuvée Jules Gaston (*D Byrne & Co; Gerard Harris; Victoria Wine Company*).

Faugères La Cave des Vignerons les Crus Faugères (*Eldridge Pope*).

La Clape Vignerons du Val d'Orbieu (*Bibendum; Wines from Paris*); Ch Braquilanges (*Oddbins*).

Vin de Pays de l'Hérault Domaine de Mas de Daumas Gassac (*widely available*); Domaine de St-Macaire (*Waitrose*); Domaine du Chapitre (*Morris & Verdin*); Cante-Cigale Syrah (*Waitrose*); Domaine des Lenthéric (*Majestic*).

Vin de Pays des Collines de la Moure Abbaye de Valmagne (*Eldridge Pope; La Réserve; Willoughbys*).

Vin de Pays des Coteaux de Murviel Domaine de Ravannes (*Oddbins; Christopher Piper Wines*); Domaine de Limbardie (*Fulham Road Wine Centre; Harrods; Lay & Wheeler; Morris & Verdin; Smedley Vintners*).

LANGUEDOC (AUDE)

Cabardès Ch Ventenac (*Majestic*).

Corbières Ch de Montredon (*D Byrne & Co*); Ch les Palais (*Victoria Wine Company*); Ch de Montrabech (*Lay & Wheeler; Tanners*); Ch des Ollieux (*Bibendum; D Byrne & Co; Thos Peatling*); Ch Vaugelas (*Majestic*); Ch de Luc (*Majestic*); Ch du Grand Caumont (*Fulham Road Wine Centre*); Ch de Lastours (*Cadwgan Fine Wines; Thresher – some branches; Winecellars*).

Fitou Chantovent (*D Byrne & Co; Tanners*); Caves de Mont-Tauch (*Les Amis du Vin; J E Hogg; Marks & Spencer, Wine Growers Association*); Cave Pilote Villeneuve-des-Corbières (*Eldridge Pope; Ian G Howe; Wines from Paris*); Ch de Nouvelles (*Gare du Vin*); Mme Claude Parmentier (*widely available*); SARL Bouffet (*Majestic*); Terre Natale (*Berkmann Wine Cellars/Le Nez Rouge; Findlater Mackie Todd; Christopher Piper Wines; Smedley Vintners*); Les Vignerons du Val d'Orbieu (*Tanners*).

Minervois Ch de Gourgazaud (*J Sainsbury; Tanners*); Domaine de Ste-Eulalie (*Adnams; Davisons; Lay & Wheeler; Tanners; Thresher*); Domaine Maris (*Majestic*); Ch de Paraza (*Blayneys; Oddbins; Wizard; Wine Warehouses*); Domaine du Pech André (*Wine Schoppen*).

Vin de Pays de la Vallée du Paradis (*Adnams; Grape Ideas; Oddbins; J Sainsbury*).

Vin de Pays du Val d'Orbieu (*Adnams*).

Vin de Pays de l'Aude Foncalieu Cabernet Sauvignon (*La Réserve; Waitrose; Wizard Wine Warehouses*); Tesco Vin de Pays de l'Aude (*Tesco*); Domaine du Puget (*Corney & Barrow; Oddbins; Waitrose; Wizard Wine Warehouses*); Campagnard (*Thresher*); Chardonney A Barolet (*Tesco*).

ROUSSILLON (PYRÉNÉES-ORIENTALES)

Côtes du Roussillon and Côtes du Roussillon Villages Caramany (*Tanners; Winecellars*); Ch de Corneilla (*Eldridge Pope*); Full French Red Côtes du Roussillon (*Marks & Spencer*); Côtes du Roussillon (*J Sainsbury*); Ch de Jau (*Oddbins*).

Vin de Pays d'Oc Listel Cabernet Sauvignon and Chardonnay (*D Byrne & Co; Willoughbys*); Vin de Pays d'Oc, Domaine d'Ormesson (*Christopher Piper Wines; La Réserve*); Syrah (*Hungerford Wine Company*).

Vin de Pays des Côtes Catalanes (*Blayneys; Ian G Howe; Oddbins*).

Best buys from The Midi

WHITE

Chasan Vin de Pays des Côtes de Thongue (*Lorne House Vintners*)

Listel Domaine de Villeroy Blanc de Blancs sur lie (*William Addison; Chaplin & Son; G M Vintners*)

Marsanne Vin de Pays de l'Hérault, Domaine de la Gardie 1988 (*The Wine Society*)

Chardonnay Vin de Pays de l'Hérault, Domaine de la Source (*Wizard Wine Warehouses*)

Vin de Pays d'Oc Chardonnay, Hugh Ryman (*Majestic*)

ROSÉ

Listel Gris de Gris, Vin de Pays des Sables du Golfe du Lion (*Augustus Barnett, Premier Wine Warehouse*)

RED

Ch de Lastours 1986, Corbières (*Barnes Wine Shop; Great Northern Wine Co; Wine Rack*)

Corbières 1985, Dame Adelaide (*Oddbins*)

Vin de Pays Catalan Cabernet, Mas Chichet (*Ian G Howe*)

Listel Domaine du Bosquet-Canet Cabernet Sauvignon 1985 (*David Alexander*)

Minervois Domaine Ste-Eulalie 1987 (*Thresher*)

Domaine de Limbardie 1988, Vin de Pays des Coteaux de Murviel (*Adnams; Majestic*)

Ch de l'Ile 1986, Corbières (*Frank E Stainton*)

Vin de Pays de l'Hérault, Domaine de Clairac (*Ubiquitous Chip Wine Shop*)

Cabardès 1986, Domaine de St-Roch (*Andrew Gordon; George Hill; Winecellars*)

Côtes de la Malapère 1986, Domaine de Fournery (*Ingletons*)

Coteaux du Languedoc 1986, Abbaye de Valmagne (*James Aitken & Son; Eldridge Pope; Villandry*)

Ch du Grand Caumont 1986, Corbières (*Fulham Road Wine Centre*)

Ch de Paraza, Cuvée Spéciale (*Fullers*)

Coteaux du Languedoc 1986, Alain Roux (*Bibendum*)

Vin de Pays de l'Aude 1986, Domaine du Puget Merlot (*Waitrose*)

Fitou 1986, Cave Pilote (*widely available*)

Faugères 1987, Les Crus Faugères (*Whiteside's of Clitheroe*)

Vin de Pays des Collines de la Maure, Domaine de Mirabeau (*Hedley Wright; Pugsons Food and Wine*)

Specialist stockists

Bibendum; Bordeaux Direct; Cachet Wines; Eldridge Pope; Peter Green; Haughton Fine Wines; Oddbins

PROVENCE

Reds steal the show

More and more parts of Provence are producing wines of great style and excitement. Although the area is probably better known locally for its rosés, for us it is the reds that are stealing the show.

The region is blessed with the best vinous climate in France; it is dry, with a low risk of disease; the summers can almost be guaranteed; and much of the land is fertile enough to give satisfyingly large yields to those who believe in quantity. The dryness of the climate, moreover, accounts for the high incidence of organically produced wines from the area: where pests and diseases are few, the need to spray is minimised.

In the past, farmers have felt quite happy to produce pretty ordinary wine for the folk who throng the beaches on the Côte d'Azur – and to charge high prices for it. But, as in parts of nearby Italy, the efforts of a number of individualists have pushed some estates in all the appellations of Provence into the front rank.

They have done many of the usual things: introduce new technology, bring in Cabernet Sauvignon to act as what the French so accurately call a cépage améliorateur (that is, a grape variety which gives life and interest to what might have been dull), and boost interest in the two grape varieties that can give quality to the wines of the South-East of France – Syrah and Mourvèdre.

The Syrah is often discussed in connection with the Rhône and, latterly, Australia. But the Mourvèdre is a local variety that has been neglected because it is pretty temperamental even in the good climate of Provence. It has a low yield and ripens late. The wines need time to mature properly, but then they make a rich, spicy wine, with flavours of truffles and black cherries, which can last for many years. This is the grape used in Bandol (see below) which many regard as the finest red wine of Provence.

While the reds are making the running in Provence, the quality of the ubiquitous rosés in their skittle-shaped bottles has improved simply by the use of modern technology to bring out the fruit and acidity and to cut down the flabbiness. There is certainly much pleasure, in the right circumstances, in drinking well-chilled rosé. Don't forget, of course, that all Provence rosé is definitely dry.

The whites are still in a tiny minority in this area. They have

tended to suffer from the dullness of the constituent grapes –
Ugni Blanc, Clairette and Macabeo. But – as with the reds – the
use of less popular varieties – Rolle, Marsanne and Rousanne, as
well as the much-travelled Chardonnay – are bringing quality to
what new technology is at least turning into clean, fruity wines.

Where's where in Provence

Bandol Traditionally, the finest appellation of Provence, making
reds and dry whites and rosés. The reds, made from the
Mourvèdre grape, are the most impressive. And while the wines
are not cheap, they have some unusual spicy, peppery flavours
worth experiencing.

Bellet A tiny area of white wine production in the mountains
north of Nice. Most of the wine is consumed in the area,
although one or two are available in Britain.

Cassis A dry white wine, with a delicious buttery taste, made
from Clairette, Ugni Blanc, Marsanne and Sauvignon grapes.
Small production means high prices.(Nothing to do with the
blackcurrant liqueur.)

Coteaux d'Aix-en-Provence This, with Coteaux des Baux en
Provence (see below), is the most interesting area of Provence.
Mainly reds and rosés, with a few whites – the reds are the
best. While the usual southern grape varieties predominate,
some enterprising producers are using Cabernet Sauvignon as
well. An area where the name of the estate is of great
importance.

Coteaux des Baux en Provence This area is rapidly hitting the
number one spot for the quality of its reds. While they are more
expensive than those from nearby Aix-en-Provence, they are
also achieving greater things. The best producers, many of
whom practise organic farming methods, use Cabernet
Sauvignon and Syrah grapes.

Côtes de Provence Catch-all appellation that takes in most of
southern Provence. Whites, reds and rosés are made. The whites
are getting better and cleaner, and the same can be said for the
rosés (by far the bulk of production), which have tended to be
dry and on the full side, but some of the better wines now have
fruit as well – quite an innovation. Reds, too, are much better,
due to the use of imported grape varieties like Syrah and
Mourvèdre. However, the huge quantities of wine produced
here mean that quality can vary from pretty good to pretty dire.
Nor are prices particularly good.

Palette Small appellation making long-lasting whites and reds covering an impressive range of tastes, but which perhaps lack immediate drinkability.

Coteaux Varois A VDQS zone with large-scale production (30 million bottles) and variable quality, making individual producers important.

Vins de Pays regions These include the reds and rosés of the Bouches du Rhône. Mont Caume encompasses the lesser offerings from Bandol, plus some Cabernet Sauvignon wines. Vin de Pays des Maures is around St-Tropez, mainly making red. The Vin de Pays d'Oc region covers Provence and the rest of the Midi.

Vintages in Provence

The quality in vintages varies little in the sunny South of France. Drink most whites and rosés – except those from top producers or from specialist areas like Bandol and Palette – in the year after the vintage. Reds from Côtes de Provence need two or three years, while those from Bandol, Coteaux d'Aix and Coteaux des Baux need at least four or five years, and will go on maturing for ten or more.

Who's who in Provence

Bellet Ch de Crémat (*Yapp Brothers*).

Bandol Domaine Tempier (*La Réserve; Windrush Wines; The Wine Society*); Ch Vannières (*Cadwgan Fine Wines; Corney & Barrow; La Réserve; La Vigneronne*); Mas de la Rouvière (*Les Amis du Vin; Ian G Howe; La Réserve; Yapp Brothers*); Domaine de la Bastide Blanche (*The Wine Society*); Domaines Ott (*Cadwgan Fine Wines; Harrods; Majestic; La Vigneronne; Willoughby's*); Domaine de Cagaloupe (*Cadwgan Fine Wines; La Réserve*); Domaine de Pibarnon (*Berkmann Wine Cellars/Le Nez Rouge; Christopher Piper Wines*).

Cassis Clos Ste-Magdelaine (*Les Amis du Vin; Ian G Howe; Yapp Brothers*); Domaine du Paternel (*The Wine Society*).

Coteaux d'Aix-en-Provence Commanderie de la Bargemone (*Barwell & Jones; La Réserve*); Ch de Fonscolombe (*Adnams; Blayneys; Harrods; Lay & Wheeler; La Réserve; Tanners*); Domaine de la Crémade (*Yapp Brothers*); Ch Vignelaure (*D Byrne & Co; Rose Tree Wine Co; La Vigneronne*); Ch de Beaulieu (*Les Amis du Vin; Wine Growers Association*); Ch Bas (*Welbeck Wines*); Ch La Gaude, Baron de Vitrolles (*Ian G Howe; Yapp Brothers*); Ch La Gordonne (*Thresher*); Domaine les Bastides, Jean Salen (*Berkmann Wine Cellars/Le Nez Rouge*); Marquis de Saporta (*Eldridge Pope*); Domaine de Ch Pigoudet (*H Allen Smith; Tesco*); Ch la Coste (*Cairns & Hickey; Richmond Wine Warehouse*).

Coteaux des Baux en Provence Domaine de Trévallon (*Les Amis du Vin; La Vigneronne; Yapp Brothers*); Domaine des Terres Blanches (*H Allen Smith; Gare du Vin; Gerard Harris; George Hill of Loughborough; Ian G Howe; La Vigneronne; Winecellars*); Mas de Gourgonnier (*Haughton Fine Wines*); Mas de la Dame (*Augustus Barnett*).

Côtes de Provence L'Estandon (*Yapp Brothers*); Domaine des Hauts de St-Jean (*Yapp Brothers*); Domaines Ott (*D Byrne & Co; Fortnum & Mason; Gerard Harris; Harrods; Majestic; La Vigneronne; Willoughbys*); Les Maîtres Vignerons de la Presqu'île de St-Tropez (*Berkmann Wine Cellars/Le Nez Rouge; Majestic; Christopher Piper Wines; Wizard Wine Warehouses*); St-André de Figuière (*Morris & Verdin*); Domaine de St-Baillon (*Bibendum*); Ch Grand'Boise (*available in a few restaurants in the Leeds area*); Domaine des Hauts de St-Jean (*Yapp Brothers*); Domaine Richaume (*Yapp Brothers*); Ch Montaud (*Wine House*); Commenderie de Peyrassol (*Redpath & Thackray*); Domaine Gavoty (*Redpath & Thackray*).

Palette Ch Simone (*La Réserve; La Vigneronne; Yapp Brothers*).

Coteaux Varois Domaine des Chaberts (*High Breck Vintners*); Domaine St-Estève, Gassier (*Ad Hoc Wine Warehouse*); Domaine du Deffends (*Redpath & Thackray*).

PROVENCE VIN DE PAYS

Bouches du Rhône Domaine de Boullery (*Wine Growers Association*); Vignerons Provençaux (*Marks & Spencer*).

Mont Caume Bunan (*Victoria Wine Company; Yapp Brothers*).

Maures Domaine d'Astros (*Bibendum*).

Best buys from Provence

WHITE

Coteaux d'Aix-en-Provence 1988, Ch de Fonscolombe (*Adnams; S H Jones; Lay & Wheeler; Tanners*)

Coteaux d'Aix-en-Provence 1988, Domaine de Paradis (*Berry Bros & Rudd*)

ROSÉ

Coteaux d'Aix-en-Provence, Ch de la Gaude 1988 (*Yapp Brothers*)
Coteaux Varois Domaine des Chaberts 1988 (*High Breck Vintners*)
Coteaux d'Aix-en-Provence 1988, Ch de Fonscolombe (*Adnams; S H Jones; Lay & Wheeler; Tanners; J Townend*)

RED

Côtes de Provence 1985, Domaine St-André de Figuière (*Hurt & Daniel; Morris & Verdin*)
Ch de Pampelonne Rouge 1988, Maîtres Vignerons de la Presqu'Ile de St Tropez (*Berkmann Wine Cellars/ Le Nez Rouge*)
Ch la Coste Rouge, Coteaux d'Aix-en-Provence (*Cairns & Hickey; Richmond Wine Warehouse*)
Ch Pigoudet 1985, Coteaux d'Aix-en-Provence (*H Allen Smith*)
Côtes de Provence 1987, Domaine du Jas d'Esclans (*Ravensbourne Wine Co*)
Mas de Cadenet Côtes de Provence (*Windrush Wines*)
Coteaux des Baux en Provence 1986, Mas de Gourgonnier (*Haughton Fine Wines; Organic Wine Company*)

Specialist stockists
Adnams; Berkmann Wine Cellars/Le Nez Rouge; Redpath & Thackray Wines; La Vigneronne; Wine House

THE NORTHERN RHÔNE

Small quantities, high demand

Things aren't cheap in the northern Rhône any more. High prices elsewhere in France, the small amount of wine made and the keen interest from the rest of the world have all conspired to push up the prices of some of the most fascinating and complex red wines in the world. As for the few whites made in the area, some are still excellent value, although one or two command stratospheric prices as well.

We talk prices before quality in this area, but not for the same reasons as we do in Bordeaux or Burgundy, because although prices have risen, the quality and price relationship seems to be fair, somewhat unusually for France.

Apart from demand, it is easy to understand why northern Rhône wines are now expensive. Any visitor to the region will see at a glance that the vineyards are not kind to husbandry.

471

Vertiginous slopes don't lend themselves to mechanical pruning or harvesting: probably only in Germany are vineyards so inaccessible. The geography of the northern Rhône inevitably means that yields are low.

So why plant vines here at all? Because of their exposure to the sun: for instance, Côte Rôtie literally roasts in the summer sun. The hill of Hermitage, jutting out into the plain, has sunshine virtually all day, while the steep slopes of Cornas face south and a little west to get the best of the sun in the hottest part of the day. And when the vine is the Syrah, here at the northern extremity of its successful cultivation, all the sunshine hours a vineyard can get are essential.

What's what in the northern Rhône

The area is dominated by two grape varieties – one widely planted, the other a rare breed indeed.

The Syrah, the only red variety used in the northern Rhône, is the driving force behind the great wines of Hermitage, Côte Rôtie and Cornas; and behind the more immediately accessible – and affordable – wines of St-Joseph and Crozes-Hermitage.

In white wines, the Marsanne is used widely in Hermitage and Crozes-Hermitage Blanc and in St-Péray, while the rarer Roussanne is also used in the blend, but the most famous white grape is the Viognier which goes to make the whites of Condrieu and Ch Grillet, dry but full of ripe, southern, peachy flavours. They command immense prices because so little is produced. The Viognier is also used to soften the Syrah in Côte Rôtie.

Where's where in the northern Rhône

Clairette de Die See the Sparkling wines section on page 639.

Condrieu A tiny appellation of 35 acres which produces small quantities of intensely lush white wines from the Viognier grape. Although the wines are dry, they have such ripe, peach-and-apricot tastes that they almost seem sweet. An experience, even if an expensive one.

Cornas Huge, robust red wines made from 100 per cent Syrah in a small vineyard area on steep hillsides south of Hermitage. The size of the vineyard area means that the prices are on the increase, but they probably deserve their recognition anyway.

Côte Rôtie The 'roasted slope' is the most northerly Rhône appellation. The old vineyards that make superb reds from the

Syrah grape, with a little white Viognier, are on the steep hillside tumbling down to the River Rhône. The terms Brune and Blonde are used to describe the principal slopes, from which the best wines come. New plantings on the top of the hill threaten to dilute the quality.

Crozes-Hermitage These vineyards currently represent the best value for money in the northern Rhône. They lie on the lower slopes and flatter land around the hill of Hermitage (see below). Less intense or punch-packing than Hermitage, they are nevertheless often of good quality, displaying the dry fruit and spicy flavours of Syrah. Whites, made from Marsanne and a little Roussanne, are improving all the time.

Ch Grillet The smallest French appellation (a mere 7.5 acres) producing a more intense version of Condrieu (see above). Very expensive, difficult to find, and not as good as its owner likes to make out. You would be better off buying Condrieu instead.

Hermitage The hill of Hermitage (so called because a knight, returning from the Crusades, built a hermit's cell on the top of the hill), dominates the towns of Tain l'Hermitage and Tournon. The wines traditionally had the reputation of being the finest in France long before Bordeaux became top dog. When young, they are the epitome of the almost inaccessible fruit of the Syrah, softened here with up to 15 per cent of white grapes, but they develop into rich, powerful, smooth maturity. White wines are also made in small quantities, mainly traditional in style and with considerable ageing ability.

St-Péray Sparkling wines from the Marsanne and Roussanne grapes, made by the Champagne method. Not very exciting and not often seen in Britain.

St-Joseph A lighter more delicate version of Hermitage which is approachable younger and doesn't last as long. New vineyards, as with Côte Rôtie, may lower the general quality. Like Crozes-Hermitage, they are still reasonable value for money.

Northern Rhône vintages

1988 As they say in France every few years, a vintage of the century. It was certainly good, even great, with an early spring, a long, hot summer, and perfect conditions at harvest time. The colour, flavour and taste of the reds are huge, and the whites are rich and sumptuous.

1987 Rain during the harvest meant that the red wines will be quite light and will mature quickly. Whites, picked before the rain, will be much more powerful and high in alcohol.

1986 A medium-term vintage, classic rather than great, with wines that will mature between five and ten years old.

1985 Although not one of the very greatest Rhône vintages, the wines are not far off the quality of the 1983s. The best areas are Côte Rôtie, Cornas and St-Joseph. Hermitage made some great wines, but also some that were less good. The whites are powerful but lack acidity.

1984 Elegance and early maturity are the hallmarks of this vintage. Côte Rôtie has lower alcohol and tannin and less concentration than usual, while Hermitage is a middle-range wine. The whites have high acidity, especially those made from the Viognier grape. Drink whites and Crozes-Hermitage now, the top appellations in a couple of years.

1983 A very great year, especially for reds – concentrated, rich wines that will last for 20 years or more without any difficulty. Hermitage and Côte Rôtie will last very well, Crozes-Hermitage and Cornas will mature in eight years' time. The whites, too, are rich and will last.

1982 Too many grapes and too hot temperatures during fermentation have dogged this vintage. While some wines are fine and will last for 10 to 15 years, others lack structure and their fruit is too 'hot' and jammy. Most whites, except Hermitage, should have been drunk by now.

1981 Careful selection is necessary in the reds for this lean year. Good growers, though, made decent wine which is good value.

1980 Well-balanced wines, much better than those of northern France, are now mature. Crozes-Hermitage and St-Joseph should be drunk now, but keep other reds a bit longer. Most whites have faded.

1979 Much better vintage than generally thought, overshadowed by 1978. Most reds are now mature (although keep Hermitage and Cornas a while yet). A good value vintage.

1978 Magnificent wines that are still almost infants! Hermitage and Côte Rôtie won't really be mature until the turn of the century, if then. Other reds will mature sooner, but don't touch them yet. Whites are still going strong.

Earlier vintages 1976 and 1971 are still at their peak, as are the 1969s. Other vintages of the early 1970s need to be bought with care.

Growers and négociants

Firms below are listed under the area in which their main production is located. Négociants, of course, make wines from a number of different appellations.

RED WINES

Cornas

G de Barjac Very concentrated wines, highly tannic and never quite softening out. Give them years to mature.
Adnams; Lay & Wheeler; Nobody Inn; Tanners; La Vigneronne

Clape One of the finest producers in the Rhône. Deep, long-lasting wines of impenetrable blackness when young. Also makes some sparkling St-Péray.
Adnams; Nobody Inn; Yapp Brothers

Marcel Juge Very traditional producer, although his wines are lighter than some from this appellation.
Whittalls Wines

Michel Old-fashioned family holding whose wines need plenty of time.
Bibendum

N Verset Product of small amounts of wine, with the classic, rich, impenetrable Cornas tastes.
Bibendum

Côte Rôtie

Albert Dervieux-Thaize Very traditional wines from the President of the local growers. Look for his La Vallière single vineyard wine.
Lay & Wheeler; La Vigneronne; Winecellars

Marius Gentaz-Dervieux Long-lasting wines that should be left for ten or twelve years before being broached. Look for La Garde, Côte Brune and Viaillère.
Hampden Wine Co; Raeburn Fine Wines & Foods

Guigal A specialist in wood-ageing of wines, Guigal keeps his wines in barrel for three years. Look for La Landonne and La Mouline, also Côte Rôtie Brune et Blonde and white Hermitage. They also make top quality Hermitage and own Vidal-Fleury (see below).
Adnams; Les Amis du Vin; Berry Bros & Rudd; Bibendum; Eldridge Pope; Alex Findlater; Harrods; S H Jones; Lay & Wheeler; Michael Menzel Wines; Oddbins; Sebastopol Wines; Tanners; T & W Wines; The Wine Society

Jasmin The greatest individual vineyard producer making classic but not heavy wines. Look for La Chevalière d'Ampuis.
Adnams; S H Jones; Lay & Wheeler; La Vigneronne; Yapp Brothers

Rostaing Another young producer whose deep-flavoured wines receive at least two years in cask. Look for La Landonne Côte Brune. Also makes St-Joseph.

Vidal-Fleury Now owned by Guigal, this is the largest firm in Côte Rôtie. Long-lasting wines which need at least ten years. The top wine is La Chatillonne, but they also make Hermitage.
Berkmann Wine Cellars/Le Nez Rouge; Christopher Piper Wines; Sebastopol Wines; La Vigneronne

Hermitage

Chapoutier One of the two big négociants in the region. Makes very traditional wines in Hermitage, Crozes-Hermitage, St-Joseph and also in Châteauneuf. The white Hermitage Chante Alouette is remarkable.
Adnams; Lay & Wheeler; Nobody Inn; Oddbins; La Vigneronne; The Wine Society; Yapp Brothers

Chave The greatest of the single vineyard growers. Long-lived reds and whites.
Adnams; Lay & Wheeler; Nobody Inn; Oddbins; La Vigneronne; The Wine Society; Yapp Brothers

Delas Frères Growers and négociants with vineyards in Hermitage, Cornas, Côte Rôtie and Condrieu. The top Hermitage is Cuvée de la Tourette.
Averys; Old Street Wine Company; Wizard Wine Warehouses

Desmeure Père et Fils A small plot of land in Crozes-Hermitage. The white Hermitage is regarded as better than the red, and the Crozes better than both.
Bibendum; S H Jones

Bernard Faurie Rated as one of the up and coming stars of the area. Tiny production of red and white Hermitage and St-Joseph.
La Vigneronne

Jaboulet Aîné The other big négociant house that's setting the pace for the area. In Hermitage they own La Chapelle for red and Chevalier de Sterimbourg for white. Also make Crozes-Hermitage, St-Joseph (La Grande Pompée), Côte Rôtie (Les Jumelles), Tavel, Châteauneuf and the famous Côtes du Rhône (Parallèle 45).
Widely available

H Sorrel Owners of a small parcel of land on the Le Méal vineyard on the Hermitage hill. Look for wines after 1983 or before 1978.
Bibendum; Stapylton Fletcher

Co-operative of Tain l'Hermitage A reliable producer, making 25 per cent of the appellation's wines, in a modern, fairly light style. Also produce white Hermitage and Cornas.
Asda; Peter Dominic

St-Joseph

Pierre Coursodon Red and white wines from the southern (better) end of the appellation. Look for Le Paradis, St-Pierre and L'Olivaie.
Lay & Wheeler

E Florentin Quite light red wines, although more recent vintages (1983 on) seem to have gained some weight. Also make a very long lived white wine. Their vineyard is Clos de l'Arbalestrier.
Adnams; Bibendum; Thos Peatling; Prestige Vintners; Raeburn Fine Wines & Foods

Jean-Louis Grippat Makes a light, early-maturing (five years) wine.
Adnams; Yapp Brothers

Crozes-Hermitage

Names to look for are Domaine Pradelle (*Thresher*); Domaine des Clairmonts (*Ellis Son & Vidler; Waitrose; Yapp Brothers*); Desmeure (*Bibendum*); Albert Bégot, who makes wine organically (*Mayor Sworder & Co*); Tardy & Ange (*Bibendum; Christopher Piper Wines; Prestige Vintners*); Jaboulet Aîné, Domaine de Thalabert (*widely available*); Chapoutier (*Adnams; Fullers; Ian G Howe; Lay & Wheeler*); Fayolle (*Chesterford Vintners*).

WHITE WINES

Condrieu and Ch Grillet

Ch Grillet The single-estate appellation which makes famous, if over-priced, wines.
Averys; Nobody Inn; La Vigneronne; Yapp Brothers

Guigal The Côte Rôtie négociant makes deliciously fresh Condrieu wines.
Adnams; Lay & Wheeler

Château du Rozay Paul Multier's young-style wine made mainly in stainless steel with a little wood, although a little traditional wine is made from old vines. Absolutely catches the flavour of the Viognier grape.
The Wine Society; Yapp Brothers

Georges Vernay Largest producer of Condrieu, making wines for a quick sale and a fresh drink.
Les Amis du Vin; Eldridge Pope/Reynier Wine Libraries; Peter Green; Lay & Wheeler; T & W Wines; Wizard Wine Warehouses; Yapp Brothers

White Hermitage and Crozes-Hermitage

Good producers include: Chapoutier (*Adnams; Peter Green; Ian G Howe; Michael Menzel Wines; Willoughbys*); Guigal (*Eldridge Pope/ Reynier Wine Libraries; Harrods; Nobody Inn*); Jaboulet Aîné, Le Chevalier de Sterimbourg and La Mule Blanche (*Les Amis du Vin; Ellis Son & Vidler; Peter Green; Harrods; Hungerford Wine Company; Lay & Wheeler; Tanners; T & W Wines*); Chapoutier (*Adnams; Berry Bros & Rudd; Grape Ideas; Peter Green; Ian G Howe; Michael Menzel Wines*); Vidal-Fleury (*Berkmann Wine Cellers/Le Nez Rouge*); Tardy & Ange (*Christopher Piper Wines*); Pascal (*Peter Dominic*).

Vin de Pays

Very little vin de pays is produced in the area, the exception being the Vin de Pays de l'Ardèche.
(*Red*): Vin de Pays les Sables (*Lorne House Vintners*); Les Terres Fines, Cépage Syrah (*Tesco*); Vin de Pays des Coteaux de l'Ardèche (*Adnams; Eldridge Pope/Reynier Wine Libraries; Welbeck Wines; Yapp Brothers*); Vin de Pays des Coteaux de l'Ardèche Gamay, Cave Co-opérative de St-Désirat (*Yapp Brothers*); (*white*): Coteaux de l'Ardéche, Chardonnay, Louis Latour (*Ian G Howe*).

Best buys from Northern Rhône

WHITE
Crozes-Hermitage La Mule Blanche, Jaboulet Aîné (*O W Loeb; Oddbins*)
Hermitage Chante-Alouette, Chapoutier (*D Byrne & Co; Direct Wine Shipments*)

RED
Côte Rôtie 1986, Levet (*Whittalls Wines*)
Crozes-Hermitage, Domaine de Thalabert 1986, Jaboulet Aîné (*widely available*)
Syrah Vin de Pays de l'Ardèche 1987 (*Hadleigh Wine Cellars*)

Terres Brunes Vin de Pays d'Oc, Vallouit (*Helen Verdcourt Wines*)
St-Joseph Clos de l'Arbalestrier (*Bibendum*)
Crozes-Hermitage 1986, Tardy et Ange (*widely available*)

Specialist stockists
Adnams; Berry Bros & Rudd; Bibendum; Restaurant Croque-en-Bouche; J E Hogg; S H Jones; Justerini & Brooks; Kurtz & Chan; Lay & Wheeler; O W Loeb; Reid Wines; T & W Wines; Helen Verdcourt Wines; La Vigneronne

THE SOUTHERN RHÔNE

The good and the bad

If the northern Rhône is associated with tiny quantities and some great wines, the southern Rhône means large quantities and a mixed bag of wines – some great, some rather mediocre. There is nothing nastier in red wines than a cheap Côtes du Rhône, nor, for that matter, than a cheap Châteauneuf-du-Pape. But there's no better value than a good example of either of these appellations, or of wines like Gigondas or Lirac, or even Côtes du Rhône Villages.

The problem with quantity is that the flat plains of the southern Rhône encourage high yields from the growers who sell their grapes to supply the co-operatives or to merchants from Burgundy. Here is where négociants come when they need to supply a wine buyer with safe red wine at a price. The names are familiar, they sell, and who's to worry if the wine has little flavour, tastes thin and acid and looks, with its pale and interesting colour, as though it came from much further north? It's cheap, and that's what matters, isn't it?

Maybe things will change a little in the wake of the round of price rises at the end of 1987 and beginning of 1988. There was a sudden panic in France when grape growers started pushing up prices for wines after a superlative harvest. It certainly seems we will have to pay more even for Côtes du Rhône from the 1988 vintage. But if we can get a better quality as well, wouldn't that justify an extra 50p a bottle?

As for poor old Châteauneuf, there's a name that has been taken in vain for too many years. Again, the problem was that merchants bought up the wine, transported it to their cellars, maybe in Burgundy, maybe somewhere else in France, and then bottled it. Quality, careful ageing and careful handling of the grapes all went by the board. But things have begun to change,

479

as estates and domaines in the areas have taken to bottling their own wine. The clue to these wines are the indication on the label that it comes from a single domaine or estate – and the coat of arms embossed on the bottle.

Look to the whites

Perhaps the biggest change in the southern Rhône in the past year or so has been the dramatic improvement in the quality of the white wines. White Côtes du Rhône, dismissed not so long ago as heavy and oxidised stuff is now tasting fresh, fruity and pleasantly refreshing. White Châteauneuf, made in increasing quantities, is a notch higher in quality, and worth looking out for.

What's what in the southern Rhône

The grape varieties of the southern Rhône are legion. There are 13 different permitted grape varieties which can be used to produce a Châteauneuf-du-Pape. The same varieties, in differing combinations, turn up all round the flat, sprawling southern Rhône vineyards. They're the varieties of the South of France – the Grenache, Cinsault, Carignan, Mourvèdre are the predominant grapes for the reds; for the whites, it's Clairette and Picpoul, Marsanne, Roussanne and Bourboulenc.

But the southern Rhône red wines now also have increasing amounts of Syrah, acting just as Cabernet Sauvignon does elsewhere in France, as a cépage améliorateur – a noble grape variety used to lift the quality of the local wine. And it is the Syrah which is behind much of the fine wine production in the area.

Where's where in the southern Rhône

Brézème Tiny appellation in the gap between northern and southern Rhône vineyards, making wines from the Syrah grape.

Châteauneuf-du-Pape It may be a much abused name but there is also a top level of very high quality, at attractive prices. There are big, chewy reds with lots of ripe fruit which mature quite fast and then go down hill slowly. Although only a small (if increasing) amount of white Châteauneuf is made (using any blend of Clairette, Bourboulenc, Roussanne, Grenache Blanc, Picpoul and Picardin), the modern style of vinification does bring about some attractive, early-drinking wines. Don't keep them for more than a couple of years.

Côtes du Luberon A newly established VDQS area in the south of the southern Rhône vineyards. One or two producers are using new technology to make some robust reds and fresh whites and rosés. Very good value.

Côtes du Rhône The basic appellation of the region. Large vineyard areas produce plenty of basic quaffing red wine, some of it terrific value, even more best avoided. Producers are important here because some growers (and co-operatives) are outstanding (see below). Prices are likely to rise with the 1988 vintage.

Côtes du Rhône Villages A more closely controlled wine than simple Côtes du Rhône, this comes from specific villages which have better sited vineyards. More flavour and concentration make some of these Villages wines very good. Names to look for: Cairanne, Vacqueyras, Beaumes-de-Venise (yes, they don't just grow Muscat there), Rasteau (also sweet Muscat), Sablet, St-Gervais, Séguret, Valréas, Visan.

Coteaux du Tricastin Fast-maturing reds, which should be drunk within two or three years of the harvest. Smooth wines of excellent value which are worth seeking out.

Côtes du Ventoux A relatively new appellation which makes light, fresh reds, with a hint of pétillance. Delicious drunk slightly chilled.

Côtes du Vivarais Lighter than straight Côtes du Rhône, the reds from this VDQS area are made using the same grapes as Côtes du Rhône with additional Syrah and Gamay.

Gigondas An earthier version of Châteauneuf, from a village that until 1971 was just another part of the Côtes du Rhône Villages. Southern-tasting wine, ideal for barbecues and rich foods, quite long-lasting, but not terribly subtle. So what's wrong with that?

Lirac Excellent value wines from south of Châteauneuf. Full but really fruity reds are generally well made. Rosés are dry and quite powerful.

Tavel Famed rosé, the delightful colour belies the fact that this is strong stuff. Dry but with good fruit, these can be some of the best French rosés.

For the two fortified wines of the region, Muscat de Beaumes-de-Venise and Rasteau, see the separate section on page 665.

Southern Rhône vintages

Apart from Châteauneuf and Gigondas, with occasional Côtes du Rhône Villages, southern Rhône wines are not for laying down. Wines earlier than 1978 should certainly have been drunk by now.

1988 This vintage may be the exception to prove the rule that southern Côtes du Rhône do not age. The high colour and extract all over the region suggests that these are wines to keep. Small quantities of basic wines – as well as the quality – are the cause of a rise in prices. The whites from this vintage are going to be delicious.

1987 A light vintage, with even the top areas producing wines which will be ready to drink soon.

1986 A big vintage, with some rot at harvest time. Drink the fresher reds now, but leave top areas such as Châteauneuf for some time.

1985 A fine harvest both for quality and quantity was aided by just the right amount of rain in June and July and fine sunny weather thereafter. Châteauneuf is full of fruit and looks set to mature well.

1984 Light, mid-range wines in both Châteauneuf and Gigondas. They will be drinking well in a couple of years' time.

1983 Light reds in Côtes du Rhône, but elsewhere in Châteauneuf and Lirac the wines will take plenty of time to mature fully. Gigondas is heavier and slower to develop.

1981 Châteauneuf is very drinkable with firm, structured wines. Some Gigondas are a little acid and watery, but some good ones are to be found as well.

1978 Long-lasting Châteauneuf is still maturing and will keep. Lots of fruit and tannin need time to soften together. The same goes for Gigondas. A great year.

Other vintages Try 1972 and 1970 in Châteauneuf.

Who's who in the southern Rhône

Brézème

Jean-Marie Lombard From a tiny appellation between the main Côtes du Rhône vineyards and the northern Rhône.
Nobody Inn; Yapp Brothers

Châteauneuf-du-Pape

TOP ESTATES

Château de Beaucastel An organically run estate producing what many consider the area's finest and certainly longest-lived reds.
Adnams; Les Amis du Vin; Berry Bros & Rudd; Lay & Wheeler; Nobody Inn; Oddbins; Sebastopol Wines; Tanners; Winecellars; Wizard Wine Warehouses

Domaine de Beaurenard Light-style wines which are attractively full of fruit.
Victoria Wine Company

Le Bosquet des Papes Medium-sized estate, producing rich, classic wines that can last a decade in good vintages.
Sebastopol Wines

Domaine des Cabrières Bang up-to-date producer making wines which are intensely commercial, but also particularly good in poor vintages.
Peter Dominic

Les Cailloux, Brunel Wines which manage to combine great fruit with an ability to age, and which benefit from an extra input of Syrah in the blend. Brunel also produces wines under his own name. Les Cailloux (*Upper Crust*); Domaine André Brunel (*J Sainsbury*).

Les Cèdres, Jaboulet Aîné Medium-weight wines that mature quite quickly, made from grapes purchased by the northern Rhône négociant firm.
Grape Ideas; Hungerford Wine Company; Michael Menzel Wines; Thos Peatling; T & W Wines; La Vigneronne; Welbeck Wines

Domaine Chante-Cigale Classic, old-style wines, weighty and tannic when young. The name of the estate means 'the singing grasshopper'.
Lay & Wheeler; Yapp Brothers

Domaine Chante Perdrix Another singer, this time a partridge. Wines from this estate are rich and perfumed, age well but also taste good when young.
Old Street Wine Company

Château des Fines Roches The home estate of Domaines Musset, a large négociant firm. Rich wines which develop early.
Unwins

Château Fortia The estate of Baron Le Roy, the originator of the modern rules governing Châteauneuf-du-Pape. Very correct winemaking, and classic wines.
Fullers; Oddbins

Domaine de Marcoux Fruit is the main character of these highly enjoyable wines which age over the medium term.
John Harvey & Sons; Welbeck Wines

Domaine de Mont-Redon Enterprising estate which has plantings of all Châteauneuf's 13 grape varieties. Some wine is aged in oak casks, but most is made in a traditional manner brought up to date.
Eldridge Pope/Reynier Wine Libraries; Harrods; Majestic; Smedley Vintners; Stapylton Fletcher; La Vigneronne

Domaine de Nalys One of the other estates that plants all 13 grape varieties. The wine is designed to be drunk young.
Peter Green; Ian G Howe

Château de la Nerthe One of the area's oldest estates, which has recently undergone considerable modernisation. The wines are traditionally heavy and long-lasting.
Mayor Sworder & Co

Clos de l'Oratoire des Papes Soft, commercial wines that mature quickly.
Michael Menzel Wines

Clos des Papes One of the top producers in the region making very rich wines that live a long time.
Bibendum; Lay & Wheeler; Thos Peatling

Château Rayas Very traditional and expensive wine that most experts agree justifies its reputation for long-lived wines.
Adnams; Peter Green; Nobody Inn; La Vigneronne

Domaine du Vieux Télégraphe To many, the greatest estate in Châteauneuf, making quite modern-style wines which age quickly but also have great elegance.
Adnams; Ian G Howe; S H Jones; Lay & Wheeler; Michael Menzel Wines; Nobody Inn; Tanners

OTHER CHÂTEAUNEUF ESTATES

Vieux Lazaret (*The Wine Society*); Château St-André (*Safeway*); Domaine de St-Préfert (*Vintage Wines; Wine Growers Association*).

White Châteauneuf-du-Pape

Château de Beaucastel (*Tanners; Winecellars*); Domaine Font de Michelle (*Davisons; Ellis Son & Vidler; Lay & Wheeler; Master Cellar Wine Warehouses; Thresher*); Domaine du Vieux Télégraphe (*Adnams; Michael Menzel Wines; Tanners*); Château de la Nerthe (*Mayor Sworder & Co*); Les Arnevels (*Tesco*); Domaine André Brunel (*J Sainsbury*); Domaine de la Roquette (*Christopher Piper Wines; Tanners*); Domaine de Valori; La Pontificale (*Blayneys*).

Côtes du Luberon

Domaine Val Joanis (*Asda; T & W Wines; Willoughbys*); Domaine Chancel (*Harrods*); Cellier de Marrenon (*Hungerford Wine Company; Safeway; Stapylton Fletcher*).

Côtes du Rhône

La Serre du Prieur (*Oddbins*); Ch du Grand Moulas (*Adnams; S H Jones; Lay & Wheeler; Tanners;*); Jaboulet Aîné Parallèle 45 (*Peter Green; Lay & Wheeler; Michael Menzel Wines; T & W Wines; Wizard Wine Warehouses*); Cave des Vignerons de Vacqueyras (*Tanners; Wizard Wine Warehouses*); Cru du Coudoulet (*Les Amis du Vin; Sebastopol Wines*); Cave des Vignerons de Rasteau (*Borg Castel; Celtic Vintner*); Domaine Rabasse-Charavin (*Berkmann Wine Cellars/Le Nez Rouge*); Fonsalette (*Les Amis du Vin; La Vigneronne*); Domaine Ste-Anne, Notre Dame des Cellettes (*Tanners*); La Vieille Ferme (*Sebastopol Wines*); Paul Coulon (*Ian G Howe*); Guigal (*Adnams; Averys; Berry Bros & Rudd; Bibendum; Harrods; Lay & Wheeler; Michael Menzel Wines; Oddbins; T & W Wines*); Château du Bois de Garde Musset (*Asda*); St-Apollinaire (*J Sainsbury*); Domaine Bel-Air (*Peter Dominic; Richard Harvey Wines*); Domaine St-Estève (*Ellis Son & Vidler*); Domaine du Grand Prieur (*Oddbins*); Didier Charavin (*Le Viticulteur*); Domaine de Mont-Redon (*Majestic*); Château de Ruth (*Edward Sheldon*).

Côtes du Rhône Villages

In this list we give the name of the village first, followed by the producer's name or estate. Village wines without the name of a particular village are a blend of wines from two or more villages.

Côtes du Rhône Villages Côtes du Rhône Villages, Jaboulet Aîné (*Fullers; Peter Green; Hungerford Wine Company; Majestic; The Wine Society*); Sainsbury's Côtes du Rhône Villages (*J Sainsbury*).

Beaumes-de-Venise Domaine de Coyeux (*Adnams; Asda; Ellis Son & Vidler; Ian G Howe; Lay & Wheeler; Marks & Spencer*); Beaumes-de-Venise, Ch Redortier (*Victoria Wine Company; Welbeck Wines*); Domaine Goubert, Jean-Pierre Cartier (*Ian G Howe; Sebastopol Wines*).

Cairanne Domaine de l'Oratoire St-Martin (*Redpath & Thackray*).

Rasteau Cave des Vignerons de Rasteau (*Oddbins; Winecellars*); Domaine Charavin (*Berkmann Wine Cellars/Le Nez Rouge; Lay & Wheeler*); Domaine de Grangeneuve (*Nobody Inn*).

St-Gervais Domaine Ste-Anne (*Adnams; Lay & Wheeler*).

Vacqueyras Domaine de la Couroulu, Ricard Pierre (*Berry Bros & Rudd; Thos Peatling*); Clos des Cazaux (*Winecellars*); Vacqueyras Jaboulet Aîné (*Averys; Fullers; Peter Green; Lay & Wheeler; Oddbins; Thos Peatling; T & W Wines*); Vacqueyras la Fourmone Réserve du Paradis (*Thresher; La Vigneronne*); Ch de Montmirail (*Hopton Wines*).

Vinsobres Caves Jaume (*The Wine Society*); Domaine du Moulin (*Majestic*).

Visan Domaine de la Cantharide Cuvée de l'Hermite (*Alex Findlater*).

Coteaux du Tricastin

Domaine de Grangeneuve (*Ian G Howe; Yapp Brothers*); Domaine du Vieux Micocoulier (*Thos Peatling; Sebastopol Wines; Stapylton Fletcher; Welbeck Wines*); Asda Coteaux du Tricastin (*Asda*).

Côtes du Ventoux

La Vieille Ferme (*Les Amis du Vin; Berkmann Wine Cellars/Le Nez Rouge; Bibendum; Christopher Piper Wines; Sebastopol Wines; Wine Growers Association; Wizard Wine Warehouses*); Domaine des Anges (*Adnams; Bibendum; Lay & Wheeler; Tanners*); Sainsbury's Côtes du Ventoux (*J Sainsbury*); Jaboulet Aîné (*Fullers; Hungerford Wine Company; Majestic; T & W Wines*); Cave des Vignerons la Tour d'Aigues (*Les Amis du Vin*).

Côtes du Vivarais

Producteurs Réunis Ardéchois (*Yapp Brothers*).

Gigondas

Guigal (*Anthony Byrne Fine Wines*); Domaine de la Fourmone (*Lay & Wheeler*); Domaine de St-Gayan (*Oddbins; Yapp Brothers*); L'Oustau Fauquet (*Tanners*); Domaine du Grand Montmirail (*Davisons; Ian G Howe; Master Cellar Wine Warehouse; Old Street Wine Company; Yapp Brothers*); Les Gouberts (*Arthur Rackhams; Sebastopol Wines*); Les Pallières (*Bibendum; Ian G Howe; Michael Menzel Wines; Nobody Inn; Thos Peatling; Christopher Piper Wines*); Domaine Raspail-Ay (*Harrods; Whighams of Ayr*); Pierre Amadieu (*Reid Wines*); Domaine de la Longue-Toque (*Barwell & Jones; Redpath & Thackray*).

Lirac (red, rosé and white)

Domaine de Ch St-Roch (*Lay & Wheeler*); Domaine de Castel-Oualou (*Peter Green; Ian G Howe; Michael Menzel Wines*); Domaine Maby (*Berry Bros; Harrods; Hungerford Wine Company; The Wine Society; Yapp Brothers*); Les Queyrades (*Berry Bros & Rudd*).

Tavel

La Forcadière (*Thos Peatling; Yapp Brothers*); Caves des Vignerons (*Oddbins*); Domaine Maby (*Harrods*); Ch d'Aqueria (*Redpath & Thackray*).

Vin de Pays

Vin de Pays des Bouches du Rhône, Domaine de la Forêt (*Eldridge Pope/Reynier Wine Libraries*); St Michael Vin de Pays des Bouches du Rhône (*Marks & Spencer*); Vin de Pays des Collines Rhodaniennes, de Vallouit (*Les Amis du Vin*); Vin de Pays du Vaucluse (*Fullers; Tesco*).

Best buys from Southern Rhône

WHITE

Côtes du Luberon Cellier de Marrenon (*Ad Hoc Wine Warehouse*)
Côtes du Luberon La Vieille Ferme (*widely available*)
Côtes du Vivarais Blanc 1988, Vignerons Ardéchois (*Chesterford Vintners*)

RED

Châteauneuf-du-Pape 1986, Ch de Beaucastel (*widely available*)
Côtes du Ventoux La Vieille Ferme (*widely available*)
Côtes du Rhône 1985, Guigal (*widely available*)
Côtes du Rhône 1986, Parallèle 45, Jaboulet Aîné (*J E Hogg*)
Côtes du Rhône Vacqueyras 1985, Jaboulet Aîné (*Whiteside's of Clitheroe*)
Gigondas 1985, Pierre Amadieu (*Reid Wines*)
Côtes du Rhône 1987, Domaine de la Renjardière (*Eldridge Pope*)
Côtes du Rhône Tradition 1987, Ch St-Estève d'Uchaux (*G M Vintners*)
Ch Val-Joanis 1986, Côtes du Luberon (*widely available*)
Côtes du Rhône 1986, Cru du Coudoulet (*widely available*)
Côtes du Vivarais 1987, Domaine de Belvert (*Adnams*)
Côtes du Rhône Ch du Grand Moulas 1987 (*widely available*)
Coteaux du Tricastin 1986, Domaine du Vieux Micocoulier (*Gerard Harris*)
Côtes du Luberon 1987, Domaine des Baumelles (*Tesco*)
Côtes du Ventoux, Domaine des Anges (*Bibendum; Pavilion Wine Co*)

Specialist stockists

Bibendum; D Byrne & Co; Restaurant Croque-en-Bouche; S H Jones; Lay & Wheeler; Redpath & Thackray Wines; J Townend & Sons; Helen Verdcourt Wines

SAVOIE

This is the region of mountain wines with a tang of fresh air.
Invigorating and crisp, they have become more popular in the
shops as drinkers seek them out after returning from their
skiing holidays. The problem is one of availability: those skiers
have too big a thirst après-ski for vast quantities to leave their
home territory.

Red, white and sparkling wines are all made in Savoie. The
grapes used are a mix of local and more widely grown varieties:
Chardonnay, Chasselas (the Swiss Fendant), Jacquère, Altesse
(or Roussette), Bergeron (the southern Rhône Roussanne) and
Molette for the whites, Mondeuse and Gamay for the reds.

The appellation system is complex for such a small vineyard
region, with nine appellations:

Crépy Dry sparkling wines made from Chasselas grapes.
Roussette de Savoie Dry white wines made from Roussette and
Chardonnay.
Roussette de Savoie Cru Wines from four communes which can
add their name to ordinary Roussette.
Seyssel Dry white wines made from Altesse grapes.
Seyssel Mousseux Sparkling wines made from Altesse and
Chasselas.
Vin de Savoie Appellation covering the whole region; can be
red, dry white or rosé.
Vin de Savoie Cru Wines from 15 communes which can add
their name to Vin de Savoie.
Vin de Savoie Ayze Mousseux Sparkling wine made in the
commune of Ayze.
Vin de Savoie Mousseux White and rosé sparkling wines made
anywhere in the region.

Most wine to reach the UK is Vin de Savoie, some a Cru wine
from Apremont. The most widely known sparkling wine is a
Seyssel Mousseux from Varichon et Clerc.

Best buys from Savoie

Vin de Savoie Apremont (*Tesco; Winecellars; Wizard Wine
Warehouses*)
Seyssel Mousseux Varichon et Clerc (*Corney & Barrow; Davisons;
Unwins*)

THE SOUTH-WEST OF FRANCE

The wines of the regions of France south and east of Bordeaux come in two distinct styles. There are the wines that follow closely the model of the Bordeaux vineyard itself, making reds based on Cabernet Sauvignon and whites on Sémillon and Sauvignon. And there are the wines – further away from Bordeaux – which follow no model other than their own distinct traditions.

In both styles, however, this is a region where tastes are usually strong and distinctive, and where there is great variety, from the driest of reds to the sweetest of whites. Often – especially if you are looking for Bordeaux look-alikes – they provide good value for money.

In this survey, we take first the regions around Bordeaux, and then move further afield.

ENVIRONS OF BORDEAUX

Some of these vineyard areas (Bergerac, Duras, Côtes du Marmandais) were once considered part of the Bordeaux vineyard. Unluckily for them, they were on the wrong side of the departmental boundaries when the extent of Bordeaux was set as the *département* of Gironde.

So while Bordeaux prospered and recovered from phylloxera at the turn of this century, these other vineyard regions of the South-West slipped into a slow decline. Only in the last couple of decades have they started forging an independent identity of their own.

BERGERAC

The first region to expand its horizons and look to the export markets was Bergerac. It was also caught up in the scandal early in 1988 which involved the re-labelling of some Bergerac as Bordeaux. In some cases the wine was preferable to basic Bordeaux – which shows how alike Bergerac is to claret – but the French fraud squad had a field day.

Bergerac is the biggest of the appellations near Bordeaux, and produces a complete range of wines. It is an eastward extension of the St-Emilion vineyards at the beginning of the Dordogne valley. There are nine appellations, ranging from dry red through dry white to sweet white. The wines most likely to be found here are Bergerac (red, rosé and dry white), Côtes de Bergerac (red and medium sweet white) Monbazillac (sweet white) and Pécharmant (very fine red).

Vintages in Bergerac

Our advice is to drink the youngest dry whites and rosés – the 1987 or 1988 vintages. Ordinary red Bergerac also should be drunk within three years. Côtes de Bergerac red and Pécharmant last longer – vintages to look for are 1983, 1985 and, for keeping, 1986. Sweet Monbazillac is best in warm, ripe years – try the 1983s and keep the 1985s for a year or two.

Who's who in Bergerac

DRY WHITES

Ch la Jaubertie (*Adnams; Booths; D Byrne & Co; Fullers; Lay & Wheeler; Selfridges; La Vigneronne; Wines from Paris*)
Ch Court-lès-Mûts (*Bibendum; Sookias & Bertaut*)
Ch du Treuil de Nailhac (*Sookias & Bertaut*)
Ch de Belingard (*Barwell & Jones; Harrods; Selfridges*)
Ch le Fagé (*M & W Gilbey; Thos Peatling*)
Ch du Chayne (*Les Amis du Vin; Christopher Piper Wines; Safeway*)

SWEET WHITES

Ch de Treuil de Nailhac (*Sookias & Bertaut*)
Ch de Belingard (*Barwell & Jones; Selfridges*)
Cave Coopérative de Monbazillac (*La Vigneronne*)

REDS

Ch la Jaubertie (also make rosé) (*Adnams; D Byrne & Co; Chaplin & Son; Fullers; Peter Green; Lay & Wheeler; Majestic; Selfridges; La Vigneronne; Wines from Paris*)
Ch de Tiregand (*J Sainsbury; Sookias & Bertaut; Tanners; Wines from Paris*)
Domaine de Plaisance (*Grape Ideas*)
Ch Jaquet Montcharme (*Peter Dominic*)
Ch Court-les-Mûts (also make rosé) (*Bibendum; Sookias & Bertaut*)
La Pelissière (*Berkmann Wine Cellars/Le Nez Rouge*)
Persigny de Bergerac, Mahler-Besse (*Averys; Majestic*)
Ch Boudigand (*Ellis Son & Vidler*)
Ch Fayolle (*Oddbins; Old Street Wine Company*)

CÔTES DE BUZET

These vineyards are on the left bank of the River Garonne, south-east of the Bordeaux region. Whites and rosés are made, but virtually only the reds reach the UK. They have some ageing potential, with jammy fruit and some tannin. The grape varieties used are Cabernet Franc, Cabernet Sauvignon, Merlot and Malbec. Much of the wine is made at the co-operative which dominates production in the area.

Who's who in Côtes de Buzet

Ch de Gueyze (*Hilbre Wine Co; Thos Peatling; Arthur Rackhams; Tanners*)
Domaine Roc de Cailloux (*Old Street Wine Company; Prestige Vintners*)
Les Vignerons Réunis, Cuvée Napoléon (*Safeway*)
Sainsbury's Buzet (*J Sainsbury*)
Côtes de Buzet (*Peter Dominic*)
Ch Sauvagnères (*Sookias & Bertaut*)
Ch des Jonquilles (*Sookias & Bertaut*)

CÔTES DE DURAS

It really is only an accident of politics that the Côtes de Duras is not part of Bordeaux. The soil is an extension of the Entre-Deux-Mers vineyards; but the departmental boundary of the River Gironde runs on the wrong side of the vineyards. The reds produced from the Cabernet Franc, Cabernet Sauvignon, Merlot and Malbec grapes are light (often made by the carbonic maceration method of Beaujolais Nouveau) and are made to drink early: they're delicious chilled. The dry whites from the Sauvignon (look for the grape name on the label) are typically fresh.

Who's who in Côtes de Duras

WHITES
Asda Côtes de Duras (*Asda*)
Ch la Place (*Majestic*)

REDS

Le Seigneuret (*Waitrose*)
Domaine Mau Michau (*Duras Direct*)
Ch la Pilar (*H Allen Smith; Alex Findlater; Majestic*)
Poulet Père et Fils (*Grape Ideas*)
Domaine de Laulan (*Hungerford Wine Co*)
Ch du Moulin (*Desborough & Brown*)

CÔTES DU MARMANDAIS

The wines produced in this area are soft, easy reds for early drinking and come at good prices. Most wine is produced by one or other of the two co-operatives.

Who's who in Côtes du Marmandais

Côtes du Marmandais Cave de Cocumont (*widely available*)

BEYOND BORDEAUX

These are the appellations that sometimes (but not always) use the Bordeaux grape varieties, but owe much less to its influence. While some of the larger ones are regaining an importance they once had, others are struggling to survive, often kept alive only by the efforts of the co-operatives.

This is also the home of some of the strange grape varieties with which the South-West abounds. In these days when everybody seems to want to plant Cabernet Sauvignon and Chardonnay, it is exciting to find such rarities as Manseng, Tannat, Fer, Auxerrois, Jurançon Noir, Meslier, Mauzac, Courbu, Baroque. These are tastes which need to be experienced.

CAHORS

The most important appellation outside the Bordeaux environs, this vineyard area has had a chequered history, which almost finished with the frosts of 1956 and 1957. It is only with the replanting since then that the region has come into its own. Now the success of the area is becoming apparent with a doubling of growers since 1971, and an increasing interest in estate-bottled top quality wines.

Modern Cahors ranges from fresh wines which have been made for early drinking to those which are fairly tough and tannic, ideal for rich, spicy foods and some bottle-ageing – for as much as 15 to 20 years in some cases.

The grape varieties used here are the Malbec, called locally the Auxerrois (to provide the concentration), the Merlot (to soften the Auxerrois and give extra alcohol) and the Tannat (to provide tannin). The ultra-modern co-operative, Côtes d'Olt, makes much of the wine but there are also 90 individual growers.

Who's who in Cahors

Clos la Coutale (*Christopher Piper Wines; Windrush Wines*)
Ch de Haute-Serre (*Harrods; The Wine Society; Wizard Wine Warehouses*)
Les Côtes d'Olt (*widely available*)
Domaine de la Pineraie (*Raeburn Fine Wines & Foods; Sookias & Bertaut*)
Domaine de Gaudou (*Adnams; Raeburn Fine Wines & Foods; Sookias & Bertaut; Winecellars*)
Domaine du Single (*Old Street Wine Company*)
Ch Didier-Parnac, Rigal et Fils (*Lay & Wheeler; Martinez Fine Wine; Wines from Paris*)
Clos Triguedina (*Raeburn Fine Wines & Foods*)
Ch de Chambert (*Gerard Harris; Prestige Vintners*)
Domaine Eugénie (*Eldridge Pope/Reynier Wine Libraries; Touchstone Wines*)
Domaine des Grauzils (*Thos Peatling*)
Domaine de Meaux (*Majestic*)
Ch les Bouysses (*J Sainsbury*)
Ch Cayrou d'Albas (*Unwins*)
Domaine des Savarines (*Sookias & Bertaut*)
Domaine de Mériguet (*Les Amis du Vin*)
Ch de Cayrou (*Bibendum; Sookias & Bertaut; Tanners*)
Clos de Gamot (*Raeburn Fine Wines & Foods; Sookias & Bertaut*)

CÔTES DU FRONTONNAIS

Red and rosé wines are made in this small area to the north of Toulouse, where the local grape is the Negrette. They're excellent value for everyday drinking, although quantities available in this country tend to be small. Drink them young as quaffing wines.

Who's who in Côtes du Frontonnais

Ch Flotis (*Sookias & Bertaut*)
Ch Bellevue la Forêt (*Berkmann Wine Cellars/Le Nez Rouge; Alex Findlater; Oddbins*)
Ch Montauriol (*Barwell & Jones*)
Ch la Palme (*Laytons; André Simon*)
Ch Montauriol (*Oddbins*)

GAILLAC

Red, white and sparkling wines are produced here. Gaillac Perlé is the name given to a slightly sparkling wine made from Mauzac Blanc and Len de l'El. While there are some good examples of this fresh taste, more interesting in the sparkling line are the Mousseux wines made by a traditional technique known as the 'méthode gaillaçoise', which produces wines of a good, peppery, fruity quality with lots of flavour.

Dry whites are also made, tending towards dullness, although good examples are likewise worth seeking out. Sweet Gaillac Doux can be superb. Reds are fresh, light and some are made by carbonic maceration to bring out the fruit in the local Fer, Duras and Negrette grapes, blended with Syrah.

Who's who in Gaillac

Jean Cros – for high quality, traditional wines, including a méthode gaillaçoise sparkler, and a good, dry white and red, Ch Larroze (*H Allen Smith; David Baillie Vintners; Chaplin & Son; Alex Findlater; Findlater Mackie Todd; Richard Harvey Wines; Lay & Wheeler; Sookias & Bertaut; Stapylton Fletcher; Tanners; Winecellars*)
Cave Coopérative de Labastide de Lévis (*Balls Brothers; Bordeaux Direct; Majestic*)
Domaine de Labarthe, Jean Albert (*Sookias & Bertaut*)

JURANÇON

While much dry white Jurançon Sec is best drunk along the nearby Atlantic coast at Biarritz, there are still small pockets of the old-fashioned sweet wines, called Jurançon Moelleux, on which this area's reputation used to rest. Surprisingly their rarity value does not make them expensive. Sparkling Jurançon Brut is also made.

Who's who in Jurançon

Cru Lamouroux sweet and medium dry (*Richard Harvey Wines; La Vigneronne*)

Jurançon Brut sparkling, Caves Vinicoles de Gan (*Bordeaux Direct*)

Clos Guirouilh dry and sweet (*Matthew Gloag; Peter Green; Prestige Vintners; Upper Crust*)

Domaine Cauhapé dry and sweet (*Les Amis du Vin; Eaton Elliot Winebrokers; Morris & Verdin; Sookias & Bertaut; Tanners; La Vigneronne; Winecellars; The Wine Society*)

Ch Jolys sweet (*Tanners*)

MADIRAN AND PACHERENC DU VIC-BILH

Heady stuff, these two names. In reality, though, while Madiran (from the Tannat grape) is a fine, red wine often dark in colour and often very tannic when young (although there are lighter wines around as well), Pacherenc du Vic-Bilh is a straightforward, rather pricy white, most of which is drunk locally. Both come from the Armagnac country of Gascony.

Who's who in Madiran and Pacherenc

Madiran

Ch d'Arricau-Bordes (*Sookias & Bertaut*)

Ch de Peyros (*Eaton Elliot Winebrokers*)

Domaine Bouscassé (*Haughton Fine Wines*)

Alain Brumont Ch Montus (*Raeburn Fine Wines & Foods; Sookias & Bertaut*)

Domaine Pichard (*Old Street Wine Company; Prestige Vintners; Tanners*)

Domaine de Margalide (*Wright Wine Co*)

Domaine de Diusse (*Oddbins*)

Coopérative Union des Producteurs Plaimont (*Desborough & Brown Fine Wines; Sebastopol Wines*)

Pacherenc du Vic-Bilh

Domaine du Crampilh (*Les Amis du Vin; Sookias & Bertaut*)

LESSER REGIONS OF THE SOUTH-WEST

While there are many more small demarcated wine areas in the South-West, production is often tiny, so not many of their products reach our shops. Here is a selection of the better ones which do.

Côtes de St-Mont

Good, simple rough red wines from the edge of the Armagnac region. The local co-operative, Producteurs Plaimont, have a good value example (*Adnams; Haynes Hanson & Clark; Lay & Wheeler; Tanners*).

Entraygues et du Fel

A VDQS area on the southern slopes of the Massif Centrale in the Lot Valley. Look for Jean Marc Viguier's wines (*Sookias & Bertaut*).

Irouléguy

Right on the Spanish border at the western end of the Pyrenees, this makes red, white and rosé. Try the red Irouléguy from the co-operative (*Ad Hoc Wine Warehouse*).

Marcillac

Deep-coloured reds from a small VDQS area also in the Lot valley. Look out for Laurens Teulier (*Sookias & Bertaut*) and Cave de Valady (*Bordeaux Direct/Taste Shops*).

Tursan

Perfumed dry whites and soft reds from the heart of Gascony. Look out for Domaine de Perchade-Pourruchot, Dulucq et Fils (*Sookias & Bertaut*).

VINS DE PAYS OF THE SOUTH-WEST

The most important vins de pays, as far as we are concerned, are Côtes de Gascogne, Côtes du Tarn, de la Dordogne, and des Pyrénées Atlantiques. All make good, everyday drinking wines. The whites, especially those from Côtes de Gascogne made using modern high tech equipment, have excited considerable interest.

Who's who in the vins de pays of the South-West

Vin de Pays des Pyrénées Atlantiques (white) Coopérative de Gan (*Eldridge Pope; Richard Harvey Wines*)

Vin de Pays des Côtes de Gascogne (white) Look especially for wines labelled Cépage Colombard, a grape which gives great flavour.
Domaine de Tariquet (*Barnes Wine Shop; Drunken Mouse; Eaton Elliot Winebrokers; Alex Findlater; Stapylton Fletcher; Thresher; La Vigneronne*)
Domaine de Tariquet, Cuvée Bois (wood-aged) (*Oddbins*)
Domaine de Planterieu (*Waitrose*)
Domaine des Rieux (*Adnams; Chaplin & Son; Eaton Elliot Winebrokers; Alex Findlater; Gerard Harris; Mayor Sworder & Co; Thos Peatling; Tanners*)
Domaine de St-Lanne (*Oddbins*)
St Michael Côtes de Gascogne (*Marks & Spencer*)
Domaine d'Escoubes, Grassa (*Tesco*)
Domaine le Puts (*Majestic*)
Producteurs Plaimont, Cépage Colombard (*S H Jones*)

Vin de Pays des Côtes de Thongue cépage Merlot (red) (*Stapylton Fletcher*)

Coteaux du Quercy (red) (*Martinez Fine Wine; Oddbins; Upper Crust; Winecellars; Wizard Wine Warehouses*)

Best buys from South West

DRY WHITE

Vin de Pays des Côtes de Gascogne, Domaine d'Escoubes (*Tesco*)
Vin de Pays des Côtes de Gascogne, Domaine le Pûts (*Majestic*)
Vin de Pays des Côtes de Gascogne, Domaine de Tariquet Cuvée Bois (*Thresher*)
Vin de Pays des Côtes de Gascogne, Domaine de Rieux (*widely available*)
Bergerac Blanc 1988, Ch Court-les-Mûts (*Bibendum*)
Gaillac Blanc Sec 1988, Domaine de Labarthe (*Sookias & Bertaut*)
Bergerac Sec Blanc 1983, Domaine de Grandchamp (*Peter Green*)
Ch Le Raz Sauvignon Blanc 1987, Bergerac (*John Harvey & Sons*)

SWEET WHITE

Monbazillac 1982, Ch La Fage (*Lamb Wine Co*)

ROSÉ

Ch La Jaubertie Rosé 1987, Bergerac (*Villeneuve Wines*)

RED

Madiran 1985, Caves Quercynoises (*Alba Wine Society*)

Côtes de Buzet 1984, Cuvée Napoléon (*G M Vintners*)

Côtes de Mont Rouge 1986, Producteurs Plaimont (*Cachet Wines*)

Madiran 1985, Domaine de Fauron (*Martinez Fine Wine*)

Côtes du Frontonnais 1988, Ch Flotis (*Sookias & Bertaut*)

Madiran 1983, Ch Peyros (*Eaton Elliot Winebrokers*)

Gaillac 1986, Ch Larroze Rouge, Domaine Jean Cros (*Alex Findlater; Moffat Wine Shop*)

Clos la Coutale 1986, Cahors (*Windrush Wines; Christopher Piper Wines*)

Specialist stockists

Bibendum; Desborough & Brown Fine Wines; Haughton Fine Wines; Oddbins; Pennyloaf Wines; Sookias & Bertaut; Upper Crust

Germany

Where are the great wines?

One of the most interesting tastings we went to last year was
organised by a group of Mosel producers calling themselves the
Grosser Ring der Prädikatsweinversteigerer von Mosel–Saar–
Ruwer. Just in case that was getting a little dense, underneath
the producers had added a slogan: 'Great wines from great
vineyards, 100% Riesling'.

And that said it all. It was a fascinating and memorable
tasting of some of the finest wines from the Mosel–Saar–Ruwer,
from some of the best producers. We left full of good intentions
to write about these wines, and say that they surely showed
that Germany can make fine wines – and that the German grape
which makes these fine wines has to be the Riesling.

Disillusion followed. In this Guide we do not recommend
wines unless they are available in Britain, and very few of those
superb wines were. A case here, perhaps, one wine from a
producer there – but the slate was mainly blank. So was our
report.

This sums up the problem of Germany quickly and sadly. The
Germans do make great wines, but the British just don't know
about them or buy them. Those few wine merchants who
maintained a good German list for the fallow years in which

only Liebfraumilch and its ilk was sold must have been near to despair that things would ever change.

Wines from great villages

It is still too early to say whether things will improve, and whether we will wake up to the best that Germany can offer, rather than the worst. There are hopeful signs: one was the launch in 1989 of a range of German village wines by one of the better-known shippers, Deinhard. With this Heritage Selection, they concentrated on providing wines which gave the true character of wines from the vineyards of that village.

But when we then say that those villages included Piesport, Bernkastel and Nierstein, perhaps Deinhard's challenge is put into perspective. To most interested wine drinkers, those names spell cheap sugar water, rather than fine wines. And that is because of the confusion behind German wine names: to us a wine called Nierstein is much the same as one called Niersteiner Gutes Domtal. That the Nierstein wine comes from the vineyards in the immediate vicinity of the village, and that the Gutes Domtal comes from a wide area much further away from the River Rhine (much the same country that also supplies Liebfraumilch) – such subtlety is lost on us.

One of the major tragedies of the German wine scene is the way that great names have been abused. And the irony of it is that most drinkers of Piesporter Michelsberg and Niersteiner Gutes Domtal neither know nor care that those villages produce famous wines: they just know that the wine they are drinking is cheap and relatively palatable.

There have been other signs that the good German producers, sufficiently worried about the reputation of German wines, are trying to do something about it. For instance, organisations like the Charta group of Rheingau producers are making some excellent wines to go with food. Some producers are experimenting with barrel-ageing – the addition of strong wood tastes to German wines doesn't work with whites wines, although it does with some reds and at least it's worth a try.

We have to pay the price

The problem with any fine German wine is that it has to overcome two hurdles in getting acceptance outside a tiny band of connoisseurs. One is that it is competing with the Liebfraumilch image. The other is that it is relatively expensive. Germany's position at the northern edge of vine cultivation (meaning that harvests can vary wildly – from 15 million hectolitres in 1982 to 5 million in 1985), the premium attached to

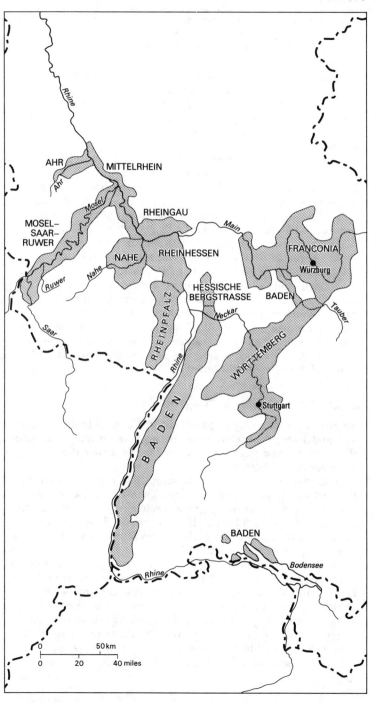

a select band of vineyards which attract just the right amount of sun, and the high costs of farming vineyards where the slope may be 1 in 3 – all combine to make Germany's great wines an expensive proposition.

Another area in which Germany has been suffering is in the relationship between her wines and food. Traditionally, beer has been the drink for food, and wine has been drunk away from the table, as an aperitif or just for the pleasure of drinking it on a warm day. It's very fruitiness has militated against its partnership with food.

This has worried German producers. They have watched the trend towards drinking wine with meals, and have seen that the French, the Italians, the New World producers have all been in a better position, with their less aromatic wines, at the dinner table. The Germans have pointed out, quite rightly, that their ordinary wines have been sweet only since the War – before that, only a tiny percentage of great dessert wines were sweet, while the rest of what they made was fruity, yes, but dry.

It is no coincidence that both the Deinhard wines we have mentioned, and the Charta wines, and many wines from the great estates of the Rheingau (like Schloss Vollrads) are all now dry. It's much more difficult to make a dry wine than a sweet wine in Germany – the residual sugar can mask plenty of mistakes which the dryness exposes. So, again, we will have to accept that they are expensive, but they surely represent the wines of the future for Germany.

Lower yields – and classed growths

There's still a long way to go to make the change to drier styles, and to distance themselves from the sugar water image, it seems that German producers are going to have to change their attitudes in a number of ways.

First, they are going to have to accept that high yields are not the best way to produce good wines. German philosophy has always been to get as many grapes from a vine as possible, and then sort out the problems in the vinification. That's fine for Liebfraumilch, but not for much else. So farmers need to be offered higher prices for low-yield vines.

Then, the emphasis must return to the great grape varieties of Germany. The Riesling is the King of German vines, but it is low-yielding and therefore not so profitable as many newer strains. Again, a premium for Riesling grapes would be the answer to encourage more reliance on this superb variety. The Silvaner, too, as grown in Franconia, should be encouraged. And, equally, the Müller-Thurgau should be discouraged.

Thirdly, there should be a more sensible classification of

German vineyards. In theory, any German vineyard is the equal of another – they can all produce quality wines, right up to the highest grade (see below for definitions) if the weather conditions are right. In practice, of course – as with any wine country – some vineyards are much better than others. This should be recognised in some form of classification, so that we know which are the top crus, which the second, and which are fairly ordinary. Such a classification would not necessarily be a guarantee of quality, but it would help point us in the right direction.Then, in return for these efforts on the part of the producers, we, the consumers, should offer to consider maturing the wines we buy for a while. We tend to think of German wines as ready for drinking almost as soon as they are bottled. But a few months, even a year or so in bottle, helps even the lesser German wines – and certainly the great estate wines – to give more depth of flavour and less tart, green and sulphury fruit.

If all these changes come to pass – a big if, we know – German wines could begin to enjoy the sort of reputation they had when they could command higher prices than many wines from Bordeaux.

German thoroughness

Germany is nothing if not thorough in giving information on the label about the wine inside the bottle, which will be tall, and green if it comes from Mosel–Saar–Ruwer and brown from elsewhere; except Franconia which has dumpy green bottles. Some wines from the Rheingau now come in blue bottles.

1 The label will indicate which category of wine it falls into: Tafelwein, the most basic; Landwein, a sort of German vin de pays; *Qualitätswein bestimmter Anbaugebiete* (QbA), the lowest quality wine level; or at the top level *Qualitätswein mit Prädikat* (QmP, which has six sub-divisions). As an indication of what Germans mean by quality wine, 90 per cent of their total production falls into a quality category. To get real quality, you need to go to the level of QmP wines.

QmP wines are divided by sweetness: Kabinett (the driest), Spätlese, Auslese, Beerenauslese and Trockenbeerenauslese (the sweetest). Eiswein, made from frozen grapes, can be either Beerenauslese or Trockenbeerenauslese quality.

2 Next, the wine region. **Tafelwein** can come from four big districts: Rhein–Mosel, Bayern (Bavaria), Neckar, Oberrhein (basically Baden). **Landwein** districts number 15, but little is sold in Britain.

Quality wine areas (for QbA and QmP wines) are (from north to south: Ahr, Mittelrhein, Mosel–Saar–Ruwer, Nahe, Rheingau, Rheinhessen, Hessische Bergstrasse, Franken, Württemberg, Rheinpfalz, Baden. In the UK we see wines from all areas (although in small quantities from Ahr, Mittelrhein, Hessische Bergstrasse and Württemberg).

3 The label will tell you which sub-region (*Bereich*) it comes from, which district (*Grosslage*), which village in that district (*Gemeinde*) and which single vineyard (*Einzellagen*).

Which of these categories is indicated will depend on the quality of the wine. The best wines will have single vineyard names, the most straightforward simply a Bereich name.

4 Other information will include:

The AP number given to the wine after it has been tested by a central testing station (useful to know only if something's wrong with the wine).

The degree of dryness (relates to QbA wines only): Trocken (dry), Halbtrocken (less dry), Diabetikerwein (for diabetics) or nothing (for standard styles).

The grape variety: not compulsory, but always included if the *Riesling* (the finest German variety) is predominant. Other grapes you might see are *Müller-Thurgau* (still the most widely planted), *Silvaner* (in Franconia especially), *Scheurebe* (which produces a highly scented wine), *Kerner* (a stylish grape with some similarity to Riesling), *Spätburgunder* or *Blauer Portugeiser* (if you are looking for a red wine – not often seen in Britain).

The vintage: see below for details of recent vintages.

The producer: if the wine has been estate-bottled it will bear the term Erzeugerabfüllung.

The bottler: if the wine is not estate-bottled it will carry the name of the merchant or shipper who bottled it.

That's certainly more information than any other country offers on its labels. However, perhaps because it *is* so complicated, most of us are totally confused and end up buying Liebfraumilch.

German sparklers

Sekt is the German name for sparkling wines. Deutscher Sekt is sparkling wine made from German grapes. Some of the best Sekts are made from the Riesling,and this will normally be indicated on the label. The word Sekt, without the prefix

Deutscher, means that the base wine may come from anywhere in Europe – often Italy, sometimes France.

Some of the biggest German merchants – Deinhard, Kupferberg, Sichel (of Blue Nun fame) – make sparkling wines. The Deinhard brands are very good, as are some which go under estate names: Schloss Rheingarten, Schloss Böchingen, Fürst von Metternich. For more details, see the Sparkling wines section on page 639.

Harvests – wide variety

German harvests can vary considerably in quantity as well as quality. The early 1980s produced the biggest harvests on record, and on the whole, harvests are now much bigger than they used to be – the most obvious result of high yields. Most ordinary QbA wines need to be drunk within 1-2 years or they will lose their freshness, but QmP wines start to mature after 2-3 years (for Kabinett wines).

Recent harvests all made some decent wines in the lower categories, but only rarely are there many wines in the top very sweet ones. Before 1983, the most recent star vintages for these great sweet wines were 1976, 1959, 1945 and 1921.

1988 Considered to be the best vintage of the 1980s so far, with many estates making 90 per cent of their wines as Prädikat wines. The best qualities are Kabinett and Spätlese, with only tiny amounts of Auslese and above. However, the quality does mean that most 1988 wines will be long-lasting, and should not be drunk too young.

1987 After a poor start to the growing season, a fine September and October saved the harvest, giving an average crop, with 75 per cent standard QbA wines, and 21 per cent QmP wines, most of which are of Kabinett level. The vintage is characterised by clean, fresh wines.

1986 A mixed bag of a vintage, with bad weather during the harvest and only small quantities of the wine likely to be at the higher QmP levels, but good acidity has resulted in plenty of easy-drinking wines.

1985 Good quality, especially for the Riesling. As much as 60 per cent reached Prädikat levels (mainly Kabinett). But quantity has been cut by as much as half because of frost in the early part of the year. The Kabinett wines are good to drink now, but keep higher Prädikat wines.

1984 Little but QbA wines were made in a poor year. These should be drunk by now.

1983 A very fine year, with some good wines up to Auslese quality, but little above. A very large crop, especially in the Mosel–Saar–Ruwer. Keep the top qualities for at least four years, and enjoy the rest now and for a while yet.

1982 A year of huge quantities, caused by high rainfall during the harvest, so only QbA wines were produced – most should have been drunk.

1981 Some of the Spätlese wines are still definitely worth drinking, and a few will keep.

1976 The top quality wines from this vintage are German classics. If you find a bottle of Spätlese or above in the QmP wines, buy it and save it for drinking with some appreciative friends.

1975 Some consider these wines just as fine as 1976 although slightly lighter. Again, any wines of Auslese and above that you spot are worth savouring.

Who's who in Germany

This selection of German producers includes some of the best estates and also some of the merchants whose wines are regularly seen in Britain.

Anheuser, Weingut Okonomierat August E Large estate of 60 hectares in the Nahe, making racy wines mainly from the Riesling grape.
Corney & Barrow

Aschrott'sche Erben, Geheimrat High quality estate in Hochheim in the Rheingau. Almost entirely Riesling wines.
Berry Bros & Rudd; O W Loeb; Raeburn Fine Wines & Foods; The Wine Society

Badischer Winzergenossenschaft, Zentralkellerei A long name for the main co-operative of Baden, making 400 to 500 different wines. High standards for a co-operative.
Booths; Peter Dominic; Oddbins; Thresher; Victoria Wine Company; Waitrose; Willoughbys; Yorkshire Fine Wines

Balbach Erben, Burgermeister Anton, Weingut One of the great estates in Nierstein in Rheinhessen with a modern outlook to winemaking.
Lay & Wheeler

Bassermann-Jordan, Weingut Geheimer Rat Dr von Rheinpfalz estate, founded in the 13th century, with vineyards in many of the best sites of Deidesheim and Forst.
Barnes Wine Shop; Bibendum; Richard Harvey Wines; S H Jones; Lay & Wheeler; Raeburn Fine Wines & Foods

Bergweiler-Prum Erben, Zach Small Mosel–Saar–Ruwer estate with vineyards in Graach, Bernkastel, Wehlen and Zeltingen–Rachtig.
Alex Findlater

Bischöflichen Weinguter, Verwaltung der Four estates (105 hectares) of ecclesiastical origin in Mosel–Saar–Ruwer, based in the city of Trier. Other ecclesiastical names you will see are Bischöfliche Priesterseminar and Bischöfliche Konvikt.
Berry Bros & Rudd; Alex Findlater; S H Jones; Lay & Wheeler; The Wine Society; Yorkshire Fine Wines

Brentano'sche Gutsverwaltung, Baron von Good Rheingau estate, whose holdings of ten hectares include part of Winkeler Hasensprung.
Lay & Wheeler

Breuer, Weingut G Small estate, part of the merchant company of Scholl & Hillebrand (see below). The main holdings are in Rüdesheim on the Rheingau.
Alex Findlater; La Vigneronne

Buhl, Weingut Reichsrat von Great Rheinpfalz estate, with a dynamic young American in charge, making wines from vineyards in Forst, Deidesheim and Ruppertsberg.
Berry Bros & Rudd; Eldridge Pope; O W Loeb; Arthur Rackhams; Raeburn Fine Wines & Foods

Burklin-Wolf, Weingut Dr Large estate based at Wachenheim in the Rheinpfalz making very fine wines.
Adnams; Berry Bros & Rudd; Lay & Wheeler; O W Loeb; The Wine Society

Castell'sches Domänenamt, Fürstlich Estate owned by the former rulers of the tiny state of Castell in Franconia. Wines made of the Rieslaner (a cross between Silvaner and Riesling) grape are a great speciality.
Andrew Gordon Wines; Tanners

Crusius, Weingut Hans Very high standards at this family-run estate in the Nahe, which has holdings in the Traiser Bastei and Rotenfels.
George Hill of Loughborough; The Wine Society

Deinhard & Co Wine merchant and vineyard owner based in Koblenz. Vineyards in Mosel–Saar–Ruwer (where they own most of the Bernkasteler Doktor vineyard), Rheingau and Rheinpfalz. Apart from estate wines, Deinhard make good branded wines (Green Label) and sparkling wine (Lila Imperial) – and the Heritage Selection (see the beginning of this section).
Adnams; Berry Bros & Rudd; Alex Findlater; Fortnum & Mason; Tanners; Willoughbys; Yorkshire Fine Wines

Diefenhardt'sches Weingut Estate of 12.2 hectares on the Rheingau with vineyards in Eltville, Martinsthal and Rauenthal.
H Allen Smith

Drathen KG, Ewald Theodor Large-scale exporters of cheap table wine.
Oddbins; Waitrose

Eltville, Verwaltung der Staatsweinguter The German state's holdings on the Rheingau and Hessische Bergstrasse, comprising 160 hectares in many of the best sites, including all of the walled Steinberg vineyard.
Adnams; Eldridge Pope; Lay & Wheeler

Fischer, Weinguter Dr Saar estate with holdings in Ockfen, Saarburg, Herrenberg.
John Harvey & Sons; The Wine Society

Friedrich-Wilhelm-Gymnasium, Stiftung Staatliches Estate founded by the Jesuits with 45 hectares of vineyard in the Mosel–Saar–Ruwer, based in Trier.
Adnams; Barnes Wine Shop; Bibendum; Alex Findlater; Richard Harvey Wines; Tanners; The Wine Society

Geltz Zilliken, Weingut Forstmeister A Saar estate with holdings in Ockfen and Saarburg, and the deepest cellar in the region.
Lay & Wheeler

Guntrum-Weinkellerei GmbH, Louis Wine merchant and vineyard owner based in the Rheinhessen. Many wines from top vineyards as well as more straightforward ones.
Widely available

Hallgarten GmbH, Arthur Firm of wine exporters selling estate-bottled wines as well as brands and standard wines. Linked with the Pieroth group (see below).
Selfridges; Unwins; Victoria Wine Company

Hovel, Weingut von One of the principal estates in the Saar, making classically delicate wines in rare good years.
O W Loeb; Windrush Wines

Huesgen GmbH, A Firm of wine merchants based in Traben–Trarbach in the Mosel–Saar–Ruwer. Specialising in inexpensive wines.
Berry Bros & Rudd; Booths; D Byrne & Co; Davisons

Juliusspital-Weingut Charitable hospital in Wurzburg, Franconia, dating from the 16th century. Makes excellent examples of Franconian wines.
O W Loeb

Kesselstatt, Weingut Reichsgraf von Four estates at Graach, Piesport, Kasel and Oberemmel in Mosel–Saar–Ruwer.
Eldridge Pope; O W Loeb; Raeburn Fine Wines & Foods; The Wine Society

Lang, Weingut Hans Small estate based in the Rheingau, with holdings in Kiedrich and Hattenheim. Lists old vintages.
George Hill of Loughborough; Mayor Sworder & Co

Langenbach Large-scale producers whose wines include Black Tower Liebfraumilch. Now owned by a joint Allied-Lyons and Whitbread company.
Widely available

Liegenfelder, Weingut K & H Estate at the northern end of the Rheinpfalz.
Adnams; Alex Findlater; Fortnum & Mason; La Vigneronne

Loeb GmbH, Sigmund Exporter owned by O W Loeb in London (see *Where to Buy* section), dealing in high quality estate-bottled wines.
O W Loeb

Loosen-Erben, Weingut A Mosel estate with vineyards at Erden and Ürzig.
Berry Bros & Rudd; Alex Findlater; Fortnum & Mason; Gerard Harris; John Harvey & Sons; Oddbins

Müller GmbH, Rudolf Wine merchant and estate owner, based in Mosel–Saar–Ruwer, selling branded wines by the name of Bishop of Riesling.
Corney & Barrow; Davys of London; Fullers; Tanners

Müller-Scharzhof, Weingut Egon Old Saar estate making fabulous wines in good years.
Bibendum; Corney & Barrow; O W Loeb

Nagler, Weingut Dr Heinrich A small Rüdesheim (Rheingau) estate, still using casks for maturing the wine.
O W Loeb

Niederhausen-Schlossböckelheim, Verwaltung der Staatlichen Weinbaudomänen German state holdings in the Nahe producing some of the best wines from this region.
Lay & Wheeler

Pauly KG, Weingut Otto Mosel–Saar–Ruwer estate with holdings in Graach and Bernkastel, making wines of good quality.
Wizard Wine Warehouses

Pieroth, Weingut Weinkellerei, Ferdinand One of the largest wine merchants in Germany, specialising in doorstep sales of QmP wines to consumers by the 16-bottle case. Despite being sold direct, wines are generally expensive for what they are. Pieroth own a large number of subsidiary companies.

Plettenberg'sche Verwaltung, Reichsgräflich von A large Nahe estate, producing a wide range.
O W Loeb; Majestic; The Wine Society

Prum, Weingut J J One of the finest Mosel–Saar–Ruwer estates, with holdings all the way along the Middle Mosel.
Corney & Barrow; O W Loeb; Tanners; The Wine Society

Reh & Sohn, Franz Large wine merchant with some vineyard holdings in the Mosel–Saar–Ruwer, mainly exporting standard wines.
Augustus Barnett; some Co-op stores

Ress KG, Balthasar Family firm owning vineyards in the central Rheingau, including leaseholding of Schloss Reichhartshausen. Classic Rheingau wines, with specially commissioned label illustrations.
Richard Harvey Wines; Windrush Wines

Richter, Weingut Max Ferd Old-established family estate producing top quality wines from a 15-hectare estate. Eiswein a speciality.
Bibendum; Summerlee Wines

Riedel, Weingut Rheingau estate with vineyards in Hallgarten.
Alex Findlater

St Ursula Weingut and Weinkellerei Firm of wine merchants based in Bingen which make Goldener Oktober branded wines, and one of the few drinkable low-alcohol wines.
Rodney Densem Wines; Oddbins; Victoria Wine Company

Schloss Groenesteyn, Weingut des Reichsfreiherrn von Ritter zu Groenesteyn Estate founded in the 14th century concentrated around Rüdesheim on the Rheingau.
Berry Bros & Rudd; Eldridge Pope; Lay & Wheeler

Schloss Johannisberg Most famous name on the Rheingau, making wine from its 35-hectare estate in Johannisberg. Not to be confused with Bereich Johannisberg wines, which can come from anywhere in the Rheingau.
Alex Findlater; Hilbre Wine Company

Schloss Reinhartshausen Large estate of 67 hectares on the Rheingau, owned by descendants of the German Emperors. Holdings at Erbach, Hattenheim, Kiedrich, Rauenthal and Rüdesheim.
Berry Bros & Rudd; Eldridge Pope

Schloss Schönborn, Domänenweingut Rheingau estate with vineyards in Oestrich, Winkel, Rüdesheim, Geisenheim, Hochheim, Hattenheim, Johannisberg and Erbach.
D Byrne & Co

Schloss Vollrads, Graf Matuschka-Greiffenclau'sche Guterverwaltung Estate dating from the 12th century, still owned by the same family which has been very active in promoting dry wines for food. Makes some very fine wines.
Averys; Eldridge Pope; Alex Findlater; Hilbre Wine Company; Reynier Wine Libraries

Schloss Westerhaus Rheinhessen estate with vineyards in Ingelheim.
Alex Findlater

Schmitt, Weingut Hermann Franz Ancient family-owned estate in the Rheinhessen, whose main holdings are at Nierstein.
Morrisons

Scholl & Hillebrand One of the firms in at the founding of the Rheingau Charta group (see the beginning of this section). Their brand is called Riesling Dry, but they produce a range of fine estate wines.
Berry Bros & Rudd; Alex Findlater; Thos Peatling; J Sainsbury; Victoria Wine Company; La Vigneronne

Schubert'sche Gutsverwaltung, C von Ancient estate near Trier on the Ruwer, first mentioned in the 10th century, which produces great wines in good years.
S H Jones; Lay & Wheeler

Sichel Söhne GmbH Producers of Blue Nun, but also selling estate wines.
Widely available

Simmern'sches Rentamt, Freiherrlich Langwerth von A large Rheingau estate owned by the same family since 1464. Its vineyards are at Erbach, Hattenheim, Rauenthal and Eltville.
Lay & Wheeler

Simon, Bert A recently (1968) established estate with land at Serrig, Eitelsbach, Mertesdorf and Kasel, all in the Mosel–Saar–Ruwer.
Les Amis du Vin; Berry Bros & Rudd; Mayor Sworder & Co

Strub, Weingut J & H A 17-hectare estate in Rheinhessen, with land at Dienheim and Nierstein, including part of the famous Rheinterrasse (the slope facing the river) at Nierstein.
Eldridge Pope; Mount Bay Wine Co, Bread Street, Penzance, Cornwall

Wagner Dr Heinz Mosel–Saar–Ruwer estate making some interesting and unusual dry wines.
Alex Findlater

Weil, Weingut Dr R Estate with holdings in Kiedrich on the Rheingau.
Eldridge Pope; Alex Findlater

Best buys from Germany

WHITE

Bernkasteler Bratenhof Kabinett 1982, Reichsgraf von Kesselstatt (*Anthony Byrne Fine Wines*)

Kaseler Kehrnagel Riesling Auslese 1983, Reichsgraf von Kesselstatt (*Gerard Harris*)

Trierer St Mattheiser Riesling Spätlese 1983, Max Erben (*Averys of Bristol*)

Winkeler Hasensprung Riesling Kabinett 1983, Deinhard (*Christchurch Fine Wine*)

Riesling Dry, Deinhard (*Richard Granger*)

Trittenheimer Apotheke Riesling Kabinett 1986, Clüsserath-Weiler (*Peter Green*)

Gau Odernheimer Herrgottspfad Riesling Kabinett 1986, Grode Erben (*Wine Schoppen*)

Schloss Westerhaus Riesling Trocken QbA, Rheinhessen (*Alex Findlater*)

Sainsbury's Baden Dry (*J Sainsbury*)

Doktor Richter Riesling Halbtrocken (*Russell & McIver; Summerlee Wines*)

Dorsheimer Beerenauslese 1971, Weingut Dr Josef Höfer (*Douglas Henn-Macrae*)

Piesporter Michelsberg Riesling 1987, Hans Reh (*Wine House*)

RED

Grossgartacher Grafenberg Lemberger 1984, Heuchelberg
Kellerei (*Douglas Henn-Macrae*)

Specialist stockists

*Adnams; Berry Bros & Rudd; G E Bromley; D Byrne & Co;
Christchurch Fine Wine; Dennhöfer Wines; Eldridge Pope; Alex
Findlater; Findlater Mackie Todd; Peter Green; Gerard Harris;
Douglas Henn-Macrae; S H Jones; Justerini & Brooks; Lay &
Wheeler; O W Loeb; J Townend & Sons; A L Vose; Peter Watts
Wines; Wine House*

Greece

It is strange that Greek wines have not caught on more in this country. After all, enough of us visit the country each year. If the examples of France, Italy and Spain are anything to go by, returning holidaymakers should be beating a path to their wine merchants, demanding that they stock the Greek wine they enjoyed so much on holiday.

Or maybe not. Not, that is, if reports of the quality of taverna wine in Greece is anything to go by. Perhaps we prefer to forget – or buy beer or ouzo instead. It certainly seems that the abiding memory of Greek wines most people have is of retsina – the wine flavoured with resinated pine – which you either hate or love.

Apart from some good examples of this very acquired taste, there are only a few quality wines in the shops to show what Greece's potential could be if she decided that exporting wine seriously was worth it (something we doubt at the moment).

A series of controls has been applied to what was seemingly uncontrollable. Since entering the European Community in 1981, Greece has designated regional wines along the lines of the French AC and VDQS rules. There are now 28 of these, and a strange collection some of them make: all of the eight AC wine areas, for instance, produce only sweet wines. With two exceptions, the Greeks have simply delimited existing areas, but have added regulations about yields, grape varieties and sugar content.

Of these, it is the islands that produce some of the sweet dessert wines, made from the Malvasia and Muscat grapes. Samos makes the best-known Muscats, while Crete has a luscious Malvasia. Sweet red wines are a speciality of the Peloponnese, of which the Mavrodaphne of Patras is the most widely known.

And then there are the few quality estate wines. Much attention has recently been focused on the efforts of Greek tycoon John Carras who has flown in the famous Professor Peynaud from Bordeaux to advise on making a French-style wine in one of the Khalkidhiki peninsulas in northern Greece. Château Carras is the result, made from the Bordeaux grapes, and a very well made wine it is. The white Domaine Porto Carras, made from Sauvignon grapes, is less successful.

Equally interesting are two wines from the island of

Cephalonia: both prove that native Greek grape varieties can produce some decent wines if only somebody tries. John Calliga's two red wines (Monte Nero, made from Agioritiko grapes, and, especially, the Calliga Ruby (– don't be put off by the asymmetrical bottle) are wines that should begin to make us take Greece more seriously.

What's what in Greece

Brand, rather than company, names rule in Greece.

John Calliga Try his red Monte Nero and Calliga Ruby. The white Robola is less interesting.
Peter Green; Hicks & Don; Tanners

Château Carras This is the top wine produced by the Domaine de Porto Carras. Others, going under the name Côtes de Méliton, are a dry white Blanc de Blancs, Sauvignon, Grand Vin Blanc, Grand Vin Rouge. Some examples of the reds in this country are too old – the 1979 vintage still around tastes past it.
Booths; Celtic Vintners; Cumbrian Cellars; Hicks & Don; Market Vintners; Reid Wines; J Sainsbury; Ubiquitous Chip; Victoria Wine Company; The Wine Society

Mavrodaphne of Patras Sweet red wine, akin to the Reciotos of Italy, but not as good. A good example is made by Tsantali.
Cumbrian Cellars; Victoria Wine Company

Muscat of Samos Sweet dessert wines made from the Muscat grape on the island of Samos. The most widely available comes from the island's co-operative.
Cumbrian Cellars; Peter Green; Majestic; Oddbins; Tanners; Victoria Wine Company

Retsina Metaxas Produced by the firm which is best known for brandies. A good example of this style of wine.
Adnams

Retsina Attiki Another good example from Attica.
Thresher

Tsantali Lousy labels hide some tasty wines – there are fresh grapes there. Try Red Superb, Golden Delicious sweet Samos (no apples), Mavrodaphne, Naoussa.
Davenport & Son, The Courtyard, 52 Market Street, Ashby de la Zouch, Leics; Lees's Wine Shop, 21 High Street, Crediton, Devon; Sandra's Wine Shop, Market Precinct, Carmarthen, Dyfed

Best buys from Greece

WHITE WINES

Sainsbury's Retsina (*J Sainsbury*)
Mavrodaphne of Patras, Tsantali (*Cumbrian Cellar*)

RED WINE

Château Carras (if younger than 1979) (*Cumbrian Cellar; Hicks & Don; Nobody Inn; Reid Wines*)
Monte Nero 1981 (*Tanners*)
Calliga Ruby 1981 (*James Aitken & Son*)
Demestica, Achaia Clauss (*Peter Dominic*)

Specialist stockists

James Aitken & Son; Cumbrian Cellar; Peter Green

Hungary

Nothing changes

Very little seems to change on the Hungarian scene. Bull's Blood, the country's most familiar wine, gets less and less interesting all the time – it certainly wouldn't put heart into any 16th-century Magyar warriors now. Other wines continue on their commercially soft, slightly sweet, slightly dirty way.

It is only with Tokay that Hungary keeps herself firmly on the world's wine map. Tokay is one of the world's great dessert wines, and is still extremely good value for money as well as being a memorable wine: look for the top qualities of sweetness (Tokay Aszu 5 Puttonyos) or, justifiably more expensive, Tokay Aszu Essencia, which is made only from the free-run juice of grapes carrying noble rot.

All very sad, when we consider the potential that Hungary has for making highly enjoyable wines. She has at her disposal a range of grape varieties which could make some suitably fiery, peppery wines to go with her own cuisine; and a variety of wine climates and soils, some of which – especially around Eger (home of Bull's Blood) and Sopron on the Austrian border – should encourage good wine production.

Hungary has a long and proud tradition of winemaking, but we seem to be getting wines that are not as good as they were. Looking at it another way, we are getting wines which have been made to a marketing man's formula: the British like medium sweet wines, so that's what we will make for them. These turn out to be vaguely sweet white wines from the Welsch Riesling grape (absolutely no relation of the great Rhine Riesling of Germany), or slightly sweet – because soft and spineless – red wines made out of local grapes with unmemorable names and forgettable tastes.

The comparison must inevitably be with neighbouring Bulgaria, which has chosen the route of quality and value, bringing rich rewards. Hungary seemed to start out that way before Bulgarian wines reached us, but now has fallen by the wayside.

What's what in Hungary

The Hungarian language is like no other (apart, it seems, from Finnish). A useful rule of thumb is that place names tend to come with the suffix 'i', followed by the grape name.

Badasconi Quality wine district, producing mainly white wines, on the northern shore of Lake Balaton.

Balaton Wines from Lake Balaton, the Hungarian 'inland sea' which enjoys a favourable microclimate.

Egri Wine from the district of Eger in the north of the country. Source of the red Bull's Blood brand.

Furmint Hungarian white grape variety making crisp, clean, slightly peppery wines. Can be fresh, but too often dull.

Kadarka Red grape making a full-bodied, gutsy wine that goes well with stews.

Nagyburgundi (or **Kisburgundi**) A light, slightly peppery red, made from the Pinot Noir.

Somló Small district to the west of Lake Balaton. Furmint appears to be the grape most commonly grown here.

Sopron District on the border with Austria. Much of the wine is red, made either from the Kékfrankos grape or from a Hungarian version of the Gamay. In whites, look for wines from the Tramini (Gewürztraminer) grape, which have a rich, sometimes botrytised style.

Tokay The great dessert wine area in the east of Hungary (see above). Grapes are the Furmint, Hárslevelü and Muskotály. The top wines will keep for years, while others can be drunk straight from the shop. Some dry whites – Tokay Furmint and Tokay Szamorodni – are also made, but are rather flabby and dull.

Vilány Red-wine growing district south of Lake Balaton. Some wines made with Pinot Noir (here called Nagyburgundi or Kisburgundi – see above) can be good.

Best buys from Hungary

WHITE WINES

Tokay 5 Puttonyos (*Adnams; Berry Bros & Rudd; Peter Green; Harrods; Lay & Wheeler; Oddbins; Christopher Piper Wines; Tanners; T & W Wines; Victoria Wine Company; Willoughbys; Wines from Paris; The Wine Society; Wines of Westhorpe*)
Somló Furmint (*Peter Green*)

RED WINES

Vilány Kisburgundi (*Peter Dominic*)
Hungarian Merlot (*Asda; Wines of Westhorpe*)
Sopron Nagyburgundi (*Peter Dominic*)
Safeway Hungarian Merlot (*Safeway*)

Specialist stockist
Wines of Westhorpe

India

New wine country

Despite India's vast production of table grapes, only one Indian wine reaches us – and it's surprisingly good.

But it has French technology behind it. Omar Khayyam sparkling wine is the result of a joint venture by Indian entrepreneur Shyam Chougule with expertise imported from Champagne.

The wine, a more than adequate brut sparkling wine, made using Champagne technology, is not cheap, but it's definitely a wine to start a conversation going.

Adnams; Fortnum & Mason; Fullers; Oddbins; Majestic; Selfridges; Tanners; Willoughbys

Israel

The success of the Golan Heights wines remains the one shining example of Israel's potential as a wine-producing nation if the vineyard site is right and care is taken in production.

There, in a 400-acre vineyard that is growing on the site of a major battleground of the Yom Kippur war of 1973 – and from which 250 tank carcases had to be removed before planting could take place – they produce wines under the Yarden and Gamla brand names. Those available in this country include the white Yarden Mount Hermon white, cold fermented and fruity in the modern tradition; Gamla White, a medium dry wine, also modern and fruity; and varietal wines (by far the most interesting) – Gamla Cabernet Sauvignon and Yarden Sauvignon Blanc. While these wines are not cheap, at least they're good; and orthodox Jews can be reassured that they are made according to strict Kosher rules.

Best buys from Israel

Yarden Sauvignon Blanc (*various vintages from Grape Ideas and Harrods*)
Gamla Cabernet Sauvignon, Galilee (*various vintages from Grape Ideas; Harrods; Master Cellar Wine Warehouse; Nobody Inn; Victoria Wine Company*)

Specialist stockist
La Reserva Wines

Italy

A buzz of excitement is going around the Italian wine scene at the moment. It was particularly noticeable at last year's annual Verona Wine Fair, Vinitaly, which brings together producers from all over this hugely diverse country. Cheek by jowl, you can find the exhibitors from Piedmont, Tuscany, Sicily, even a few from Basilicata. It is difficult ever to say that Italians have anything in common, but this year they did share one feeling, at least: confidence.

Of course, not everything is right with Italian wines: plenty of producers are still making rather ordinary – even unpleasant – stuff, and some crazy decisions are still being made – more about these under the regional reports which follow. But when one of the major British supermarket wine buyers can report back to base that 'there are some stunning wines and excellent prices', he seems to be summing up what most people feel about Italy at the moment.

It was perhaps symptomatic of the luck that Italy is enjoying at the moment that a minor wine scandal in Piedmont (a producer had been adding ascorbic acid to some Dolcetto) was completely swamped by the Bergerac/Bordeaux scandal which broke in France at exactly the same time. The Italians weren't exactly rubbing their hands, but they weren't downhearted by this turn of events, either.

Conversation among the increasing band of exciting Italian wine producers now centres around such subjects as the concentration of the wine, the clones used to produce it, the latest wine release from a competitor, whether famous wine zones should be divided up into quality classifications. These are subjects suitable for an innovative wine country, not one which is in trouble.

The cloud on the horizon

Inevitably one small cloud on the horizon threatens to spoil this idyllic scene, one which the Italians must beware of it before it gets too big. That is the question of prices.

The traditional view of Italian wines in the British wine trade has been of cheap and cheerful plonk. It's a view still perpetuated in many Italian restaurants in Britain, where price is the determining factor, not quality. But, on the whole, wine

Italy – White Wines

Chardonnay
Gewürztraminer
Goldmuskateller
Müller–Thurgau
Pinot Bianco
Rhine Riesling
Sylvaner

Arneis
Asti Spumante
Gavi
Moscato d'Asti
Verbesco

Lugana
Pinot-based
sparkling wines

VAL
D'AOSTA

SOUTH TYROL
(ALTO
ADIGE/
TRENTINO)

LOMBARDY

Picolit
Pinot Grigio
Tocai del Piave
Tocai di Lison

FRIULI–
VENEZIA-
GIULIA

Bianco di Custoza
Chardonnay
Prosecco
Soave

PIEDMONT   Po

VENETO

EMILIA-
ROMAGNA

LIGURIA

Arno

Albana di Romagna

Bianco Vergine
della Valdichiana
Chardonnay
Galestro
Montecarlo
Pomino
Trebbiano
Vernaccia di San Gimignano

TUSCANY

Verdicchio

MARCHES

UMBRIA

Tiber

Bianco d'Arquata
Orvieto

LATIUM

ABRUZZI

Est! Est!! Est!!!
Frascati

MOLISE

SARDINIA

CAMPANIA

Locorotondo

APULIA

Fiano di Avellino
Greco di Tufo
Lacryma Christi

BASILICATA

CALABRIA

SICILY

Bianco di Alcamo
Moscato di Pantelleria

| 0 | 100 | 200 km |
| 0 | 50 | 100 miles |

Italy – Red Wines

Casteller
Lago di Caldaro
Lagrein
Santa Maddalena
Sorni
Teroldego
Valdadige

Barbaresco
Barbera
Barolo
Carema
Dolcetto
Ghemme
Grignolino
Nebbiolo
Spanna

Franciacorta
Oltrepò Pavese
Riviera del Garda Bresciano
Valtellina

Cabernet/Merlot di Friuli
Cabernet/Merlot di Pramaggiore
Colli Orientali del Friuli
Collio

Bardolino
Breganze
Colli Berici
Colli Euganaei
Lison–Pramaggiore
Piave
Valpolicella/Recioto di Valpolicella

VAL
D'AOSTA

SOUTH TYROL
(ALTO
ADIGE/
TRENTINO)

FRIULI–
VENEZIA-
GIULIA

PIEDMONT

LOMBARDY

VENETO

Po

LIGURIA

EMILIA-
ROMAGNA

Colli Bolognesi
Gutturnio dei Colli Piancentini
Lambrusco
Sangiovese di Romagna

Arno

TUSCANY

Rosso Cònero

Brunello di Montalcino
Carmignano
Chianti
Morellino di Scansano
Rosso di Montalcino
Vino Nobile di Montepulciano

MARCHES

Colli Altotiberini
Colli del Trasimeno
Montefalco
Torgiano

UMBRIA

Tiber

LATIUM

ABRUZZI

Montepulciano d'Abruzzo

Biferno

MOLISE

Castel del Monte
Salice Salentino

SARDINIA

Cannonau

CAMPANIA

Taurasi

APULIA

BASILICATA

Aglianico del Vulture

CALABRIA

Cirò

SICILY

0   100   200 km

0   50   100 miles

merchants are now becoming aware of the wide variety and value for money – not the same thing as cheapness – which Italian wines are currently providing.

But then we learn that since 1984 – the year it received the DOCG (of which more below) – Chianti has risen three-fold in price; Alto Adige wines, seen as terrific bargains only four years ago, now seem to be commanding quite high prices for what they are; 'designer' wines (the ones with pretty labels and expensive bottles) are a regular phenomenon in most areas.

Italians, we know, have suffered from high inflation. To get the quality in their wines, they have had to keep the yields from the vineyards down, with a consequent increase in the price of grapes. Labour costs are high (and so are the repayments on all the new equipment). But much of this is true of any vineyard area in the world. What makes Italy different at the moment is that the producers are trying to become like Bordeaux or Burgundy, not just in quality, but in price as well – and in five years rather than several hundred.

It's probably true that much good quality Italian wine has been too cheap. But if the Italian producers want to retain their new markets – and their new reputation – they should try and put the brakes on price increases and think in the long and medium term, rather than in the short (a hard thing to do in a country which lives by fashions and crazes).

Concentrating the wines

We've already mentioned that one of the topics of current conversation in Italian wine circles is the concentration of a wine, its depth of flavour. The greater the depth of flavour, the more likely is it that the producer has cut the yield from his vines down well below the legal requirements.

The yield from vines is a contentious issue in Italy. Late in 1988, there was a demand from some Valpolicella producers that the maximum legal yield should be increased. These producers' vineyards are on the flat plain, south of the true heartland of Valpolicella Classico. Nevertheless, they are making Valpolicella and their vines could produce more grapes than the present legal maximum, so if they could up their yields they could get more quick-and-easy cash from the local co-operative.

This had already been permitted in neighbouring Soave (and for the same reasons). But by the time the Valpolicella producers got wise to the idea, the authorities had, too. There were numerous representations from Italian wine organisations both in Italy and abroad. The gist of their argument was that Valpolicella was only just pulling itself out of the mire of two-litre screw-cap bottles: the results of increased yields – thin and weedy wines – would push it right back. Permission was refused.

Valpolicella is also in the middle of another – much more positive – debate. That concerns the question of vineyard classification. In the continuing quest for fashionable ideas, many Italian producers are making single vineyard wines, rather than just sticking all their grapes into a big vat and calling it plain Valpolicella, Barolo, or whatever, as they had done in the past.

Obviously, this trend applies particularly to estate-owning producers. But even merchants who buy in grapes are promoting particular vineyard sites. The reason for this promotion, of course, is that those particular sites happen to be good.

Now there are calls to regularise the roll call of these top vineyards and to have some form of classification of the best sites in a DOC or DOCG zone (see below for definitions of these initials). The idea makes sense in Barolo, where many producers now sell their best wines as single vineyard wines. It makes equal sense in Chianti, where there are suggestions that the different communes, with their different characters should receive individual recognition (see under Tuscany).

It is talk like this – with its general concern about how to apply the new-found general quality of Italian wine, rather than how to achieve that quality - that created the positive atmosphere at the 1989 Vinitaly. And, as always, figures prove that the quality message is getting through to us in Britain. We imported 17 per cent more Italian wine in 1988 than in 1987 – in a year when German imports fell, and those of Spain stagnated. If only the prices can stay right, that figure could easily be repeated over the next few years.

The Italian wine label

There are three quality designations in Italy:

Vino da tavola This can refer to the rock-bottom local wines or to the finest designer wines from a top producer which do not conform to the DOC or DOCG regulations.

Denominazione di Origine Controllata (DOC) This indicates that the wine comes from a specified zone and has been made in accordance with the rules of that zone. It is like the French AC in that it is a guarantee of origin only, not of quality.

The name of the DOC may appear in a number of ways: as a geographical name for a region (Frascati); as the name of a village (Barolo); or it may appear as a grape variety attached to a geographical name (Barbera d'Asti – wines made from the

Barbera grape in the town of Asti). It may appear as a combination of geographical name and a fantasy name (Oltrepò Pavese Buttafuoco – Oltrepò Pavese the geographical name, Buttafuoco the fantasy name). Occasionally, the name may be sheer fantasy (Est! Est!! Est!!!).

Denominazione di Origine Controllata e Garantita (DOCG)
This is the top Italian controlled quality level. The 'garantita' part of the title means that the wine has been tested by government-appointed officials and conforms to the rules they have set out. It applies to six areas, five reds and one white: Barolo, Barbaresco, Brunello di Montalcino, Vino Nobile di Montepulciano, Chianti, and the white Albana di Romagna.

With the accession of Albana di Romagna (a relatively undistinguished wine from Emilia-Romagna) to the canon of DOCG, there was much grumbling about the way the DOCG was being put into disrepute, particularly as it was beginning to prove its worth with the five red wines (especially in improving the quality of Chianti and Vino Nobile). So now the whole system is in abeyance until more realism – and fewer politics – reigns.

Other terms on the label

Abboccato: Medium sweet.
Amabile: A little sweeter than Abboccato.
Amaro: Bitter.
Annata: Year or vintage.
Azienda agricola, azienda vitivinicola: Farm or wine estate.
Bianco: White wine.
Bottiglia: Bottle.
Cantina: Winery.
Cantina Sociale: Co-operative.
Casa vinicola: A wine house, usually one which buys in grapes to make wine.
Chiaretto: Rosé.
Classico: The heartland of a particular region, not necessarily – but generally – where the best wines of a particular type come from.
Consorzio: A voluntary grouping of producers to control standards of production.
Dolce: Sweet.
Etichetta: Label.
Fattoria: Central Italian term for farm or estate.
Fermentazione: Fermentation.
Frizzante: Lightly sparkling.
Imbottigliato da: Bottled by.

Invecchiato: Aged.
Metodo champenois/metodo classico: The Champagne method.
Passito: Strong, generally sweet wines made from semi-dried grapes.
Produttore: Producer.
Riserva: Applied to DOC or DOCG wines that have undergone specific ageing, generally in barrel. Riserva Speciale means even longer ageing.
Rosato: Rosé wine.
Rosso: Red wine.
Secco: Dry.
Spumante: Sparkling wine, usually, but not always, sweet.
Superiore: A DOC wine that meets higher standards (alcohol, ageing, area of production) than the norm.
Tenuta: Another word for farm or estate.
Vecchio: Old.
Vendemmia: The year of the harvest.
Vigna, vigneto: Vineyard.
Vino novello: New wine (as in Beaujolais Nouveau).

Italian vintages

Most Italian white wines (unless they are matured in wood) are designed for immediate consumption, so comment on vintages here refers only to red wines.

1988 A small harvest throughout Italy. In Piedmont, rain may have spoiled the harvest for red wines, but Moscato wines like Asti are delicious. In the Veneto, there is average to good quality. In Tuscany and Friuli, the quality is very high. The dry summer meant very low quantities – and also poor quality – in southern Italy.

1987 The vintage was at its best in Piedmont, with lighter wines like Dolcetto and Barbera, but Barolos and Barbarescos were patchier. In the Veneto, the vintage was average to good for Valpolicella and other regional reds. In Chianti, some good-to-average wines were made, the first of which are ready for drinking now. Quality was good in the south.

1986 Very good in Piedmont, excellent in Chianti and the Veneto, above average for Brunello and Vino Nobile di Montepulciano. Another vintage – certainly in Tuscany – for relatively early drinking.

1985 A superb year all round. After dreadful winter frosts which had killed huge swathes of olive trees in Tuscany, the vines came through to make some of the best wines of the decade. The Chianti Riservas are just coming on stream, but they and all Barolos and Barbarescos need plenty of time yet.

1984 A disaster of a vintage after the wettest summer for years. Only in the Veneto was anything approaching quality produced. If buying '84s, check very carefully on the producer's track record.

1983 These are the Chianti Riservas to drink in 1990. In Piedmont and in the Veneto, the wines are quite forward, and not for keeping, but for fruity enjoyment now.

1982 A big year. High quality from the best producers in Tuscany and Piedmont, with some wines needing years to emerge from their wood and tannin tastes. The Veneto was much worse off, and should be avoided unless the producer's name guarantees some quality.

Other vintages in **Tuscany** to watch for: 1981, 1979, 1978, 1977.
Other vintages in **Piedmont** to watch for: 1980, 1978, 1974, 1971.
Other vintages for **Recioto della Valpolicella**: 1979, 1978, 1977.

PIEDMONT

Value and fruit

There are probably better value red wines to be had from Piedmont than from any other Italian wine region at the moment. To many, that may come as a surprise, considering the (justifiably) high cost of the Nebbiolo-based Barolo and Barbaresco. But they seem to be making better and better wine all the time from two other grapes, the Dolcetto and the Barbera, high-yielding workhorse varieties.

What the producers are doing is bringing out the fruitiness of these wines. At one time even Dolcetto seemed to lurk behind a mask of wood tannin. Now the freshness and attractiveness of this grape, Italy's answer to Beaujolais, is plain for all to see. Even the Barbera, which seemed once to have more acidity than fruit, is being allowed to blossom with rich flavours.

The increasing emphasis on fruit is also being seen in some Barolos and Barbarescos. There is much discussion in Piedmont about the new style (emphasising the fruit and leaving the wine in wood for a relatively short time) and the old (leaving the wine in wood for five or so years and then a couple more for luck). The new style makes wines that mature more quickly, but if you are prepared to wait for ten years or so, the old style can provide great experiences.

What's what in Piedmont

RED AND ROSÉ WINES

Barbaresco Nebbiolo-based wine from three villages near Alba. Long-lived wines, if less powerful and more accessible than those from neighbouring Barolo.

Barbera The grape lends its name to a number of wine towns. Look especially for Barbera d'Asti (soft, full and rounded), Barbera d'Alba (rich and long-lived) and Barbera del Monferrato (the lightest of the three).

Barolo Considered by many as Italy's finest red, traditional Barolo needs years to mature. More modern styles exhibit the complex violet and truffles fruit of the Nebbiolo grape.

Brachetto Usually sparkling red wines, with a Muscat-like taste, but can also be still.

Carema Mountain vineyards producing Nebbiolo-based wines which can be elegant; they need five or six years from the vintage.

Dolcetto The fruitiest wine of Piedmont. It attaches its name to those of villages: look out for Dolcetto d'Alba and Dolcetto d'Asti (the lighter of the two), and the lesser-known but richer Dolcetto di Diano d'Alba.

Freisa Another sparkling red wine.

Gattinara Medium-lived red from the Vercelli hills, based on Nebbiolo (called here Spanna).

Ghemme Another Nebbiolo wine, this can also be blended with Bonarda to make small quantities of elegant wine.

Grignolino Generally a light, rosé.

Nebbiolo The great grape of the region is also found in the name of wines. Look for Nebbiolo d'Alba and Nebbiolo del Piemonte (the lesser of the two).

Spanna The Nebbiolo is called Spanna around Novara, where it makes good value everyday wines, with some exceptional quality as well.

WHITE WINES

Arneis Small production of rich, and complex wine from the Roeri hills north of Alba.

Favorita Very dry, light wine from the Langhe hills near the Barolo vineyards.

Gavi Highly priced and fashionable wine, also known as Cortese di Gavi. Gavi dei Gavi is the top wine.

Moscato Delicious sweet still and sparkling (spumante) wines. The most familiar is Asti Spumante, but Moscato d'Asti often produces better wines.

Verbesco A wine from red grapes (Barbera) which are vinified to make a white (by avoiding skin contact) rather in the manner of Champagne. Fizzy and of little interest.

Who's who in Piedmont

(For details of Asti Spumante and Moscato Spumante producers not also making still wines, see the Sparkling wines section on page 640.)

Fratelli Alessandria Good value Barolo producers. Wines: Barolo Vigneto Monvigliero.
Willoughbys; Wine Growers Association

Altare Make non-DOC wines in the Barolo region, using small French barriques for ageing. Wines: Nebbiolo Vigna Arborina, Barbera Vigna Larigi.
Winecellars

Ascheri Rich, powerful Barbaresco which still manages to preserve the fruit.
Valvona & Crolla; Winecellars

Duca d'Asti Wide-ranging company with a large portfolio of wines: Barbaresco, Barbera d'Asti, Barbera del Monferrato, Cortese di Gavi, Dolcetto d'Ovada, Nebbiolo d'Alba; Granduca Brut sparkling.
Berry Bros & Rudd; Eaton Elliot Winebrokers; Oddbins; Tesco; Waitrose; The Wine Society

Giacomo Borgogno e Figli Renowned producers of Barolo, specialising in old vintages. Wines: Barbera d'Alba, Barolo, Dolcetto d'Alba.
A&A Wines; selected Asda stores; David Alexander; Averys; Chaplin & Son; Eldridge Pope; Lay & Wheeler; Millevini; Tanners; Valvona & Crolla; Wine Growers Association; Winecellars

Agostino Brugo Good examples of the Nebbiolo in their Ghemme and Gattinara wines. Wines: Ghemme, Gattinara, Spanna.
David Alexander; Eldridge Pope; Lay & Wheeler; Millevini; Oddbins; Seckford Wines; Valvona & Crolla; Victoria Wine Company; Wine Growers Association

Castello di Neive Produce small amounts of fine Barbaresco, also very good white wines. Wines: Barbaresco, Barbera d'Alba, Dolcetto d'Alba, Moscato d'Asti, Arneis.
Alex Findlater; Martinez Fine Wine; Millevini; Valvona & Crolla; La Vigneronne; Winecellars; Wines from Paris; Wine Schoppen

Fratelli Cavallotto Own the renowned Bricco Boschis vineyard in Barolo. Wines: Barbera d'Alba, Barolo, Dolcetto d'Alba, Favorita, Grignolino, Nebbiolo.
Market Vintners; Valvona & Crolla; Winecellars; Wines from Paris

Ceretto A producer of ripe, fruity, plummy Barolos in a fresher, less traditional style. Top quality, especially for single vineyard wines (called bricco). Wines: Barbaresco, Barbera d'Alba, Barolo, Dolcetto d'Alba, Nebbiolo d'Alba. Try Barolo Bricco Roche and Barbaresco Asiy.
Berry Bros & Rudd; Corney & Barrow; Laytons; The Wine Society

Pio Cesare Traditional producer making very fine wines. Wines: Barbaresco, Barbera d'Alba, Barolo, Dolcetto d'Alba, Nebbiolo d'Alba, Grignolino, Gavi, Cortese di Gavi.
Alex Findlater; La Vigneronne; Willoughbys

Aldo Conterno Makes Monforte d'Alba and Barolo Bussia Soprana and Colonello di Bricco Bussia. Look out especially for his Dolcetto. Wines: Barbera d'Alba, Barolo, Dolcetto d'Alba.
H Allen Smith; Tanners; Winecellars

Giacomo Conterno Makes a single vineyard Barolo Monfortino. Very traditional, heavy wines: Barbera d'Alba, Barolo, Dolcetto d'Alba.
Valvona & Crolla; Winecellars

Guiseppe Contratto Specialises in spumante (sparkling) wine. Wines: Asti Spumante, Contratto Brut, Riserva Bacco d'Oro, Gavi.
Only available through restaurants. For further information contact Belloni & Co Ltd, Belloni House, Albert Street, Parkway, London NW1

Cordero di Montezemolo Small estate in La Morra. Wines: Barolo Enrico VI, Barolo Monfalletto.
Millevini; Winecellars

Carlo Deltetto Makes some attractive white wines. Wines: Favorita, Gavi, Arneis.
Winecellars

Luigi Ferrando e Figli Producers of pricy Carema Black Label, of marvellous quality.
D Byrne & Co; Cadwgan Fine Wines; Millevini; Valvona & Crolla; Winecellars

Fontanafredda An estate founded by the son of King Victor Emmanuel II. Make fine spumante as well as accessible Barolo. Some of their single vineyard Barolos are excellent, if pricy. Wines: Asti Spumante, Barbaresco, Barbera d'Alba, Barolo, Dolcetto d'Alba, Brut Spumante Contessa Rosa.
H Allen Smith; D Byrne & Co; Classic Wine Warehouse; Peter Dominic; S H Jones; Frank E Stainton; Upper Crust; Valvona & Crolla; La Vigneronne; Wizard Wine Warehouses

Franco-Fiorina Believers in stainless steel rather than oak who buy in grapes. Wines: Barbaresco, Barbera d'Alba, Barolo, Dolcetto d'Alba, Nebbiolo d'Alba.
Valvona & Crolla

Gaja The guru of Piedmont who makes the most expensive and some of the finest, if most controversial, Barbarescos. Wines: Barbaresco, Barbera d'Alba, Dolcetto d'Alba, Nebbiolo d'Alba, Vinot, Chardonnay, Cabernet Sauvignon.
Adnams; Valvona & Crolla; La Vigneronne

Bruno Giacosa Fine aged reds, including single vineyard wines. Wines: Barbaresco, Barbera d'Alba, Barolo, Dolcetto d'Alba, Grignolino d'Alba, Nebbiolo d'Alba, Arneis, Moscato d'Asti.
Barwell & Jones

Marchese di Barolo A long-established firm, recently sold by its founding family. Wines: Asti Spumante, Barbaresco, Barbera d'Alba, Barolo, Cortese di Gavi, Dolcetto d'Alba, Freisa d'Alba, Nebbiolo d'Alba.
Valvona & Crolla

Mascarello Producer of top quality Barolo Monprivato.
Thos Peatling; Winecellars

Luigi Nervi e Italo Make reasonably quick maturing Gattinara.
Lay & Wheeler

Pasquera-Elia Producer of some superbly fruity Barbaresco, Dolcetto and the rare Roero.
Winecellars

Alfredo Prunotto Traditional style of wine and single vineyard Barolo. Wines: Barbaresco, Barbera d'Alba, Barolo, Dolcetto d'Alba, Nebbiolo d'Alba.
Cantina Augusto

Renato Ratti Rich but also elegant wines. Minimum ageing in cask ensures good fruit. Wines: Barolo Marcenasco, Dolcetto.
Adnams; Tanners; The Wine Society

Terre di Barolo A large co-operative which makes a lighter style of wines. Wines: Barbera d'Alba, Barolo, Dolcetto d'Alba, Dolcetto di Diano d'Alba, Nebbiolo d'Alba.
D Byrne & Co; Davisons; Ubiquitous Chip; Victoria Wine Company

Vietti Make wines for drinking young, as well as some more serious wines for ageing. As many as possible of their wines are from designated vineyards. Wines: Barbaresco, Barbera d'Alba, Barolo, Dolcetto d'Alba, Nebbiolo d'Alba, Freisa, Moscato d'Asti.
Chiswick Wine Cellars

Villadoria Large-scale producer of commercial wines. The Barberas are best.
For further information contact Fiandaca, 78 Chandos Crescent, Edgware, Middx

Best buys from Piedmont

For Sparkling wine best buys, see page 21.

Barbaresco 1983, Arione (*Millevini*)
Barbaresco 1984, Pasquero (*Winecellars*)
Spanna del Piemonte 1987, Brugo (*Wine Growers Association*)
Spanna del Piemonte 1986, Dessilani (*Wine Emporium*)
Dolcetto d'Alba 1987, Ascheri (*Oddbins; Winecellars*)

LOMBARDY

More interest than there was

The commercial heartland of Italy, as well as one of its richest agricultural provinces, Lombardy tended until recently to feature low on the list of interesting wine regions. It has certainly not reached the top of the list yet, but there's much more interest – and quality and value – than there was. Wine growing is spread through the region, from the mountainous northern half to the Apennine foothills in the south. Inevitably, the wide Po Valley in the middle produces almost nothing of any note.

Where's where in Lombardy

Franciacorta Zone on the southern edge of the Alps north of Brescia where both still and sparkling whites based on Pinot Bianco and Pinot Nero, Pinot Grigio and Chardonnay are produced. There are finer reds, made mostly of the unusual combination of Barbera, Cabernet Franc, Nebbiolo and Merlot. Can be very good in the right hands.

Lugana Fresh-tasting white wine from the southern shores of Lake Garda. Similar in style to Soave, but often better value.

Oltrepò Pavese In the south-west of the region, this area is home to some of Italy's top sparkling wines (made from Pinot Grigio and Pinot Nero as well as some Chardonnay) and to a range of varietal reds made from Barbera and the local Bonarda (rustic, bitter cherries fruit). Also look for the red bubbly, Buttafuoco.

Riviera del Garda Bresciano A large zone on the western shore of Lake Garda making red and rosé for early drinking.

Valtellina Right in the north of Lombardy, near Switzerland, this zone makes reds mainly from Nebbiolo. Valtellina Superiore is better wine, with fearsome names like Grumello, Inferno, Sassella and Valgella.

Who's who in Lombardy

Ca' del Bosco Producer of very fine Chardonnay-based spumante, also Franciacorta. Wines: Franciacorta Pinot, Franciacorta Rosso, Rosa Ca' del Bosco sparkling.
Valvona & Crolla; Winecellars

Enologica Valtellinese Very fine Valtellina wines. Wines: Grumello, Sassella, Inferno, Sforzato.
Winecellars; Wine Growers Association

Fugazza, Castello di Luzzano The Fugazza sisters make excellent Oltrepò Pavese wines on their organically run vineyard. Part of the vineyard is just in Emilia-Romagna and so makes Gutturnio. Wines: Oltrepò Pavese Bonarda, Oltrepò Pavese Barbera, Colli Piacentini (Emilia-Romagna).
Millevini; Oddbins; Valvona & Crolla; Wine Growers Association; Wines from Paris; Winecellars

Longhi-de Carli A Franciacorta producer using Cabernet, Merlot, Nebbiolo and Barbera. Wines: Franciacorta.
Asda; Millevini; Winecellars; Wine Growers Association

Nino Neri Makes wine in Valtellina. Wines: Sassella, Inferno, Grumello.
D Byrne & Co; Ostlers

Santi Soave producer who also makes Lugana.
D Byrne & Co; Classic Wine Warehouse; Tanners; Upper Crust; Valvona & Crolla; Wizard Wine Warehouses

Zenato Producer of Lugana and Riviera del Garda as well as Soave.
H Allen Smith; Davisons; Arthur Rackhams; Tanners; Threshers; Waitrose; Winecellars

Best buys from Lombardy

For Sparkling wine best buys, see page 21.

WHITE

Tocai di San Martino della Battaglia 1988, Zenato (*Davisons*)

RED

Valcalepio Rosso 1985, Tenuta Castellodi Grumello (*Millevini*)
Ronco di Mompiano 1985, Pasolini (*Winecellars*)
Franciacorta Rosso 1986, Contessa Martinoni (*Alistair's Grapevine; City Wines*)
Bonarda Oltrepò Pavese, Luzzano (*Peter Green*)

TRENTINO

The beginning of the Mediterranean

Trentino is the northern outpost of Italy. Travellers coming south over the Brenner Pass go through the essentially German Südtirol before bursting through a narrow gorge and into the wider plain of the Trentino, where Italy – and the Mediterranean – take over.

In the past few years, this region has seemed to be in the shadow of the more go-ahead Alto Adige (Südtirol). But it makes an interesting range of wines in its own right, with standards as high as those of its neighbour just up the Adige Valley. Judging by the efforts its local wine trade is making, we may see more of its wines in the shops quite soon. It does, however, suffer from the same fault as the Alto Adige: high yields, which can make many of the more ordinary wines seem distinctly thin and uninteresting.

Where's where in Trentino

While most wines in the Trentino are named after grape
varieties, there are a number of DOC zones. Trentino DOC is
region-wide, and produces red, white and rosé wines.

Then there are a number of smaller DOC zones: Sorni (for
whites), Teroldego Rotaliano (red and rosé), Valdadige (red,
white and rosé) and Casteller (red).

The main grape varieties found in the Trentino include:

Whites: Chardonnay, Pinot Bianco, Pinot Grigio, Müller-
Thurgau, Riesling Renano, Riesling Italico, Moscato Gaillo, and
the local grape, Nosiola.

Reds and rosés: Lagrein, Pinot Nero, Merlot, Cabernet Franc,
Cabernet Sauvignon, Schiava, and the local specialities,
Teroldego and Marzemino.

Trentino is also famed for its sparkling wines, most made by
the Champagne method, and some of world-class quality. For
more details of these, see the Sparkling wines section on
page 640.

Who's who in Trentino

Càvit The main Trentino co-operative, making 70 to 77 million
litres of wine a year. Quality tends to vary widely; the
Chardonnay and Teroldego Rotaliano wines are best. Wines:
Casteller, Teroldego Rotaliano, Vicariati (a premium red made
from Cabernet Franc and Merlot), Valdadige, Chardonnay, Pinot
Grigio.
Majestic; Victoria Wine Company; Wine Society

Fedrigotti A 75-acre family-owned vineyard south of Trentino.
Their top wines are both vini da tavola. Wines: Cabernet and
Merlot Trentino; Foianeghe Bianco and Rosso Vini da Tavola.
Millevini; Wine Growers Association

Gaierhof A small estate at the northern end of the region.
Wines: Riesling Italico, Pinot Bianco, Pinot Grigio, Müller-
Thurgau, Teroldego Rotaliano, Caldero, Schiava.
Majestic; Waitrose

Pojer & Sandri Top producer in Trentino specialising in white
wines. Wines: Chardonnay, Müller-Thurgau.
Alex Findlater; Valvona & Crolla; Winecellars

Stockists given in *italic* type after wines in this section will be found in
the WHERE TO BUY section earlier in the book.

Santa Margarita Large producer who also makes wine in other regions. Good, commercial standards. Wines: Valdadige Bianco and Rosso.
Valvona & Crolla

Roberto Zeni Trento winemaker specialising in Teroldego Rotaliano. Wines: Chardonnay, Teroldego Rotaliano.
Millevini; Tanners; Valvona & Crolla; Wine Growers Association

Best buys from Trentino

Pinot Grigio Ca'Donini (*Valvona & Crolla*)
Teroldego Rotaliano 1986 Ca'Donini (*Gare du Vin*)

ALTO ADIGE

It's still there

We don't seem to be hearing as much about the Alto Adige (or the Südtirol as many of the locals call it) as we did four or five years ago. Then it was the flavour of the year as we discovered the fresh, tangy, varietal white wines, and the strange tastes of the reds. Since then, some of those producers have not made the headway in Britain everybody expected, while others have become so much a part of our everyday wine scene that we just take them for granted.

One of the problems was that we were spoilt by the superb 1984 vintage for white wines. That was the year the Alto Adige really took off. It was followed by wines from the fatter, less zesty 1985 vintage, and our interest slackened. Quantities of the 1986 vintage were low and prices started to rise. Fashion moved on to Australia, and the Alto Adige took a back seat.

There has also been some concern about the yields from some vineyards, which are extraordinarily high by Italian standards, and nearer to German levels. It has been suggested that the high yields decrease the concentration and fruit flavours of the wines, but better producers are cutting down on the yields and producing piercingly fragrant white wines.

But we should not forget this northernmost Italian region, more German than Italian, which produces white wines from German grape varieties, in an Italian - in other words dry – way. The analogy with Alsace in France is the most obvious. They have also moved into Chardonnay (and more recently Sauvignon Blanc) production in a big way, and with both the unoaked and the newer generation of barrique-aged Chardonnays, they are coming up with some finely delicate and fruity wines.

Where's where in the Alto Adige

While we are more familiar with the white wines, 70 per cent of production is red, much of it exported to Switzerland and Austria in tanker loads, very little to other parts of Italy.

Although Alto Adige wines are all labelled varietally, the labels can sometimes be confusing, because they are mainly in German rather than Italian. They may describe themselves as Qualitätswein rather than DOC. Only the small print, Produce of Italy, will show that they are not from Austria or Germany.

There are a number of DOCs in the region, most of them based on the grape variety. Thus you get Alto Adige Cabernet, Alto Adige Chardonnay, Alto Adige Riesling Renano (Rhine Riesling), and so on. There are 19 different varietals under this general DOC.

There are also more localised wines.

Caldaro/Kaltersee A red quaffing wine from south of Bolzano.

Goldmuskateller A vino da tavola, made in small quantities, with a true muscat smell and taste.

Santa Maddalena/Sankt Magdalener Once rated by Mussolini as one of Italy's three greatest wines (along with Barolo and Barbaresco), this is more prosaically a dry, rounded wine from Bolzano, made from the local Schiava/Vernatsch grape.

Valle Isarco/Eisacktaler Northernmost end of the region, near the Brenner Pass, producing mainly varietally labelled white wines. Look for Sylvaner and Müller-Thurgau.

Who's who in the Alto Adige (Südtirol)

Arunda Makes brut spumante high up in the Alps of the Alto Adige. One of the finest Italian sparklers. Wines: Arunda Brut. *H Allen Smith*

J Hofstätter Some of his wide range of wines – especially reds – age remarkably well. Wines: Pinot Grigio, Rhine Riesling, Gewürztraminer, Schiava, Cabernet Sauvignon. *Wine Society*

Kettmeir Makes the full range of varietal Alto Adige wines. Now part of the Santa Margherita company (see below). *Valvona & Crolla*

Alois Lageder Family-owned company making a wide variety of wines in the Alto Adige. One of the top two producers of the region. Wines: Chardonnay, Moscato (sweet), Pinot Grigio,

Sauvignon, Gewürztraminer (from the village of Tramin, claimed to be the home of this grape), Schiava, Cabernet Franc.
Berry Bros & Rudd; Eldridge Pope; Oddbins; Christopher Piper Wines; Winecellars

Santa Margherita Firm based in the Veneto which has considerable interests in the Alto Adige, including the Kettmeir company (see above). Makes a top quality white vino da tavola called Luna dei Feldi.
Valvona & Crolla; Willoughbys

J Tiefenbrunner One of the two top Alto Adige producers, Tiefenbrunner is proud owner of the highest vineyard in Europe, called Feldmarschal, planted with Müller-Thurgau. Look for his barrique-aged wines. Wines: makes every varietal in Alto Adige, all of very high quality.
Adnams; H Allen Smith; Hungerford Wine Company; S H Jones; Millevini; Tanners; Valvona & Crolla; Willoughbys; Whitesides of Clitheroe

Viticoltori Alto Adige The main co-operative of the Alto Adige, with very high standards. There are associated co-operatives at St Michael in Eppan and Terlan. Wines: Sauvignon, Gewürztraminer, Rhine Riesling, Chardonnay, Pinot Bianco, Lagrein Dunkel, Cabernet Franc, Schiava.
A&A Wines; Peter Dominic; G Hush; Lay & Wheeler; Tanners; Ubiquitous Chip; Valvona & Crolla; Wine Growers Association

Best buys from Alto Adige

Chardonnay di Appiano 1988, Cantina Sociale di Appiano (*Wine Growers Association*)
Pinot Grigio Kettmeir 1988 (*Chiswick Wine Cellar*)

VENETO

Source of innovation

While still producing much wine that is mediocre, the home of the terrible two - Soave and Valpolicella – is also the source of much innovation, and some wine styles that are uniquely Italian.

The good producers in the western Veneto are busy fighting a rearguard action to save the name of what have become synonymous with industrialised grape juice. The problem has been the rapid expansion of the vineyard areas, particularly of Soave and Valpolicella, on to the plains and away from the hillsides which were the traditional vineyard areas. This has resulted in a huge increase in production, so that today, for instance, the old heartland of Soave produces only 25 per cent of the total. The plains produce wines from high-yielding vines (at 220 hectolitres per hectare, they are well above the DOC maximum of only 98 hectolitres per hectare – but nobody stops them producing at that rate), which have lost character and only achieved cheapness.

Luckily that heartland is still recognisable on the label of the wine: look for the word Classico, and there will at least be some guarantee of quality (the same goes for Valpolicella, where another useful word to look for is Superiore). It is really only in the last few years that we have become aware that some producers are still making quality wines – some of them world-class. We have seen a growth of interest in single vineyard wines, here as in the rest of Italy and we have watched the development of super vini da tavola.

We have also learned about the great Veneto contribution to Italian winemaking - the Reciotos, which come from both Valpolicella and Soave. The Valpolicella Reciotos are huge red wines made from partly dried grapes. Deep, rich, bitter tasting when dry – called Amarone – or smooth and creamy in their sweet version, Amabile, they are some of the finest red wines of Italy. Rarer, but equally exciting, are the sweet white Recioto Soaves, made in the same way.

Where's where in the Veneto

The Veneto is not just Soave and Valpolicella – in the UK we are beginning to discover many more DOCs right round the region (of course we have known some – like Bardolino, for a long time).

Bardolino Often seen as poor man's Valpolicella, this actually has a lighter, fresher, early-drinking style all its own. Also attractive as a rosé, when it is known as Chiaretto.

Bianco di Custoza A near neighbour of Soave, producing wines that are often more reliable than run-of-the-mill Soave, at only slightly higher prices.

Colli Berici This area, south of Vicenza, makes seven varietal wines (including Pinot Bianco, Tocai Italiano, Merlot, Pinot Noir).

Breganze To the north of Vicenza, Breganze also makes varietal wines, including, unusually, good Pinot Nero and Bianco (based on Tocai Friuliano). Look too for Cabernet Franc and Merlot.

Colli Euganaei This area near Padua makes seven types of varietal wine, of which the best are Cabernet, Rosso (Cabernet, Merlot, Barbera and Reboso) and Pinot Bianco.

Gambellara White wine zone east of Soave, producing wines of a similar, if lighter, style.

Lison-Pramaggiore A DOC area that combines Tocai di Lison and the Cabernet and Merlot di Pramaggiore. Twelve different wines (including the very dry Verduzzo) are produced in this flat plain north-east of Venice.

Piave Big DOC area north of Venice producing the usual range of varietals. Look especially for red Raboso.

Prosecco Produces sparkling wines in the Valdobbiadene, which are made in quantity but not always quality.

Who's who in the Veneto

Allegrini Old-fashioned family firm. Excellent Valpolicella and Amarone. Wines: Valpolicella Classico Superiore, Recioto Amarone.
Alex Findlater; Market Vintners; Martinez Fine Wine; Oddbins; Valvona & Crolla; Winecellars; Wine Schoppen

Anselmi One of the top Soave producers. Wines: Soave, Recioto di Soave, Soave Capitel Croce. Vino da tavola: Capitel Foscarino (Soave-style wine aged in oak), red Realda (Cabernet Sauvignon).
Anthony Byrne Fine Wines; Oddbins; Valvona & Crolla; Winecellars

Bertani Traditional family company specialising in old Valpolicella Amarone. Wines: Bardolino, Soave, Valpolicella, Valpolicella Recioto.
The Great Northern Wine Company; Harrods; S H Jones; Selfridges; Tanners

Bolla Well-established company whose wines are widely available in Britain. Look for single vineyard Soave (Castellaro) and Valpolicella (Jago Bolla). Wines: Soave, Valpolicella, Bardolino, Amarone.
Chiswick Cellars; Valvona & Crolla

Boscaini A family firm with increasingly exciting wines, now also specialising in single vineyards wines. Wines: Soave, Valpolicella, Bardolino, single vineyard Soave (Cantina di Monteleone), single vineyard Valpolicella (Vigneti di Marano)

and single vineyard Bardolino (Tenuta Le Cane). Red super vino da tavola, Le Cane.
A&A Wines; Berry Bros & Rudd; Safeway; Seckford Wines; Ubiquitous Chip; Wine Growers Association; Wines from Paris; Winecellars

Maculan High quality wines from Breganze. Look for sweet white Tercolato, and a new Chardonnay. Wines: Breganze Cabernet, Rosato Tercolato.
Adnams; D Byrne & Co; Alex Findlater; Tanners; Winecellars

Masi One of the best Valpolicella and Soave producers. Also associated with Boscaini. Wines: Bardolino, Soave, Valpolicella, Amarone. Also single vineyard wines (Serego Alighieri is a fine Valpolicella), red super vino da tavola (Campo Fiorín) and white (Masianco).
Adnams; D Byrne & Co; Alex Findlater; Oddbins; Christopher Piper Wines; Tanners; Valvona & Crolla; Winecellars; Wines from Paris

Pieropan Often reckoned to be the finest Soave producer. He makes a number of single vineyard Soaves as well as a wider blend. Taste his wines, and Soave will never be the same. Wines: Soave and Recioto Soave.
Adnams; Eaton Elliot Winebrokers; Alex Findlater; Millevini; Oddbins; Valvona & Crolla; Winecellars; Wine Schoppen; Wines from Paris

Portalupi Producer of Bardolino and rosé Chiaretto. Another who sets the standards against which other Bardolino producers must be marked.
Adnams; Bibendum; Alex Findlater; Market Vintners; Millevini; Oddbins; Thos Peatling; Valvona & Crolla; Winecellars

Giuseppe Quintarelli Traditional firm making small amounts of high quality wines. Their Reciotos are sensational. Wines: Valpolicella Recioto Amabile and Amarone.
Adnams; Winecellars

Santa Margherita The large merchant house is based in the Lison area and makes a number of wines under this DOC, as well as Piave and Prosecco.
Peter Dominic; Valvona & Crolla

Santa Sofia Sound quality wines from around Lake Garda. Wines: Bianco di Custoza, Soave, Valpolicella, Bardolino.
Eaton Elliott Winebrokers; Majestic

Santi A medium-sized producer of Soave.
D Byrne & Co; Upper Crust; Waitrose; Willoughbys

Tedeschi A specialist in Recioto-style wines, and some top quality vini da tavola. Wines: Bianco di Custoza, Soave, Valpolicella, Bardolino, Recioto, Capitel San Rocco super vini da tavola white and red.
A&A Wines; Adnams; David Alexander; Harrods; G Hush; Lay & Wheeler; Millevini; Oddbins; Seckford Wines; Valvona & Crolla; Wine Emporium; Wine Growers Association

Venegazzù-Conte Loredan-Gasparini The Loredan family are descendants of Doges of Venice and the wines still sport the Doge's cap of office on their label, although the firm is now owned by a businessman. Produce highly reputed vini da tavola, although standards of recent vintages seem more variable than they should be. Wines: Venegazzù della Casa, Venegazzù Etichetta Nera (Cabernet Sauvignon), Venegazzù Rosso; sparkling Venegazzù Prosecco Brut.
D Byrne & Co; Alex Findlater; Peter Green; Millevini; Frank E Stainton; Tanners; Valvona & Crolla; La Vigneronne; Willoughbys

Zenato Makes very good whites around Lake Garda, plus Valpolicella. Good value. Wines: Soave, Valpolicella, Bianco di Custoza.
Davisons; Arthur Rackhams; Tanners; Waitrose; Winecellars

Best buys from Veneto

WHITE

Soave Classico 1988, Guerrieri-Rizzardi (*widely available*)
Soave Classico Superiore 1987, Anselmi (*Summerlee Wines*)
Bianco di Custoza, Portalupi 1987 (*Cadwgan Fine Wine Merchants*)
Soave Classico Monte Tenda, Tedeschi (*Oddbins*)
Safeway Pinot Grigio 1987 del Triveneto (*Safeway*)

RED

Bardolino Classico 1986, Guerrieri-Rizzardi (*widely available*)
Valpolicella Classico Superiore Vigneti di Jago, Bolla
(*G E Bromley*)
Valpolicella Classico Superiore 1986, Vigneti Marani, Boscaini
(*Safeway*)

Find the best new wine bargains all year round with our newsletter, *Which? Wine Monthly*, available for just £19 a year from: Dept WG90, Consumers' Association, FREEPOST, Hertford SG14 1YB – no stamp is needed if posted within the UK.

FRIULI–VENEZIA–GIULIA

Taking notice again

Suddenly, we're beginning to take notice of what's going on in this far north-eastern outpost of Italy. We're discovering producers whose wines far outshine what we already knew, and we're realising that here is a new area waiting to be discovered.

Or rediscovered, we should say. We knew their wines some years ago, and those from one or two producers have always been around. But they seemed to fade a little – the quality wasn't as good, perhaps, or, more likely, we found out about the Alto Adige and forgot about Friuli.

There are certain similarities between the two regions. Both are frontier regions, once part of the Hapsburg Empire and before that of the Venetian Republic. Their wine traditions are different from the rest of Italy. Their insistence on varietal labelling is the same – and this certainly helps us to find our way around. As with the Alto Adige, Friuli uses German and French grapes as well as Italian varieties, and even has one all its own.

But the Friuli producers are also following trends in other parts of Italy: the single vineyard wines are an example, as is the use of barriques for some white as well as red wines.

What they are producing is interesting – and getting more so each year. But while there are claims that the region makes Italy's best white wines, we would prefer to say that they make some of Italy's most reliable white wines – and the same also goes for the reds. What the wines lack is the tingle of excitement buzzing around in some other regions – the Veneto or Tuscany – where the range of quality from the best to the worst is much wider, but where the peaks are higher as well.

Where's where in Friuli–Venezia–Giulia

There are two levels of DOC: the wide regional one (Grave del Friuli), and the smaller ones for more specific areas. The five DOC areas to look out for are Collio Goriziano, Colli Orientali del Friuli, Collio, Grave del Friuli and Aquileia. Collio and Colli Orientale are generally reckoned to be the best. They all have a range of grape varieties which can carry the DOC designation.

The whites that can do this are Tocai, Traminer, Pinot Bianco, Pinot Grigio, Riesling Italico, Verduzzo and the new imports of Sauvignon and Riesling Renano (Rhine Riesling). The rare

Picolit, making a sweet wine, is less often seen than talked about.

In the reds, Cabernet Franc and Merlot make reliable, good value wines, provided they are not over-cropped. Also look out for some examples of Pinot Nero (Pinot Noir) and the local Refosco, which often makes the most interesting wines.

Who's who in Friuli–Venezia–Giulia

Collavini Wines from the Collio and Grave del Friuli. Look out for their unusual white Ribolla and red Schioppettino, both local grape varieties. Wines: varietals from Grave del Friuli and Collio. Also a good cheap sparkler, Il Grigio.
A&A Wines; Lay & Wheeler; Millevini; Pimlico Dozen; J Sainsbury; Valvona & Crolla; Victoria Wine Company

Giovanni Dri Wines from Colli Orientali. Look especially for Verduzzo di Romondolo (a dessert wine) and Refosco.
Valvona & Crolla

Livio Felluga Wines from both Collio and Collio Orientale del Friuli. Look for some of their single vineyard wines.
Valvona & Crolla

Gradnik Wines from the Collio DOC area, with great varietal character and intensity. All 12 varietals are made, but look especially for the Tocai.
Cadwgan Fine Wines; Millevini; Valvona & Crolla

Silvio Jermann Internationally recognised wines from the Collio DOC. Also makes some top-class vini da tavola. Look for the Moscato Rosa and Vintage Tunina.
Millevini; Valvona & Crolla; Winecellars

Fratelli Pighin New firm which has already established a reliable reputation. Wines: varietals from Collio Goriziano and Grave del Friuli. One of the best Picolits.
Valvona & Crolla; Waitrose

Russiz Superiore Makes wines in the Collio DOC area. Wines: varietals from Collio.
David Baillie Vintners; Corney & Barrow; Harrods; Lay & Wheeler; Laytons; Winecellars; Yorkshire Fine Wines

Mario Schiopetto Collio producer making the full range of varietals. Look for his Tocai and Pinot Bianco.
Valvona & Crolla; Winecellars

Tenuta Ca' Bolani Estate in Aquileia owned by the Zonin family. Look for their Tocai Friuliano.
Willoughbys; Winecellars

Volpe Pasini Clean, true-to-type wines from the Colli Orientali. *Windrush Wines*

Best buys from Friuli-Venezia-Giulia

Pinot Grigio Isonzo 1987, Angoris (*Cantina Augusto*)
Refosco Calunghetta 1986 (*Moffat Wine Shop*)

TUSCANY

One grape, many names

Hands up those who know the connection between Sangiovese di Lamole, Brunello, Prugnolo Gentile and Sangiogheto? The answer – for those who are a little unsure – is that they are all clones of the Sangiovese vine, and they all grow in Tuscany. Add to that the Sangiovese di Romagna, and it seems that the Sangiovese – the Chianti grape that some reckon has the greatest potential for world-class status of any Italian variety – is proving pretty elusive to pin down.

The search is on in Tuscany for the best Sangiovese to make the best wines. Not – as it was in the 1960s – the best

Sangiovese to make as much wine as possible (that proved to be the inferior Sangiovese di Romagna). Quality, not quantity, is what they are talking about in Tuscany today.

What is particularly interesting at the moment is that the talk of quality seems more and more centred on Sangiovese, and that Cabernet Sauvignon, at a time heralded as the salvation of Tuscany, is being put on one side. A sigh of relief is going up that the threatened internationalisation of Tuscan wines has been avoided. They are going for a strictly Italian solution.

The chance to make that solution work has never been better in Tuscany. For a start, Chianti is now fetching prices that were undreamt of a few years ago, when to most people it was the wine that came in wicker flasks. The advent of DOCG in 1984 has meant a considerable fall in the total production of Chianti and – on the whole – a great increase in quality.

So now there is the money to carry out the replanting programme necessary in many of Chianti's vineyards which were last planted in the 1960s. The opportunity to replant these vineyards with the highest quality clones of Sangiovese will mean that many of the problems which have beset the Tuscan vineyard for the past 20 to 25 years (low quality and high yields being the main ones) will be a thing of the past.

On top of the choice of clones, there is now much talk in Tuscany about viticultural regions. There are discussions, for instance, in Chianti Classico (the heartland zone of Chianti, home of many of the finest estates) about the differences between the communes and the need for some sort of village categorisation. The experts suggest, for instance, that Castellina and Radda in the southern Classico zone produce much richer, longer-lived wines than those in the northern part of Classico around Greve – and that these differences should be recognised on the label and in the bottle.

But as Chianti gets more quality-conscious, an awful lot of wine is left which can only be declassified to basic vino da tavola (not to be confused with the super vini da tavola – see below). There is much talk in Chianti of a second, lesser wine, with a DOC to control its quality, but, as is the way in Italy, not too much action.

However, there are good examples in the other two Tuscan DOCG zones. In Montalcino, the second wine of the famed (and often too heavily wood-aged) Brunello is the much more approachable Rosso di Montalcino. In Montepulciano, the junior partner to the greatly improved Vino Nobile is Rosso di Montepulciano, which saw life for the first time with the 1988 vintage – so it is too early to say how this will turn out. But the principle in both cases is sound – and is something which should be emulated in Chianti as well.

While we traditionally associate Tuscany more with reds than with whites – after all, there is no white Chianti – things are looking up on the white scene as well. Galestro, a modern-style wine from some of the top Chianti houses, is proving a considerable success. And of course every producer now thinks he (or she) ought to make a Chardonnay-based wine. But there are still neglected areas of white wine production. One of them is the Vernaccia di San Gimignano, often a maligned wine because of the usual problems of over-production in the vineyard, but in the hands of the right producer, a deliciously nutty, almondy-fresh wine. And over in Montepulciano, the producers who no longer use their white grapes as part of the blend of the red wine have developed a Bianco Vergine della Valdichiana, which is a pleasant if undemanding drink.

And if this is not enough, there is the clutch of super vini da tavola. Every self-respecting estate, especially in Chianti Classico, makes one: Antinori's Tignanello and Solaia, and Incisa della Rochetta's extremely expensive Cabernet Sauvignon Sassicaia or Vinattieri, another 100 per cent Cabernet Sauvignon wine. Others in this group include Prima Vigna from Castello Vicchiomaggio, Sangioveto di Coltibuono, Palazzo Altesi of Altesino, Ser Niccolò of Serristori, Ghiaie della Furba of Capezzana, Coltassala of Castello di Volpaia – and many others. And while many of the producers have used varying quantities of Cabernet Sauvignon in their wines, they are increasingly returning to the virtues of the Sangiovese to produce truly Tuscan wines.

There's also a new grouping of super vini da tavola from some estates, under the name Predicato. These producers make their vini da tavola following certain rules. These include low yields from vineyards at least 150 metres above sea level, earliest release dates for the wines, and tastings by fellow members of the group before the wines can be described as Predicato. Members of the group include top houses such as Antinori, Frescobaldi and Ruffino. The name Predicato is followed by a village name, such as Predicato di Cardisco, Predicato di Biturica. Red and white wines are being made using Cabernet Sauvignon, Chardonnay, Pinot Bianco and Sauvignon as well as Italian grape varieties.

What's what in Tuscany

RED WINES

Brunello di Montalcino The top Tuscan wine, made from the Brunello grape, commanding high prices and great esteem. It needs many years to mature, due particularly to the way in which it is aged in wood – often, some would say, for too long.

Carmignano Small area to the south-west of Florence recognised as the world's oldest controlled zone (from 1716). The wine is a superior Chianti, with some Cabernet in the blend.

Chianti An enormous area, stretching from the hills south of Pisa to the border south of Arezzo. It is divided into a number of zones: Chianti Classico and Chianti Rufina are generally considered the best; Chianti Colli Fiorentini, Chianti Montalbano and Chianti Lucchesi come next in rank; while Chianti Colli Aretini and Chianti Colline Pisani rank as the lightest and shortest-lived. All, however, have the DOCG denomination.

Morellino di Scansano New DOC in the hills near Grosetto in southern Tuscany. It shares with Brunello di Montalcino the distinction of being the only Tuscan red which may be made entirely from Sangiovese grapes. The quality is good and improving.

Rosso di Montalcino The second wine of Brunello di Montalcino (see above).

Rosso di Montepulciano The second wine of Vino Nobile di Montepulciano (see below).

Vino Nobile di Montepulciano Made from Prugnolo Gentile (a clone of Sangiovese), this wine has had its ups and downs over the past years, but is now improving splendidly, aided by professional winemaking and better production methods. And still the prices are good value.

WHITE WINES

Bianco Vergine della Valdichiana From south-east Tuscany, much of this wine comes from Montepulciano producers, with some of the better ones making quite an enjoyable wine.

Galestro New-style white made by some of the top Chianti producers. Low in alcohol (for an Italian wine), it relies on high technology for its production.

Montecarlo Zone east of Lucca making wines which include Sémillon, Pinot Bianco, Pinot Grigio, Sauvignon, Vermentino and Roussanne in the blend to give character to the Trebbiano.

Pomino White wine area in Chianti Rufina, based on Pinot Bianco and Chardonnay with some Trebbiano.

Vernaccia di San Gimignano Traditional white, made in the hill town of San Gimignano, which used to be golden in colour and designed for ageing, but is now cleaner, fresher, sometimes wood-matured, and more acceptable to the modern palate.

Vin Santo Tuscany makes the incomparable Vin Santo, a
Sherry-style wine but unfortified, of great character and interest.
A few examples are available:

Villa di Vetrice (*Valvona & Crolla; Winecellars*); Frescobaldi
(*Christopher & Co; S H Jones; Valvona & Crolla*); Capelli (*Harrods;
The Wine Society*); Antinori (*Cantina Augusto; Valvona & Crolla*);
Montellori (*Camisa Delicatessen, Old Compton Street, London W1;
Luigi's Delicatessen*).

Who's who in Tuscany

Altesino Make some fine Brunello di Montalcino. Wines:
Brunello; super vini da tavola: Palazzo Altesi, Alte d'Altesi.
H Allen Smith; Valvona & Crolla; La Vigneronne; Winecellars

Antinori One of the great names of Chianti. Makes Chianti and
fine vini da tavola like Tignanello. A new Chianti Classico is
Peppoli. Also makes some of the best Orvieto (see under
Umbria). Wines: Chianti Classico, sparkling Brut, Tignanello,
Solaia, Galestro.
*H Allen Smith; Berry Bros & Rudd; Direct Wine Shipments;
Alex Findlater; Lay & Wheeler; Laytons; Majestic; Oddbins;
J Sainsbury; Tanners; Thresher; Unwins; Valvona & Crolla;
Winecellars; Wine Society; Yorkshire Fine Wines*

Argiano Brunello di Montalcino producer whose cellars are in a
spectacular crumbling castle. Wines: Brunello di Montalcino,
Rosso di Montalcino.
Peter Dominic

Avignonesi Producer of some of the best and longest-lived Vino
Nobile di Montepulciano; super vini da tavola: Il Marzocco, Grifi.
*Berry Bros & Rudd; Laytons; Arthur Rackhams; Reid Wines;
Valvona & Crolla; Waitrose*

Badia a Coltibuono Expensive Chianti Classico producer who
seems to be having problems maintaining quality. Wines:
Chianti Classico Riserva, Chianti Classico; super vino da tavola:
Sangioveto di Coltibuono.
D Byrne & Co; Alex Findlater; Valvona & Crolla; Winecellars

Biondi-Santi (Il Greppo) The godfathers of Brunello di
Montalcino – they invented it. Their wines command enormous
prices, not always justified by the quality.
Valvona & Crolla; Willoughbys

Tenuta Caparzo One of the currently top two or three Brunello
di Montalcino producers. Wines: Rosso di Montalcino, Brunello
di Montalcino.
Valvona & Crolla; Winecellars

Tenuta di Capezzana One of the most important producers in Carmignano DOC, of which this estate was the creator. Wines: Carmignano, Barco Reale; super vino da tavola: Ghiaie della Furba.
Peter Dominic; Alex Findlater

Castelgiocondo Large producer of Brunello di Montalcino. A more modern style – with lesser prices – than Biondi-Santi (see above). Wines: Brunello di Montalcino, Rosso di Montalcino.
S H Jones; Valvona & Crolla

Castellare A producer of high quality Chianti Classico; super vino da tavola: I Sodi di San Niccolo.
Valvona & Crolla; Winecellars; Wine Growers Association

Castello di San Polo in Rosso Chianti Classico made by one of the best winemakers in Tuscany. Ought to be great, but sometimes disappoints; super vino da tavola: Centinaia.
H Allen Smith; Demijohn Wines; J Sainsbury

Castello Vicchiomaggio Fine winemaking, bringing together modern and traditional methods. Wines: Chianti Classico; super vino da tavola: Prima Vigna; also new, modern-style white and oak-aged white.
James Aitken & Son; David Baillie Vintners; Great Northern Wine Company; S H Jones

Castell' in Villa Rounded, rich style of Chianti Classico, especially good in Riservas; super vino da tavola: Santa Croce.
Tanners; Turl Wine Vaults, Turl Street, Oxford

Castello di Volpaia Top estate based around a hilltop village. Wines: Chianti Classico; super vini da tavola: Coltassala (Sangiovese), Mammolo (aged in small barrels).
Adnams; Eaton Elliot Winebrokers; La Vigneronne

Luigi Cecchi Producer of considerable quantities of rather undistinguished Chianti, much of which is sold under own labels. The estate wine is better: Villa Cerna.
Budgens; Fullers

Col d'Orcia Brunello producer now owned by Cinzano. Wine: Brunello di Montalcino.
Barwell & Jones

Fattoria Selvapiana Chianti Rufina producer, whose wines tend to leanness and austerity. Single vineyard Vigna Bucerchiale.
Winecellars

Fontodi Chianti Classico estate in the heart of the region. Wines: Chianti Classico; super vino da tavola: Flaccianello.
Wine Society

Frescobaldi Long-established firm (since the 13th century) producing all their wines from their own estates. Wines: Chianti Rufina (Nipozzano, Montesodi), Chianti Classico, Pomino Chardonnay, sparkling brut, rosé, Galestro, Vin Santo.
Adnams; D Byrne & Co; Alex Findlater; Gare du Vin; Lay & Wheeler; Nobody Inn; Christopher Piper Wines; Selfridges; Unwins; Valvona & Crolla; Winecellars

Grati Producers in Chianti Rufina, making some good value wines. Wines: Chianti Rufina Poggio Galiga, Villa di Monte.
Bibendum; D Byrne & Co; Winecellars

Isole e Olena Small, high quality Chianti Classico producer; super vino da tavola: Borro Cepparello.
Haynes Hanson & Clark; Valvona & Crolla; La Vigneronne; Winecellars

Mellini Large producer in Chianti Classico. Makes some single vineyard wines. Wines: Vernaccia di San Gimignano, Chianti Classico, Brunello di Montalcino, single vineyard Chianti (La Selvanella and Granaio). Super vino da tavola: I Coltri (Sangiovese and Cabernet Sauvignon).
Chiswick Cellars; Valvona & Crolla

Pagliarese Makes good commercial quality Chianti Classico, and very fine Riservas. Wines: Chianti Classico, Cipresso del Cucco (very fresh wine from young vines).
David Alexander; Oddbins; Seckford Wines

Poggio Antico Modern-style Brunello di Montalcino; also Rosso di Montalcino.
Valvona & Crolla

Poliziano Producer of top Vino Nobile di Montepulciano. Wines: Vino Nobile, Chianti; super vino da tavola: Elegia.
Valvona & Crolla

Le Pupille Producer of Morellino di Scansano, the new high quality DOC from south-west Tuscany.
Alex Findlater; Oddbins; Valvona & Crolla; Winecellars

Ricasoli The Baron Ricasoli was the inventor of modern Chianti in the 19th century. While the estate has had its ups and downs (more downs recently), it is getting better. Wine: Chianti Classico.
D Byrne & Co; Majestic; Millevini

Rocca della Macie Superb fruity Chianti Classico, designed to be drunk in two or three years at good value prices. Wines: Chianti Classico, Chianti Classico Riserva; white, Numero Uno.
Widely available

I L Ruffino Large scale producer with a very fine Chianti Classico Riserva. Wines: Chianti Classico, Riserva Ducale, Torgaio, Galestro.
Peter Dominic; Morrisons; Safeway; Whiteside's of Clitheroe

San Felice Big, full-bodied wines from south-east Chianti Classico near Castelnuovo Berardenga. Wines: Chianti Classico, Chianti Classico Riserva, Il Grigio.
Valvona & Crolla

San Quirico Producer of classic Vernaccia di San Gimignano.
J Sainsbury; Thresher; Wine Growers Association

Sassicaia The Marchesi Incisa della Rocchetta makes this legend-in-its-lifetime 100 per cent Cabernet Sauvignon from unlikely wine country south of Livorno. Small quantities of highly priced wines.
Harrods; Lay & Wheeler; Laytons; Selfridges; Tanners; Yorkshire Fine Wines

Conti Serristori The property includes the house where Machiavelli lived in exile. Wines: Chianti Classico, Riserva Machiavelli; super vino da tavola: Ser Niccolò; white wine, I Pianacci.
Chiswick Cellars; Davisons

Teruzzi e Puthod Currently regarded as the best Vernaccia di San Gimignano producer. Look also for the wood-aged white Terre di Tufo.
Valvona & Crolla; Winecellars

La Torre Good quality Vernaccia di San Gimignano.
(Case sales only) Giordano Ltd, 28/40 Windmill Street, London, W1

Val di Sugo Brunello di Montalcino which is approachable reasonably early. Wines: Brunello, Rosso di Montalcino.
Marks & Spencer

Villa Banfi Highly successful firm of Riunite (producers of Lambrusco) have branched into Montalcino with a huge estate mainly designed for sparkling Moscato wines, but also a little red. Wines: Brunello di Montalcino, Rosso di Montalcino, Chianti Classico.
Augustus Barnett; Anthony Byrne Fine Wines; D Byrne & Co; Alex Findlater; Oddbins; Valvona & Crolla; Willoughbys

Villa Cafaggio Chianti Classico producer with a 28-hectare estate. Makes a rich style of wine.
Marks & Spencer

Vinattieri A red vino da tavola, made from Sangioveto and Brunello grapes and aged in French oak, with high quality results. (A white is also made, which comes from the Südtirol/ Alto Adige.)
Bibendum

Best buys from Tuscany

WHITE

Galestro Rocca delle Macie 1986 (*Millevini*)
Vin Santo della Toscana, Lucignano (*Demijohn Wines*)
Galestro 1987, Antinori (*David Baillie Vintners; Direct Wine Shipments*)

RED

Chianti San Vito 1987 (*Vinceremos*)
Sangioveto del Borgo, Carlo Citterio (*Bibendum*)
Chianti 1987, Fattoria dell'Ugo (*Pimlico Dozen*)
Chianti Classico Santa Cristina 1987, Antinori (*Smedley Vintners*)
Chianti Classico Castell'in Villa 1983 (*Whighams of Ayr*)
Chianti Rufina Banda Blu, Grati (*Ellis Son & Vidler; Winecellars*)
Rosso di Montalcino 1987, Altesino (*Oddbins*)
Ser Gioveto, Rocca delle Macie 1986 (*Valvona & Crolla*)
Chianti Rufina Remole 1987, Frescobaldi (*Celtic Vintner; Upper Crust*)
Chianti Classico Riserva 1982, Castello di San Polo in Rosso (*J Sainsbury*)
Vino Rosso di Massaciuccoli 1987, Seidler (*Vintage Roots*)
Rosso di Montalcino, Villa Banfi 1985 (*J E Hogg*)

EMILIA–ROMAGNA

Not just Lambrusco

While this region is best known for the ubiquitous Lambrusco, there are patches of more serious winemaking on the hills away from the flat Po Valley.

Emilia–Romagna is also home to a fascinating agricultural experiment that may change the face of vineyard management. Integrated Pest Management (or, in Italian, Lotta Integrala) is a scheme which aims to reduce the use of chemicals in the war against vineyard pests by prevention rather than cure. It's a bold move, started in the 1970s, when few people thought in Green terms - and, even more encouraging, it is proving successful. By 1990, 50 per cent of Emilia–Romagna's vineyards and orchards will come under the scheme.

Where's where in Emilia–Romagna

Albana di Romagna White DOCG area of uneven quality, based in the hills south of Forli. The grape is the Albana, which can – in the right hands – make some peachy sweet wines as well as more neutral dry wines.

Colli Bolognesi Just south of Bologna, this zone makes red and white wines from Barbera, Cabernet Sauvignon, Merlot, Pinot Bianco, Riesling Italico and Sauvignon.

Colli Piacentini Area in the south-west of the region, bordering on the Oltrepò Pavese area of Lombardy. Makes red wines from Barbera, Bonarda and Pinot Nero, with Gutturnio a blend of Barbera and Bonarda. Whites planted include Chardonnay, Malvasia, Sauvignon.

Lambrusco The Coca Cola of Italy, made from the Lambrusco grape, normally found in a sweet version, but it can also be dry (more traditional and more interesting). The DOC zones are Lambrusco di Sorbara (the best), Lambrusco Salamino di Santa Croce, Lambrusco Reggiano, Lambrusco Grasparossa di Castelvetro. Cheaper Lambrusco is non-DOC and can come from outside Emilia–Romagna.

Sangiovese di Romagna The red partner to Albana di Romagna, generally producing straightforward quaffing wine, occasionally hitting greater heights.

Trebbiano di Romagna Neutral white wine, with only modern clean vinification to justify buying it.

Who's who in Emilia–Romagna

Cantine Romagnoli Good quality Gutturnio. Wines: Gutturnio dei Colli Piacentini.
Valvona & Crolla

Castello di Luzzano The Fugazza family (who also make Oltrepò Pavese on the other side of the hill) make top quality Gutturnio in the Colli Piacentini DOC. Super vino da tavola: Sagitarrio (from Bonarda).
Millevini; Valvona & Crolla; Wine Growers Association; Wines from Paris

Cavacchioli Makes top quality dry Lambrusco (various DOCs); also white Lambrusco.
D Byrne & Co; Oddbins; Wine Growers Association

Fattoria Paradiso Good quality red Sangiovese wines, and the best white Albana di Romagna. Look also for the unique – and beefy – red Barbarossa (from grapes only found in this vineyard). Wines: Sangiovese di Romagna, Barbarossa, Albana di Romagna.
Millevini; Valvona & Crolla

Pasolini Fruity, good value Sangiovese. Wines: Sangiovese di Romagna, (white) Trebbiano di Romagna.
Gerard Harris; Harrods; Michael Menzel; André Simon Wines

La Stoppa Colli Piacentini producer making fine Chardonnay, Sauvignon and Pinot Nero. Super vino da tavola: Macchiona (Barbera and Bonarda blend).
Winecellars

Best buys from Emilia-Romagna

Sangiovese di Romagna Conavi (*Cantina Augusto*)
Safeway Lambrusco dell'Emilia (*Safeway*)

THE MARCHES

Getting serious

Things are looking up all round in the Marches, the coastal region which takes in some of Italy's most popular seaside resorts. Away from the hot sandy beaches, they are making impressive improvements to the region's most famous Verdicchio – and coming up with some fine reds as well.

Once upon a time all we knew about Verdicchio was that it came in a funny-shaped bottle (like an amphora) and went hand in hand with Soave and Frascati as Italy's bulk-produced (and eminently forgettable) white wines. Now a new note of seriousness has crept in. Barrique-ageing, single vineyard wines, all the attributes of the Italian new wave are to be found here. And the results show that there is more to Verdicchio than the bottle (less and less used anyway now), and that perhaps its traditional reputation as a perfect seafood partner is justified.

The red of the region, Rosso Cònero, has suddenly stopped being just another red made from the Montepulciano grape – of which there are so many on Italy's east coast. Again, just as with Verdicchio, producers are suddenly coming out with really exciting wines, some from single vineyards (here they're called

Vigneti). They shouldn't be left around too long, though – three to five years is ideal.

What's what in the Marches

Rosso Cònero Red, made from the Montepulciano grape in vineyards on Monte Cònero near Ancona. From a fairly ordinary base, the top wines are improving all the time.

Verdicchio Two main areas make white wine from the Verdicchio grape: the larger Verdicchio dei Castelli di Jesi (look especially for wines from the Classico zone) and the smaller Verdicchio di Matelica.

Who's who in the Marches

Bianchi Make a delicious Rosso Cònero. Wines: Rosso Cònero, Verdicchio.
D Byrne & Co

Bucci One of the Verdicchio producers who uses a Burgundy bottle for his wine. The weight and quality seems to reflect the change in bottle shape. Wine: Verdicchio dei Castelli di Jesi.
Michael Menzel; Pimlico Dozen; Wine Growers Association

Colle del Sole The brand name of the main Verdicchio co-operative. Wines: Colle del Sole, Coste del Molino, Monte Schiavo – all Verdicchio.
Chiswick Cellars; A H Colombier; Grape Ideas; Arthur Rackhams; Waitrose

Fazi-Battaglia The inventors of the amphora bottle, but they, too, seem concerned to improve the quality. Wines: Titulus Verdicchio dei Castelli di Jesi, Rosso Cònero.
Berry Bros & Rudd; Alex Findlater; Haynes Hanson & Clark; Hungerford Wine Company; Stapylton Fletcher; Tanners; The Wine Society

Marchetti Weighty, comparatively long-lasting Rosso Cònero. Wines: Rosso Cònero, Verdicchio.
H Allen Smith; Valvona & Crolla

Mecvini Well-balanced Verdicchio from a private producer, plus good straightforward Rosso Cònero.
Barwell & Jones

Pagliano Producer of Verdicchio from the smaller region of Matelica. Wines: Verdicchio di Matelica.
Time for a Drink, 182 Kingston Lane, Teddington, Middx

Umani Ronchi Good quality wines which have suddenly shot ahead in quality. Look especially for their single vineyard wines. Wines: Verdicchio dei Castelli di Jesi, Rosso Cònero (single vineyard San Lorenzo), vino da tavola Cumaro; also use brand name CaSal di Serra.
Peter Dominic; Fulham Road Wine Centre; Millevini; André Simon Wines; Valvona & Crolla; Wine Emporium; Winecellars

Best buys from the Marches

Verdicchio dei Castelli di Jesi Classico 1988, Bucci (*Wine Growers Association*)
Rosso Cònero 1982, Vigneto San Lorenzo, Umani Ronchi (*Oddbins; Wizard Wine Warehouses*)

UMBRIA

The forgotten grape varieties

Umbria is the attractive backwater of central Italy: few big cities, miles of rolling green hills and a magical light that derives from lack of pollution. There are patches of wine production going on right round the region, isolated from each other, all doing their own thing.

It's hardly surprising, therefore, to find two grape varieties in Umbria which have been almost ignored and forgotten, but which are now being used to transform two DOC areas into something rather interesting.

The most familiar wine of Umbria is the white Orvieto. Dominated by the ubiquitous and boring Trebbiano grape, it used to be dull and flabby, and is – even now – too often just neutral and clean. But in the permitted blend there is one grape variety – the Grechetto – which is now being used in super vini da tavola and which shows just how good Orvieto can be if the Grechetto is given its head. Antinori's Cervaro della Sala is a blend of 25 per cent Grechetto and 75 per cent Chardonnay, a heady mixture, fermented in barrels – a new star wine. The same is true of Bigi's Marrano, which is 100 per cent Grechetto.

The other change which has shown up the promise of Orvieto is the development of single vineyard wines, and both Bigi and Antinori have released some top-notch wines from their own estates.

Across the hills in the centre of Umbria, south of Assisi, can be found the other unappreciated grape of the region. This is a red wine grape – the Sagrantino – rich, tannic, intense. It is used in the DOC of Montefalco Rosso, and also in the sweet red Sagrantino Passito, which is made from dried grapes.

One of the great catalysts in Umbria has been Lungarotti who dominates the Torgiano red DOC near Assisi. He seems to have overcome old problems with varying quality between bottles, and now his standard Rubesco di Torgiano is a well-crafted wine. Look also for his single vineyard white and red and his Riserva wines, which set very high standards.

What's what in Umbria

Bianco d'Arquata White made just south of Perugia from Grechetto and Trebbiano grapes. Made famous by one producer, Adanti.

Colli Altotiberini New DOC from the north of region, making red, rosé and white wines. The reds, from Merlot and Sangiovese, are best.

Colli del Trasimeno Both red and white wines from a large area around the shores of Lago di Trasimeno. Not much of a reputation yet.

Montefalco Two DOC zones in the mountains near Foligno, of which the inky-black (and sometimes sweet) Sagrantino di Montefalco is better than the Montefalco Rosso.

Orvieto This wine nearly went the way of Soave and others, but its reputation is being revived by attention from some good producers. Both sweet (abboccato) and dry (secco) styles are made – the sweet is the more traditional.

Torgiano Small DOC area dominated by the Lungarotti firm. Reds are from Sangiovese, Canaiolo and Montepulciano grapes, white from Trebbiano and Grechetto.

Who's who in Umbria

Adanti Makes white Bianco d'Arquata and red Montefalco.
Valvona & Crolla; Winecellars; Wine Schoppen

Antinori The great Tuscan firm also has vineyards in Orvieto. The Orvieto is reliable, but their star wines are a single vineyard Castello della Sala and the Grechetto/Chardonnay Cervaro della Sala.
H Allen Smith; David Baillie Vintners; Corney & Barrow; Lay & Wheeler; J Sainsbury; Tanners; Winecellars

Barberani Producer of some top quality Orvieto Classico.
Mitchells of Lancaster; Wine Growers Association

Luigi Bigi Commercial, reliable wines on the one hand and some exciting single vineyard Orvieto on the other. Wines: Orvieto, Vigneto Torricella, Vigneto Orzalume, Colli del Trasimeno (also makes Est! Est!! Est!!! from Latium and Chianti).
Adnams; D Byrne & Co; Peter Dominic; Majestic; Market Vintners; Oddbins; Upper Crust; Valvona & Crolla; La Vigneronne; Wizard Wine Warehouses

Lungarotti The creator of the Torgiano DOC and generally considered one of Italy's finest winemakers. Wines: Rubesco di Torgiano, Cabernet Sauvignon di Miralduolo, Chardonnay, Solleone (a Sherry-like wine).
Adnams; H Allen Smith; David Baillie Vintners; Berry Bros & Rudd; Corney & Barrow; Alex Findlater; Lay & Wheeler; J Sainsbury; Tanners; Valvona & Crolla; The Wine Society

Best buys from Umbria

WHITE

Grechetto d'Arquata, Adanti (*Oddbins*)

RED

Rosso di Montefalco 1986, Caprai (*Marske Mill House*)
Rosso di Montefalco 1985, Adanti (*Valvona & Crolla*)

LATIUM

Frascati – becoming good

Frascati – another of those much-abused Italian wines – is at last beginning to show why it was so popular in the first place. While there is still too much thin, badly made stuff around, selling too cheaply, we now have access to a regular supply of the real thing as well.

Frascati is a surprisingly delicate wine. Its flavours sort of steal up on you. A good Frascati will taste slightly honeyed, aromatic, perfumed. It should also taste fresh. And one of the problems has been that the grape that lends Frascati its character, the Malvasia, oxidises quickly without the aid of modern technology. In the past, most producers cut out the Malvasia and just used boring old Trebbiano, which produces large amounts of watery grapes – hence the dullness of most

Frascati. Now, with cold fermentation and stainless steel, that can change, and we can all be thankful.

Traditional Frascati, made almost entirely from the honeyed Malvasia grape, was semi-sweet and frankly, an acquired taste. But at least it travels and at least it's drinkable.

So not only are we now getting a few Frascatis made using bags of Malvasia, but also single vineyard wines of surprising quality.

As for the other major DOC of Latium, the notoriously named Est! Est!! Est!!!, nothing seems to have improved here, and our advice is still to avoid it.

Apart from these two familiar white wines, we can also happily recommend a wine that is not a DOC at all, but a top quality vino da tavola (see below).

Who's who in Latium

Colli di Catone The best Frascati available in the UK is made by Antonio Pulcini. Look for his single vineyard Villa Catone, the white-bottled Bottiglia Satinata, and the semi-sweet sparkling Carlo V. Wines: Frascati Superiore.
Augustus Barnett; Alex Findlater; Chaplin & Son; Oddbins; Christopher Piper Wines; Tanners; Valvona & Crolla; Winecellars; Wine Growers Association; Wines from Paris

Bruno Colacicchi Maker of the legendary Torre Ercolana, a blend of Cabernet Franc, Merlot and the local Cesanese. Only about 200 cases made a year, so count your buys in single bottles. Wines: Torre Ercolana vino da tavola.
David Alexander; Cliff & Co, 49 Simon Street, London SW3; Valvona & Crolla; Wine Growers Association

Fontana Candida A large-scale Frascati producer, whose best wine is the single vineyard Vigneto Santa Teresa.
Classic Wine Warehouse; Rodney Densem Wines; Majestic; Upper Crust; Valvona & Crolla; La Vigneronne; Wizard Wine Warehouses

Best buy from Latium

Frascati Superiore 1988, Villa Catone (*J Townend & Sons*)

The Wine Development Board is a small organisation with the responsibility of encouraging more people to drink wine. They may be able to supply literature and general promotional material. Contact them at: Five Kings House, Kennet Wharf Lane, Upper Thames Street, London EC4V 3BH; TEL 01-248 5835.

ABRUZZO AND MOLISE

The land of the Montepulciano

There's only one grape that matters in these two mountainous regions on the east coast level with Rome: the Montepulciano. In the Abruzzo, the DOC is Montepulciano d'Abruzzo, and at their best the wines can be rich and elegant; at their least they are full of good, peppery fruit. In Molise, look for the Biferno DOC for good bargain reds.

There's also some charming rosato – rosé – wine made with the Montepulciano grape. It's called Cerasuolo, because of its cherry colour.

The whites – made of the Trebbiano grape – are normally as dull as only that grape can make them. One producer, Valentini, does something better – but he knows he does, and his prices have shot up accordingly.

Who's who from the Abruzzo and Molise

Barone Cornacchia Makes red and very good rosé. Wines: Montepulciano d'Abruzzo, rosé.
Millevini; Valvona & Crolla; Winecellars

Ramitello Luigi de Majo's organically produced red Biferno is the only wine from this Molise DOC to reach the UK. Wines: Di Majo Norante Biferno.
The Wine Club

Cantina Sociale di Tollo Make widely available vino da tavola. Wines: Montepulciano d'Abruzzo, (red) Colle Secco.
H Allen Smith; Valvona & Crolla; Winecellars

Edoardo Valentini Makes one of the few decent Trebbiano d'Abruzzo wines, as well as Montepulciano.
Millevini; Valvona & Crolla

Vini Citra A large co-operative in the Abruzzo making robust, peppery reds. Wines: Montepulciano d'Abruzzo, vino da tavola Castel Citra.
John Harvey & Sons; Pimlico Dozen; Wine Growers Association

Best buys from Abruzzo and Molise

Montepulciano d'Abruzzo 1985, Barone Cornacchia (*Millevini*)
Montepulciano d'Abruzzo 1987, Umani Ronchi (*Ad Hoc Wine Warehouse*)
Montepulciano d'Abruzzo 1987, Tollo (*Augustus Barnett*)

CAMPANIA

The viticultural desert

Some say that viticulturally this region has never recovered from the Fall of the Roman Empire, when Falernum (from north-west of the region) was a favoured tipple. Now all it can offer is the ludicrous white Lacryma Christi (now under the DOC of Vesuvio) as its main claim to fame.

Serious wine drinkers would be better off looking instead at the smaller white wine areas of Greco di Tufo and Fiano di Avellino (the better of the two, and another favourite of the Romans).

There is really only one red that has more than local renown and that's Taurasi. Made from the Aglianico grape (see also Basilicata below), in the hands of Antonio Mastroberardino, the wine has a plummy, almost sweet richness that leaves awe and puzzlement on the faces of those who taste it for the first time.

Who's who in Campania

Mastroberardino A great producer of both white and red wines – at a price. Wines: Fiano di Avellino; Greco di Tufo, (red) Taurasi.
David Baillie Vintners; D Byrne & Co; Lay & Wheeler; Tanners; Valvona & Crolla

PUGLIA (APULIA)

This is the home of the wine lake. And to look at the vast acres of vineyards on the flat plains stretching for two hundred miles down the heel of Italy, it's hardly surprising that few really good wines emerge. But some producers are making very fine wines and a few – too few – are available in the UK. There's a whole range of DOCs, but, as often, the vini da tavola are just as good.

Who's who in Puglia

Cantine Sociale di Locorotondo Makes what is sometimes called the best white in the region, from Verdeca and Bianco d'Alessano grapes. Wines: Locorotondo Bianco.
Millevini

Leone de Castris Family firm which was the first in Italy to bottle a rosato. Wines: Salice Salentino, Locorotondo, Five Roses rosato.
For further information contact Fiandaca, 78 Chandos Crescent, Edgware, Middx

Rivera Best known for rosato, but also makes a good red. Wines: Castel del Monte Rosso and Rosato.
Stapylton Fletcher

Taurino The wines from this family firm come from deep inside the heel of Italy in the Salentino peninsula. They are heavy and full-bodied and need time to soften. Wines: Salice Salentino, Rosso di Salentino, Rosso Brindisi.
Majestic; Millevini; Oddbins; Winecellars; Wine Growers Association

Torre Quarto Run by Belgians, making their best wines from French grapes. Wines: Torre Quarto Rosso (made from Malbec), DOC Rosso di Cerignola; vini da tavola.
Millevini; Winecellars

Best buys from Puglia

WHITE

Locorotondo Bianco Leone de Castris (*Luigi's Delicatessen*)
Arpi Sauvignon 1988, Cantina Sociale Foggia (*Wizard Wine Warehouses*)

RED

Torre Quarto (*Millevini*)
Salice Salentino Riserva 1982, Taurino (*Oddbins; Wine Growers Association*)

BASILICATA

The land of the lone DOC

A wider variety of wines made in Basilicata than this small, neglected region's one DOC would suggest. But only one wine is available in Britain – Aglianico del Vulture, a serious, somewhat austere red, sometimes described as the best red from southern Italy.

Who's who in Basilicata

Fratelli d'Angelo Small family company, by far the best producer of Aglianico del Vulture.
Averys; David Alexander; Millevini; Wine Growers Association; Winecellars

Best buys from Basilicata

Aglianico del Vulture, d'Angelo (*Wine Growers Association*)

CALABRIA

A few characters

The Greeks called this Enotria, the land of wine. Things may have slipped since then (although that the Greeks watered their wine may say something for its quality), but a few characterful wines – of which the best is red and white Cirò – are to be found in the toe of Italy.

Who's who in Calabria

Librandi The only producer of more than local renown. The Cirò Rosso is better than the Bianco, and there is a good Riserva.
Cliff & Co, 4a Simon Street, London SW3; Millevini; Pimlico Dozen; Wine Growers Association

Best buys from Calabria

Cirò Classico Rosso 1985, Librandi (*Millevini; Wine Growers Association*)

SICILY

The wine revolution

If any region has profited by the revolution in Italian wine, it must be Sicily. From the dark, murky products of less than 20 years ago, the region is now at the forefront of high tech wine-making, and is capable of churning out huge quantities of modern, squeaky clean wines, much of it without great character, although some offers good value and interest.

Much of the innovation is being done outside the DOC system, so many of Sicily's interesting wines are vini da tavola. But they're not of the super vino da tavola type found in Tuscany, where they are the top of a range which includes DOC wines. Here, the main production is of ordinary vini da tavola from the more go-ahead companies – and brand names are important (see below under Who's who).

Of course, there are DOC wines – Alcamo is one of the more interesting, while Etna tends to be drunk by the holidaymakers on the beaches of Taormina.

(For Marsala, see the section on Fortified wines on page 662.)

Who's who in Sicily

Corvo, Duca di Salaparuta Modern winery making modern-tasting, straightforward wines of good quality. Wines: Corvo Bianco and Rosso, Corvo Bianco Colombina Platino.
D Byrne & Co; Peter Dominic; Lay & Wheeler; Millevini; Tanners; Valvona & Crolla; Willoughbys

Donnafugata Red and white vini da tavola from an estate owned by the Rallo (Marsala producer) family. Rising stars for quality and character. Wines: Donnafugata Bianco and Rosso.
Bromley Wine Centre, Bromley, Kent; Gerry's Wines, Old Compton Street, London W1; Master Cellar; Selfridges; Valvona & Crolla

Rapitalà Make much better whites than their Alcamo DOC would suggest, while the red and rosato are well-crafted wines. Wines: Rapitalà Bianco di Alcamo DOC, Rapitalà Rosso, Rapitalà Rosato.
Hicks & Don; Valvona & Crolla

Regaleali This estate produces the star among Sicilian table wines. Both red and white are top class and good value. Wines: Regaleali Rosso, Regaleali Bianco, Rosso del Conte.
G M Vintners; Valvona & Crolla; Wine Growers Association

Sambuca di Sicilia A co-operative in south-west Sicily, making a good value red, rosé and white vino da tavola. Wines: Cellaro Rosso, Rosato, Bianco.
Berry Bros & Rudd; Valvona & Crolla; Winecellars

Settesoli Co-operative making light, fruity wines on the southern coast. Wines: Settesoli Bianco, Rosso, Rosato.
Valvona & Crolla

Best buys from Sicily

WHITE

Cellaro Bianco (*Rose Tree Wine Co; Winecellars*)
Regaleali Bianco 1987 (*Del Monicos*)
Settesoli Bianco (*Demijohn Wines*)
Josephine Doré, de Bartoli (*Oddbins*)

RED

Cellaro Rosso (*Rose Tree Wine Co; Winecellars*)
Settesoli Rosso (*A & A Wines; Demijohn Wines*)

SARDINIA

Italy's largest wine estate

By far the most interesting wines from this region come from one go-ahead company, Sella e Mosca, which owns one of Europe's largest wine estates at Alghero in the north-west of the island. They make a big range of innovative vini da tavola, using local grapes such as the white Vermentino, and the red Cannonau, as well as lesser varieties such as the white Torbato.

Elsewhere, the production is mainly in the hands of co-operatives, of whom the best are making some good-value DOC wines.

Who's who in Sardinia

Cantine Sociale di Dolianova Three good-value DOC wines. Wines: (red) Monica di Sardegna, Cannonau di Sardegna; (white) Vermentino di Sardegna.
H Allen Smith; Chiswick Cellars; Waitrose; Winecellars

Sella e Mosca The innovators in Sardinia, whose total production equals that of the whole Côte d'Or of Burgundy, yet they manage to make distinctive wines. Virtually all are vini da tavola, rather than DOC. Whites: Riviera del Corallo, Vermentino di Alghero, Torbato di Alghero, Terre Bianche. Reds: Cannonau di Alghero, Tanca Farra. Dessert wine: Anghelu Ruju.
Averys; Harrods; Majestic; Millevini; Winecellars; Wine Growers Association

Best buys from Sardinia

WHITE

Vermentino di Sardegna, Cantina Sociale di Dolianova (*Winecellars*)

RED

Selvatico Rosso (*Luigi's Delicatessen*)
Cannonau di Sardegna 1986, Cantina Sociale di Dolianova (*Winecellars*)

Specialist stockists (for all regions)

Ad Hoc Wine Warehouse; Adnams; H Allen Smith; Bibendum; D Byrne & Co; Demijohn Wines; Alex Findlater; Peter Green; J E Hogg; Luigi's Delicatessen; Marske Mill House; Millevini; Raeburn Fine Wines and Foods; Reid Wines; Selfridges; Tanners Wines; Upper Crust; Valvona & Crolla; La Vigneronne; Windrush Wines; Wine Growers Association; Wine House

Lebanon

Wine has been made in the Lebanon since grapes were first fermented, and but for the war there would probably be a flourishing export industry. As it is, our knowledge of Lebanese wines has developed only because of one remarkable man, Serge Hochar.

We had a letter from M. Hochar's British agent while this edition was being prepared to say that he had hoped to be at the major wine show in Bordeaux in June, but that 'we have had no message from him for some time'. It is part of the tragedy in the Lebanon that a dedicated winemaker is prevented from even seeing his vineyards because they are in territory held by Muslim fundamentalists, yet still manages to produce world-class wines.

M. Hochar was trained in Bordeaux and uses a blend of French grapes (Cabernet Sauvignon, Syrah and Cinsault), varying them according to the year, in order to make Château Musar. It is powerful, rich, elegant and long-lasting: 20-year-old wines are still full of fruit. In the years of civil war, with Château Musar's vineyards in the Bekaa Valley and the winery across at least two front lines in the Christian area north of Beirut, only one vintage (1984) has been completely missed, although 1985 only just made it.

In the UK we see only Château Musar (*widely available*), although M. Hochar also produces a second wine, Cuvée Musar, and a white. Old vintages of Château Musar are occasionally available, and this is a wine which repays laying down.

Specialist stockists
Barnes Wine Shop; Peter Green; Upper Crust

Luxembourg

Vineyards grow on either side of the Mosel River as it flows through the Grand Duchy of Luxembourg. They produce very light German-style wines which need to be drunk young but can be quite refreshing. A small amount reaches our shops.

A greater quantity of Luxembourg sparkling wine is also available. While some of this is made from Luxembourg grapes, much of it is based on cheap Italian wine to which is added some Luxembourg air (a habit the Luxembourgeois have picked up from their German neighbours). So read the small print carefully on a label – it should indicate where the wine has come from. If it is simply described as 'bottled in Luxembourg', that means the wine has come from elsewhere.

The best wines are all white. They are officially classified, in ascending order of quality, as: marque nationale, vin classé, premier cru and grand premier cru. Two producers send their wines here: the co-operative of Wormeldange (*Luxembourg Wine Company*) and Bernard Massard (*Eldridge Pope/Reynier Wine Libraries*).

Grapes on the label

Auxerrois Fairly neutral but pleasant wine which can be quite full and almondy in good years from good sites.

Elbling Light, fresh, crisp wines.

Gewürztraminer Very little is grown, but it makes good, fresh, only slightly spicy wines.

Pinot Gris Little is grown, but it makes full, soft wines.

Riesling Makes flowery wines, with good varietal character, thin in poor years but clean and delicate in better ones.

Rivaner The Müller-Thurgau under another name. Makes soft, fruity, sometimes medium dry but often dry wines.

Specialist stockists

Eldridge Pope/Reynier Wine Libraries; The Luxembourg Wine Company

New Zealand

Making the headlines

For a small industry from a small country a long way away,
New Zealand wines have managed to make plenty of headlines
in the last year (and increase exports to Britain by 45 per cent in
the last six months of 1988). They have pushed with a
vengeance into the New World white wine slot previously
occupied by Australia, earning superlatives for Chardonnay and,
especially, Sauvignon Blanc. Even the reds – dismissed only two
short years ago – are being praised for their clean, straight-
down-the-middle tastes.

Fruit is the thing in New Zealand. Probably more even than
Australia, NZ wines taste of fruit – direct, uncomplicated and
delicious. This is helped by the country's latitude, enabling the
production of what the New Zealanders themselves call 'cool
climate wines'. What this means is that there is a long ripening
season, giving intense flavours to the fruit, nicely balanced
acidity and a refreshing taste to the wines.

New Zealand's wine industry has moved fast in the past
decade. Not all of it has been forward. There was a
Government-sponsored vine-pull system when it was found that
the country could not consume enough of the wine that was
being made (unlike Australia, NZ wine drinking is low and
falling). Then, when they found success on the export markets,
they realised that they did not have enough of the magic pair of
Chardonnay and Sauvignon Blanc, and new plantings had to be
rushed in. Now we are waiting for those plantings to mature
before the supply situation can get properly back on course.

The last frontier

New Zealand has started out in the international wine scene as
the last frontier. Although the wine industry began in the
middle of the last century, it really only started moving ahead in
the 1970s. What this has meant is that there are no rules, no
traditions, and that NZ can learn from the rest of the world's
mistakes.

New Zealand has been helped in the learning process by
Australia, not just in technology, but in people. Many of the
most talented winemakers in New Zealand today are

Australians – Cloudy Bay Sauvignon is made by an Australian, as are Morton Estate wines – and there are now several joint venture deals with Australian firms. And many Australian wine producers are buying New Zealand grapes (especially Sauvignon) because they recognise that the quality is better.

Putting vines to places

Although the country might seem to be wide open to vine planting, it is already apparent that certain areas and certain varieties are better at it. So, in North Island, while the earliest vines were planted in the Auckland area, right at the north (and therefore warmest) end of the island, it now seems that Hawkes Bay is best for classic reds like Cabernet Sauvignon, Gisborne for high-cropping vines for jug wines, and Auckland itself for robust reds. And in South Island, Marlborough is proving home to great Sauvignon Blanc and Chardonnay. There are smaller areas as well – Martinborough in North Island, Christchurch and Otago in South Island – where the discoveries of which vines do best where still have to be made.

Of course, while we talk of the different areas of New Zealand, and the variety of styles they can produce, the size of the industry must always be borne in mind. An annual total national grape crop of 60,000 tons is less than the crop from the Hunter Valley in Australia, one of the smaller wine-producing areas of that country. With the opening up of completely free trade between New Zealand and Australia in 1990, we must hope that all those grapes don't just go into Australian vats, and that there's still plenty of that beautiful, pure, varietal taste left to bottle to send to us.

The taste of New Zealand

WHITE WINES

The principal grape variety in terms of acreage is still the Müller-Thurgau. Occasionally it is used unblended, but normally it provides the basis of the slightly sweet blends which still form the staple part of New Zealand wine production.

More important, in terms of quality, are the Chardonnay and the Sauvignon Blanc. Both produce wines with those intense fruit tastes already mentioned. The Chardonnay seems to succeed best with a touch of wood taste to balance its clean flavours. The Sauvignon just reeks with herbaceous, grassy flavours. Coming up fast on the outside are Gewürztraminer and Rhine Riesling, including late-harvest wines.

All four produce wines that are best drunk young – 1987 for Chardonnay and 1988 or 1989 for Sauvignon (except for late harvest) are the vintages worth considering in 1990.

RED WINES

Cabernet Sauvignon, making a soft and definitely blackcurrant-flavoured wine is the most frequently found red variety, but some Pinot Noir wines – especially in the cooler South Island – are beginning to display delicious strawberry fruit, while the Pinotage is showing good Rhône character.

New Zealand vintages

1989 A top quality harvest in all areas, with great richness of fruit and good quantities. The warm weather will probably benefit the reds and the Chardonnay more than the Sauvignon Blanc.

1988 A late harvest with reduced quantities, due to cyclones. Quality is good for most varieties, except Gewürztraminer which suffered from heavy spring rains. Red wines will be particularly good.

1987 A year with a late harvest, and mixed quality for whites, with Müller-Thurgau, Sauvignon and Chardonnay the most successful. Reds should be good.

1986 Low yield but high quality. The whites (except Chardonnay and Gewürztraminer) are beginning to fade, but the reds are now mature.

1985 Another good year. Drink the reds and any Chardonnays.

1982 Reds are the only wines worth drinking now. It was a very good year, and the pricier Cabernet Sauvignons should still be good.

Where's where in New Zealand

Names to look for on labels include Hawkes Bay (for Cabernet Sauvignon) and Marlborough (for Chardonnay and Sauvignon Blanc). Gewürztraminer and Pinot Noir are grown in most areas, but site selection is important. Pinotage is grown around Auckland.

Please write to tell us about any ideas for features you would like to see in next year's edition or in *Which? Wine Monthly*.

Who's who in New Zealand

Babich Wines (Henderson, Auckland). Descendants of Dalmatian settlers. Their Cabernet Sauvignon, Pinot Noir and Gewürztraminer are regular prize-winners. Wines: Chardonnay, Irongate Chardonnay, Gewürztraminer, Müller-Thurgau, Pinot Noir, Pinotage, Cabernet Sauvignon.
Davisons; Alex Findlater; Fullers; Peter Green; Harrods; Hedley Wright; Master Cellar Wine Warehouse; Michael Menzel Wines; Nobody Inn; Oddbins; Selfridges; Tanners; Victoria Wine Company

Cloudy Bay (Marlborough, South Island). Western Australian producer, Cape Mentelle, makes superb (but pricy) Sauvignon Blanc, and has now launched a Chardonnay of equal quality.
Adnams; Averys; Fullers; Grape Ideas; Lay & Wheeler; Majestic; Nobody Inn; Raeburn Fine Wines & Foods; La Vigneronne; Winecellars

Collard Brothers (Auckland and Gisborne). Mainly fruity Germanic-style wines, but also some reds and a Chardonnay.
Bibendum

Cooks/Corbans (Te Kauwhata, North Island). One of the biggest producers, and one of the best distributed in British shops. Luckily, quality is good as well. The premium Stoneleigh range comes from their Marlborough vineyards. Wines: Cooks New Zealand Medium White and Dry White, Chardonnay, Gewürztraminer, Dry Red, Hawkes Bay Cabernet Sauvignon; Stoneleigh Marlborough Rhine Riesling, Chardonnay, Sauvignon Blanc, Cabernet Sauvignon.
Widely available

Delegats Vineyard (Henderson and Hawkes Bay, North Island). Family winery producing award-winning whites (especially Chardonnays) and fine dessert wines. Wines: Chardonnay, Sauvignon Blanc, Fumé Blanc, Reserve Semillon, Müller-Thurgau Auslese.
Les Amis du Vin; Alex Findlater; Grape Ideas; Peter Green; Hungerford Wine Company; Kiwifruits; Master Cellar Wine Warehouse; Nobody Inn; Thos Peatling; La Vigneronne; Welbeck Wines; Winecellars

Hunters Estate (Blenheim, South Island). Ultra-modern winery making some high-class crisp white wines from Marlborough. Wines: Rhine Riesling, Gewürztraminer, Sauvignon Blanc.
J C Karn

Kumeu River Wines (Kumeu, Auckland, North Island). Family winery, with red wines, made by Australian-trained winemaker,

the stars. Wines: Merlot/Cabernet, Pinot Noir, Chardonnay, Semillon.
Adnams; Ellis Son & Vidler; Alex Findlater; Thos Peatling; Sebastopol Wines

Matua Valley Wines (Auckland and Hawkes Bay). Modern winery in Auckland making some exciting white wines. Wines: Sauvignon Blanc, Cabernet Sauvignon.
Adnams; Berry Bros & Rudd; Alex Findlater; Peter Green; Hedley Wright; Hungerford Wine Company; Kiwifruits; Nobody Inn; Thos Peatling; Welbeck Wines; Wizard Wine Warehouses

Mission Vineyards (Hawkes Bay). As its name suggests, a vineyard run by a religious order. Quality has improved recently. Wines: Sauvignon Blanc, Cabernet/Merlot.
Alex Findlater; Hedley Wright; Kiwifruits

Montana Wines (Gisborne, North Island and Marlborough, South Island). The pioneer of vineyards in the South Island. The experiment has paid off with some good crisp whites (including an excellent Sauvignon) that are widely available in British shops. Wines: Gisborne Chardonnay, Sauvignon Blanc, Fumé Blanc, Pinotage, Cabernet Sauvignon.
Widely available

Morton Estate (Hawkes Bay, North Island). Talented young winemaker specialising in white wines. Wines: Sauvignon Blanc, Chardonnay, Chardonnay Reserve.
Alex Findlater; Lay & Wheeler; Christopher Piper Wines; Sebastopol Wines; Wizard Wine Warehouses

Nobilo (Auckland, North Island). Red wine specialists who make a good Pinot Noir, but are also at home with white wines. Quality can be variable. Wines: Riesling/Sylvaner, Chardonnay, Pinotage, Cabernet Sauvignon, Pinot Noir.
Asda; Averys; Alex Findlater; Peter Green; Harrods; Majestic; Nobody Inn; Arthur Rackhams; Selfridges; Stapylton Fletcher

Selaks Wines (Auckland, North Island). One of the longest-established New Zealand producers. Wines: Chardonnay, Sauvignon Blanc/Semillon, Rhine Riesling.
Ellis Son & Vidler; Alex Findlater; Thos Peatling; Willoughbys; The Wine Society

St Nesbit (South Auckland, North Island). New winery making an exciting Cabernet Sauvignon.
Alex Findlater

Te Mata (Hawkes Bay). High-class small winery, with one of the best NZ red wines. Wines: Castle Hill Sauvignon Blanc, Elston Chardonnay, Coleraine Cabernet/Merlot.
Alex Findlater; Lay & Wheeler; Selfridges; La Vigneronne

Villa Maria Well-priced, rich wines, which seem to gain plenty of medals at local shows. Look especially for barrique-fermented Chardonnay. Wines: Chardonnay, Sauvignon Blanc, Gewürztraminer, Cabernet Sauvignon.
Alex Findlater; Michael Menzel Wines; Winecellars

Best buys from New Zealand

WHITE

Montana Sauvignon Blanc/Chenin 1987 (*widely available*)
White Cloud Müller-Thurgau, Nobilo (*Averys of Bristol*)
Montana Sauvignon Blanc 1988 (*widely available*)
Bakers Creek Crackling (*Kiwifruits*)

RED

Tolaga Bay Dry Red, Cooks (*Wessex Wines*)
Cooks Cabernet Sauvignon 1986, Hawkes Bay (*Hampden Wine Company*)
Babich Pinot Noir 1986 (*J C Karn*)
C J Pask Cabernet Sauvignon/Merlot/Cabernet Franc 1988 (*Kiwifruits*)

Specialist stockists

Averys of Bristol; City Wines; Claridge Fine Wines; Drunken Mouse; Alex Findlater; Haughton Fine Wines; J C Karn; Nobody Inn; La Reserva Wines; Upper Crust

North Africa

Once over half the world's wine trade was in wine from North African countries, especially Algeria and Tunisia. While the French ran the vineyards, the Muslim locals didn't touch the stuff, and it all went abroad. Some of it was sold in its own right, but the majority went into blending vats in France, quite possibly in Burgundy, certainly at points further south. After independence, because of official indifference, the quality of the wines – mainly red – tended to decline; and when the European Community banned foreign blending, the bulk trade of North African wines dried up.

But, more recently, one or two decent ranges of good, robust, quaffing wines have turned up in our shops at competitive prices.

Morocco, which was never involved in the bulk export market to the same extent as Algeria and Tunisia, is the country which has managed to keep up quality most successfully. But it is Algeria which has come up with new wines, based on grape varieties from the Rhône and Bordeaux. One Algerian wine even beat all-comers in a national newspaper tasting. And rumblings from Tunisia suggest that we will see some of their wines soon, successful Muscats in particular.

Who's who in North Africa

Morocco

Tarik – a red blend of Cinsault, Carignan and Grenache.
Sidi Brahim – straight Cinsault and better quality.
Welbeck Wines

Algeria

Wines produced by the state monopoly under a variety of
names: Medea Rouge, Coteaux de Zaccar, Dahra, Coteaux de
Mascara and Cuvée du Président (regarded as the top wine).
Grape Ideas; Peter Green
Coteaux de Tiemcen Red Infuriator. A good, basic, powerful red
wine.
Peter Dominic

Portugal

It was raining in Oporto the last time we visited. It was raining the time before that – and the time before that. We've been at most times of the year, and it has always been raining.

Now this is not a tale of woe of ruined holidays, but a reflection on the fact that, apart from the area south of Lisbon, much of Portugal gets as much rain as Manchester – and more than London. It's certainly warmer than either British city, but it's just as wet. Which means, as far as vines are concerned, that it is much fairer to compare Portugal as a growing area with Bordeaux or the Loire (despite the greater heat) than with the dryness of Rioja or other major Spanish areas.

If that suggests to you that Portugal has probably greater potential than Spain as a quality wine producer, you would be right. Not only does the climate lend itself to high quality wines – because the balance between heat and moisture is just about right – but Portugal's vine varieties are much more exciting and useful than all but a handful from Spain.

Portugal's vines rejoice in arcane names. There's the Baga of Bairrada, the Periquita of Arrábida and Alentejo (and the same grape in Ribatejo where it's known as João de Santarem), the Touriga Francesa and Touriga Nacional of the Douro, the Alvarinho of Vinho Verde. Hardly names to trip off the tongue, but between them – and with many more like them – they can produce a fascinating set of flavours and tastes that keeps Portugal firmly on a path of its own.

We can't wait 20 years

The problem at the moment is that in many cases the wines are not being given the chance to yield their flavours. They are being swamped and stifled by old-fashioned wine-making techniques that may be splendid if you are willing to wait 20 years for a wine to mature, but are of little use in a world which wants to drink its wines sooner rather than later.

Most books explain away this heavy reliance on tradition in Portugal as a result of consumer demand. Statistics show that Portugal is second to none in Europe as a drinker of wines, above all preferring its own wine – as anybody who has tried to buy anything other than Portuguese in a restaurant or wine shop will testify. That means that, compared with any other European country, the pressure on Portuguese producers to export is pretty low.

So producers are likewise under no pressure to improve their production processes. And the consumer is left with little choice but to drink what's there or do without. Maybe the older generation of Portuguese wine drinkers likes old, tannic, dried up reds – and pretty much the same (with the addition of oxidised fruit) in whites – but we suspect that the younger generation, like wine drinkers all over Europe, wants more fruit and less dirty wood.

Certainly, of those wines whose firms do export seriously, it's the ones with fruit and clean flavours that do consistently well in tastings, while those from areas and producers that rely heavily on 'tradition' do worst. But tradition is a double-edged sword: when *Which? Wine Monthly* ran a tasting of Portuguese reds earlier in 1989, the top wine was one that is still being made in old earthenware amphorae of the same design that the Romans used – but the process was clean, the choice of grapes was excellent, and great care was taken.

Under the rule of co-operatives

There is a world of difference from an estate like that of Rosada Fernandes in Reguengos de Monsaraz (the name of that tasting's top wine) and most of the Dão wines in the same tasting, which had lost what fruit they ever had. But they were made by the cartel of co-operatives which controls virtually all Dão production (selling finished wine to merchants rather than grapes) and which continues to insist that Dão needs to spend a long time in wood *after* it has spent an equally long time in cement tanks – thereby ensuring that little or no fruit is left for the consumer.

Co-operatives dominate a number of Portuguese areas in a way which they do in few other wine-producing areas in western Europe. Not that they are a completely malign influence: the co-operative at Arruda dos Vinhos in the Estremadura has managed to create a whole market for cheap and cheerful red wines by working closely with a British supermarket to come up with a properly fruity Beaujolais-style of wine for around £2. Similarly, the co-operative of Reguengos de Monsaraz makes very accessible red wines at excellent prices, and the co-operative of Ponte de Lima in the Vinho Verde makes one of the best examples of the fresh, dry tingling style of this white wine.

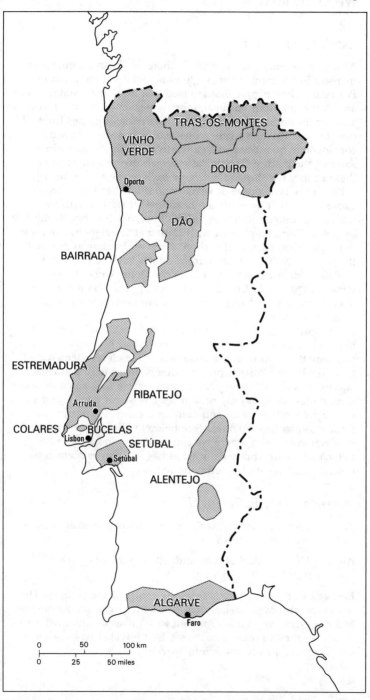

Portugal

Estates and regions

At the other end of the spectrum, there has been an interesting increase in the number of single estate wines coming out of Portugal. When people first realised that more than Mateus Rosé and Port came from Portugal, most wines on offer were made by a merchant house which bought either wine or grapes from all over the country and made a blended, branded product in considerable quantity and to a relatively high standard. Indeed, some of the mature Garrafeiras (special reserve) wines from these firms gave stupendous value back in the late 1970s.

But in the last couple of years or so it has been the single estate wines that have hit the headlines. It started with the oddball Quinta da Bacalhôa (oddball because it is one of the few estates in Portugal planted with Cabernet Sauvignon) from the Arrábida region south of Lisbon. Then we became aware that the best Vinho Verdes came from estates such as Paco de Anha or Palacio da Brejoiera. Then from the Douro came the estate wines of Quinta do Cotto. And then it dawned on us that all over Portugal there were estate wines of great interest – and often terrific value.

And now there's more news from this traditionalist country: more areas are going to become demarcated. Not very exciting, you may think, until you realise that of the eleven demarcated areas (including Port) at present, one is down to one vineyard, another has almost disappeared, another is a tiny patch on some sand dunes, another only recognises one sweet wine – and so on. So recognition of up-and-coming areas like Ribatejo and – most importantly – Alentejo (see below) will show where the new action is – and where we can expect to find a more outward-looking approach in what has sometimes seemed a determinedly old-fashioned wine industry.

Where's where in Portugal

There are ten **demarcated table wine regions** in Portugal, some of very minor significance.

Algarve High-in-alcohol reds and whites seen only in the holiday resorts of the Algarve.

Bairrada Good quality reds from the centre of the country. The red grape, the Baga, makes rich, soft wines, with plenty of fruit and not excessive tannin. An area with great potential, whose wines are now in many shops (see Best Buys). There are also some whites, mostly made into sparkling wine.

Bucelas Dry white wines from near Lisbon, sometimes with a slight prickle. They have a tendency to oxidise.

Carcavelhos Almost impossible to find this slightly sweet fortified wine, made near Lisbon (buildings cover almost all the vineyards).

Colares Colares wines are made from vines grown in sand dunes (so they don't have to be grafted, because the phylloxera louse can't cope with sand). Only a few firms make this wine now: it suffers from the true Portuguese red astringency and toughness in youth (and also from the dominance of one co-operative), but given many years matures into an amazingly perfumed wine.

Dão A strange system operates in Dão, whereby only farmers are allowed to make wine which they then sell to the merchants and négociants (rather than letting the big companies buy in grapes and use sophisticated equipment to make the wine). This has meant that the vast majority of the wine from the area is disappointing. The only Dão which gets round this problem is Grão Vasco from the producers of Mateus Rosé who control and buy the production of one co-operative. There is also a single estate wine, Conde de Santar, which is better than most. The whites are best avoided.

Douro Only about 40 per cent of the wine from here is made into Port, the rest becoming rather fat and oily white or much better red. Indeed, what is often regarded as Portugal's finest wine – Barca Velha, made by Ferreira – is produced here, but only in very good years, and in limited quantities. Another Port producer, Champalimaud, makes a red that's Californian in its intensity, although it is made with Portuguese grape varieties. Other, cheaper, Douro wines are more variable, although the grapes used – the Port grape varieties – mean that this is an area to watch.

Moscatel de Setúbal Fortified dessert wines (see the section on Fortified wines on page 661).

Vinho Verde Largest demarcated region, producing a quarter of all Portugal's wine. Slightly pétillant, crisp dry whites and acid reds. The initial success of vinho verde in Britain was as slightly sweet branded white wine – an alternative to Liebfraumilch, in fact. But gradually people are becoming aware that true vinho verde as drunk in Portugal is bone-dry, with a cooking-apple acidity. A few wines of this style available in the shops (see Best Buys), and they are definitely worth snapping up for cool summer drinking.

However, many of the currently **undemarcated areas** are of equal – if not more – interest.

Alentejo The vast southern plains of Portugal. There are three main wine areas: Portalegre in the north which makes reds and whites; Borba and Reguengos de Monsaraz for reds; and Vidgueira and Beja for whites. Of these, Reguengos is promising to make some of the country's finest and best value wines. All the towns mentioned are to be demarcated.

Arrábida Hilly country to the west of Setúbal. Production here is dominated by the firms of J M da Fonseca and João Pires (see under Who's who), two of the most go-ahead producers in Portugal.

Arruda The town of Arruda dos Vinhos in Estremadura to the north of Lisbon is dominated by its wine co-operative which supplies wines to Sainsbury's under the Arruda name. Value and quality seem to be good.

Estremadura Vast area to the north of Lisbon, centred on the town of Torres Vedras, whose co-operative makes 2.5 per cent of all Portugal's wines. Much goes into merchants' blends. There are plans to make six demarcated regions in this area – Arruda, Torres Vedras, Alenquer, Alcobaça, Gaeiras, Encostas de Aire.

Palmela Area inland from Setúbal, near Arrábida, with the small town of Azeitão at its centre.

Ribatejo Huge, flat vineyard area on the east bank of the Tagus. Another source for merchants' blends. Some areas are about to be demarcated areas (Coruche, Cartaxo, Almeirim, Santarem, Chamusca, Tomar).

Tras-os-Montes The remote north-east province, north of the Douro. Chaves and Valpaços (both dominated by comparatively go-ahead co-operatives) are to be demarcated.

What's what in Portugal

Some names that appear on Portuguese labels:

Colheita Vintage.
Engarrafedo Bottled (by).
Garrafeira A wine merchant's best wines, generally selected after some years in cask and bottle. This will normally be a branded wine, and can be a blend of vintages.
Região Demarcada Demarcated region, similar to AC or Italian DOC (see above for list).
Reserva Another term for an older wine, but, unlike Garrafeira, one from a demarcated region.
Velho (or **Velha**) Old.

Vintages in Portugal

These notes apply to red wines only.

1988 A disastrous year, with crop quantities down by as much as two-thirds. What little was made turned out to be of average to good quality, so prices for these wines will inevitably rise.

1987 Heavy rains during the harvest have either meant a ruined crop or a crop of swollen grapes. Most areas made light wines, not for keeping. Only in the Alentejo were there better things.

1986 Small quantities were made after spring frosts. Only in the south, in Ribatejo and Alentejo, are quality and quantity good.

1985 A great year all round. Everybody did well although in the Alentejo quantity was down because of the dry summer.

1984 A light vintage, which will be ready to drink soon.

1983 A classic vintage in the north. Average quality and small quantities in Ribatejo and Alentejo.

1982 Another classic vintage, this time right across the country. These wines are for keeping.

1980 A good start to the decade with long-lived wines being made right round the country.

Older vintages: 1978, 1975, 1974, 1971, 1970.

Who's who in Portugal

Names of some producers and estates to look for:

Quinta da Abrigada Estate in the Estremadura region in Alenquer. Very fruity reds which can develop well.
Bibendum; Oddbins

Caves Acacio Bairrada producer who makes a good Reserva.
Blayneys

Caves Aliança A whole range of good quality wines from vinho verde, Dão, Bairrada and Douro.
Chiswick Wine Cellers; Majestic

Quinta da Aveleda Producer of a straightforward vinho verde (Aveleda) and a superior estate-bottled wine (Quinta da Aveleda).
(Aveleda only): Augustus Barnett; Davisons; Morrisons; Unwins; Quinta da Aveleda available only through hotels and restaurants

Julio Bastos Alentejo producer of an elegant red, under the name of his estate, Quinta do Carmo.
For further information contact Wineforce (01-538 2512)

Borges e Irmão Make the best-selling vinho verde, Gatão, but also a drier style and Dão wines.
Marks & Spencer's own label; Victoria Wine Company (Gatão)

Carvalho, Ribeiro e Ferreira A major table wine producer, specialising in branded and Garrafeira wines of high quality mainly from the Ribatejo. Brands include Serradayres.
Lisboa Delicatessen, 54 Goldborne Road, London, NW10

Champalimaud Single vineyard Port producer (see under Ports) who also makes some top quality Douro table wines. Names are Cotto Grande Escolha, Quinta do Cotto. Also make good Vinho Verde, Paço Texeiro.
Adnams; Bibendum; Alex Findlater; Peter Green; J E Hogg; Oddbins; Tanners; Winecellars; Wines from Paris

Adega Cooperativa de Chamusca An enterprising co-operative in the Ribatejo, making good, tarry reds.
Selected Co-op branches; Oddbins

Conde de Santar The only single vineyard Dão; its quality shines out against other Dãos.
For further information contact Wineforce (01-538 2512)

Caves Dom Teodosio Garrafeiras under the brand name Casaleiro are huge, peppery and long-lasting.
For further information contact Vinicave (01-969 9771)

Ferreira Port producers who also make Douro table wines. Their finest wine, Barca Velha, is made only in exceptional years. The less expensive brand, Esteva, is now widely available.
Oddbins; Thresher

J M da Fonseca One of the best wine firms in Portugal. A whole range of branded wines include Camarate, Periquita, Pasmasdos and Garrafeiras. Also the major producer of Moscatel de Setúbal. Now making a good wine from Reguengos de Monsaraz in the Alentejo (José de Sousa Rosada Fernandes).
Adnams; H Allen Smith; Alex Findlater; Hungerford Wine Company; Majestic; Nobody Inn; Christopher Piper Wines; La Reserva Wines; Tanners; Ubiquitous Chip; La Vigneronne; Waitrose; Winecellars; The Wine Society

Adega Cooperativa de Mealhada Another reliable quality co-op in Bairrada.
Waitrose

Luis Pato Regarded as one of the top Bairrada producers, combining ultra-modern methods with the best of the traditional.
H Allen Smith; Bibendum; Eaton Elliot Winebrokers; Hampden Wine Company; Alex Findlater; Peter Green; Touchstone Wines; Winecellars

João Pires Source of some fine branded red and white wines made in a brand-new, space age winery. Reds include Tinto da

Anfora and Quinta do Santa Amaro, whites João Pires. Also make the claret-like Quinta da Bacalhôa, one of the few Cabernet Sauvignon-based wines in Portugal.
(Bacalhôa): J Sainsbury; (for other wines): H Allen Smith; Davisons; Hungerford Wine Company; Majestic; Oddbins; Christopher Piper Wines; Arthur Rackhams; Tanners; Ubiquitous Chip; Unwins; Waitrose; Winecellars

Adega Cooperativa de Reguengos de Monsaraz Good quality co-operative wines from the best wine town in the Alentejo.
Selected Co-op branches; Dinis Off-Licence, 195 Holborn Road, London, SE3; Hampden Wine Company

J Serra Bairrada producer of reliable wines.
Les Amis du Vin; The Winery

Quinta de São Francisco Small estate in the Palmela region which makes Moscatel de Setúbal and the red Cepa de Serra.
Dinis Off-Licence, 195 Holborn Road, London, SE3; Ferreira Delicatessen, 40 Delancey Street, London, NW1

Caves São João Good red wines under the Frei São João name.
Anthony Wine Cellars, 67 Regents Park Road, London, NW1; D Byrne & Co; W & T Palmer, 47 West Way, Botley, Oxford; Selfridges

da Silva Chitas Colares producer who also makes a number of Vinho da Mesa (table wines) which have the Colares style without the necessary Colares waiting period. Wines: Casa de Azenha, Beira Mar.
Vintage Wines, 116 Derby Road, Nottingham

Sogrape Producers of Mateus Rosé and Mateus White *(widely available)*. They also make Grão Vasco Dão wines.
(Stockists for Dão): Asda; Averys; Davisons; Eaton Elliot Winebrokers; Grape Ideas; Irvine Robertson Wines; David Scatchard

Quinta do Tamariz Single estate Vinho Verde.
Bentalls of Kingston; G Hush; Selfridges; Upper Crust; Wine Emporium; Wine House; Wine Schoppen

Adega Cooperativa de Valpaços One of the two good co-operatives in the Tras-os-Montes region. Douro-style wines, with plenty of acidity, and the curious sweet Jeropiga.
John Islip Wines, John Islip Street, London, SW1; La Reserva Wines

Caves Velhas Sole remaining producers of the Bucelas wines. Also make Dãos and some good Garrafeiras under the Romeira name.
Lisboa Delicatessen, 54 Goldborne Road, London, NW10; Tesco

Best buys from Portugal

WHITES

Vinho Verde, Paço de Texeiro, Champalimaud (*Bibendum*)
Vinho Verde Solar das Boucas (*La Réserve*)
João Pires Branco (*H Allen Smith*)

REDS

Reguengos de Monsaraz 1983, José de Sousa Rosada Fernandes
(*Peter Green; Hungerford Wine Company; Tesco*)
Quinta de Camarate 1983, J M da Fonseca (*Peter Green; Majestic*)
Sainsbury's Arruda (*J Sainsbury*)
Pasmados 1981, J M da Fonseca (*H Allen Smith; D Byrne & Co;
Christopher Piper Wines; Tanners*)
Tinto da Anfora, João Pires (*Augustus Barnett*)
Bairrada 1980, Caves Aliança (*Majestic*)

Specialist stockists

*H Allen Smith; City Wines; Peter Green; Hampden Wine Company;
Oddbins; La Reserva Wines; Selfridges; Tanners Wines; Upper
Crust; Wine House*

Rumania

Rumania has come up with an unexpected vinous treat this year, even while her reputation politically and economically has plummeted. We tasted a red wine that was both inexpensive and very acceptable. It was fruity, pleasantly mature, vegetal and velvety. And it was made from one of the most notoriously difficult grapes to deal with successfully – the Pinot Noir.

There must be something to Rumanian viticulture after all, we thought, as we tasted this wine. But it is difficult to find out, because so little is exported. Maybe that Pinot Noir was an attempt to increase wine exports as a way of gaining hard currency to get the country out of its economic mess. In which case, they have a long way to go to catch up with the example of their southern neighbour, Bulgaria.

The potential for good wine-making is certainly there. There is a long tradition, never interrupted (as it was in Bulgaria) by Moslem prohibitions on alcohol. The most familiar wines are from Transylvania and are white: Pinot Gris, Furmint (the Hungarian grape) or Traminer. But traditionally the best wines come from further east – from Murfatlar near the Black Sea which makes a sweet Muscat wine.

The one wine for which Rumania should be famous is Cotnari, a white dessert wine from Moldavia and the equivalent of the Hungarian Tokay. It used to be all the rage in Paris at the turn of the century but is difficult to find anywhere now.

A few other wines have made their way to the UK. Of the reds, there is a good fruity Merlot from the Dealul Mare region of the Carpathians (the source of our Pinot Noir) and the Minis brand of Cabernet Sauvignon.

Of the whites, look for the medium dry Tirnave made in the Dracula country of Transylvania, a reasonable Laski Riesling and a wine made from the local grape variety, the Fetească (also called by the German name of Mädchentraube), which makes an aromatic, grapy wine.

Best buys from Rumania

Classic Pinot Noir, Dealul Mare (*Booths; Peter Dominic; Arthur Rackhams*)
Murfatlar (sweet white) (*Europa Foods; Vintage Off-Licence, 33 Angel Road, Norwich, Norfolk*)

Specialist stockist

Touchstone Wines

Spain

A serious risk

The renaissance of Spain as a serious wine-growing nation is currently at risk. It is threatened by two factors: one is price, the other is quality. Often the two go hand in hand.

That link might not be immediately apparent. We are not about to complain about high prices for Spanish wines (although that will come later – see under Rioja), but about prices which are impossibly low.

This year we have tasted a fairly disparate array of cheap Spanish wines, although the bulk have come from Valencia and La Mancha. Their cheapness seemed to be their only virtue: more often than not, they tasted of rather dirty, over-ripe fruit, baked in hot sun and then treated without adequate care or attention, bottled and sold to us as the bargain of the week.

Well, thank you very much, we don't want 'bargains' like this. If we did, we could go to the South of France, to Bulgaria, to Portugal. We have come some way since price was the sole determining factor when buying a bottle of wine: now we want quality *and* value for money – and that doesn't necessarily mean cheapness.

Spain

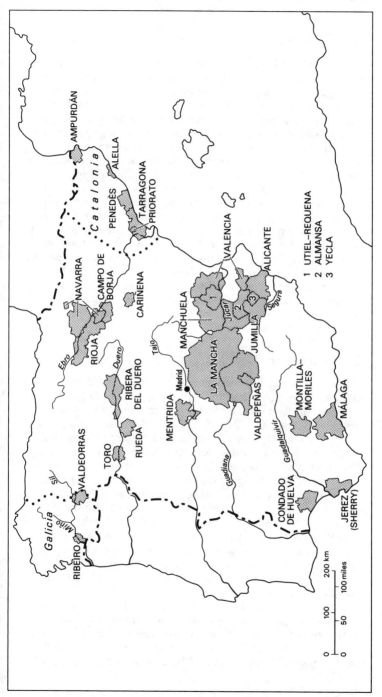

Neutral whites

So far, we have been talking here about Spain's red wines. With whites, it is, on the whole, a different story – not a problem of poor quality (or sloppy wine-making), more one of dullness. The new generation of Spanish whites has left the days of hangover-inducing Spanish Chablis far behind. The bodegas have turned enthusiastically to modern technology to produce perfectly fresh clean wines. But they lack character, individuality, soul – all the things the Italians are managing to reintroduce into their white wines at comparable prices.

So what is Spain's problem? One answer is certainly that traditional attitudes die hard. Although many co-operatives are starting to pick grapes before they are fully – and alcoholically dangerously – ripe, there are still plenty who pay their growers on sugar content (the higher the better). And the co-ops still dominate many areas of Spain – even in Rioja, some 30 per cent of the wine comes from co-ops, while in neighbouring Navarra, most of the wine does. Their temptation – especially with conservative farmers as members – is to leave well alone. It's only when pressurised by more enterprising merchant houses that quality can improve.

Dull grape varieties

The second problem concerns the grape varieties in Spain. Most commentators agree that the black Tempranillo has great potential (it is, of course, the basis of the finest Riojas and Spain's priciest wine, Vega Sicilia), and that Viura is a pleasant enough white grape which can give character to a wine. But there's not much else: the rapid-oxidisation grape, the Garnacha, and the Bobal, Monastrell and the Cariñena – they rarely reach great heights. And in the whites, there's Airen, dubbed the world's most boring grape, and also the world's most widely planted, carpeting vast areas of La Mancha. With such undistinguished raw material, small wonder that much of Spain's wine production is, shall we say, of lesser quality.

Of course, Spain has potential. The French were quite right to be concerned when Spain was about to enter the EC, and promptly set up as many restrictions as they could. After all Spain has the largest vineyard area in the world – 15 per cent of the total – even though, because of low rainfall and methods of planting, her production is only fourth in the world league.

And she has her world-class wines. The example of Torres in Penedés is always quoted, but there are others, including the top bodegas of Rioja, much of Ribera del Duero, a number of other producers in Catalonia, and one-offs like the Marqués de Grignon near Toledo. But the list is short – and it doesn't ever seem to get any longer. There's neither the excitement of Italy, nor the growing potential of Portugal (with its much more interesting grape varieties) - just acres of vines which could, if pushed, come up with some adequate middle-brow wines, but which are still a long way away from fulfilling even that potential.

Last year, we wrote that the revolution in Spanish winemaking was beginning. This year we are much less sure. At the moment, we are still holding our breath. When the revolution does get going, the world should watch out. But the time is not now.

What's on the Spanish label

Like every country, Spain has its own set of terms to describe the wine inside the bottle. Here are a few of the most common.

Abocado Medium sweet.
Anejado por Aged by.
Año In the past Spain has used terms like 2 año and 3 año which indicate that the wine was bottled in the second or third year after the vintage – *not* that it is two or three years old. This term is banned by the Common Market so only older wines will now carry it.
Blanco White.
Bodega Winery.
Brut Dry – generally used for sparkling wines.
Cava A generic term for sparkling wine made by the Champagne method (the word means cellar) – see section on Sparkling wines, page 641.
Con crianza Means that the wine has been aged in wood. Each region has different regulations concerning wood-ageing.
Cosecha Harvest; vintage.
Criado por Blended and/or matured by.
Denominación de Origen (DO) Like appellation contrôlée in France – the official system of quality control.
Dulce Sweet.
Elaborado por Made/blended/matured by.
Embotellado por Bottled by.
Espumoso Sparkling wine made by any method.
Generoso Fortified or dessert wine.
Gran Reserva Top quality wine aged in the winery for a specified period – the highest quality grading for the finest wines. Normally, it means two years in wood and three in bottle, or the other way round (ie a minimum of five years in

total). Generally used for reds, but can apply to whites or rosés, in which case the rules specify at least six months in wood and four in bottle.

Reserva Good quality wine, aged (in Rioja) for one year in wood and two in bottle – or the other way round (a minimum of three years). Whites and rosés need at least six months in wood and 18 months in bottle.

Rosado Rosé.

Seco Dry.

Semi-seco Medium dry.

Sin crianza Without wood-ageing. A wine that is made to be drunk young.

Tinto Red wine.

Vendimia Vintage; the gathering of the grapes.

Viña Literally means vineyard, but is often used to refer to a wine as part of a brand name.

Vino de mesa Table wine.

Vintages in Spain

1988 A pretty disastrous year for many areas. In some parts, like La Mancha, Valencia and Levante, 65 per cent of the crop was lost due to mildew, late frost and hailstorms. In Rioja, mildew occurred but was dealt with and the vintage has proved better than forecasts. But, even here, because of a dry summer, quantities are down; the same is true of Navarra and Penedés.

1987 Low quantity but good quality was the norm for this harvest. A hot, dry summer meant that yields were low, and that red wines will be much better than whites. Only in Ribera del Duero did quantities approach normal.

1986 Good reds in the north of Spain – Rioja, Navarra, Penedés – but less satisfactory for whites. Further south, a good all-round harvest.

1985 Good generally. Very good, with good quantity as well, in Rioja and Navarra.

1984 Average to good quality, much better for whites than reds. Quantities and quality badly down in Rioja.

1983 Good, but not great. Whites fared better than reds again – especially in Penedés. The reds are unlikely to last long.

1982 A great year, with some very fine reds on the way, especially in Rioja, Penedés and Ribera del Duero.

1981 Light reds, but very high quality. Some ageing potential in the Reservas. Best wines from Navarra for a decade.

1980 Variable generally. Very good in La Mancha, good in Rioja and Penedés, average in Navarra.

1979 Good to average vintage. Rioja and La Mancha good, Navarra average.
1978 Good vintage everywhere, very good in Navarra and La Mancha.

RIOJA

Lucky farmers – not so lucky consumers

Some of the luckiest grape farmers in Spain live in the Rioja. They have watched their region become internationally renowned, and, at home, seen demand soar. Not surprisingly, they want a share of the profits that are coming in the direction of the bodegas to whom they sell their grapes. So they've asked for more money – something like 100 per cent more for the 1987 harvest, and more again in 1988.

Now that may enhance the lifestyle of the Rioja farmer, but it's not going to help sales of Rioja when the inevitable price increases come through. We've already learnt to be more cautious about the quality of the wine that is coming from what must still be called Spain's premier wine region – high prices on top are going to drive us right away.

Much has changed in Rioja from the days when it was hailed as the discovery of the decade. The oaky, vanilla tastes of the long-lived Reservas and Gran Reservas – at silly prices – were a palate-opener for many fledgling wine drinkers at the time when wine was just taking off.

Of course, those fabled bottles have been drunk up, but what replaced them? Certainly not more of the same – even at higher prices. There now seems to be an enormous amount of Rioja without any wood-ageing (sin crianza it will say on the label, or nothing at all), which is fruity, yes, but no more or less fruity than wines from many other, lesser, regions, and which doesn't age.

Reservas and Gran Reservas are still produced. But with those Gran Reservas, which should represent the peak of excellence, there seems to be a willingness on the part of the bodegas to lower standards and to use fruit and wine (sometimes from indifferent vintages) which, in the past, would never have got past simple Reserva or even basic crianza status – just to get the higher prices the Gran Reserva tag achieves.

It's no way to maintain a reputation. So while we would still recommend crianza and Reserva Riojas, we would suggest that you buy Gran Reservas only from a handful of the very best bodegas – and then only in the best vintages.

Who's who in Rioja

Bodegas Alavesas Soft, light but concentrated reds made from grapes grown in the Rioja Alavesa. Also a young, deliciously fruity red. Brand name: Solar de Samaniego.
Arriba Kettle; Laymont & Shaw; Mi Casa Wines; Moreno Wines

Bodegas Berberana Use of new barrels in maturation gives these wines a strongly woody, somewhat one-dimensional quality. But early bottling prevents them losing their fruit. Brand name: Berberana.
David Alexander; Arriba Kettle; Ellis Son & Vidler; Andrew Gordon Wines; Gerard Harris; Moreno Wines; Reid Wines; La Reserva Wines; Sherborne Vintners; Willoughbys

Bodegas Beronia Good, soft, oaky reds and fresh whites. Brand name: Beronia.
Bibendum; D Byrne & Co; Alex Findlater; Laymont & Shaw; Moreno Wines; Oddbins; Sherborne Vintners; Upper Crust

Bodegas Bilbainas An old-fashioned family firm, making wines in the old style. Brand names: Viña Pomal, Viña Zaco.
Arriba Kettle; Moreno Wines; La Reserva Wines; Sherborne Vintners

Bodegas Campo Viejo One of the largest bodegas, making reds in a plummy, fruity style. The top wines, Marqués de Villamagna and the Gran Reserva Campo Viejo, are very good. Brand name: Marqués de Villamagna, Campo Viejo.
David Alexander; Bibendum; D Byrne & Co; Gateway; Grape Ideas; Hedley Wright; Mi Casa Wines; Moreno Wines; La Reserva Wines; Sherborne Vintners; Ubiquitous Chip; Upper Crust; Victoria Wine Company

CVNE (Compañia Vinícola del Norte de España) Produce an excellent range of old style Riojas, including a white called Monopole. The Gran Reservas and Reservas are outstanding. Brand names: Imperial, Monopole. The company's name is often pronounced as if it were spelt CUNE.
Widely available

Bodegas Corral A new bodega whose best wine is its Don Jacobo Reserva.
The Grape Ideas, 14 Market Street, Winslow, Bucks; Hanslope Wines, 18 Gold Street, Hanslope, Milton Keynes; Wine Growers Association

Bodegas El Coto Medium-sized bodega making light, soft, fragrant wines. Brand name: El Coto.
Laymont & Shaw; La Reserva Wines; Sherborne Vintners

Domecq The famous Sherry and brandy producers have established a reputation for good quality Rioja from their own vineyards. Brand: Domecq Domain.
D Byrne & Co; La Reserva Wines; Sherborne Vintners; Victoria Wine Company; Yorkshire Fine Wines

Bodegas Faustino Despite the terrible fake dust on the bottles, these are good wines, at all quality levels. Whites, including the Viura-based Faustino V, is fresh in the modern style; red Reservas are very good. Brand name: Faustino.
D Byrne & Co; Peter Dominic; Peter Green; Moreno Wines; Mi Casa Wines; La Reserva Wines; Sherborne Vintners

Bodegas Lagunilla Reliable reds, including a reasonable Gran Reserva, but a rather dull white. Brand name: Lagunilla.
Peter Dominic; La Reserva Wines; Upper Crust

Bodegas Lan Modern producers of good young wines. The white is fresh, the red is fragrant. Brand name: Lan.
H Allen Smith; Premier Wine Warehouse; La Reserva Wines; Sherborne Vintners

Laserna Single estate wine, one of the few in Rioja. Brand name: Contino.
David Baillie Vintners; Cadwgan Wines; Mayor Sworder & Co; Unwins

Bodegas Lopez de Heredia Old-fashioned bodega (in the best sense). Virtually everything – including fermentation – is done in wood. The results are glorious whites, more delicate reds. Brand name: Tondonia.
Hedley Wright; Laymont & Shaw; Majestic; Martinez Fine Wines; Moreno Wines; La Reserva Wines; Sherborne Vintners; Tanners; La Vigneronne

Bodegas Marqués de Cáceres Pioneer of the new-style whites and softer modern reds. Still some of the best of their type around. The Reservas age remarkably well for such modernity. Brand name: Marqués de Cáceres.
Widely available

Bodegas Marqués de Murrieta The finest white Riojas, made in the old style and superbly long-lasting, the nearest Spain gets to white Burgundy. The reds, less interesting, are still very good and age well. Brand name: Marqués de Murrieta, Castillo de Ygay.
Widely available

Which? Wine Guide does not accept payment for inclusion, and there is no sponsorship or advertising.

Marqués de Riscal A bodega that continues to disappoint, despite its fine reputation. Its white is not from Rioja but from Rueda (and none the worse for that), the red tends to be on the thin side and with harsh edges. Brand name: Marqués de Riscal. *David Baillie Vintners; D Byrne & Co; Mi Casa Wines; Moreno Wines; Nobody Inn; La Reserva Wines; Tanners; Willoughbys; Victoria Wine Company*

Bodegas Martinez Bujanda A century-old firm in one of the region's newest bodegas. Makes a young, fruity red using carbonic maceration (in the style of Beaujolais Nouveau), as well as good Reservas. Wines: Conde de Valdemar Reserva/Gran Reserva. *Arriba Kettle; The Wine Club*

Bodegas Martinez Lacuesta An old family firm making fairly standard whites and reds, but some very good Reservas. Brand names: Campeador, Reserva Especial. *Moreno Wines*

Bodegas Montecillo Ultra-modern bodega making very good commercial wines. Brand names: Viña Monty, Viña Cumbrero. *Barwell & Jones; Peter Green; Laymont & Shaw; Ubiquitous Chip; Wines from Paris*

Bodegas Muga Much better for reds, which are delicate and elegant, than for whites. Traditional methods still in operation. Brand name: Muga. *H Allen Smith; Arriba Kettle; D Byrne & Co; Blayney's; Bottle & Basket; Hungerford Wine Company; Laymont & Shaw; Andrew Mead Wines; Mi Casa Wines; Moreno Wines; Sherborne Vintners; Upper Crust; Willoughbys*

Bodegas Olarra Brand new bodega making some excellent reds, including a very good Reserva at a knock-down price. Brand names: Reserva Cerro Añon, Olarra. *D Byrne & Co; Oddbins; La Reserva Wines; Sherborne Vintners*

Bodegas Palacio Medium-sized bodega, making good, younger-style red as well as an interesting white, using Sémillon. Wines: Reserva Glorioso, Bodas de Oro Reserva Especial. *Oddbins*

Bodegas Federico Paternina Vast, modern bodega but a long-established firm, whose wines have been going through a bad patch. Reds are better than the whites. Brand names: Banda Azul (red), Banda Dorada (white). *D Byrne & Co; Peter Dominic; La Reserva Wines; Sherborne Vintners; Victoria Wine Company*

Remelluri One of the few Rioja bodegas to estate-bottle their wines from their own vineyards. Make perfumed, rich, soft wines. Brand name: La Bastida de Alava.
Arriba Kettle; Lay & Wheeler; Laymont & Shaw; La Reserva Wines; Sherborne Vintners; Tanners; Willoughbys

Bodegas La Rioja Alta A traditonalist producing one of the most reliable ranges in Rioja. Great heights can be reached in the Reservas and Gran Reservas. Brand names: Metropol (white), Viña Alberdi, Viña Arana, Viña Ardanza, Reserva 904.
Widely available

Bodegas Riojanas The influence of the French founders of this bodega can still be felt in the elegance of the wines. Quite a lot of old-fashioned reds. Brand names: Viña Albina, Monte Real.
Peter Green; Majestic; Mi Casa Wines; Moreno Wines; La Reserva Wines; Sherborne Vintners

Viña Salceda Small family bodega making only red wines. Wine: Conde de la Salceda.
Arriba Kettle; Lay & Wheeler; La Reserva Wines; Sherborne Vintners; Tanners

Bodegas Santiago Lightweight wines which can be drunk young. Brand name: Gran Condal.
Eldridge Pope; La Reserva Wines; Sherborne Vintners

Bodegas Sierra Cantabria
Prestige Vintners

Bodegas Unidas Large firm, also known as AGE, under American ownership, making reliable wines. The Siglo is sold in a distinctive sacking cover. Brand names: Marqués de Romeral, Siglo, Fuenmayor.
Marks & Spencer; Mi Casa Wines; Moreno Wines; Reid Wines; Sherborne Vintners

Best buys from Rioja

WHITE

Monopole Seco Blanco 1985, CVNE (*Hungerford WineCompany*)
Faustino V Blanco 1987 (*A&A Wines*)
Rioja Blanco 1984, Marqués de Murrieta (*Waitrose*)
Añares Blanco 1985 (*Abbey Cellars*)

RED

Rioja Artadi Tinto 1988, Cosecheros Alavesas (*Arriba Kettle*)
Rioja Reserva 1981, Beronia (*Raeburn Fine Wines and Foods*)
Rioja 1981, Samaniego (*Bottle and Basket*)

Rioja Señor Burgues (*Blayneys*)
Rioja Tinto 1985, CVNE (*D'Arcys*)
Rioja Reserva 1985, Faustino V (*Charles Hennings*)
Rioja Gran Reserva Campo Viejo 1978 (*widely available*)
Rioja Montecillo Cumbrero 1985 (*Barwell & Jones*)
Rioja Gran Reserva 1980, Montecillo Viña Monty (*Wine House*)
Rioja Muga 1984 (*Wizard Wine Warehouses*)

CATALONIA AND PENEDÉS

Blending with foreigners

Despite the reputation of its reds, Penedés – the main wine-
producing area of Catalonia – is much more concerned with
white wines. While the bulk of production goes into the
sparkling cavas (see the section on Sparkling wines, page 634) of
which 130 million bottles are made each year, there are also
many more interesting still white wines coming out of this
region than from anywhere else in Spain (apart, of course, for
the wines of Jerez – see the section on Fortified wines, page
643).

The local white grapes, the Xarel-lo, Parellada and Macabeo,
form the bulk of production. Of these, the Parellada seems to
have the most character, and the Viña Sol of Miguel Torres (see
below under Who's Who) is one of the best examples of wines
from this grape.

The reds in the Penedés tend to more variability. While some
which use the Garnacha and Cariñena grapes can be good when
drunk not too old, there is little that can equal the Reservas of
Rioja until the Tempranillo comes into play.

However, it is in the judicious blending of Spanish and more
international varieties – Chardonnay, Cabernet Sauvignon,
Muscat, Gewürztraminer, Pinot Noir – that Penedés (and
Catalonia in general) leads the way. While pioneering work has
been undertaken by Torres, other firms have followed closely.
The 'foreign' varieties generally form a small part of a blend,
although some of the region's top wines come from 100 per cent
Cabernet Sauvignon or 100 per cent Chardonnay. But even in
small quantities, they give a depth of flavour which the Spanish
varieties on their own seem to lack.

Apart from Penedés, other wine DOs in Catalonia include
Alella (a small zone making some white wines); Ampurdán—
Costa Brava (fairly alcoholic rosados); Tarragona and Terra Alta

(best known for communion wines); Priorato, home of intensely flavoured and intensely alcoholic reds; and Costers del Segre (source of the top quality wines of Raimat – see below).

White wines from Penedés should in general be drunk young. Look for the 1988 vintage now. The only exceptions to this are some of the wines produced by Torres and Jean León (see below).

Reds also should be drunk younger than they would be from Rioja. Three-year-old wines are at their best, but some wines repay keeping for five or six years – again, those from Torres and Jean León being the best keepers.

Who's who in Catalonia

Alta Alella Company producing the best whites from the Alella DO. Wines: Marqués de Alella.
Moreno Wines; Sherborne Vintners

René Barbier Under the same ownership as the sparkling Conde de Caralt, this estate makes a fresh white and some reliable reds. Also sells wines under the Canals & Nubiola name. Wines: Kraliner (dry white), red, Canals & Nubiola.
Mi Casa Wines; La Reserva Wines; Sherborne Vintners; Unwins

Ferret i Mateu Good value Penedés wines. Wine: Viña Laranda.
Prospero Wines, 2 Warrington Crescent, London W9

Jean León Run by a Spaniard based in California. The influence shows in both his wines, which are 100 per cent varietals. His Chardonnay is especially interesting. Wines: Chardonnay, Cabernet Sauvignon.
Alex Findlater; Fortnum & Mason; Laymont & Shaw; Majestic; Moreno Wines; La Reserva Wines; Sherborne Vintners; Tanners; La Vigneronne

Marqués de Monistrol Makes a range of sound table wines. Part of the Martini e Rossi Italian company. Wines: Blanc de Blancs, Reserva.
David Alexander; Sherborne Vintners

Masía Bach Best known for its sweet wine which some regard highly, others dislike. Also makes a good red wine and a less good dry white. Wines: Masía Bach red, Extrísimo Bach sweet white.
Majestic; Moreno Wines; La Reserva Wines; Sherborne Vintners; The Wine Society

Mont Marçal Goodish whites, better reds from the Penedés.
Moreno Wines

Raimat Large showplace estate in Lerida in western Catalonia, owned by sparkling wine producers Codorníu, making Cabernet Sauvignon and Chardonnay wines and an excellent blended red called Abadía. Also a Chardonnay sparkler (see under Sparkling wines on page 642).
D Byrne & Co; Fortnum & Mason; Laymont & Shaw; Majestic; La Reserva Wines; Victoria Wine Company; The Wine Society; also J Sainsbury for Raimat Abadía

Manuel Sancho Best known for both modern and old-style white wines. Wines: red Mont Marçal Añada and oaky, aged but well-balanced Mont Marçal Blanco Reserva.
Arriba Kettle; Sherborne Vintners

Jaume Serra Makes a top Muscat wine in Alella.
Cantina Augusto; Eldridge Pope; Lorne House Vintners; Sherborne Vintners; Stapylton Fletcher; The Wine Society

Torres The most famous firm in Penedés, and probably in Spain. Their reputation is based on the skills of Miguel Torres Jr in blending European grape varieties – Chardonnay, Sauvignon, Gewürztraminer, Muscat, Pinot Noir, Cabernet Sauvignon and Cabernet Franc – with local Spanish varieties to create innovative wines. Wines: Viña Sol, Tres Torres, Coronas, Sangredetoro. The French/Spanish blends are: Gran Viña Sol (Chardonnay and Parellada), Gran Viña Sol Green Label (Parellada and Sauvignon), Viña Esmeralda (Gewürztraminer and Muscat), Viña Magdala (Pinot Noir and Cariñena), Gran Coronas (Cabernet Sauvignon and Tempranillo) and Gran Coronas Black Label (Cabernet Sauvignon and Cabernet Franc). A 100 per cent Chardonnay wine, Milmanda, was released last year, along with Mas de la Plana (100 per cent Cabernet Sauvignon) – both in small quantities from single vineyards.
Widely available

Best buys from Catalonia and Penedés

WHITE

Chardonnay 1987, Raimat (*Gare du Vin*)

RED

René Barbier Tinto 1986 (*Alba Wine Society*)
Coronas 1985, Miguel Torres (*widely available*)
Sangredetoro 1986, Miguel Torres (*widely available*)
Raimat Abadía 1986 (*Gare du Vin; Victoria Wine*)

NAVARRA

Trying hard

Navarra has suffered from being right across the river from Rioja – and from not producing such fine wines. Much of her production has been in rosado (rosé) made from the Garnacha grape. Only in the past few years have producers here recognised that they needed to progress in reds and whites to get anywhere on foreign markets.

The producers of Navarra deserve to succeed in improving the quality of their wines – they are trying hard enough. They have banned plantings of the lesser Garnacha grape and are encouraging the Tempranillo in an effort to move away from reds (and rosados) that faded fast. They have established Spain's best viticultural station at Olite, and have even authorised small plantings of some foreign varieties – Pinot Noir, Cabernet Sauvignon and Chardonnay – for use as refining and blending material.

They've certainly made great progress in the reds – about the whites we are less sure. Navarra wines are never going to reach the heights of good Rioja, but at the middle and lower price range they are better value. The rosados, we feel, are best left to the Spaniards who seem to like these things.

One major problem has still to be overcome. Much of the production remains in the hands of indifferent co-operatives who sell in bulk to local merchants or foreign buyers. Few co-operatives bottle their own wines, so the incentive for improvement is still at least two removes away from the growers. Until that changes, progress will be slower than the Navarra authorities would like.

Terms in Navarra

Vinos de Crianza Red wines which have spent at least one year in barrel.

Reservas Aged for at least three years, at least one year of which must have been in barrel.

Gran Reservas Aged for two years in wood, then three in bottle.

Who's who in Navarra

Bodegas Bardon Owned by Olarra, the Rioja bodega. Produce two young reds and one Reserva style. Wines: Togal, Larums, Don Luis.
Sherborne Vintners

Cenalsa Marketing consortium producing good modern-style whites, rosés and reds. Wines: Agramont brand.
Fullers

Julián Chivite Fresh, clean, well-made wines. Wines: Gran Feudo range, Gran Vino Aniversario 125.
Laymont & Shaw; Majestic; La Reserva Wines; Sherborne Vintners; La Vigneronne

Bodegas Gurpegui Good nouveau-style red, and other good reds. Wines: Monte Ory brand.
H Allen Smith; Corney & Barrow; Winecellars

Bodegas Irache Make a good aged Reserva. Wines: Gran Reserva, Reserva.
Sherborne Vintners; Sherston Wine Company

Nuestro Padre Jesus del Perdón Nothing like invoking a top name to protect this, probably the best of the Navarra co-operatives. Their reds are much better than their whites. Wines: Nuevo Vino (red), Casa la Teja (white)
Majestic; La Reserva Wines

Bodegas Ochoa Lighter style reds and whites.
La Reserva Wines; Tanners; La Vigneronne; The Wine Society

Señorio de Sarria One of the best producers in the region. A spectacular new-style red, plus oak-aged wines of some class. Wines: Viña Ecoyen, Viña del Perdón, Gran Viña.
Arriba Kettle; Laymont & Shaw; La Reserva Wines; Sherborne Vintners; La Vigneronne; The Wine Society

Vinícola Navarra Owned by the same company as Campo Viejo in Rioja, this firm is the largest exporter of Navarra wines. Wines: Castillo de Olite, Castillo de Tiebas.
Bibendum

Best buys from Navarra

Gran Reserva 1978, Gran Plané (*B H Wines*)
Castillo de Tiebas Reserva 1975 (*Grape Ideas Wine Warehouse*)
Monte Ory Reserva 1978 (*Premier Wine Warehouse*)
Ochoa Reserva 1978 (*Frank E Stainton*)

RIBERA DEL DUERO

Since Robert Parker, the American wine guru, discovered Ribera
del Duero, prices of wines from some producers in this area
have shot to sky-high levels. One bodega, Vega Sicilia, always
did command high prices because its wines are so good and in
such short supply.

Of course, Robert Parker is right in praising the wines from
the Duero Valley just east of Valladolid (the Duero, by the way,
crosses the frontier into Portugal where soon after it becomes
the Douro of Port fame). In this small area, very hot in summer,
freezing cold in winter, the Tempranillo of Rioja (which is called
here the Tinto Fino or Tinto del Pais) makes some of Spain's
finest red wines. They are rich, almost sweet in their intensity
and heavy with perfumed, peppery but elegant fruit. It is an
expanding area, too, as more bodegas – and the local co-
operative – realise that they are in a region where fine wine can
be made. If any area could threaten the supremacy of Rioja in
Spanish wine terms, this is it.

Who's who in Ribera del Duero

Bodegas Victor Balbas Small family firm, making elegant wines.
Wine: Balbas.
Majestic

Bodegas Alejandro Fernandez Founded in 1970, this estate
makes red wines which are aged in small Bordeaux barriques
for up to two and a half years. Described rather too
enthusiastically by Robert Parker as the Château Pétrus of
Spain – but they are good. Wine: Pesquera.
*Adnams; Andrew Gordon Wines; Laymont & Shaw; La Reserva
Wines; Sherborne Vintners; Tanners; The Wine Society*

Bodegas Mauro Small bodega making a rich, heavy wine with
considerable ageing ability. Wine: Mauro.
Davisons; Moreno Wines; The Wine Society

Bodegas Peñalba López A privately owned bodega whose wines
can be some of the most immediately approachable in Ribera
del Duero. Wine: Torremilanos.
Majestic; La Reserva Wines; Willoughbys

Ribera del Duero Co-operative Old established but with a newly enhanced reputation. At the moment the younger wines are the best, but increased winemaking quality should improve the Protos Gran Reserva. Wines: Protos Gran Reserva red, Ribera Duero, Peñafiel.

H Allen Smith; D Byrne & Co; Laymont & Shaw; Moreno Wines; Oddbins; La Reserva Wines; Sherborne Vintners

Bodegas Vega Sicilia They say that the wine here needs 30 years to reach its peak. Mainly a blend of Cabernet Sauvignon, Merlot and Malbec, it has enormous reserves of fruit which are intensely tannic and chewy when young, but still full of tobacco-rich flavours which emerge after ageing in bottle. It is made only in the best years and is then available only in small quantities at a high price. A second wine, Valbuena, made every year, is more approachable but still expensive. Production is being expanded under new ownership. Wines: Vega Sicilia, Valbuena.

Adnams; H Allen Smith; Laymont & Shaw; Majestic; Moreno Wines; La Reserva Wines; Sherborne Vintners; Tanners; La Vigneronne

Best buys from Ribera del Duero

Peñalba 1985, Bodegas Ribera Duero (*Augustus Barnett*)
Tudela del Duero 1984, Mauro (*Fulham Road Wine Centre; Master Cellar Wine Warehouse*)
Viña Valduero 1985, Foux & Read (*Mi Casa Wines*)
Ribera del Duero Tinto 1985, Bodegas Ribera Duero (*Peter Green; Moreno Wines*)

OTHER REGIONS OF SPAIN

JUMILLA

Because of the high organic content of the soil in this region inland from Valencia, the phylloxera louse never struck, so the vines are ungrafted. The result is some very rich reds, which, when the alcohol is lowered by early picking, are good drunk young. An area with potential. Wines available in the UK include Condestable (*Bibendum; Laymont & Shaw; Lorne House Vintners; Sherborne Vintners*) and Castillo Jumilla (*Alba Wine Society; Europa Foods shops in London*).

RUEDA

This region seems to be making some of Spain's best white wines, thanks to new technology and the fact that the local white grape, the Verdejo, has some character. The region is also high in the plateau of Castille, so night temperatures are low, which white grapes like.

Who's who in Rueda

Marqués de Riscal This white is the best known wine from the area. It's a modern-style wine, made for the Rioja bodega by Vinos Blancos de Castilla.
Adnams; David Baillie Vintners; Laymont & Shaw; Moreno Wines; La Reserva Wines; Thresher

Bodegas de Crianza de Castilla la Vieja Wines from here are more of a find. The bodega has used the talents of the Bordeaux-based Professor Peynaud to make a top-class modern white and an outstanding oak-aged red (made near Toledo using Cabernet Sauvignon). Wines: Marqués de Grinon red and dry white.
Adnams; H Allen Smith; Booths; D Byrne & Co; Hungerford Wine Company; Laymont & Shaw; Majestic; La Reserva Wines; Sherborne Vintners; Tanners

TORO

This small area, close to Ribera del Duero, has been showing some promising signs, with one wine – the Gran Colegiata – attracting particular attention for its good value. The red grape used in this wine is the familiar Tempranillo (called here the Tinto de Toro), and because the area has a lower altitude than Ribera, the wines are heavier and less acidic, and therefore develop and fade more quickly.

Who's who in Toro

Bodegas Farina Producer of Tinto Colegiata and Gran Colegiata.
Adnams; Tanners; La Vigneronne

VALDEPEÑAS

This region lies within the larger denominación of La Mancha.
Valdepeñas produces some very good reds and less interesting
whites at very good prices.

Two bodegas are making above-average wines.

Cosecheros Abastecedores Produce good reds, especially at
Reserva and Gran Reserva levels at amazingly good prices.
Wine: Señorio de los Llanos.
*Arriba Kettle; Peter Dominic; Alex Findlater; Laymont & Shaw; Mi
Casa Wines; Moreno Wines; La Reserva Wines; Sherborne Vintners*

Bodegas Felix Solis Make a good red called Viña Albali.
Sherborne Vintners; Upper Crust

VALENCIA

The fertile coastal plain of Valencia, besides being the source of
most of our Spanish oranges, is also one of the largest wine-
producing areas in the country, with massive bodegas in the
city of Valencia and vineyards in the hinterland of Utiel–
Requena. Not that we would know, because most of the wine is
exported in bulk and blended, for selling as rock-bottom cheap
Spanish red. But some bottled wine is now finding its way to
our shops, and we are now becoming familiar with good value
sweet Moscatel-based wines such as Moscatel de Valencia
(*Marks & Spencer; J Sainsbury*). There's also plenty of very
inexpensive red such as Casa lo Alto red (*Safeway*) and Castillo
de Liria (*Tanners*).

GALICIA

Galicia is the north-west corner of Spain, north of Portugal.
Being right in the line of the Atlantic low fronts that also hit
Britain, it is very wet. It is green, mountainous and makes
piercingly crisp white, and tart red, wines, which have a close
affinity with the Vinhos Verdes of Portugal – indeed, they are
called Vinos Verdes.

The best Galician white wines are made from the Albarino grape (the top quality Alvarinho of Portuguese Vinho Verde), but a number of other grape varieties (of which the most important are the Treixadura and the Torontes) are also used. Denominated areas are Valdeorras (which specialises in red wines), the coastal Rias Baixas and, just inland, Ribeiro.

Producers include Bodegas Campante (*Moreno Wines; La Reserva Wines*); and Bodegas Chaves (*Laymont & Shaw; La Reserva Wines*).

Best buys from other regions

Valdepeñas 1988, Marqués de Gastanaga (*H Allen Smith*)
Valdepeñas Señorio de los Llanos Gran Reserva 1978 (*widely available*)
Marius Reserva 1982, Bodegas Piqueras, Almansa (*Findlater Mackie Todd*)
Altos de Pio 1987, Jumilla (*Laymont & Shaw*)
Castillo de Almansa Gran Reserva 1981, Almansa (*Fullers*)
Campo Seco, Jumilla (*Alastair's Grapevine*)
Castillo de Alhambra Tinto 1988 (*Martinez Fine Wine; Oddbins*)
Condestable Tinto 1986, Señorio de Condestable, Jumilla (*Laymont & Shaw; Moreno Wines*)
Vega de Toro Tinto Reserva 1981, Luis Mateos (*Moreno Wines*)
Gran Colegiata 1985, Bodegas Farina (*widely available*)

Specialist stockists (for all regions)

A & A Wines; Ad Hoc Wine Warehouse; H Allen Smith; Arriba Kettle; Bottle and Basket; Cadwgan Fine Wines; Peter Green; Laymont & Shaw; Martinez Fine Wine; Master Cellar Wine Warehouse; Mi Casa Wines; Moreno Wines; La Reserva Wines; Sherborne Vintners; Upper Crust; La Vigneronne; Wine House

Switzerland

We have tasted no Swiss wines this year, probably because we haven't been to Switzerland: unlike most wine-producing countries, it is pretty rare to see examples of Swiss viticulture over in Britain.

That is hardly surprising: Swiss wine is expensive. There are plenty of reasons – the high cost of land, the impossibly steep slopes which are hugely labour-intensive to work and, of course, the famously stable Swiss franc.

Anyway, the Swiss are extremely fond of their own wines, as well as importing considerable quantities from other countries. A recent succession of large harvests, though, has meant that more wine has been available for export, and at least one firm is now working actively to encourage us to try Swiss wine.

Wine is made all over the country. The German speakers make German-style wines in the north-east of the country. In the south, the Italian speakers in the Ticino make red wines based on the Merlot grape. And in the west, it is the French speakers who produce wines in the Vaud around Lake Geneva, in the Valais and in Neuchâtel.

The most important areas, as far as we are concerned, are the French-speaking areas, since these are where most wine is made, and from which most is exported. The smallest of the three is Neuchâtel, which specialises in light rosé wines called Oeil de Perdrix (partridge's eye) made from the Pinot Noir. White Neuchâtel is made from the Chasselas grape.

In the Vaud, production is much larger, and it is here that the white Chasselas grape, almost the national grape of Switzerland, comes into its own. The large expanse of Lake Geneva keeps the temperature in the summer warmer than the surrounding areas, and vines are planted on the hillsides leading down to the lake. The wine-growing area is divided into three sub-zones: Chablais, Lavaux and La Côte. Inevitably production costs on these valuable areas of real estate are high.

The Valais to the east and near the source of the River Rhône is the largest production area. Chasselas (here called Fendant) and Sylvaner (called Johannisberg) produce the white wines, Pinot Noir and Gamay the reds. A blended red, made from the two grapes, is called Dôle.

Swiss wines are not complex, being quite delicate in flavour. The whites from the Chasselas tend to lack acidity but can age well. The reds are light and attractive when slightly chilled.

Who's who in Switzerland

Valais

Alphonse Orsat (*Eldridge Pope/Reynier Wine Libraries; Peter Green*).

Vaud

Testuz Try the top estate white, Arbalète Dézaley Premier Cru (*Eldridge Pope/Reynier Wine Libraries; La Réserve*).

Bernard Bovy Makes a very expensive St-Saphorin La Roche aux Vignes (*La Réserve; Swiss Centre*).

Hammel Large négociant and estate owner. Wines come from individual estates in the La Côte region of the Vaud: Ch de Trêvelin, Domaine de la Bolliattaz, Clos du Châtelard, Les Closailles, Réserve de la Harpe, Ch de Pictet-Lullin (*Tanners*).

Neuchâtel

Samuel Chatenay (*Eldridge Pope/Reynier Wine Libraries; La Réserve*). Also the attractive rosé Oeil de Perdrix from the **Caves des Coteaux Cortaillod** (*Swiss Centre*).

Other areas

Schaffhausen In eastern Switzerland (Steiner Beerliwein Faleberg, a red from Pinot Noir) (*Swiss Centre*).

A selection of other wines, including Merlots from Ticino (the Italian area's best style) should usually be available at the *Swiss Centre, Leicester Square, London WC2.*

Turkey

A range of Turkish wines was introduced by one of London's major department stores in 1989. We will spare that store its blushes by not naming it: we can only assume that it was an aberration in an otherwise excellent range, because the wines themselves were dreadful – old, tired, fruitless – we could hardly bring ourselves to taste them. We gather the wines were not a success, and are no longer listed.

In any case, they were not necessarily representative of what Turkey makes in the way of wine. There is nothing of high quality, but some of the wines mentioned below are at least drinkable in a simple, hearty sort of way, and just right for rich food like stews and kebabs.

Turkey has the fifth largest area under vine in the world, but under five per cent of the grapes are made into wine – the rest are table grapes. It is in the regions with the strongest European links – in the small area of Thrace, which is Turkey in Europe, and on the Aegean coast – that the wine industry flourishes. The only other area to produce wine is around the capital, Ankara.

The best Turkish wines are red. New technology has not made a big enough impact to make decent white wines possible. Branded names are the thing, even though the wine may come from a specific area, and most exports go through the state monopoly.

What's what in Turkey

Buzbag Branded wine made on the Anatolian plateau near Ankara.

Trakya A light red wine, made in Thrace.

Villa Doluca Regarded as the most interesting Turkish wine. Produced in Thrace from Gamay grapes.

To try these wines, your best bet would be to visit a Turkish restaurant in London, such as Efes Kebab House, 80 Great Titchfield Street, London W1, or Topkapi, 25 Marylebone High Street, London W1, or one of the many Turkish food shops/off-licences in London N1 and N16.

The United States

CALIFORNIA

Keeping pace

You need to move fast to keep up with what happens in California. Every year seems to come up with a new trend, a new fashion, a new discovery. This year, the buzz-word is appellation, that good old French term used to designate a particular area as good for making wines of a certain type.

And, surprise, surprise, that is exactly how the Californians are using it. Although the US Bureau of Alcohol, Tobacco and Firearms (an unholy alliance if ever there was one), which controls the US wine industry, has been designating viticultural areas since 1978 (one of them, the Ohio River Valley, spans four states, so you can see how precise they are), California now wants to go one better and designate specific appellations within those viticultural areas.

Deserving appellation

The first area to apply for designation is the one that deserves it most. The twin vineyard areas of Rutherford Bench and Oakville Bench in the centre of the Napa Valley are the heart of the California wine industry to many people. They are the home of some of the finest Cabernet Sauvignon vineyards (the Mondavi/ Rothschild Opus One is produced here), as well as being perhaps the area most densely planted with vines anywhere in the state.

Once the most obvious appellation is created, there is every reason why the idea should be extended to other prime areas – Carneros, for instance, or parts of Sonoma County. The names will appear on the labels and, just as in Europe, we will begin to recognise the premium growing areas of California.

It's a far cry from the time, only three or four years ago, when the Californians seemed to be saying that where the vines grow is much less important than what happens in the winery. Now they have realised that grapes and vineyards are inextricably tied together, that some vineyards are better at growing certain grape varieties than others, and that not every site can support grapes – at least for premium wine production.

Other buzz-words are going the rounds, as well. Fashion has affected the standing of the two great grape varieties – Chardonnay and Cabernet Sauvignon. Now they have become mainstream, so are no longer exciting. The 'in' grapes are currently Sauvignon Blanc (or the wood-aged variant Fumé Blanc), Merlot (either as a straight varietal wine, or blended with Cabernet Sauvignon in a Bordeaux-style blend) and that old workhorse of the California vineyards, Zinfandel, either as a Blush (or pink) wine or in its proper character of a good, big, beefy red.

Not just premium wines now

What we see in the UK in the way of California wine is the tip of a huge mountain of grapes which the state produces every year. Much of the production is still of Thomson seedless grapes which are used not only for table grapes but for production of many of the cheaper 'jug' wines in the Central Valley, a hot plain away from the moderating breezes and fogs of the Napas and Sonomas of this world.

Until not so long ago, California seemed to be finding difficulty in producing wines somewhere between the top varietal wines and the jug wines. Now all that is changing. With good quality wine much more widely available (as a result of wider planting of good varietals and also a fall in demand within the United States), enterprising producers – led, as far as the British market is concerned, by Robert Mondavi – are starting to come up with medium-priced wines that can fill the gap. The result is that California can become more competitive on price – and quality – with Australia.

California wines came to Britain in the late 1970s and early 1980s, full of excitement, and we all thought that French wines were about to be knocked off their pedestal. Of course, no such thing happened: California wines shot up in price as the exchange rate went against the pound, exports to Britain declined - and France went on as before as number one.

Then along came Australia. Conditions were just right for the Aussies to make substantial inroads into the British market. Australia managed to come up with quality and good prices, a combination California has found hard to achieve, so her wines were left out in the cold.

The pendulum swings

Now the pendulum has swung the other way. While Australia suffers from grape shortages, and consequent risk of price rises, California is sailing in with good-value medium-priced wines which are attracting major supermarkets and off-licences, just as Australia did a year or two ago. Imports of California wines in 1987 were 97 per cent higher than in 1986 – and went up by nearly half as much again in 1988. The result is actually good for both countries, because it establishes 'New World' more strongly than ever as an important category in any wine merchant's listings.

Certainly, looking at new wines being offered by the major retailers, 1990 could be the year in which California makes its comeback. And if we can find another source of good quality and good value, we shall be the first to cheer. But we must hope that – as with Australia – small harvests in 1987 and 1988 don't mean an end to the value we are now seeing.

The Californian label

Californian labels are generally informative and can reveal a great deal about the wine in the bottle: when the grapes were picked, how they were fermented, when the wine was bottled.

There is also considerable detail on the front label, such as the name of the vendor of the wine: so and so's vineyard. Whether the vendor actually made the wine or just bottled it from wine made elsewhere will be identifiable from the information at the bottom. If a vineyard is indicated on the label, 95 per cent of the grapes in the wine must come from that vineyard.

The phrases 'estate grown' or 'grown, produced and bottled by' mean that the wine has been made by the vendor entirely from his own grapes; if 'produced and bottled by' appears, he will have bought in the grapes – no bad sign, as many winemakers prefer to leave grape growing to grape growers as well as wanting to take advantage of the best grapes, wherever they may have been grown. If the phrases are simply 'bottled by' or 'cellared and bottled by', the vendor will have bought in the wine and just matured and bottled it.

You may also see the phrase 'contains sulfites' (or sulphites, as they are known in the UK). This is the result of new legislation which requires American wine producers to state if sulphur dioxide was used during the wine's vinification. Since virtually all wine uses sulphur at some point, all wines have to have the phrase on their labels. There is nothing special about American wines in this respect – European wines also contain sulphur (and when exported to the United States also have to state 'contains sulfites' on their labels).

In the United States, there is pressure for more information to appear on wine labels, in particular that the ingredients of a wine should be listed. In California, there have been demands for warnings to pregnant women that alcohol can damage the health of their babies; and that wine contains a carcinogen (ie ethyl alcohol).

While some of this information may be of use to the consumer (ingredient listing is something we would support), much of the current ferment in wine labelling is an over-reaction to the problem of alcoholism, which California producers fear is leading to neo-prohibitionism and a refusal to understand the central place of wine in western culture. We must hope that such bigotry does not reach European shores.

The varietal taste

While there is a growing interest in blended wines (either at the basic level of California white and red branded wines, or at the higher level of claret look-alikes which are blends of Merlot and Cabernet Sauvignon), many top wines in California are still labelled varietally. By law, at least 75 per cent of such a varietal wine must consist of that grape. Below that percentage the wine will be regarded as a blend and will have a brand name (and a description saying which grapes go into the wine).

WHITE GRAPES

Chardonnay The grape variety on which much of California's reputation has been built. It used to make wines that tasted more of new wood than ripe, creamy fruit. Now they're more delicate, but still have the characteristic overtones of tropical fruits.

Sauvignon Blanc (or **Fumé Blanc**) The currently fashionable flavour from California. A grape variety that lends itself well to the trend for lighter, more acidic wines. Can be full of zing and freshness.

Chenin Blanc Lighter wines are beginning to bring out flavours from this often dull grape. Good, appley acidity is a characteristic. Blended with Chardonnay, it makes fuller, richer wines.

Johannisberg Riesling (also known as **White Riesling**) Makes wines that are fuller than their German models and so don't have the same delicate balance of acidity and sweetness. But it also produces some marvellous sweet dessert wines from grapes affected by noble rot. New categories have been devised to describe the degree of sweetness of these wines: *Early Harvest* equals the German Kabinett with a slight sweetness but no noble rot; *Late Harvest* equals the German Auslese; *Select Late Harvest* equals Beerenauslese; *Special Select Late Harvest* equals Trockenbeerenauslese.

RED GRAPES

Cabernet Sauvignon As much of a success story as Chardonnay in the whites. The fruit can be over-ripe and a touch sweet, but more recent wines have become drier and less heavy. They're tannic when young, but tend to mature more quickly than Cabernet Sauvignon in Bordeaux.

Pinot Noir California is at last coming to grips with the elusive Burgundian grape variety. It needs the lighter treatment and less continuous sunshine that much of California provides, but areas like Carneros (a sub-district of the Napa Valley), with its climate more affected by the fogs of San Francisco Bay, are well suited to this grape variety.

Merlot More and more fashionable as a straight varietal wine, with very fine results sometimes. Also used as a part of a blended wine.

Petit Syrah Makes rather coarse wines which rely on strength rather than character.

Zinfandel California's own grape variety, producing wines that range from the early-maturing (rather like Beaujolais) to the rich, ripe and peppery. It is also used as the basis for the Blush or White Zinfandel wines. An exciting grape that we are now learning to appreciate more.

California vintages

1988 A disastrous vintage in terms of quantity, especially for Merlot, Cabernet Sauvignon and Sauvignon Blanc. Quality is average rather than good for these varieties. For Chardonnay, things were better, both in terms of quantity and quality. Coupled with the poor quantity in 1987, price rises for grapes – and therefore finished wines – have been steep.

1987 A small harvest of high quality. Amounts of Cabernet Sauvignon were particularly small – down by 20 per cent on average.

1986 A very good vintage – the third success story in a row. A cool summer gave a very long ripening period which was good for white grapes and even suited the reds.

1985 An outstanding vintage, with very concentrated grapes after low rainfall. White wines are rich but with enough acidity, but the reds are the real stars - powerful Cabernet Sauvignon and Merlot and high quality Pinot Noir.

1984 Whites suffered from the heat in this vintage, and most are rather blowsy. Reds are uneven, but all are ready to drink now. Cabernet Sauvignon did best, Pinot Noir worst.

1983 Medium-bodied whites are fading. Pinot Noir reds are available and at the time were some of the best yet from that grape variety. Other reds will keep a little longer.

1982 Few whites are still worth drinking, although the occasional Chardonnay will still keep. The Cabernet Sauvignons are very mature and the Pinot Noirs and Zinfandels are fading.

1980 Whites should have been drunk, except for top Chardonnay, but reds will continue to mature, especially Cabernet Sauvignons.

1978 and before Only top Cabernet Sauvignons and some Zinfandel from 1978, 1976, 1974, 1973 and 1970 are likely to last. Other wines should be approached with caution – if you find any, that is.

Where's where in California

As vineyards in California mature, so different areas develop different wine styles. Certain areas produce outstanding wines while others are better at jug wines. Here are those areas where the wines have some consistency and quality.

Livermore Area to the east of San Francisco Bay.

Mendocino County The northernmost wine-growing region. Sub-regions are Anderson Valley, Ukiah Valley, Potter and Redwood Valleys.

Monterey County A cool area inland from Monterey Bay. Sub-regions are Arroyo Secco, Carmel Valley, Greenfield, the Pinnacles, Salinas Valley.

Napa Valley The biggest quality wine area. Sub-regions include Calistoga, Carneros, Chiles Valley, Stag's Leap, Silverado Trail, Pope Valley, Mount Veeder, Yountville, Oakville, St Helena and Spring Mountain.

San Joaquin The Central Valley, which produces large quantities of jug wines from the biggest vineyard area in California.

San Luis Obispo Up-and-coming area. Sub-regions include Paso Robles, Edna Valley, Shandon.

Santa Barbara To the north of Los Angeles. Sub-regions are Santa Maria and Santa Ynez.

Santa Clara Vineyard area south of San Francisco. Sub-regions are Hecker Pass and Santa Cruz.

Sonoma County between Napa and the ocean north of San Francisco, and approaching Napa in fame and quality. Sub-regions are Sonoma Valley, Kenwood, Russian River Valley, Dry Creek, Alexander Valley, Knight's Valley.

Who's who in California

Acacia In Carneros, Napa Valley. Has achieved a big reputation for its Pinot Noirs. Wines: Chardonnay, Pinot Noir.
H Allen Smith; Les Amis du Vin; Barnes Wine Shop; Bibendum; D Byrne & Co; Alex Findlater; La Vigneronne; Yorkshire Fine Wines

Adler Fells Small, do-it-yourself winery in Sonoma, whose star is a Sauvignon. Wines: Chardonnay, Fumé Blanc.
Oddbins

Alexander Valley Sonoma valley winery, famous for its Chardonnay, but also making good Cabernet Sauvignon. Wines: Chardonnay, Gewürztraminer, Cabernet Sauvignon.
Averys

Almadén Range of standard varietals from one of the largest California producers. Based in San José south of San Francisco Bay. Wines: Chardonnay, Chenin Blanc, Cabernet Sauvignon, Zinfandel.
D Byrne & Co; Chaplin & Son; Peter Dominic; Upper Crust

Beaulieu One of the pioneering wineries of the Napa Valley, still making very fine wines. Wines: Chardonnay, Pinot Noir, Cabernet Sauvignon; the top wine is called Georges de Latour Private Reserve Cabernet – pricy but outstanding.
Bottoms Up; Peter Dominic; Gateway; La Reserva Wines; J Sainsbury; The Wine House

Beringer Vineyards Medium-sized Napa Valley producer whose wines are improving after a recent decline. Wines: Chardonnay, Cabernet Sauvignon, Fumé Blanc and Riesling.
D Byrne & Co; Victoria Wine Company

Buena Vista Sonoma winery under German ownership producing straightforward commercial wines. Wines: Fumé Blanc, Zinfandel.
David Alexander; Les Amis du Vin; Barnes Wine Shop; D Byrne & Co; Peter Green; Willoughbys

Calera Small winery at San Benito, inland from the Salinas Valley, making some of California's best Pinot Noirs. Wines: Jensen Vineyard Pinot Noir, Zinfandel.
Adnams; David Alexander; Les Amis du Vin; Bibendum; Hungerford Wine Company; La Vigneronne; Winecellars

Carmenet New Sonoma winery making top quality blends, the reds including Cabernet Sauvignon, Cabernet Franc and Merlot. Wines: Sauvignon Blanc, Carmenet Sonoma Red Table Wine.
H Allen Smith; Les Amis du Vin; Peter Dominic; La Vigneronne

Chalone Vineyards Another winery, based in Monterey County, that has made top-class Pinot Noir and Chardonnay. Wines: Chardonnay, Pinot Blanc, Pinot Noir.
Les Amis du Vin; Fortnum & Mason

Ch St Jean White wine producer specialising in noble-rot Rieslings. Wines: Frank Johnson Chardonnay, Robert Young Vineyard Chardonnay, Riesling.
Les Amis du Vin; D Byrne & Co; La Vigneronne

Christian Brothers A Napa winery, run by a religious order, whose reputation – after a poor period of stagnation – is reviving, helped by new investment. Wines: Fumé Blanc, Chardonnay, Cabernet Sauvignon, Gamay Noir.
Marks & Spencer

Clos du Bois Northern Sonoma producer with vineyards in Alexander Valley and Dry Creek, making very good Merlot and Chardonnay. Top Chardonnays are named after vineyards: Calcaire, Flintwood. There is also a top quality red blend, Marlstone. Wines: Sauvignon Blanc, Chardonnay, Pinot Noir, Cabernet Sauvignon, Merlot.
Widely available

Clos du Val Wines made by a Frenchman whose father was manager of Ch Lafite in Bordeaux, and whose brother makes wine at the Taltarni winery in Australia. Wines: Merlot, Chardonnay, Zinfandel, Pinot Noir, Cabernet Sauvignon.
David Alexander; David Baillie Vintners; Berry Bros & Rudd; Alex Findlater; Nobody Inn; Reid Wines; Ubiquitous Chip; Upper Crust; The Wine House; Wizard Wine Warehouses

Conn Creek Elegant Cabernet Sauvignons from this St Helena, Napa winery. Wines: Chardonnay, Zinfandel, Cabernet Sauvignon.
David Baillie Vintners

Cuvaison Top quality producer in the Napa Valley. Wines: Cabernet Sauvignon, Chardonnay, Zinfandel.
Barnes Wine Shop; Anthony Byrne Fine Wines

Diamond Creek Minute quantities of top class single vineyard Cabernet Sauvignons in the Napa valley. Wines: Gravelly Meadow Cabernet Sauvignon, Red Rock Terrace Cabernet Sauvignon, Volcanic Hill Cabernet Sauvignon.
Windrush Wines

Dominus The new winery owned by the Moueix family who run Ch Pétrus in Pomerol. Their new red wine is called Dominus – and it's very expensive.
Adnams; Corney & Barrow; Haynes Hanson & Clark; Lay & Wheeler

Dry Creek Vineyards Good whites, especially the Fumé Blanc. Wines: Cabernet Sauvignon, Fumé Blanc, Chenin Blanc.
Les Amis du Vin; Barnes Wine Shop; Bibendum; D Byrne & Co; La Vigneronne; Yorkshire Fine Wines

Edna Valley Vineyards Producer of rich, full-flavoured Chardonnay. Wines: Pinot Noir, Chardonnay.
H Allen Smith; Les Amis du Vin; Barnes Wine Shop; Bibendum; D Byrne & Co; Peter Dominic; Majestic; La Vigneronne; Yorkshire Fine Wines

Far Niente Highly priced wines from Napa in superb packaging. Wines: Chardonnay, Cabernet Sauvignon.
T & W Wines

Fetzer Vineyards Good, middle-range blended wines from Mendocino – good value as well. Their second label is Bel Arbres. Wines: Premium red and white, Cabernet Sauvignon, Chardonnay.
Alex Findlater; Majestic; Safeway; J Sainsbury; Tesco; Waitrose

Firestone Vineyard Famous for its big, rich wines from the Santa Ynez Valley. Wines: Chardonnay, Cabernet Sauvignon, Pinot Noir, Merlot.
Les Amis du Vin; D Byrne & Co; Ellis Son & Vidler; Alex Findlater; Peter Green; Hicks & Don; Majestic; J Sainsbury; Ubiquitous Chip; La Vigneronne; Willoughbys

Freemark Abbey Well-established producer of expensive, high quality Cabernet Sauvignon and Chardonnay. Also produce Edelwein (dessert wine).
Averys; Barnes Wine Shop; D Byrne & Co; Drunken Mouse

Frog's Leap Small winery, outside St Helena in Napa, built on a former frog farm. High reputation in the US. Wines: Sauvignon, Chardonnay, Cabernet Sauvignon.
Lay & Wheeler

E & J Gallo The world's largest winery, in Central Valley, turning out a quarter of a million cases a day. Quality is, not surprisingly, reliable rather than inspired, although the premium varietals are made in small quantities and come up with some good quality.
Peter Green; La Reserva Wines; Victoria Wine Company; Wessex Wines

Glen Ellen Good value wines from Sonoma, with fine varietal flavours. Wines: Merlot, Chardonnay, Cabernet Sauvignon, Sauvignon Blanc, Proprietor's Reserve range.
Oddbins

Grgich Hills Cellar Big wines from Rutherford, Napa. Wines: Cabernet Sauvignon, Chardonnay, Fumé Blanc, Zinfandel.
Eldridge Pope

Hanzell Vineyards Old-established winery in Sonoma which has a high reputation for its Pinot Noir. Wines: Chardonnay, Pinot Noir.
Windrush Wines

Heitz Wine Cellars Famous small Napa producer of single vineyard wines. Quality seems to have slipped recently. Wines: Martha's Vineyard Cabernet, Bella Oaks Cabernet, Chardonnay.
Adnams; Les Amis du Vin; Alex Findlater; Peter Green; Lay & Wheeler

Inglenook Vineyards A Napa winery that has had some bad times recently, but is on the rebound again. Wines: Cabernet Sauvignon, Cabernet Sauvignon Reserve Cask, Chardonnay, Merlot.
Peter Dominic; Fullers; Hilbre Wine Company; Victoria Wine Company

Iron Horse Light, often austere wines from Sonoma; also good sparkling wines. Wines: Cabernet Sauvignon, Chardonnay.
Berry Bros & Rudd; D Byrne & Co; Christopher & Co

Jekel Vineyard Monterey County winery with vineyards in Arroyo Seco, making particularly good Johannisberg Rieslings. Wines: Chardonnay, Cabernet Sauvignon, Riesling.
David Alexander; Barnes Wine Shop; Oddbins; J Sainsbury

Jordan Winery Sonoma winery making expensive Cabernet Sauvignon (blended with Merlot) and Chardonnay.
David Alexander; Fortnum & Mason; Lay & Wheeler; Yorkshire Fine Wines

J Lohr San Jose owner with vineyards in Napa, Sacramento, Monterey and San Luis Obispo. Wines: Cabernet Sauvignon, Sauvignon Blanc, Chardonnay.
For further information contact Geoffrey Roberts Associates, 19 Charlotte Street, London W1

Paul Masson Mass producer in Santa Clara of the carafe wines whose containers now sprout more cut flowers than any other

wine bottle. Wines: varietal wines under the Pinnacle name, as well as the red, white and rosé carafes.
G E Bromley & Sons; Rodney Densem Wines; Andrew Gordon Wines; Victoria Wine Company; Willoughbys

Matanzas Creek Small Sonoma winery making some very good Chardonnays. Wines: Chardonnay, Merlot, Sauvignon Blanc.
Haynes Hanson & Clark; Windrush Wines

Mayacamas Vineyards Tiny producer in the Napa of top quality Chardonnay and Cabernet Sauvignon. They need ageing for a long time.
David Alexander; Les Amis du Vin; Alex Findlater

Robert Mondavi Winery Often described as the guru of Californian wine-making, Robert Mondavi and his family make some of the best, most reliable wines in the State. Co-producer of the expensive Opus One with Philippe de Rothschild of Bordeaux. What Mondavi does this year, others follow next. Recently, his RM range of quality medium-priced wines set the pace again. Wines: Opus One, Fumé Blanc, Chardonnay, Cabernet Sauvignon, Riesling, Robert Mondavi California red and white.
Widely available

The Monterey Vineyard Part of the group which also owns Paul Masson. Make a range of good inexpensive blended wines, and more serious varietals. Wines: Classic range.
H Allen Smith; Rodney Densem Wines; Alex Findlater; Oddbins

Monticello Cellars Southern Napa producer of distinguished Chardonnay. The winery house is modelled on Jefferson's house in Virginia. Wines: Cabernet Sauvignon, Chardonnay.
David Alexander; Les Amis du Vin; Berry Bros & Rudd; Winecellars

Newton Vineyard Small high quality vineyard, owned by an Englishman in a spectacular position in Napa. Wines: Merlot, Sauvignon, Chardonnay, Cabernet Sauvignon.
Laytons

Pedroncelli Dry Creek vineyard in Sonoma, established in 1904, and still family-run. Wines: Sauvignon, Chardonnay, Cabernet Sauvignon.
Lay & Wheeler

Joseph Phelps Vineyard One of the great producers of California, Phelps makes a huge range of wines, all of good quality, although not the highest. Wines: Riesling, Gewürztraminer, Chardonnay, Cabernet Sauvignon, Zinfandel.
Adnams; H Allen Smith; Les Amis du Vin; D Byrne & Co; Alex Findlater; Peter Green; Raeburn Fine Wines & Foods; Tanners; La Vigneronne; Yorkshire Fine Wines

Andrew Quady Producer in Madera in the Central Valley who has done wonders with the Muscat-based fortified wines, Essensia and Elysium.
Fortnum & Mason; Harrods; Selfridges; Yorkshire Fine Wines

Ridge Vineyards Single vineyard wines from Santa Cruz, with a reputation for longevity. Wines: Zinfandel, York Creek Cabernet Sauvignon, Monte Bello Cabernet Sauvignon (high reputation, but scarce).
Adnams; Les Amis du Vin; D Byrne & Co; Peter Green; The Wine Society

Rutherford Hill Winery A Napa winery that has leapt back to success with a new winemaker. Wines: Chardonnay, Merlot, Cabernet Sauvignon.
Cliff & Co; Drunken Mouse; George Hill of Loughborough; La Vigneronne

Saintsbury Winery Carneros (Napa) producer of fine Pinot Noir. Wines: Pinot Noir, Chardonnay.
Adnams; Bibendum; Haynes Hanson & Clark; Majestic; The Wine Society

Sanford Santa Barbara winery producing a widely acclaimed Sauvignon Blanc; also Chardonnay.
Les Amis du Vin

Schramsberg Vineyards Napa Valley producer of top quality (and expensive) sparkling wines made by the Champagne method. Wines: Blanc de Blancs, Blanc de Noirs.
Adnams; Les Amis du Vin; La Vigneronne

Simi Winery Small winery in Sonoma making some superb Chardonnay. Wines: Cabernet Sauvignon, Sauvignon Blanc, Alexander Valley Chardonnay.
David Alexander; Corney & Barrow; Lay & Wheeler

Sonoma-Cutrer Small northern Sonoma winery which has built its reputation on Chardonnays. Wines: Chardonnay Cutrer Vineyard, Chardonnay Les Pierres, Chardonnay Russian River Ranches.
Averys; Barnes Wine Shop; Fulham Road Wine Centre; Hampden Wine Company; Harrods

Stag's Leap Wine Cellars Small producer of top quality Chardonnay and Cabernet Sauvignon, both worth the high price. They make a second wine (in the style of Bordeaux châteaux) called Hawk Crest. Wines: Chardonnay, Cabernet Sauvignon, Merlot.
David Alexander; Bibendum; Corney & Barrow; La Vigneronne; Windrush Wines

Sterling Vineyard A spectacular winery in the northern Napa Valley. Wines: Diamond Mountain Ranch wines; Cabernet Sauvignon.
La Vigneronne

Tjisseling Dutch-owned winery in Mendocino making wines in a full, open style. Wines: Chardonnay, Cabernet Sauvignon.
Alex Findlater; Harrods; Wizard Wine Warehouses

Trefethen Vineyards (Napa) Good value wines with high quality. The Chardonnays are very good, and the blended wines are very reliable. Wines: Chardonnay, Pinot Noir, Cabernet Sauvignon, Eshcol branded wine (red and white).
Adnams; Les Amis du Vin; Bibendum; D Byrne & Co; Alex Findlater; Peter Green; Majestic; Tanners; La Vigneronne; The Wine Society

Vichon Napa winery, now owned by Mondavi (see above), being used to make premium white varietals. Wines: Chevrignon (a blend of Semillon and Sauvignon Blanc), Chardonnay, Cabernet Sauvignon.
For further information contact Geoffrey Roberts Associates, 19 Charlotte Street, London W1

Wente Brothers Large-scale producer of middle-range wines. Good, reliable quality, with some good aged Zinfandels. Wines: Sauvignon Blanc, Chardonnay, Riesling, Cabernet Sauvignon, Zinfandel.
David Alexander; Peter Green; La Reserva Wines

Mark West Vineyards Elegant wines from the Russian River Valley. Wines: Chardonnay, late harvest Riesling.
H Allen Smith; Les Amis du Vin; D Byrne & Co; Peter Green; Hicks & Don

William Wheeler Dry Creek vineyard (Sonoma), making wine from its own land and from bought-in grapes (Chardonnay from Monterey). The quality gets better as the vines get older. Wines: Chardonnay, Sauvignon, Cabernet Sauvignon.
Les Amis du Vin; D Byrne & Co; Fortnum & Mason; Hungerford Wine Company

ZD Wines Lush, rich wines made from grapes bought in from other vineyards. Wines: Cabernet Sauvignon, Chardonnay, Pinot Noir.
Barnes Wine Shop; D Byrne & Co; Alex Findlater; Harrods; Wizard Wine Warehouses

Best buys from California

WHITE

St Michael California Sauvignon Blanc, Buena Vista (*Marks & Spencer*)

Sanford Sauvignon Blanc 1987 (*Ubiquitous Chip Wine Shop*)

Sauvignon Blanc 1986, Gallo (*Gare du Vin; Rex Norris; Wessex Wines*)

Semillon Reserve 1987, Bird Label, R H Phillips (*Claridge Fine Wines*)

Sonoma White, Pedroncelli (*Lay & Wheeler*)

Chardonnay 1986, Firestone Vineyard (*Upper Crust*)

RED

Monterey Vineyard Classic Red 1984 (*Bentalls of Kingston*)

Glen Ellen Cabernet Sauvignon 1987 (*Augustus Barnett*)

California Red, Geoffrey Roberts (*Les Amis du Vin; Hilbre Wine Company*)

Glen Ellen Merlot 1986, Sonoma (*Oddbins*)

Hawks Crest Cabernet Sauvignon 1985, Napa Valley (*Askham Wines*)

Zinfandel 1982, Inglenook Vineyard (*Victoria Wine Company*)

Fetzer California Zinfandel 1985 (*Tesco*)

Lost Hills Red, San Joaquin Valley (*Bibendum*)

Pinot Noir 1987, Saintsbury Winery, Carneros (*Haynes Hanson & Clark*)

Specialist stockists

Adnams; David Alexander; Les Amis du Vin; Averys of Bristol; Bibendum; Haynes Hanson & Clark; Haughton Fine Wines; Nobody Inn; Oddbins; Selfridges; T & W Wines; Windrush Wines; Wine Growers Association

NEW YORK STATE

There are two areas of wine production in New York State. By far the larger area is the Finger Lakes near the Great Lakes in the north of the state. Much of the production from here is of *Vitis labrusca* (the American grape used in Europe as a grafting root for the classical *Vitis vinifera*). But there are also well-made, flavoursome *Vitis vinifera* wines, with higher acidity than most West Coast whites, of which the Chardonnay is particularly good. The sparkling wine is more interesting than outstanding.

The Long Island vineyards at the eastern end of Long Island are much younger. With its maritime climate, the area has cooler summers and warmer winters than the Finger Lakes. So far, white wines are better than reds. Virtually all the grapes planted are the *Vitis vinifera*, especially Chardonnay, Sauvignon and Riesling.

Who's who in New York State

Gold Seal Vineyards Winery which pioneered New York 'Champagne' in its Blanc de Blancs, and also the use of *Vitis labrusca* vines. Now makes good Blanc de Blancs and Chardonnay.
Great American Wine Company, Office 13, J O Sims Building, Winchester Walk, London SE1

Lenz Winery Long Island winery making aromatic wines like the Gewürztraminer as well as Sauvignon Blanc.
Great American Wine Company (see above for address)

PACIFIC NORTH-WEST

This is the area – covering the states of Oregon, Washington and Idaho – which can produce the cool-climate wines that are much more difficult to make in California further south. The cooling influence of the Pacific Ocean and a more northerly latitude combine to produce conditions which are ideal for Pinot Noir and Chardonnay, as well as for light, elegant Cabernet Sauvignon.

Idaho

A very new wine state, with vineyards high up in the Snake River Valley in the Rocky Mountains.

Who's who in Idaho

Covey Rise Tiny vineyard owned by a fishmonger. Wines: Chardonnay.
David Alexander; Bibendum; Windrush Wines

Rose Creek Snake River vineyard which also buys in grapes from Washington State. Wines: Chardonnay, Cabernet Sauvignon.
Windrush Wines

Oregon

Most of the vineyards are south of the state capital of Portland in the Willamette River valley, in the lee of the small Coast Range of hills. Despite being south of Washington State, Oregon's vineyard climate is cooler, and it is best at varieties like Riesling, Sauvignon Blanc and Pinot Noir.

Who's who in Oregon

Alpine Vineyards Family-owned vineyard in Willamette Valley making small quantities of wine. Wines: Chardonnay, Pinot Noir, Cabernet Sauvignon.
Windrush Wines

The Eyrie Vineyards Pioneer Oregon vineyard that has won medals in France for its Pinot Noir. Wines: Pinot Gris, Pinot Noir, Chardonnay.
David Alexander; Windrush Wines

Elk Cove Small-scale family business making delicious Pinot Noir. Wines: Chardonnay, Riesling, Pinot Noir.
Windrush Wines

Knudsen Erath One of Oregon's largest producers who also makes sparkling wine. Wines: Pinot Noir.
Great American Wine Company, Office 13, J O Sims Building, Winchester Walk, London SE1; Wizard Wine Warehouses

Tualatin Top quality Chardonnay and consistent Pinot Noir; also Sauvignon Blanc.
Windrush Wines

Tyee Wine Cellars Tiny new winery making excellent Chardonnay.
Windrush Wines

Washington State

Of the three north-west states, it is Washington which has been making the running this past year as far as the British market is concerned. The producers organised a major tasting in London at which a large range of their wines were on show. From what we tasted, it seems that, while they can make very correct Chardonnay and Cabernet Sauvignon, they seem to shine much more at Pinot Noir, Sauvignon Blanc, Riesling and Merlot. Among other oddities, the German red wine variety, Lemberger, has come out with some very attractive peppery, fruity wines.

Most of the vineyards in this northernmost Pacific state are in the warmer areas to the east of the Cascade Mountains, on lands which need irrigation in the summer, but which have a long growing season. A few growers are on the wet, cool, western side, where they produce German-style wines. The state is now second in the US to California in production of *Vitis vinifera* wines, and prices seem to be getting more competitive.

Who's who in Washington State

Arbor Crest Specialist in late harvest wines. Wines: Riesling Select Late Harvest, Merlot, Chardonnay, Sauvignon.
Reid Wines; Windrush Wines; Yorkshire Fine Wines

Château Ste-Michelle The state's largest winery, making wines under its own name (more serious, some from single vineyards) and under the Columbia Crest name (lighter, softer style). Wines: Fumé Blanc, Chardonnay, Cabernet Sauvignon, Merlot.
David Baillie Vintners; Harrods; John Harvey & Sons; Mitchells of Lancaster; Oddbins; Selfridges

Chinook Another small winery, making white wines with some up-and-coming reds. Wines: Sauvignon Blanc, Chardonnay, Merlot.
Reid Wines; Windrush Wines

Columbia Formerly known as Associated Vintners, this has a high reputation for its white wines. Wines: Chardonnay, Cabernet Sauvignon.
Windrush Wines

The Hogue Cellars Ex-spearmint grower (for chewing gum), Warren Hogue makes a range of mainly white wines. Best are Fumé Blanc, Chardonnay, Riesling.
Great American Wine Company, Office 13, J O Sims Building, Winchester Walk, London SE1; Tesco; Wizard Wine Warehouses

Kiona Specialises in German grape varieties. Wines: Late Harvest Riesling, Dry White Riesling, Chardonnay, Lemberger, Cabernet Sauvignon.
Oddbins

Salishan Vineyards Small winery whose star is a Pinot Noir. Also Chardonnay and Chenin Blanc.
Irvine Robertson Wines; Windrush Wines

Snoqualmie Unpronounceable winery making good whites, especially Semillon; also Lemberger and Fumé Blanc.
David Alexander; Windrush Wines; Yorkshire Fine Wines

Stewart Vineyards Winery particularly renowned for its botrytised Riesling. Wines: Late Harvest White Riesling, Chardonnay.
Douglas Henn-Macrae; Windrush Wines

Best buys from the North-West

WHITE

Chardonnay Covey Rise 1986, Idaho (*Windrush Wines*)
Fumé Blanc 1985, Ch Ste Michelle Washington State (*David Baillie Vintners*)
Columbia Crest Sauvignon Blanc 1986, Washington State (*Oddbins*)
Kiona Chenin Blanc 1987, Washington State (*Oddbins*)

RED

Salishan Pinot Noir Reserve, Washington State 1985 (*Philip Eyres Wine Merchant*)

Specialist stockists
David Baillie Vintners; Douglas Henn-Macrae; Windrush Wines

TEXAS

The lone star state may not seem a likely candidate for a burgeoning wine industry, but there are now two dozen wineries and 4,000 acres under vine. Even though the state is on the same latitude as North Africa, it seems that with the right irrigation in the vineyards, a careful matching of vine and soil types, and the use of the most modern technology, much can be achieved.

The Texans use the familiar varietal approach, with some additional varieties to the usual Cabernet Sauvignon and Chardonnay: Chenin Blanc, Riesling, Gewürztraminer, French Colombard.

Wineries whose wines are available here are Fall Creek and Llano Estacado (*Douglas Henn-Macrae*), and you may also come across wines from Texas Vineyards, Pheasant Ridge and Sanchez Creek.

California and North–West U.S.A.

USSR

In November 1988, members of the British wine trade went to Georgia and Moldavia to look at what was going on in the fifth-largest (some say fourth-largest) wine producer in the world. If they found much to horrify them (two wines with the same label but made in wineries several thousand miles apart; impossibly unhygienic bottling lines; white wines stored in tanks for two or more years instead of being bottled – tricks of the trade that the West dispensed with many years ago), they also found that the Soviet Union produces sparkling wines (the well-known Champanski) that at least rival the cheaper fizz we can buy in Britain. And they found a willingness to learn and to change which suggests that, in time, much could come from the Soviets' new eagerness to export.

At the moment, though, little has happened. In Britain, the best place still to find examples of the wines is the *Russian Shop, High Holborn, London WC2*. Otherwise, there is Ruby of Crimea, described as a beefy, dry red (*Peter Dominic*).

Yugoslavia

We have been delighted that the Yugoslav wine we have been tasting most often recently is not the Laski Rizling (note the new spelling under EC rules of Yugoslav wines made from the Italian Riesling grape), but a red wine, Milion, made from the Merlot grape. It is chunky, and comes across slightly sweet.

It shows that Yugoslavia can produce more than just the dull, often over-sulphured white Laski Rizling wines with which we are most familiar. As an alternative to Liebfraumilch, these don't have much going for them except their price. And they take account of 95 per cent of all Yugoslav wines to reach the UK.

As elsewhere in Eastern Europe, French grape varieties have made inroads into Yugoslav vineyards: Cabernet Sauvignon, Merlot, Pinot Noir, Sauvignon, Gewürztraminer. The Cabernet Sauvignon is less successful than it is in Bulgaria, but the Merlot makes some very good wines.

White wines made in Slovenia from the Sauvignon, the Gewürztraminer and the Rhine Riesling (as distinct from the Laski Rizling) are lively with good, fresh acidity, reminiscent in a somewhat coarser way of the Italian Alto Adige. They tend to be softened and sweetened for the UK market – a pity.

Of native Yugoslav varieties, the most famous and interesting are the red wines made from the Vranac (the word means 'black stallion') in Montenegro – rich, robust and dark in colour (this wine will improve with some ageing). The white Zilavka from Herzegovina is a steely dry wine.

What's what in Yugoslavia

Beli Burgundec The Pinot Blanc grape.
Fruška Gora Quality white wine area of Serbia.
Faros A red wine from Hvar, with high acidity but a soft, slightly sweet finish.
Modri Burgundec The Pinot Noir grape.
Strem (Stremski Karlovci) Formerly called Carlowitz, this area once famous for reds now makes some good whites as well. Traminer and Sauvignon are worth looking out for.

Best buys from Yugoslavia

Milion Merlot (red) (*Ellis Son & Vidler; Alex Findlater; Oddbins; Selfridges; Waitrose*)
Pinot Noir 1986, Krajina (red) (*J E Hogg*)
Modri Cabernet Sauvignon (red) (*D Byrne & Co*)

Specialist stockist
Wine House

Zimbabwe

Old Southern Rhodesia hands will know that there has been a small wine industry in what is now Zimbabwe for many years. Now a small selection of the wines has arrived in Britain. They are possibly more of a curiosity than something to rush out to buy, but the quality is acceptable, and likely to get better.

Who's who in Zimbabwe

Flame Lily Brand name for wines from Philips Central Cellars of Harare. Wines: Dry white, Medium white, Premium white/red.
Peter Green; Nicolas Wines; Wessex Wines; Wine Spot

Specialist stockist
Vinceremos

Sparkling wines

Sparkling wines – other than Champagne – have enjoyed a boom in the past year, partly because Champagne has gone up in price, but also because the range and quality of these other sparklers has improved. As in many other vinous areas, Australia has set the pace, but Spanish Cava, Crémant from Burgundy and Alsace and Saumur from the Loire are all now providing a viable alternative to Champagne itself. In many cases, it is better to buy a Champagne alternative than some of the young, tart, green Champagnes that are on offer at basic prices.

Here we recommend a selection of the main styles of sparkling wines available in Britain. The vast majority of these wines are made in the same way as Champagne with the second fermentation in the bottle in which the wine is eventually sold: the only exceptions are sweeter wines like the Italian spumantes and some from southern France.

Terminology on the labels of these wines can be confusing if you are looking for wines made in the same way as Champagne. It is now forbidden for producers of these wines to say 'méthode champenoise' or 'Champagne method' on the label. So they either say nothing, leaving it up to the consumer to work out that, say, all Cava is made in this way, or they use phrases like the Italian 'metodo classico', or the New World 'second fermentation in this bottle' or 'bottle-fermented'. Price is a good but not infallible clue to the method used – you are unlikely to find anything made by bottle fermentation under £4–£4.50.

AUSTRALIA

Australians have taken on the sparkling wine market with great force and style. They are making some attractive sparklers which can be quite full, almost tropical, but can also have considerable refinement and elegance. A country to watch for sparkling wines – just as it has been for still.

Angas Brut, from Hill-Smith in the Barossa Valley (*Les Amis du Vin; Davisons; Drunken Mouse; Harrods; Oddbins; Waitrose; Wine Growers Association*)

Yalumba D – one of the top Australian sparklers (*Les Amis du Vin; Drunken Mouse*)

Seppelts Great Western Imperial Reserve (*David Baillie Vintners; Alex Findlater; J Sainsbury; Selfridges; Thresher; Upper Crust*) and Chardonnay Brut (*Drunken Mouse; Gare du Vin; Selfridges; Thresher*), both from Victoria.

Thomas Hardy Grand Reserve Brut (*H Allen Smith; Averys; Alex Findlater*)

Tyrrell's Pinot Noir Brut, Hunter Valley (*Alex Findlater*)

Yellowglen Brut, from Victoria (*Drunken Mouse; Alex Findlater*)

Sainsbury's Australian Sparkling Wine (*J Sainsbury*)

Rosemount Chardonnay Brut, from New South Wales (*Booths; Alex Findlater*)

Seaview Brut, Seaview Pinot Noir, Seaview Blanc de Blancs, from South Australia (*Augustus Barnett; Drunken Mouse; Alex Findlater; Fullers; Gare du Vin; Lay & Wheeler; Majestic; Oddbins; Peter Green; Selfridges*)

Minchinbury Grande Cuvée (*Oddbins*)

St Michael Australian sparkling wine, from Penfolds in South Australia (*Marks & Spencer*)

CHILE

Miguel Torres, the Spanish wine producer who has vineyards in Chile making still wines, now produces a sparkling wine as well.

Miguel Torres Chile Brut Nature (*Celtic Vintners; Gerard Harris; Master Cellar Wine Warehouse; Arthur Rackhams*)

ENGLAND

There are now at least two English sparklers on the market. More are promised.

Carr Taylor Dry (*Selfridges; Tanners*)

Lamberhurst Vineyards Brut (*Ridge Farm, Lamberhurst, near Tunbridge Wells, Kent*)

FRANCE

Details of **Champagne** will be found on page 427.

ALSACE

Alsace's sparkling wines are called Crémant d'Alsace. Unlike Champagne, where the term Crémant means a lower pressure and hence fewer bubbles, in Alsace it simply means a straightforward Champagne method sparkling wine. The wines can be made from the local grape varieties – Sylvaner or Riesling are used – or from Chardonnay. They are some of the best sparklers in France outside Champagne, but are not cheap.

Crémant d'Alsace, Dopff et Irion Cuvée Extra (*Cadwgan Fine Wines; Eldridge Pope/Reynier Wine Libraries; Hilbre Wine Company*)
Crémant d'Alsace, Dopff au Moulin (*Peter Green; Lay & Wheeler; La Vigneronne*)
Crémant d'Alsace, Willy Gisselbrecht (*Martinez Fine Wine*)
Crémant d'Alsace, Marc Kreydenweiss (*La Vigneronne*)
Crémant d'Alsace, Willm (*Harrods; Selfridges; London Wine*)

BLANQUETTE DE LIMOUX

With a claim to have been sparkling even before Champagne, at their best these are attractively appley green wines. They are made from a blend of the local Mauzac grapes with some Clairette and Chardonnay to give body. They come from the South-West near Carcassonne and all the brands available are dry.

Blanquette de Limoux, Cuvée Alderic (*Gare du Vin; Matthew Gloag; Harrods*)
Christopher's Blanquette de Limoux (*Les Amis du Vin; Wine Growers Association*)
Blanquette de Limoux, Ets Salasar (*Master Cellar Wine Warehouse*)

BURGUNDY

Burgundy's sparkling wine production was organised in 1975. The appellation is called Crémant de Bourgogne and the grapes used are Pinot Noir (for reds - not often seen in our shops), and Pinot Blanc, Aligoté and Chardonnay (for whites). There is also a lower category of sparklers, called Vins Mousseux, some of them good value.

WHITE

Crémant de Bourgogne, Caves de Bailly (*H Allen Smith; Fullers; Peter Green; Harrods; Raeburn Fine Wines & Foods; Upper Crust; Waitrose*)
Crémant de Bourgogne, Cave de Viré (*Davisons; Majestic; Master Cellar Wine Warehouse; Thresher; Winecellars; Wines from Paris; Wizard Wine Warehouses*)
Crémant de Bourgogne, Cave de Lugny (*Alex Findlater; Haynes Hanson & Clark; Marks & Spencer*)
Asda Crémant de Bourgogne (*Asda*)
St Michael Sparkling White Burgundy (*Marks & Spencer*)
Blanc de Blancs, Dominique Charnay, Vin Mousseux (*Bibendum*)

RED AND ROSÉ

Crémant de Bourgogne Rosé, Bailly (*Fullers; Upper Crust; Waitrose; Wines from Paris*)
Chanson Père et Fils, Crémant de Bourgogne, Red (*Tanners*)
Prosper Maufoux, Crémant de Bourgogne, Red (*Harrods*)
Sainsbury's Crémant de Bourgogne Rosé (*J Sainsbury*)

SAUMUR

The major source of sparkling wine on the Loire is the town of Saumur, whose cellars, carved out of chalk cliffs, are reminiscent of Champagne – so reminiscent, in fact, that many Champagne houses have bought up companies in Saumur. Quality is reliable, but the wines, made from Chenin Blanc, seem to lack great individuality. Flavours should be clean and refreshing. Rosés are made as well as Blanc de Blancs.

La Grande Marque (*Adnams; Balls Brothers; Lay & Wheeler; Tanners*)
Bouvet Ladubay (*Davisons; Harrods; Martinez Fine Wine; Master Cellar Wine Warehouse; Thos Peatling*)

Gratien et Meyer (*Booths; Peter Dominic; Harrods; Hilbre Wine Company; Justerini & Brooks; Oddbins; Christopher Piper Wines; Arthur Rackhams; Selfridges; The Wine Society*)

Langlois-Chateau (*Averys; Peter Green; Gerard Harris*)

Cuvée de Chevalière, Cave des Vignerons de Saumur (*H Allen Smith; Old Street Wine Company*)

De Neuville (*Gare du Vin; Grape Ideas; Victoria Wine Company*)

Sainsbury's Sparkling Saumur (*J Sainsbury*)

Tesco's Sparkling Saumur (*Tesco*)

Asda Saumur Brut (*Asda*)

Ackerman, Saumur 1811 (*Augustus Barnett; Chaplin & Son; Davisons; Alex Findlater; Fullers; Master Cellar Wine Warehouse*)

There is also a much wider appellation, Crémant de Loire, of which production is more strictly controlled than that of Saumur, but the grapes for which can come from anywhere along the Loire.

Crémant de Loire, Marcel Neau (*Majestic*)

Crémant de Loire, Gratien & Meyer (*The Wine Society*)

Crémant de Loire Brut, Domaine Richou (*Old Street Wine Company; Prestige Vintners*)

VOUVRAY AND MONTLOUIS

Upstream from Saumur, in Touraine, the twin wine towns of Vouvray and Montlouis both produce sparkling wines. They tend to be fuller than Saumur, and some producers also make a sweet style. There is little difference between Vouvray and Montlouis – perhaps the wines of Vouvray have more intensity, while those of Montlouis are softer.

Vouvray

Aigle d'Or, Prince Poniatowski (*La Vigneronne*)

Marc Brédif (*Yapp Brothers*)

Foreau Clos Naudin (*O W Loeb*)

Huet Brut (*Bibendum; Oddbins; Prestige Vintners; Raeburn Fine Wines & Foods; The Wine Society*)

Daniel Jarry (*Yapp Brothers*)

Roger Félicien Brou (*Stapylton Fletcher*)

Le Peu de la Moriette Crémant (*Tanners*)

Montlouis

Montlouis Brut and Demi-Sec, Berger (*Prestige Vintners; Yapp Brothers*)
Montlouis Brut, Gilles Verley (*Vinceremos*)

Other sparkling wines from the Loire

Blanc Foussy de Touraine (*Victoria Wine Company*)
Beauvolage Blanc de Blancs, Touraine Brut (*Cadwgan Fine Wines*)
Cuvée JM93, Monmousseau (*Wine Growers Association*)

OTHER FRENCH SPARKLING WINES

Clairette de Die Tradition: a sweet Muscat-based sparkler from the Alps (*Alex Findlater; Lay & Wheeler; Vinceremos*)
Clairette de Die Tradition Demi-Sec, Archard-Vincent (*Vinceremos; Yapp Brothers*)
Brut de Listel: straightforward wine (*Grape Ideas*)
Varichon et Clerc Blanc de Blancs: produced in Seyssel in Savoie (*Davisons; Hungerford Wine Company; Lay & Wheeler; Tanners; Windrush Wines; The Wine Society*)
Vin de Bugey Blanc de Blancs: made east of Lyons (*The Wine Society*)
Diane de Poitiers, Blanc de Blancs Chardonnay Brut: made in Haut-Poitou (*Adnams; Lay & Wheeler; Majestic; Stapylton Fletcher*)
Ryman Brut, made at Ch La Jaubertie in Bergerac (*Wines from Paris*)
Cavalier Brut Blanc de Blancs (*Oddbins; Wizard Wine Warehouses*)

GERMANY

The best German sparklers are made from the Riesling grape. Deutscher Sekt is made from German grapes; the word Sekt on its own indicates that the wine is not German, even though the bubbles are.

Deinhard Lila Riesling Imperial (*Alex Findlater*)
Deinhard Sparkling Mosel (*Gerard Harris*)
Schloss Vollrads Sekt (*Eldridge Pope/Reynier Wine Libraries*)
Burgeff Rheingau Riesling (*Oddbins*)
Wehlener Hofberg Riesling Brut Sekt (*Hilbre Wine Co*)

INDIA

Some surprisingly good sparkling wine – if expensive – is made in Maharashtra state, near Bombay.

Omar Khayyam (*Adnams; Booths; Fullers; Gare du Vin; Majestic; Oddbins; Selfridges; Tanners; Vinceremos*)

ITALY

The most familiar sparkling wine from Italy is sweet and based on the Moscato grape. It appears under the name Asti Spumante or the slightly cheaper but often better quality Moscato d'Asti or Moscato Spumante. It needs to be very fresh and young to show off its delicious honey and fruit taste.

Italy is also making more serious dry sparkling wines, some of very high quality. Some use the classic Champagne blend of Pinot Noir and Chardonnay, others go for local grapes like Prosecco from the Veneto. 'Metodo classico' on the label indicates that the wine was made in the same way as Champagne.

For details of **Lambrusco**, see page 555.

Asti Spumante and Moscato sparklers

St Michael Asti Spumante (*Marks & Spencer*)
Asti Spumante Fontanafredda (*widely available*)
Moscato d'Asti, Moscatel Vej, La Spinetta (*Adnams*)
Asti Spumante Sandro (*Waitrose*)
Asti Spumante, Tosti (*Findlater Mackie Todd*)
Asti Spumante Calamandrina (*Wine Growers Association*)
Asti Spumante, Cinzano (*Peter Dominic*)
Asti Spumante, Viticoltori dell'Acquese (*Winecellars*)
St Michael Moscato Frizzante, fewer bubbles than standard Spumante (*Marks & Spencer*)

Dry sparkling wines

Arunda Extra Brut (*H Allen Smith*)
Brut Pinot Oltrepò Pavese, Villa Banfi (*mainly available in restaurants*)
Ca' del Bosco, Franciacorta (*Adnams; Valvona & Crolla*)
Mompiano Spumante Brut (*Adnams; Winecellars*)

Carpene Malvolti Chardonnay and Brut Metodo Classico (*Valvona & Crolla; Winecellars*)
Verbesco Duca d'Asti (*Battersea Wine Co*)
Cuvée Imperiale Brut, Berlucchi (*Cantina Augusto; Valvona & Crolla; The Wine Case Place*)
Marchese Antinori Nature, Cuvée Royale (*Valvona & Crolla*)
Ferrari Gran Spumante Brut (also rosé) (*Oddbins; Selfridges; Valvona & Crolla; Wine Growers Association*)
Frescobaldi Brut (*Les Amis du Vin; Matthew Gloag*)
Prosecco di Conegliano (*Valvona & Crolla*)
Loredan Gasparini Brut di Venegazzù (*Morrisons; Valvona & Crolla*)

LUXEMBOURG

Luxembourg's small wine industry produces some good Champagne method sparklers.

Bernard Massard (*Eldridge Pope/Reynier Wine Libraries; Selfridges*)

PORTUGAL

Portugal's sparkling wine industry has only just begun to export anything. Some examples have considerable bottle age and a tendency to oxidise – not unattractive but an acquired taste.

Sainsbury's Portuguese Sparkling Wine (*J Sainsbury*)

SPAIN

The generic name for Champagne method sparkling wines in Spain is Cava (meaning cellar). The main centre of production is in Catalonia in the Penedés area west of Barcelona, although Cava wines can come from anywhere in the country. While quality of all these wines seems to be getting better, the taste of Penedés Cava is peppery and quite full. Cavas need to be drunk young or the fruit tends to fade. They work better with food than without. Other wines vary widely in style: one uses Chardonnay.

Castellblanch Brut Zero (*Sherborne Vintners*)
Codorníu Premier Cuvée (*Adnams; Fullers; Gare du Vin; Laymont & Shaw; Moreno Wines; Selfridges; Victoria Wine Company*)
Freixenet Cordon Negro (*widely available*)
Sainsbury's Spanish Cava (*J Sainsbury*)
Parxet Cava Extra Brut (*Wine House*)
Cavas Manuel Sancho, Mont Marçal (*Arriba Kettle; Harrods*)
Raimat Chardonnay (*widely available*)
Segura Viudas Blanc de Blancs (*Moreno Wines*)
Marqués de Monistrol Brut (*Booths; Fullers; Martinez Fine Wine; Moreno Wines; Thos Peatling; Unwins*)
Juve y Camps Brut Reserva de la Familia (*Harrods; Laymont & Shaw; Moreno Wines; La Vigneronne*)

USA

More of the many American sparkling wines are now available in the UK. Prices tend to be on the high side, often above the level of Champagne.

Domaine Chandon, the Californian arm of the giant Moët et Chandon Champagne house (*Adnams*)
Schramsberg Blanc de Blancs and Blanc de Noirs (*Adnams; Les Amis du Vin; Harrods; Hilbre Wine Company; Wine Growers Association; La Vigneronne; The Wine Society*)
Iron Horse (*Les Amis du Vin; Gare du Vin; Victoria Wine Company*)
Gold Seal, New York State (*Great American Wine Company*)
Wente Brothers Brut Vintage (*Matthew Gloag; Selfridges*)
Paul Masson Brut Reserve (*Safeway*)

Fortified wines

The fortified wines covered in this section are all great originals, many with fascinating histories behind them, and often involving the British. But at a time when lightness in a wine is considered a vital property, such wines, which tend to be heavy and quite high in alcohol, would seem to be on a losing wicket. Sherry, particularly, is in the doldrums at the moment, but others have surmounted the problem by changing their image from one of fusty dowdiness to one of class, quality and – to a certain extent – rarity value.

Fortified wines differ from table wines in that brandy has been added to them, either to stop fermentation or at the end of fermentation. The practice originated in the days when this was the only practical way of transporting wine over long distances by sea.

SHERRY

Of the two major fortified wines (Sherry and Port), Sherry is the one with the problems. Shipments in 1988 were back at the level of 1975. Its principal market, Britain, is still shrinking, and other export markets are not taking up the slack (although the Spaniards themselves, never previously great Sherry drinkers, are taking to it more and more). Its name is taken in vain by products which do not come from Spain (British, Irish and Cyprus 'Sherry'), and until relatively recently, its image tended to be that of a sweet drink consumed entirely by maiden aunts who did not see it as really alcoholic.

The Sherry producers in Jerez de la Frontera may indeed be worried that they have enormous stocks of the stuff sitting unsold in cool, dark bodegas, but in some ways they should be thankful because the type of Sherry that is selling less – the sweet, dark style – is just the sort of Sherry that has given it a bad name. Rather, they should be encouraged by the increasing interest in fino, the driest style of Sherry, particularly in the top quality versions. If they can respond by selling less, but better, they would be mirroring the new trend in European drinking habits very closely. And it would do much to lessen the image problem at the same time.

As for the question of the abuse of the name of Sherry, it must rankle, and justifiably so, that concentrated grape must diluted with local tap water (British and Irish) and a Sherry style that comes from a thousand or so miles further east (Cyprus) should still be allowed to carry the same name. It must be especially galling because two of the biggest Sherry companies in Jerez (Allied Lyons and Grand Metropolitan) just happen to make the British products as well (guess which is the more profitable).

The Jerezanos plan to raise the question with the European Commission when the time limit on the use of those names comes up in 1995. In the meantime, they have dreamt up a commendable slogan in British advertising – 'Real Sherry comes only from Spain'.

The solera system

This is the system by which Sherry is matured and prepared for bottling. An individual solera is a series of sherry butts (barrels) containing wine of similar maturity. A series of criaderas (nursery wines) feeds a solera from which wine is drawn for bottling. The barrels are never emptied, but topped up with younger wines which quickly take on the character of the older wine already in the barrel. Thus the continuity of style is preserved.

The Sherry label

Styles of Sherry available in the UK can be divided into three main categories: light, medium and full.

THE LIGHT SHERRIES

We use the term 'light' deliberately here, because although these are fortified wines, they are much lighter than they used to be. Even ten years ago, all dry Sherry used to reach our shops at 20 per cent alcohol. Then it went down to 17 per cent and now it's down to 15.5 or even 15 per cent. That's the strength it is drunk in Spain – and that's the way it should taste.

However, the lowering of strength has had one side effect. The wine, once bottled, begins to tire and oxidise sooner in bottle, so it needs to be drunk fresh. Firms are now sending over small consignments of dry Sherry (more and more in half-bottles – hurrah!), and some major supermarkets (*Tesco* and *Safeway*) have started putting 'drink-by' dates on the labels. The more we get fresher dry Sherry, the more we will enjoy it.

Manzanilla The driest, lightest style of all, applied only to wines made in Sanlúcar de Barrameda by the Atlantic coast. Tasters detect a whiff of sea-salt on the nose and in the flavour. The wines certainly have a lighter, more pungent flavour than those from Jerez itself. Serve manzanilla chilled.

Fino The classic dry Sherry. The flor yeast which protects the wine from oxidation in the barrel gives this wine its yeasty flavour. The palate is dry and full of tangy flavour. Serve it chilled.

Fino Amontillado A fino which has been left to age in cask under its layer of flor until the flor dies. It is darker in colour than a fino, nuttier and more pungent.

Manzanilla Pasada The manzanilla equivalent of fino amontillado.

THE MEDIUM STYLES

Amontillado True amontillados are aged finos which have taken on an amber colour and nutty taste. They are dry, but much amontillado we see in Britain is sweet and not a patch on the real thing. Real amontillado will probably be labelled dry amontillado or 'amontillado secco', and will be more expensive than commercial sweetened stuff. Worth paying more for it.

Palo Cortado A rare intermediate style between amontillado and oloroso (see below). They are amber-coloured wines which started out growing a flor, but suddenly changed course in mid-life and veered towards oloroso. They should be dry.

THE FULL STYLES

Oloroso Wines which never grew flor. They should not be too sweet, but full of richness and flavour. Most are sweetened, but there are some Old Dry Olorosos around which make good winter aperitifs.

Cream and Pale Cream Marketing Man's Sherry. Cream is oloroso with extra sweetening, and delicious poured over ice-cream. Pale Cream (a British invention) is sweetened fino and the one style that would never be drunk in Spain.

Other terms on the label

Amoroso A sweetened oloroso style

Brown A rich, dessert Sherry

Viejo and Muy Viejo Old and very old. A term used at the discretion of a producer.

Who's who in Sherry

Because Sherry is a heavily branded product, most major
retailers sell an own-label Sherry range. Some are good - it all
depends on the quality of the retailer. Our recommendations are
indicated in the Where to buy section under each merchant's
entry. Here, we list those producers who sell under their own
name. Many of them also supply the merchants' own-label
Sherries.

Tomas Abad A small bodega in Puerto de Santa Maria selling
its own good quality brands and some Sherries from other small
producers. Quality can be variable. Wines: Tomas Abad, Don
Tomas.
Bordeaux Direct

Barbadillo, Antonio Based in Sanlúcar and recognised as
manzanilla specialists, although they handle other styles of
Sherry, too. Wines: Manzanilla, Fino de Balbaina, Principe
(manzanilla pasada); also a table wine called Castillo de San
Diego, made from the same Palomino grapes as are used in
Sherry.
Widely available

Bertola Best known as producers of sweet Sherry. Wines: Bertola
Cream.
Peter Green

Bobadilla Large company with good value, inexpensive fino.
Peter Green; Moreno Wines

Burdon Two ranges one of good value Sherries of commercial
character, the other superior with wines of much greater style.
Wines: Puerto Fino, Heavenly Cream, Don Luis Amontillado.
*D Byrne & Co; Martinez Fine Wine; Oddbins; Selfridges; Upper
Crust*

Croft British-owned firm whose main product is a Pale Cream
Sherry – they were the inventors of this style – plus a range of
other styles. Wines: Delicado Fino, Palo Cortado, Original Pale
Cream.
Widely available

Diez-Merito Firm which makes one of the best older finos.
Wines: Don Zoilo range, Diez Hermanos range.
*D Byrne & Co; Fulham Road Wine Centre; Harrods; Laymont &
Shaw; Moreno Wines; Russell & McIver; J Sainsbury (own-label);
Selfridges; Willoughbys*

Domecq One of the largest Sherry bodegas, producing a range of top quality wines. Their new, low-strength (15.5 per cent) La Ina is a revelation. Wines: La Ina (fino), Botaina (dry amontillado), Rio Viejo (dry oloroso), Amontillado 51 -la (dry amontillado), Sibarita (Palo Cortado), Venerable (very sweet, luscious wine from Pedro Ximénez grapes), plus the less classy Double Century sherries.
Widely available

Duff Gordon Old-established bodega, founded by a Scot in 1768. Wines: Fino Feria, Club Dry, El Cid Amontillado, Santa Maria Cream.
J Sainsbury (own-label); Selfridges

Duke of Wellington A very good light fino from Bodegas Internacionales, one of the most spectacular of the modern Jerez bodegas. Other Sherries in the range are less exciting but good.
D Byrne & Co; Peter Green; Selfridges

Findlater Despite being the name of a British wine merchant, this has become a more widely available brand than just an own-label. Wines: Dry Fly, May Fly, River Fly, La Luna, Amontillado Fino Viejo.
Findlater Mackie Todd; Major Sworder & Co; Selfridges; Unwins; Willoughbys

Garvey Make superb fino and an equally good range of other styles. They have recently introduced a lower-priced 'popular' range, which is not nearly so interesting. Wines: San Patricio Fino, Tio Guillermo Amontillado, Ochavico Dry Oloroso, Extra Dry, Amontillado Medium Dry, Pale Cream, Cream.
Widely available

Gonzàlez Byass Large firm owning some of the best-known brand names, which tend to do well in tastings (rare examples of brand leaders in a market coming out on top). Wines: Tio Pepe (fino), Elegante (fino – less expensive), La Concha (medium amontillado), San Domingo (pale cream), Apostoles (dry oloroso), Amontillado del Duque Seco (dry).
Widely available; older Sherries from Oddbins

Harveys The biggest-selling Sherry range in Britain. The top brand is a cream Sherry. The quality of the standard range is strictly commercial, but they have also launched a much more interesting premium range, 1796. Wines: Luncheon Dry (fino), Bristol Cream, Bristol Milk, John Harvey (mixer Sherry); also 1796 Manzanilla, Fino, Amontillado, Palo Cortado, Oloroso. Harvey's also have a rare range of late-bottled Sherries which are available in small quantities and worth looking out for.
Widely available; older Sherries from John Harvey & Sons

Hidalgo Small firm specialising in good quality manzanilla. They supply many of the own-label Sherries to wine merchants. Wines: La Gitana Manzanilla, Jerez Cortado Hidalgo, El Cuadrado Fino.
Adnams; Findlater Mackie Todd; Haynes Hanson & Clark; Lay & Wheeler; O W Loeb; Tanners; Waitrose; Windrush Wines

Lustau, Emilio A leading independent company known for its range of almacenista Sherries. These are individual Sherries purchased from small producers and then aged in separate lots by Lustau; they are known by number rather than names and vary according to availability. Lustau's standard range (the main brand is Dry Lustau – fino) has been somewhat variable recently, which is a pity. They have also just introduced a range of Landed Age Sherries: these are exported from Spain in wooden butts and given some time in cellars in London before bottling. They also have a limited availability.
Widely available

Marqués de Real Tesoro Small bodega making a rather good set of old Sherries. Wines: Fino Ideal, Almirante Oloroso Secco, Solera 1850 (amontillado).
Mayor Sworder & Co

Osborne A large independent company, based in Puerto de Santa Maria, making a top-class fino and a full range of other styles. Famous in Spain for the use of their bull symbol on hoardings. Wines: Fino Quinta, Coquinero (amontillado), Bailen (dry oloroso), Osborne Cream.
J Sainsbury (own-label); Willoughbys

Palomino y Vergara Small bodega, now part of Harveys, but making its own high quality fino. Wines: Tio Mateo (fino).
Gare du Vin

Sánchez Romate A small, privately owned bodega, mainly concerned with brandy, but also producing a good manzanilla and fino. Wines: Petenara Manzanilla, Marismeno Fino, Don José Oloroso, Iberia Cream.
H Allen Smith; Tesco (own-label, Premium range)

Sandeman The same firm as the Port producers with the famous symbol of the cloaked Don. They have a fine range of old Sherries. Of their standard range, the Don Fino is much improved, and the Royal Esmeralda is a lovely nutty old amontillado, but the Character Amoroso (a medium-style) is a disappointment. Wines: Bone Dry Amontillado, Dry Old Palo Cortado, Royal Ambrosante, Old Amoroso, Royal Corregidor, Imperial Corregidor, Pale Cream.

Alex Findlater; Fortnum & Mason; Oddbins; Selfridges; Upper Crust; La Vigneronne

De Soto A privately owned company which, unusually, makes wines only from its own vineyards. Wines: Fino Soto, Manzanilla, Amontillado Maravilla, Dry Oloroso, Amontillado Viejo.
D Byrne & Co; Mi Casa Wines; Moreno Wines

De Terry Although mainly concerned with making brandy, De Terry also produce a fairly commercial range of Sherries. Wines: Maruja Fino.
Mi Casa Wines

Valdespino Family company producing some fine Sherries which show well in tastings. Their fino (which unusually is a single vineyard wine) is especially good, and they also have a range of old Sherries. Wines: Inocente (Fino), Tio Diego (amontillado), Don Tomas (amontillado), Don Gonzalo Old Dry Oloroso, Manzanilla Deliciosa.
Les Amis du Vin; D Byrne & Co; Ellis Son & Vidler; Alex Findlater; Haynes Hanson & Clark; Mayor Sworder & Co; Oddbins; La Réserve; La Vigneronne; Willoughbys; The Wine Society

Williams & Humbert One of the more spectacular bodegas, now owned by Barbadillo. They specialise in richer, darker styles of wine. Wines: Pando (fino-amontillado), Dry Sack (amontillado), Canasta Cream, A Winter's Tale, Dos Cortados Palo Cortado.
H Allen Smith; Alex Findlater; Mayor Sworder & Co; Oddbins; Russell & McIver; Selfridges; Unwins; Willoughbys

Wisdom & Warter One of the Sherry firms with British origins, who make a wide range of Sherries. Wines: Fino Oliva, Manzanilla la Guapa, Amontillado Royal Palace, Wisdom's Choice Cream.
Unwins

Best buys in Sherry

Dry Old Oloroso, Garvey (*Frank E Stainton*)
Apostoles Oloroso Abbacado, Gonzalez Byass (*Del Monicos*)
Valdespino Inocente Fino (*Cairns & Hickey; Classic Wine Warehouses; George Hill*)
Solear Manzanilla Pasada, Barbadillo (*Alex Findlater*)
Sainsbury's Premium Sherries (*J Sainsbury*)
Osborne Fino Quinta (*D Byrne & Co*)
Manzanilla La Gitana, Hidalgo (*Philip Eyres Wine Merchant; Pavilion Wine Co*)

Puerto Fino Superior Dry, John William Burdon (*La Reserva Wines*)
Tanners Mariscal Fino (*Tanners*)
Manzanilla Pasada, Herederos Argueso (*David Baillie Vintners*)

Specialist stockists

Bin Ends; Cumbrian Cellar; Alex Findlater; Peter Green; John Harvey & Sons; Hicks & Don; High Breck Vintners; S H Jones; Justerini & Brooks; Laymont & Shaw; Moreno Wines; Pond Farm Wines; La Reserva Wines; Tanners Wines; Wine House

PORT

If any wine style should be in decline, it ought to be Port. It's sweet, dark, alcoholic, expensive: everything that is frowned on today.

But on the contrary, Port is booming. The Port trade has skilfully avoided the troubles in Sherry and has managed to project itself into the 1990s without too many compromises to its integrity.

How? The answer lies in careful marketing as much as in the quality of the product, although the fact that so much Port is so good does help. The style of Late Bottled Vintage was invented, a clever balancing act using the name, Vintage, which was associated with the greatest Ports, and price, which was on the cheap side for Port. Whatever one may think of Late Bottled Vintage (and the closely related Vintage Character), it is this style that has saved Port, and enables us to continue to enjoy the fine vintage Ports.

Moreover, the arrival of another style, aged tawny, in greater quantities than a few years ago, has opened up a whole new dimension, and has widened the appeal of Port to those drinkers who never appreciated the vintage style.

For a drink which likes to cultivate an old-fashioned image, there is frenetic activity in Portugal. New vineyards are being created, old ones replanted (all with help from the World Bank, anxious to improve the local economy in Portugal's poorest region). New bottling complexes are being opened, white-coated laboratory staff are learning to analyse the relationship between soil and different types of grapes (unheard of in the Port-producing area, where the traditionally permitted 40 or so varieties could be planted anywhere), clonal selection of grapes has arrived. The Port trade is moving fast, catching up with the rest of the wine world in a few short years.

The classification of Port

Port is one of the most closely controlled wines anywhere. The vineyards are in the large but tightly defined area of the Douro Valley in north-east Portugal. They are classified on a number of scales, according to productivity (low yields are best), altitude (somewhere around 400—500 metres above sea level is the most favourable), soil (schist is best, granite worst), geographical position (based on a pre-determined set of locations), how well the vineyard is maintained, the variety of grapes planted (see below for the best types), the gradient (the steeper the better), shelter, the age of the vines (up to the best at 25 years old), the distance root to root of the vines (too close is no good), the nature of the land and, finally, the aspect of the vineyard.

The marks from all these are added up. Any vineyard that gets over 1201 is graded as A, the best, down to F for vineyards which get fewer than 400 points (including minus scores). On the basis of this grading the maximum number of litres of juice per 1,000 vines which can go to Port is determined; the rest must go as table wine.

Controls don't stop there. Each year, representatives from the various controlling bodies in the Port trade (the exporters, the Casa do Douro and the Instituto do Vinho do Porto) meet together and determine how much each Port house can make, based on the exports by that firm in the previous year. Any Port which leaves the Port shippers' lodges at the mouth of the Douro in Vila Nova de Gaia has to have permits, and any wine bottled in Portugal (as most is nowadays) has to have a seal over the cork to guarantee its origin.

Now if some of these regulations stem from a surprising Portuguese love of bureaucracy (and passivity in the face of it), they have the result that the general quality level of most Port is high, and getting higher.

Port grapes

Forty-eight different types of grapes are allowed in the Port vineyards. Most of them are still cultivated but in dwindling quantities as the six major varieties take over. These are: Touriga Naçional, making a soft, spicy wine; Touriga Francesa, producing very fruity wine with good acidity; Tinta Cão, giving elegant wine; Roriz, making soft, smooth, broad wines; Barroca, giving tannic, hard wines; Mourisco, producing light, slightly tannic wines.

Port is a blend of any or all of these grape varieties in a combination that gives a shipper the style he wants.

White Port (see below) is made from Malvasia Fina and Malvasia Grossa.

Styles of Port

Port comes in a vast range of styles, some of which seem to overlap, at least in name. There is particular argument about whether the terms Late Bottled Vintage and Vintage Character can confuse the drinker into thinking he or she is buying true vintage wine, and there are calls for clarification of the whole issue.

White Port Usually put last in a listing of styles because is has never taken off. We suggest it should because it makes a marvellous aperitif, served chilled. It's made from white rather than red grapes, but is fortified in the same way. A new, lighter, drier style is being developed.

Ruby The most basic quality. Youthful, simple wine. Widely available.

Tawny This term has two completely different meanings. One is an alternative to ruby, of basic quality. But there are also aged tawnies – 10-year-old, 20-year-old, etc – which are some of the finest Ports available. This second type of tawny has a lighter style than a ruby, and is delicious slightly chilled, drunk as an aperitif or after a meal.

Colheita A tawny style of which the base is wine from one particular year. The wine is kept in wood and bottled ready for drinking. However, the casks are topped up in the interim with wine that can come from any year, and so a Colheita wine really becomes more of a solera-type wine, like Sherry.

Crusted A blend of wines either from different years or from a single vintage, bottled after three to four years in wood. It matures reasonably quickly in bottle – generally five or six years from bottling (this date should be on the label). It tends to throw a sediment – hence the name – and therefore needs decanting. There is still argument over the legal definition of crusted, but for the time being we can certainly recommend it as a good value alternative to expensive vintage Port.

Late Bottled Vintage (LBV) The poorer man's vintage Port, kept in wood for four to six years and then bottled. This means that it is virtually ready to drink when bottled. The vintage will be on the label, but not the bottling date. While LBVs are seen as an alternative to much pricier vintage Ports, they are really more like superior rubies than true vintage wines.

Late Bottled or **Vintage Character** Similar to Late Bottled Vintage in style, but not from one year.

Single Quinta Port Up until now, single quinta Port has been wine from one estate made in a year which the shipper hasn't considered quite good enough for a general vintage declaration (see vintage Port below and vintage information). It is bottled and sold after two years, and needs some years to mature in bottle. Now single quinta Ports also come from smaller producers who make wine from a single vineyard.

Vintage The finest of Ports – and the most serious. A vintage will be 'declared' only in the best years and is traditionally bottled after two years in wood. It needs many years to mature, because wine ages more slowly in glass than in wood. Decant vintage Port before serving it. Some of the Portuguese houses leave their vintage Ports in cask longer, and these tend to be ready to drink sooner.

The great vintages

1985 This is likely to be a great vintage year since the weather was boiling hot right through the summer. The wines were bottled in early 1987, and are rather expensive.

1983 Well-coloured, aromatic wines. The majority of shippers have declared this vintage. The wines are quite forward and should be ready in the mid-1990s.

1982 Declared by a minority of shippers. The wines are maturing quite fast, and are full of fruit. They should be ready by the 1990s.

1980 A longer-lasting vintage. Good quality wines from many of the oldest-established shippers will be ready in the late 1990s. Excellent value for money.

1977 The classic vintage since 1963, much admired. Keep it until the turn of the century.

1975 A light vintage. Drink now.

1970 Much better than originally considered, this vintage is still underpriced.

1966 Wines from this year started off by being underrated, but the world has caught on to their quality and now, though good, they are over-priced.

1963 Great post-war vintage, the best since 1945. Keep those you have and grab any you can. They will keep for years.

In addition to these general vintage years, single quinta Ports (see above) were made by shippers in 1983, 1980, 1978, 1976, 1974, 1972, 1968 and 1967.

Who's who in the Port trade

Cálem A Portuguese house which surprised the world by making one of the best 1985 vintage Ports. The quality of all their wines has improved enormously in the past few years, and prices are still relatively inexpensive. Single quinta: Quinta da Foz.
Safeway (own-label); Selfridges; Wine Growers Association; The Wine Society

Churchill Graham Small, independent family firm making extremely good wines, selling under the brand name Churchill. Single Quinta: Quinta do Agua Alta.
Adnams; H Allen Smith; Averys; Berry Bros & Rudd; Corney Barrow; Ellis Son & Vidler; Alex Findlater; Findlater Mackie Todd; Haynes Hanson & Clark; Laytons; Tanners (own-label); Upper Crust

Cockburn Biggest firm on the British market with Special Reserve. Some good tawnies, and underrated vintages.
Widely available

Croft Specialise in LBV and Distinction brands, also Gilbey's Crown Triple Port. Single quinta: Quinta da Roêda.
Widely available

Delaforce Owned jointly with Croft, but still managed by the family. His Eminence Choice and Vintage Character as well as lighter vintage styles. Single Quinta: Quinta da Corte.
Arriba Kettle; Averys; Berry Bros & Rudd; Corney & Barrow; Peter Dominic; Alex Findlater; Fortnum & Mason; Selfridges; Upper Crust; Willoughbys

Dow One of the leading vintage houses. High quality wines have a powerful, dry and nutty style. Single quinta: Quinta do Bomfim.
Widely available

Ferreira The leading Portuguese Port house (as opposed to those owned by British families), producing some of the finest tawnies. They also produce table wines, of which the best is called Barca Velha (see under Portugal). Duque de Bragança

Tawny Port is famous. Single Quinta Tawny: Quinta do Porto.
Fulham Road Wine Centre; Thresher; Unwins; Upper Crust

Fonseca Company with a very high reputation. Their best-known brand is Bin 27, but they also make long-lasting vintage Ports. Their Late Bottled Vintage Port is one of the best. Single quinta: Quinta du Panascal.
Widely available

Forrester A famous name in Port, known until recently as Offley Forrester. Their aged tawnies, such as Baron Forrester 10-year-old, are now very good. The vintage Port is called Boavista.
Bibendum; Laytons; O W Loeb; Oddbins; Tanners

Gould Campbell Part of the same group as Dow and Graham, making middle-weight wines. Good 10-year-old tawny, Finest Old Tawny and Vintage Character.
H Allen Smith; Averys; Berry Bros & Rudd; Davisons; Eldridge Pope; Haynes Hanson & Clark; Laytons; Mayor Sworder & Co; Russell & McIver; Willoughbys; Windrush Wines

Graham Big, luscious vintage Ports. Other styles emulate these qualities. Single Quinta: Quinta do Malvedos.
Widely available

Martinez Associated with Cockburn. They produce some very attractive Ports at good prices.
Adnams; Averys; Corney & Barrow (own-label); Alex Findlater; Laytons; Majestic; La Réserve; Russell & McIver; Selfridges; Upper Crust; La Vigneronne; Waitrose; Willoughbys

Niepoort Firm with Dutch origins specialising in Colheita Ports.
Bibendum; Celtic Vintner; Selfridges; Wessex Wines

Quarles Harris Another small Port house, part of the Symington group, which also owns Dow, Graham and Warre.
Adnams; Averys; Berry Bros & Rudd; Ellis Son & Vidler; Findlater Mackie Todd; Haynes Hanson & Clark; Upper Crust; La Vigneronne

Quinta do Cotto A single quinta Port, made by the Champalimaud family (who also make rather good table wines). Quite unlike most other Ports in its jammy richness.
Alex Findlater

Quinta do Noval High quality Ports are made in one of the finest Douro vineyards (although not all their production is actually grown there). Late Bottled is their best-known brand. They also make the rare (and very expensive) Nácional Port from ungrafted vines.
Widely available

Ramos Pinto Small, go-ahead Portuguese house making a range of light Ports good quality. Single Quinta Tawny Ports: Quinta da Bom Retiro; Quinta da Ervamoira.
Berkmann Wine Cellars/Le Nez Rouge; Andrew Gordon Wines; Peter Green

Rebello Valente Brand name of Robertson Brothers, a small Port house, now owned by Sandeman.
Adnams; Averys; Berry Bros & Rudd; Caves de la Madeleine; La Réserve; Upper Crust; Winecellars

Royal Oporto The largest Port producer, controlling 20 per cent of the trade. They make light-style wines, including vintage Ports every year. Many of their wines are sold under own-label brands. Single quinta: Quinta dos Carvalhos.
H Allen Smith; Alex Findlater; Mayor Sworder & Co; Tesco; Unwins; Winecellars

Sandeman A range of Ports in all styles is made by this firm, which is linked to the Sandeman Sherry firm. Aged tawnies are their best.
Widely available

Smith Woodhouse Fragrant, fruity wines, with particularly successful vintage wines that are not too expensive. Also His Majesty's Choice 20-year-old tawny.
Widely available

De Sousa Small family firm whose finest wines are the vintage Colheitas.
Richmond Wine Warehouse

Taylor Expensive, top quality Ports. Late Bottled Vintage is widely available, but is not as good as it was. Taylor also produce aged tawnies of a high standard. Single quinta: Quinta de Vargellas.
Widely available

Warre The oldest Port house, now jointly owned, along with Graham and Dow, by the Symington group. Single quinta, Quinta da Cavadinha.
Widely available

Best buys in Port

Martinez Fine Crusted Port (*Adnams*)
Niepoort Colheita Port 1975 (*Premier Wines*)
Quinta da Ervamoira 10-year-old tawny, Ramos-Pinto (*Berkmann Wine Cellars/Le Nez Rouge; Lamb Wine Co*)
Dows Crusted Bottled 1985 (*Oddbins*)
Quinta da Roêda, Croft (*Andrew Gordon Wines*)

Wood Port 1978, De Souza (*Richmond Wine Warehouse*)
Messias 10-year-old tawny (*Ad Hoc Wine Warehouse*)
Calem 10-year-old tawny (*Wine Growers Association; Wine Schoppen*)
Russell & McIver's Finest Crusted Port, bottled 1986 (*Russell & McIver*)
Booths Fine Crusted Port (*Booths*)

Specialist stockists

William Addison (Newport); Adnams; Berry Bros & Rudd; Classic Wines; College Cellar; Davisons; Eldridge Pope; Fortnum & Mason; Matthew Gloag & Son; Harrods; John Harvey & Sons; Justerini & Brooks; Richard Kihl; Kurtz & Chan; Lay & Wheeler; Master Cellar Wine Warehouse; Nickolls & Perks; Old Street Wine Company; Thos Peatling; Premier Wines; Edward Sheldon; Selfridges; Turville Valley Wine; La Vigneronne; Whittalls Wines

MADEIRA

Consider that the island of Madeira has only 400 square miles of land – most of it mountainous – to support a population of 250,000. Consider also that there are only 200 hectares of vineyard on the island, that bananas are a much better cash crop, and that the bulk of the wine produced on the island is a rather unpleasant table wine made entirely for local consumption. It is perhaps a minor miracle that any Madeira wine is made at all.

But it is – and we must be very thankful. Madeira is a unique taste. It is a fortified wine, but it is also a cooked wine – and that is where Madeira gets its special taste. After the brandy has been added, the wine is heated up to 40°C in an *estufa* or stove, and then cooled. The whole process can last for up to a year. Such a strange way of treating a wine derives from the 18th and 19th centuries when it was discovered that the heat in the holds of ships improved the wine no end.

The resulting wine has three characteristics – a burnt, caramel taste, oxidation (hence the word for a wine that has been oxidised – maderised) and considerable acidity because of high volatility. This is an unlikely range of tastes to make a great wine, but with the essentially rich base they all work together.

The styles of Madeira

Because the island of Madeira is part of Portugal, Madeira wine is often equated with Port, but a better comparison would be with Sherry: there is a range of styles, from comparatively dry to very sweet. Moreover, Madeira can be drunk in the same circumstances as Sherry.

The driest style is Sercial, which makes an excellent aperitif, just like Fino Sherry. Verdelho is also an aperitif wine, but being slightly fuller will also go well with food like soups, rather like Amontillado. Both Bual and Malmsey make magnificent after-dinner drinks, like the richest Oloroso Sherries.

The grapes of Madeira

Those wine names are also the names of the best quality grapes grown on the island. There are two other quality varieties – Terrantez and Malvasia – both of which are grown in tiny quantities, and which make superb and fascinating wines.

However, these 'noble' varieties account for only a small proportion of the island's vines. A much larger area of vineyard is occupied by a variety called Tinta Negra Mole, and another large area of vineyard is planted with American vines which rejoice in names like Black Spanish and Barrete de Padre. Until recently, all these varieties used to be chucked into Madeira, which was still sold as Sercial or Malmsey regardless of the fact that those grape varieties might have made up only ten per cent of the whole.

With the arrival of Portugal in the EC, that had to stop (the wine laws of the European Community do have some uses). The new rules specify that 85 per cent of the wine in a bottle of Sercial must be made from Sercial grapes. If it isn't, it must be called Dry. The same, of course, applies to other grape varieties, so we are now getting the genuine article. And the farmers are being encouraged to plant more of the noble varieties in place of the lesser types.

Categories have been developed and will be indicated on the label:

Reserve: over five years old

Reserva Velho: over ten years old

Special Reserve: over 15 years old

Fresqueira (vintage): wine from a specified year that has been in cask for over 20 years.

Wine that lasts for ever

We've already indicated something of the taste of Madeira. What is also so special about the cooking process (known as the *estufagem*) is that it has the effect of allowing the best wines to last seemingly for ever without really ageing. It is possible (but very expensive) to drink vintages of Madeira that date from well into the last century – there are still some 1795 wines on the island that have plenty of fruit. While that's a characteristic of the top wines, ordinary Madeiras are wines which are at their best when they are bottled and are not designed to improve in bottle.

If you plan to open a bottle of Madeira, don't be worried that it may fade if it is not finished at one sitting. Unlike any other wine, a bottle of Madeira once opened will survive unchanged for months.

Who's who in Madeira

Barbeito Family-owned firm which has a superb collection of vintage wines. Sadly, all we see is the basic range: Rainwater Dry, Island Dry, Island Rich, Crown Malmsey.
Les Amis du Vin

Blandy Brothers One of the most famous Madeira companies, which also owns Reid's Hotel, one of the island's top hotels. Wines: Duke of Sussex Sercial, Duke of Cambridge Verdelho, Duke of Cumberland Bual, Duke of Clarence Malmsey, 5-year-old and 10-year-old wines.
Augustus Barnett; D Byrne & Co; Davisons; Peter Dominic; Fortnum & Mason; Peter Green; Lay & Wheeler; Mi Casa Wines; La Réserve; Selfridges; Thresher; Unwins; Upper Crust; La Vigneronne; Willoughbys

Cossart Gordon Producer of classic Madeira, often in a light style. Top quality wines. Wines: Good Company Sercial, Cossart Rainwater, Good Company Bual and Malmsey, 5-year-old Reserve, 10-year-old Special Reserve.
Widely available

Harveys Part of the famous Sherry firm, whose Madeiras are produced for them by Henriques & Henriques. Wines: Very Superior Old Dry Sercial, Royal Solera Verdelho, Old Bual, Old Rich Malmsey.
Asda; John Harvey & Sons; Safeway; Tesco; Victoria Wine Company

Henriques & Henriques Large producer who makes wines under a number of different labels. Wines: Henriques & Henriques, Belem, Casa dos Vinhos de Madeira.
Les Amis du Vin; D Byrne & Co; Alex Findlater; Peter Green; Arthur Rackhams; La Réserve; La Vigneronne

Leacock Rich, deep Madeiras which are balanced by clean fruit. Wines: Leacock St John Reserve Sercial, Verdelho and Bual, Special Reserve Malmsey.
Adnams; La Vigneronne; The Wine Club

Lomelino The oldest Portuguese Madeira house. Wines: Imperial Sercial, Verdelho, Reserve 5-years, Special Reserve.
Russell & McIver; La Vigneronne

Rutherford & Miles Very stylish wines in quite a light style. Wines: Old Custom House Sercial, La Reina Verdelho, Old Trinity House Bual, Reserve, Special Reserve.
D Byrne & Co; Eldridge Pope; Fortnum & Mason; Peter Green; Haynes Hanson & Clark; Hicks & Don; Martinez Fine Wines; Mayor Sworder & Co; La Réserve; Tanners; Willoughbys; Windrush Wines; Wizard Wine Warehouses

Veiga Franca The largest exporters of Madeira, much of which goes to France. They supply a number of wines to British shops under own labels.
Findlater Mackie Todd; Majestic; Tesco

Best buys from Madeira

Most houses stock small quantities of vintage solera wines which make for memorable drinking. Of the more widely available Madeiras, here are our best buys:

Tesco Malmsey Madeira (*Tesco*)
Finest Old Malmsey, Five Year Old Reserve, Cossart Gordon (*Farthinghoe Fine Wine and Food*)
Finest Old Sercial, Cossart Gordon (*Averys of Bristol; Lay & Wheeler*)

Specialist stockists

Alastair's Grapevine; Averys of Bristol; Berry Bros & Rudd; Eldridge Pope; Fortnum & Mason; Peter Green; Old Street Wine Company; Premier Wines; Russell & McIver; Turville Valley Wines; La Vigneronne; Willoughbys

OTHER PORTUGUESE FORTIFIED WINES

Apart from Port and Madeira, Portugal makes other fortified wines. The one we see in Britain is Muscat de Setúbal, which comes from the Muscat grape, and is produced just south of Lisbon. The style is normally quite heavy.

Muscat de Setúbal, J M da Fonseca
H Allen Smith

MONTILLA AND MORILES

Despite their similarity to the middle range and cheaper Sherries, these are not in fact fortified wines - they just taste like it. The heat from the sun in the vineyards right in the centre of southern Spain near Córdoba has the effect of pushing up the sugar content of the grapes to such an extent that an effortless 15 or 16 degrees of alcohol is achieved without any aid from brandy.

The word 'Montilla' was borrowed by the Jerez Sherry producers and used in the description 'amontillado'. Rather unfairly, the law now forbids Montilla to use its own name in describing its wines, so they are simply labelled 'dry', 'medium' or 'cream'.

Although they don't have the sophistication of top Sherries, Montilla wines are probably better value at the lower price and quality levels. Most of the Montilla available in the shops is own-label, so the quality varies according to the quality of the stockist.

Moriles produces slightly lighter wines than Montilla, but the style is very similar. Try the two that *Tesco* stock.

Who's who in Montilla and Moriles

Apart from the readily available own-label wines, classier examples of Montilla are available in the UK.

Alvear The biggest and the most modern bodega in the region, supplying much of the own-label market.
Davisons; J Sainsbury (own-label); Tanners; Unwins

Tomás Garcia Small company (in Montilla terms), but probably making the best wines in the area. Wines: Solera Fina 1, Flor Montilla, Tomás Garcia.
J Sainsbury (own-label); Tesco (own-label)

Perez Barquero This firm has greatly improved the quality of its wines in recent years, especially in the dry styles. Wines: Dos Reinos Dry, Los Amigos, Los Palcos.
Oddbins; Safeway (own-label)

MÁLAGA

Málaga is sweet, fortified wine from the middle of Spain's south coast to the east of Jerez. It is made from a blend of Moscatel and Pedro Ximenez grapes. At its best, it can be complex, either a sort of cross between old tawny Port and fino sherry or darker, very nutty and intense. It's best drunk as a dessert wine.

The top quality Málaga is known as Lagrima, simply made from the free-run juice of uncrushed grapes (as in Tokay in Hungary). Other styles are Pajarete (more of an aperitif style), a pale semi-dulce and a darker Moscatel.

Who's who in Málaga

Scholtz Hermanos The great name in Málaga, making a whole range of styles. Wines: Solera Scholtz (light brown dessert wine), Seco Añejo (dry), Lagrima.
Alex Findlater; Findlater Mackie Todd; Fortnum & Mason; Fulham Road Wine Centre; Peter Green; Majestic; Martinez Fine Wine; Moreno Wines; Arthur Rackhams; Selfridges; Upper Crust; La Vigneronne; Winecellars

Bodegas Barcelo Family firm making reasonably priced wines. Wines: Bacarles Solera Vieja, Gran Malaga (very sweet), Lagrima, Gran Vino Sanson (a lighter version of Lagrima).
Mi Casa Wines; Moreno Wines

MARSALA

This fortified wine from Sicily seems to have become much better known as an essential ingredient in that favourite in Italian restaurants, zabaglione, rather than as a drink in its own right.

Cooking is what most Marsala is probably best for, but recently there has been a revival of interest in quality in this dusty Sicilian port, and the new Marsalas are worth seeking out.

The nearby island of Pantelleria is home of two fascinating

wines. Moscato di Pantelleria can be either fortified or unfortified, but both styles rely on the raisiny richness of the Moscato grape for their sweetness. Moscato Passito di Pantelleria is made from sun-dried Moscato grapes, and is normally fortified, giving an intensely luscious wine.

The styles of Marsala

There are a number of gradations of quality in Marsala, which are now governed by Italian DOC regulations. There is no control over dryness or sweetness, although the best styles are normally dry.

Fine Basic Marsala, light, generally sweet and best for cooking. Also known by the initials IP (Italy Particular) because it is the style sold in Italy. It is sweetened with a strange concoction of syrup made from cooked grapes.

Superiore Stronger than Fine and more likely to be sweetened with semi-dried grapes than the syrup used in Fine. Dryness or sweetness depends on the producer. Also known as Superior Old Marsala (SOM), London Particular (LP) – because it was sold to Britain – or Garibaldi Dolce (GD).

Vergine and Vergine Stravecchio The top category, always dry wines with none of the sweetening agents used in the other two styles. Vergine is matured in wood for five years, Vergine Stravecchio for ten. This is the category that is of most interest as a drink rather than as a recipe ingredient.

Speciale This category includes all the strangely flavoured Marsalas (such as eggnogs) that have given Marsala a bad name. They cannot be called Marsala, but are allowed to say on the label that they are made from Marsala wine.

Who's who in Marsala

De Bartoli The best producer in the region. Wines: Joséphine Doré (very dry), Vecchio Samperi (like an amontillado Sherry), Marsala Superiore (sweet and raisiny). De Bartoli also makes great wines from Pantelleria (see above).
Adnams; Fortnum & Mason; Oddbins; Winecellars

Other producers of Marsala include: Florio; Pellegrino and Rallo.
Oddbins; J Sainsbury; Selfridges

Best buy in Marsala

Bukkuram Moscato Passito di Pantelleria, De Bartoli (*Winecellars*)

FORTIFIED WINES FROM AUSTRALIA

Outside the classic fortified areas of Port, Sherry and Madeira, Australia produces the best fortifieds in the world. The best are made from Muscat grapes (Liqueur Muscat) or from Muscadelle grapes (known in Australia as Liqueur Tokays, but in Europe as Liqueur Muscadelle or Liqueur Tokay). Both styles have great intensity and lusciousness, derived partly from blending with small quantities of very old wines. Every producer has a range of styles, some with indications of age, some without. The very best come from Rutherglen in North-East Victoria.

Port and Sherry styles are also made in Australia, but we rarely see them in the UK.

Who's who in Australian fortifieds

All Saints Liqueur Muscat (*D Byrne & Co; Hicks & Don; Willoughbys*)
Campbells Old Rutherglen Muscat (*D Byrne & Co; Alex Findlater; Fortnum & Mason; Harrods; Hicks & Don; Reid Wines; La Réserve; Upper Crust*)
Morris of Rutherglen Liqueur Muscat (*Averys; Alex Findlater; Peter Green; Oddbins; Wizard Wine Warehouses*)
Chambers' Rosewood Vineyards Special Liqueur Muscat (*Adnams; Averys; D Byrne & Co; Chaplin & Son; Alex Findlater; Fulham Road Wine Centre; Haynes Hanson & Clark; Hicks & Don; La Réserve; Selfridges; La Vigneronne; Willoughbys*)
Seppelt Rutherglen Show Muscat (*Alex Findlater*)
Stanton & Killeen Rutherglen Liqueur Muscat (*Averys; D Byrne & Co; Fortnum & Mason; Majestic; Russell & McIver; Selfridges; Tanners; La Vigneronne*)
Yalumba Museum Show Reserve, S Smith & Son (*Les Amis du Vin*)
Brown Brothers Liqueur Muscat (*Adnams; Alex Findlater; Majestic; Willoughbys*)
Bullers Rutherglen Muscat (*Alex Findlater; Upper Crust*)

Best buys from Australia

Verdelho 6-year-old, Bleasdale, Langhorne Creek (*Barnes Wine Shop; Fulham Road Wine Centre*)
Baileys Founders Award Liqueur Muscat, Glenrowan (*Whiteside's of Clitheroe*)

FORTIFIED WINES FROM FRANCE

Vins doux naturels

These are wines from the arc of southern French vineyards along the Mediterranean coast. There are a number of styles: white wines are made from Muscat grapes, and red from the Grenache. While all whites are sweet, reds vary from dry to sweet. Some reds called Rancio, which are aged in cask for a long time, are the nearest thing to Port made in France.

Who's who in Vins Doux Naturels

WHITE

Muscat de Beaumes-de-Venise, Cave Coopérative (*Les Amis du Vin; Asda; D Byrne & Co; Caves de la Madeleine; Davisons; Peter Dominic; Lay & Wheeler; Majestic; Oddbins; Selfridges; Unwins*)
Muscat de Rivesaltes, Ch de Jau (*D Byrne & Co; Oddbins*)
Muscat de Rivesaltes, Domaine de Bresson (*Adnams; Oddbins*)
Cuvée José Sala, Vin de Liqueur (*Eldridge Pope; Majestic; Selfridges; Tesco; Willoughbys; Wizard Wine Warehouses*)
Muscat de Frontignan, Cave Coopérative (*Tanners*)
Ch De Corneilla (*Cadwgan Fine Wines*)
Muscat de St-Jean de Minervois, Domaine Simon (*Mayor Sworder & Co*)
Muscat de Beaumes-de-Venise Domaine de Durban (*Eldridge Pope; La Réserve; Russell & McIver; Victoria Wine Company; Yapp Brothers*)
Muscat de Rivesaltes, Aphrodis (*Eldridge Pope*)

RED

Banyuls, R Dutres (*David Alexander; Oddbins*)
Rasteau, Cave Coopérative de Rasteau (*Cadwgan Fine Wines*)
Banyuls, Dr Parcé (*La Vigneronne*)

Pineau des Charentes

From the Cognac vineyards in western France also come red, white and rosé fortified wines, which are made by stopping the fermentation of the wines with local brandy (Cognac). Many would argue that the sweet result is better for its brandy content than for its wine, but as an aperitif, Pineau does have its advocates.

Who's who in Pineau des Charentes

Ch de Beaulon (*Berkmann Wine Cellars/Le Nez Rouge; Harrods*)
Plessis (*Addison Avenue Wine Shop; Alastair's Grapevine; Great Northern Wine Company*)
Gautier (*Eldridge Pope*)
Mme Raymond Ragnaud (*Dell Fines, Claymark House, 63 Stalker Lees Road, Sheffield; Peter Lunzer Fine Wines, 309 Old Street, London EC1*)
Jules Robin (*David Alexander; D Byrne & Co; Oddbins; Tesco; Unwins; Upper Crust*)

FORTIFIED WINES FROM CALIFORNIA

California makes a large quantity of fortified wines, most of which are cheap and cheerful Sherry styles and facing a declining market. More recently, a few producers have started to make more serious fortifieds (including Port styles) and a couple of examples, based on Muscat grapes, are available in the UK.

Who's who in California

Ca' Togni, Philip Togni (*Windrush Wines*)
Elysium Black Muscat, Quady (*Jeroboams*)
Essencia California Orange Muscat (*Asda; Findlater Mackie Todd; Majestic; La Réserve; Selfridges*)

Organic Wines

Below we list merchants whose entries appear in the WHERE TO BUY section and who stock at least some organically produced wines. Those firms dealing entirely in organic wines are indicated with an 'O'.

Adnams
Barwell & Jones
Bentalls of Kingston
Berry Bros & Rudd
B H Wines
Bibendum
Bin Ends
Bin 89 Warehouse
Cadwgan Fine Wines
Chaplin & Son
City Wines
Cumbrian Cellar
Demijohn Wines
CCG Edwards (O)
Fullers
G M Vintners
Haughton Fine Wines (O)
Gerard Harris
Hungerford Wine Company
Lay & Wheeler

Lorne House Vintners
Organic Wine Company (O)
Pallant Wines
Premier Wines
Premier Wine Warehouse
Ravensbourne Wine Co
C A Rookes
Sapsford Wines
Sebastopol Wines
Stones of Belgravia
J Townsend & Sons
Ubiquitous Chip Wine Shop
Helen Verdcourt Wines
La Vigneronne
Vinature (O)
Vinceremos (O)
Vintage Roots (O)
A L Vose (O)
Wessex Wines
West Heath Wines

Pudding wines

Merchants who stock a particularly wide range of sweet dessert wines include:

Barnes Wine Shop
Battersea Wine Company
Berry Bros & Rudd
Christchurch Fine Wine
College Cellar
Restaurant Croque-en-Bouche
Fulham Road Wine Centre

Justerini & Brooks
Lay & Wheeler
Nobody Inn
Reid Wines
Tanners Wines
La Vigneronne

Old and rare wines

Specialist stockists include:

Ballantynes of Cowbridge
Nigel Baring
Benson Fine Wines
Butlers Wine Cellars
Classic Wines
College Cellar
Eldridge Pope
Farr Vintners

Justerini & Brooks
Richard Kihl
Kurtz & Chan
Reid Wines
La Réserve
Turville Valley Wines
T & W Wines
La Vigneronne

Special bottle sizes

Large bottles

For celebrations or for finer wines which age well in larger
bottles, you may find the following stockists' lists particularly
rewarding:

William Addison (Newport)
Adnams
Berry Bros & Rudd
Bibendum
Champagne and Caviar Shop
Farr Vintners
Hungerford Wine Company

Jeroboams
Lay & Wheeler
Edward Sheldon
Stones of Belgravia
Tanners Wines
T & W Wines
La Vigneronne

Half-bottles

Although you may find odd half-bottles at many merchants, the
following stockists make a point of carrying a good number. It's
a practice we think every merchant should adopt.

Adnams
Bibendum
D Byrne & Co
Caves de la Madeleine
Celtic Vintner
Eldridge Pope
Jeroboams

Lay & Wheeler
Nobody Inn
Christopher Piper Wines
Raeburn Fine Wines and Foods
Tanners Wines
T & W Wines
La Vigneronne

Find out more about wine

There is more activity than ever before for those who want to find out more about wine. You can join wine clubs and wine societies, you can go on wine courses, or you can travel to the vineyards in the company of like-minded enthusiasts. In this section we list a wide variety of what's available.

Some of these activities are organised by wine merchants themselves – and in the listings that follow this is plainly indicated by a reference back to the WHERE TO BUY section of the Guide. Others are run independently or (in the case of some wine courses) in conjunction with auction houses or cookery schools.

WINE CLUBS

Alba Wine Society
Proprietors Alba Wine, Leet Street, Coldstream, Borders TD12 4BJ TEL (0890) 3166
Membership to this Scottish mail order wine society is by an initial fee of £10. Thereafter, membership is free so long as at least one case of wine is bought each year. In addition, members are offered a variety of tutorial events and tastings including the annual Alba Wine Society Tasting. (See also the WHERE TO BUY section.)

Les Amis du Vin
19 Charlotte Street, London W1P 1HB TEL 01-636 4020
Life membership £15. Discounts: five per cent off all wines, ten per cent off unmixed cases, free delivery for 2+ cases or over £75. Priority booking for tastings. Regular newsletter and special offers including en primeur. (See also the WHERE TO BUY section.)

Averys Bin Club
7 Park Street, Bristol, Avon BS1 5NG TEL (0272) 214141
Members join the Club by committing themselves to subscribing a minimum monthly amount of £30 by Bankers Order. Members may use the Club for buying wines for investment purposes, for everyday drinking and en primeur for future drinking; also Averys will choose wines for laying down

when the opportunity arises on behalf of members. Members may also purchase wines at five per cent discount off prices in Averys' current wine list, receive a regular newsletter, special offers at discounted prices, tastings and en primeur offers and tasting notes by Master of Wine John Avery. New members receive a Bin Club Cellar Book and membership certificate. (See WHERE TO BUY section under Averys of Bristol.)

Christchurch Fine Wine Co

1-3 Vine Lane, High Street, Christchurch, Dorset BH23 1AE
TEL (0202) 473255
Membership costs £5, which is refunded upon the purchase of one case of wine. Members receive a monthly newsletter, invitations to tutored tastings and five per cent discount off the basic wine list. (See also the WHERE TO BUY section.)

Coonawarra Club

Mike McCarthy (secretary), 224 Minard Road, Catford, London SE6 1NJ TEL 01-828 2216 (work), 01-698 2504 (home)
Membership £5, renewal £2 per annum. Tastings of Australian wines, sometimes tutored. Occasional dinners with appropriate wines. Mike McCarthy also runs the Zinfandel Club (see below).

Howells of Bristol Limited Bin Club

Wickwar Trading Estate, Station Road, Wickwar,
Gloucestershire GL12 8NB
TEL (0272) 277641 TELEX 449443 (CRES HO) FAX (0272) 277095
This club, with over 1,100 members, run by Jim Hood and Rodney Holt, specialises in the laying down of wines 'under the ideal conditions of Howells' fine old cellars, so that customers can buy wines at opening prices, gradually build up a cellar and then enjoy their wines at a later date when they are properly mature'. There is a once-only membership fee (£15) and then payment is made by monthly subscription (recommended minimum £35). On joining, a cellar book is provided and cellar cards follow each purchase of wine. (See also the WHERE TO BUY section under Bin Club.)

The International Wine & Food Society

108 Old Brompton Road, London SW7 3RA TEL 01-370 0909
Director Hugo Dunn-Meynell. Enrolment fee £10. Membership terms on application; special rates for members under 25. The President is Master of Wine Michael Broadbent. The London headquarters has a library, club facilities and worldwide contacts. Nearly 200 regional branches organise dinners, tastings, lectures and visits. The twice-yearly journal and quarterly newsletters are free of charge.

Lay & Wheeler

6 Culver Street West, Colchester, Essex CO1 1JA
TEL (0206) 764446 FAX (0206) 564488
A series of popular wine workshops are held in the Colchester
Garrison Officers Club: during 1989 the world renowned
speaker Len Evans presented a selection of his wines from the
Petaluma and Rothbury Estates in Australia. Monthly
workshops are also held at Lay & Wheeler's Wine Market in
Colchester. These workshops are presented by members of Lay
& Wheeler's buying team and external speakers such as Señor
Javier Hidalgo on his famous Sherries from Sanlúcar. Other
topics include white Burgundy, and wines from Alsace,
California and the Rhône. (See also the WHERE TO BUY section.)

Lincoln Wine Society

12 Mainwaring Road, Lincoln, Lincolnshire LN2 4BL
TEL (0522) 542077
Chairman Christine Austin. Monthly talk and tasting sessions,
sometimes with guest speakers. Fine wine evenings held three
times a year, regular newsletters and an annual trip to a wine
region. Membership £5 annually (£8 joint membership).

Methuselah's

29 Victoria Street, London SW1H 0EU TEL 01-222 0424/3550
Annual subscription £15. Tutored tastings usually held every
second Monday of the month. Priority bookings for events.
Two-course dinner with coffee at £8.50 a head available after
tastings.

Martin Mistlin's Fine Wine Dining Club

41 Kingsend, Ruislip, Middlesex HA4 7DD TEL 01-427 9944 (day)
The Club specialises in wine and food events such as tastings,
dinners, wine tours, etc. The subscription for 1990 is
approximately £8.50–£9.50.

Le Nez Rouge Wine Club

Berkmann Wine Cellars, 12 Brewery Road, London N7 9NH
TEL 01-609 4711
Manager Charles Savage. Annual membership £11.75. Reduced
prices, special offers, regular tastings, dinners, etc. Members are
sent the Club's wine list twice a year. (See also the WHERE TO
BUY section under Berkmann Wine Cellars.)

North East Wine Tasting Society

Terry Douglas (Secretary), 3 Bemersyde Drive, Jesmond,
Newcastle-upon-Tyne, Tyne & Wear NE2 2HL TEL 091-281 4769
Monthly tastings held in Newcastle, some of them tutored.
Annual membership £10.

Northern Wine Appreciation Group

D M Hunter, 21 Dartmouth Avenue, Almondbury, Huddersfield, West Yorkshire HD5 8UR TEL (0484) 531228

Weekly meetings in West Yorkshire from September to June, 'to taste, assess and extend the members' experience of wine and food'. The relationship between food and wine leads to the planning of the meals which form part of the group's activities. Graded tutored tastings are held for new members.

Ordre Mondial des Gourmets Dégustateurs

Details from: Martin Mistlin, 41 Kingsend, Ruislip, Middlesex HA4 7DD TEL 01-427 9944

This is a French wine guild with a British chapter (the headquarters are in Paris). Its aims are the promotion of the knowledge of good wines and spirits. Varied regular tastings and dinners are held with access to meetings abroad. The subscription in 1989 was £65 for professionals, £45 for amateurs.

Private Wine Club

309 Old Street, London EC1V 6LE TEL 01-729 1768

This is a 'non-profit-making wine club consisting entirely of wine lovers' run by John Corliss. Membership is by contribution to Capital Radio's Help a London Child Appeal (minimum £5). This brings a quarterly newsletter, an invitation to the Grand Annual Tasting in November and to the Great Beaujolais Breakfast. Other tastings in 1989 included the wines of Paul Jaboulet Aîné, Brunello di Montalcino, Rhône wines in magnum and Burgundy versus Bordeaux.

Tanglewood Wine Society

'Tanglewood', Mayfield Avenue, New Haw, Weybridge, Surrey KT15 3AG TEL (09323) 48720

This club, with over 70 members, is now in its fifth year. Membership costs £6 per person or £10 for a couple at the same address. A charge is made for each tasting, averaging £6 per head.

Helen Verdcourt Wines

Spring Cottage, Kimbers Lane, Maidenhead, Berkshire SL6 2QP TEL (0628) 25577

Two local clubs meet monthly, one in Maidenhead, the other in Englefield Green, for tastings tutored by Helen Verdcourt. No membership fees, tastings charged at cost. Helen Verdcourt also tutors for two terms of Adult Education at Beaconsfield College in Wine Appreciation. Other clubs meet occasionally. (See also the WHERE TO BUY section and WINE TOURS.)

La Vigneronne

105 Old Brompton Road, London SW7 3LE TEL 01-589 6113
The tutored tastings of fine and rare wines held twice a week
(usually Monday and Thursday) are very popular. No
membership fee. (See also the WHERE TO BUY section.)

Vintner Wine Club

Winefare House, 5 High Road, Byfleet, Surrey KT14 7QF
TEL (09323) 51585
Initial enrolment fee and annual membership £14. The Vintner:
James Rackham. Quarterly newsletter. Comprehensive list of 300
wines and individual tasting notes. Members can get a discount
on single bottles at every branch of Arthur Rackhams.
Gastronomic programme of monthly tutored tastings and
dinners in West End and Surrey restaurants. La Grande Taste –
weekend members' tastings at Arthur Rackhams. (See also
Arthur Rackhams in the WHERE TO BUY section.)

The Wine Club

New Aquitaine House, Paddock Road, Reading, Berkshire
RG4 0JY TEL (0734) 471144
Also known as The Sunday Times Wine Club. Mail order only.
President Hugh Johnson, Secretary Jillian Cole. Annotated wine
list, tastings, tours, Vintage Festival, and a lively quarterly
magazine. Tours vary from long weekends to seven-day tours of
wine-growing regions. (See also Bordeaux Direct in the WHERE
TO BUY section.)

The Wine & Dine Society

96 Ramsden Road, London SW12 8QZ TEL 01-673 4439
Weekly tastings of wines from all over the world, including fine
and rare bottles. Guest speakers. Dinners in London follow an
ethnic theme.

Wine and Gastronomic Societies (WAGS)

Martin Mistlin, 41 Kingsend, Ruislip, Middlesex HA4 7DD
TEL 01-427 9944 (day)
This society comprises the Alsace Club of Great Britain
(President Hugh Johnson), the Cofradia Riojana and the Gallo
Nero Club of Great Britain (President The Hon Rocco Forte). A
joining fee of £12 allows members to attend tastings and dinners
featuring wines from these regions plus occasional events based
on other wine regions. (No annual subscription.) Wine tours
abroad and wine weekends in the UK will feature in the clubs'
activities.

Wine Mine Club

Peter Dominic, Astra House, Edinburgh Way, Harlow, Essex
CM20 2BE TEL (0279) 451145
This Club was in abeyance as we went to press. Tastings may
be resumed in 1990. (See also Peter Dominic in the WHERE TO
BUY section.)

The Wine Society

Gunnels Wood Road, Stevenage, Hertfordshire SG1 2BG
TEL (0438) 741177; DELIVERIES (0438) 741010; FAX (0438) 741392;
ORDER OFFICE (0438) 740222 or 01-349 3296; TELEX 826072 (IECWS).
(See the WHERE TO BUY section.)

The Winery

4 Clifton Road, Maida Vale, London W9 1SS TEL 01-286 6475
Manager Marcus Titley. Offers a large selection of fine wines,
particularly from the New World (the range has been further
enlarged to include many older wines, especially clarets).
Tastings are organised by Les Amis du Vin (see above).

The Winetasters

P B Beardwood (Secretary), 44 Claremont Road, London
W13 0DG TEL 01-997 1252
Annual subscription £3 (£1.50 if you live more than 50 miles
from London). Non-profit-making club which organises tastings,
seminars, dinners and tours (the major tour in 1989 was to
Northern Italy – the next major tour, in 1991, will be to a French
wine-growing area). The club grew out of the Schoolmasters'
Wine Club.

Winewise

Michael Schuster, 107 Culford Road, London N1 4HL
TEL 01-254 9734
Promotes all aspects of tasting, understanding and appreciating
wines and spirits. Regular tastings include two wine courses: a
Beginners' Course (£75 for six evenings) and an Intermediate
Course (£108 for six evenings). Each course is limited to 16
participants. Other tastings are held on individual properties
('vertical') and vintages ('horizontal') and on comparisons of fine
wines from round the world. There are blind tastings each
spring, workshops on Saturday mornings and many fine wine
tastings on late Sunday afternoons. A brochure of tasting details
is mailed regularly on request.

Zinfandel Club

Mike McCarthy (Secretary), 224 Minard Road, Catford, London SE6 1NJ TEL 01-828 2216 (work), 01-698 2504 (home)
Membership fee £5. Sporadic meetings to taste California wines, sometimes tutored. Occasional dinners with appropriate wines.

WINE COURSES

David Baillie Vintners School of Wine

The Sign of the Lucky Horseshoe, 86 Longbrook Street, Exeter, Devon EX4 6AP TEL (0392) 221345
This West Country wine merchant plans to repeat his School of Wine course in 1990. The course is run once a year at Exeter University Conference Centre, and comprises seven three-hour evening sessions of tastings and lectures given by experienced members of the wine trade, with an optional exam at the end, leading (for those who pass) to a Certificate from the David Baillie School of Wine. Cost in 1990, £120. (See also the WHERE TO BUY section.)

Christie's Wine Course

63 Old Brompton Road, London SW7 3JS TEL 01-581 3933
Principals Michael Broadbent MW and Steven Spurrier, Secretary Caroline de Lane Lea. Christie's run two wine courses: Part 1 is an introduction to wine tasting through the principal wines of France and is run four to five times a year; Part 2 consists of specialised tastings of Burgundy, Bordeaux, Port and Madeira, and is run once or twice a year. Both courses take place on five consecutive Tuesday evenings, lasting roughly two hours, for 45 students. Discussion and tasting are conducted by top wine experts (in 1989 the roll included Michael Broadbent MW, Serena Sutcliffe MW, David Peppercorn MW, Pamela Vandyke Price and Steven Spurrier). Part 1 costs £115 and part 2 £143.75, but the latter can be taken as five separate evenings, each at £30.

Corney & Barrow's Wine Course

12 Helmet Row, London EC1V 3QJ TEL 01-251 4051
In 1989 a course of four sessions was offered. Aimed particularly at Corney & Barrow's younger customers and those within the hotel/restaurant trade, the cost of the course – £20 per session or £75 for all four – covered the cost of wines, tuition, information sheets, maps and glasses. Numbers are restricted to a maximum of 20. Further details from Judy Emerson at the above address. (See also the WHERE TO BUY section.)

Ecole du Vin, Château Loudenne, Bordeaux

Ecole du Vin, Château Loudenne, St-Yzans-de-Médoc, 33340
Lesparre, France TEL 33 (56) 090503 FAX 33 (56) 090287
Six-day courses (starting on Monday) are held for a dozen
students five times a year at Gilbey's Ch Loudenne, under the
direction of Charles Eve MW. Accommodation and cuisine of
very high standard in the château. Aimed at the public and
professionals in the trade, the lectures and tastings cover all
aspects of viticulture and vinification. Visits are arranged to
other Bordeaux areas and châteaux. Cost (in 1989) £860, plus
travel to France.

The Fulham Road Wine School

The Fulham Road Wine Centre, 899–901 Fulham Road, London
SW6 5HU TEL 01-384 2588
A selection of courses from the straightforward introduction to
identifying flavours and styles through to tastings covering
grape types and classic wine regions in greater detail. Also how
to match food and wine, and Saturday workshops. (See also the
WHERE TO BUY section.)

German Wine Academy

P O Box 1705, 6500 Mainz, Federal Republic of Germany
A 12th-century monastery is the setting for courses (delivered in
English), which include lectures by wine experts, vineyard visits
and tastings. The basic seven-day course is run throughout the
year (DM1640) per person and is supplemented by more
advanced courses and an extended culturally oriented course
conducted at a more relaxed pace. Further information from the
German Wine Information Service, 114 Cromwell Road, London
SW7 4ES TEL 01-244 7558.

Leith's School of Food and Wine

21 St Alban's Grove, London W8 5BP TEL 01-229 0177
Some of Leith's wine courses are for students of the School only,
as part of their food and wine studies. However, at least two are
available to others: five two-hour evening sessions starting in
January 1990, leading to the Leith's Certificate (if you pass the
exam, that is); and a ten two-hour evening session starting in
October, leading to Leith's Advanced Certificate of Wine,
examined by Leith's Master of Wine, Richard Harvey. This is
roughly analogous to the Wine and Spirit Education Trust's
Higher Certificate, without the sessions on licensing and
labelling laws, and with particular stress on tasting. Cost £140
and £225 respectively. Other courses, such as specialist
evenings, are also sometimes available.

The Lincoln Wine Course

Christine Austin, 12 Mainwaring Road, Lincoln, Lincolnshire
LN2 4BL TEL (0522) 42077
Wine courses offered for both trade and public at Yarborough
Adult Education Centre, Lincoln, starting in September each
year. Wine and Spirit Education Trust Certificate and Higher
Certificate courses are offered. A Diploma study group is also
being planned. A two-term course (two hours a week) is also
offered, with the emphasis on tasting as well as gaining a good
general knowledge of wine. Cost is approximately £42 per term.
Specialist evenings are sometimes held.

Sotheby's

Wine Evenings with Sotheby's, 34–35 New Bond Street, London
W1A 2AA TEL 01-408 5272; Wine Department now at Unit 5,
Albion Wharf, London SW11 4AN TEL 01-924 3287
As we went to press, Sotheby's had temporarily halted their
Wine Evenings. However, there were plans for a new series in
autumn 1989. Contact David Molyneux-Berry MW for further
details.

Tante Marie School of Cookery

Woodham House, Carlton Road, Woking, Surrey GU21 4HF
TEL (048 62) 26957
Conal Gregory MW, MP, organises wine appreciation courses,
generally during the autumn and winter, on three weekday
evenings (lasting two hours), aimed at those with modest
knowledge and including extensive tutored tastings.

WINE TOURS

Arblaster & Clarke Wine Tours

104 Church Road, Steep, Petersfield, Hampshire GU32 2DD
TEL (0730) 66883
This is a small family-run specialist tour operator in its fourth
year. Tours in 1990 will include five Champagne weekends, the
eastern Loire, Burgundy, Alsace and Mosel and Portugal. In
addition there will be tours to Rioja, the Duero and Penedés
in Spain, central Loire, Bordeaux and California. The tours are
suitable for all ages whether alone or in a group. Prices range
from £139 for a long weekend in Champagne to £499 for eight
days in Portugal.

Allez France

27 West Street, Storrington, West Sussex RH20 4DZ TEL (09066) 2345; VINEscapes Bespoke Wine Holidays TEL (09066) 5793
In 1989 Allez France launched their 'VINEscapes' brochure for the independent traveller in France. Most of the wine-growing areas are covered – Alsace, Champagne, Burgundy, Rhône/ Provence, Bordeaux, Cognac, the Loire and Midi. The itinerary is completely flexible and travel is by car ferry, Motorail or fly-drive. Accommodation is at vineyard hotels and châteaux. All bookings include literature on the wine regions and the opportunity to visit growers.

Australian Tourist Commission

Heathcoat House, 20 Savile Row, London W1X 1AE
The Tourist Commission can provide information on tours and holidays available through Australian travel firms. For more specific information on wine tours, contact South Australia House, 50 Strand, London WC2N 5LW TEL 01-930 7471, and see also Victour below.

Blackheath Wine Trails

13 Blackheath Village, London SE3 9LD TEL 01-463 0012
In 1989, eleven wine tours were offered: Burgundy and Chablis, Bordeaux, Champagne, Loire Valley, Lisbon Coast, Switzerland, Madeira and Wine Festival, Madrid and La Rioja, Northern Portugal and the Douro, Seville and Jerez, and Tuscany. Tours vary from three to seven days and prices range from £210 to £675. All are air/coach except Champagne, which is ferry/coach.

DER Travel Service

18 Conduit Street, London W1R 9TD TEL 01-408 0111
As well as Rhine cruises, DER arranges air and rail holidays in German and Austrian hotels, guest houses or apartments, many of them in wine-growing areas: with your own car you can tour the wine-growing areas of the Rhine and Mosel on the 'Wine Regions Tour'. An eight-night tour in 1989 cost from £168 (for five adults travelling) to £208 (for two adults travelling).

English Vineyards

Many English vineyards are open to the public offering guided tours, tastings and sales. For further information contact The English Vineyards Association, 38 West Park, London SE9 4RH TEL 01-857 0452

Eurocamp

Edmundson House, Tatton Street, Knutsford, Cheshire
WA16 6BG TEL (0565) 3844
(Reservations only: 28 Princess Street, Knutsford, Cheshire
WA16 6BG)
Eurocamp arranges self-drive camping and mobile home
holidays at 179 sites in Europe, many of which are 'almost
among the grapes – and the more well-known grapes at that'.
These include the Gironde, Saumur, Meursault, Bergerac,
Cahors, Mosel, Bordeaux and Rhineland.

Eurocamp Independent

(at the above address) TEL (0565) 55399 offers a ferry/pitch
reservations 'package' for campers and touring caravan owners
to over 200 sites in Europe.

Francophiles

Ron and Jenny Farmer, 66 Great Brockeridge, Westbury-on-
Trym, Bristol, Avon BS9 3UA TEL (0272) 621975
The Farmers offer France 'lovingly packaged' on their personally
escorted holidays of discovery in the regional heartlands. Their
clients are 'not usual coach holiday travellers but ones who
appreciate in-depth, unhurried visits and structured tastings'. In
1990 they offer Alsace, Burgundy, Provence, Savoy, Auvergne,
Cévennes, Charentes and the Dordogne and special and general
interest holidays with wine appeal.

Hide-a-Way Wine Holiday in Burgundy

Maureen and Ken Deeming, Oak Lodge, Ambleside Road,
Keswick, Cumbria CA12 4DL TEL (07687) 72522
Vacancies in Maureen and Ken Deeming's 'small, renovated
two-hundred-year-old Burgundian cottage' run weekly from 1
July to 30 September. Price is approximately £175 per person per
week (maximum 10 people) and consists of bed and continental
breakfast and three evening meals with house wine. Guided
visits include a selection of the vineyards of Côte de Nuits, Côte
de Beaune, the Chalonnais, Mâconnais and Beaujolais.

KD German Rhine Line

G A Clubb Rhine Cruise Agency, 28 South Street, Epsom,
Surrey KT18 7PF TEL (037 27) 42033
In 1989, a week-long cruise left from Nijmegen, visited
vineyards on the Rhine, the Mosel and in Alsace, and included
lectures and tutored tastings by Dr Hans Ambrosi, Director of
the Eltville State Vineyards. This 'floating wine seminar' ended
in Basle.

Moswin Tours

P O Box 8, 52b London Road, Oadby, Leicestershire LE2 5WX
TEL (0533) 719922/714982 FAX (0533) 716016
Fully inclusive tours, by air or coach, to the Mosel Valley and its
wine festivals with sightseeing excursions, wine tastings and
visits to vineyards in the autumn. These range from 4 to 11
days. Also available are independent tailor-made wine tours to
the Mosel Valley (budget to luxury) with an option of staying
with a wine farmer (May to October) and wine seminars to
other wine-growing regions of Germany and France.

Premier Wine Tours

4 Elms Crescent, London SW4 8RB TEL 01-622 3735
This is a newly formed company specialising in 'wine tours to
the great wine-producing regions of the world'. Groups vary
between 15 and 25 people and tours can be tailor-made. In 1989
the choice of regions included Champagne, Bordeaux,
Burgundy/Rhône Valley, Central Italy, Northern Spain, Australia
and California. The aim is to provide a 'special interest holiday
for discerning people blending wine, good food, history, art and
scenery'.

Alastair Sawday's Tours

17 Cornwallis Crescent, Clifton, Bristol BS8 4PJ TEL (0272) 741812
This six-year old company specialises in tailor-made land tours;
they also specialise in barging (they recently took over the
European Canal Cruises business). Recent tour proposals for
both individuals and groups have incorporated six nights
aboard a barge in the Burgundy area, including wine tastings
and vineyard visits, and stays in private châteaux in the Loire
area.

Special Interest Tours

1 Cank Street, Leicester, Leicestershire LE1 5GX
TEL (0533) 531373
Coach tours (with convenient joining points: Leicester,
Birmingham, Coventry, Sheffield, London etc) visit French wine
regions for five, six and seven days tours, which include
tastings.

Tanglewood Wine Tours

'Tanglewood', Mayfield Avenue, New Haw, Weybridge, Surrey
KT15 3AG TEL (09323) 48720
In 1989 tours were offered of four nights to Burgundy and the
Loire Valley. Travel was by luxury coach with accommodation
in comfortable hotels situated centrally in Dijon and Saumur
respectively. There was also an additional Champagne weekend
based in the centre of Reims. (See also WINE CLUBS.)

Helen Verdcourt Wine Tours

Spring Cottage, Kimbers Lane, Maidenhead, Berkshire SL6 2QP
TEL (0628) 25577
During 1989 two 4-day tours to the Champagne area were being
planned. (See also the WHERE TO BUY section and WINE CLUBS.)

Victour

Tourist Office, Victoria House, Melbourne Place, Strand,
London WC2B 4LG TEL 01-240 3974 or 01-836 2656
The Victoria Tourism Commission produce a good wine and
food guide to Victoria with helpful notes on wineries and ideas
for self-drive visits. They also have details of various rail and
coach tours including brochures for Australian Wine Tours,
Peter Heath's Unique Winery Tours, Winery Walkabout and
Bogong Jack Cycling Winery Tours. The Commission will also
assist in planning group tours around the state's 115 public
wineries.

Vintage Wine Tours

8 Belmont, Lansdown Road, Bath, Avon BA1 5DZ
TEL (0225) 315834/315659
Concentrates on designing tours for groups (10–40 people) by
air and coach, and will arrange tours to any destination,
including gourmet meals, sightseeing excursions and any special
requirements. A brochure is available to spark off ideas.

Wine Tours by Helen Gillespie-Peck Travel Services

103 Queen Street, Newton Abbot, Devon TQ12 2BG TEL (0626)
65373 or (0803) 34672
Helen Gillespie-Peck has been teaching and dealing with wines
for the last 15 years. On offer in 1989 were tours to Dordogne/
Bergerac, Languedoc/Roussillon, Loire, Alsace/Champagne,
Burgundy, Bordeaux and Rioja. Tours were by ferry and luxury
coach. Numbers are limited to a maximum of 32 per departure.

World Wine Tours

4 Dorchester Road, Drayton St Leonard, Oxfordshire OX9 8BH
TEL (0865) 891919
World Wine Tours, run by Liz and Martin Holliss, offer a wide
range of quality wine tours for the novice and connoisseur alike,
each lasting from four to eight days. All tours are led by wine
experts and most are led by a Master of Wine. A maximum of 30
bookings are accepted on to any one tour (the average is 20
clients per tour). Tours in 1990 will run throughout the year and
will visit: Alsace, Bordeaux, Burgundy, Chablis, Champagne,
Germany, Loire Valley, Madeira, Penedés, Rhône Valley, Rioja,
Tuscany and Umbria. Inclusive prices range from £395–£850 per

person. Specially tailored tours can be arranged both for private groups of wine enthusiasts and as corporate incentives/ hospitality. Also on offer: stays in historic private châteaux throughout France, cruises in luxury hotel barges in the Alsace, Burgundy or the Midi, self-catering on a wine estate in Tuscany, art history tours in wine regions and a series of wine weekends in the UK.

Storing and serving wine

While wine is best kept in a dark cellar at a constant temperature of around 50°F, it is not the end of the world if you have no access to such a place. Keeping wine in the kitchen is not the best place (it gets too hot and steamy and then too cold), but the cupboard under the stairs, the broom cupboard or the top of a wardrobe are all places where wine can be stored and survive unscathed, certainly if it has been bought for drinking within a few weeks or even months.

Only a couple of rules apply. One is to avoid storing the bottle upright (the cork dries out, shrinks and the wine oxidises); the other is to avoid too many extremes of temperature (which age a wine prematurely).

Long-term storage of fine wines is different. If you have no access to a cellar, we suggest you make use of a wine merchant's cellaring service (we indicate whether cellaring is available in the WHERE TO BUY section). Most merchants charge £3 or more a year per case – and for fine wine the investment is certainly worth it.

Serving wine

All wine benefits from being served sympathetically. There are, of course, no hard and fast rules and, for many people, just pulling the cork is sufficient to produce all the pleasure a wine can give. But taking just a little extra care with the correct temperature of a wine and the glasses in which it is served will enhance that pleasure immeasurably. Here we give a few suggestions.

Temperature White and rosé wines should be served chilled, with rosé wines cooler than white, say, after a couple of hours in the fridge. If you need to chill a bottle more quickly, 20 minutes in a freezer will have the same effect, but don't forget the bottle or it will eventually explode; or use ice in a bucket of cold water.

Generally speaking, the finer the wine, the less cool it should be: so that a good white Burgundy or a fine German wine should be somewhat warmer than your basic white from the corner off-licence. This allows a fine wine the chance to give off its taste and aromas which would be muted if too cold. Fino

Sherry should be chilled in the same way as any fine white wine.

Once chilled, the wine can be kept cool by being placed in an ice bucket (half and half water and ice), in a plastic insulating sleeve, in an insulated picnic bag – or back in the fridge.

Red wine should normally be served warmer than white wine. The books say 'room temperature', but modern centrally heated rooms are too hot – around 60°F is a good temperature. Ideally they should be warmed by being stood in the room for an hour or so, but if you are desperate decant the wine into a warm decanter. Heating the wine on a stove will simply heat one part of a bottle and not another, but holding the bottle under running warm water is effective. Otherwise, simply cup your glass of wine in your hand for a moment or two before drinking.

A few red wines – Beaujolais Nouveau and similar fruity wines are good examples – are often attractive lightly chilled. Be prepared to experiment with chilling red wines to see which work.

Glasses Experience suggests that the ideal glass is one that curves in at the upper edges and is big enough to hold a reasonable amount. Thin, fine glass is a greater pleasure to drink from than thicker glass. Engraving or colour in the glass means that it is difficult to see the colour or clarity of a wine.

Fill a glass half to two-thirds full. This leaves enough space at the top for the aromas to gather before being sniffed as you drink – which is half the pleasure of drinking a good wine. It also means you can swirl the wine in the glass without much risk to the tablecloth.

Apart from normal wine glasses, special tall flutes can be used for Champagne and sparkling wines – avoid the flat Champagne coupes which release the bubbles too fast. For Sherry, the tulip-shaped copita is the traditional glass used (and not the narrow-waisted and rather ugly Elgin glass).

Opening Remove the foil or plastic capsule completely, or cut it well underneath the bottle tip, so that it cannot possibly come into contact with the wine: this would be just messy with modern aluminium foil or plastic, potentially poisonous in the long term if it's the old-fashioned lead variety! If the cork won't budge, hold the neck for a minute or so under fairly hot running water and try again. For corks that drop into the bottle, there's a long spindly-legged plastic gadget called a 'Decorker'; you may have to resort to a coffee filter or a sieve if you make unacceptable quantities of cork crumbs.

Champagne corks Twist the bottle by holding it firmly at the base: don't twist the cork or it may break. Hold the top firmly and be careful where you point the bottle: people have lost eyes through flying corks. If the mushroom top breaks off as you twist the bottle, carefully use a corkscrew. Always disturb the bottle as little as possible beforehand, and keep a glass on hand to catch accidental fountains.

Checking the quality Pour some for yourself first to check that it is sound before serving your guests; and don't forget to check subsequent bottles. There may be a difference between two bottles of a quite simple wine, so make sure that any wine connoisseurs among your guests have finished up the dregs of one bottle in their glass before serving them from the next; they may be deeply shocked if you mix bottles, especially of different wines! Non-winos will think this nonsense – so just top them up.

Decanting

There are no hard and fast rules about whether to decant or not. It's a favourite subject for argument in the wine magazines – especially in the letters columns. But a consensus does emerge about when it can be an advantage.

● When a bottle of wine has a sediment in the bottom, decanting is essential unless you want to end up with the last glasses full of unpleasant black sludge.

● Strong red wines, which may have spent some time in wood before bottling – Barolo, some Portugese reds, Gran Reserva Rioja or Rhônes, for example – will benefit from some decanting, especially if they are quite young.

● Conversely, old vintages of any wine will suffer positive harm if decanted – the remains of the fruit will combine with oxygen and the whole delicious fragrance of mature wines will disappear.

● The only reason for decanting everyday reds will be to get rid of some of the sulphury smells that may still linger in the bottle. A few minutes in a glass will achieve the same effect.

● Some whites – particularly those which have been in wood and are still quite young – will benefit from an hour in a decanter before serving. Make sure the decanter is cool before pouring wine in and then keep it in a cool place or in the fridge.

The only time when care needs to be taken over decanting is when the wine has thrown a sediment and the purpose of decanting is to leave this in the bottle and the clear wine in the decanter. Before decanting, stand the bottle upright for two or three hours to allow the deposit to collect in the bottom. Draw the cork and pour the wine carefully into the decanter. If the bottle is dusty from the cellar, a light shining through from below will help identify when the sediment reaches the neck of the bottle. If you're at all worried about letting the sediment pass into the decanter, despite all your efforts, a coffee filter paper should solve the problem.

Keeping wine fresh

If you don't want to drink a bottle of wine in one session, keeping white wine in the fridge helps, or you could decant wine of either colour into two half-bottles as soon as it is opened.

Alternatively, various devices are available which keep the wine fresh either by creating a vacuum in the bottle or by pumping a layer of inert gas on top of the wine.

The cheapest is the Vac-u-Vin (which sells for about £6.99 in many off-licences and wine merchants). This system consists of rubber stoppers and a small plastic pump which pumps the air out of the bottle, creating a vacuum. Wine treated this way should stay pretty fresh for three or four days, and, depending on how full the bottle is, up to a week.

Another system is more elaborate and expensive. It consists of pumping inert gas from a cylinder into the wine through a special stopper. Although it is effective and can keep wine fresh for longer than Vac-u-Vin, its price, we feel, makes it unnecessary for the normal wine drinker at home.

A third system, the Wine Preserver, consists of a gas squirted from a canister on to the open bottle of wine. In some cases the canisters have exploded. We suggest you avoid this system.

How the law can help you

If you buy a bottle that is bad or isn't what the label says it is, the law offers you some protection and redress. Barrister JENI MCCALLION *sets out just what the law can do to assist you.*

In the eyes of the law, if not the connoisseur, wine is any liquor obtained from the alcoholic fermentation of fresh grapes or the must of fresh grapes. Wine can, of course, be made from other fruits or vegetables, but in this case an indication of the type of fruit or vegetable used must appear on the label immediately before the word wine: apple wine or elderberry wine, for example.

There are a number of laws which protect you when you buy and drink wine. Civil laws cover things like getting a bottle of Burgundy when you ask for a bottle of Bordeaux. It's generally necessary to enforce your civil rights through court action. Criminal offences include selling adulterated wine and false or misleading labelling – and are matters for your local trading standards department. Some things may infringe both the Criminal and Civil law. So if the pickled remains of a snail drop into your glass as you drain the last of your bottle of Châteauneuf-du-Pape, and you are violently ill as a result, the seller may be guilty of a criminal offence, under the Food Act, and you might also be able to sue the seller or the manufacturer for damages.

Here are some of the things that you might need to know:

1 *You see a very attractive wine offer in a magazine. A delivery time of 28 days is given and you send off your order, along with a cheque for the full amount. Your cheque is cashed, but six weeks later you're still waiting for the wine to arrive. What should you do?*

Write to the company concerned giving them an ultimatum – either they deliver within the next, say, 14 days, or you will consider the order cancelled. If you get your wine within the specified time, all well and good; if not, you should write to the advertising manager at the publication in which the advertisement appeared. The advertising manager should see that your complaint is investigated. Your legal rights when buying goods by mail order are the same as those when buying from a shop. So if the company fails to deliver the goods, you are entitled to your money back, plus any additional cost in getting the same wine elsewhere.

2 *You buy a bottle of inexpensive red wine at a local supermarket. It tastes like vinegar and is quite undrinkable.*

It's usually true that you get what you pay for – and there's a world of difference between a good bottle of St-Emilion and a litre of vin de table. Leaving aside the finer distinctions that exist between a good and a mediocre bottle of wine, the law says that wine must be of 'merchantable quality' and that it must be 'fit for human consumption'. So even the cheapest plonk must be drinkable.

3 *You buy a bottle of wine which, when opened, turns out to be way past its best. What can you do?*

Not much, apart from putting it in the boeuf bourguignonne. Unlike some foods, the law doesn't insist that wine bottles be labelled with a 'sell by' or 'best before' date (although some supermarkets are beginning to introduce this information on their own-label wines).

4 *You buy a bottle of wine and share it with friends. The next day all who indulged are violently ill – suggesting that the wine may have been contaminated.*

It is a criminal offence to sell or to offer for sale food or drink which is intended for human consumption, but which is unfit. If you suffer as a result, inform your local trading standards department who will consider bringing a prosecution. As the actual buyer of the wine, you are entitled to redress for a breach of contract. Until a couple of years ago, the unfortunate consumer who suffered injury as a result of faulty goods, but didn't actually buy them, could get compensation only if he or she could prove negligence. The Consumer Protection Act 1987 should make things easier. Under this Act, your friends wouldn't have to prove negligence, only that the wine was defective and that they were ill as a result.

5 *You buy a bottle of '1868 Vintage Port' at auction, but you subsequently discover that it's really an injudicious mixture of supermarket vintage character Port and Lambrusco-style home brew. What can you do?*

Deliberately setting out to fake something (be it a bottle of vintage Port or a Constable painting) and then passing it off as the real thing is fraud and the seller will be liable to criminal prosecution. But in sales by auction (as opposed to buying from a wine merchant) any undertaking as to merchantable quality or conformity with description or sample can be excluded. It's also worth noting that your rights are generally against the seller rather than the auctioneer, which could make if difficult to get redress if the wine does happen to be faulty in some way (although, as we suggest in the section on buying wine at auction, most auction houses will help in negotiations with the seller).

6 *You're having a quick lunch-time drink at a local wine bar, so you order by the glass, rather than the bottle. Your second glass of house white is noticeably smaller than the first, but you're charged exactly the same. Is it legal?*

Unfortunately, the law is extremely slack on wine glass measurements. At the moment, there are no standard quantities for wine, unlike those for beer and spirits. There is, however, a purely voluntary code which says, among other things, that quantities of wine should be given alongside prices, and that no bar or restaurant should sell wine by the glass in more than two measures and that the difference between these two measures should be at least two fluid ounces (or 50ml). However, few wine bars or restaurants seem to follow this voluntary code.

7 *You order a bottle of 1985 Chablis Premier Cru at a local restaurant. The waiter brings the bottle to your table, and allows you a cursory glance before opening it. When you taste the wine, you realise immediately that you're drinking a lesser quality 1987 Petit Chablis. What should you do?*

Strictly speaking, the fact that you had an opportunity to inspect the label before the bottle was opened might weaken your legal position and your right to insist on getting exactly what you ordered. But in most cases, a bar or restaurant should exchange without too much hassle. If you proceed to consume the whole bottle before noticing the difference, you can't then complain and reasonably expect to get your original order.

8 *What do you do if you think you've been over-charged for a bottle of wine?*

A restaurant must display a menu and wine list outside, or immediately inside the entrance. Wine lists containing six or fewer items must state the price (inclusive of VAT) for each wine available. Establishments with a larger selection must show at least six items, but they don't have to display a comprehensive list. You should always check your bill carefully and query anything which doesn't add up.

Sour grapes? – how to complain

The Criminal Laws mentioned above are usually enforced by public authorities. So if you've been sold a bottle of wine which contains something unpleasant or positively harmful to health, you should report the matter to the environmental health department of your local authority. False or misleading descriptions are a matter for the trading standards department of your local authority. If you want to bring a civil action for damages, you should seek legal advice.

Wine Bookshelf

Wine books continue to pour off the presses. This is a selection from the past three years or so which we have found most interesting and useful.

General

The Story of Wine – Hugh Johnson (Mitchell Beazley, £25)
This book puts wine into a cultural perspective by looking at its development from ancient Egypt right up to the present.

Vintage Timecharts – Jancis Robinson (Mitchell Beazley, £19.95)
The life-cycle of famous wines up to the year 2000, vividly presented in graphic form with tasting notes and analysis of each vintage as well as the methods of the wine-makers.

Sotheby's World Wine Encyclopedia – Tom Stevenson (Dorling Kindersley, £30)
Packed with information, listings, illustrations and useful maps, this is valuable reference material to all the major wine areas of the world.

The Wine Companion – Hugh Johnson (Mitchell Beazley, £14.95)
A complete revision of the widest-ranging guide to wine regions of the world and the producers who work in them. Essential reference.

Webster's Wine Guide (1990 edition) – edited by Oz Clarke (Webster's, £9.95)
A guide to the price you should expect to pay for wine at merchants and in the supermarkets, coupled with brief articles on the state of the market in the regions of production.

Pocket Wine Book (1990 edition) – Hugh Johnson (Mitchell Beazley, £5.95)
The annual update of the book most wine merchants put in their pockets when they travel or even when they meet customers.

Understanding Wine – Michael Schuster (Mitchell Beazley, £9.95)
A review of wine-tasting techniques, the major grapes and their tastes, and the practicalities of wine and wine drinking.

Liquid Gold, Dessert Wines of the World – Stephen Brook
(Constable, £14.95)
The first book ever devoted entirely to sweet wines. Covers the
world, but devotes most detail to France and Germany. Well
written, with good profiles of producers and a detailed study of
the way the wines are made.

The World Atlas of Wine – Hugh Johnson (Mitchell Beazley,
£22.50)
A revision of the best-selling book which now includes greater
detail on the New World wine areas as well as Italy and Spain.

Vines, Grapes and Wines – Jancis Robinson (Mitchell Beazley,
£16.95)
A book that goes back to origins – the vine – and explores the
character of each variety and the types of wine it produces.
Beautiful line drawings.

The Demon Drink – Jancis Robinson (Mitchell Beazley, £9.95)
Ms Robinson wants to show other wine lovers how wine and
health go together, if both are treated in the right way. This is
full of scholarly research and information about the way alcohol
affects us. Essential reading.

Sainsbury's Book of Wine – Oz Clarke (Websters/Sainsburys,
£4.95)
Terrific value for a well-written, beautifully produced guide to
the world's wines. Plenty of information and plenty of opinions.

Specialist

AUSTRALIA

Complete Book of Australian Wine – Len Evans (J M Dent & Sons,
£25)
Complete is the word – every winery, small and large, is there,
with tasting notes and technical information galore.

The Pocket Guide to Australian and New Zealand Wines – Jane
MacQuitty (Mitchell Beazley, £5.95)
A wide-ranging guide to the wines and wineries of these two
emerging wine-producing nations.

CHILE

Chilean Wines – Jan Read (Sotheby's, £19.95)
The first English book on the wines from this exciting wine
country. Jan Read – an expert on Spanish wines – gives a wide-
ranging portrait of history, present conditions and producers.

ENGLAND

A Taste of English Wine – Hugh Barty-King (Pelham Books, £15.95)
A history of English wines from the Romans to the present day, coupled with a survey of what is happening now and a foretaste of the future.

The Vineyards of England – Stephen Skelton (S P and L Skelton, £9.95)
A guide to the vineyards of the British Isles, with information on the wines made and when the vineyards are open (plus useful road directions).

FRANCE – GENERAL

Sainsbury's Guide to French Red and Rosé wines – Oz Clarke (J Sainsbury, £2.95)
Alphabetical encyclopedia of the names you are likely to encounter on French wine labels. Witty text and good illustrations.

Sainsbury's Guide to French White wines – Oz Clarke (J Sainsbury, £2.95)
Companion volume to the above.

French Wine Atlas – Hubrecht Duijker and Hugh Johnson (Mitchell Beazley, £16.95)
A complete guide to visiting French vineyards: route maps, lists of producers, where to eat and drink, where to stay, places of interest. Well written and good for reading at home as well as taking with you.

The Pocket Book of French Regional Wines – Roger Voss (Mitchell Beazley, £4.95)
In the familiar Pocket Book format, a guide to the wines and producers of all the regions of France apart from Bordeaux, Burgundy and Champagne. Tasting information and vintage reports, plus detailed information on all the AC and VDQS areas of France.

The Traveller's Guide to the Wine Regions of France – Hubrecht Duijker (Mitchell Beazley, £5.95)
A pocket-sized guide to the French wine regions, with information on where to eat and stay. Handy reference.

The Wine Lovers' Guide to France – Michael Busselle (Michael Joseph, £14.95).
Beautiful photographs of the vineyard areas, but also useful information for tours and visits (including details from *Michelin* maps).

Traveller's Wine Guide, France – Christopher Fielden (Waymark, £9.95)
Informative text and useful listings marred by uninformative maps.

FRANCE – ALSACE

The Wines of Alsace – Liz Berry (The Bodley Head, £10.95)
Sub-titled *A Buyer's Guide*, this book is full of tasting notes and information on individual producers and vintages.

FRANCE – BORDEAUX

Château Bordeaux – Jean Dethier (Mitchell Beazley, £25)
A beautifully illustrated guide to the splendid buildings of the Bordeaux estates, coupled with an environmental plea to preserve them.

Pocket Guide to the Wines of Bordeaux – David Peppercorn (Mitchell Beazley, £4.95)
Following the standard Pocket Book style, this covers the whole of Bordeaux with a tightly written guide to the main areas and estates. Tasting notes cover recent vintages.

The Wines of Bordeaux (revised edition) – Edmund Penning-Rowsell (Penguin, £12.95)
Anybody who knows how comprehensive and useful previous editions of this guide to Bordeaux have been will want to buy this new version.

Bordeaux – The Definitive Guide – Robert Parker (Dorling Kindersley, £12.95)
Despite its aggressive title, this is indeed a major guide to Bordeaux, packed full of Robert Parker's tasting notes on individual châteaux.

The White Wines of Bordeaux – William Bolter (Octopus Books, £4.95)
Part of a new series of guides to the wines and producers, containing a regional description plus a guide to producers.

The Red Wines of Bordeaux – William Bolter (Octopus Books, £4.95)
Companion volume to the above.

FRANCE – BURGUNDY

White Burgundy – Christopher Fielden (Christopher Helm, £12.95)
A village-by-village study of the most highly priced white wines in the world. Mean production, but interesting opinions.

Pocket Guide to the Wines of Burgundy – Serena Sutcliffe (Mitchell Beazley, £4.95)
A guide to the minefield of Burgundian wines, based on the Pocket Book formula with directory-style entries for producers and villages. Plenty of opinions, too.

The White Wines of Burgundy – Jasper Morris (Octopus Books, £4.95)
Information about the region, plus guided tours of each village and the best producers. Illustrated with maps and photographs.

The Red Wines of Burgundy – Mark Savage (Octopus Books, £4.95)
Companion volume to the above.

FRANCE – CHAMPAGNE

The Story of Champagne – Nicholas Faith (Hamish Hamilton, £17.95)
The fascinating history of Champagne is told with scholarship and style. There's nothing romantic about this view, either – there are warts a-plenty among the Champenois. Details on the way Champagne is made and a directory of producers follow.

A Celebration of Champagne – Serena Sutcliffe (Mitchell Beazley, £20)
Celebration is the word, as this book covers the finest Champagnes and their makers and history, leaving the more sordid details to other writers. A beautiful production.

Champagne – Tom Stevenson (Sotheby's, £19.95)
An authoritative guide to everything there is to know about Champagne – the producers, the villages, the history, the taste, the vintages, how to drink and store the wines.

RHÔNE AND PROVENCE

The Wines of the Rhône Valley and Provence – Robert Parker (Dorling Kindersley, £14.95)
A guide to the producers in both regions, accompanied by copious tasting notes. Plenty of reputations are pricked here, as well, but there are also exciting discoveries.

GERMANY

Atlas of German Wines – Hugh Johnson and Ian Jamieson (Mitchell Beazley, £14.95)
A guide to the German vineyards, with listings of all the different estate names and regions. Good for touring (if a bit big) and for reference.

ITALY

The Wines of Italy – David Gleave (Salamander Books, £8.95)
Considering its size, this is an astonishingly full and

informative account of what is happening in Italian wine, written with authority. Includes recommendations of the best producers.

Life Beyond Lambrusco – Nick Belfrage (Sidgwick & Jackson, £7.95)
Packed full of information on Italian wines, with easy cross-referencing and plenty of background information. Wines and producers are described, the main styles are analysed and what each area produces listed.

NEW ZEALAND

The Wines and Vineyards of New Zealand – Michael Cooper (Hodder & Stoughton, £19.95)
A revised edition to everything you could possibly want to know about New Zealand's wines, plus some beautiful photography.

Pocket Guide to the Wines of Australia and New Zealand (See under Australia.)

PORTUGAL

The Wines of Spain and Portugal (See under Spain below.)

SPAIN

The Wine and Food of Spain – Jan Read and Maite Manjon (Weidenfeld and Nicolson, £12.95)
The top experts on Spanish food and wine cover the country, looking at the different regions, their wine, the local cuisine. Includes information on restaurants and hotels.

The Wines of Spain and Portugal – Charles Metcalfe and Kathryn McWhirter (Salamander Press, £7.99)
A region-by-region view of the wines of the two Iberian countries, liberally illustrated with maps and colour photographs.

The New Wines of Spain – Tony Lord (Christopher Helm, £12.95)
A review of the rapid developments that have taken place in Spain over the past few years, plus a regional guide to who is doing what where.

SPARKLING WINES

Pocket Guide to Champagne and Sparkling Wines – Jane MacQuitty (Mitchell Beazley, £4.95)
Exhaustive guide to the sparkling wines of the world – from New Zealand to Oregon and Champagne to Chile. Directory-style entries, full of tasting notes and opinions.

FORTIFIED WINES

Pocket Guide to Fortified and Dessert Wines – Roger Voss (Mitchell Beazley, £9.95)
A detailed guide to fortified wines round the world, with special sections on Port, Sherry, Madeira and Australia; plus a shorter survey of major dessert wines.

Port – an Essential Guide to the Classic Drink – Andrew Jefford (Merehurst Press, £9.95)
A slim volume, but one which packs in plenty of information about Port production, and short company profiles. There are some good illustrations as well.

Sherry and the Sherry Bodegas – Jan Read (Sotheby's Publications, £19.95)
The history of the Jerez region plus Bodega profiles and chapters on the way Sherry is made, go to make the most comprehensive book on Sherry for 25 years.

Index

This index covers the WHAT TO BUY section only. Names from the lists of 'Who's Who' in each country have been indexed only if they also appear in the main text. Maps have not been indexed.

Report to the Editor *Which? Wine Guide*

This report is

a new recommendation ☐

a comment on existing entry ☐

please tick as appropriate

name of establishment

address

tel no:

please continue overleaf

date of most recent visit
_____

signed
_____

I am not connected directly or indirectly with the management or proprietors

name   *in block letters, please*
_____

address
_____
_____

Send to: Which? Wine Guide, Freepost, London NW1 4DX
(please note: no postage required within UK)

Report to the Editor *Which? Wine Guide*

This report is

a new recommendation ☐

a comment on existing entry ☐

please tick as appropriate

name of establishment

address

tel no:

please continue overleaf

date of most recent visit

signed

I am not connected directly or indirectly with the management or proprietors

name   *in block letters, please*

address

Send to: Which? Wine Guide, Freepost, London NW1 4DX
(please note: no postage required within UK)

Report to the Editor *Which? Wine Guide*

This report is

a new recommendation ☐

please tick as appropriate

a comment on existing entry ☐

name of establishment

address

tel no:

please continue overleaf

date of most recent visit
_____

signed
_____

I am not connected directly or indirectly with the management or
proprietors

name   *in block letters, please*
_____

address
_____
_____

Send to: Which? Wine Guide, Freepost, London NW1 4DX
(please note: no postage required within UK)

Report to the Editor *Which? Wine Guide*

This report is

a new recommendation ☐

a comment on existing entry ☐ *please tick as appropriate*

name of establishment

address

tel no:

please continue overleaf

date of most recent visit

signed

I am not connected directly or indirectly with the management or proprietors

name   *in block letters, please*

address

Send to: Which? Wine Guide, Freepost, London NW1 4DX
(please note: no postage required within UK)

Report to the Editor *Which? Wine Guide*

This report is

a new recommendation ☐

please tick as appropriate

a comment on existing entry ☐

name of establishment

address

tel no:

please continue overleaf

date of most recent visit
_____

signed
_____

I am not connected directly or indirectly with the management or
proprietors

name   *in block letters, please*
_____

address
_____
_____

Send to: Which? Wine Guide, Freepost, London NW1 4DX
(please note: no postage required within UK)

Report to the Editor *Which? Wine Guide*

This report is

a new recommendation ☐

a comment on existing entry ☐

please tick as appropriate

name of establishment

address

tel no:

please continue overleaf

date of most recent visit

signed

I am not connected directly or indirectly with the management or proprietors

name   *in block letters, please*

address

Send to: Which? Wine Guide, Freepost, London NW1 4DX
(please note: no postage required within UK)

Report to the Editor *Which? Wine Guide*

This report is

a new recommendation ☐

please tick as appropriate

a comment on existing entry ☐

name of establishment

address

tel no:

please continue overleaf

date of most recent visit
_____

signed
_____

I am not connected directly or indirectly with the management or proprietors

name   *in block letters, please*
_____

address
_____
_____

Send to: Which? Wine Guide, Freepost, London NW1 4DX
(please note: no postage required within UK)

Report to the Editor *Which? Wine Guide*

This report is

a new recommendation ☐

a comment on existing entry ☐

please tick as appropriate

name of establishment

address

tel no:

please continue overleaf

date of most recent visit
_____

signed
_____

I am not connected directly or indirectly with the management or
proprietors

name   *in block letters, please*
_____

address
_____
_____

Send to: Which? Wine Guide, Freepost, London NW1 4DX
(please note: no postage required within UK)